Colonialism and Development

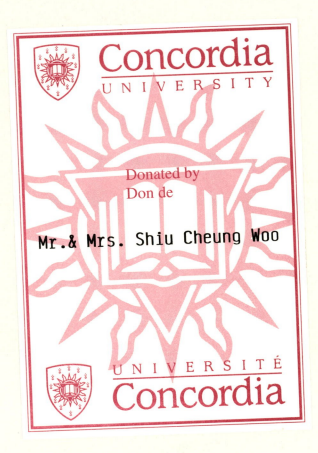

Colonialism and Development

Britain and its tropical colonies, 1850–1960

Michael Havinden and David Meredith

London and New York

First published 1993
by Routledge
11 New Fetter Lane, London EC4P 4EE

Simultaneously published in the USA and Canada
by Routledge
29 West 35th Street, New York, NY 10001

Typeset in 10 on 12 point Baskerville by Florencetype Ltd, Kewstoke, Avon
Printed in Great Britain by T.J. Press (Padstow) Ltd., Cornwall

British Library Cataloguing in Publication Data
A catalogue record for this book is available from the British Library

Library of Congress Cataloging in Publication Data
Havinden, Michael Ashley.
Colonialism and development : Britain and its tropical colonies, 1850–1960 /
Michael Havinden and David Meredith.
p.   cm.
Includes bibliographical references and index.
1. Great Britain—Colonies—Economic conditions.   2. Great
Britain—Colonies—Economic policy.   3. Economic development.
I. Meredith, David (David George)   II. Title.
HC259.H38   1993
338.9′009171′241—dc20   92–40809

ISBN 0-415-02043-3

For my wife, Kate

M.H.

For my parents, William and Edith

D.M.

Contents

Tables

Preface

Now that Third World development problems have become such a universal concern and have assumed such an alarming aspect, there is a tendency to look back to the colonial period with renewed interest in the hope that it may shed some light on the nature of the development problem or alternatively be made the scapegoat for current difficulties. It can be argued that if the colonial powers had been more successful in developing the economic and political structures of their colonies, contemporary problems would be less severe and intractable. Conversely, others would claim that the legacy from the colonial period can be overestimated; that it occurred too long ago to have had any very powerful influence on current problems – which stem rather from the inequality and instability of the world's trading economy and the failure of developing countries to adjust adequately to the responsibilities of independence, than to any alleged shortcomings in colonial rule. Indeed it might be argued that the conditions of relative peace and stability which prevailed in much of the colonial period were more conducive to development than the instability and uncertainty which has afflicted the Third World since the 1960s. These matters are highly controversial and will no doubt always remain so. They have already generated a vast polemical literature, and it is not our intention to add to it. Instead we hope that by attempting an analysis of the aims, activities, achievements and shortcomings of one major colonial power (Great Britain) in its tropical colonies over a period of a little over a century, we may be able to bring into sharper focus the specific problems and obstacles to development as they unfolded; and to assess the usefulness, or otherwise, of policy decisions and initiatives as they were taken.

Such an aim may perhaps be considered modest in relation to modern development problems, but analysing and absorbing the lessons of history is never a simple process; and one of the more distressing aspects of contemporary Third World experience has been a tendency to repeat mistakes previously made through an inadequate knowledge and understanding of past activities. If we can lessen that danger, and can highlight some of the achievements and shortcomings of past performance, we might be able to help clarify the planning agenda which developing countries need to elaborate, and to help to set it more firmly in the context of previously hard-won experience.

Despite many studies of British imperialism (the most important of which are discussed in what follows) there is still a gap in the literature concerning the long-range development of the tropical colonies during the colonial period (or at any rate from the mid-nineteenth century). It is this gap which we attempt to fill. The official and unofficial sources are voluminous and there is no way in which every relevant source could have been consulted. We have concentrated on a range which seemed the most useful for our purposes, which is a mixture drawn in the main from official government archives, contemporary accounts, official trade statistics and government publications. We have analysed the official trade statistics in some detail, using the records from the colonial customs offices, as printed in the annual governors' reports, or the Blue Books, and cited the reports themselves. We have also used original material from the Colonial Office, the Board of Trade, the War Office, the Foreign Office, the Treasury and the Cabinet Office in the Public Record Office; and a wide range of official publications and reports relating to colonial affairs.

In addition, we have sought to illuminate the picture by citing contemporary accounts of the colonies such as Anthony Trollope's travels in the West Indies in 1859 and accounts of East Africa, c. 1905, by Sir Harry Johnston and Sir Charles Eliot. We are conscious that much more could have been done in this respect, but limitations of space curtailed what was possible. We are also aware that our sources tend to bias our account towards the official British version. This is unfortunate, but in the present state of knowledge, more or less inevitable. We are sure that more research will be carried out in the future by historians in the former colonies, which will illuminate the economic impact of imperialism from a local perspective, leading eventually to a more balanced assessment of British colonial rule.

Acknowledgements

We would like to thank all those librarians and archivists who have assisted us, and in particular Stuart Macwilliam, Susanna Guy and Martin Myhill at Exeter University Library and the librarians of the Inter-Library Loans Department of the Social Sciences and Humanities Library, University of New South Wales: Margot Zeggelink and Ruth Arentz.

We are also most grateful to our research assistants Gerard D'Sousa and Philip Wallace who helped collect the foreign trade statistics and to Susan Millward, Ray Burnley and Janine Rabe of the Exeter University Social Studies Data Processing Unit who analysed them. We also thank the Exeter University Research Fund for financial assistance and the Department of Economic and Social History at Exeter for encouragement and for typing, which was cheerfully carried out by Celia Manning, Susan Murch and Jane Ashby. Kate Havinden also provided much support and also a lot of typing. At the University of New South Wales we wish to thank the Dean of the Faculty of Commerce and Economics for financial assistance to research; Anne Bolding for valuable research assistance in London and Sydney; members of the Department of Economic History who commented on early drafts; and Mrs Charleen Borlase who expertly processed so many words, so many times.

Our thanks are also due to Professor A.G. Hopkins for discussing many of the issues and for invaluable comments. He is of course in no way responsible for our views and conclusions.

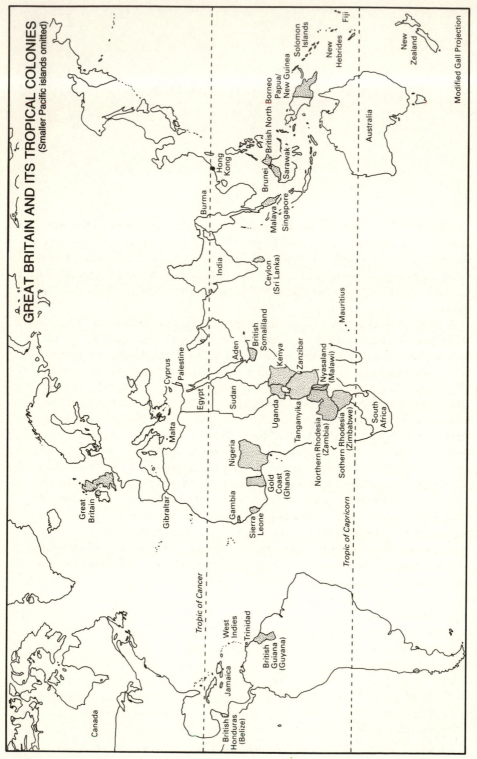

GREAT BRITAIN AND ITS TROPICAL COLONIES
(Smaller Pacific islands omitted)

Modified Gall Projection

Modified Gall projection. Equatorial scale 1 : 110,000,000.

1

Introduction and framework

THE DEVELOPMENT PROBLEM IN ITS HISTORICAL CONTEXT

The basis of our approach stems from an examination of the plans for colonial development which were gradually evolved by British statesmen and administrators from the late nineteenth century onwards. For although Britain may have started with a fairly laissez-faire attitude to the economic progress of its colonies, increasingly from the 1880s onwards, the need for positive plans was realised. At first these remained general and poorly articulated, but as experience grew, refinements were added, until by the 1920s quite ambitious and far-reaching plans for colonial economic development had been framed. No doubt by modern standards they were too partial and limited. Nonetheless they far exceeded the performance on the ground. It is in the analysis of the way in which these plans evolved, and the reasons why they failed to achieve more than a relatively small part of their objectives, that we believe that much of the interest in the present study lies.

The two sides to this evolution affected theory and practice. Initially the way in which the plans grew and were changed illustrates the way in which the actual course of development and the obstacles to it, influenced the growth of theory and led to its ever-growing elaboration. It also reveals how the limited intellectual horizons and prejudices of past periods affected the development of thinking and hampered action. But, although this development of theory is of considerable interest it is of less importance than the second aspect, which concentrates attention on the specific achievements and failures of policy in the different countries concerned, and seeks to assess how this has affected their current development situation. This analysis tends to place much more emphasis on things that were not done (perhaps especially the failure to provide more than a rudimentary infrastructure, and to make more than derisory progress with industrialisation) than it does on criticism of specific initiatives, though there were of course some glaring examples of these – such as the misconceived groundnut scheme in Tanganyika in

1

the early 1950s and the lesser known, but equally disastrous, Gambian egg scheme of the late 1940s.[1]

It may be objected at this point that it would have been unrealistic to expect any balanced development under conditions of imperial control, and by extension, under the conditions of so-called 'neo-colonialism' which have succeeded it. It can be argued that, although formal colonial rule has ended, the dominance which the developed countries, with their world-wide multinational companies, have on the international economy is such that they will never permit more than an unbalanced development in Third World countries. This would enable the developed countries to extract food and raw materials cheaply, and to sell some surplus production in Third World markets, but would not allow the development of competing industries or trade and financial networks. There is clearly much force in this argument and it would be foolish to deny the strength of vested interests in the international economy, but at the same time to give too much weight to such a proposition also has its dangers, since it consigns all hope of development to some far off date when the developed world may have changed its character; and it has the effect of demoralising development initiatives in the Third World. In fact the recent economic history of Europe has shown that trade between industrialised countries grows more quickly than trade between industrial and non-industrial countries, because of the general widening and deepening of the market which comes from greater all-round prosperity; and there seems no good reason for believing that what applies to intra-European trade would not apply equally well to world-wide trade. It is true that breaking out of their relative dependence will not be easy for Third World countries, and will involve a much greater degree of economic cooperation and mutual assistance than they have hitherto been able to achieve; but the advances which the Organisation of Petroleum Exporting Countries (OPEC) were able to make in the 1970s (while admittedly exceptional) perhaps indicate that there is more scope for cooperative progress than has hitherto been realised. Even if this scenario seems too optimistic it is well to reflect that a century ago Japan was regarded as a poorly developed country, not well endowed with natural resources. Yet it is amazing what organisation, national independence, and determination can achieve. To sum up this line of argument, we are not suggesting that world conditions make Third World development easy or simple; but merely that history suggests that even under the relatively unfavourable conditions of colonial control quite a lot of development (admittedly unbalanced) was achieved, and that it is not helpful to exaggerate the importance of negative factors.

It is also important to remember that a great deal of development commences by its very nature from an initial unbalanced concentration on one product (often a staple export) and that this can continue for a long time before a more balanced development begins. Australia provides one of many examples. Between 1820 and 1930 it relied overwhelmingly on the export of wool (and to lesser extent gold and wheat) to generate its economic growth. Some significant, but still small, progress towards industrial development and 'balanced' growth occurred between 1860 and 1930, but it was not until the late 1930s that really significant structural change and diversification took place. It is true that conditions in the self-governing Australian settler colonies were very different from those in the dependent tropical colonies, but the lesson that a country can escape from over-dependence on one staple export is still valid.[2]

To return to the aims of the present study, it may be useful to explain more clearly what we mean by 'tropical colonies' and what are the geographical limitations involved in this definition. Initially it seemed an attractive idea to try to comprise the whole of British imperial experience in the study, but we soon realised that this was impractical for a variety of reasons. In the first place the experience of the settlement colonies (later to become dominions) of Canada, Australia, New Zealand and South Africa was so fundamentally different from that of the other parts of the empire that their inclusion would have contributed little to our central concerns, quite apart from the problems that would have arisen from expanding the scope of the study beyond what could be sensibly covered in one book. To some extent similar considerations applied to India. In a sense the inclusion of India would have been desirable. Much of it is tropical, and it was sometimes used as an experimental laboratory for policies later to be tried out elsewhere in the colonial empire. On the other hand, the Indian Empire was always a separate organisation with its own ethos and traditions, and with an exclusive civil service whose members were not normally employed elsewhere in the colonial empire; so that the spin-off from their experience was limited. This factor, coupled with the immense amount of space which would have had to have been accorded to India (at the expense of the Colonial Office's tropical colonies) made us decide reluctantly to leave India out, except where the transfer of specific experiments from India called for discussion.

Essentially, we decided that more than enough material was available for our purposes from the large number of colonies that were under the direct control of the Colonial Office; and for this reason two African colonies not administered by the Colonial Office were also excluded. These were Zimbabwe (formerly Southern Rhodesia) a settlement colony administered by the British South Africa Company; and the Sudan (formerly the Anglo-Egyptian Sudan) a condominium jointly administered by the British Foreign Office and the Egyptian government.

At this stage it will also help to clarify our aims if we allude to some of the interesting issues connected with British imperialism which we do not attempt to address, except in passing. Recently much interest has been shown in the question of the costs and benefits of imperialism to Britain,[3] especially since the publication in 1986 of the pioneering work of Lance Davis and Robert Huttenback, *Mammon and the Pursuit of Empire: The Political Economy of British Imperialism, 1860–1912*. This massive study of British investment in the empire of course throws up many fascinating problems relating to development in the colonies, but these aspects are not central to the authors' aims. They specifically state that they have made no attempt to measure the economic, social or psychological effects of imperialism on the inhabitants of the colonies, which is one of our principal aims.[4] Instead they are centrally concerned with the economic effects of the empire on Britain. We thus regard their study as complementary to ours, while remaining somewhat sceptical of their conclusion that Britain contributed more to the empire than vice versa. In a penetrating review of *Mammon and the Pursuit of Empire*, Andrew Porter has noted that they regarded trade 'as not of overwhelming significance' (p.190) for their analysis, whereas we share his view that it is one of the main reasons for imperial expansion.[5] However, their new estimates of British imperial investment, based on the analysis of the accounts of 482 companies, refines previous estimates, even though they ignore direct investment through investment groups.[6]

Decolonisation is another topic which has attracted a good deal of research recently, and which obviously had an economic dimension, but which we do not discuss in any detail, since it is essentially outside the scope of our study.[7]

Moreover, we could not, for reasons of space, have attempted to write a detailed economic history of each colony. A few, like Nigeria, Kenya and Malaya, have been reasonably well researched, but many others have not, partly because until recently the colonial period was, understandably, not a major historical research priority for post-independence scholars.[8] Above all, our book is concerned with government colonial development policy and practice, because only the government was in a position to formulate, inspire and direct development policy, even if it relied to a considerable, but gradually decreasing, extent on private enterprise for much of its implementation.

Like all historical researchers we rely heavily on the existing literature on the subject for the foundation on which we seek to build. A few examples are the classics by the early pro-consuls, such as Sir Harry Johnston's, *The Opening Up of Africa* (1911), Sir Frederick (later Lord) Lugard's immensely influential *The Dual Mandate in British Tropical Africa* (1922) which argued that Britain had a duty to develop the tropics, not just for its sake or theirs, but for the benefit of the whole world; and Sir

Frank Swettenham's, *British Malaya, an Account of the Origin and Progress of British Influence in Malaya* (1906); and of course many more.

Recent scholarship has much refined these pioneering (and not by any means unself-interested) accounts. Of the many popular histories of the British Empire, Bernard Porter's, *The Lion's Share, a short History of British imperialism, 1850–1970* (1975), is one of the best and most entertaining. A major re-interpretation of imperial history has recently been undertaken by Peter Cain and Anthony Hopkins in two seminal articles in the *Economic History Review*, of which the second, 'Gentlemenly Capitalism and British Expansion Overseas II: New Imperialism, 1850–1945' (1987) refers to our period.[9] Their emphasis is however different from ours, in that they are primarily concerned with British motives for imperial expansion and the empire's effect on Britain. This is naturally an oversimplification of a complex argument, which will be elaborated in a two-volume study to be published in 1993 entitled *British Imperialism: A Re-interpretation*, which promises to be a major landmark, not only in imperial, but in British history as well. Unfortunately it was not available for us to consult.

Of recent works which touch more closely on the history and development of the tropical colonies, particularly in the later colonial period, mention must be made of Stephen Constantine's, *The Making of British Colonial Development Policy, 1914 to 1940* (1984) which is a very useful study, and the two volumes of documents, *British Imperial Policy and Decolonisation, 1938–64* (1987 and 1989)) edited by Andrew Porter and A. J. Stockwell, which is essential for the post-war period in particular. Perhaps the most valuable of all for our purposes though, is David J. Morgan's five volume, *Official History of Colonial Development*, which covers the period 1925 to 1971, drawing on the Colonial Office's and other official government sources.

It is necessary at this point to define what is meant by 'development'. Many treatises have been written on this subject, and social scientists are by no means fully agreed on every aspect. However, certain characteristics are generally agreed. There should be a rise in average living standards which involves not merely an increase in material goods, but an enlargement of social and cultural opportunities and widespread access to education, health and recreational facilities. As a starting point this will involve economic growth, but this must take the form not merely of an increase in national production, but of increased production per head of population. Economic growth which merely keeps pace with population growth, or worse still, falls behind it, can of course make little contribution to development. There is a further problem with economic growth. It is normally measured as gross national product (GNP) or gross national income (GNI) using methods of national accounting which were invented for developed countries. Essentially these techniques measure commercial transactions, and it is well known that they are not very appropriate for underdeveloped areas with large subsistence, or non-market sectors. This was a problem throughout the colonial period, and we have frequently had to fall back on the growth of foreign trade as the only available (and not very reliable) proxy for economic growth. A further problem is that national accounting techniques do not always take proper account of environmental damage, resource depletion and pollution, which often accompany the cruder forms of economic growth, and need somehow to be offset against it.

It is sometimes assumed that economic growth will inevitably be overtaken by an expanding population, and although this is an obvious danger, there is no reason why population growth should outstrip economic growth. In fact, in many of Britain's tropical colonies the major problem was shortage of people, especially in Africa, and increasing populations from the 1950s onwards provided both the means as well as the need for accelerated development.

Another weakness with conventional measurements of GNP or GNI is that they measure averages for the whole population, which can sometimes conceal wide gaps in income distribution between the very wealthy and poorer groups who were becoming increasingly proletarianised by the drift to the towns which typically accompanied the break-up of traditional agrarian societies. Some colonial societies had what might be described as almost a 'feudal' income distribution pattern which was not necessarily altered by economic growth, at least not in its early stages. In addition some leakage of wealth out of the colonies to the 'mother country' was inevitable, so that in many cases the principal beneficiaries of more rapid economic growth were traditional rulers plus British shareholders and, possibly, British workers. Income distribution cannot be measured in any exact way for the colonies, but it is important to note that the quickening of economic activity which was visible in most of the colonies at various times did not automatically mean that incomes per head were rising for the majority of the population. Such a situation depended on their degree of participation in the growing parts of the economy, whether as entrepreneurs, 'peasant' producers or merely as wage labourers. It also depended on the extent to which some of the new wealth (usually in the form of enhanced customs duties) was translated into social and welfare services, such as hospitals, electricity supplies, piped water and drainage and, above all, schools, since education rapidly became a major ambition of colonial peoples. This was in general a slow and incomplete process. Acceptance by Britain that it had an obligation to provide welfare services came about only gradually, and even then local funding of such services remained dominant.

Beyond all this, however, is the vital question of structural change in the colonial economies. Economic growth tended to lead (inevitably to

6

begin with) to a dependence on a narrow range of unprocessed primary exports and, indeed, prior to the First World War, this was a rational way for the undeveloped tropical colonies to integrate into the world economy, especially given their ties to Britain. The very success of reaching this initial level of economic development led the colonies to get stuck in a rut for the next few decades or even to the end of the colonial epoch. Yet 'development' had to include the stimulation of a diversity of industries and occupations for the colonial inhabitants, the growth of a buoyant domestic market for locally made products as well as imports, rises in the productivity of traditional agriculture, shifts of labour and capital from (low productivity) agriculture into (higher productivity) manufacturing and services, the transformation of traditional handicraft industries towards mechanised ones and the establishment of conditions for mass consumption including adequate infrastructure for domestic distribution and marketing. The transformation of a undeveloped economy to an industrial one is a long drawn out process lasting, in Britain's case, for several centuries, and even in Japan's case, it took nearly a century from the 1860s. There were also service industries – tourism, entrepôt facilities, communications – where the colonial economies could diversify. At the time when they were integrated into the world economy the tropical colonies might have seemed to have possessed a comparative advantage only in producing primary products. They undoubtedly did have a comparative advantage in producing some tropical agricultural commodities and minerals, and they were no doubt wise to base their economic progress on maintaining and intensifying this position. Comparative advantage, however, is not static: government and private capital (guided by government, perhaps) often act to alter comparative advantage. State assistance to economic development was normal in the economic history of the developed nations of today, Britain included. Although the period of colonial rule was generally less than 100 years, it was long enough for British colonial policy to have had a major impact on economic development and it is not unreasonable to expect the colonial regime to have played a significant role in this sense. How and to what extent this was tackled remains a major topic of this book.

We must turn now from these general issues to a brief survey of the far-flung and heterogeneous group of territories that made up Britain's empire in the tropics.[10]

THE TROPICAL COLONIES

Britain eventually came to possess colonies in every part of the tropics, extending from the old colonies in the Caribbean, through Africa to Asia and across large stretches of the Pacific Ocean. Their area, population, density, approximate land use and capital cities are summarised (*c.* 1956) in Table 1.1. This was the period when the colonial empire was at its maximum extent, just prior to its dissolution (though Sri Lanka (Ceylon) had already achieved independence in 1948). The tropical colonies comprised some 1.8 million square miles (compared with Great Britain's 94,000) and had a population in 1956 of about 87.7 million (compared with Great Britain's 50.2 million). But although this was, in Joseph Chamberlain's words, an immense 'estate' for Britain to administer, it was far from conveniently located or rationally laid out. Instead it was an incredibly varied group of countries strung around the globe with representatives in every continent. The distances from London are immense. Going west it is 4,700 miles to Jamaica. Southwards to Nigeria in West Africa is 3,000 miles, and to Zambia in southern Africa is 4,800 miles. Going southeastwards to Asia via East Africa the distances are as follows: to Kenya 4,250 miles, to Sri Lanka (Ceylon) 5,430 miles, to Malaya 6,700 miles and to the Solomon Islands in the Pacific Ocean about 12,000 miles. Distant Fiji and the remote Kiribati and Tuvalu (Gilbert and Ellice) Islands in the Pacific Ocean are actually slightly closer, at about 11,000 miles when approached from the west through the Panama Canal. In 1956 a boat from London to Suva in the Fijian Islands took about 35 days; in the nineteenth century it was considerably longer.

There is also a vast variety in size and importance between the different colonies, as can be seen in Table 1.2 where the 16 most important (comprising 84 million people, or 96 per cent of the total) are grouped in rank order according to the size of their population (c. 1956). We could place the 16 in four divisions, similar to a football league. In the first division Nigeria would reign supreme and alone, with its 31.2 million people it was about four times as populous as the leaders of the second division, Tanganyika and Ceylon. In addition to its large population Nigeria was also important in the international economy, being one of the world's largest suppliers of groundnuts, palm oil, palm kernel nuts and cocoa, as well as being a substantial producer of cotton, hardwoods and tobacco. This was of course before petroleum oils had been discovered in economically viable quantities.

The second division was dominated by East Africa and Asia. Britain had been trying to federate the three contiguous East African colonies of Kenya, Uganda and Tanganyika since 1929. In the 1950s some progress was being made, and, they had (with Zanzibar) a combined population of just under 20 million; and had this federation been successfully achieved (it fell apart in the 1960s) the new country would have moved into the first division. The East African grouping appeared to have considerable economic advantages. Uganda was a major cotton producer and had hydro-electric power from the Falls on the Nile at Jinja. Tanganyika

Table 1.1 British tropical colonies (and **Sri Lanka**) c. 1956: area, population, land use and capital city (in rank order of population, by region)

	Area (sq. miles)[a]	Population (to nearest 1,000)	Density (per sq. mile)	Approximate land use (%)				Capital city
				Arable and Orchard	Permanent grassland	Forest and woodland	'Waste' (city areas, 'bush fallow', water, etc.	
AFRICA								
West Africa								
Nigeria	373,250	31,170,000	84	23.1	–	32.0	44.8	Lagos
Gold Coast (Ghana)	91,843	4,118,000	45	22.3	–	63.9	13.8	Accra
Sierra Leone	27,925	2,100,000	75	50.7	30.4	4.2	14.8	Freetown
Gambia	4,003	277,000	69	21.4	–	29.8	49.2	Bathurst (Banjul)
East Africa								
Tanganyika (Tanzania)	342,706	8,196,000	25	11.5	16.0	38.3	34.2	Dar-es-Salaam
Kenya	219,730	6,000,000	27	2.8	20.6	2.2	74.4	Nairobi
Uganda	80,292	5,425,000	68	11.7	–	7.1	81.2	Kampala
Nyasaland (Malawi)	37,374	2,545,000	68	23.0	4.7	14.2	58.0	Zomba
Northern Rhodesia (Zambia)	287,640	2,128,000	7	40.6	–	49.7	9.7	Lusaka
British Somaliland	68,000	640,000	9	0.4	48.9	46.4	4.4	Hargeisa
Zanzibar & Pemba (Tanzania)	1,020	264,000	259	51.1	8.0	0.8	40.2	Zanzibar
ASIA								
Ceylon (Sri Lanka)[b]	25,332	8,104,000	320	23.0	–	53.8	23.1	Colombo
Malaya	50,680	6,200,000	123	17.0	–	74.0	9.0	Kuala Lumpur
Singapore	280	1,467,000	5,239	21.0	–	27.0	52.0	Singapore
Total: Malaya/Singapore	50,960	7,667,000	–	–	–	–	–	–

Table 1.1 (continued)

	Area (sq. miles)[a]	Population (to nearest 1,000)	Density (per sq. mile)	Approximate land use (%)				Capital city
				Arable and Orchard	Permanent grassland	Forest and woodland	'Waste' (city areas, 'bush fallow', water, etc.	
Hong Kong	391	2,340,000	5,985	12.9	0.4	33.7	53.5	Victoria
British Borneo	79,134	1,035,000	52	17.7	0.8	74.4	7.1	
North Borneo	29,837	361,000	12	–	–	–	–	Jesselton
Brunei	2,226	60,000	27	–	–	–	–	Brunei
Sarawak	47,071	613,000	13	–	–	–	–	Kuching
Mauritius	720	539,000	749	45.7	23.6	19.4	11.3	Port Louis
Seychelles Islands	156	47,000	237	42.0	1.0	10.0	47.0	Victoria
CARIBBEAN								
West Indies Federation								
Jamaica	4,411	1,532,000	347	15.2	20.8	17.7	46.2	Kingston
Trinidad & Tobago	1,980	698,000	353	33.6	1.2	45.7	19.7	Port of Spain
Windward Islands	821	303,000	368	35.0	3.7	32.7	28.5	
Grenada	133	85,000	639	–	–	–	–	St George's
St Lucia	233	83,000	356	–	–	–	–	Castries
St Vincent	150	[a]73,000	487	–	–	–	–	Kingstown
Dominica	305	61,000	200	–	–	–	–	Roseau
Barbados	166	221,000	1,331	65.2	11.6	–	23.2	Bridgetown
Leeward Islands	438	126,000	287	34.0	10.1	12.8	43.1	
St Christopher, Nevis & Anguilla	168	49,000	292	–	–	–	–	Basseterre
Antigua, Barbuda & Redonda	171	46,000	269	–	–	–	–	St Johns
Montserrat	32	14,000	438	–	–	–	–	Plymouth

Table 1.1 *(continued)*

	Area (sq. miles)[a]	Population (to nearest 1,000)	Density (per sq. mile)	Approximate land use (%)				Capital city
				Arable and Orchard	Permanent grassland	Forest and woodland	'Waste' (city areas, 'bush fallow', water, etc.	
Virgin Islands	67	7,000	104	–	–	–	–	Road Town
British Guiana (Guyana)	83,000	474,000	6	0.6	5.0	77.0	17.4	Georgetown
Bahama Islands	4,404	85,000	19	1.2	–	25.4	73.4	Nassau
British Honduras	8,867	81,000	9	5.1	0.6	–	94.5	Belize
PACIFIC								
Fiji Islands	7,183	332,000	47	7.9	52.0	40.0	z[c]	Suva
British Pacific Islands					Not available			
British Solomon Islands	11,500	100,000	9		Not available			Honiara
Tonga Islands	270	56,000	207		Not available			Nuku'alofa
New Hebrides (Br-Fr condominium)	5,700	52,000	9		Not available			Vila
Gilbert, Ellice & misc. islands	369	38,000	103		Not available			Tarawa
Totals	1,819,585	87,692,000						
For comparison: UK								
England	50,327	41,148,000	817					
Scotland	30,405	5,096,000	168					
Wales	8,015	2,597,000	324	29.1	50.4	6.6	13.9	
N. Ireland	5,238	1,371,000	262					
Total	93,985	50,212,000						

[a] 1 sq mile = 2.58995 sq kilometres 640 acres and 258.9952 hectares.
[b] Independent from 1948.
[c] Included in other groups.

Table 1.2 Colonies with populations of over 0.5 million by size groups (*c.* 1956)

Number of colonies			Population (millions)
		I	
1	1.	Nigeria	31.2
		II	
	2.	Tanganyika	8.2
	3.	Ceylon	8.1
	4.	Malaya & Singapore	7.7
	5.	Kenya	6.0
	6.	Uganda	5.4
6	7.	Gold Coast	4.1
		III	
	8.	Nyasaland	2.5
	9.	Hong Kong	2.3
	10.	Northern Rhodesia	2.1
	11.	Sierra Leone	2.1
	12.	Jamaica	1.5
6	13.	British Borneo	1.0
		IV	
	14.	Trinidad & Tobago	0.7
	15.	British Somaliland	0.6
3	16.	Mauritius	0.5
16			84.0[a]

[a] i.e. 96% of total population of all British tropical colonies.

admittedly was poor in natural resources and extent of development; but Kenya was an important exporter of coffee and produced a wide range of agricultural products and had made a start with industrial development. The major problem was that Kenya was still dominated politically by a small group of European settlers, entrenched in the Legislative Council; and as long as this privileged position continued, neither Uganda nor Tanganyika could be expected to cooperate whole-heartedly in the federation. Tragically, the division created then (and earlier) spilled over into the post-colonial period, and even when the issue of white domination was no longer an obstacle, these divisions, wedded to different perceptions of where their economic interests lay, combined to frustrate plans to continue the federation once independence had been achieved by the participants. The economic costs of this failure have been heavy for all three countries, but in different degrees.

Two small, but densely populated, Asian countries occupied the middle of the second division. These were Ceylon and Malaya (including

Singapore). Both were considerably more developed than any of the African colonies, with more extensive infrastructures, and with the beginnings of some industrial growth – but both were still heavily dependent on a narrow range of staple exports. In Ceylon it was tea and copra; in Malaya, tin and rubber. For tea, tin and rubber these two countries were amongst the world's most important producers.

Finally, a single West African country, the Gold Coast (shortly to become independent as Ghana in 1957) completed the second division. Ghana was at this time the most economically developed of all the West African countries (French as well as British colonies), though its export economy was overwhelmingly concentrated on cocoa beans – of which it, almost unbelievably, grew about half the quantities entering the world trade in the 1950s.

The third division consisted of colonies with small populations ranging from one to two-and-half million. Some, like Hong Kong and Jamaica, were densely populated. Others, like Northern Rhodesia (now Zambia) and the British territories in Borneo, were almost uninhabited over large stretches of their territory. Zambia was poorly developed agriculturally but had rich resources of copper to export, while British Borneo likewise relied on a mineral export – petroleum oil. Nyasaland (now Malawi) in Southeast Africa, and Sierra Leone in West Africa were two smallish colonies in which indigenous agriculture was fairly well developed, but which had not established any important export staples. Sierra Leone produced palm kernels on a small scale, and had recently become important for alluvial diamonds; while Malawi was a supplier of migrant labour to the Zambian copperbelt and the gold mines of South Africa.

The fourth division comprised three small colonies, one of which, British Somaliland, largely consisted of desert. Of the other two, Trinidad was important for its petroleum oil fields, and densely populated Mauritius for its exports of sugar.

The remaining tropical colonies, with only 4 per cent of the population, were mostly groups of small islands, such as the Windwards and Leewards in the West Indies, the Seychelles in the Indian Ocean, and the widely scattered coral atolls of the Pacific Ocean. Beyond a possible potential for tourism, or as military bases, or airplane refuelling depots, their scope for any kind of economic activity beyond the most basic, was severely limited; and although subsistence agriculture was often sufficiently productive to yield their inhabitants a reasonably happy lifestyle (as witness Sir Arthur Grimble's attractive picture of life in the Gilbert Islands, 1914–19)[11] geographical constraints placed firm limits on most opportunities for changing the pattern.

Another way of categorising the tropical colonies is to divide them into types based on their socio-economic structure. Thus we have the old plantation colonies, located mainly in the Caribbean, dominated by a small white-settler 'aristocracy' of plantation owners, and a large work force of ex-slaves of African descent. Barbados, Jamaica and Trinidad were the largest and most important of these. Some cocoa, oranges, limes and bananas were grown for export, but in almost every case the cultivation of sugar cane dominated the economies of these islands.

Next there were the newer plantation colonies, like Mauritius and Ceylon in the Indian Ocean, Malaya and British North Borneo in Southeast Asia and a scatter of Pacific islands like the Solomons and Fiji. Their socio-economic structure was similar to the old plantation economies except that the labour force was usually of Indian (or in Malaya, partly of Chinese) origin; and considerably more capital was invested in them than in the Caribbean. In addition to plantation crops like sugar in Mauritius and Fiji, tea in Ceylon and rubber in Malaya, the export of minerals was also important, such as petroleum oil from North Borneo, and especially tin from Malaya.

Another category of colonies were those which exported cash crops grown by indigenous farmers, usually, though not always, on fairly small holdings. These were mainly in West Africa, where cocoa production was important in Ghana (formerly Gold Coast) and Nigeria. Sierra Leone and Nigeria also produced palm oil and palm kernel nuts, and Gambia and Northern Nigeria specialised in groundnuts (peanuts). Nigeria also produced cotton as did Uganda in East Africa. Minerals were also important in a few of these colonies (produced by European-owned firms) such as the tin of Nigeria, the iron ore and diamonds of Sierra Leone, and the manganese, industrial diamonds and gold of Ghana.

Finally, the last category of tropical colonies were the relatively new settler colonies in East and Central Africa, like Kenya, Nyasaland (Malawi) and Northern Rhodesia (Zambia). In these places relatively large areas of the best land had been taken from the local population and 'reserved' for European settlers, who operated extensive farms, employing native labour. These farms were not exclusively devoted to export crops, though Northern Rhodesia exported tobacco, and Kenya exported coffee, tea and sisal. They relied to some extent on supplying food for the internal market, particularly for capital cities like Nairobi in Kenya and Lusaka in Northern Rhodesia. The latter city was the centre of an extensive copper mining industry (European owned) and Northern Rhodesia's economy was heavily dependent on the export of copper. (See Appendix 3 for details.)

It can be seen that the economies of Britain's tropical colonies were linked to the world economy by a relatively small group of export commodities, which were sent principally to Europe and the United States (and in much smaller quantities to India, South Africa, Australia

and New Zealand). These export commodities consisted largely of agricultural raw materials, foodstuffs and minerals (both metals and non-
metals).

The most important of the raw materials were rubber (mostly from
Malaya) used mainly for the manufacture of automobile tyres; palm oil
used in the nineteenth century for the lubrication of machinery, and
subsequently for the manufacture of soap, cosmetics and associated
products, and cotton for the textile industry. Less important were
tobacco for cigarettes and sisal for ropes, cordage and heavy textiles.

Occupying a half-way house between raw materials and foodstuffs
were the palm kernel nuts and groundnuts produced mainly in West
Africa. Both the palm kernels and the groundnuts were crushed (not
locally) for their high quality oils which were used for the manufacture
of margarine and cosmetics, etc.; and for their residues which were used
to make high-protein cake for dairy cattle. European milk production
relied heavily on these products.

Amongst the foodstuffs, sugar and tropical fruits had a wide range of
uses. The beverages, cocoa, coffee and tea enjoyed growing popularity.
Spices like pepper, cloves (from Zanzibar) ginger and cinnamon were
somewhat less important; but some of the basic tropical foodstuffs, like
tea, coffee, bananas, oranges and chocolate were staples of European
and American diet.

The range of mineral exports was more limited, but still important.
Potentially the most important was petroleum oil, but this was not well
developed in the colonial period, except in Trinidad. Much more important were tin and copper, which were widely used throughout
European and American industry – tin primarily for canning, and
copper for electrical wiring. Malaya, and to a lesser extent Nigeria were
important sources of tin, with copper coming from Northern Rhodesia.
Gold was found in various places but was only important in Ghana. The
small West African colony of Sierra Leone had rich deposits of iron ore
and high quality gem diamonds, both of which began to be mined in the
1930s. Coal was not abundant (or much needed in the tropics) but was
mined in eastern Nigeria for the railways, and in a few other places, like
Labuan in Borneo.

All the products of the tropical colonies shared one critical weakness.
They were all subject to competition from other tropical (and in the case
of minerals, non-tropical) countries, and in many cases were produced
in relatively small quantities by thousands of producers. This led to over-
production in times of boom, and under-production in times of slump
and war, with the concomitant sharp rises and falls in prices. This
instability in the international markets was quickly transferred to the
colonial economies, producing an unwelcome volatility, which neither
they, nor Britain, could readily control.

Mining represented a particular problem, both because minerals are wasting assets, and because the sophistication of the technology involved almost always led to foreign ownership and control (not always British). This was a sensitive area for Britain where the Colonial Office was conscious of the problems, but had difficulty in establishing coherent policy.

Another problem arose from the contemporary belief, reflected by authors like Benjamin Kidd in his book *The Control of the Tropics* (1898) that the inhabitants of the tropics had *no right* to their resources, which must be developed for the use of the world as a whole (which effectively meant Europe and North America). This was still being reflected in modified form by Lord Lugard as we have previously noted, in his *The Dual Mandate in British Tropical Africa* as late as 1922, even though he cared passionately for the welfare (as he conceived it) of the tropical colonies. This ambivalence of view clearly influenced the formation of the British government's colonial policy.

Finally, it may be helpful to survey in broad terms the possible scope for development and what might reasonably have been expected in terms of the climatic, agricultural, mineral and human resources of the tropical colonies; as well as some of the more serious impediments, both natural and man-made, which frustrated progress.

POSITIVE FACTORS FOR DEVELOPMENT

Tropical climates are a mixed blessing for economic development. Lord Leverhulme once described Nigeria (*c.* 1920) as a huge natural greenhouse with free heat and water, and it is true that despite generally poor soils impoverished by leaching, tropical agriculture can be remarkably productive when the distribution of heat and rainfall is propitious. Swamps which are naturally irrigated by springs and streams can yield three crops of rice in a year; and a luxuriant variety of roots, vegetables and fruits can be grown with amazing rapidity. Things are, however, not so simple. There is also a bewildering variety of plant, animal and human diseases, some of which have recently been brought under control, such as yellow fever and, to some extent, malaria; while others like the deadly trypanosomiasis in cattle, and 'swollen shoot' in cocoa continue to wreak economic havoc on a massive scale. Moreover, substantial progress in disease control has been mainly an achievement of the period since 1945. During much of the colonial period the population of the tropical colonies (particularly in Africa) was kept well below its economic optimum by diseases, of which those which caused widespread debilitation in humans and livestock may have been even more harmful than the more widely publicised lethal ones, like yellow fever. As Pierre Gourou put it in 1966:

16

the development of the tropical world has been much delayed since the industrial and scientific revolution. Progress in the conquest of infectious diseases and in the maintenance of soil fertility has been realized in the temperate zone, through the agency of research workers born and living in the temperate zone; such discoveries have been but slowly transferred to the tropical zone, because the natural conditions are there so different. Scientists of tropical origin have been rare, and those from the temperate zones have needed much time to accustom themselves to the conditions of the tropics.[12]

Nevertheless, the widespread use of quinine as an anti-malarial medicine after the 1850s, and the discovery by Ross in 1898 that malaria was spread by the *Anopheles* mosquito, and that this could be reasonably easily controlled by spraying paraffin on its freshwater breeding places, reduced the disease problem to manageable proportions, and opened up bright new possibilities for development. These were most promising in Africa and Malaya, where there was ample scope for increasing populations to be combined with abundant land – and especially where mineral exports were also available to encourage outside investment, as with tin in Malaya and Nigeria and gold in the Gold Coast, and later on, copper in Zambia.

Ironically the very sparseness of the population in so many tropical colonies, which had clearly been a cause of economic backwardness in the pre-colonial period, represented one of the most favourable elements in their growth potential; for one of the easiest ways to encourage the first steps in economic development, is to facilitate the spread of population into lands which have hitherto been more or less unoccupied. The population figures for the pre-colonial and early colonial periods are notoriously unreliable in detail, but there can be no doubting that in general pre-colonial populations were very much smaller than they later became. Rapid population expansion, rather than being a source of anxiety as today, was on the contrary welcomed; and where indigenous growth was insufficiently rapid was assisted by immigration, as with the Chinese into Malaya, the Indians into East Africa and the Lebanese (Syrians) into West Africa. This of course sowed the seeds of future trouble, but greatly assisted economic development at the time it occurred (primarily between the 1890s and 1914).

The sparse population (especially urban) and the associated lack of transport facilities and infrastructure in general, meant that most of the tropical colonies were in a situation in which the provision of even modest transport links (such as steamships on the river Niger in Nigeria, or a railway from Singapore to Kuala Lumpur and Pahang in Malaya), could yield very substantial initial dividends, especially when large areas of new country were rapidly 'opened up' to staple export crops. In effect the model of economic development that was applicable at this time was a variant of the 'staple theory' first applied to Canadian, and later to Australian, economic development.[13] Further details of the working out of this model are provided in later chapters. Here it is only the general points which need to be considered.

In the case of the tropical colonies it was apparent that the local market was too small, scattered, and poor to encourage a move away from mere subsistence production into a more sophisticated mode of production which would allow a division of labour and the associated rises in productivity and ultimately incomes per head that spring from it. In the circumstances it was necessary to find export staples which would be saleable in Europe and America, and whose proceeds could be used to finance the loans and investments needed, both to pay for the necessary infrastructure, and to expand the area from which the staples were drawn.

This, of course, is where a tropical location did prove advantageous for, generally speaking, the agricultural and forestry products which could be most easily produced in the tropics (such as palm oil, cocoa, rubber, citrus fruits and spices amongst many others) did not have temperate zone substitutes – and hence enjoyed great growth potential if only the costs of the long sea journeys to market could be lowered. Here again progress was likely to be cumulative (and was in the period up to the 1920s) since each expansion of the market for tropical produce called for larger, faster and more efficient ships (sometimes refrigerated) and with each addition of such ships, the *unit cost* of transport fell, and the resulting profits could be used to finance yet another expansion in the size and efficiency of the transport network. The fact that the extensive colonial trade routes were by and large protected by the worldwide patrols of the British navy (at least prior to 1939, with the exception of the First World War) meant also that the rate of expansion was governed purely by economic factors and was not inhibited by extraneous strategic considerations.

In these circumstances expansion could continue until overseas markets were glutted, or succeeded in producing substitutes, as continental Europe did with beet sugar in the late nineteenth century, at the expense of tropical cane sugar producers in the West Indies, Mauritius and Fiji. To some extent this problem was lessened when the staple exports were minerals. Being in the tropics obviously made no difference here, (and there were in fact very few colonial minerals which could not be found elsewhere) but even so, at important periods in their history it was difficult to find substitutes for Zambian copper or Malayan tin, and to that extent producers enjoyed some natural protection.

The other main feature of the pre-colonial economies was the pronounced shortage (amounting in some cases to virtual absence) of capital and technology. Here again injections of very small quantities initially could produce results out of all proportion to the amounts supplied. A very good example of this was the introduction of cocoa seedlings into Ghana. The initial cost of the trees (cocoa not being found indigenously in Ghana) must have been trivial, yet within a few years this tiny investment (of the 1890s) had led to the growth of million of trees and the development of a massive world-wide trade in cocoa beans. Furthermore the savings of thousands of cocoa farmers meant that Ghana was soon in a position to generate some of its own indigenous sources of capital, and to lessen its dependence on outside investment.[14]

It is true that in the backward conditions existing during the early years of colonial rule, injections of the most modern European technology would hardly have been appropriate, yet it remains the case that in principle the opportunities for the transfer of new technology were greatly enhanced by the much closer contact with Europe which colonial rule provided.[15] However in this area the development prospects were certainly more latent than actual; except in the case of railways, which were introduced fairly rapidly in the two decades before 1914, even if still on a restricted scale.

It is obvious from the previous discussion that the conditions for a fairly rapid (even if still very unbalanced) economic expansion existed for the tropical colonies, on the basis of export staples, whether agricultural or mineral, in the period when the overseas demand for such staples was still growing rapidly, as it was up until the late 1920s; and when the tropical colonies themselves could derive the maximum benefit from the relatively minimal input of infrastructure. The difficulties would arise when the easy growth path, based on export staples, became restricted, and the colonial economies would need to beat out new paths for themselves based on greater reliance on their own internal economic growth. This could in principle come from an extension and enlargement of the market which would have encouraged structural changes in their economies, leading ultimately to the partial replacement of the export staple trades by indigenous industrial and service sectors.[16]

CONSTRAINTS ON DEVELOPMENT

There are a number of major difficulties in the way of such a transformation – some economic and some political, which have already been alluded to. There were powerful vested interests, like the great trading companies, who profited from exporting the staples and also from *importing* British manufactured goods. Clearly for them the development of an indigenous manufacturing sector could have competed for domestic labour, and have possibly reduced the supply of staple exports

19

while at the same time eating into the market for imported manufactures. To some extent these companies were also helped by the colonial governments, who derived much of their revenue from taxes on imports, and who naturally did not wish to see this source of supply reduced. At that point the economic and political forces came together.[17]

However, there is more to the matter than that. In wider terms, British businessmen in general looked to the colonies for expanded markets for a wide range of goods and services and also as possible fields for future investment. It was not necessarily in their interests to see these markets monopolised by a handful of trading companies, especially when the pattern of trade appeared to be approaching stagnation. For in the 1930s, as the colonial staples were over-produced, their prices fell dramatically and the terms of trade moved sharply against the tropical colonies. Inevitably as their incomes fell, they cut down on their imports from Britain, and their value, both as markets and fields for investment were painfully reduced. Conversely if they had had more diversified and resilient economies, the damage which was done both to the British and their own economies might have been reduced. Nor is colonial control necessarily inimical to all industrial development, even industrial development behind a protective tariff, as the case of India shows. Despite widespread opposition from Lancashire cotton interests, the imperial government of India introduced such protection in the 1930s in the greater interest of India's overall economic development.

These broader issues of weighing the relative economic merits of policies designed to increase overall economic development in the colonies, in the hope of securing a *linked* expansion in Britain itself, as against policies of favouring the more limited interests of companies already engaged in colonial trade and production, bring us back to the heart of the problem. In the evolution of central colonial economic policy, a range of general themes are relevant, which it is convenient to introduce briefly now, as they constantly recur throughout the later history of the colonial development effort, like the basic themes in a symphony.

We have alluded briefly to the factors which were generally favourable to the economic development of the tropical colonies, it is now necessary to consider some of the persistent negative factors which repeatedly occurred and hampered development. Part of the failure to realise hopes and aims arose from an underestimation of the size and intractability of the obstacles to development. These were of course of many types but the more important may be grouped under five main headings. First, there were widespread illusions about the richness of the colonies' resources. Initially these illusions were not unnatural, but inevitably they caused underestimation of the likely costs of development, and the raising of unrealistic expectations. Second, there were major problems of capital supply: private capitalists were much more reluctant to invest in unfamiliar and undeveloped areas than had been hoped; and where private capital would not lead, the British Treasury was equally reluctant to pioneer with public capital. There was a further problem relating to the use to which capital was put. In the 'Chamberlain model' much emphasis was placed on railway building, which was assumed to be economically sound and beneficial, although this never seems to have been investigated and properly tested in colonial conditions. In fact railways were often extremely expensive solutions to transport bottlenecks, and, because they were mostly financed with foreign capital, they placed a burden on colonial economies to earn enough foreign exchange to service and repay the necessary loans. This in turn led to an emphasis on maximising cash-crops and mineral exports, which was not always in the best interests of the colonies' long-term development. It was another problem arising from the inexperience and pre-conceived ideas of colonial administrators. Third, there were considerable political divisions and uncertainties in Britain. There were convinced imperialists, of varying degrees of enthusiasm, in all the major political parties, but in no party could they always be sure of consistent support. Even in the Conservative Party, where they were more numerous and influential, there remained some old-fashioned free-traders and believers in retrenchment, who doubted whether colonies would ever be worth the expenses of initial development and continuing defense. Such people were more common in the Liberal Party, where they were reinforced by radicals who objected on principle to what they regarded as colonial exploitation. This attitude was also strong in the Labour Party, but was offset to some extent by feelings of paternalism, and of an obligation to extend a helping hand to people who could not realistically be expected to do very much for themselves. This melange of opinions did not assist in the formulation of a consistent policy.

Fourth, there were different views and perspectives about what type of colonial development was needed. As previously mentioned, British companies involved in colonial trade, or with mining or plantation concessions, had their own specific interests to promote, and these were not always consistent with the optimum development strategy, whether viewed from London or the colonies themselves. In the latter the views of the indigenous people were not usually accorded very high priority, but were frequently reflected, though no doubt in distorted form, by paternalistic colonial administrators, like Sir Hugh Clifford in Malaya and West Africa, and Sir Donald Cameron in Nigeria and Tanganyika, who believed deeply in the concept of 'trusteeship' under which colonial rule would protect what they conceived to be the basic interests of the local people – which often in practice meant preserving the 'traditional society' in the state in which it happened to be when they encountered it.[18] This was often reflected in a naive or confused attitude to the agricultural and trading systems in being at the commencement of colonial rule. There were two aspects to this. There was a danger that where local agricultural systems were based on shifting cultivation, British officials would regard this as wasteful and inefficient and would seek to impose permanent cultivation, based perhaps on some ideas derived from the English 'agricultural revolution', without realising the importance of shifting cultivation in maintaining soil fertility and pre-venting erosion. An example of this was the statement by the director of forests in Southern Nigeria that 'all the available forests of Southern Nigeria were in process of rapid extinction, owing primarily to the thriftless system of "shifting cultivation" by which the agricultural popu-lation were constantly burning the forest in order to obtain virgin soil'.[19] Yet in a well-regulated shifting system the burnt forest is allowed to regenerate in a 10–14 year cycle.[20] Conversely there was the possibility that officials would idealise the traditional systems and would regard them as a tropical version of 'Merrie England' as Sir Hugh Clifford seems to have done in Malaya before 1914. Lastly, and perhaps at a lower level of causation, there was too often a lack of imagination regarding development by the men on the spot, even when London was calling for initiatives after the passing of the Colonial Development Act in 1929. This arose partly because senior colonial rulers were often short-term residents (governors seldom stayed in one colony for more than four years) and hence found it difficult to formulate, let alone execute, long-term plans or projects. Their eyes were fixed on promo-tion in an imperial system which was far larger than the colony they were in at any particular time. Hence, pleasing the Colonial Office (which often meant in practice, pleasing the Treasury) was far more important than formulating expensive development plans.

It is not necessary to elaborate any further here on the various impediments to development since they form the substance of much that follows; but since the illusion of vast riches, just waiting to unfold at the touch of the British colonial administrator's wand, proved so alluring and so long-lasting, it is appropriate to end with two contemporary examples, taken from the early days of colonial enthusiasm, before any bitter experiences had a chance to tarnish the glitter. Shortly after the 'scramble' for Africa was over the prospects for development there, and even beyond in Siam and China, seemed dazzling to the *Chamber of Commerce Journal*, which could declare in June 1894 that

Africa . . . presented infinite possibilities. Its peaceful partition by Lord Salisbury and its free opening to our trade was the commer-cial event of our century. . . . If only we would dare to govern the development of such countries meant the renewal of trade on the grandest scale; and the same might be said of our relations with Siam and . . . the southern provinces of China.[21]

A few years later, when Britain was daring to govern, the young Winston Churchill, under-secretary of state at the Colonial Office, toured East Africa, and, after a brief sojourn in Uganda in 1907 declared that

> Uganda is the pearl . . . that Uganda will become one of the greatest centres of tropical produce in the world seems to me to be indubitable.[22]

Uganda did indeed become an important source of cotton in the 1920s and 1930s, though hardly of tropical produce in general; but it also exhibited that characteristic dependence on one crop which distorted the development of so many tropical colonies, and which still remains one of the most persistent problems of Third World countries.

2

The tropical colonies in the mid-Victorian age (1850–70)
Opportunities and problems

THE UNCERTAIN FUTURE OF THE TROPICAL COLONIES

The 1850s make a good starting point for an analysis of the development of the tropical empire, because they were the critical decade during which vital decisions had to be taken as to whether it was worth retaining tropical colonies at all, since the process of granting responsible government to the settlement colonies was in full swing. The economic difficulties experienced by the West Indies after the final ending of slavery in 1838, the high costs (both in money and lives) of maintaining the navy's anti-slave trade patrols off the West African coast, and the generally disease-laden and unpromising aspect of tropical areas, made many people in Britain feel that the retention of tropical colonies (let alone their expansion) was a foolish and costly enterprise. Disraeli's famous comment in 1852 about the colonies being a 'millstone around our necks' captured this mood, but in the event it proved to be only a passing phase.[1] Despite much agonising Britain did not give up its tropical colonies. On the contrary it began a process – slow and hesitating at first – of gradually expanding them, so that by 1885, (even before the scramble for Africa) the size of the tropical empire was very considerably greater than it had been in 1850.[2] The reasons for this were varied and complex and will be considered in more detail for each region in due course.

What then was the inheritance of tropical colonies whose uncertain future the Colonial Office controlled in 1850? In Table 2.1 the tropical colonies are listed with their populations in the early 1850s, and in 1881. In that period of about 30 years their population virtually doubled from around 3.1 million to 6.1 million. The Asian colonies were the most populous at both dates: Ceylon leading the way with a population of a little over 1.7 million in the early 1850s, followed by the Straits Settlements in the Malayan peninsula with just over 200,000 inhabitants and Mauritius with just under that figure. The Asian colonies increased their population from nearly 2.2 million in 1850 to 3.85 million in 1881,

24

Table 2.1 British tropical colonies c. 1850 with population
(in rank of population, by region)

		Population c. 1850	% of total	New additions	Population c. 1881	% of Total
	Caribbean					
1	Jamaica	377,433			580,804	
2	Barbados	135,939			171,860	
3	Brit. Guiana	127,695			257,940	
4	Trinidad	68,600			153,281	
5	Antigua	37,136			34,963	
6	Grenada	32,671			43,757	
7	St. Vincent	30,128			40,548	
8	St Lucia	24,123			40,154	
9	Dominica	22,220			28,211	
10	St Kitts	20,741			29,137	
11	Tobago	14,378			18,051	
12	Nevis	9,571			11,864	
13	Montserrat	7,053			10,296	
14	Virgin Is.	6,689			5,287	
15	Brit. Honduras	4,500			27,452	
16	Turks & Caicos Is.	*included in Jamaica*			4,778	
	TOTAL	918,877	29.5%		1,458,383	23.9%
	Asia			Fiji (1874)	130,270	
1	Ceylon	1,713,738			2,763,984	
2	Straits Settle.	202,540/(1857)			423,384	
3	Mauritius	192,503			370.766	
4	Hong Kong	36,788			160,402	
5	Labuan	1,150			5,833	
	TOTAL	2,146,719	68.9%		3,854,639	63.0
	Africa			Lagos (1861)	75,270	
1	Sierra Leone	44,472			60,546	
2	Gambia	5,502			15,150	
3	Gold Coast	1,200		Protectorate (1874)		
	TOTAL	51,174	1.6%		800,966	13.1
	GRAND TOTAL	3,116,770			6,113,988	100

but their relative share amongst the tropical colonies fell slightly from 68.9 per cent to 63 per cent, although they still remained by far the most important group numerically.

The biggest relative gainers were the West African colonies. With only 51,174 inhabitants in the early 1850s, they had only 1.6 per cent of the population, and were an insignificant group, widely believed to be on the point of abandonment by the British government.

Indeed, with the ending of the American Civil War in 1865, and the belief that this would lead to the final cessation of the slave trade (it did not because slavery continued in Brazil and Cuba almost until 1900)[3] the House of Commons set up a select committee to provide the evidence that the retention of the West African colonies was no longer necessary. To many people's surprise the committee was unable to make the unequivocal recommendation that some of its members had hoped for. As always the facts were found to be much more complicated than most people had thought.

The committee reported on 26 June 1865, as follows:

That it is the opinion of this Committee:

1 That it is not possible to withdraw the British Government, wholly or immediately, from any settlements or engagements on the West African Coast.

2 That the settlement on the Gambia may be reduced by M'Carthy's Island, which is 150 miles up the river, being no longer occupied; and that the settlement should be confined as much as possible to the mouth of the river.

3 That all further extension of territory or assumption of Government, or new treaties offering any protection to native tribes, would be inexpedient; and that the object of our policy should be to encourage in the natives the exercise of those qualities which may render it possible for us more and more to transfer to them the administration of all the Governments, with a view to an ultimate withdrawal from all, except, probably Sierra Leone.

4 That this policy of non-extension admits of no exception, as regards new settlements, but cannot amount to an absolute prohibition of measures which, in peculiar cases, may be necessary for the more efficient and economical administration of the settlements we already possess.[4]

Essentially the committee came up against three intractable, and linked, problems. These were (1) the need to sustain the settlement of Christian Africans around Freetown in Sierra Leone, who had been liberated from the slave ships at sea, and to keep Sierra Leone as long as the slave trade continued; (2) to suppress the slave trade; and (3) to stimulate 'legitimate' trade (basically a trade in palm oil at this time) in order both to finance the administration of the British forts and settlements and to provide an alternative trade to replace the slave trade.

These points were well illustrated in the evidence which Richard Burton, the famous explorer, gave to the committee. First he was reassuring about the economic prospects for the palm oil trade especially from the coast round Lagos, which had been annexed by Britain in 1861.

> *Question*: What is the present amount of the palm oil trade? *Answer*: I believe it is between 2,000 and 3,000 tons.

> *Question*: And do you think it could be raised up to 100,000 tons? *Answer*: I think so.[5]

But on the intractable problems of suppressing the slave trade (an essential pre-requisite for increasing legitimate trade) he was far less reassuring.

> *Question*: Proceeding to the Gold Coast territory, from the Volta to the Assinee, do you consider, with our present objects in view namely, the suppression of the slave trade, as well as the extension of commerce, that we could do that work with fewer ports than the four or five which we now maintain? *Answer*: If the export of slaves continues in demand, and we remove those forts, the Ashantees will necessarily come down to the coast and they will be in a position to export any number of slaves; on the other hand, supposing the country to be relieved of that export of slaves, we might do without them.

> *Question*: So long as the demand for slaves continues, you think that we cannot do without our present forts? *Answer*: Certainly not without Cape Coast, Accra and Annamaboe, and we ought to re-establish the settlement of Addah on the Volta to have two ports at the mouth of the Volta. I was there in 1862, and I found 400 slaves in the barracoon.[6]

Thus, even though Burton was personally in favour of withdrawal, he seemed to recognise that it was not a practical option.[7] Instead the Lagos colony and the Gold Coast protectorate were added to them, so that by 1881 they had over 800,000 inhabitants and comprised 13.1 per cent of the population. They were soon to be joined by Nigeria.[8]

THE WEST INDIES

The most numerous, and the oldest, of the colonies were the West Indian Islands, which had slightly over 900,000 inhabitants in 1850 and nearly 1.5 million in 1881 falling from 29.5 per cent to 23.9 per cent of the total. However, as can be seen from Table 2.1 most of the islands had insignificant populations, and only four of them had more than 100,000 inhabitants by 1881. Of these Jamaica, with over half a million, was much the most populous, followed by British Guiana, Barbados and Trinidad. The West Indian colonies were a source of sore perplexity to

27

the Colonial Office. Their great age as English colonies, going back to the seventeenth century, their vociferous English planter-settlers organised in Parliament in the West India Committee, and their past importance as naval bases, made their abandonment extremely difficult: but the steady decline of their sugar exports after the equalisation of Britain's sugar import duties in 1854, wreaked havoc with their economies. The loss of the protection they had previously enjoyed made it very difficult for them to compete with sugar from Cuba and Brazil, which was still being produced by slave labour until the 1880s.[9]

As the largest and most populous of the island colonies (excluding mainland British Guiana) Jamaica appeared to have more potential in the 1850s than any other except perhaps Trinidad: but with an area of 4,411 square miles Jamaica was well over twice as large as Trinidad (see Table 2.1). An island of great beauty, and a British colony since 1655, Jamaica had long been famous for its sugar production; and yet had a rugged and mountainous terrain which made communication and internal transport difficult, as noted by the novelist Anthony Trollope who visited the West Indies in 1859, to help reorganise their decrepit postal system. Of Jamaica, he wrote that despite its fame for sugar cane

> one may travel for days in the island and see only a cane piece here and there. By far the greater portion of the island is covered with wild wood and jungle – what is there called bush. Through this, on an occasional favourable spot, and very frequently on the road-sides, one sees the gardens or provision-grounds of the negroes. These are spots of land cultivated by them, for which they neither pay rent, or on which, as is quite as common, they have squatted without payment of any rent.
>
> These provision-grounds are very picturesque, They . . . contain cocoa-trees, breadfruit trees, oranges, mangoes, limes, plantains, jock fruit, sour-sop, avocado pears, and a score of others.

In addition there were yams, a West African root which formed the staple food, and occasionally patches of coffee, arrowroot and sugar cane.[10]

The existence of these small-holdings lay at the root of what the European planters (and many in the Colonial Office) perceived to be Jamaica's fundamental economic problem; for they had rendered the former slaves to a considerable extent self-sufficient in food, and hence partly independent of wage-labour, especially at the very low rates being offered by the planters. Hence the sugar planters were afflicted not only with low prices and foreign competition, but with a labour force which was only prepared to work irregularly, and which could not be compelled to turn out at critical periods like planting-time and harvest; though the planters no doubt much exaggerated this reluctance. As a

Table 2.2 Jamaica sugar exports (in tons), 1829/33–1853/55

Yearly average	Tons
1829–33	69,206[a]
1835–38	52,004[a]
1842–45	33,895[a]
1853–55	22,950[b]

[a] To UK only.
[b] To all destinations.

combined result of all these factors sugar exports in the mid-1850s were less than one-third of what they had been in the final days of slavery in the early 1830s, as can be seen from Table 2.2.

Clearly Jamaica's future lay in a diversification away from sugar production to other types of activity. Trollope believed that meat production might be the answer:

I saw various grazing farms – pens they are here called . . . and I could not but fancy that grazing in Jamaica should be the natural and most beneficial pursuit of the proprietor . . . I never saw grass to equal the guinea grass in some of the parishes; and at Knockalva I looked at Hereford cattle which I have rarely, if ever, seen beaten at any agricultural show in England. At present the island does not altogether supply itself with meat; but it might do so, and supply, moreover, nearly the whole of the West Indies. Proprietors of land say that the sea transit is too costly. Of course it is at present; the trade not yet existing; for indeed, at present there is no means of such transit. But screw steamers now appear quickly enough wherever freight offers itself; and if the cattle were there, they would soon find their way down to the Windward Islands.[11]

Here Trollope put his finger on one of the biggest problems facing West Indian colonies; the absence of an adequate transportation system. Local trade was insufficient to make such a system profitable, but without such a system diversification out of sugar was highly unlikely, especially in view of the strong prejudices which most planters still clung to. Trollope states that it would be highly unwise to advise the planters to give up sugar 'if you give such advice in a voice loud enough to be heard, the island will soon be too hot to hold you. Sugar is loved there, whether wisely loved or not. If not wisely, then too well'.[12]

Trollope also complained about the bad state of the roads, and the miserably unsanitary condition of the towns, especially Kingston, the largest town, but not the capital city (which was at nearby Spanish Town). His pessimism was shared by Governor Sir Charles Grey, who in his annual report to the colonial secretary for 1852, wrote that

> The revenue does not fully meet the authorised public expenditure, although within the period of my government that expenditure . . . had been reduced by nearly one third of the whole.[13]

He had reduced it from £304,658 in 1847 to £218,648 in 1850, but owing to an outbreak of cholera, and other necessary expenses, the government's debt had increased substantially, and then stood at 'between £700,000 and £800,000'. With a falling revenue he foresaw difficulties in meeting future interest payments.[13] He was forced to say 'with a feeling of great regret that the colony still remains in a very languishing and depressed condition'.[14]

The island of Trinidad, although smaller and less developed than Jamaica, seemed to offer brighter prospects. Situated about 10° north of the Equator and only a few miles offshore from Venezuela, it was much flatter than Jamaica, although it had some mountains, and hence offered more scope for agriculture and improved communications. However it is quite small, being about 50 miles from north to south, and 37 miles from east to west and comprising 1,863 square miles in all. In the 1850s it was still relatively underpopulated with slightly fewer than 70,000 inhabitants. This created a labour shortage on the sugar plantations, which was being alleviated by the importation of indentured labourers from India, thus building up potential trouble for the future.

Sugar still retained its obsessive predominance in the economy. In 1850 16,837 tons were exported compared with only 1,594 tons of cocoa, the next most important export. Trivial quantities of molasses, coffee, cotton and rum were also exported, but the staples of the future, asphalt from the famous pitch lake, and petroleum were unutilised or undiscovered.[15]

Trollope was much taken with the beauty of the island's scenery, noting in 1859 that it was an island

> great portions of which are but very imperfectly known; of which but comparatively a very small part has been cultivated. During the last eight or ten years, ten or twelve thousand immigrants, chiefly Coolies from Madras and Calcutta, have been brought into Trinidad, forming now above an eighth part of its entire population; and the consequence has been that in two years, from 1855, namely to 1857, its imports were increased by one-third, and its exports by two-thirds.[16]

Nevertheless, much of the island was still underdeveloped and Trollope spent most of his time in and around the capital, Port of Spain. He added that

> a tour through the whole of Trinidad would richly repay the trouble, though indeed, it would be troublesome. The tourist must

take his own provisions, unless, indeed, he provided himself by means of his gun, and must also take his bed. The mosquitoes, too, are very vexatious.[17]

In spite of a minuscule annual revenue of £88,660, the governor, Lord Harris, was able to report in his despatch of 10 February 1851, that

I have been enabled to effect a very decided improvement in the condition of the roads, which . . . will in a short time become general to the whole island.[18]

He had also been repairing decayed bridges and had taken precautions lest the 'fearful scourge' of cholera should spread to the island from Jamaica:

A sanitary inspector has been appointed, who is in constant communication with the police, in order to enforce the laws bearing on the subject. The wardens have been instructed to be prepared to establish hospitals and dispensaries in their wards at a moments notice, and a good supply of medicine has been secured.[19]

Perhaps not surprisingly he had been able to do little about education and reported that

I am sorry that I am not able to give a very satisfactory account of the general progress of education, the scarcity of efficient teachers being the principal impediment, and which must continue until a good normal school be established.

He regretted that he could not make proper statistical returns, and hoped that when a census had been taken, and a postal service was 'punctually at work', he would be able to remedy the defect. This was written eight years before Trollope's visit on behalf of the Post Office. Despite the paucity of his resources, Lord Harris ended by noting the rising sugar exports, and a belief 'that the material prospects of the island are good'.[20]

The largest underdeveloped colony in the Caribbean was British Guiana, occupying a chunk of the mainland of South America, just to the east of Venezuela. Situated just to the north of the Equator and comprising some 83,000 square miles, British Guiana was nearly as large as the United Kingdom (which is approx. 94,000 square miles), but was largely unexplored and very sparsely populated, with a recorded population of slightly under 128,000 people in 1851. These would have been virtually all resident on the coastal strip, and probably did not include the small, scattered Amerindian population in the remote interior. Like the Caribbean Islands British Guiana was a sugar colony, and produced little else. As late as 1951, 85 per cent of the country was virgin forest, and a further 10 per cent inland mountain savannah, so that in 1850 it is doubtful if the settled coastal belt comprised more than 2 per cent of the land area. Originally settled by the Dutch in the seventeenth century, who drained some of the coastal plain, it was occupied by Britain in 1796, and formally annexed in 1815.

Rather unexpectedly, Trollope was much taken with British Guiana (also then known as Demerara) during his short visit in 1859:

> At home there are prejudices against it I know. They saw that it is a low, swampy, muddy strip of alluvial soil, infested with rattlesnakes, gallinippers, and mosquitoes as big as turkey-cocks; that yellow-fever rages there perennially; that the heat is unendurable . . . There never was a land so ill spoken of – and never one that deserved it so little.[21]

He liked it so much, he said he would happily settle there and described it ecstatically as 'the one time and actual Utopias of the Caribbean Seas – the Transatlantic Eden'. His subsequent description hardly bore out this high praise, but he believed that there was tremendous agricultural potential inland, which would be realised when the programme of settling indentured labourers from India had been completed.[22] This had been initiated by Governor Sir Henry Barkly (1848–53) and brought moderate prosperity to the colony until the 1870s, based on rising sugar exports. In 1850 sugar exports had amounted to 37,351 hogsheads (Trollope said a hogshead of sugar was supposed to weigh one ton, but seldom did) and planters told Trollope that one million hogsheads a year could be produced in the country, which was equivalent to some 90 per cent of the world's sugar production at that time. That the world market would expand proportionately Trollope seemed to have no doubt, and the obsession with sugar continued to dominate British Guiana for many years to come.

The towns of New Amsterdam and Georgetown, the capital, impressed Trollope:

> Georgetown to my eyes is a prepossessing city, flat as the country round it is, and deficient as it is – as are all the West Indies – in anything like architectural pretension. The streets are wide and airy. The houses, all built of wood, stand separately, each a little off the road; and though much has not been done in the way of their gardens – for till the great coming influx of Coolies all labour is engaged in making sugar – yet there is generally something green attached to each of them.[23]

New Amsterdam, on the other hand, though it impressed Trollope as 'clean and orderly' had much decayed in trade owing to a sandbar across the mouth of the river Berbice on which it is situated. It was a town in which 'three persons in the street constitute a crowd, and five collected for any purpose would form a goodly club'; yet signs of renewed vigour were not lacking, for in his trip from Georgetown to New Amsterdam, Trollope had travelled for fifteen miles on a railway.[24]

Signs of economic improvement were also commented on by the governor, Sir Henry Barkly, in his despatch to the colonial secretary, sent in May 1851, where he noted that prospects were not as bleak as had been suggested by a recent Commission of Inquiry into the State and Property of the Colony.

> In reporting upon the condition and prospects of colonial agricul-
> ture . . . I myself entertain no doubt that a very decided improve-
> ment has manifested itself in the position of the planting interests.

and he ended his report by saying

> On the whole, whatever prognostications of ill the Commissioners
> of Inquiry may have indulged in . . . I must avow myself thankful
> that the colony has made much greater progress than could have
> been anticipated in so comparatively brief a space of time, and also
> far more confident than I should then have ventured to express
> myself as to its future prosperity.[25]

The last of the major colonies, and much the most densely populated, was Barbados, where in 1850 nearly 136,000 people occupied an island only slightly larger than the Isle of Wight. Barbados is 21 miles long from north to south and 14.5 miles broad at its widest point. It comprises 166 square miles and had an average population density of about 820 persons per square mile in 1850. The Barbadians believed this was denser than China and it was certainly very different from the West Indian colonies previously described, all of which were fairly thinly populated.[26]

Lying 13° north of the Equator and about 100 miles to the east of St Vincent, the nearest of the Windward Islands, the climate of Barbados is said not to be as oppressively hot as the other islands. It had a special importance as the oldest British West Indian colony, and the head-quarters of the British West Indian naval and military garrisons. It had apparently been discovered by the Spanish in 1518, who removed some of the native Indian population as slaves to their colony of Hispaniola (now the Dominican Republic). This policy may have been continued, because the island was said to be uninhabited by 1536. The Spaniards established no settlements and the island was still uninhabited when the first English settlers arrived in 1627. Subsequently Barbados was intensi-vely occupied by planters and their slaves from West Africa and was famous as a sugar island as early as the 1640s.[27]

When Trollope visited it in 1859, he commented that

But for the heat its appearance would not strike with any surprise a Englishman accustomed to an ordinary, but ugly agricultural country. It has not the thick tropical foliage which is so abundant in the other islands, nor the wild, grassy dells. Happily for the Barbadians every inch of it will produce canes; and, to the credit of the Barbadians, every inch of it does so.[28]

Communications were much better than in the larger colonies, the roads being 'excellent, but so white that they sadly hurt the eye of a stranger'[29] being made from the limestone subsoil which is prevalent in the island. The capital Bridgetown, did not impress Trollope. It was

much like a second or third rate English town . . . the streets are narrow, irregular, and crooked but it had good, respectable well-to-do shops, that sell everything, from a candle down to a coffin, including wedding-rings, corals, and widows' caps[30]

He thought the land was being strained by encouraging the growth of sugar by the use of imported guano manure, which he believed injured the soil and the sugar. Despite what he regarded as the healthy pressure of land shortage which forced the populace to work on the sugar plantations, he believed that the standard of living was quite high, commenting that

numerous as are the negroes, they certainly live an easier life than that of an English labourer, earn their money with more facility and are more independent of their masters. A gentleman having one hundred and fifty families on his property would not expect to obtain from them the labour of above ninety men at the usual rate of pay, and that for not more than five days a week. They live in great comfort, and in some things are beyond measure extravagant.[31]

It is doubtful if this optimistic picture was very accurate. It is somewhat at variance with the sombre comment of Governor Sir W.M.G. Colebrooke in his despatch to the colonial secretary a few years earlier (27 August 1851), where he stated that the effects of recent changes in the taxation system, whereby more of the revenue was raised by duties on imports, was

to throw the burden of the taxes for the most part on the consumption of the labouring classes, and, excepting where export duties are imposed, to exempt the staple products of the colonies in a great degree from taxation, and from the large amount of remittances to absent proprietors deriving their incomes from the colonies, and from the limited investments of capital in local

34

improvements, the population are held stationary in their condition, while increasing in their numbers.[32]

However, in some other respects, Barbados was improving. Trade had grown between 1949 and 1851 and the revenue had

yielded a considerable surplus on the receipts for the preceding year; and as there is every prospect that the revenue of the present year will be equally productive, I have recommended to the Assembly a reduction of the duties which press upon colonial trade.[33]

Here his high Victorian free trade principles came into conflict with his desire to improve social welfare, for in his next despatch he went on to note that, although more money had recently been spent on churches and education, and even though

this was much in advance of the other colonies, it was still inadequate to meet the growing requirements of the population, and it is important that the absent proprietors should be generally aware how very disproportionate are their own contributions towards objects so essential to the welfare of the colonies, from whence they derive their resources.[34]

When it is realised that the total expenditure of the Barbadian government amounted to only £47,060 in 1850, (about 35 pence a head) of which £23,083 went on the judiciary, the police and the prisons, the decision to reduce taxation seems all the more remarkable. The miserly sum of £1,265 spent on education sharply underlies how limited were mid-Victorian concepts of welfare.[35]

The remaining British colonies in the West Indies consisted of a chain of small islands strung out in the shape of a boomerang, and extending from the Virgin Islands, near Puerto Rico in the north down to Tobago, some twenty miles from Trinidad in the south. Most of them were mountainous and covered with luxuriant vegetation. All produced some sugar, but few had much potential for development in the days before cruise liners and jet aircraft made tourism a viable prospect. The more northerly islands were known as the Leewards and the more southerly as the Windwards. As can be seen from Table 2.1 only three of these islands supported more than 30,000 people in 1850. These were Antigua in the Leewards and Grenada and St Vincent in the Windwards.

According to Trollope, Antigua's main asset was the possession of a fine harbour:

Neither is Antigua remarkable for its beauty. It is approached by an excellent and picturesque harbour, called English Harbour, which in former days was much used by the British navy; indeed I believe it was at one time the headquarters of a naval station. Premising, in the first place, that I know very little about harbours, I would say that nothing could be more secure than that.[36]

Travelling southwards Trollope compared the British Islands of Dominica and St Lucia unfavourably with the larger French colonies of Guadaloupe and Martinique, with their cleaner and more prosperous looking towns. Continuing to St Vincent, which was 'green and pretty, and tempting to look at', he commented that

> this island is said to be healthy, having in this respect a much better reputation than its neighbour St Lucia, and as far as I could learn it is progressing – progressing slowly, but progressing – in spite even of the burden of Queens, Lords and Commons.[37]

This latter reference was to the constitutional arrangements, which existed in all the old British West Indian colonies, which Trollope much disliked. In these constitutions the Queen was represented by the governor, the 'Lords' by his nominated council, and the 'Commons' by an assembly, which was sometimes elected and sometimes appointed, and sometimes a mixture of both; but which was always mainly representative of the small minority of European planters. These assemblies often had powers to block legislation, particularly where it affected taxation; and were almost universally abolished in the later nineteenth century, except in Barbados, the Bahamas and Bermuda. Paternalistic English governors and civil servants were considered to be more efficient and progressive, and in the conditions prevailing at the time, probably were; though by definition could do nothing to encourage indigenous political initiative or experience.[38]

Some 70 miles south of St Vincent is Grenada, where Trollope again commented on faded glories.

> Grenada is also very lovely, and is, I think, the headquarters of the world for fruit. The finest mangoes I ever ate I found there; and I think the finest oranges and pineapples.

He admired the capital, St Georges, rather more than most West Indian towns, and noted that the island had been

> fertile also, and productive – in every way of importance. But now here, as in so many other spots among the West Indies, we are driven to exclaim, Ichabod! The glory of our Grenada has departed . . . the houses, though so goodly, are but as so many Alhambras, whose tenants now are by no means great in the world's esteem.[39]

That final sentence might perhaps be a fitting summary on the condition of Britain's West Indian colonies in the 1850s.

ASIA AND THE PACIFIC

The most important British tropical colonies at mid-century were those in Asia. Of these Sri Lanka (known before achieving independence in 1948 as Ceylon) was by far the most populous and developed. A large lozenge-shaped island, about 265 miles long from north to south, and about 140 miles across at its widest point from east to west, it is situated between 6° and 10° north of the Equator, and only about 20 miles from the tip of the Indian sub-continent to which it is almost linked by a chain of small islets known as Adam's Bridge. The interior of the island is occupied by hilly and mountainous country of great beauty, with rugged, jungle-clad mountains rising to nearly 8,000 feet in the south-centre. Here the climate is temperate or sub-tropical, and this region is the centre of the famous tea plantations, which have long been the backbone of the country's economy, but which did not yet exist in the 1850s.[40] The coastal plains extend inland for 20 to 50 miles, and are densely forested in the south, but give way to dry, sandy savannah lands and scrub in the northern province. The island is very fertile and has been the centre of advanced civilisations for thousands of years. Ancient irrigation works supported extensive cities, whose impressive remains have still not been fully revealed by modern archaeological investigation. The magnificent Buddhist temples at old capital cities, such as Anuradhapura (c. 437 BC) and Polonnaruwa (c. AD 1050) in the north-centre of the island, are some of the world's most impressive examples of early architecture and sculpture.

So the Europeans who conquered Ceylon were not imposing their rule on a backward and primitive people but on one with very ancient cultural traditions, though less advanced in terms of material technology than their European rulers. The British were only the last of a succession of European conquerors, although they were the only ones to establish full control over the mountainous interior. The coastlands were occupied by the Portuguese from 1518, until they were gradually driven out by the Dutch in the early seventeenth century. The Dutch held the island until 1796, when having been conquered by Napoleon, the British regarded their colonies as legitimate prizes in war. Some of the colonies seized at that time, like Java, were returned to the Netherlands at the peace of Paris in 1814–15, but Ceylon, Cape Colony in South Africa, and some places in the Malayan Peninsula were kept by the British, who were specially concerned to retain them as bases on the sea route to India. The magnificent harbour at Trincomalee on the northeast coast of Ceylon was specially important for this purpose, since all ships heading for ports in eastern India, such as Madras or Calcutta, had to pass the eastern coast of Ceylon. Moreover, Colombo was an important re-victualling and training centre, after the long voyage from Cape Town, before the opening of the Suez Canal in 1869.[41]

The Dutch East India Company had derived a profit from its monopoly of the export of cinnamon, but this trade declined in the early nineteenth century, and the British administration sought to undermine the power of the local chiefs and particularly the rulers of the inland kingdom of Kandy, by destroying the traditional agrarian system, which had been based on communal land-ownership and labour-services (known as *rajakaria*), rendered by peasants to chiefs. Private ownership of land was gradually introduced and the economy was monetised.[42] The central hill country was opened up to coffee production by European planters in the 1840s. Coffee production rose from 2,093 tons in 1839 to 16,000 tons in 1850, largely as a result of the equalisation of British import duty on coffee in 1846, which allowed coffee from Ceylon into Britain at the same duty as that from the West Indies (i.e. 6d per pound) whereas previously coffee from Ceylon and paid 9d a pound.[43] Between 1840 and 1847 some £3 million was invested in coffee, but this form of development, while good for the customs revenue, also helped to prepare future problems; for not only were the profits largely exported to Britain, but a large labour force of Tamils from south India was brought into Ceylon to work the plantations. These workers could not be integrated into traditional Sinhalese society; but when the coffee plantations were struck by disease in the 1880s, the workers remained in Ceylon to work the new tea plantations. The resentment caused by this development continued in the 1980s when the Tamil demand for an independent state in northern Sri Lanka erupted into a violent confrontation which threatened the country's economic future. It would not be appropriate to enter into the rights and wrongs of this dispute here, but there can be no doubt that its origins lie in a somewhat cavalier colonial attitude to economic development in the mid-nineteenth century.

The growth of the coffee export trade underlined the inadequacy of transport and communications in the 1850s. In his despatch to the colonial secretary of 22 April 1851, the governor, Sir G.W. Anderson, referred to the government's programme of road construction, which he said was being actively pursued, although he admitted that 'the only metalled road throughout is . . . from Colombo to Kandy'; and that a 'general scheme of roads, to be hereafter constructed, should, as soon as possible, be laid down . . . in order to quicken and economise the transit of merchandise'. He added, more pessimistically, that

There is a desire for a railroad from Colombo to Kandy, it would, so far, be a vast improvement, but still only partially, as benefiting only one or two of the great planting interests. It was not, however, on this ground that I declined to recommend to your lordship the guarantee of five per cent that was much pressed on me; but that I could by no means anticipate any such surplus revenue that would warrant the colony in coming under so serious and enduring a pledge.[44]

Clearly the governor's faith in the island's future was limited, and it was not until 1867 that Kandy was linked to Colombo by rail; and not until the last quarter of the nineteenth century that an effective railway system was built in Ceylon.[45]

The next most populous tropical colony in Asia consisted of the four small and scattered settlements on the Malayan coast, known as the Straits Settlements; and with a population hardly above 200,000 (1857) it was still very insignificant compared with Ceylon. The British were not yet taking much interest in it, and were only beginning to comprehend its immense economic potential, which was to make it by far the most valuable of the tropical colonies by 1914. This is hardly surprising since the Malay peninsula in the early nineteenth century has been described as a

scantily populated, jungle-covered wilderness politically divided into a series of small states of varying degrees of independence and isolation. Settlement was restricted to small, traditionally organised and often temporary Malay coastal and riverine *kampongs* (rural settlements) to a few diminutive mining centres in the foothills and to a shifting aboriginal population elsewhere.[46]

Transport was by river and a few single paths. Exports were confined to very small quantities of tin, gold and spices. Yet the region had immense strategic important, for the whole of the rapidly growing trade between India and China, which was an East India Company monopoly until 1833, had to pass through the narrow Straits of Malacca between Malaya and Sumatra, both sides of which were controlled by the jealous Dutch East India Company, until the British seized Malacca from them in 1795 (after the Netherlands had been conquered by France). British interest in the area in fact dated from a slightly earlier period, when a British trader, Francis Light, persuaded the Sultan of Kedah to cede the island of Pahang to the East India Company in 1786, primarily to provide a naval base for British squadrons operating in the Bay of Bengal. In protecting Madras and Calcutta, they found bases on the east coast of India were useless when the monsoon was blowing from the north east from October to May, since they could not get out of harbour.

Neither the possession of Pahang nor Malacca opened the straits, but this was achieved in 1811, when the British occupied Java and all the other Dutch possessions in Indonesia. Under the energetic governorship of Sir Stamford Raffles, the whole area was rapidly opened up to a free and growing trade, and Raffles confidently expected that these conditions would continue after the Peace of 1815. He was bitterly disappointed when Britain decided to build up the restored kingdom of the Netherlands as a bastion against future French aggression by restoring its East Indian possessions to it, including Malacca. Desperate to find a way of keeping the straits from again being closed up by the Dutch monopolists, Raffles persuaded the Sultan of Johore to cede to him the small, the sparsely populated island of Singapore in 1819, on which he built a free-trade port. With the Dutch still in Malacca, relations remained strained until 1824, when a treaty between Britain and the Netherlands effected a new division: the Dutch surrendered Malacca in exchange for a few British settlements in Sumatra. Henceforth the British yielded economic and political control of Indonesia to the Dutch, but kept the trade routes to China unimpeded by their gradual control over, and absorption of, Malaya – a process which was not completed until 1909. The British had two other small outposts on the coast. An area of Pahang called the Dindings, came with Malacca, and a stretch of coast opposite Pahang, called Province Wellesley had been ceded in 1800.[47]

In 1850 these scattered settlements were still part of the possessions of the East India Company and were administered (rather reluctantly) from Calcutta. In 1858, they passed to the India Office, when the East India Company was taken over, but it was not until 1867 that they were transferred to the Colonial Office. In the 1850s they were still small and undeveloped, though the entrepôt trade of Singapore was growing very rapidly. Its population, which had only been about 150 when Raffles arrived, had reached 57,421 by 1857 and was growing by leaps and bounds.[48]

Singapore had developed as the entrepôt for the expanding trade not only of India and China, but of the whole of Southeast Asia – a trade which had grown rapidly after Britain established trading stations off the Chinese coast at Hong Kong in 1842, and off the Borneo coast at Labuan in 1846. In 1833 the total value of Singapore's trade had been £3.625 million, but by 1860 this had risen to £11.6 million.[49] Singapore was also attractive to Chinese merchants, who settled on the island, and brought compatriots in to establish agricultural plantations for export crops. The most popular of these were black pepper and gambier, a plant from whose leaves and branches a dyeing and tanning agent was extracted. These two plants were grown on different parts of the same plantation, having complementary labour requirements. They were both exported, mainly to Britain. By 1851 there were 24,220 acres of gambier and 2,614 acres of black pepper growing on Singapore island,

and since the crops were exhausting to the soil, the Chinese cultivators were spreading into the neighbouring Malay state of Johore – a process which would in time help to draw it ever more closely into the British orbit. Nutmegs, cloves and sugar were also being grown for export, but were not very profitable, and over 75 per cent of the cultivated area of Singapore Island was devoted to gambier and pepper. The island is, however, only about 25 miles wide from east to west, and 13 miles long from north to south. Its significance lay not in its own potential for development, but in the haven it supplied for those whose capital could finance development all over Malaya.

Pahang played a similar, although less important role. An even smaller island than Singapore (a mere 15.5 by 10.5 miles) it also was attractive as a base for Chinese and European merchants financing agricultural development in the mainland colony of Province Wellesley, only about three miles across the water from Pahang. The northern part of Province Wellesley was occupied by Malay padi-rice growers, who supplied Pahang with food, while the forests and swamps farther south were being exploited by European and Chinese sugar planters. By 1858, eleven large European plantations comprised about 10,720 acres and the Chinese had another 1,000 acres. Sugar was exported to Britain and rum to India and Burma.[50]

Finally, between Pahang and Singapore was the old Dutch colony of Malacca, about 250 miles south of Pahang and about 130 miles north of Singapore. After the East India Company took over in 1825, it became 'a quiet backwater' with a hinterland of nine squabbling little Malay states, the Negri Sembilan (which means the nine states in Malay). In 1831 the company became involved in their petty quarrels and soon 'there began a series of wars between the jealous little states which kept the area in ferment for the next forty years, and prevented the Malacca merchants from exploiting their hinterland', until the 1870s, when the Negeri Sembilan became British protected states and accepted British residents. These were supposed to 'advise' the local rulers, but increasingly moved into a controlling position.[51]

In the 1850s Malacca's entrepôt trade, and its traditional tin-mining were in decline, but enterprising Chinese were beginning to develop a new product. This was tapioca, a root which was grown for export to Britain, in the form of dried flour, flakes or pearls. Grown by shifting cultivation, much jungle was cleared for it, and by 1882, some 93,000 acres had been planted. This, however, was the peak and the tapioca acreage had declined to about 10,000 acres in 1911.[52]

Malaya's subsequent prosperity rested on exports of tin and rubber but these were not developed in a major way until the 1880s and 1890s. In the 1850s Malaya was still very much 'an underdeveloped estate' and one moreover to which Britain had not yet laid more than a shadowy claim.

After the Straits Settlements, the next most populous colony in the eastern group was Mauritius with slightly over 192,000 inhabitants in 1850. A smallish island of roughly triangular shape, Mauritius is about 39 miles long from north to south and about 29 miles from east to west, and lies at a latitude of about 20° south, some 500 miles east of Madagascar. It was apparently uninhabited when visited by the Portuguese explorer, Mascarenhas, in 1505. The Portuguese claimed it, but did not settle, and the island was taken for a naval base by the Dutch in 1598, who named it Mauritius after their stadholder, Count Maurice of Nassau. The Dutch eventually abandoned the island in 1710, and in 1715 it was occupied by the French, again as a naval station to support the empire they were seeking to establish in India. Throughout the eighteenth century French fleets operating from Mauritius were a continual menace to British merchant and naval craft in the Indian Ocean, and in 1810 a military expedition captured the island. The Peace of Paris (1814) confirmed British possession.[53]

Mauritius is dramatically mountainous, well watered and has a fertile soil. The coastal lowlands are hot and humid, but there is a fertile central plateau at an altitude of between 1,000 and 1,500 feet where the climate is less oppressive. All kinds of tropical crops and fruits will grow in Mauritius but when the British took over, French planters, using slaves from Africa, had already established sugar as the dominant crop, which continued throughout the whole period of British colonial rule. However the abolition of slavery by Britain in 1834 created a temporary crisis since there was still enough unoccupied land in the island (as in Jamaica) for the ex-slaves to 'squat' as self-sufficient peasant farmers and to refuse to work for wages on the sugar plantations. It was reckoned in 1840, that of 30,000 freed slaves not more than 5,000 could be induced to work as field labourers for wages.[54] The planters' problems were solved by the importation of indentured labourers from India, for whom even the hard labour on the sugar plantations was preferable to the poverty they had to endure at home. By 1845 there were nearly 82,000 Indian immigrants in Mauritius, and sugar production was well above its level in the days of slavery, and was still rising. An average of 97,500 tons was exported between 1853 and 1855.[55]

With the equalisation of the British sugar import duties after 1846, Mauritius, with its expanding supply of cheap Indian labour, enjoyed a certain advantage over the West Indies; and a colony, which had been occupied initially for strategic reasons, began to develop a prosperous economy of its own – albeit one still dangerously dependent on the one crop as was recognised by the new governor, John Higginson in his first despatch to the colonial secretary in 1851. He wrote that 'sugar is now our only article of export' and hoped that the introduction of silk cultivation would be successful, 'as presenting a fresh channel for the development of agriculture, and offering suitable employment to many, chiefly women and children, who are incapacitated from engaging in more laborious occupations'.[56]

Higginson was remarkably optimistic about the future of Mauritius, even though he admitted that 'no new public highways have been constructed', and there were 'new lines of communication which might be opened with great advantage to some districts, but I fear they must be deferred for the present'. This referred to a shortage of funds, although he had just cut public expenditure by £18,091 since the previous year, and hoped to reduce taxation in the year to come. He certainly shared that prevalent Victorian scale of priorities which placed development far far below 'economy'. Nevertheless he ended his report on a hopeful note,

> On the whole I earnestly trust that the tide of fortune has turned, that the termination of the disasters that have pressed so heavily on the colony, has been hailed with increased energy and exertions on the part of all classes, and that the year 1850–51 . . . may not inaptly be characterised as one of recovery of progress and of promise.[57]

Britain's remaining Asiatic colonies in 1850 were the small islands of Hong Kong and Labuan. Hong Kong had been acquired in 1842 at the close of the 'opium war' (1839–41) in which Britain and other western powers forced the Chinese empire to open various ports to foreign trade, and to allow foreign merchants certain privileges. Of these ports Shanghai and Canton were by far the most important, and it was to enforce British rights in Canton and southern China that Hong Kong island was annexed.[58] The island is less than a mile from the Chinese mainland and about 80 miles southeast of Canton. It is only about 11 miles across at its widest point from east to west, and from 2 to 5 miles broad from north to south. It has the finest deepwater harbour on the China coast between Shanghai and Indo-China, and its possession was of great value to Britain for securing the valuable and expanding China trade, which was also an integral part of the India trade, since British imports from India were partly financed by exports of Indian opium to China. In 1840 it was reckoned that of total British imports from India and China, worth £9.6 million, some £3.4 million was paid for by exports of opium to China, even though this trade was supposed to be illegal![59]

When Britain occupied Hong Kong island in 1841 there were only a few fishermen and opium smugglers there, but the British founded the harbour town of Victoria, as a free-trade port, and the population increased very rapidly. In 1850 it was still under 37,000 but by 1881 this had risen to 160,402 – a very rapid rise, but still a far cry from the four million who crowd the territory today. Growth was probably slowed before 1860 because Hong Kong harbour was still subject to disturbances on the mainland. This was ended in 1860, when some land opposite Hong Kong island, known as the Kowloon peninsula, was ceded to Britain, thus insulating the whole harbour. Between 1859 and 1866 the shipping entering the harbour rose from 625,536 to 1,063,252 tons.[60]

For a tropical region Hong Kong has a relatively mild climate, especially in winter, but the island is very mountainous, so that its economic potential for long lay in its importance as an entrepôt for the huge trade of China and the western Pacific, rather than for itself – though its post-1945 industrial and commercial development has shown that under certain, admittedly rather special, conditions, even very small territories can achieve remarkable development.

Labuan's history has been very different. This little island, comprising only 35 square miles, is 6 miles off the northwest coast of Borneo, and was ceded to Britain by the Sultan of Brunei in 1846 for use as a naval base and refitting port for ships engaged in suppressing piracy, and in the Borneo trade. It seems to have been uninhabited at the time, and had only 1,150 inhabitants in 1850. It did however have coal deposits and these became important after 1850, when steam ships began to replace sailing vessels in the far eastern trade. Now part of Malaysia, its original significance was in enabling British influence to be spread along the north coast of Borneo by Sir James Brooke, the renowned 'white rajah' of Sarawak, who obtained that territory by cession from the Sultan of Brunei in 1841, and whose descendants retained it until 1946.[61]

WEST AFRICAN OUTPOSTS

Finally, the last group of tropical colonies were the British settlements on the west coast of Africa. These were, going southeastwards along the coast, the Gambia colony at the mouth of that river, the Sierra Leone colony on the peninsula of that name, and the string of forts and trading stations along the Gold Coast. The earliest of these colonies dates back to the seventeenth century, and they had all been used in the slave trade since their establishment until the abolition of the trade in 1808. The economic importance of these colonies was so minimal in the 1850s that discussion of their condition and development potential can be more conveniently left to the next chapter where the results of the 'scramble' for Africa in the 1880s and 1890s are considered.

3

Early development theory and the spread of the empire, 1870–85

SLOW EVOLUTION OF THEORY AND POLICY

Theories and attitudes to colonial development unfolded only very slowly and uncertainly in this period, which is not surprising, considering that it was a time when British attitudes to the empire as a whole, and to the tropical colonies in particular, were still confused and incoherent. On the one hand, there was what might be called the 'unofficial orthodoxy' of the Manchester school of laissez-faire dogmatism, based on the worship of free trade, which believed that, provided Britain was powerful enough to enforce free trade (or something approaching it) on tropical regions, formal colonial rule was unnecessary: and on the other hand there was the whole tribe of traders, merchants, missionaries and colonial administrators who had a vested interest in maintaining the tropical colonies, and in some cases in expanding them. Since possession is said to be nine-tenths of the law it is perhaps not surprising in retrospect that those who represented the vested interests were ultimately successful; and that the advocates of abandoning the colonies (the settlement colonies as well as the tropical ones) were eventually defeated – as much by the course of events – as by any determined new policy of expansion.[1]

However, the mere possession of colonies, or their retention to prevent someone else from acquiring them, as happened in Malaya, Nigeria and elsewhere, was soon discovered to be inadequate. Colonies cost money to administer, even on the pinch-penny principles so beloved of the Victorians, and so, even at the lowest level of policy, and ignoring any humanitarian or moral considerations about the need to combat poverty and 'backwardness', there was a necessity to increase the economic capacity of the colonies simply, in the first instance, to raise the revenue necessary to pay for their administration. Initially, this was not thought to be a very serious problem, because the believers in the Manchester school idea had a ready-made development theory. The expansion of foreign trade would lead to a quickening of economic life in the region affected. Production of tradeable goods would increase, a

45

division of labour would take place, a customs or taxation revenue would become available to finance government and public works, and the whole question of development could be safely left to the beneficent activity of the inhabitants of the region itself. It would not be necessary for the British government to do anything, except remove obstacles and obstructions to trade. Trade between the temperate and the tropical regions of the world assisted the development of both. Many Victorians believed that this was, in Lord Palmerston's words in 1842 'the dispensation of Providence', and that trade between the two regions existed so that

> the exchange of commodities may be accompanied by the . . . diffusion of knowledge – by the interchange of mutual benefits engendering mutual kind feelings . . . It is, that commerce may go freely forth, leading civilization with one hand, and peace with the other, to render mankind happier, wiser, better.[2]

In citing this passage from Palmerston, John Gallagher and Ronald Robinson in *Africa and the Victorians*, pointed out that it epitomised the authentic mid-Victorian outlook on the world, and went on to expand that view in its economic aspect:

> the trader and missionary would liberate the producers of Africa and Asia. The pull of the industrial economy, the prestige of British ideas and technology would draw them also into the Great Commercial Republic of the world. In time 'progressive' native groups within the decaying societies of the Orient would burst the feudal shackles and liberalise their political and economic life. Thus the earlier Victorians hoped to help the Oriental, the African and the Aborigine to help themselves. Many would be called and all would be chosen.[3]

The wide currency of views like these, helps to account for the reluctance with which British officials and politicians regarded the expansion of formal British colonial rule in the tropics. As long as it seemed possible to believe that the economic benefits of free trade could be obtained without the costs of colonial government, they clung to that faith. It was but gradually that bitter experience taught them that only when peace, stability and internal order had been secured, could free trade be established – and even then they probably never understood that its spin-off would be destructive and traumatic before any of the intended benefits could be expected.[4]

A few examples of this changing mentality must suffice to illustrate a wholesale transformation in the attitudes of the British official classes, from the prevailing scepticism of the mid-century to the imperial enthusiasm of the 1880s. Disraeli's opinion of the colonies in 1852, as 'mill

stones round our necks' has already been cited. W.D. McIntyre maintains that this was untypical of his real attitude, and that Disraeli had
always been in favour of close imperial ties; and that even his letter to
Lord Derby in 1866 was untypical of his real views. In this letter Disraeli
said

> Power and influence we should exercise in Asia . . . but what is the
> use of these colonial deadweights which *we do not govern* . . . Leave
> the Canadians to defend themselves; recall the African Squadron,
> give up the settlements on the west coast of Africa, and we shall
> make a saving which will, at the same time, enable us to build ships
> and have a good budget.[5]

McIntyre believed that Canada and West Africa were special cases for
Disraeli and that when, in his celebrated Crystal Palace speech of 1872,
he advocated 'reconstructing as much as possible of our colonial empire',
he was returning to his long-felt idea, which had now come back into
fashion. Even so it must remain doubtful how much real interest Disraeli
had in the British colonies. Yet he sensed that public opinion had
changed, and a rather bombastic imperial policy was pursued by his
government between 1874 and 1880, with the annexation of the Boer
Republic of the Transvaal and an expensive war in Afghanistan.[6]

Meanwhile, on the Liberal side, where scepticism about the empire
was more firmly entrenched, the course of events overseas had already
brought changes of opinion amongst the Colonial Office ministers in
Gladstone's government of 1868–74. The Earl of Kimberley, who was
colonial secretary from 1870 to 1874, and especially his under-secretary,
Edward Knatchbull-Hugesson, were responsible for a major change in
policy towards the tropical colonies, which led to important extensions of
British rule in the Gold Coast, Southern Nigeria, Malaya and Fiji.
Gladstone probably never altered his belief that 'lust for territory' was
one of the 'greatest curses of mankind'; or that when Knatchbull-
Hugesson urged a policy of colonial expansion on the House of
Commons, he was talking 'bunkum' but he nevertheless acquiesced in
Kimberley's forward policy in the tropics.[7]

John Wodehouse, first Earl of Kimberley (1826–1902) and a Norfolk
landowner, seems to have possessed the usual Liberal attitudes when he
became colonial secretary in 1870 at the age of 44. He thought that new
colonies would simply be 'multiplying the points open to attack', and that
France had been weakened by her Algerian and African empire.
Ironically, he had hoped that no British government would 'ever be mad
enough to embark on so extravagant an enterprise as the establishment
of a West African empire' in 1873, but he was soon to be responsible for
initiating major extensions of British rule in the Gold Coast and
Southern Nigeria.[8] In 1871 he also thought it 'very natural that the

Australians should wish to see the British flag flying in the Fijis', and on hearing a rumour that the Germans might be going to establish a protectorate in Malaya, he rapidly authorised the establishment of British 'residents' in some of the Malay States, writing to Prime Minister, Gladstone on 10th September 1873 that it would be 'a serious matter if any other European power were to obtain a footing on the Peninsula'.[9] It is not surprising that the imperial enthusiast Sir Charles Dilke thought that Kimberley was 'a wise man, even though he *talks* like a chattering idiot'.[10]

It seems that Kimberley's change of view was to some extent the result of the constant pressure applied by his expansionist under-secretary, Edward Knatchbull-Hugesson (1829–93, created first Baron Brabourne in 1880). Knatchbull-Hugesson believed that Britain was too involved in West Africa, Malaya and the Pacific Islands to withdraw, and that an extension of colonial rule was the only recourse. McIntyre notes that he stated this 'more clearly and persistently, almost passionately one feels, than anyone else' and that his persistence 'therefore played an important part in the new approach of the Colonial Office in the early 1870s'.[11]

Finally, the changing attitude of the permanent under-secretary, Sir Robert Herbert (1831–1905) was also important. A cousin of the Conservative colonial secretary, the Earl of Carnarvon, he had also for a short time, in 1855, served as private secretary to Gladstone; so he had wide contacts in official circles, which he assiduously cultivated in the various London clubs to which he belonged. He also served for an unusually long time, from 1871 to 1892, so had plenty of opportunity to build up a consistent view. However, he was so calm, imperturbable and diplomatic that historians have found it difficult to assess his real views. Blakely notes that he opposed annexation in Fiji and Swaziland, but favoured it in New Guinea and Matabeleland; but McIntyre believes more positively that Herbert's flexible and pragmatic approval was an important factor in the development of an expansionist policy in the tropics, especially in West Africa and Malaya.[12]

Underlying these gradual changes of attitude amongst politicians responsible for policy was the persistent pressure exercised by Britain's changing role in the world economy, and by the emergence of rival powers who increasingly began to challenge Britain's world trading supremacy. With the ending of the American Civil War in 1865, the unification of Germany in 1871 and the speedy recovery of France after its defeat in the Franco-Prussian War (in 1871), industrialisation spread rapidly in all three countries; and by 1880 Britain's position as the world's trade leader was being seriously threatened. The need to retain old markets and seek new ones was thus ever present in the minds of policy-makers even if seldom explicitly stated.[13]

This pressure was exacerbated by Britain's continually mounting defi-

Table 3.1 Balance of payments of the United Kingdom, selected years
1850–1913 in £m. All items are net balances.

Year	Merchandise trade	Overseas investment earnings	All other invisible trade	Bullion and specie	Overall balance on current account
1850	−19.6	+9.4	+21.8	−1.0	+10.6
1855	−25.9	+12.9	+34.7	−7.8	+13.9
1860	−45.5	+18.7	+48.0	+2.5	+23.7
1865	−51.2	+24.1	+68.4	−6.4	+34.9
1870	−57.5	+35.3	+76.8	−10.5	+44.1
1875	−90.5	+57.8	+89.6	−5.6	+51.3
1880	−121.1	+57.7	+96.4	+2.6	+35.6
1885	−98.5	+70.3	+90.7	−0.2	+62.3
1890	−86.3	+94.0	+99.6	−8.8	+98.5
1895	−126.5	+93.6	+87.8	−14.9	+40.0
1900	−167.0	+103.6	+109.1	−7.5	+37.9
1905	−155.9	+123.5	+120.1	−6.2	+81.5
1910	−142.7	+170.0	+146.7	−6.7	+167.3
1913	−131.6	+199.6	+168.2	−11.9	+224.3

Source: B.R. Mitchell and Phyllis Deane, *Abstract of British Historical Statistics* (Cambridge, 1962), pp.333–4.
+, excess of receipts; −, excess of payments.

cit in the balance of trade (though not in the balance of payments) in this period, which rose from a deficit of £19.6 million in 1850 to £121.1 million in 1880, as shown in Table 3.1.

In 1880 the surplus on invisible trade (at £96.4 million) fell significantly below the deficit on merchandise trade for the first time, and it was only the ever-growing surpluses from the profits of overseas investment, which enabled Britain to maintain its surplus on the balance of payments, which at £35.6 million was significantly below its 1875 figure of £51.3 million. Thus two new forces joined with many others to encourage Britain to change its attitude to overseas possessions – the need to secure new export markets and the need to find new areas for overseas investment. Admittedly these did not need to be colonies, indeed most of Britain's overseas investments went to the United States, South America and Europe, but instability in areas outside British control, such as the crisis in Argentina in 1890, which nearly brought down the great Baring Brothers bank, and sent severe shock waves through the City, must have made the need for safe British colonies in which to invest seem much more attractive. In the 1860s 36 per cent of British investments abroad were in the Empire and by 1911–13 this had risen to 46 per cent.[14] The desire for tropical colonies was also increased by changes which were taking place in British industrial technology, the rise of new industries, and their associated raw materials, which had increasingly to be imported from the tropics. Before petroleum oil was found in significant quantities in the Near East (mainly after 1900) the ever-growing quantity of British industrial machinery had to be lubricated by vegetable oils, of which palm oil from West Africa and the Far East was much the most important component. Palm oil was also much used in the tin-plate industry and by soap makers, whose production rose from about 90,000 tons a year in the early 1850s to 260,000 tons a year in 1891, led by William Lever (later Lord Leverhulme) who established his well-known Port Sunlight works near Liverpool in 1889, having started commercial soap production in Warrington in 1877.[15]

The margarine industry was another growth point which used palm-kernel and groundnut oil from the tropics, while the burgeoning retail food market demanded ever-increasing quantities of sugar, coffee, cocoa beans, oranges, lemons, bananas and countless other minor tropical products (the growth in Britain's trade with the tropical colonies between the 1850s and the early 1880s is given below (see pages 62–9). With French and German colonial rivals who did not believe in free trade, avidly seizing colonial possessions in the 1880s and 1890s (the French took most of West Africa and Indo-China, while the Germans seized Cameroon, Togo, Tanganyika and Namibia in Africa and Samoa in the Pacific) the British feared that the sources of tropical raw materials would all be swallowed up by their rivals if they did not take effective steps to secure (and expand) the areas in which British merchants had long been active. Hence the mounting pressure to secure Britain's share before it was too late, which lay behind the 'scramble' for tropical colonies in the 1880s and 1890s.[16]

Even as early as 1870 this anxiety about raw material supplies was expressed by *The Economist*:

> We have often remarked upon the great importance of a good supply of raw materials of our chief manufacturing industries as lying at the foundations of our mercantile superiority; the opening up of new colonial possessions is more important from this point of view than as forming new markets for our manufacturers.[17]

Britain's leaders were also becoming conscious of a slippage in economic power, which was almost inevitable (at least relatively) in relation to the extraordinary world dominance which Britain had enjoyed around 1850, when it had produced two-thirds of the world's coal, half its iron, five-sevenths of its steel, two-fifths of its hardware, half of its traded cotton cloth, and 40 per cent of its traded manufacturers. As rivals grew and overtook Britain, its own rate of industrial growth was also slowing down. In 1870 British steel production had been twice that of Germany, but by 1910 Germany's was more than than twice that of Britain. Between 1840 and 1870 British industrial production had grown at an annual rate of 3 per cent a year, but by 1875–94 this had slowed to 1.5

per cent a year, and British manufacturers were beginning to lose their share of the unprotected home market – a sure sign of uncompetitiveness. This sense of lessening power added a 'geo-political' dimension to Britain's search for new colonies.[18]

It is sometimes argued that economic motives cannot have been a very important cause of colonial expansion because the tropical areas which became British colonies were not very rich or developed at the time they came under British rule; but this rather misses the point – it was the fact that British businessmen and officials thought that these regions were potentially rich if they could be developed, which provided the economic component of Britain's imperial expansion.

Of course the more enlightened imperialists did not see the extension of British rule as a one-way process. Naturally, they expected it to benefit Britain but they also believed that it would be advantageous for the colonies as well. However it was one thing to believe that British rule would in some way benefit tropical regions, but quite another to have a clear view about how this might be brought about in terms of development. This also emerged slowly and unevenly during the period. The attitudes of early imperialists like Sir Charles Dilke, who wrote *Greater Britain* in 1868, after a round-the-world tour of British colonies were strongly tinged by racialism, although the origin of the later 'trusteeship' ideas can also be found there. Dilke believed that economic development would flow from trade, which followed the flag, and that British rule was essential for its health. He wrote that 'were we to leave India or Ceylon, they would have no customers at all; for falling into anarchy, they would cease at once to export their goods to us and to consume our manufactures'.[19] India and Ceylon were in fact the only tropical areas which Dilke thought it worthwhile to visit in 1867, but by 1880 he was speaking of the Niger territories in West Africa as 'new Indias of the next generation'.[20]

Similarly, the Cambridge professor, Sir John Seeley, whose book *The Expansion of England*, published in 1883, did a great deal to publicise and enthuse the growing imperialist sentiment, largely ignored the tropical colonies. He wrote that 'when we inquire into the Greater Britain of the future we ought to think much more of our Colonial [i.e. English settler colonies] than of our Indian Empire'.[21] Insofar as he thought of the development of tropical areas, his vision was still limited to India. This view was, however, already out of date in 1883. Eleven years earlier, in 1872, Edward Knatchbull-Hugesson had minuted on a letter from Sir John Pope Hennessy, the governor of West Africa to Kimberley that

England has sown the seeds of civilisation and Christianity upon these coasts, and whether for the furtherance of these great objects, or for the mere development of the resources of a country *evidently teeming with underdeveloped wealth*, her continued presence and action is most desirable in the interests of West Africa and of the world. (Our italics.)[22]

Here we also see the seeds of Lord Lugard's famous 'dual mandate' idea – that Britain had a duty to undertake the development of tropical areas, not only for their own good, and for Britain's, but for the sake of world-wide economic advancement.

So, despite all the hesitations of the 1860s and 1870s, these were decades when Britain made major extensions to its tropical empire. The most important of these were in West Africa, Malaya and Fiji.

EXPANSION IN WEST AFRICA

At first, West Africa looked like one of the least promising areas for expansion, owing to its unhealthy climate and vigorous warlike peoples, especially the Asante behind the Gold Coast and the Yoruba behind Lagos. The abolition of the slave trade by Britain in 1808 had been regarded by many people as a signal for the relinquishment of the West African colonies, and there were many influential people in Britain who had favoured that. The difficulty was that Britain had committed itself to the abolition of the slave trade and this required the operation of naval squadrons in the Atlantic to intercept illegal slavers. Such squadrons needed bases; and nor was that the end of the matter for it soon became obvious that liberated slaves could hardly be returned whence they had come (mostly from the Nigerian coast in the early nineteenth century) since they would be immediately re-enslaved and re-exported. Some place in Africa was needed where they could be resettled as free people. This place was the Sierra Leone peninsula which, with its magnificent harbour at Freetown (the best in West Africa), became the most important, as well as the most populous, British colony on the coast (prior to the 1890s).[23]

The Sierra Leone peninsula is situated about 8° north of the Equator, and sticks out into the Atlantic from the mainland. It is 24 miles long from north to south and about 10 miles wide on average from west to east. It had various advantages as a colonial location. It is almost an island, since the Bunce river and the Waterloo creek separate it from the mainland on the northeast, and the Calmont creek, with its surrounding mangrove swamps, forms a boundary on the southeast. There is a strip of land only about four miles wide between the Waterloo and Calmont creeks, and even today there is only one road from the peninsula into the interior. This road was guarded by a small British settlement called Waterloo, a village in which liberated slaves (known as 'recaptives') were settled.

The port of Freetown was also very important on several major international trade routes. About 3,500 miles south of Britain, it was a valuable stopping place for ships to revictual and obtain fresh water on the long trips around the Cape of Good Hope to India, Malaysia or Australasia before the opening of the Suez Canal in 1869. It is also about 3,500 miles from Rio Janiero on the direct route from Europe to Brazil or Argentina, or around Cape Horn into the Pacific.

As a site for settlement, it was less satisfactory. The peninsula is largely taken up by the Sierra Leone mountains, which are mostly over 1,000 feet high, and have several peaks of over 2,000 feet. They rise fairly steeply from Freetown and provide some residential sites which are considerably cooler than the oppressively hot and humid city and the coastal lowlands; but the mountains have a rocky and infertile soil and are covered by a densely impenetrable 'bush' or jungle. Consequently very few settlements have been possible in the interior of the peninsula and the villages in which the recaptives were settled are nearly all on the narrow coastal strip. As a consequence agriculture was always unimportant in the colony which had to import much of its food by trade with the neighbouring peoples. Fortunately the large number of navigable estuaries and rivers near Freetown made this relatively easy by canoes and small boats.[24]

The unusual history of the foundation of Sierra Leone as a British colony shaped all subsequent development in a unique way, making Sierra Leone quite different from all other British colonies in West Africa. Originally Freetown was founded by a private company, the Sierra Leone Company, in 1787. It was one of those strange evangelical creations in which it was hoped to combine philanthropy with profit. The slave trade and slavery not yet having been abolished in 1787, the company was founded to deal with a different problem. Many slaves in the southern states of America had fought in the British army during the American Revolution and had been promised their freedom after the war. The British defeat was an embarrassment which necessitated the shipment of these people to one of the surviving British colonies in America, namely Nova Scotia. In that cold and somewhat inhospitable environment they were naturally miserable, and many drifted to London, where they were reduced to poverty and despair. The aim of the Sierra Leone Company was to settle the 'Nova Scotians', as they later became known, and the 'black poor' of London in Sierra Leone. After many vicissitudes they succeeded and some slaves who had revolted in Jamaica, and were known as 'Maroons', joined them in 1800.[25]

To these original settlers were soon added a stream of 'recaptives', and by 1850, the total population of the colony was over 44,000 and growing rapidly, since the slave trade, though now illegal, had by no means ceased. Nearly one-third of the population lived in the town of

Freetown, which had a recorded population of 16,679 in 1850.[26] By this time the 'settlers', the 'Maroons' and the 'recaptives' were blending into a new Europeanised African people known as Creoles. Clearly scope for development in such a small colony was very limited, but it carried on an extensive trade with a hinterland which included not only the present area of Sierra Leone, but much of the coast to the north in what is now the Republic of Guinea. Tropical hardwoods formed part of this trade but its most important component was groundnuts (peanuts) which were cultivated by the peoples in the river valleys to the north of Freetown, and were brought to Freetown for export to Europe, primarily to France, where groundnut oil was used as a cheap substitute for olive oil.[27]

This trade had flourished in the 1840s, but received a setback from the French Revolution of 1848 as the governor, Norman MacDonald, reported in his despatch to the colonial secretary, of 18 August 1851.

> 1847 was the most prosperous year . . . from 1840 to 1850 both inclusive; and . . . that prosperity was in great measure, if not wholly, attributable to the vigour with which the ground-nut trade of the colony and neighbourhood was prosecuted by our resident merchants under contracts with foreigners, principally French houses.
>
> In 1848, however, the French Revolution, which has unhappily been productive of such wide-spread destruction to trade and commerce, totally paralysed that flourishing trade . . . Had nothing occurred to intercept the progressive improvement of the ground-nut trade of this colony, I know I am within bounds when I assert that it would have, by this time, quadrupled itself in extent and value. I am happy, however, to be able to point to the fact of the increase in the imports of 1849 and 1850 over those of 1848, as an indication of the return of confidence and of the improvement in that trade, which is recovering itself, though slowly.[28]

Since Sierra Leone relied on bringing produce from its hinterland to export to Europe (increasingly palm oil and palm kernels after 1850), its governors spent a great deal of time and energy in making treaties with the neighbouring tribal rulers in an effort both to abolish the slave trade and to keep the 'legitimate' trade routes open. These latter were constantly being blocked by petty quarrels and warfare. During 1851 and 1852 Governor MacDonald made nine such treaties with rulers stretching from the Rio Pongo country (now in Guinea) down to the Sherbro country on the southern coast of Sierra Leone. However, all this was in vain, and gradually between 1861 and 1881 Britain annexed the whole of the present coast of Sierra Leone; but even this failed to keep the trade routes open, and partly in response to French expansionary pressure, from both the north and the east, Britain extended a protectorate over what was left of the hinterland in 1896.[29]

The next most populous British settlement, the Gambia colony, was much smaller and less significant than Sierra Leone, having a population of only about 5,500 in 1850. Situated at the south of the Gambia river, one of the great natural waterways into the interior and navigable for 250 miles upstream by boats with a draught of up to ten feet, the colony appeared to have great trade potential but this had never been realised. At 13° north of the Equator and in the savannah belt, the Gambia had a much drier and more pleasant climate than any other British West African settlement, with an average rainfall of only about 40 inches a year, nearly all of which falls between June and October. However, it was still very unhealthy for Europeans, especially in the only town, Bathurst, which was situated on the low and swampy island of Banjul, where mosquitoes abounded (Bathurst resumed its original name of Banjul shortly after the Gambia became independent in 1965).[30]

British slave traders had been active in the river since the 1660s, but had finally abandoned their fort on James Island in 1779, after it had been repeatedly captured and recaptured in wars with the rival French up the coast in Senegal. However, with the abolition of the slave trade in 1808, a British naval base to patrol the coast was needed and the little settlement of Bathurst was founded in 1815. The colony failed to develop the expected trade up the river, partly because the hinterland did not have much to offer (small quantities of beeswax, ivory, gum and hides were exported in the 1840s) and partly because constant tribal warfare up the river disrupted trade and agriculture. It was not until after a British protectorate was established in 1889, that peaceable conditions returned, and the cultivation of groundnuts, on which the later economy was built, began to assume importance.

Some 'recaptives' had been settled near Bathurst before 1840, and their interests, plus the obstinate refusal of the slave trade to wither away, obliged Britain to maintain the colony, although there were many who believed it should be abandoned, or traded to France for something more useful. The Parliamentary Select Committee on British holdings in West Africa in 1844, however, reported that the Gambia river possessed advantages for trade 'far beyond those of any other British settlement on the coast of Africa'.[31] This was a considerable exaggeration, but the region did have potential for economic development, as was shown by the subsequent history of French Senegal; but Britain's failure either to secure the hinterland, or to exchange the colony with France, meant that this potential was never realised. The Gambia became a narrow river-strip colony cut off from its natural hinterland, but this was still far in the future in the mid-Victorian epoch.[32]

The final West African colony comprised the string of British forts and trading stations on the Gold Coast, (now Ghana) with an official population of a mere 1,220 in 1850; although many thousands of the adjacent coastal peoples had accepted a form of British protection under an agreement made by their chiefs in 1844, known as the 'Bond'.[33] The British forts were hangovers from the slave trade and their future looked fairly uncertain at mid-century; but contrary to appearances, events turned out very differently. With the unexpected expansion of British control over the hinterland, between 1872 and 1902 a prosperous colony, based on the export of cocoa beans, came into existence, which was to become in many ways the most successful of all the British tropical colonies.[34]

The Gold Coast lies between 5° and 6° north of the Equator, and directly south of Britain at a distance of about 3,150 miles by air, but some 4,000 miles by sea. A narrow strip of savannah land extends along the coast separating the dense rain forest of the interior and making it much drier and less oppressively hot and humid than its immediate hinterland. This is what had made it an attractive site for the forts of the European slave trading companies in the seventeenth and eighteenth centuries, which stretched along the coast for some 250 miles. The western end of the Gold Coast was at the entrance to the Aby lagoon in the Ivory Coast, and its eastern end was formed by the delta of the Volta river and the Keta Lagoon.[35] During the heyday of the slave trade more than 30 forts belonging to eight European countries had been scattered, intermixed, along the coast, but at the beginning of 1850, only three countries, Britain, the Netherlands, and Denmark still retained their forts, and during 1850, the Danes sold their forts to the British. By this time a considerable geographical concentration had occurred, with the British having four main forts in the central portion of the Gold Coast extending from their headquarters at Cape Coast eastwards to Accra. These two were the most important places. Between them were two smaller towns at Anamabu, a little to the east of Cape Coast, and Winneba, mid-way between Cape Coast and Accra. The Danish forts, which were transferred to Britain in 1850 were all on the eastern coast. They comprised the important castle of Christiansborg on the edge of Accra, and four small places stretching eastward to Keta.

The Dutch forts were concentrated on the western part of the coast and were centred on the historic former Portuguese settlement of Elmina, the first European outpost on the Gold Coast. The Dutch had seven forts in all, stretching westwards from Kormantin to Axim, but of these only Elmina and Secondi were of any real significance.[36] It was widely believed by the British that the Dutch carried on an illegal slave trade with the powerful inland kingdom of Asante, and that as long as this continued, the peaceful settlement of the region and the development of legitimate trade would be impossible. This was one reason why

Britain attempted a gradual withdrawal from the Gold Coast after 1865; but British merchants and missionaries had been involved in the affairs of the region for too long to make such a policy viable. Instead the British bought the Dutch forts between 1868 and 1872.[37] This soon led to a war with the Asante, in which a British military expedition sacked their capital Kumasi, in 1874. In the same year the southern part of the Gold Coast became formally a British colony. Further quarrels with the Asante finally led to the establishment of a British protectorate over Asante and the Northern Territories in 1902.[38]

The making of the 'Bond' in 1844 led to an uncertain situation between that date and 1874, during which it was not clear whether the coastal people, the Fanti, were British subjects or not. Technically they were not, but Lieutenant-Governor James Bannerman seemed to assume that they were in his despatch to the colonial secretary of 7 April 1851.

> Upon the subject of population, where no census has been taken and especially throughout such an extensive country, it would be impossible to state anything with certainty regarding actual numbers. My own opinion is that there has been exaggeration upon this point, as the country is far from being thickly populated; although taking into account the immense space over which our jurisdiction extends, even without exaggeration the number must be great.[39]

He believed that future prospects were promising. Health was improving, due he thought to the recent introduction of quinine; agriculture was improving, although trade had been depressed in 1840, this was

> more on account of over trading and excess of competition than any falling away of the resources of the country which are steadily increasing.[40]

Bannerman was in a good position to know. The son of a Scottish father and an African mother, he had been trading in a large way in Accra for some 40 years, and had married a daughter of the Asantehene (King) of Asante in 1826.[41]

By 1880 the Gold Coast protectorate had been combined with Lagos to form a new Crown colony on the model of the Straits Settlements. Officially this was still supposed to be a 'protectorate', although nobody really knew what that meant; but during 1874 an important change had been made in British policy, summarised thus by McIntyre:

> While British sovereignty was not extended in the Gold Coast the Legislative Council of the new colony (which included both Lagos

and the Gold Coast forts) was empowered to legislate for the protectorate, and the queen was proclaimed the sole authority on the Gold Coast. The colonial Government, instead of confining itself to police and judicial functions, as before, would also comprehend health, education, roads, economic and social regulation. However singular the exact legal position became, it might be said that the protectorate was 'annexed administratively' to the colony.[42]

This was followed shortly after by measures by Governor Strachan of the Gold Coast to abolish domestic slavery. These were not fully effective, but the internal slave trade was reduced and the lot of domestic slaves was said to have improved.[43] By these moves Britain declared her ultimate intention to try to develop the 'teeming underdeveloped wealth' to which Knatchbull-Hugesson had drawn attention, and which subsequent events were to show was by no means illusory, if not perhaps quite so extensive as optimists had hoped. The role of exaggerated illusions in stimulating colonial advance has also been demonstrated by Kanya-Forstner for French expansion into West Africa after 1875.[44]

Britain did not have any formal colonies in Nigeria before 1861, when Lagos was annexed, but British merchants and missionaries had been active in several places on the coast around Lagos and Calabar in Eastern Nigeria as well as inland at Abeokuta, about 50 miles north of Lagos. A British consul, John Beecroft, had resided in the Spanish island of Fernando Po in the 1840s, to keep a watch over British interests and to help coordinate the antislave trade squadrons, and further extensions of British rule occurred soon after. In 1851 the British arranged for the deposition of the ruler of Lagos for engaging in the slave trade and established a virtual protectorate; and when his successor also proved unreliable, Lagos was annexed as a colony in 1861. This was the first step in an inexorable British advance inland which was completed in 1906.[45]

THE INCORPORATION OF MALAYA

In Malaya a major extension of British control also took place between 1871 and 1877, with the appointment of British 'Residents' in the vital western coastal states between Malacca and Pahang. Going north from Malacca they were Sungai Ujong (one of the 'Negri Sembilan' or Nine States), Selangor and Perak. All were undergoing rapid development based on tin mining (largely in Chinese hands) timber extraction and agricultural expansion, and the need for law and order and internal peace was urgent, especially following riots in the tin fields in 1875 which threatened the investments of Singapore capitalists. Officially 'advisers' to the local rulers, the Residents soon became the real executive heads of their states as the Malay rulers came to realise the economic and political advantages of collaboration with them. In Cowan's words:

> the result of Colonial Office policy on the one hand and Malay acquiescence on the other was that an unsanctioned system of direct government by Residents developed which, however successful it may have been, was completely at variance with the *de jure* position. The gulf between practice and theory was only widened by the so-called Federation Agreement of 1895. For what resulted was not a Federation of Malay States, but a union with a British direct central government. This was the system under which the Federated Malay States were administered until the outbreak of the Japanese War.[46]

Since Chinese and European merchants, planters and the miners were spontaneously, 'opening up' the interior of Malaya in the late nineteenth century, it was not necessary for the colonial government, to have any very well worked out policies for economic development, other than trying to encourage and facilitate what was already happening. In his report on the Straits Settlements for 1881, the governor, Sir Frederick Weld, commented that

> attention may fairly be drawn to the continued prosperity and progress of the Colony. The population during the past ten years has been shown to have increased 37 per cent. . . . Then, too the volume of trade has grown . . . to about £34,557,124, while ten years ago the corresponding returns of trade show the value to have been £21,584,852 . . . and as the native states continue to develop their resources, the export returns of the Colony must show a marked expansion of trade. . . . Or again, as further signs of progress, it is only necessary to look to the increased revenue. . . . The Government has not failed to avail itself of this prosperous condition of the Colony. A large number of public improvements have been undertaken, and more are in course of preparation. The public departments are being strengthened where most needed. Sanitation, which carries with it great expenditure, is receiving much attention . . . the material prosperity of the Colony is beneficially affecting all classes, and . . . the promise of the future is as full of hope as the retrospect of the past is satisfactory.[47]

In fact, the sums being spent on public works and education were very small and two of the major items were a new hospital for Europeans and a new prison; but it is clear that the rising prosperity of Malaya was beginning to create the conditions in which a better balanced development policy could emerge.[48]

OUTREACH IN THE PACIFIC: FIJI

There were also important developments in the Pacific area, where the Fijian islands were annexed and became a Crown colony in 1874, after attempts to control them by informal means had failed, as had efforts to prevent the kidnapping of labourers (known as *kanakas*) from the New Hebrides, the Solomons and other islands to work in the sugar plantations which a few European settlers had established in Fiji. The Fijian islands had not initially been attractive to the British for their economic potential, but once the decision to annex had been taken the need to facilitate economic development moved to the foreground of policy.[49]

The Fijian archipelago consists of more than 300 islands and islets, of which about 205 are inhabited. They lie between 15° and 20° south of the Equator and about 1,650 miles due east of Brisbane in Queensland, Australia. There are only two islands in the group which are large enough to have any real economic significance, although some of the smaller ones are now popular with tourists. The largest island is Viti Levu, which is 98 miles long from east to west, 67 miles broad from north to south, and comprises 4,053 square miles. The capital city, Suva, is located on the southeastern tip, but it is a colonial creation, having been built in the 1880s to replace the traditional capital Levuka, which is on a small island, Ovalau, a few miles off the eastern coast of Viti Levu. The sugar plantations, which have long formed the backbone of the Fijian economy, are mainly centred in the south and east of Viti Levu. The island, though rugged and mountainous, with peaks rising to 5,000 feet, is fertile and well watered, with a heavy rainfall (up to 10 to 12 feet a year) and a climate which is fairly temperate for the tropics. The average temperature is 24°C.

The other large island is Vanua Levu, which is about 40 miles northeast of Viti Levu, and is 117 miles long from east to west and 30 miles broad from north to south and comprises 2,130 square miles. It is not so densely populated or so developed as Viti Levu. Apart from sugar, the islands grow coconuts and export copra, and they also grow a wide range of tropical fruits and food crops, like bananas, maize, pumpkins and beans, as well as small quantities of rubber and cotton.

The influx of European sugar planters, the illegal trade in *kanakas* and the rivalry between local chiefs and tribes threatened to reduce the islands to anarchy and chaos. To avoid this, one of the chiefs, Thakombau who had become a Christian in 1857, offered to cede the islands to Britain in 1874 and, after some hesitation, his offer was accepted. He had previously unsuccessfully offered the islands to the

United States in the early 1860s, and fear that they, or France or Germany might move in, helped to spur Britain's acceptance. In making his offer of cession Thakombau wrote to Queen Victoria, saying that he was ceding the land to her

> to exercise a watchful control over the welfare of his children and people, who having survived the barbaric law and age, are now submitting themselves, under her Majesty's rule, to civilisation.[50]

In accepting the cession, the colonial secretary, the Earl of Carnarvon, had drawn up a list of nine arguments in favour of cession, which were mostly humanitarian and strategic, but which also included, as number eight:

> Probably ultimately paying – like other groups of islands like Bahamas . . . which do pay even with their Assemblies. But if governed as Crown Colony it may pay better.

Nevertheless, he was anxious not to give the impression that Britain's motives were sordid, and on a letter from Sir Hercules Robinson, the governor of New South Wales, he added the notes

> But not a question of money. Mission of England. A sprit of adventure – fill up the waste places of the earth.[51]

However that may have been, the governor, Sir Arthur Gordon, soon found that it was necessary to put the colony's economy on a firmer foundation, and since the Fijians were not anxious to work in the sugar plantations, began a process of importing Indian indentured labourers, which led by the 1950s, to Indians becoming the majority community, with all the problems that has caused in recent times.

In the 1880s that was of course far in the future, but in his farewell speech to the colonists on relinquishing the governorship, Sir Arthur could point to major achievements since annexation in 1875, and a bright future. He noted that

> capital has been already introduced, to a far larger extent than most people are aware, and the results of its introduction will, during the next two years, be of a very marked character.
>
> We have an abundant supply of labour, obtained at a cheaper rate than any other free labour in the world.
>
> Three steamers now ply regularly between this port and those of Sydney, Auckland, and Melbourne, while two seagoing steamers are employed in interinsular communication, and several small ones in private hands keep up a constant communication with Suva and Rewa.
>
> Our judicial system has been excellently framed, and is adminis-

tered by a Judge of higher standing and repute than a young colony is often able to obtain.

Thanks to Ordinances introduced by that Judge, we have now a good public school in Levuka, and have provided for the creation of industrial schools for natives in another part of the group.

The revenue in 1875 was but £16,000. Last year it exceeded £67,000, and is estimated for the present year at over £80,000, whilst the Customs revenue during the same period has increased from £8,000 to £22,000.[52]

The basis of all this progress was the increase in production and trade consequent upon the establishment of peaceful and orderly conditions, and the immigration of Indian labourers.

Gordon noted that between 1876 and 1879, exports had increased from £113,459 to £191,540, and imports from £94,806 to £142,212.[53] This was all very satisfactory as far as it went, but the colony was commencing a development path which was to lead to a dangerous dependence on the export of one crop, sugar, with all the instability and unbalanced economic structure which can result from such a situation. That was, however, still some way into the future when Gordon surveyed Fiji's prospects in 1880, and was probably not foreseen by him.

So it can be seen that even before the European powers engaged in their celebrated 'scramble' for African colonies between 1885 and 1900, British colonial rule in the tropics had already become quite significant, and Britain had become committed to a policy of expansion which was probably already irreversible.

THE GROWTH OF COLONIAL TRADE, 1852–84

The economic significance of these developments cannot easily be measured accurately since a number of key indicators such as the amount of capital which had been invested, the value of domestic production and changes in labour productivity (to name only a few) are unavailable; however, to some extent the growth in overseas trade may be taken as a proxy, which gives at least an indication of the direction in which affairs were moving. By comparing the value of tropical colonial trade in the early 1850s with the early 1880s, it is possible to see that, although this was still not very significant when compared with the trade between Britain and temperate countries in Europe and the Americas, it had still shown a very healthy growth; and since most of the tropical countries were still very underdeveloped the long-term prospects for continued growth looked favourable for most of them.

The increases in the exports and imports of seven of the leading tropical colonies between the early 1850s and the early 1880s are set out

Table 3.2 The growth of the value of imports and exports (less bullion) 1852–4 to 1882–4, selected colonies (annual averages, £)

Colony	1852–4	1882–4	Increase	%	Average annual growth rate %
Exports					
Ceylon	1,382,015	3,292,625	1,901,610	137.6	4.6
Mauritius	1,256,624	3,942,333	2,685,709	213.7	7.1
British Guiana	1,132,857	2,901,000	1,768,143	156.1	5.2
Jamaica	919,921	1,500,333	580,412	63.1	2.1
Barbados	890,131	1,217,666	327,535	36.8	1.2
Trinidad	428,600	2,636,333	2,207,733	515.1	17.2
Straits Settlements	a	14,233,256	–	–	–
Imports					
Ceylon	746,857	4,011,239	3,264,382	437.1	14.6
Mauritius	1,025,312	2,875,666	1,850,354	180.5	6.0
British Guiana	909,555	2,029,667	1,120,112	123.1	4.1
Jamaica	943,721	1,504,000	560,279	59.4	2.0
Barbados	681,027	1,158,000	476,973	70.0	2.3
Trinidad	518,907	1,738,333	1,219,426	235.0	7.8
Straits Settlements	a	15,964,895	–	–	–

[a]Very small and included in East India Co. trade figures.
Source: Appendices 1 and 2

in Table 3.2, where it can be seen that growth occurred in all these colonies, though it was much more pronounced in Asia than it was in the older West Indian colonies. It is true that these trade increases started from a fairly low base, with average annual exports ranging from nearly £1.4m in Ceylon to only £428,600 in Trinidad in 1852–54, with only Mauritius having imports worth over £1 million; but the increase was not the result of inflation, rather it was based on a genuine growth in production and trade. Indeed, the period was one of deflation rather than inflation, for the general level of British agricultural and industrial prices fell by about 10 per cent (the Rousseaux index) and food and raw material prices by about 12 per cent (the Sauerbeck-Statist index).[54] This means that, had the colonial trade figures for 1882–84 been measured in the prices of the early 1850s, the increase would have been even greater than it was when recorded in current prices. These figures are also somewhat lower than the officially recorded trade figures, which include the import and export of bullion; but since bullion frequently represented capital movements, it has been removed from the trade figures where possible (that is in the import and export totals; it was not possible to subtract it from the figures relating to Great Britain's share of trade). The only exception to the removal of bullion was in relation to the Gold

Coast, where gold exports largely represented gold production, and so have been retained in the figures in later chapters.

Since exports were the principal means of paying for imports, it was the increase in the import figures which was the most significant, especially as imports played a dual role in the tropical colonies: as articles of necessity or luxury they improved the standard of living, and acted as 'inducement goods' to producers, whilst as articles of taxation (via customs duties) they provided the main source of governmental revenue, which might be used for long-term development. As can be seen from Table 3.2 the relative growth in imports between the tropical colonies varied very widely. While the West Indian colonies of Barbados and Jamaica (the old sugar colonies) recorded only a modest annual growth of imports of 2.3 and 2 per cent respectively, the more recently developed sugar and cocoa island of Trinidad was increasing its imports by an impressive 7.8 per cent a year. This achievement was, however, dwarfed by the remarkable growth of imports into the Asian colonies of Ceylon and Malaya (the Straits Settlements). Ceylon's imports grew at 14.6 per cent a year to stand at just over £4 million a year in 1882–84; while the Straits Settlements had surged ahead and were importing nearly four times as much (just under £16 million a year in the same period). The growth rate here (although it cannot be calculated) was almost phenomenal since imports in the 1850s had been trivial.

These increases were financed by imports of capital and by a massive expansion of exports. In the Straits Settlements this was based primarily on the export of tin (the rubber industry had not yet begun). There were also considerable increases in the exports of Ceylon (mainly coffee) and Mauritius (mostly sugar). The increases in Malayan trade were particularly impressive because much of the country had still not yet been opened to settlement and production in the early 1880s.

Further details of the growth in trade are given in Tables 3.3 and 3.4 where the ten leading exporting and importing colonies are listed in rank order in 1852–54 and 1882–84. It is noticeable that none of the West African colonies appear as significant exporters or importers in the 1850s and that their contribution was still modest in the early 1880s, although the exports worth £616,000 which left Lagos annually were a herald of the significant growth that would be forthcoming once the interior of Nigeria had been opened up to trade. Between 1882–84 and 1910–12 Nigeria's exports grew at 26.4 per cent a year and imports by 39.2 per cent a year!

Impressive though the growth of trade was it still retained considerable structural weakness, in that most of the colonies were crucially dependent on a narrow range of export staples; although the range of imports was naturally much more varied. Table 3.5 shows that, of the seven leading exporters in 1882–84, five were almost totally dependent

Table 3.3 Value of exports (excluding bullion) by colony (in rank order), 1852/54–1882/84

	1851–4			1882–4	
Rank	Colony	£	Rank	Colony	£
1.	Ceylon	1,382,015	1.	Straits Settlements	14,233,256
2.	Mauritius	1,256,624	2.	Mauritius	3,942,333
3.	British Guiana	1,132,857	3.	Ceylon	3,292,625
4.	Jamaica	919,921	4.	British Guiana	2,901,000
5.	Barbados	890,131	5.	Trinidad	2,636,333
6.	Trinidad	428,600	6.	Jamaica	1,500,333
7.	British Honduras	379,533	7.	Barbados	1,217,666
8.	St Vincent	193,537	8.	Nigeria (Lagos)	616,000
9.	Gambia	192,521	9.	Gold Coast	390,333
10.	Antigua	184,720	10.	Sierra Leone	387,667

Table 3.4 Value of imports (excluding bullion) by colony in rank order, 1852/54–1882/84

	1851–4			1882–4	
Rank	Colony	£	Rank	Colony	£
1.	Mauritius	1,025,312	1.	Straits Settlements	15,964,895
2.	Jamaica	943,721	2.	Ceylon	4,011,239
3.	British Guiana	909,555	3.	Mauritius	2,875,666
4.	Ceylon	746,857	4.	British Guiana	2,029,667
5.	Barbados	681,027	5.	Trinidad	1,738,333
6.	Trinidad	518,907	6.	Jamaica	1,504,000
7.	British Honduras	213,994	7.	Barbados	1,158,000
8.	St Vincent	157,224	8.	Nigeria (Lagos)	468,333
9.	Antigua	154,084	9.	Sierra Leone	417,333
10.	Grenada	133,730	10.	Fiji	416,666

on sugar and its by-products, molasses and rum (Mauritius, British Guiana, Trinidad, Jamaica and Barbados), while the other two, Malaya and Ceylon, were essentially dependent on tin and coffee, respectively. This narrow specialisation clearly held dangers for the future and the danger of having such a limited range of export staples was underlined by inter-colonial competition: the rapid rise of Mauritius as a sugar exporter (rising from around £1.19 million a year in the 1850s to £3.5 million a year in the 1880s) was to some extent at the expense of the West Indies, even though their sugar exports continued to grow, as we have seen. (See Appendix 3.)

Although the range of imports was usually more varied, it was still fairly limited. Since the colonies had virtually no industries of their own, they were dependent on Europe (mainly Britain) for industrial products and machinery; and often for fuel as well. (See Table 3.6.) For example, Ceylon imported £0.47 million of cotton goods and £0.36 million of coal

Table 3.5 Shares of the three main export commodities in the seven leading exporting tropical colonies in 1882–4, Compared with 1852–4

Colony	3 main exports	% of Exports	
		1852–4	1882–4
Straits	Tin	n.a.	11.5
Settlements	Rice	n.a.	9.3
(Malacca and	Gambier	n.a.	6.3
Pahang only)			
Mauritius	Sugar	94.3	88.7
	Rum	0.4	1.5
	Vanilla	a	0.9
Ceylon	Coffee	53.5	39.6
	Chinchona Bark	a	11.9
	Cocoa	a	11.2
British Guiana	Sugar	64.2	80.4
	Rum	24.0	9.3
	Molasses	1.9	2.5
Trinidad	Sugar	77.5	30.4
	Cocoa	12.4	13.5
	Molasses	4.5	2.6
Jamaica	Sugar	46.6	35.4
	Rum	19.6	16.5
	Coffee	8.1	8.6
Barbados	Sugar	73.0	66.5
	Molasses	5.6	12.9
	Petroleum	a	0.2

[a]None or negligible amounts

and coke in the early 1880s. Perhaps surprisingly food imports were even more important, Ceylon importing £1.82 million of rice and paddy rice, and £0.10 million of fish in the same period. (See Appendix 4.) The import of cheap goods like rice enabled Ceylon to specialise in growing the more valuable coffee, and many of the other colonies pursued a similar trade pattern.

Because the colonies operated in a free trade environment they were theoretically at liberty to conduct business anywhere they liked, but inevitably the concentration of British businesses, finance and expertise in the colonies meant that most of this trade was with Britain, although the extent of concentration varied considerably. Table 3.7 shows the change over time and reveals that there was a considerable divergence between exports and imports. Between the early 1850s and the early

Table 3.6 Shares of the main imported commodities in the seven leading importing tropical colonies in 1882–4, compared with 1852–4

| Colony | 3 main imports | % of Imports | |
		1852–4	1882–4
Straits	Tin	n.a.	13.5
Settlements	Rice	n.a.	11.2
	Cotton goods	n.a.	6.7
Ceylon	Rice	55.8	43.0
	Cotton goods	33.0	11.7
	Coal and coke	11.2	9.0
Mauritius	Rice	27.2	15.1
	Cotton manufactures	a	6.7
	Coals	a	4.2
British Guiana	Rice	n.a.	10.4
	Machinery	n.a.	8.0
	Linens, cottons, etc.	n.a.	7.1
Trinidad	Textile manufactures	20.4	18.7
	Flour and meal	7.4	7.7
	Rice	3.7	6.2
Jamaica	Cotton	11.7	20.0
	Flour etc.	10.5	9.5
	Fish	6.1	7.1
Barbados	Linens and cottons	n.a.	13.3
	Wheat, flour, etc.	9.4	9.2
	Rice	2.5	6.4

[a] Nil or negligible

1880s Britain's position as a market for colonial exports, while growing absolutely, suffered quite a sharp relative decline: Britain's share falling from 66 per cent to 35 per cent. With imports the trend was less clear, because the provenance of imports entering the Straits Settlements (the

Table 3.7 Changes in the United Kingdom's share of the trade of the tropical colonies, 1852–5 to 1882–84

| Years | United Kingdom share | |
	Exports	Imports
1852–4	66%	40%
1882–4	35%	20%[a]
Change	–31%	–20%

[a]Does not include Straits Settlements, so is an underestimate.

Table 3.8 Comparison of the value of British trade with the tropical colonies and India, 1852–4 to 1882–4 (annual averages)

	Tropical Colonies	India
Exports		
Exports to Britain, 1852–4 (£)	5,752,596	7,939,333
Total exports, 1852–4 (%)	n.a.[a]	40.7
Exports to Britain, 1882–4 (£)	11,533,525	33,629,063
Total exports, 1882–4 (%)	n.a.[a]	42.0
Increase, 1852–4 to 1882–4 (£)	5,780,929	25,689,730
Increase (%)	100.5	323.6
Average annual growth rate (%)	3.3	10.8
Imports		
Imports from Britain, 1852–4 (£)	3,185,807	9,558,263
Total imports, 1852–4 (%)	n.a.[a]	84.5
Imports from Britain, 1882–4 (£)	11,335,546	43,533,750
Total imports, 1882–4 (%)	n.a.[a]	93.1
Increase 1852–4 to 1882–4 (£)	8,149,338	33,975,487
Increase (%)	255.8	355.5
Average annual growth rate (%)	8.5	11.8

[a]Although the exports and imports of the tropical colonies cannot be calculated accurately for reasons explained in the text, the figures are available in Appendices 1 and 2 for many individual colonies. The West Indian Islands sent some 30 to 70 per cent of their exports to Britain and took some 40 to 50 per cent of their imports from Britain (with inter-island variations). By contrast the Gold Coast sent 71.9 per cent of its exports to Britain and took 91.7 per cent of its imports from Britain in the early 1880s.

largest single importing colony) is not recorded in the official statistics. Excluding the Straits Settlements, Britain's share of the tropical colonies' imports fell from 40 per cent to 20 per cent, but this may well not reflect the real overall movement of imports.

Finally, in Table 3.8 an attempt is made to set the growth of the trade of the tropical colonies in a wider perspective by comparing it with Indian trade. Ideally it would have been desirable to have compared the total value of all the exports and imports of the tropical colonies with those for India, but this is not possible because the trade of the Straits Settlements (the largest amongst the tropical colonies in the early 1880s) presents the danger of double counting. Figures for the trade of each one of the Straits Settlements exist separately, but if some of, say, Pahang's exports went to Singapore, and vice versa, adding together the combined exports of Pahang and Singapore would inflate the *total* exports from the Straits Settlements by an unknown amount; and so on with Malacca's trade. This difficulty can however be overcome if we compare, not total trade, but trade with Britain, which was separately listed in the trade returns. This is what is done in Table 3.8. It does not, therefore, tell the whole story of the development of colonial trade, but it highlights the significant role of the 'mother country' in that situation.

What emerges clearly from the comparison is that the trade both of India and the tropical colonies with Britain grew very rapidly in the third quarter of the nineteenth century. Not surprisingly, India's trade with Britain was larger than that of the tropical colonies and grew more rapidly. This was partly because it was more heavily concentrated in Britain. For instance in 1882–84 India drew 93.1 per cent of her imports from Britain. This was considerably more than most of the tropical colonies, which had much smaller proportions like Barbados's 39.1 per cent, Ceylon's 31.5 per cent and Nigeria's 66.3 per cent. Only the Gold Coast with 91.7 per cent approached India's proportion.

Comparison with a much larger country like India is in some senses unfair to the tropical colonies, and it should not conceal the very considerable rate at which their trade with Britain was expanding. Their exports to Britain of food and raw materials slightly more than doubled, rising from £5.72 million to £11.53 million, while their imports from Britain (largely of manufactures) did even better, rising by 256 per cent from £3.19 million to £11.34 million. However, if their trade is examined on a per capita basis, it compares very favourably with India, for the tropical colonies had a combined population of only 6,114,000 in 1881 compared with 253,983,000 in India. Thus Indian imports in the early 1880s represented an average of only 3s 5d (17p) per person compared with imports worth £1.17s (£1.85) per head in the tropical colonies. Looked at in this perspective the potential for growth in the tropical colonies was greater than that of India. No doubt this enhanced propensity for growth was one of the reasons why British governments abandoned their reluctance to absorb more tropical colonies in the years between 1885 and 1914; though of course there were also many other reasons. Even so the tropical colonies had proved that they were no longer 'mill stones round our necks'.

4

The colonial 'scramble' and Joseph Chamberlain's development plans, 1885–1903

CAUSES AND RESULTS OF THE EUROPEAN 'SCRAMBLE' FOR TROPICAL COLONIES

Although the tropical colonies had made some important economic advances prior to 1885, and were beginning to assume a much more important role within the British Empire, they still represented a relatively minor component of the whole in the early 1880s. The next thirty years or so, however, were to see a startling transformation, by which the size of the tropical empire was very substantially increased. Most of this expansion took place in Africa, and not surprisingly it has received the most attention and publicity, but it should not be forgotten that the celebrated colonial 'scramble' was not confined to Africa, and that important new British colonies were established – or in some cases greatly extended – in Asia and the Pacific Islands as well as in Africa, as may be seen in Table 4.1, which charts the expansion of British colonial rule by region.

Although very important extensions of British formal rule took place, particularly in eastern and southern Africa (Kenya, Uganda, Nyasaland/ Malawi, Northern Rhodesia/Zambia) and also in West Africa (Nigeria and Gold Coast/Ghana) and Malaya, this period of expansion was also, ironically, a period of reduced British influence in the tropics, for Britain was forced to relinquish the informal economic influence it had exercised in many regions to aggressive new colonial powers (especially France and Germany) who carved out extensive new colonies for themselves and thereby separated and confined the British colonies, particularly in West Africa. Thus Nigeria and the Gold Coast were separated by German control of Togo in 1884 and the French seizure of Dahomey/ Benin in 1893.[1] More seriously, the British protectorates of Sierra Leone (1896) and Gambia (1894) were severely circumscribed by the expansion of French West Africa, and were reduced to enclaves which were far too small for optimum economic development. With the benefit of hindsight, it can be seen that the British empire, and its successor West African States, have paid a heavy price for the vacillation, irresolution

70

and confusion of British colonial policy towards West Africa at that time.[2]

In Eastern and Central Africa the situation was not so serious, since the British East African Protectorate (Uganda and Kenya) was large, as was the area comprised in Nyasaland/Malawi, and Northern Rhodesia/Zambia and Southern Rhodesia/Zimbabwe, but British East and British Central Africa were separated by the large German colony of Tanganyika, from its formation in 1884 until its conquest by Britain in 1917–18. Even after Tanganyika became a British mandated territory in 1919, and hence a bridge between East Africa and Central Africa, this did not lead to the unification of those areas as some people had hoped. This proposal was rejected in 1929 in the Report of Sir E. Hilton Young's Commission on Closer Union of the Dependencies in Eastern and Central Africa.[3] It is doubtful whether in fact the unification of such a huge area, stretching from Kenya in the north to Zambia in the south, would have been a practicable proposition from the administrative point of view, but this was not the critical issue. The reason the British government rejected the plan was political. The proponents of the idea wished to subordinate the huge majority African population living in the area to the small minority of European settlers in Zimbabwe (then Southern Rhodesia) and Kenya. The British government quite correctly saw that such a proposal would lead to acute resentment and probably resistance, and that African interests should have paramountcy in East Africa.[4] Thus, although the abandonment of Closer Union avoided some serious problems, it still contributed to the ultimate 'Balkanisation' of Africa.

The motivation for the imperial partition and absorption of tropical Africa between 1885 and 1900 has attracted an immense literature, some of it highly polemical, and it is probable that agreement will never be finally reached concerning the precise mixture of commercial, financial, social, strategic and power-political forces that were involved, and their complex interrelationships.[5] It is clear in some cases, perhaps Nigeria is one, that fairly straightforward economic factors, like the protection of the palm oil trade, were prominent, though not necessarily totally dominant; in other cases, perhaps Sierra Leone, Kenya and Uganda are examples, economic forces were much less powerful than the need to prevent another power from acquiring exclusive control over important regions. Though even in the case of Uganda and Kenya, where there was a strategic reason for the extension of British rule in the desire to protect the sea route to India, both via the Cape of Good Hope and Suez Canal, and in particular to safeguard British paramountcy in Egypt by ensuring that no other power controlled the sources of the Nile, the *expected economic* potential of the region was always active in the minds of those who sanctioned the action.[6]

Table 4.1 The chronology of the colonial 'scramble' and its aftermath

WEST AFRICA

Nigeria
1885 Oil Rivers Protectorate
1886 Royal Niger Co.
1900 N. Nigeria Protectorate
1914 N. & S. Nigeria united
1919 Brit. Cameroon (mandate)

Gold Coast/Ghana
1896 N. Territoreis Protectorate
1901 Gold Coast Colony & N. Territories united
1919 British Togo (mandate)

Sierra Leone
1896 Sierra Leone Protectorate

Gambia
1894 Protectorate

EAST AFRICA

Kenya
1886 British claim
1888 British Imperial East Africa Co. chartered
1895 (Part of) British East Africa Protectorate under F.O.
1905 Transferred to C.O.
1920 Kenya Colony established

Uganda
1886 British claim
1890 Assigned to British Imperial East Africa Co.
1895 (Part of) British East Africa Protectorate
1905 Transferred to C.O.
1920 Uganda Colony established

Zanzibar
1890 British Protectorate (F.O.)
1914 Transferred to C.O.

Tanganyika
1919 British (mandate)

Somaliland
1884 British Protectorate (Ind. O)
1898 British Protectorate (to F.O.)
1905 British Protectorate (to C.O.)

SOUTHERN AFRICA

Nyasaland/Malawi
1874 Missions established
1889 British Protectorate
1893 Enlarged to be British Central African Protectorate (F.O.)
1904 Enlarged to be British Central African Protectorate (C.O.)

N. Rhodesia/Zambia
1889 British South African Co. established
1893 British Protectorate
1924 British Protectorate to C.O.

Bechuanaland/Botswana
1885 British Protectorate

Table 4.1 (continued)

ASIA AND THE PACIFIC

Malaya

1885	Johore Protectorate
1888	Pahang Protectorate
1895	Federated Malay States
1903	Kelantan, British advisor
1909	Kedah, Perlis, Kelantan
	Trengganu, Protectorate

British Borneo

1881	British N. Borneo chartered Co.
1888	Brunei & Sarawak Protectorate
1890	Labuan to British N. Borneo Co.
1906	Labuan to Straits Settlements
1912	Labuan separate colony

New Guinea

1884	Papua Protectorate
1901	Papua transferred to Australia
1901	New Guinea, British (mandate)

PACIFIC ISLANDS

1877	New Hebrides Protectorate
1878	W. Pacific High Commission over Solomon, W. Gilbert & Ellice, Tonga, etc. islands
1887	Joint Anglo-French Protectorate, New Hebrides
1888	Cook Islands Protectorate
1892	Gilbert & Ellice Islands separate Protectorate
1893	Solomon Islands separate Protectorate
1898–1990	New addition to Solomon Islands Protectorate
1906	New Hebrides, Anglo-French Condominium

From the development viewpoint the reasons which motivated the extension of British colonial rule are much less important than the policies and activities that were pursued after colonial rule had begun; except of course in those cases, of which Gambia is an extreme example, where the circumstances in which rule began were such as more or less to guarantee that economic development was going to be very limited. A country which consists simply of one river valley 250 miles long and only 12 miles wide, must of necessity find itself in an uncomfortably constrained situation from almost every point of view.[7] However, if Gambia, and to lesser extent Sierra Leone, Nyasaland and Bechuanaland/Botswana were constituted in an unsatisfactory way by the scramble, this was much less the case for Britain's other tropical colonies, some of which possessed relatively favourable population and resource endowments.

THE NEW COLONIES: NIGERIA

Nigeria was perhaps the most fortunately placed of the new colonies in terms of development potential. To the relatively small Lagos colony were added two adjacent territories in Eastern and Northern Nigeria, over which British rule was rather hesitantly extended in the 1880s, before all three were formally joined in a united Nigeria in 1914. In 1885 a British protectorate was established over the very considerable area of Southeastern Nigeria which forms the delta lands of the river Niger. This was a great centre of the palm oil trade and the British protectorate was originally named the Oil Rivers Protectorate. In 1893 it became the Niger Coast Protectorate and in 1906 was merged with the Lagos colony to become Southern Nigeria. It was, however, considerably smaller than the huge area in Central and Northern Nigeria which was assigned to a British chartered company which, after several confusing changes of name, eventually became the Royal Niger Company.[8] This company was formed by Sir George Taubman Goldie and his associates and received a royal charter in 1886. It was supposed to provide colonial rule on the cheap. British control of a valuable area would be maintained at no expense to the British government, while the company would provide policing and administration (in association with local chiefs, with whom the company signed treaties) in exchange for a charter under which certain trading rights and privileges were granted on condition that free trade was maintained in the region. It was asking rather too much that the company should be expected to pay all the administrative and military expenses of extending British rule over an immense area, and should then allow all its competitors equal trading facilities with itself. Despite the pledges given in the charter it soon became clear that the company was effectively monopolising the trade of Northern

Nigeria, and that the concept of trying to combine political and commercial activities was inappropriate, and benefited neither. In 1900 the charter was revoked and the British government bought all the company's political and administrative rights, leaving it as a purely trading organisation.[9] However, this did not immediately solve the British government's problems. Many of the peoples of Northern Nigeria resisted British rule. They had believed when they signed treaties with the Royal Niger Company that these merely concerned trade and friendly relations. When they found that the British claimed ownership of their land and political control they naturally resisted this disruption of their economic, political and social life. It was only because of the overwhelming technical superiority of his weapons (machine-guns versus spears) that Sir Frederick Lugard, the Nigerian proconsul, was able to defeat them in a series of fiercely fought battles between 1902 and 1906. Later Lugard was able to win over the support of the emirs and chiefs by buttressing their position against their own local critics and rivals in his celebrated system of ruling by 'Indirect Rule' by which British 'advisers' subtly controlled the activities of the 'traditional' rulers.[10] The British authorities thus gained the cooperation of the indigenous rulers but at the expense of 'freezing' what had formerly been a fluid customary society, with serious consequences for future development. For instance, in deference to the local rulers' Muslim susceptibilities, Christian missionaries were barred from Northern Nigeria, education remained with Koranic schools and teaching in Arabic, with the result that Northern Nigerians were later severely handicapped by their ignorance of English, with its access to modern scientific and commercial ideas.[11] However, all this is to anticipate future problems.

At the outset of colonial rule in 1906 the British had control over a country with an area of rather more than 350,000 square miles, which is three times the size of the United Kingdom, and about the same size as France and Germany put together. It is about 700 miles from east to west, and 650 miles from north to south, and lies between 4° and 14° north of the Equator. Apart from a belt of mangrove swamps along much of the coast, very little of the country is unfit for human habitation, and its estimated population of 13.6 million in 1900 was the largest of any African country (Egypt, the next most populous African country, had about 11.3 million people in 1900). With a population in the 1990s approaching 90 million, it is far larger than any other African country.[12]

Dense tropical rain forest occupied the southern part of the country for 100 miles or so inland from the coast, though in recent years it has been much reduced. It gives way to a rolling savannah plateau of between 1,000 and 2,000 feet above sea level, but which rises in a few places to heights of over 5,000 feet. The most prominent of these are the

Jos-Bauchi plateau in the north-centre of the country and the mountains which form the eastern border with Cameroon. The savannah plateau gradually gives way to desert conditions along the northern border with the Republic of Niger, but all parts of the country receive some rain in the monsoon seasons, and the true Sahara desert begins some way to the north of the border.

The Niger river flows through the country for about 730 miles from the northwest to the south-centre, and about 225 miles upstream from its mouth it is joined by the Benue river, which flows southwestwards for some 400 miles from its source in Northern Cameroon. The two rivers are immense and provide Nigeria with navigable arteries which stretch for hundreds of miles. With some coal in the southeast near Enugu and with extensive tin deposits on the Bauchi plateau, Nigeria had some scope for mining and mineral development, but its chief assets were in the agricultural sector, where a wide range of tropical crops and forest products supported a vigorous and adaptable people, who had learned to overcome even the disadvantages of a hot humid climate and the presence of disease-carrying mosquitos and tsetse flies. Yet despite considerable earlier advances in agricultural specialisation and urban culture, the country was still relatively underpopulated at the outset of the colonial period and the scope for rapid increases in production and commercialisation was extensive.[13]

THE NEW COLONIES: THE GOLD COAST (NOW GHANA)

The other West African colony with a promising development potential was the Gold Coast, lying about 140 miles to the west of Nigeria. The establishment of a formal colony in 1874 had extended British rule over a considerable area in the south of the country, but the precise relationship between the British authorities and the native states had been left vague, and even the boundaries of the colony had been left indeterminate.[14] The powerful inland forest state of Asante had been defeated in 1874 by Sir Garnet Wolseley, but had not been incorporated in the colony. Relations remained strained and it was not until after another war in 1896, and mounting encroachments from the French and the Germans, that Britain finally staked out a claim to the Gold Coast hinterland by establishing protectorates over Asante and the Northern Territories in 1902. This latter area lay roughly between 8° and 11° north of the Equator in the savannah and comprised numerous peoples of whom the Gonja, the Dagomba, the Mamprusi, and the Talensi were perhaps the most numerous.

The result was that by 1902 the British had established a large, rectangular colony stretching along the coast for 334 miles, and inland for some 450 miles at its greatest extent. The area was approximately

78,650 square miles, comprising 23,490 square miles in the original Gold Coast colony, 24,560 square miles in Asante and 30,600 square miles in Northern Territories. In 1919 part of the former German colony of Togo, was added to the eastern Gold Coast under a League of Nations mandate, adding a further 13,040 square miles to the colony, making a grand total of 91,690 square miles – about the same size as the United Kingdom.[15]

The territory was very sparsely populated. The first attempt at a complete census was made in 1911, when just over 1.5 million people were counted, although this census was admitted to be inadequate. For instance, in the Northern Territories, according to the *Gold Coast Handbook, 1923* many villages could not be counted

> owing to the wildness of the inhabitants. One finds that in parts of the Tumu area, even in 1921, the only practical method of enumeration was extremely primitive. The Chief's messengers brought the District Census Officer calabashes filled with beans, groundnuts and stones representing the numbers of males, females, and children in the more remote villages.[16]

The average density of population in 1911 was just under 19 people per square mile compared with 359 in Great Britain.[17]

In the 1890s the means of communication were limited to small boats on the rivers and narrow bush paths through the jungle, though a wider network of trading waterways existed in the northern savannah lands. The agricultural and forest potential of the country was largely untapped, though there were small exports of palm products, rubber and lumber. Between 10,000 and 20,000 tons of palm oil and palm kernels were exported during the 1890s, but the once booming rubber exports had declined to a mere three tons in 1898.[18] What had really interested the British in the country had been gold, and a mini-gold rush had taken place in the early 1880s, but although there are important gold mines in the country their value was greatly overestimated. No fewer than 476 companies with a nominal capital of nearly £43 million were registered for gold mining and exploration in West Africa (mainly in the Gold Coast) between 1880 and 1904, but at that date there were only four Gold Coast companies whose output of gold was worth more than £10,000 a year.[19]

Ironically it was not gold, but a tropical tree from the Americas which was virtually unknown on the Gold Coast before 1881 – the cocoa tree – on which the country's considerable export growth in the first half of the twentieth century was to rest; but this development was only just beginning when British colonial rule was established in the Gold Coast, and was certainly not foreseen by the authorities.[20]

THE NEW COLONIES: UGANDA AND KENYA

The other tropical colonies which seemed to have promising development potential were the East African colonies previously referred to. They comprised a large area lying athwart the Equator and stretching some 600 miles from north to south and over 800 miles from east to west, which initially lay within the British East Africa Protectorate, though they eventually became the separate colonies of Uganda and Kenya. Although linked together by geographical proximity and an extensive railway (some 650 miles long) which connected Uganda to the Indian Ocean at the Kenyan port of Mombasa, they were in fact very different both in their climate and resource endowments and in their earlier history. The highlands of Kenya were thought to be attractive for European settlers, but initially it was not Kenya which seemed to hold out the best hopes for economic development, but Uganda, which was occupied by a vigorous and relatively advanced population, especially in the state of Buganda on the shores of Lake Victoria.[21]

Buganda was unusual among tropical African states. It was a fertile and fairly densely populated country (estimates of the 1890s put its population at around one million, though these were essentially informed guesses and may have been exaggerated) with a relatively advanced agriculture, a hierarchical political system based on chiefs who held landed estates to finance their rule, and a monarch, called the Kabaka, with very extensive powers. As such it contrasted fairly strongly with the majority of the surrounding peoples, most of whom were only loosely organised politically and some of whom were cattle-keeping nomads, such as the Masai in Central Kenya and the Karamajong in Northeastern Uganda. These people practised a lifestyle which was very finely attuned to the arid and inhospitable environment in which they lived. Their migrations in sympathy with the changing patterns of rainfall and aridity were in fact the optimum response to their harsh environment; but almost inevitably this was misunderstood by the early colonial officials, who thought that the land was 'empty' and unutilised, and could therefore be given to European settlers without harming the nomads. The consequences of this mistake were later to prove very severe as the nomads were forced off the best land, and the remainder became seriously overstocked and degraded. The full nature of this calamity did not become fully understood until the 1930s.[22]

As stated earlier, British economic interests in East Africa were more latent than actual prior to 1903. British consuls, like Dr (later Sir) John Kirk (1847–1922) had resided in Zanzibar and had tried to influence its sultans to abolish the slave trade, which their subjects carried on all over East Africa to serve markets in Arabia and surrounding countries, and had built up some 'legitimate' trade (mainly with India) but it was not very extensive. Additionally, British and French missionaries who had penetrated to Uganda before 1890 had had a remarkable success in converting leading chiefs to their respective versions of Christianity (Anglican and Roman Catholic). This unfortunately led to internal conflict, exacerbated by Muslim and pagan factions, so that the missionaries lives were soon in danger. Finally, Britain perceived a need to control the headwaters of the Nile, which flowed out of Lake Victoria Nyanza at Jinja in Uganda, lest a rival European power (Germany from Tanganyika or France from French Congo) should cut off Egypt's water supply and endanger British control there. This fear was probably fanciful, but combined with the other causes, and the hope of future economic development, was sufficient to propel a rather reluctant British government to supersede the bankrupt British Imperial East Africa Company, which had tried, but failed, to play in Uganda the role which the Royal Niger Company had performed in Nigeria. So in 1894 a British protectorate was established in Uganda, and Parliament was induced to vote a small sum of money for a railway survey.[23] Sir Charles Eliot, who governed the British East Africa Protectorate from 1900 to 1904, summarised subsequent events, as follows:

in 1895 the Company sold their remaining rights to the Government for £250,000, and the East Africa Protectorate was constituted. An Official notice of August 31, 1896, declares that 'all the territories in East Africa under the Protectorate of Her Majesty, except the islands of Zanzibar and Pemba, and the Uganda Protectorate, are for the purposes of administration included in one Protectorate, under the name of the East Africa Protectorate'. It was decided to construct the Uganda Railway. The first rails were laid in 1895, and the first train reached the Lake in December 1901.[24]

The lakeside terminus was at Port Florence, now Kisumu, on the Gulf of Kavirondo, whence cargo and passengers proceeded by steamer either to Entebbe or to Port Bell, the port of Kampala, the capital of Buganda.

Although Uganda did not initially have much to export, except ivory, which was a declining trade, its population was numerous and industrious and eager for European goods. Sir Harry Johnston, who was sent to Uganda as a special commissioner, reported in 1900 that they were 'greedy for cloth and for almost every manufactured article up to a phonograph and a brougham'.[25] Optimists believed that agricultural exports would soon be found since the soil was fertile and well watered. Cotton grew wild and coffee and rubber also looked like good prospects. Johnston dreamed that by uniting Uganda and Kenya a new India could be created. Kenneth Ingham in *The Making of Modern Uganda* notes that he wrote enthusiastically

> to the Foreign Secretary on February 18, 1900, to say that he had already found an excellent site for a joint capital on the Mau plateau near mile 475 on the Uganda Railway. Mombasa, he added gaily, would be the Bombay of the new, united Protectorate and should remain the capital of the coastal region. Entebbe, the Uganda capital, would be the Calcutta of East Africa, and Fort Portal with its snowy Ruwenzori mountains in the background would be its Darjeeling. The new capital, high on the rolling plateau, would then become the Simla of the United Protectorate.[26]

He could hardly have chosen anyone less likely than Lord Salisbury, who was prime minister as well as foreign secretary, to be enthusiastic about such flights of fancy, and not surprisingly he got a cool reply.

The protectorates remained separate and pursued different courses. Each was in truth quite large enough on its own. Uganda comprised some 94,000 square miles (though 14,000 of these were in Lake Victoria Nyanza) and was thus nearly as large as Great Britain. Much of the country was a rolling plateau between 4,000 and 5,000 feet above sea level, so that, although on the Equator, it was not excessively hot. To the north the savannah lands suffered from periodic drought, but a network of lakes and rivers such as the Nile, Lake Kyoga and Lake Albert, provided fairly good inland communications by water. Distance from the sea was the problem as far as trade was concerned, but once the Uganda railway had been opened in 1901 the prospects for the beginning of development via export crops looked quite promising – as indeed they proved to be with Uganda's booming cotton exports in the decade before 1914, (see next chapter for details).

Kenya represented a different problem. Over twice as large as Uganda (containing a land area of 219,730 square miles) it comprised a series of sharply contrasting regions, ranging from a narrow strip of mangrove forest along the coast, through a baking and inhospitable desert to the great rolling highlands of Central Kenya with forested and snow-covered peaks like Mount Kenya, the Aberdare ranges and Mount Elgon on the Uganda border, rising to heights between 10,000 and 17,000 feet. There were no navigable rivers of any significance, and transport depended on painfully slow foot porterage. It took Lugard and his caravan over four months from 6 August to 18 December 1890 to proceed from Mombasa to Kampala.[27] Much of the country was sparsely inhabited and the nomadic Masai occupied the great rift valley which separate the settled, agricultural people, the Kikuyu, who occupied the forested country to the south of Mount Kenya and the

Aberdares, and the Luo peoples, who were settled in the west of Kenya around the Kavirondo Gulf and the shores of Lake Victoria, growing maize, sorghum and other grains.[28]

As we have seen, the British were only interested in Kenya initially as the route to Uganda, but it soon became evident that the central highlands were cool and fertile enough to be suitable for European settlers, and almost from the beginning, hopes of development were concentrated on that area. Sir Charles Eliot in the preface to his book *The East Africa Protectorate* (1905) wrote that

> my special object has been to point out the opportunity which it offers for European colonization and the interesting effect which such a colony may have on the future development of Africa.[29]

After describing the mineral, agricultural and commercial advantages in some detail he concluded by saying that

> closely connected with European colonisation is the question of native rights. This difficulty is lessened in East Africa by the paucity of the native population, and I think that the obstacles which it has been supposed to present to European settlement exist in prejudiced imaginations rather than in reality. Natives must be protected from unjust aggression, and be secured sufficient land for their wants; but with this proviso, I think, we should recognise that European interests are paramount. Nomad tribes must not be allowed to straggle over huge areas which they cannot utilise, nor ought the semi-settled natives to continue the wasteful and destructive practice of burning and clearing in the woods, using it for a few years, and then moving on and doing the same elsewhere.[30]

The misunderstanding about the *rotational* nature of African bush-fallow farming revealed here was then compounded by another, equally serious. Eliot continued:

> there is no real opposition between European and native interests, or cause for hostility. There is land enough for both, and the East African tribes are not sufficiently numerous to feel the pressure of European immigration.[31]

It is true that Kenya was not densely populated in 1905, and a series of epidemics, both animal and human, had recently decimated its peoples; but it was certainly not true that there would be no competition for land between European settlers and African farmers. Moreover this matter was compounded by the question of a labour supply for the European settlers. These were not working farmers, but aristocrats like Lord Delamere, who proposed to lease or sell vast estates to 'gentlemen settlers' who would require an African labour force to work them. Thus vast acreages were alienated for European settlement (5,028,142 acres by 1914 in 3,068 holdings, average 1,639 acres) so that the local Africans became landless and were forced to work for the settlers. The ill-feeling caused by this policy rankled for years and lay at the heart of the Kenyan Africans resistance to British rule from as early as the 1920s.[32] While it is probable that the inhabitants of Kenya received some indirect benefits from the settlement of the so-called White Highlands it is also true that the ensuing conflicts diverted the development of the Kenyan economy along a path which had ultimately to be abandoned. The history of the early development experience of Kenya is thus rather less instructive than that of colonies where the problem of European settlement did not arise. The same of course applies to Southern Rhodesia/Zimbabwe, where the ensuing conflict was much more prolonged and serious.[33]

THE NEW COLONIES: MALAYA AND SINGAPORE

A rather different experience was occurring in Malaya, which was also the scene of a major expansion of British control in this period, although in Malaya, the process was not effectively completed until 1909. The confidence with which Governor Weld had completed his report in 1881 (see Chapter 3, p.59) was fully borne out in the succeeding years. Tin-mining in the western states of Perak and Selangor continued to expand rapidly, and was accompanied by forest and agricultural development; but in Malaya the development process was more complex than in Africa. It was not European settlers, but Chinese and Tamils from Southern India, who provided one of the spurs to growth, coupled with the import of European capital for trading, mines and plantations.[34] Most of the Chinese and Indians went into the tin mines and new plantations of sugar, pepper, gambier, tapioca and, increasingly after 1895, of rubber, which was to become the great export staple of the colonial Malayan economy. It was hoped that the Malayan peasant farmers operating on a semi-subsistence basis would specialise in rice, vegetable and fruit production to feed the rapidly growing new towns like Kuala Lumpur and Port Swettenham; but huge quantities of imported rice from Burma, Thailand and Indo-China kept the price of rice low, and encouraged the local Malays either to quit agriculture for more lucrative jobs or to retreat to the remoter districts and to continue with subsistence production.[35] The economic development of Malaya thus became more and more unequal, with the non-Malayan immigrants benefiting greatly while the local Malayan population were threatened with increasing marginalisation in their own country. As early as 1901, the 299, 740 Chinese and 548,210 Indians already outnumbered the 312,490 Malays, even though the Malay population had probably doubled since the 1870s.[36]

The further extension of British control over the Malayan peninsula took place in stages, partly because this assisted economic development, and partly because Britain feared the ambitions of France and Germany, and felt that if they were able to establish footholds in the peninsula (which at various times seemed possible) they would be in a position to threaten the huge British trade with China which passed via Singapore to Hong Kong, Shanghai and other Chinese ports. Thus, when domestic conditions seemed appropriate Britain took the opportunity to extend its control through the Resident system to all the Malay states in the southern part of the peninsula.[37]

It began with Johore, the state immediately across the straits from Singapore, in 1885, when that state accepted official British protection, but because the Sultan of Johore was so friendly to Britain, and acted so closely with the Governor of the Straits Settlements, it was not necessary to place a formal British Resident in his capital until the international crisis of 1914. Northwest of Johore were the Negri Sembilan, which were closely involved in the economic expansion around Malacca, and one of which, Sungai Ujong, was already a British protected state; and to the northeast was Pahang, the largest, and one of the least developed of the Malayan states, which extended about 100 miles up the east coast and over a large area of the central jungle.[38] The rulers of the Negri Sembilan and Pahang both accepted British Residents in 1888. This extended British control from Singapore to Pahang, but in a way which was too uncoordinated to be convenient; so in 1895, Perak, Selangor, Negri Sembilan and Pahang were joined together as the Federated Malay States. But as Cowan comments

> the so-called Federation soon became in effect a union, with the Resident-General as the Chief executive officer. The relations of this officer with the Residents meant that most of their control over policy quickly passed into his hands, and the development of large-scale European investment in tin and rubber after 1895 resulted in the proliferation of the specialist departments such as Public Works, Mines, Railways, Posts and Telegraphs, and so on, with their headquarters at the Federal capital of Kuala Lumpur.[39]

Britain now had in effect two linked colonies in Malaya – the Straits Settlements of Pahang, Province Wellesley, Dindings (carved out of the Perak coast in 1824) Malacca and Singapore, with their capital at Singapore, and the Federated Malay States, with their capital at Kuala Lumpar, connecting Malacca to Pahang – while the gap between Malacca and Singapore was filled by the allied and protected state of Johore.

In 1909 a further advance north and eastwards took place when Thailand was persuaded to relinquish its somewhat shadowy control over the west coast states of Kedah and Perlis, which lay opposite, and to the north of Pahang; and over the northeast coastal states of Kelantan and Trengganu. These latter were still relatively undeveloped (but occupied a strategic position) while Perlis and Kedah not only occupied a critical location in relation to Pahang and Province Wellesley, but were vital suppliers of rice and other foods to both.[40]

The extension of political control in 1909 coincided with the completion of the west coast railway from Singapore to Butterworth, opposite Pahang, and left Britain with control over an area in the Malay peninsula comprising some 52,000 square miles, and stretching for about 470 miles from Singapore to Northern Perlis, and for about 200 miles from coast to coast at its maximum width between Perak and Trengganu, some 250 miles north of Singapore. Most of the coastlands of Southern Malaya are low-lying, flat, and very fertile, providing scope for a wide range of tropical crops, being both hot and well watered by monsoonal rains. Part of the interior is mountainous, with some peaks in the Cameron Highlands in the west-centre of the country rising to heights somewhat over 6,000 feet. Malaya thus provided excellent scope for forest and agricultural development, in addition to its considerable wealth in tin.[41]

As well as the major tropical colonies, which were obtained or expanded in the 'scramble' there were a number of minor colonies. These included places with small populations, like Nyasaland/Malawi and Sierra Leone in Africa, or Fiji, the Solomons and Tonga in the Pacific; and the older, depressed colonies like the West Indies, some of which had larger populations, but whose economies had become stagnant.

THE NEW COLONIES: NYASALAND (NOW MALAWI)

Of the minor African colonies, Nyasaland/Malawi had become a British protectorate between 1889 and 1893, largely to suppress slave trading and protect the Scottish missionaries who had established stations at and around Blantyre in the hills which lay to the south of Lake Nyasa and to the east of the Shiré river, which flows out of Lake Nyasa, southwards to the Zambesi in Mozambique, about 90 miles upstream from its mouth. Stretching along the west side of Lake Nyasa and down the Shiré river almost to its junction with the Zambesi, the Nyasaland Protectorate was about 520 miles long from north to south and varied in width from 50 to 100 miles. It comprises 37,374 square miles of land and lay between 9° and 17° south of the Equator. Much of the land was over 3,000 feet high, and parts of the protectorate were relatively densely populated by the standards of nineteenth-century Africa. The development potential was, however, fairly limited since there was little to trade, and communications were poor because the Shiré river was broken by rapids, making water communication between the lake and the sea very difficult. Slaves and ivory had been the early exports, but with their demise, the country could offer only maize and sorghum, for which there was no demand, and mountain timber, such as the Malanje cypress, which was too expensive to transport. Cecil Rhodes' British South Africa Company was given a charter to search for minerals and develop mining in 1884, but by 1903 had little to show for its efforts.[42]

MINOR COLONIES, OLD AND NEW

Far away on the west coast, the Sierra Leone Protectorate, established in 1896, offered rather better prospects. Although only covering 27,925 square miles, making it a little smaller than Scotland, but a little larger than Eire or Sri Lanka, it possessed some fertile rain forest on its eastern side, with a good potential for the export of palm oil, palm kernels, kola nuts and eventually cocoa. In Freetown it had potentially the best port in West Africa, and palm kernels and kola nuts were shipped down many rivers and then coastally to Freetown in the 1890s. In 1900 exports were worth £172,000 and £79,000 respectively. A railway was commenced in 1895 to proceed eastwards from Freetown into the palm belt, and it was confidently expected that exports would increase as it neared its destination, as indeed they did. The railway reached its eastern terminus in 1908, at a town called Pendembu, 277 miles from Freetown, near the border with Liberia; and by 1913, the tonnage of palm kernels exported had increased two and a half times, and their value had risen five-fold. This rise in trade provided the government with an enhanced revenue with which to commence further improvements to the infrastructure, health measures and education. It was all still very limited in 1900, but the future was beginning to look more promising than it had for many years past.[43]

By contrast, the economic situation in the West Indies had deteriorated. Still largely dependent on sugar exports, they had suffered acutely from competition from Mauritius and from European beet sugar, which enjoyed protective tariffs and bounties. The need to revitalise their economies was one of the problems with which Joseph Chamberlain wrestled when he took over the Colonial Office in 1895, as we shall see.[44]

The scatter of Pacific islands which Britain had acquired during the scramble were generally too small and remote to possess any great development potential, with the exception of Fiji, where the importation of Indian indentured labourers to grow sugar (both on plantations and on their own account) was beginning to show signs of success. The sugar was mostly exported to New Zealand and Australia, under the auspices of an Australian enterprise, The Colonial Sugar Refining Company, which was founded in 1880.[45] The population of Fiji had reached 120,000 by 1901 and exports (mostly sugar) were valued at £549,000. The development of the internal market, however, seems to have lagged behind, if the value of imports may be taken as a guide. They were worth only £351,000 in 1901 – far less than the value of the exports.[46]

The protectorates over the more remote Pacific islands were primarily undertaken to appease fears in Australia and New Zealand that they would be colonised by France or Germany, and thus threaten Australasian security. The Cook Islands, a group of small atolls lying between Tonga and Tahiti, about 20° south of the Equator, were thus taken over in 1888; as were the rather more important Solomon Islands in 1893. The Solomons, of which Guadalcanal is the most important, lie to the east of Papua-New Guinea, between 5° and 10° south of the Equator. Rather more important than either of these was British North Borneo, which was awarded to the British North Borneo Company under a charter of 1882. It was believed to have some value as a source of tropical produce, but it was also occupied to counter Spanish claims from their colony in the Philippines, to suzerainty over the local sultanates of Sulu and Brunei.[47] The small, but ancient sultanate of Brunei was regarded as being in a loose British 'sphere of influence' (it accepted British protection in 1888) since it bordered the British colony of Labuan and the state of Sarawak, which had been ruled by the Brooke family as 'independent', but as British rajahs, since 1841.[48] The British North Borneo Company was another attempt at annexation on the cheap, Lord Granville, the foreign secretary, assuring the House of Lords on 13th March 1882 that British commercial interests would thereby be promoted 'with an absence of reasonable ground for apprehending military or financial burdens'.[49] British protection was extended to North Borneo in 1883, and the company continued to administer the territory until the Japanese occupation in 1941. In 1946 it became a Crown colony.

JOSEPH CHAMBERLAIN'S COLONIAL DEVELOPMENT POLICIES, 1895–1903

Thus, when Joseph Chamberlain moved into the Colonial Office in June 1895, he was confronted with a mixed bag of tropical colonies and dependencies, some of which were in a flourishing condition, and others of which showed every sign of neglect or decay. He immediately set out to survey his responsibilities and to lay plans for a major step forward in colonial development policy. It may be a source of some surprise that a politician of Chamberlain's eminence and importance (as the most prominent and energetic of the Liberal Unionists) should have been interested in the mundane subject of colonial development, which had not hitherto excited any interest amongst major Victorian statesmen; especially when Lord Salisbury had offered him any office he wanted, including the Treasury, on the formation of the Unionist government in June 1895.[50] The answer is not altogether clear, but was no doubt influenced to some extent by pressure from Chamberlain's Birmingham constituency, where his supporters in the metal trades were finding competition from German and American rivals very difficult, both at home and in colonial markets, and who were already pressing for tariff protection within the empire, and seeking new markets.[51] But probably more important was Chamberlain's fear that Britain's power, wealth and prestige were on the wane, and that unless it could be restored through imperial union and development, the future would lie with larger and more powerful rivals like Germany, the USA and Russia.[52] This view is well summarised in the extract from Chamberlain's letter of 13 June 1902 to Sir George Reid premier of New South Wales 1894–9 and of Australia 1904–5, cited by Kesner, which has a truly prophetic ring to it. Chamberlain wrote that

> I feel sure that the time for small kingdoms has passed away. The future is with the great Empires and it rests with us to say whether our own shall be counted for many years to come as one of the greatest or whether we shall split up into minor comparatively unimportant nationalities.[53]

Clearly the expense of maintaining and defending an empire which was as large and as far-flung as the British, was going to be great, and threatened to become even greater.[54] Therefore, what was needed were prosperous and contented subjects within all parts of the empire, Crown colonies as well as dominions, which were capable of raising sufficient revenues, both to contribute to the defence of their territories, and to generate sufficient investment capital to set their domestic economies on a path of self-continuing growth. Thus Chamberlain's policies, while designed primarily to serve Britain's interests, had the potential merit of also being beneficial to the colonies, if they could be achieved. Canada, Australia, and to some extent New Zealand, South Africa, and India, showed signs of autonomous economic development (though most of them obstinately refused to contribute to imperial defence). The tropical colonies were, however, a more difficult problem, as Chamberlain was well aware.

While still in opposition, in March 1895, Chamberlain had told the Birmingham Jewellers Association that

> it is not enough to occupy certain great spaces of the world's surface unless you can make the best of them – unless you are

willing to develop them. We are landlords of a great estate; it is the duty of a landlord to develop his estate.[55]

After taking office in June 1895 he set to work to survey his domains and was soon able to amplify his plans. On 22 August he told the House of Commons that the

> underdeveloped estates could never be developed without Imperial assistance . . . cases have already come to my knowledge of colonies which have been British Colonies perhaps for more than a hundred years in which up to the present time British rule has done absolutely nothing . . . I shall be prepared to consider very carefully myself, and then, if I am satisfied, confidently submit to the House, any case which may occur in which by the judicious investment of British money those estates which belong to the British Crown may be developed for the benefit of their population and for the benefit of the greater population which is outside.[56]

However, his optimism was soon to be cooled by a douche of cold water from the Treasury, which resolutely refused to invest public money in colonial development on to guarantee loans raised on the commercial money market; and without a Treasury guarantee, such loans could only be raised at rates of interest which were far higher than most colonies could reasonably be expected to pay – especially for long-term loans.[57]

Chamberlain was determined to overcome these obstacles and after repeated rebuffs from the Treasury to his requests for funds for railway building in various parts of the colonial empire, he hit upon what appeared to be an ingenious scheme. The shares in the Suez Canal, which Disraeli had purchased for Britain in 1875, passed into full government ownership in 1st July 1895. Their net cost had been a little over £2 million, but by 1895 they had appreciated to £24 million – a gain of some eleven-fold – and were yielding an annual income of £670,000. This was money which was derived to a considerable extent from dues on imperial trade, so what more appropriate, thought Chamberlain, than that it should be used to set up a guarantee fund for loans for 'railways, bridges, harbours and irrigation' in the colonies. He circulated a memorandum to the Cabinet on 8 January 1896:

> It is certain that in many cases progress has been delayed, and in some cases absolutely stayed, because the only methods by which improvement could be carried out were beyond the scope of private resources . . . In Dominica, in British Honduras, and in British Guiana for instance, there are untold possibilities of natural wealth in the shape of gold and other minerals, dye woods and timber, and all tropical productions, which neither the colonies themselves nor individual adventurers are in a position to open up. Crown

estates of immense extent and undoubted intrinsic value are waiting a purchaser because there are no proper means of access.
Individual enterprise will till the fields and cut the timber, and
work the mines; but Government and Government alone can make
the roads and the railways. This is the true province of
Government in new countries, and until it is recognised by Great
Britain she will not have fulfilled her obligations to the dependencies which the she holds under her rule.[58]

Chamberlain had high hopes that his scheme would be successful,
especially as it was supported by the prime minister, Lord Salisbury, and
the leader of the House of Commons, Arthur Balfour; but the
Chancellor of the Exchequer, Sir Michael Hicks Beach was adamant in
his refusal to accept it. He argued that the Suez shares had been
purchased with public money, under parliamentary authority, and that
any diversion of income derived from them to the colonies would be
illegal. Furthermore, he would have to raise new taxes to replace the lost
revenue. Hicks Beach won his argument in cabinet, ably supported by
memoranda from officials like Edward Hamilton, the assistant secretary
of the Treasury (who had formerly been Gladstone's private secretary).
Salisbury later lamented ruefully that 'the influence which the
Gladstonian garrison of the Treasury have upon Beach's mind is very
disastrous'.[59]

Chamberlain was not, however, a man to give up a struggle in which
he believed, and he entered into negotiations with the Treasury
designed to find another route to his end. After long and tortuous
negotiations, a Colonial Loans Act was passed in 1899, which enabled
Crown colonies to raise guaranteed loans from the Treasury for fairly
long periods at relatively low rates of interest ($3\frac{1}{4}$ per cent for 30 years,
$3\frac{1}{2}$ per cent for 40 years, and $3\frac{3}{4}$ per cent for 50 years). There was
however a rub. The colonies had to pass laws making the repayment
(and the interest) a first charge on the local revenues. This was not only
very restrictive, but tended to discourage any future lenders. The
Colonial Office decided therefore more or less to ignore the Act, and
only to use it in emergencies. It appeared that the Treasury's determination to control Chamberlain's development expenditures had undermined him yet again.[60] But once more he fought back, and finally in
1900, with the passage of the Colonial Stocks Act, he secured a measure
which went some way towards giving him what he wanted.

Under the Colonial Stocks Act 1900, the colonies were given the
privileges of being empowered to issue loan stock with trustee status (i.e.
trustees could invest their funds in it), which was tantamount to an
imperial guarantee. However this still did not solve the problem because
even with the low interest rates then prevailing most colonies could not

afford to borrow money. What they needed were development grants – a concept which was anathema to the 'orthodox' financial mandarins whose views still dominated governmental thinking. Chamberlain was able to make a very small breach in this wall by reviving grants-in-aid, such as the £30,000 which was given in 1897–98 to build roads in Dominica and settle peasant proprietors in St Vincent, and several others; but in relation to the development needs of the colonies these were trivial.[61]

The tendency of modern historians has been to play down Chamberlain's success in what has come to be known as 'constructive imperialism', and to stress the limitations of his achievements. Andrew Porter notes that 'Chamberlain's own haste, lack of detailed preparations, and economic ignorance had much to do with his limited success, both on the ground and in attempts to convert the Treasury to his faith'.[62] Nevertheless, while it is true that Chamberlain was sometimes a better publicist than performer, it is also true that he went quite a long way towards loosening the restrictive coils which had hitherto bound colonial development; and that after his tenure at the Colonial Office, the development issue was fixed permanently on the British government's agenda.

His specific achievements may have been limited, but as Kesner maintains, measures like the Imperial Penny Postage Act, steamer and cable subsidies, and many railway, irrigation, drainage, sanitation and health programmes, initiated during Chamberlain's years at the Colonial Office, did make a real difference.

> These policies and pieces of legislation allowed these colonies some of the essential elements upon which the local population and foreign industrial and commercial elites could build new enterprises. For certain colonies, such as Lagos, British Guiana, Cyprus and Gold Coast, these circumstances led to a major economic transformation.[63]

It has also to be remembered that Chamberlain's accession to the Colonial Office in 1895 coincided with the ending of the long downswing of prices and trade of the 1880s and early 1890s, so that his policies for the tropical colonies were assisted by the general upswing of business activity which characterised the later 1890s and the early twentieth century.[64]

5

First fruits
Colonial development, 1903–14

A NEW ERA IN COLONIAL DEVELOPMENT

With the ending of the prolonged agony of the Boer War by the Peace of Vereeniging (31 May 1902) the Colonial Office could once again turn its attention to the development programme initiated by Chamberlain; and indeed the years between 1903 and 1914 saw some of the most effective advances yet recorded in the tropical colonies.[1] Of course, compared with modern assessments of what was required these achievements were still very limited. The Colonial Office's development philosophy still depended upon the belief that once the state had provided a framework of ordered government and a basic infrastructure, private entrepreneurs and private capital could be relied upon to initiate and carry out a steady programme of economic advance. That the development problem was not as simple as this was partly obscured by the initial achievements of private capital, both imported and domestic, as a response to the very simple infrastructural attainments of this period. Just because so many of the tropical colonies were so deficient in the elementary infrastructural needs such as railways, roads, bridges, harbours, currencies, banks and telecommunications, the response to their initial provision seemed almost miraculous – particularly in the field of foreign trade, as we shall see. This encouraged the illusion that the problems of economic development were relatively simple, and concealed the fact that further investments in infrastructural growth were unlikely to yield dramatic returns.

The advances of the Edwardian period were also facilitated by some fortuitous factors. After the prolonged pause in world-wide economic advance between 1873 and 1896, known at the time as the 'Great Depression' (though it seemed very mild to later generations) the world economy in general and the British economy in particular, entered into a period of boom and growth. Production and trade surged forward, and the prices of colonial agricultural and mineral produce rose in sympathy with this renewed demand. Thus, the provision of the new colonial infrastructures geared in very well with changes in the world

91

economy, and enabled the colonial response to take place in favourable conditions. Furthermore, the Edwardian world was generally peaceful, trade was not much obstructed by tariff or financial restrictions; and until the international situation began to darken significantly around 1911, the period was one of hope and optimism.[2] But, even allowing for these favourable exterior conditions, the economic achievements of many, though not all, the tropical colonies were still impressive.

THE EXPANSION OF COLONIAL TRADE, 1884–1912

The economic achievements of the tropical colonies can be most clearly seen if we compare their trade performance in the early 1880s with that of the period just before the First World War (i.e. 1910–12). For in this period the growth in overseas trade continued on a very large scale. As in the period from the early 1850s to the early 1880s there were considerable variations in the performance of the tropical colonies, and there were even a few sugar colonies, like Barbados, British Guiana, St Lucia and Mauritius, whose trade contracted; but this was insignificant compared with the surging growth in Malaya, Ceylon, Nigeria, the Gold Coast and the new East African colonies. The growth in exports and imports between 1882–4 and 1910–12 is shown in Table 5.1 for seven of the leading tropical colonies. The West African colonies of the Gold Coast and Nigeria had the fastest growing exports with annual growth rates of 29.4 per cent and 26.4 per cent respectively in the twenty-eight year period; but they started from very low bases, and the total exports of the West African leader, Nigeria, at £5.2 million in 1910–12 were far overshadowed in value by the £40.5 million from the Federated Malay States and the £12.2 million from Ceylon. The best performance in the West Indies came from Trinidad and Tobago with exports worth just over £4 million (nearly double those of Jamaica) while the new colony of Southern Rhodesia (now Zimbabwe) in South-central Africa was not far behind with exports worth £3.1 million.

The import figures are similar to the export ones. Again Malaya was far in the lead with the Straits Settlement increasing their imports by a relatively massive (for the period 1910–12) figure of £28.9 million over 1882–4, with a respectable growth rate of 6.5 per cent a year, but again this was overshadowed by the West African late starters, Nigeria and the Gold Coast. The Gold Coast increased its imports over seven-fold and Nigeria recorded more than a ten-fold growth. Its annual average increase was an extraordinary 37.9 per cent. Ceylon, the Federated Malay States, Trinidad and Tobago and Southern Rhodesia all substantially increased their imports by amounts ranging from £10.7 to £2.8 million year in 1910–12 (annual averages).

As in the earlier period these were real, not inflationary, gains and

Table 5.1 The growth of exports and imports by value (less bullion) 1882–4 to 1910–12, selected colonies (annual averages)

Colony	1882–84 £	1910–12 £	Increase £	%	Average annual growth rate (%)
Exports					
Straits Settlements	14,233,256	40,491,333	26,258,077	184.5	6.6
Fed. Malay States	a	14,548,333	–	–	–
Ceylon	3,292,625	12,168,000	8,875,375	269.6	9.6
Nigeria	616,000[b]	5,171,000	4,555,000	739.4	26.4
Trinidad & Tobago	2,681,999	4,014,000	1,342,001	50.0	1.8
Gold Coast	390,333	3,363,667	2,973,334	761.7	29.4
S. Rhodesia	a	3,105,433	–	–	–
Imports					
Straits Settlements	15,964,895	44,900,666	28,935,771	181.2	6.5
Fed. Malay States	a	7,794,666	–	–	–
Ceylon	4,011,239	10,703,667	6,692,428	166.8	6.0
Nigeria	468,333[b]	5,436,333	4,968,000	1,060.8	37.9
Trinidad & Tobago	1,780,666	4,514,666	2,734,000	153.5	5.5
Gold Coast	365,334	2,996,000	2,630,666	720.1	25.7
S. Rhodesia	a	2,849,866	–	–	–

[a] Separate figures not available; quantities small
[b] Lagos only
See Appendices 1 and 2 for details

took place in a period of remarkable price stability – the indices for food, raw materials and industrial prices remaining almost stationary throughout this period.[3] Once again it was the Asian colonies; led by Malaya and Ceylon, which captured by far the largest share of the growing trade as can be seen in Tables 5.2 and 5.3 where the ten leading exporters and importers in 1882–4 and 1910–12 are listed in rank order of the value of their exports and imports. The recently developed African colonies had moved well up the tables by 1910–12 as we have already seen at the expense of some of the other colonies, especially in the West Indies. As exporters Jamaica and British Guiana had fallen to ninth and tenth places respectively, whilst Barbados had dropped out of the first ten. In relation to imports the story was very similar with much the same rank order. Mauritius, as already noted, had also suffered a trade decline, in absolute as well as relative terms, and had fallen from third to ninth place in the import table, with a decline in imports from £2.9 million in 1882–4 to £2.4 million in 1910–12.

However, not all the West Indian colonies suffered a decline. Trinidad's economy had begun to grow rapidly, and taken together the West Indies, British Guiana (now Guyana) and British Honduras (now

Table 5.2 Value of exports (excluding bullion) by colony (first ten in rank order)

	1882–4 (£)			1910–2 (£)	
1.	Straits Settlements	14,233,256	1.	Straits Settlements	40,491,333
2.	Mauritius	3,942,333	2.	Fed. Malay States	14,548,333
3.	Ceylon	3,292,625	3.	Ceylon	12,168,000
4.	British Guiana	2,901,000	4.	Nigeria	5,171,000
5.	Trinidad	2,636,333	5.	Trinidad & Tobago	4,024,000
6.	Jamaica	1,500,333	6,	Gold Coast	3,105,433
7.	Barbados	1,217,666	7.	Southern Rhodesia	3,105,433
8.	Nigeria (Lagos)	616,000	8.	Mauritius	2,576,333
9.	Gold Coast	390,333	9.	Jamaica	2,575,000
10.	Sierra Leone	387,667	10.	British Guiana	1,653,668

Table 5.3 Value of imports (excluding bullion) by colony (first ten in rank order)

	1882–4			1910–12	
1.	Straits Settlements	15,964,895	1.	Straits Settlements	44,900,666
2.	Ceylon	4,011,239	2.	Ceylon	10,703,667
3.	Mauritius	2,875,666	3.	Fed. Malay States	7,794,666
4.	British Guiana	2,029,667	4.	Nigeria	5,436,333
5.	Trinidad	1,738,333	5.	Trinidad & Tobago	4,514,666
6.	Jamaica	1,504,000	6.	Gold Coast	2,996,000
7.	Barbados	1,158,000	7.	Southern Rhodesia	2,849,866
8.	Nigeria (Lagos)	468,333	8.	Jamaica	2,843,666
9.	Sierra Leone	417,666	9.	Mauritius	2,407,333
10.	Fiji	416,666	10.	British Guiana	1,675,666

Belize) increased their value of their exports by 12 per cent in this period but managed to increase the value of their imports by 62 per cent. This discrepancy arose because they had imported considerably less than they had exported in the early 1880s, but reversed the process in the 1910–12 period, when they imported goods worth nearly £1.6 million more than they exported. Inward capital flows, perhaps to the expanding Trinidad oil and asphalt fields, just being developed, may have allowed them to pay for the import surplus.

The export expansion of the tropical colonies continued to depend on a limited range of staples, although it was not quite as narrowly based as it had been in the 1880s. In particular sugar was far less dominant, as can be seen from Table 5.4. Tin from Malaya was still of prime, and increasing, importance, but it had been joined by the booming rubber industry (already accounting for well over a third of the exports from the Federated Malay States in 1910–12) and still growing fast. Tea had dramatically replaced coffee in Ceylon, where rubber was also import-ant; and the new West African staples of cocoa and groundnuts had joined the traditional exports of palm oil and palm kernels.

Table 5.4 Shares of the three main exports in the seven leading exporting tropical colonies in 1910–12 compared with 1882–4

Colony	3 Main exports	% of Exports	
		1882–4	1910–12
Straits Settlements	Tin	11.5	26.4
	Rice	9.3	11.6
	Rubber	a	7.2
Federated Malay States	Tin	a	56.4
	Rubber	a	37.8
	Copra	a	1
Ceylon	Tea	a	45.3
	Rubber	a	21.3
	Coconut oil	a	7.5
Nigeria	Palm kernels	46.9[b]	50.4
	Palm Oil	34.2[b]	32.8
	Rubber	a	4
Trinidad & Tobago	Cocoa	13.5[c]	33.7
	Sugar	30.9[c]	15.2
	Balata gum	a	8.7
Gold Coast	Cocoa	a	40.9
	Gold	15.4	32.6
	Palm kernels	16.1	5.6
Southern Rhodesia	Gold	a	81.7
	Chrome	a	3.5
	Tobacco	a	1.5

[a]Not available
[b]Lagos only
[c]Trinidad only

The structure of imports still remained much the same as it had been in the earlier period, with basic foodstuffs like rice and simple manufactures like cotton cloths and various types of metal hardware predominating in most colonies (see Table 5.5). The import structure of the Straits Settlements was distorted by the fact that they were not yet politically integrated with the Federated Malay States so that articles like tin were imported from interior regions, like that around Kuala Lumpur, to be re-exported from the ports of Pahang and Malacca. Likewise Singapore's huge entrepot trade meant that many of its imports and exports were goods in transit. The opium, which was produced in India and which passed through Singapore en route for China, was probably a case in point; although increasing quantities of opium were being imported into Malaya as demand grew strongly amongst the many Chinese who were working in the tin mines.

95

Table 5.5 Shares of the main imports in the seven leading importing tropical colonies in 1910–12 compared with 1882–4

Colony	Main imports	% of Imports	
		1882–84	1910–12
Straits Settlement	Tin	13.5	22.1
	Rice	11.2	13.3
	Cotton Manufactures	6.7	6.6
Ceylon	Rice	43	30.2
	Coal and coke	9	8.7
	Cotton Manufactures	11.7	7.2
Federated Malay States	Rice	a	22.9
	Opium	a	8.8
	Hardware	a	6.9
Nigeria	Cotton goods	43.5[b]	16
	Spirits	15.4[b]	7.6
	Iron, steel, Manufactures	a	6.4
Trinidad & Tobago	Apparel, etc.	18.7[c]	10.9
	Balata gum	a	7.7
	Flour	7.7[c]	5.3
Gold Coast	Provisions	a	5.7
	Apparel, etc.	38.5	3.4
	Rum	17.9	2.3
Southern Rhodesia	Iron Manufactures Machinery & Railway materials	a	15.0
	Cottons & apparel	a	10.7

[a]Nil or negligible
[b]Lagos only
[c]Trinidad only

Generally speaking the trade pattern remained the classical one of exports of raw materials and foods and imports of a wide range of manufactured goods and fuels. Without any industries of their own the tropical colonies remained a buoyant market for the industrial exports of Britain and Europe. Unfortunately this structural imbalance was to be continued into the 1920s and 1930s, when it became increasingly inappropriate as the markets for colonial food and raw material exports became glutted.

In terms of their dependency on the 'mother country' for their exports the tropical colonies widened their trading network slightly, reducing their dependence on Britain as an export market from 35 per cent to 31 per cent, as the German and American markets expanded more rapidly than the British. Changes in the sources of their imports are more difficult to determine owing to uncertainties in the statistics for the Straits Settlements for the 1880s, but by 1910–12 the tropical colonies were taking about one quarter of their imports from the UK, which probably represented a slight reduction in their dependence. (See Table 5.6.)

Table 5.6 Changes in the United Kingdom's share of the trade of the tropical colonies, 1882–4 to 1910–12

| Years | United Kingdom share | |
	Exports	Imports
1882–4	35%	20%[a]
1910–12	31%	24%
Change	–4%	+4%

[a]Does not include Straits Settlements so is probably an understatement.

In comparison with India the tropical colonies had become pace-setters in the growth of trade with Britain even though starting from a much smaller base and with a considerably smaller total trade. As can be seen from Table 5.7 they increased their exports to Britain from £11.5 million in 1882–4 to £32.1 million in 1910–12, an increase of £20.6 million or 178.3 per cent (an average annual growth of 6.45 per cent) compared with an increase of only £4.45 million from India, or 13.2 per cent. Although in the early 1880s the tropical colonies' exports to Britain had been worth only one-third of India's exports, by 1910–12 their £32.1 million was not far behind India's £38.1 million. As a supplier of food and raw materials to Britain they had become a very significant addition to India.

As a market for British exports they continued to be less important than India, though their annual growth rate of imports in this period was about twice that of India's (4.2 per cent compared with 2.4 per cent) so that their relative importance had increased significantly. At an annual average of £24.6 million in 1910–12 their imports from Britain were only about one-third of India's £72.9 million, but as most of the tropical colonies remained much more underdeveloped than India their scope for future growth was obviously much greater.

There remained also wide variations amongst the tropical colonies in their trading relations with Britain. In 1910–12 most of the West Indian and Asian colonies sent about one-quarter to one-fifth of their exports to Britain and received about the same proportion of their imports from her (see Table 5.8) though of the very large total of imports entering the Straits Settlements only 11 per cent came from Britain. The African

Table 5.7 Comparison of the value of British trade with the tropical colonies and India, 1882–4 to 1910–12 (annual averages, £)

Exports	Tropical colonies	India
Exports		
Exports to Britain, 1882–4	11,533,525	33,629,063
% of total exports	n.a.[a]	42
Exports to Britain, 1910–12	32,099,862	38,078,333
% of total exports	n.a.[a]	26.4
Increase, 1882–4 to 1910–12	20,566,337	4,449,270
% of total increase	178.3	13.2
Average annual growth rate (%)	6.4	0.5
Imports		
Imports from Britain, 1882–4	11,335,546	43,533,750
% of total Imports	n.a.[a]	93.1
Imports from Britain, 1910–12	24,551,274	72,897,666
% of total imports	n.a.[a]	81.9
% Increase, 1882–4 to 1910–12	13,215,728	29,363,916
% of total increase	116.6	67.5
Average annual growth rate (%)	4.2	2.4

[a]Although the exports and imports of the tropical colonies cannot be calculated accurately for reasons explained in the text, the figures are available in the appendices for many individual colonies. A few examples are given in Table 5.8. See Appendices 1 and 2 for details.

Table 5.8 Proportions of the trade of selected tropical Colonies with Britain, 1910–12

Colony	Exports (%)	Imports (%)
Trinidad	25.7	27.2
Jamaica	17.1	43.8
British Guiana	47.0	49.7
Ceylon	47.9	28.4
Straints Settlements	24.8	11.0
Southern Rhodesia	85.8	52.6
Gold Coast	64.6	88.7
Nigeria	59.9	76.9

See Appendices 1 and 2 for details.

colonies on the other hand, traded much more exclusively with Britain. No fewer than 85.8 per cent of Southern Rhodesia's exports went to Britain, while the Gold Coast and Nigeria drew 88.7 per cent and 76.9 per cent of their imports respectively from thence.

Although analysis of the trade figures reveals an important aspect of colonial development in this period, it has to be remembered that this was still a very one-sided and unbalanced process, which benefited only a minority of the population. By levying tariffs on trade, the colonial governments' increased their revenues quite appreciably, and hence their potential for a more balanced economic and social development, if these revenues could be invested in socially fruitful ways. This trade growth was a useful, but not sufficient basis for further progress. To understand more clearly the nature and significance of the growth in overseas trade it is desirable to look at some individual countries in more detail, albeit still fairly briefly. There is not space to consider every example, but a selection of the more important countries will illuminate the main features satisfactorily. For this purpose we may look at Nigeria and Ghana in West Africa, Uganda in East Africa, and Ceylon and Malaya in Asia.

THE GROWTH OF THE NIGERIAN ECONOMY

Nigeria had one of the most dramatic development records of the period 1900-14, as has already been shown in the trade figures. The value of its exports rose from £1,887,000 in 1900 to £6,799,000 in 1913, and in the same period the value of its imports rose from £1,735,000 to £6,332,000.[4] In other words both exports and imports rather more than tripled in value in the short space of thirteen years; and this at a time when parts of the country were still troubled by warfare (for instance, rebellions in the south-centre by the Tiv near Mukurdi on the Benue river, and by some of the Fulani near Sokoto in the extreme northwest in 1906, threatened to disrupt the whole country, though in the event they were easily suppressed).[5]

The provision of even the most basic infrastructure resulted in quite remarkable increases in local production, and consequently in income. As we have seen Southern Nigeria had been producing and exporting palm oil, palm kernels, cocoa and wild rubber in appreciable quantities before 1900, but the productive capacity of Northern Nigeria had hardly been tapped owing to the absence of a cheap and efficient transport system. The rural population could produce their basic subsistence needs by working much less than a whole year. They had time on their hands which could have been put to productive use if certain exterior conditions could be met. Two of the most important of these were that there should be a market for any surplus produce they grew, and and that there should be desirable products available which they could purchase with any money thus earned. In fact, as Hopkins points out this 'vent-for-surplus' theory considerably oversimplifies the real situation, in which a number of complex forces were at work; but emphasises the most important economic variables.[6]

Thus, the extension of the railway from the port of Lagos into Northern Nigeria between 1896 and 1911 was critically important. Produce could now be cheaply shipped away for export, and the multitudinous products of industrial Europe could be cheaply and easily distributed by trading companies with the assistance of itinerant traders and village shopkeepers. Axes, saws, hammers, kettles, bottles, guns, bicycles and bedsteads were amongst the hosts of items for which there was a ready demand. It remained to find the export. The British hoped it would be cotton, and tried to persuade the farmers, but it turned out to be groundnuts, (more commonly known as peanuts), for which there was a burgeoning demand in Europe, and which were also a valuable local food. In Europe they had a double use. They could be pressed for their oil, which was the main ingredient in the growing margarine industry; and the residue could be used as a high-protein cattle cake for dairy cows. The prices for both these products remained generally buoyant in the Edwardian years, and the transport needs were met by the Nigerian railway, which reached Kano, the centre of the Northern Nigerian groundnut area (711 miles to the north) in 1911.[7] The effect was almost miraculous, with groundnut exports rising from 790 tons in 1905 to 19,288 tons in 1913 and soaring to 127,226 tons in 1925 (see Table 5.9).

Table 5.9 Nigerian groundnut exports, 1905–25 (selected years)

Year	Long tons exported	Value (£)
1905	790	7,000
1912	2,518	19,000
1913	19,288	175,000
1916	50,368	474,000
1925	127,226	2,394,000

Source: Gerald K. Helleiner, *Peasant Agriculture, Government and Economic Growth in Nigeria* (Homewood, Illinois, 1966), Table 1VA-A-7 and 8.

The effect of the railway was not fully felt in 1912, but already by 1913 the tonnage exported had leapt nearly seven-fold and by 1916 by a further two and a half times; and this would no doubt have been even more if wartime shipping shortages had not artificially restricted the trade. Of course these rapid increases cannot be attributed purely to the railway. As Hopkins points out,

The Kano area had long produced grain and cotton for the market so agriculture was far from being stuck in a subsistence groove. Farmers were keen to develop a profitable export crop in order to pay taxes, to finance their trading activities in the dry season, and generally to expand their purchasing power. Agriculture in the

Kano region was a subtle mixture of shifting and permanent cultivation, the latter being associated with manuring, water and soil conservation, and, wherever possible, irrigation.[8]

It was also important that traditional systems of land tenure did not prevent the farmers from retaining the profits, and that there was a small group of Hausa traders who were able to provide finance and advice. They had long been engaged in the trans-Sahara trade in cloth and salt, and in the Kola nut trade with the south and were always looking for new opportunities.

> They contacted their established agents and suppliers in the villages around Kano, persuaded farmers to grow more groundnuts, or to grow them for the first time, offered financial assistance, and gave guarantees regarding the purchase of the harvest. The fact that the farmers were prepared to trust the Hausa traders and to treat them as opinion leaders was vital to the success of the the enterprise.[9]

This was a classic case of local enterprise responding quickly and favourably to the provision of infrastructure, in the way that Chamberlain had predicted. It also had a desirable knock-on effect, because Nigeria's main source of revenue came from customs duties, and the growth of trade increased the customs revenue, which provided the finance for further extensions of the infrastructure. Governor-General Lugard began a new oceanic port in eastern Nigeria, Port Harcourt, which was opened in 1911; and planned the railway connecting it to Northern Nigeria at Kaduna, which was opened in 1926.[10] Government revenue and expenditure grew rapidly in these years with revenue rising from £639,000 in 1900 to £3,327,000 in 1913, and expenditure rising from £735,000 to £2,916,000 in the same period (see Table 5.10).

Table 5.10 Nigerian government revenue and expenditure (selected years)

Year	Gross revenue (£)	Customs revenue (£)	Gross expenditure (£)
1900	639,000	601,000	735,000
1907	1,673,000	1,262,000	1,716,000
1913	3,327,000	1,773,000	2,916,000

Source: Helleiner, Peasant Agriculture, Table V-E-3.

The total sums involved were still relatively small, but the rates of growth were impressive, and were not affected by inflation as we have seen. The rising revenue also enabled the Nigerian government to borrow money in London under the Colonial Stocks Act, and by 1914 £9,656,476 had been spent on railways alone by this means. The total debt stood at nearly £10.8 million in 1919.[11] In addition to railways the

101

government had built 2,000 miles of motorable roads by 1914, had begun electricity undertakings in Lagos, had opened coal mines in Enugu in Eastern Nigeria and had introduced a postal and telegraph system and a uniform currency.[12]

THE COCOA TRADE AND THE DEVELOPMENT OF THE GOLD COAST (GHANA)

Like Nigeria, Ghana was also making rapid progress in this period, in some ways even more impressive than in Nigeria, although more narrowly based, since Ghana's economic growth was increasingly dependent on one export, cocoa beans, (although gold was also important) whereas Nigeria's exports were more evenly spread amongst palm produce, cocoa, groundnuts, timber and tin. Just as Nigeria had found an important new export in groundnuts, so Ghana had in cocoa; and the case of cocoa was even more remarkable because unlike groundnuts it was not an indigenous crop, but an import from the Americas.[13] The Basel missionaries had introduced trees experimentally in the early 1860s at their agricultural station at Akropong in the forested hills 30 miles to the north of Accra, but these trees had failed. Cocoa was first successfully introduced to Ghana on a commercial basis by an Accra goldsmith, Tetteh Quarshie, who smuggled in some seeds from the Spanish island of Fernando Po, and grew them successfully at his farm at Mampong, near Akropong. Interestingly Quarshie had been educated by the Basel missionaries, and seems to have been encouraged by them to experiment with cocoa cultivation.[14]

However that might be, farmers in the Akropong area, who had previously exported palm oil, were looking for a new product and began to take an interest in cocoa in the 1890s. They migrated in groups westwards into Akim Abuakwa, where they purchased unoccupied forest land, and planted cocoa trees. From the beginning the farms were quite large, and the operation engendered the growth of local capitalism in Southeastern Ghana.[15]

The demand for chocolate in Europe and America was strong, prices were good, and European trading companies were soon actively buying. The government assisted with the distribution of seed, and built a railway north of Accra, which helped with transport (it carried 20,648 tons of cocoa in 1911);[16] but compared with the enterprise and initiative of the local cocoa farmers, the contribution of expatriate agencies was minimal.[17] The responsiveness of the local farmers exceeded all expectations, with the value of cocoa exports rising from £27,000 in 1900 to £2,489,000 in 1913, and to £8,222,000 in 1925 (see Table 5.11).

At the same time, gold mining, which was an enclave sector, entirely dependent on foreign capital, raised its export earnings from £596,000

Table 5.11 Gold Coast cocoa exports (selected years)

Year	Tons exported	Value (£s)
1900	500	27,000
1907	9,500	515,000
1913	51,300	2,489,000
1916	72,000	3,848,000
1925	218,000	8,222,000

Source: Geoffrey B. Kay, *The Political Economy of Colonialism in Ghana* (Cambridge, 1972), pp.334–6.

in 1905 to £1,626,000 in 1913, but saw its share of total export earnings fall from 43.9% in 1905 to 33.9% in 1913. In 1913 cocoa accounted for 51.9% of export earnings.[18]

As with Nigeria, the rapid growth in overseas trade was reflected in government revenue, and expenditure, both of which roughly doubled between 1904 and 1913 with revenue rising from £682,000 to £1,302,000, and expenditure from £537,000 to £1,193,300 (see Table 5.12).

Table 5.12 Gold Coast government revenue and expenditure (selected years)

Year	Gross revenue (£)	Customs revenue (£)	Gross expenditure (£)	Development expenditure (£)
1904	682,000	384,000	537,500	10,600
1907	709,000	414,000	530,900	34,000
1913	1,302,000	780,000	1,193,300	228,100

Source: As for Table 5.11, pp.348 and 360.

Impressive though these growth rates were, they still represented very small sums in per capita terms. For instance in 1911, Gold Coast government expenditure amounted to only £0.46 per head, and Nigerian only £0.165, and inevitably the amount of development which could be financed from such small sums was strictly limited. Nevertheless, a start was being made in countries where almost nothing had been done before.

Kay sums up the development situation in Ghana between 1898 and 1919 as follows:

The construction of a railway system was the main economic activity of the colonial government during this period, which opens with the construction of the Secondi–Kumasi line (1898–1904). Between 1909 and 1917 the second line was built, from Accra to Kumasi, and by 1920 there were 250 miles of track open in the colony. Expenditure on railways accounted for 24 per cent of total

103

government expenditure and 88 per cent of expenditure on economic services during this period. Health and education accounted for 9.7 and 2.4 per cent respectively of total government expenditure. A rough estimate of the development of these services by 1920 is that the health service provided hospital facilities for about 0.02 per cent of the population, while one child in more than 200 had the opportunity of attending school.[19]

CHANGE IN EAST AFRICA: UGANDA

On the other side of Africa, Uganda enjoyed an experience similar to that of Northern Nigeria. Much of the country is over 600 miles from the sea at Mombasa, and like Kano, Kampala was connected to the coast by a single-line railway, which proved to be the lifeline which made possible the development of an extensive export trade, this time in cotton. At the time that it became a British protectorate in 1894, Uganda was something of an embarrassment, because its economy was extremely simple, and the amount of revenue which could be raised by taxation was minuscule in relation to the costs of administration – even when these were kept to an absolute minimum. In consequence a grant-in-aid from the imperial Treasury was required, and although this was always quite modest, its elimination remained a priority of the British government. For instance in 1900–1 the Ugandan Government spent £252,000, of which it was able to raise only £82,000 in local taxation, and received a grant-in-aid of £204,000. The total value of its exports, which consisted mainly of ivory, was a mere £25,000.[20] Clearly if the Ugandan government was going to spend any money on development, let alone pay its yearly running costs, some means of dramatically increasing its revenue needed to be found, and an export crop was the obvious and essential starting point.

Initially no one knew what this should be and many recommendations were made. Cotton was amongst these at a time when a world shortage had almost doubled its price between 1903 and 1904. The Ganda chiefs were attracted by the idea that their people should grow a cash crop, much of whose value could be transferred to them; so they pressed their tribesmen into cotton cultivation with such success that by 1914–15 the value of cotton exports had reached £369,999 out of total Ugandan exports of £523,000. This raised the government's revenue to £282,000 and reduced the grant-in-aid to a mere £10,000.[21] This was a remarkable achievement which was obtained within a single decade. Nevertheless, the lack of internal transport facilities in Uganda remained a severe problem. The railway to the coast began at Kisumu in Kenya, and although steamers on Lake Victoria Nyanza provided cheap transport from Uganda to Kisumu, cotton and other produce had still to be expensively carried to the lakeshore ports by foot porters carrying head loads since the prevalence of tsetse flies made it impossible to keep draught animals and there were as yet no roads for motor lorries (or any lorries either).[22]

This was a problem which had been worrying the Colonial Office for some time, and was highlighted by the visit of Winston Churchill, then under-secretary of state, to Uganda in 1907. Churchill was struck by the need for better transport, and realising that private companies were unlikely to be interested at the time when the cotton export trade was not yet properly established, he advocated government-owned railways, saying rather surprisingly that he was in favour of 'a practical experiment in State Socialism'. The colonial secretary, Lord Elgin eventually agreed to ask the Treasury for a loan of £500,000 from the Local Loans Fund to build a railway from the port of Jinja on the lake, westwards to Kasese, near the border with the Belgian Congo, to encourage cotton production. The officials in the Colonial Office did not think this scheme had much chance of overcoming Treasury caution and were quite surprised when a loan of £200,000 was finally agreed in 1909. This was not enough to finance the railway to Kasese but was sufficient to build a line 46 miles northwards from Jinja to the nearest navigable port on the Nile at Namasagali. This railway was opened in 1912, and greatly facilitated transport in an area where cotton cultivation was spreading rapidly. It showed that some development risks were worth taking.[23]

In his summary of the Uganda experience Cyril Ehrlich notes that although it was still very limited before 1914, there were definite signs of progress, which had diffused widely amongst the small farmers, who were the most numerous class in Uganda. The old fear of famine had been banished, and the men had exchanged warfare and political intrigue for cotton cultivation, (food crops were still produced by women). The people were 'consistently, if not more nutritiously fed, better clothed, and better housed'. In addition they 'enjoyed the small but significant luxuries of oil-lighting, sugar, tea, perhaps a bicycle'.[24] They were also beginning to have some access to another much-coveted need – European-style education, which many of them felt was the key to entering the modern world of science and technology, which had broken so suddenly and unexpectedly upon them. Uganda is another example of a country where a very limited infrastructural investment before 1914 had brought a most gratifying return, even if it was still quite modest.

CEYLON (NOW SRI LANKA) AND THE TEA TRADE

Across the Indian Ocean in Ceylon, economic development was also progressing quite rapidly in the Edwardian era, although there it was not so firmly based on the indigenous peoples. After the failure of coffee cultivation, owing to attacks of coffee leaf disease in the 1880s, the European planters in the central hill area switched to new crops, of which tea and rubber were the most important. The expansion of tea cultivation and tea exports was extremely rapid. Starting from virtually nothing in the 1880s, tea exports were worth £5,660,000 in 1911, when they far surpassed all rivals in value. The average share of the leading exports in the years 1907–11 inclusive was tea 52.4 per cent, rubber 9.9 per cent and coconut oil 9.0 per cent. Between 1903 and 1912 the total value of Ceylon's exports rose from £7,251,000 to £12,135,000, and imports rose from £7,751,000 to £10,960,000 (1911). This was of course reflected in the government's revenue, which was primarily derived from customs duties. It rose from £1,962,000 in 1902 to £3,498,000 in 1913, and enabled the government to borrow relatively extensively for development projects like railways, irrigation, roads and education. By 1911 Ceylon's outstanding debt under the Colonial Stocks Act stood at £5,426,000.[25]

The main development need was for transport and communications since the expanding tea industry was located in the mountainous centre of the country, south of Kandy, and this area was extremely inaccessible without railways, which were needed not only for shipping tea to the port of Colombo, but also for transporting the many articles needed by tea planters and their employees. These latter were mainly Tamil labourers, imported from South India, who required to be fed. The expansion of tea and rubber cultivation thus had an indirect spin-off advantage for the indigenous Sinhalese cultivators, since the domestic market for their food production was greatly enlarged. They thus increased the production and sale of their traditional crops, vegetables and fruits. The staples were rice, coconuts (whose oil was used for cooking) plantains, yams, manioc, peas and beans. In addition chillies, onions, breadfruit, pawpaws and citrus fruits were widely grown. Because so many people were vegetarians, and because animal diseases like rinderpest were rife, the demand for livestock produce was fairly small, but the production of eggs, chickens, goats and fish was considerably expanded.[26]

With buoyant tea prices after 1895, demands for an expansion of the transport network into the interior were strong, and proposals for a major expansion of the railway network by Governor West Ridgeway were sympathetically received at the Colonial Office, whose officials urged the Treasury not to oppose the scheme. Kesner illustrates this by quoting a memorandum of 1895 by Charles Lucas, then a first class clerk in the Colonial Office and a rising man. Lucas wrote that

Ceylon and the other Eastern Colonies are countries in the making or remaking and the greatest happiness of their inhabitants is it seems to me promoted not by economising, unless it is absolutely necessary, nor by doing away with taxes, but by laying out money on water, roads, railways, and other works.[27]

Even so, Joseph Chamberlain found it necessary to reduce the scope of the governor's railway scheme and in April 1898 he

> asked the governor to accept a less expensive rail network combined with a programme of economic diversification. In this regard, he looked to the future, advocating the adoption of a plan that would meet Ceylon's immediate needs for better transport while providing later colonial administrations the fiscal flexibility to pursue other types of economic development progress.[28]

Under the approved scheme Ceylon's railway operating mileage was more than doubled, increasing from 297 miles in 1901 to 671 miles in 1914. During the same period the quantity of freight carried on the island's railways also virtually doubled, rising from 520,639 tons to 999,943 tons.

Expenditure on other aspects of development was not on such a large scale, but problems of health and education were concerning the more conscientious officials serving in Ceylon, as is revealed by the well-known author, Leonard Woolf in his autobiography. His view is particularly interesting as he was later a prominent member of the Fabian Society and a trenchant critic of imperialism in his book *Empire and Commerce in Africa* (1920). He was assistant government agent in the poor and remote district of Hambantota in Southern Ceylon between August 1908 and May 1911. He became devoted to the place and its people and wrote that

> I rarely thought of anything else except the District and the people, to increase their prosperity, diminish the poverty and disease, start irrigation works, open schools.[29]

He was particularly proud of his work in connection with education and his last act before leaving Ceylon was to visit some schools in Hambantota, where 'I had built and opened a Government Tamil school in the town and had made primary education compulsory'.[30]

PROGRESS IN MALAYA

Finally, we may look briefly at Malaya, the tropical colony whose export sector was in many ways the richest and most highly developed of all in 1914. This can be seen if we compare the five tropical colonies which had

Table 5.13 The five tropical colonies with the highest revenues in 1911

Country	Revenue (£m)	Population (m)	Revenue per head (£m)
Malaya[a]	6.147	2.653	2.32
Ceylon	3.022	4.106	0.74
Nigeria	2.571	17.131	0.15
Jamaica	1.352	0.831	1.63
Gold Coast	1.112	1.502	0.74

[a]Includes the Straits Settlements, the Federated Malay States, and the Protected Malay States. The revenue of Trengganu is not known but has been estimated at one-half that of neighbouring Kelantan, which had roughly twice the population. The Trengganu revenue is thus estimated at £25,000. Even if this is too large it is still a trivial proportion of the total Malayan revenues.

Sources: B.R. Mitchell, *International Historical Statistics, Africa and Asia (London, 1982)*; Richard Kesner, *Economic Control and Colonial Development* (London, 1981), and *The Oxford Survey of the British Empire*, Vol. II, *Asia* (Oxford, 1914).

the largest governmental revenues just before the First World War, where Malaya's £6,147,000 was more than double Ceylon's £3,022,000 and was well ahead of Nigeria's £2,571,000, Jamaica's £1,352,000 and the Gold Coast's £1,112,000 (see Table 5.13).

The Malayan revenue and population has been obtained by adding together those of the Straits Settlements of Singapore, Pahang, Malacca and the Dindings with the Federated Malay States of Perak, Selangor, Negri Sembilan, and Pahang, and the Protected Malay States of Johore, Kedah, Perlis, Kelantan and Trengganu; for despite the variations by which British control was exercised they were all being effectively merged into one economic unit by the extension of British commercial law, currency and banking, telegraphs, railways and all the other socio-economic links which were being developed between them.

The contrast between Malaya and Ceylon is even more in Malaya's favour if the comparison is made on a per capita basis, for each Malayan yielded £2.6s.4d (£2.32) in taxation, and each Sinhalese only 14s.8d (£0.74). In neither case of course were any considerable direct taxes paid, the great bulk of both colonies' revenues being derived from customs duties. It has to be remembered of course that revenue per head is not the same thing as income per head, and as the population of the Federated Malay States, where the great majority of the tin mines and rubber plantations were located, rose from 678,600 in 1901 to 1,037,000 in 1911, (52.8 per cent) it is quite possible that income per head did not rise at all, illustrating once again that increases in foreign trade, no matter how impressive, made only a very one-sided contribution to development. This is emphasised by the fact that much of the population growth came from Chinese and Indian labourers who were paid very low wages.[31]

The growth of the Malayan economy was very rapid in the Edwardian

Table 5.14 World rubber exports, 1911–14 (in tons)

Year	Wild rubber		Cultivated rubber		
	South America	Africa	Malaya	Others[a]	Total
1911	58,271	18,283	10,800	6,300	93,654
1912	62,025	18,918	20,300	11,800	113,070
1913	50,493	15,986	33,600	19,800	119,879
1914	40,867	7,19	47,000	28,700	124,286

[a] Mainly Indonesia and Ceylon
Source: Adapted from John H. Drabble, Rubber in Malaya 1876–1922 (OUP, Kuala Lumpur, 1973) p. 106.

period, especially in the Federated Malay States (FMS) after they were joined together in 1895, because it was in these states that the great majority of the tin mines and rubber plantations were located and on whose remarkably rapid growth the economy depended. The trade of the Straits Settlements also grew very rapidly in this period, but this was principally based on exports from and imports to the FMS. The huge rise in the population of the FMS came mainly from the immigration of Chinese and Indian labourers to work in the tin mines and rubber plantations, but the Malay population also increased by 34.3 per cent at the same time.[32]

The growth of the economy was most clearly reflected in the trade statistics, as previously noted. Tin ore exports from the FMS had grown strongly in the 1890s, reaching 47,475 tons in 1901 and they levelled out in the next decade, and were slightly lower in 1911, at 44,148 tons; but the slack was more than taken up by the booming rubber industry. No rubber had been exported from Malaya in 1901, but by 1911 exports had reached 10,800 tons and by 1914 had leapt to 47,000 tons. In 1911 Malaya's share of world rubber exports was already 11.5 per cent. By 1914 it had soared to 37.8 per cent. Malaya's rise was mainly at the expense of South America and Africa (see Table 5.14).

A number of factors were responsible for Malaya's rise as a rubber producer. Expanded demand for motor car tyres was reflected in rapid price rises. The London average price rose from 3s 6d (£0.17½) per pound in 1897 to 8s.9d (£0.75¾) in 1910, before sinking to 2s 3½d (£0.11½) in 1914, but by that time the huge increase in the acreage of rubber trees guaranteed continued high production, despite falling prices.[33] On the supply side, the Malayan government provided access to virgin land at low prices, and freely distributed the seeds of the *Hevea* rubber trees (developed at Kew Gardens from Brazilian originals). In addition investors in London and Singapore were anxious to supply capital and management, while Tamil labourers from South India were willing to come to Malaya to work on the plantations and were actively encouraged by the Indian and Malayan governments to do so. The rise in the acreage of rubber trees in Malaya was remarkable. In 1897 there were only 345 acres, all in the FMS. By 1914 there were 1,168,000 acres with some in every Malayan state, ranging from 471,050 in the FMS to 1,802 in Trengganu the last state to take up rubber plantations.[34]

The construction of roads, railways, hospitals, and water supplies, etc. was an essential part of the process and one where the state was prepared to take the lead ahead of developments, in order to ensure that expansion continued.[35] Sir Frank Swettenham, who was Resident-General in the FMS from 1896 to 1901, and governor and commander-in-chief of the Straits Settlements from 1901 to 1904, summed up this aspect of his work in the FMS in 1906:

> a country which, in 1874, had no post office and had never seen a postage stamp, in 1904 dealt with about 10,000,000 covers, issued money orders to the value of over $1,250,000 [Straits $ worth 2s 4d] had $275,000 in the Post Office Savings Banks, and maintained over 2,000 miles of telegraph wires. In the same year the prisons received 10,000 prisoners, the hospitals treated 46,000 in-patients and 130,000 out-patients at a cost of over £50,000 a year, and the schools were attended by over 13,000 scholars. In 1875 the States did not possess a mile of first class road, but in 1904 there were over 2,500 miles, the greater part of which will compare favourably with the roads in any country, while 340 miles of the railway, built at a cost of $32,000,000, were open for traffic, and, when the present extensions are completed, the Federation will have constructed and equipped close on 500 miles of railways, out of current revenue, without borrowing a farthing. Indeed, the Government balances at the end of 1905 amounted to no less than $22,000,000. It may be questioned whether it is possible to find, in the history of British administration over-seas, a parallel to this record.[36]

Sir Frank Swettenham was certainly not a man to hide his light under a bushel, but he did have cause for some legitimate pride, and all the indicators he mentioned continued to expand up to 1914. For instance, the railway mileage had reached 822 miles by that date.[37]

On the other hand, it is clear that most of the advantages of economic development were being realised by the European, Chinese, and Indian communities, and that the advantages to the indigenous Malayan population were rather more indirect. They were no doubt alarmed to note that by 1911 they were no longer a majority in the FMS. At that date the census revealed that there were 420,840 Malays (40.5 per cent of the total population) compared with 433,200 Chinese (41.8 per cent) and 172,500 Indians (16.6 per cent; see Table 5.15).

The British authorities repeatedly stated that their aim was to benefit the Malayan people and no doubt they had to derive what reassurance they could from that; and from the indirect economic benefits that came with development. The Malays were primarily farmers on a small scale, and the expansion of the food market, especially for rice, vegetables and fruits, in the growing towns like Singapore, Kuala Lumpur and Pahang, enabled them to participate in the new export economy at a supporting level, and to increase their incomes by raising cash crops. In Swettenham's words 'The Malays are rice growers and planters of cocoa-nuts [sic] and other fruit trees, and it is very satisfactory to know that in the last thirty years these cultivations have been enormously extended'.[38] However, as noted in the previous chapter, the Malayan farmers were not as successful as rice growers as Swettenham liked to believe, and the alienation of much of their best land for foreign-owned tin mines and rubber plantations made the rapid commercialisation of the Malayan economy a very mixed blessing for many of them.

But it was the phenomenal growth of rubber cultivation in the years before 1914, which was the motor powering Malayan economic develop-ment; and in his final comments (in 1973) on its effects on the economy, Drabble noted its two-sided role. On the one hand it had led to a huge growth in commercial activities and services, and to the impressive infrastructural development already described; but on the other

it is somewhat ironic that Malaya's leading role in rubber-growing, one of the outstanding agricultural enterprises of the twentieth century, at the same time placed her firmly in the group of primary producing countries which are today categorised as less-developed[39]

However, in the heady days between 1905 and 1914, the tangible advantages of rapid economic development would have been much more prominent.

THE NATURE OF EARLY DEVELOPMENT: SUCCESSES AND IMPEDIMENTS

With the benefit of hindsight it is now clear that the years before 1914 represented something of a high point in the development of the tropical colonies. The markets for their exports had been rapidly grow-ing and the undiversified nature of their economies had not yet become a problem: when cheap manufactures were so easy to import from Britain, Europe and America, the absence of indigenous industries did

Table 5.15 Ethnic composition of the population of the Federated Malay States in 1911

	No.	%
Malays	420,840	40.5
Chinese	433,200	41.8
Indian	172,500	16.6
European	3,290	0.3
Eurasians	2,650	0.25

Source: *Oxford Survey of the British Empire*, vol. II, *Asia*, p.481.

not seem so important, especially as their exports of primary products were expanding so satisfactorily and were bringing so much prosperity with them; even if this was not equally distributed. Even so with much export income going to peasant producers (as with Gold Coast cocoa, Nigerian groundnuts and Ugandan cotton, for instance) the distribution of the gains was more equal than it was in places like South America, where large estate owners were considerably more prominent.

There were, however, some signs that the rapid development of the pre-war years might not be sustained. In particular there is some evidence that capital supplies, curiously enough from Britain in particular, were becoming difficult to obtain. For instance, between 1910 and 1913 the Admiralty became worried about oil supplies for the navy (which had recently converted from coal-fired to oil-fired ships) and wished to develop oil fields which would be firmly under British control in the event of war (as the then important Rumanian oil fields were not). The Persian (Iranian) oil fields were operated by a British company (the Anglo-Persian Company) but the fields were still undeveloped and not in British territory, so Trinidad seemed like a good prospect as it was a British colony which was very poor, and in need of an export staple. The difficulty was to find a British company which would undertake to develop the oil fields. The main contender was a consortium of companies, known as the United British West Indies Petroleum Syndicate Ltd, which included a number of foreign interests about whom the Admiralty were worried. In particular they were concerned that the Shell Company, which was 60 per cent Dutch owned, was involved; since the possibility of the Germans buying out the Dutch share was taken seriously at the time.

The Admiralty tried to circumvent the syndicate by entering into negotiations with two British companies, Consolidated Gold Fields of South Africa, chaired by Lord Harris, and S. Pearson and Son, chaired by Lord Cowdray, in the hope that they would be prepared to develop the oil fields, but both declined on the grounds that they would be unable to market the oil without Shell's cooperation. In the event the

Admiralty's fears about the foreign elements in the syndicate (which were French and Russian as well as Dutch) proved groundless and a lease of 200,000 acres was made to them in 1913 for a fifty-year period with the right to negotiate for thirty more years. As a result of the Colonial Office's rather weak bargaining position it was not able to obtain very good terms for Trinidad. For instance, royalties were only two shillings a ton on the first 100,000 tons, and one shilling and sixpence on all higher tonnages. A rent of fifteen shillings an acre was paid on all land being worked for oil, but the Trinidad government agreed not to tax oil exports, or oil underground values, and not to exercise its right of pre-emption (on which the Admiralty had insisted) except in war or emergency.[40]

Another example relates to British Guiana, where a Mr Evan Wong, a citizen of the colony, had been granted exclusive rights to mine bauxite and had sold these to two American companies, the Maritime Chemical Company of Boston, Massachusetts and the Southern Aluminium Company of Whitney, North Carolina. When war broke out in 1914, the Colonial Office became worried that the then neutral American companies might sell aluminium from British Guiana to the Germans who could use it in armaments production. The Colonial Office therefore wanted a British company to buy the rights back from the American companies. However, all the British companies with whom the Colonial Office negotiated refused to invest money in British Guiana. Eventually a Canadian company, the Northern Aluminium Company of Canada, which was also registered in Britain, was persuaded to enter into an agreement with the two American companies whereby they entered a 'British' consortium.[41]

Even when British companies were willing to invest capital in the tropical colonies, the colonial administrators' concept of 'trusteeship' sometimes caused them to block such proposals. One of the best known examples of this occurred when William Lever, the great soap magnate, sought to obtain concessions of land in Nigeria and Sierra Leone in 1907 to develop palm oil plantations, but the colonial governments refused to agree, and he turned instead to the Belgian Congo where he was granted a substantial concession in 1911.[42] In defence of the colonial governments, though, it has to be remembered that peasant production of palm oil and palm kernels was very buoyant at that time, and alienation of land in the relatively densely populated palm belts of Southern Nigeria and Sierra Leone would have created resentment and political unrest for which there was no strong justification at that time; even if the case for plantations became stronger after 1920, when Congolese, Malayan and Indonesian plantations offered powerful competition to peasant producers.[43]

These examples not only illustrate the difficulties of procuring capital

113

for colonial development, but also show that the problem of dependence on international capital supplies is by no means a new one.

Finally, how should the record of development under colonial rule in the years before 1914 be assessed? These were the early years for many of the colonies, especially the African ones, and it might thus seem that it would not be surprising if achievements were rather limited, but paradoxically for many of the colonies this was the period when their economies grew more rapidly than before or since. Of course fast growth does not necessarily mean development, although it can be a very helpful pre-condition for it. It has to be remembered that the world's trading economy was expanding very quickly in the period 1903–14 anyway, and that the demand for many tropical products was strong, so that to some extent these areas would have been involved in economic growth even if they had not become colonies.

On the other hand colonial rule certainly speeded up their integration into the world economy by providing a stable political environment and by providing a very basic infrastructure of railways, roads, telegraphs, banks, currency, hospitals, schools, etc. The fact the private capital could not be induced to build railways in the colonies, and that the colonial governments were forced to do it, suggests that without colonial rule economic development might have been considerably slower.

Conversely proconsuls like Swettenham and Lugard tended to exaggerate the importance of the innovations which they introduced, and to equate mere trade growth with the much more complex problem of achieving balanced and comprehensive development. Even in this period of rapid trade growth the incomes of most of the inhabitants of the tropical colonies remained pitifully small and their standard of living abysmally low. Also trade growth tended to benefit some regions more than (and sometimes at the expense of) other regions, transferring labour and capital to the more favoured regions, often coastal, at the expense of the interior parts. The resulting regional disparities were often very severe and made the problem of securing a balanced and equitable development more difficult.

So in conclusion, while it is important to recognise the role that colonial rule played in laying down a basis for future development, it is also necessary to acknowledge the very limited nature of the achievement, even before 1914, in the period which was in many ways the heyday of colonial rule.[44] Unfortunately many of the one-sided aspects of development which commenced in this period were never overcome, with serious consequences, to which we must now turn.

6

The impact of the First World War and its aftermath

In the twenty-five years prior to the First World War the extension of colonial rule by European conquest in the tropics had accelerated the process of integration of these lands into the expanding global economy. The external trade of the British colonial territories kept pace with the growth of international trade generally and doubled in value between 1901 and 1913. In the three years preceding the outbreak of the war, growth in colonial trade outpaced that of the world economy and colonial exports increased to about 3.7 per cent of world exports of primary products (Tables 6.1 and 6.2). This era of fairly rapid expansion came to an end in 1914. The war created considerable problems for the newly established colonial economies. In the short run there were severe difficulties with external trade as transport links were disrupted and markets deteriorated. Colonial government revenues were also adversely affected and the colonies' terms of trade tended to decline. In the longer run the economic plight of Britain after the war made the provision of public capital for development less certain while at the same time focussing attention on how developing the 'colonial estate' might be harnessed to assist Britain's recovery. The redistribution of German and Turkish colonies as 'mandates' to the Allies at the Paris Peace Conference in 1919 revived concerns about the content of British imperial trusteeship and the appropriate balance between development and welfare. These themes dominated colonial economic policy in the post-war era.

ECONOMIC IMPACT OF THE WAR

The war affected the colonial economies in various ways and to some extent the nature of the changes was determined by the country's integration with the British and continental European economies, the distance from its external markets and the particular mix of its export products. Few of Britain's tropical colonies were much dependent upon German demand for their export earnings or upon a German supply of

115

Table 6.1 Comparison of growth of world trade and colonial trade, 1896/1900–1911/13

Period	Annual average rate of growth of world trade (%)	Annual average rate of growth of colonial trade (%)[a]
1896–1900	5.6	6.4
1901–5	4.8	1.2
1906–10	5.0	7.0
1911–13	7.4	9.3

[a] Excludes India, Australia, New Zealand, South Africa and Canada.
Sources: World Trade: J. Tinbergen, *Business Cycles in the United Kingdom, 1870–1914*, (2nd edn, 1956), Table 1A; League of Nations, *Industrialisation and Foreign Trade*, (1945), pp.157–67; Colonial Trade: 1896–1900: *Statistical Abstract of the British Empire*, No. 48; 1901–1913: *Statistical Abstract of the British Empire*, No. 52.

Table 6.2 Comparison of growth of world exports of primary produce and colonial exports 1901–13

Period	Average annual value of world exports of primary products (£m)	% change	Average annual value of colonial exports (£m)	% change
1901–5	1659.9		55.1	
1906–10	2140.0	28.9	72.1	30.6
1911–13	2703.2	26.3	101.1	38.8

Source: League of Nations, *Industrialisation and Foreign Trade*, pp.166–7; *Statistical Abstract of the British Empire*, No. 52.

imports. France, Belgium and Holland were generally even less significant as trading partners. Overall Germany supplied about 3.5 per cent of the tropical colonies' imports in the period 1911–13, and took approximately 9 per cent of their total exports. In only two cases was German trade really important – Sierra Leone sold 56 per cent of its exports (chiefly palm kernels) to Germany in 1911–13, and Nigeria 47 per cent, and took approximately 9 per cent of their total exports. For virtually all other colonies the removal of Germany and its allies from the international market during the war was little more than a minor setback. Britain, on the other, was an important market and supplier of imports for nearly all the countries in the colonial empire. Britain supplied about 26 per cent of the colonial empire's total imports in 1911–13 and took about 32 per cent of its exports. More detailed figures are shown in Table 6.3 for the major tropical colonies.

The war caused supplies of British imports to be disrupted and to rise sharply in price. Price inflation was partly the result of increased ship-

Table 6.3 Trade between Britain and selected tropical colonies, 1911–13

Colony	Annual average of total imports (£m)	% from UK	Annual average of total exports (£m)	% to UK
Nigeria	6.43	68.4	6.27	48.7
Gold Coast	4.27	70.0	4.50	63.9
Sierra Leone	1.47	67.6	1.53	17.9
Jamaica	2.93	42.4	2.70	15.1
Trinidad	2.73	35.0	2.67	19.5
British Guiana	1.63	53.8	1.97	41.5
Fiji	0.93	17.9	1.25	3.5
Federated Malay States	8.90	13.4	16.33	22.6
Straits Settlements	51.63	10.6	43.00	23.8
Ceylon	12.13	28.0	13.70	47.2
Mauritius	2.40	33.2	2.50	21.1
Kenya–Uganda	2.57	27.3	1.40	37.9
Northern Rhodesia	0.23	48.3	0.15	41.8
Total	98.25	23.7	97.97	30.2

Source: *Statistical Abstract of the British Empire*, No. 57.

ping costs, but it was also due to higher levels of inflation in Britain as a result of the way in which the war was financed and shortages caused by the diversion of production to war goods. Exports to Britain were affected by higher shipping costs, shipping shortages, the desire of the British government from 1916 to purchase supplies in the cheapest (which usually meant the nearest) market and distortions in demand for particular commodities as production was switched from civilian to military use.[1] In some colonies, heavy investment in production and transport facilities in the years immediately prior to the war led to large increases of produce being available which resulted in price falls. In other cases export prices rose as certain commodities were strategic for the war effort or, as occurred with sugar, were affected by the removal of Germany as an exporter.

The value of colonial exports doubled between 1914 and 1918 whilst the cost of imports more than doubled (Table 6.4). Average growth per year between 1914 and 1918 of the value of total colonial trade was 14 per cent, compared to about 10 per cent between 1909 and 1913. However, in many colonies this was due more to price inflation than to physical increases, especially of imported manufactured goods. The immediate effect of the war was to depress nearly all colonial export prices as demand was uncertain and supply was increasing. By 1915 a number of commodities were below their pre-war price levels: cotton, copra, groundnuts, bananas, palm products, rubber and tin (Table 6.5).

Table 6.4 Imports, exports and balance of trade, selected colonies, 1911–21 (£000)

Colonies	1911	1912	1913	1914	1915	1916	1917	1918	1919	1920	1921
Imports											
West Africa	9622	10946	11899	11428	9844	11862	11059	12917	21150	42574	20914
East Africa	2636	3321	3881	3002	3025	5856	7165	6500	8326	12118	5161
Central Africa	435	515	465	408	419	686	693	1102	1015	1173	1372
Eastern	57348	63797	68445	57708	63495	79427	89097	96360	125350	165460	84958
Caribbean	9257	9306	9172	8754	8827	11132	13120	14862	18049	29794	18877
Pacific	854	903	843	893	836	848	933	1128	1032	1652	1484
Total	80152	88788	94705	82193	86446	109811	122067	132869	174922	252771	132766
Exports											
West Africa	9345	10229	12647	10966	10375	12115	14855	14573	27239	33795	15852
East Africa	2227	2314	2667	1843	1533	2629	4083	5359	10136	8378	4841
Central Africa	294	270	419	351	335	450	373	876	939	1205	976
Eastern	53053	57373	61222	56586	68494	81655	96518	89774	148891	143027	83789
Caribbean	8595	7961	8417	9119	10737	12783	13171	13069	19237	25890	12804
Pacific	1275	1059	1426	1391	1474	2254	2068	1655	1871	2876	2538
Total	74789	79206	86798	80256	92948	111886	131068	125306	208403	215271	120800
Balance											
West Africa	-277	717	748	-462	531	253	3796	1656	6179	-8779	-5062
East Africa	-409	-1007	-1214	-1159	-1492	-3227	-3082	-1141	1810	-3640	-320
Central Africa	-141	-245	-46	-57	-84	-236	-320	-226	-76	32	-396
Eastern	-4295	-6424	-7223	-1122	4999	2228	7421	-6586	23541	-22433	-1169
Caribbean	-662	-1345	-755	365	1910	1651	51	-1793	1188	-3904	-6073
Pacific	421	156	583	498	638	1406	1135	527	839	1224	1054
Total	-5363	-9582	-7907	-1937	6502	2075	9001	-7563	33481	-37500	-11966

Total exports and imports excluding bullion and coin.
West Africa: Gambia, Gold Coast, Nigeria, Sierra Leone;
East Africa: Kenya–Uganda, Zanzibar;
Central Africa: Northern Rhodesia, Nyasaland;
Eastern: Ceylon, Mauritius, Straits Settlements;
Caribbean: Barbados, British Guiana, British Honduras, Jamaica, Trinidad.
Source: *Statistical Abstract for the British Empire*, No. 57, (1909–23).

Table 6.5 Effect of the war on colonial export prices, 1913–21 (indices of unit values, 1909–13 = 100)

Commodity/colony	1913	1914	1915	1916	1917	1918	1919	1920	1921
Bananas/Jamaica	100.0	108.2	87.1	76.5	111.8	109.4	138.8	171.8	153.9
Cocoa/Trinidad	122.0	97.4	141.0	128.4	99.3	109.7	159.3	192.0	67.7
Cocoa/Gold Coast	118.3	99.5	113.5	128.4	83.2	64.9	113.0	193.8	86.1
Coffee/Kenya	119.6	103.7	108.7	103.2	82.7	99.5	237.0	165.8	147.5
Copra/Kenya	122.4	95.9	94.1	109.2	105.5	84.4	192.0	159.8	120.7
Copra/Ceylon	116.0	102.0	90.0	103.0	76.1	62.2	170.7	193.9	110.4
Cotton/Uganda	100.3	82.7	70.9	129.7	202.2	268.1	408.1	481.7	129.7
Cotton/Nigeria	96.0	102.2	80.0	125.2	170.0	251.5	275.3	365.0	110.3
Groundnuts/Nigeria	105.1	122.2	94.0	109.1	163.7	187.2	206.0	286.1	253.0
Hides/Kenya	127.9	128.5	115.8	103.9	133.6	132.0	213.3	176.7	63.3
Maize/Kenya	91.0	114.4	109.5	129.4	154.2	—	264.0	215.7	148.8
Palm kernels/Nigeria	121.7	106.9	75.5	73.7	94.9	107.5	155.9	188.8	126.3
Palm oil/Nigeria	106.7	102.9	95.2	99.1	120.0	143.8	200.0	262.9	149.5
Rubber/Fed. Malay States	51.6	37.9	44.8	50.2	50.5	31.7	37.9	37.7	15.2
Rubber/Straits Settlements	53.4	39.3	44.7	50.1	47.5	31.1	37.2	38.8	14.1
Rubber/Ceylon	62.9	42.9	42.0	49.0	47.0	34.8	50.9	35.5	15.2
Sisal/Kenya	99.5	169.8	264.1	319.8	366.0	340.9	372.0	274.5	255.7
Sugar/British Guiana	103.3	121.3	145.9	168.9	180.3	180.3	244.3	409.8	159.0
Sugar/Trinidad	90.1	87.3	146.5	157.8	164.8	163.4	176.7	376.7	216.4
Sugar/Mauritius	96.8	119.7	142.6	179.6	170.8	176.1	246.5	406.7	267.6
Sugar/Fiji	102.5	101.8	116.0	131.7	142.2	145.1	146.9	267.3	263.5
Tea/Ceylon	104.1	105.1	128.9	117.4	111.2	104.4	190.1	148.6	158.2
Tin/Straits Settlements	114.2	85.9	88.6	99.6	122.4	173.5	144.3	172.3	92.7
Tin/Nigeria	109.0	92.2	89.1	98.1	120.0	171.8	138.7	181.7	102.6

Source: Statistical Abstract of the British Empire, Nos. 55, 57.

Only sugar, cocoa and sisal were substantially above pre-war levels. Prices increased more rapidly in 1917 and 1918 as production was cut back and the rate of inflation in Britain and the United States accelerated. The entry of the latter into the war in May 1917 further improved the demand for colonial primary exports. By 1918 most were above their 1909–13 levels (Table 6.5), though not cocoa (Gold Coast), copra and rubber.

A similar acceleration in the prices of imported commodities can be seen in the last two years of the war, though import prices had generally advanced more by 1915 than had export prices (Table 6.6). A pattern in trade which seemed to affect many tropical colonies was for export volumes to rise faster than export prices during 1915 and 1916 whilst in 1917 and 1918 volume slowed or fell back but prices accelerated. Similarly, physical quantities of imports were curtailed as their prices rose in 1917 and 1918. For most colonies the war produced a worsening of their terms of trade, which had been improving in many cases in the immediate pre-war years. Of the colonies shown in Table 6.7, all suffered declining terms of trade by 1918, except Mauritius, most of whose trade was with India and East Africa rather than Europe. Declining terms of trade meant that imports had to be restricted and/or export volumes greatly increased, as happened with rubber for example. In either case, it involved greater effort for relatively less reward and in some colonies by 1918 resulted in export sectors which were operating at a loss. A third course was to run up foreign debt, but borrowing in London was not permitted and in fact capital was repatriated during the war: between 1909 and 1913 total imports (measured cost insurance freight (cif) and including specie movements) exceeded total exports by some £26 million for the colonial empire as a whole, which may be taken as a rough guide to capital inflow to the colonies. Between 1914 and 1919, however, exports exceeded imports by £78.7 million, or three times as much.

Price distortions in international trade were much more severe after the war ended than during it. In the three post-war years the colonial empire's import trade increased in value by 116 per cent whilst exports rose by 103 per cent. As indicated by Tables 6.5 and 6.6 most of this increase was due to price rises, but import prices tended to rise more than export prices so the terms of trade continued to deteriorate for some, though not all, of the tropical colonies (Table 6.7). The postwar boom was short-lived and trade values in 1921 returned to their levels of 1918. Some export prices fell to pre-war levels: cocoa, hides and skins (Kenya) and tin, whilst rubber prices reached new lows of about 15 per cent of their 1909–13 levels (Table 6.5). Many imported goods also fell in price in 1921 (Table 6.6), though again they tended not to fall as much as the prices of exported commodities, causing a

Table 6.6 Effect of the war on colonial import prices, 1913–21 (indices of unit values, 1901–13 = 100)

Commodity	Colony	1913	1914	1915	1916	1917	1918	1919	1920	1921
Coal	Ceylon	105.4	106.3	108.0	143.8	178.6	279.5	282.9	104.6	182.1
	Nigeria	112.3	119.2	212.7	307.5	309.1	458.2	573.2	804.2	475.3
	Straits Settlement	111.8	110.9	110.0	184.6	291.8	512.7	411.8	463.6	330.0
	Trinidad[a]	98.5	95.6	113.2	178.5	242.9	361.0	330.7	243.9	472.2
Cotton Piece Goods	Kenya–Uganda	95.2	99.3	104.1	130.8	187.0	265.8	341.8	391.1	268.5
	Mauritius	107.3	103.2	120.4	134.6	172.1	235.8	314.8	324.9	347.2
	Straits Settlement	100.1	100.1	90.0	112.1	154.0	209.9	157.0	423.5	234.7
	Trinidad[a]	97.1	109.6	92.9	133.9	173.2	282.0	287.0	493.7	236.8
Fish	Jamaica	105.7	117.9	122.1	135.7	179.3	230.0	287.7	265.7	180.0
	Nigeria	100.3	105.8	152.5	185.8	106.4	141.0	151.9	272.5	198.9
	Straits Settlement	106.6	109.2	109.9	106.1	113.9	124.0	157.0	236.9	185.1
Flour	Jamaica	95.4	98.2	113.6	137.3	236.4	268.2	251.8	318.2	227.3
	Kenya/Uganda	105.5	123.6	127.3	125.5	169.1	209.1	318.2	294.6	240.0
Gin	Nigeria	106.5	106.5	147.0	220.0	326.0	608.8	903.5	974.1	866.7
Kerosene	Ceylon	105.0	109.3	124.2	162.3	170.0	165.5	182.1	201.8	138.4
Petroleum	Kenya–Uganda	93.2	115.1	130.1	201.1	210.6	282.6	308.3	384.5	369.1
	Mauritius	95.6	95.6	91.7	106.9	101.6	104.6	112.4	121.7	97.3
Rice	Ceylon	100.0	104.4	104.4	113.3	113.3	120.0	183.8	234.2	117.1
	Jamaica	105.4	108.8	137.8	180.3	243.2	304.4	355.4	454.1	190.5
	Kenya–Uganda	110.4	108.3	114.6	131.3	170.8	212.5	360.4	350.0	227.1
	Mauritius	102.3	122.7	127.3	136.4	143.2	197.7	184.1	288.6	111.4
	Nigeria	112.0	104.0	148.0	186.0	261.4	406.0	358.0	636.0	284.0
	Straits Settlement	102.6	94.1	93.4	98.4	107.9	142.9	283.1	486.0	176.7
Rum	Gold Coast	100.5	109.0	123.2	162.3	229.3	298.5	341.0	1383.5	1274.3
Salt	Nigeria	113.2	119.7	257.9	344.7	411.2	590.1	611.8	664.5	599.3
Soap	Mauritius	110.9	111.9	113.9	139.6	173.3	271.3	278.2	263.4	195.1
Tobacco	Kenya–Uganda	104.8	120.9	135.9	167.2	172.2	216.4	408.9	435.1	361.3
	Mauritius	99.0	110.8	191.4	268.4	284.6	308.4	291.9	393.4	266.5
	Nigeria	97.2	100.1	108.9	121.3	139.5	180.4	243.5	304.0	393.0

a 1912–3 = 100.
Source: As for Table 6.5.

Table 6.7 Terms of trade, selected colonies, 1913–1921 (1909–13 = 100)

Colony		1913	1914	1915	1916	1917	1918	1919	1920	1921
Nigeria[a]	E	–	–	100.0	106.3	131.6	158.9	200.0	259.7	158.9
	I	–	–	100.0	109.0	137.0	202.2	250.0	355.9	307.0
	T	–	–	100	97	96	79	80	73	52
Kenya	E	114.5	108.1	99.1	117.8	159.3	175.3	296.1	293.3	102.8[c]
Uganda[b]	I	97.6	105.0	113.7	138.0	184.5	246.6	347.6	393.8	267.3[c]
	T	117	103	87	85	86	71	85	75	39[c]
Mauritius[d]	E	96.8	119.7	142.6	179.6	170.8	176.1	246.5	406.7	267.6
	I	103.3	105.4	111.0	128.1	151.5	233.1	201.1	256.7	136.0
	T	94	114	129	140	113	76	123	158	197
Ceylon[d]	E	97.6	90.7	102.2	106.0	102.7	86.3	105.0	89.2	74.3
	I	100.6	104.7	108.4	124.2	132.1	156.0	203.8	232.9	129.3
	T	97	87	94	85	78	55	52	38	58
Straits	E	103.4	77.7	80.8	90.9	109.1	148.3	125.3	148.7	78.8
Settlement	I	103.4	98.4	96.4	110.5	121.7	189.4	254.2	440.3	489.4
	T	100	79	84	82	90	78	49	34	16
Trinidad[e]	E	103.8	99.2	127.3	121.9	109.8	117.3	168.8	237.0	120.9
	I	98.6	99.6	110.6	133.2	207.3	271.2	258.0	296.6	240.3
	T	105	100	115	92	53	43	65	80	50

[a] 1915 = 100; [b] 12 months ended 31 March year following; [c] 9 months ended 31 December 1921; [d] Unit values at pre-war parity; [e] 1912–13 = 100; E, weighted index of the unit value of principal exports; I, weighted index of the unit value of principal imports; T, terms of trade: E divided by I × 100.
Source: As for Table 6.5.

further fall in the terms of trade in a number of colonies (Table 6.7).

The economic impact of the war and post-war boom–slump on each colony differed. Some export industries which were small but growing rapidly before the war – rubber, cotton, sisal, groundnuts, coffee, cocoa (West Africa) and tin (Nigeria) – continued to do so and by the early 1920s had become major export commodities. Some of these were stimulated by high prices during the war and post-war boom – sisal and cotton especially – whilst rubber prices plummeted. Other export industries which had been established longer and which were not expanding very rapidly pre-war, declined in output despite some years of high prices: palm oil and kernels, maize, hides and skins, tin (Straits Settlements), tea, copra, and bananas. Sugar prices by 1920 were two to three times their pre-war levels, yet physical exports remained at or below the pre-war point. The war distorted the external trade of most of these colonies and the stimulus of high export prices was often offset by even higher import prices. Transport costs, especially of international shipping, greatly increased and capital inflow was reversed. Above all, the war brought to an end the steadily increasing demand of the industrial and industrialising economies for tropical raw materials and foodstuffs on which the colonial economies – and strategies for their development – had been based. It was inevitable that the economic problems of the industrial economies in the post-war period should fundamentally affect the tropical primary producers as well.[2]

The outbreak of the war put pressure on colonial public finances by threatening their major source of revenue, import duties, and by cutting off borrowing in the London market. All colonies were informed in December 1914 by the secretary of state that they would not be permitted to raise funds in Britain for the duration of the war.[3] The drying-up of public capital flows caused a cessation of public works programmes in most colonies and the fear of falling revenues from trade led to stringency in recurrent expenditure. A number of colonies were in the middle of major transport development programmes when the war came and these experienced long delays in completion. Sir F.D. Lugard, governor of Nigeria, commented in December 1915. 'The war has hit us hard, and instead of a large surplus we anticipate a deficit of fully half a million sterling.'[4] New taxes were imposed to boost revenues: in all colonies, import duties increased, particularly ad valorum duties as prices rose, and in some colonies there was an extension of head tax, income tax and export duties.[5] Most of the burden of these tax increases fell on the indigenous producer and wage-earner. The impact on government revenues was not as serious as anticipated in 1914. Higher values of imported goods and new taxes raised revenues whilst expenditure cuts ensured most colonies broke even or obtained a budget surplus by 1916 (Table 6.8).

Direct costs to colonial governments for the war consisted of contributions to the imperial government for the war effort and the payments in connection with troops and non-combatants sent to colonial war theatres – for example, West African forces sent to East Africa. These costs varied with the geographical location of the colony and its ability (and willingness) to make cash contributions to Britain, but in most cases these costs were not heavy.[6] Inflation became a problem in all colonies from 1916. Price rises were caused by higher prices of imported goods, shortages of locally produced commodities because of labour and/or imported inputs shortages, and higher levels of taxation. Serious food shortages developed at the end of the war in many cases and in several colonies government controls over food production, distribution and prices were imposed.[7] Silver coin tended to disappear from circulation as hoarding took place and in the end new alloy tokens were circulated in some colonies. Exchange problems were experienced by Ceylon,

Table 6.8 Colonial budgets, 1914–19 (£m)

Colony	1914	1915	1916	1917	1918	1919
Straits Settlements	447	460	732	966	851	−93
Federated Malay States	−2065	−241	2235	2879	2702	170
Ceylon	−402	93	660	195	−68	−52
Mauritius	62	−1	99	135	163	−40
Fiji	−21	−9	85	35	46	−25
Uganda	−6	2	26	41	28	45
Kenya	−167	93	337	−122	−22	−447
Nigeria	−649	−831	−767	198	504	430
Gold Coast	−240	−14	27	263	−18	958
Sierra Leone	−4	−43	18	23	39	45
Jamaica	−69	−135	66	70	−103	356
Trinidad	−56	33	47	10	49	34
British Guiana	−39	29	24	−1	85	−28

Current revenue minus current expenditure; − denotes expenditure exceeds revenue
Source: *Statistical Abstract of the British Empire*, No. 57.

Malaya and Kenya as the rupee appreciated against sterling, causing a permanent exchange rate rise of 50 per cent in 1919 (15 rupees to the pound in 1914; 10 to the pound in 1919).[8] Export trades were chiefly affected by shipping shortages and the imposition of – and changes in – import restrictions by Britain and the United States. By 1917 many of Britain's imports were controlled and those on the 'essential list' were given priority in shipping; a number of major colonial agricultural exports dependent upon the UK market were, however, considered 'inessential' and in some cases produce was left to rot on the colony's wharves.[9] Businesses owned by African indigenous traders found these problems particularly acute and many went under.[10]

Foreign trading patterns changed as Britain declined as a market and supplier and the United States, Japan, India and Australia took its place. The war offered some opportunities for import substitution but this occurred to only a limited extent. The main obstacles were shortages of machinery, of labour and in the case of foodstuffs the difficulty of diverting farmers' energies from export cash crops despite the uncertainty surrounding the their ultimate sale. Labour shortages were experienced in most tropical colonies at times during the war, though in several urban unemployment also increased as external trade and internal development stagnated. All colonies lost British officials and managers who returned to Britain to join up. Some also lost large numbers of labourers conscripted as carriers for the campaigns in the German colonies and the Middle East and some also experienced shortages of skilled artisans who were sent out of the colony to fight or act as support. Widespread disruption and shortages resulted in East and Central Africa as large numbers of adult males were conscripted as

124

soldiers and carriers.[11] The European staff were not replaced by local personnel to any great extent and most colonies were attempting to run their administrations with half or two-thirds of their peacetime complement of British officials by 1918. As the cost of living rose real wages fell and all colonial governments were obliged to pay war bonuses to at least some of their employees by the end of the war. Wages generally, however, did not keep pace with prices, which led to outbreaks of strikes and other forms of protest, including some riots, in many colonies.[12] The post-war boom in prices stimulated economic activity but inflation grew worse during 1919 and the first half of 1920 as demand outstripped supply of both imported goods and domestic produce. The high prices paid for nearly all colonial export commodities called forth a great increase in production, and revealed the inadequacies of the transport systems which five years of neglect had exacerbated. Exports would have been greater during the boom in some cases if the railways and harbours had been able to cope more adequately.[13]

Whatever the adverse short and longer term effects of the war were on the tropical colonial economies, none suffered to any extent compared with Europe and Britain, except possibly parts of East and Central Africa. There was a sense of relief and even amazement in many colonial reports at the end of the war at how comparatively little damage had been done:

> It is probable that no country has been so free from trouble during the war as British Malaya. (Federated Malay States, 1918).

> the Colony, far from feeling the effects of a war which is devastating Europe, has actually benefitted from the war. (Straits Settlements, 1917)

> speaking generally, the War has had little effect on the prosperity of the Colony. (Fiji, 1916)

> the Gold Coast, with its agricultural population, suffered comparatively little from the world-wide catastrophe of 1914–1918, in so far as the personal comfort of the masses was concerned. (Gold Coast, 1919)

> The war, which has brought such calamity and disaster to other lands, has touched these West Indian Islands with a very light hand. (Trinidad, 1917).[14]

In East and Central Africa the loss of life and property was much more serious and the war had an important lasting effect in that it strengthened the economic and political power of the white settlers, particularly in Kenya.[15] Although many governors were grateful that the war was relatively mild in its impact the interruption to growth and development which it caused focussed attention on the need for reconstruction, made especially urgent when the post-war trade boom collapsed in mid-1920. As colonial governments looked to the future in 1920 they appreciated the problems of economic development to a greater extent than before the war and particularly the need for new equipment, technical staff, transport and communications improvements and, above all, more capital investment. It was also apparent that the tasks of reconstruction and future economic growth could not be accomplished without material assistance from the imperial government, which seemed to some colonial inhabitants to be more relevant to their everyday lives as a result of the shared experience of world war.[16]

TERRITORIAL ADJUSTMENTS AND THE MANDATES SYSTEM

At the outset of the war the Royal Navy implemented its pre-war strategy of hampering German ocean trade and attacking its colonies.[17] The German Pacific islands were invaded by Japanese, Australian and New Zealand forces in August 1914, South Africa launched an attack on German Southwest Africa, British and French troops on Togoland and the Cameroons and British and Indian forces on German East Africa.[18] Germany's African colonies were not heavily defended and its forces could do little more than retreat into the interior and hold out there for as long as possible.[19] The Pacific islands were quickly captured. The German authorities in Togoland surrendered at the end of August 1914 to troops from the Gold Coast and Nigeria.[20] The Cameroons port of Duala was captured by British West African forces in September 1914 and an invasion mounted from the coast. French and Belgian units also invaded from Gabon and the Congo. German Cameroons surrendered in February 1916. The South African attack on German Southwest Africa prompted an uprising by some elements of the Boer population in the Union and its forces had to be diverted to quelling these rebels. This achieved, German Southwest Africa was invaded by land and sea and the German government there surrendered in June 1915. The Germans were strongest in German East Africa where an army of 3,000 white and 12,000 African troops under General Lettow von Vorbeck resisted invasion until the beginning of 1916. In February 1916 a large force of British, Indian and African troops under the command of South African General Jan Smuts invaded from Kenya and by September had captured the central railway and – together with Belgian forces from the Congo – controlled some 90 per cent of the territory's population. Von Vorbeck retreated slowly to the south, finally crossing into Portuguese Mozambique in November 1917. From there his forces carried out raids into Northern Rhodesia and the former German colony until the end of the war in Europe.[21] The German East Africa campaign involved the use of some 50,000 African troops (half from West Africa) and over 600,000 carriers and other non-combatants. Recruitment was only nominally voluntary and in Kenya itself conscription was formally adopted in August 1915. The death rate among African troops was high (20 per cent) and for all Africans employed in the campaign the death rate was estimated at 10 per cent. Large-scale conscription of adult males into the service of the armed forces caused severe dislocation and labour shortages in Kenya, Uganda, Nyasaland, and Northern Rhodesia which hampered food and export production.[22]

These conquests of German colonies by Allied forces formed the basis for territorial adjustments at the Paris Peace Conference in 1919. Jan Smuts in a speech to members of both Houses of Parliament in May 1917 told his audience

> one of the by-products of this war has been that the whole world outside Europe has been cleared of the enemy. Germany has been swept from the seas, and from all continents except Central Europe. . . . When peace comes to be made you will have all these parts in your hand, and you can go carefully into the question of what is necessary for your future security and your future safety as an Empire, and you can say, so far as it is possible under war circumstances, what you are going to keep and what you are going to give away.[23]

The exact distribution of ex-German colonial territory amongst the Allies was determined by wartime treaties and agreements between Britain and France, Britain, France and Italy and Britain and Japan. In February 1916 France was offered most of Togoland and the Cameroons by Britain, chiefly as a means of boosting French morale in the face of lack of progress on the western front.[24] This agreement split both German colonies into a British and French sphere (the French share in both cases amounted to about four-fifths), a division which remained in force until the end of the colonial era. In March 1916 the Sykes–Picot Agreement divided Turkish territory in the Middle East between Britain and France. The Treaty of London between Britain, France and Italy signed in April 1915 promised Italy territorial compensation in Africa in the event that France and Britain 'extend their colonial possessions in Africa at the expense of Germany'.[25] Finally, Britain agreed with Japan in February 1917 to support the latter's claim to the German Pacific islands north of the Equator which Japan had conquered, in return for Japan's support of Australia's claim to German New Guinea and its eastern islands and New Zealand's claim to German Samoa. Despite Lloyd George's comment that 'war plays havoc with the refinements of conscience', and Asquith's that 'at the time the treaty with

Italy was made the French and ourselves were fighting for our lives on the western front', these wartime agreements were to be fully honoured at the Peace Conference.[26]

As the war dragged on and the military stalemate on the western front took on an air of desperate permanency, the question of the future of the German colonies became more complicated. With the prospects of an outright military victory for the Allies fading at the end of 1916 and the beginning of 1917, the likelihood of a negotiated peace became more real. In such a circumstance, argued Lord Curzon in the Imperial War Cabinet, Germany might have some of its colonies returned in order, for example, to secure the return to France of Alsace and Lorraine.[27] The entry of the United States into the war against Germany in May 1917 greatly increased the practical influence of President Wilson in the eventual peace terms.[28] It soon became clear that, whatever the British and dominion governments thought in private, public statements to the effect that Germany would not have its colonies restored would not be tolerated by the President of the United States. In November 1917 the British government wished to announce that Germany would definitely not receive German East Africa back in order to encourage Africans working with von Vorbeck's forces to desert. Colonel House, Wilson's adviser in London, was consulted and 'resolutely opposed' a public statement to the effect either that Germany would not receive German East Africa back or that Britain would retain it. However, 'Colonel House was not opposed to us keeping the country eventually and thought it was in our interest not to tie our hands publicly at this moment'.[29]

Such statements were also to be avoided for domestic political reasons. As civilian weariness with the war increased, pressure grew for the announcement of more specific war aims and ones which embodied more worthwhile purposes for the sacrifices of the British people than mere imperial expansion.[30] Organised labour could not be ignored by the coalition government and indeed the War Cabinet included a member of the Labour Party executive, Arthur Henderson. He dissented, appropriately enough on May Day, 1917, from Cabinet's decision to endorse a memorandum by Lord Curzon which argued that all of Germany's colonies, except possibly those in West Africa, should be retained by Britain and the dominions along with Palestine and Mesopotamia. This amounted to annexation, said Henderson, and was therefore against party policy.[31] In December 1917 Russia concluded a separate peace with Germany and published the Allies' secret war treaties and agreements concerning the distribution of the Central Powers' territories. Austria–Hungary also put forward peace proposals on Christmas Day, 1917, to which the Allies felt a need to respond.

These domestic and international pressures prompted the prime minister to make a statement to a meeting of trade unionists on 5 January 1918 which went further than any previously announced war aims in avoiding the appearance of territorial aggrandisement. The objective, Lloyd George told the Cabinet, 'was to issue a declaration of our war aims which went to the extreme limit of concession, and which would show to our own people and to our Allies, as well as to the peoples of Austria, Turkey and even Germany, that our object was not to destroy the enemy nations'. The 'most difficult point' was the German colonies, since Britain was anxious not to appear to be 'merely trying to annex more territory to an over-gorged Empire'. Lloyd George's solution was to extend the principle of 'self-determination' which President Wilson (among others) had already urged as the basis for political settlement in Europe after the war, to the German colonies. 'Precisely how the principle was to be applied need not now be discussed, but there were chiefs and heads of tribes who could be consulted'.[32] Thus in his address to the trade unions on 5 January 1918, the prime minister declared the German colonies

> are held at the disposal of a Conference whose decision must have primary regard to the wishes and interests of the native inhabitants of such colonies. . . . The governing consideration . . . in all these cases must be that the inhabitants should be placed under the control of an administration acceptable to themselves, one whose main purpose will be to prevent their exploitation for the benefit of European capitalists or Governments. The natives live in their various tribal organizations under chiefs and councils who are competent to consult and speak for their tribes and members, and thus to represent their wishes and interests in regard to their disposal. The general principle of national self-determination is therefore as applicable in their case as in those of occupied European territories.[33]

Lloyd George's speech somewhat upstaged that of President Wilson to a joint session of Congress three days later in which the 'Fourteen Points' were announced.[34] Point Five read.

> A free, open-minded, and absolutely impartial adjustment of all colonial claims, based upon a strict observance of the principle that in determining all such questions of sovereignty, the interests of the populations concerned must have equal weight with the equitable claims of the government whose title is to be determined.[35]

Neither of these pronouncements, in fact, called for the internationalisation of German and Turkish colonies, but they made it more difficult to contemplate direct annexation of German colonies at the end of the war, even if the Allies were in a position to dictate the peace terms to Germany.

The colonies passed from Germany at the Paris Peace Conference with little discussion: the Germans were accused of mistreating the indigenes, not controlling the troops raised in East Africa during the campaign there and of planning to use colonies in the future as submarine bases.[36] The British prime minister accepted the idea of 'mandates' which would guarantee the open-door and non-militarisation – and claimed that this was, in fact, British colonial practice already – but urged that in the case of German Southwest Africa, East Africa, Samoa and Nauru 'frank annexation' was preferable.[37] The prime ministers of Australia, New Zealand and South Africa argued for outright annexation of the German colonies their troops occupied, chiefly on the basis of strategic proximity, but also as compensation for wartime losses and with an eye on the possibilities for commercial advantage.[38] France also supported direct annexation of Togoland and the Cameroons on the basis of the 1916 agreement with Britain.[39] President Wilson observed that all this might well appear to the outside world as 'the mere distribution of spoils' and insisted that the German colonies be held as mandates under the auspices of the (as yet non-existent) League of Nations.[40] The United States government also insisted on mandates in order to prevent Japan from annexing the German North Pacific islands which lay across United States lines of communication.[41] Lloyd George had no wish to wreck the peace conference in its first month over the relatively unimportant issue of the dominion governments' claims.[42] Smuts and Lord Robert Cecil[43] then devised a formula whereby there would be a three-fold division of the German and Turkish territories: first, Turkish territories in the Middle East which could be expected to become independent in the foreseeable future; second, the German colonies in Central Africa to which the open-door and non-militarisation should apply; and, third, the German colonies presently held by the dominions which would be annexed by them.[44] Wilson agreed to the creation of different types of mandate, but not that the third type should involve annexation. A member of the Australian delegation, Melbourne lawyer John Latham, suggested a definition for the third type of mandate which would give the dominions what they wanted – a closed door in trade and immigration – while still stopping just short of outright annexation and which would have the additional advantage of preventing Japan from annexing the German North Pacific islands.[45] This formula was put to Wilson on 30 January 1919.

> there are territories, such as South West Africa and certain of the Islands in the South Pacific, which owing to the sparseness of their population, or their small size, or their remoteness from the

centres of civilization, or their geographical continuity to the mandatory state, and other circumstances, can be best administered under the laws of the mandatory state as integral portions thereof, subject to the safeguards above-mentioned in the interests of the indigenous people.[46]

These 'safeguards' were

the prohibition of such abuses as the slave trade, the arms traffic and the liquor traffic, and the prevention of the military training of the natives for other than peace purposes, and the establishment of fortifications or military and naval bases

President Wilson agreed to these proposals as forming the basis of a settlement but refused to sanction the assignment of mandates to particular nations until the Peace Treaty was signed and the League in place. Lloyd George and the dominion prime ministers continued to press Wilson for allocation of the mandates, however, and in May 1919 the mandates were assigned, though Wilson was still 'very anxious to avoid the appearance of a division of the spoils being simultaneous with the Peace'.[47] France and Britain received mandates for Togoland and Cameroons, the exact boundaries to be decided 'according to the Anglo-French Agreement of 4th of March, 1916'. Britain received a mandate for German East Africa, South Africa for German Southwest Africa, Australia for all German islands in the Pacific south of the Equator except Nauru and German Samoa, New Zealand for German Samoa, and Japan for all German Pacific islands north of the Equator. The tiny but phosphate-rich Pacific island of Nauru went to the British Empire, its fertiliser output to be divided between Australia, Britain and New Zealand only.[48]

In the end the Great Powers achieved most of their aims: Britain obtained German East Africa (and thus fulfilled Rhodes' dream of 'Cape to Cairo') and kept the French from imposing a closed-door in the ex-German West African colonies; Britain protected its strategic and economic interests in the Middle East by obtaining a division of the Turkish territories with France as 'A' mandates, thereby maintaining a 'Cairo to Calcutta' route also.[49] France added the Cameroons' seaboard and excellent harbour of Duala to its equatorial African territory, together with some 2.8 million inhabitants.[50] The British dominions were able to incorporate nearby German territory into their own regimes and by acquiescing to the mandate principle prevent Japan from annexing the German North Pacific islands. President Wilson obtained a colonial settlement which was based on mandates rather than outright annexation and which involved a degree of international scrutiny by the League of Nations. On the other hand, the mandates system did not formally impinge upon existing colonial policy and practice and the content of the 'sacred trust' was vague beyond the specified prohibitions on slavery, alcohol and the like. Article 22 read:

> To those colonies and territories which as a consequence of the late war have ceased to be under the sovereignty of the States which formerly governed them and which are inhabited by peoples not yet able to stand by themselves under the strenuous conditions of the modern world, there should be applied the principle that the well-being and development of such peoples form a sacred trust of civilization and that securities for the performance of this trust should be embodied in this Covenant.[51]

Nor did it convince many commentators that any fundamentally new principles had entered into the theory of colonial rule. Article 22 might contain internal contradictions: a major driving force behind the mandates concept was the idea of the open-door, the purpose of which was to secure equal access for the industrial nations to the tropical colonies' resources. Even critics of imperialism such as Henry Noel Brailsford subscribed to this view, which descended, in fact, from Benjamin Kidd's *Control of the Tropics* published in 1898. Brailsford wrote in 1920 in relation to Mesopotamia, 'The sparse tribes of half-nomad Arabs and Kurds who live around Mosul have no right to deny its resources to the rest of mankind.'[52] What exactly were the 'strenuous conditions' which the indigenes were to be given protection from by the mandate system? And would open-door cushion or exacerbate the impact of these conditions? Open-door was a principle adopted in the interests of the industrial countries, not of the colonial inhabitants, and whether the colonial economies themselves would benefit, and if so, how, by the imposition of open-door was not a question which was addressed.[53] The principle of self-determination invoked by Lloyd George and President Wilson in January 1918 was not implemented,[54] allocation of the mandates to the various Allies was clearly on the basis of their wartime conquests, and the fundamental problems of colonial economic backwardness and poverty were never discussed. Finally, it remained to be seen whether the Permanent Mandates Commission of the League of Nations would be able to act effectively and in what directions its actions would go.[55]

COLONIAL DEVELOPMENT POLICY

The economic crisis of the war highlighted the degree to which Britain was dependent upon overseas supplies of foodstuffs and raw materials and how vulnerable these lifelines were to enemy attack. Although the United States was Britain's main supplier during the war, the economic links between Britain and the empire were strengthened during the conflict. Examination of problems of wartime supply focussed attention on both the importance of secure sources of supply in the future and on the apparent potential for economic development in the dominions, India and the colonies. In June 1916 the Allies met in Paris to discuss post-war economic plans. It was agreed that ex-enemy countries would, at least for a period, be denied most-favoured-nation status and that the Allies would conserve their raw materials supplies for their own use during the reconstruction period. Long-term the Allies would attempt to be as independent as possible of the present enemy countries as regards supplies and markets and would, therefore, trade with each other to a greater extent.[56]

The new coalition government formed by Lloyd George in December 1916 was dominated by imperialists whose appeals to the nation had been rejected in the general election of 1906, but who were now in a position to attempt to create a greater degree of imperial economic cohesion: Lord Curzon, Viscount Milner, Leopold Amery, and W.A.S. Hewins.[57] The twin pillars of their economic policy were a common imperial tariff structure and the concentration of resources on empire economic development. The first series of meetings of the Imperial War Cabinet which included the dominions' prime ministers and a representative of the Indian government took place in March and April 1917, and in June 1917 General Jan Smuts was called from his campaign against von Vorbeck in East Africa to join the War Cabinet as a permanent member. An Imperial War Conference was held in April 1917 which passed resolutions concerning imperial preference and development of empire resources:

> Having regard to the experience obtained in the present War, this Conference records its opinion that the safety of the Empire and the necessary development of its component parts require prompt and attentive consideration, as well as concerted action, with regard to the following matters:
> 1. The production of an adequate food supply and arrangements for its transportation when and where required, under any conditions that may reasonably be anticipated.
> 2. The control of natural resources available within the Empire, especially those that are of an essential character for necessary national purposes, whether in peace or in war.
> 3. The economical utilisation of such natural resources through processes of manufacture carried on within the Empire.

and

> The time has arrived when all possible encouragement should be

given to the development of Imperial resources and especially to making the Empire independent of other countries in respect of food supplies, raw materials and essential industries. With these objects in view this Conference expresses itself in favour of:

1. The principle that each part of the Empire, having due regard to the interests of our Allies, shall give specially favourable treatment and facilities to the produce and manufactures of other parts of the Empire.
2. Arrangements by which intending emigrants from the United Kingdom may be induced to settle in countries under the British flag.[58]

These resolutions were accepted by the Imperial War Cabinet and sent to a ministerial committee on trade relations which reported to a second Imperial War Conference held in June 1918 which in turn reaffirmed them and called on the United Kingdom to introduce imperial preference into any customs duties which it imposed in the future.[59] This was, in fact, implemented in the budget brought down in 1919, though the customs duties affected only a small number of imported commodities and the margin of imperial preference was slight.[60] The particular problem of raw materials was highlighted by the Committee on Commercial and Industrial Policy after the war chaired by Lord Balfour of Burleigh. In February 1917 this committee passed the following resolution:

> In the light of experience gained during the War, we consider that special steps must be taken to stimulate the production of food-stuffs, raw materials and manufactured articles within the Empire wherever the expansion of production is possible and economically desirable for the safety and welfare of the Empire as a whole.[61]

The government's concern to retain British control of raw materials produced in Crown colonies was indicated by its decision in May 1917 to restrict the ownership of the Malayan rubber industry to British subjects in order to prevent United States and Japanese expansion in the industry.[62] On a more grandiose scale altogether was the propaganda work of the Empire Resources Development Committee (ERDC) formed in October 1916 under the auspices of Lord Milner. This was a parliamentary lobby group with close connections with the British South Africa Company. It claimed support from over 200 members of Parliament including Neville Chamberlain, Lord Curzon, William Ormsby-Gore and Sir William Joynson-Hicks as well as from such figures as L.S. Jameson and Rudyard Kipling. The ERDC's ideas were variously expressed, but essentially it proposed that certain of the empire's assets should be taken over and exploited on a large scale by the

British government, and the profits so made be used to pay off Britain's war debts. The committee was confident that there was enormous scope in the empire for this sort of activity. H. Wilson Fox, the secretary of the ERDC stated in January 1918, 'It is obvious . . . that the surface of the subject has only been scratched, and that the opportunities offered by our vast Empire for profitable development are practically unlimited'.[63] State investment, organisation and control were essential features of the committee's proposals, and their most novel ones, at least as far as previous peacetime experience was concerned. Their basic tenet was laid down by Lord Milner in 1916 when he referred to 'the development of the State by the State and for the State – the development of our national and Imperial property'.[64] This policy would involve the state in the development of selected assets of the empire, as the committee's manifesto put it, 'under such conditions as will give the State an adequate share of the proceeds . . . by concentration on . . . assets ripe for development for the common good of the Empire'.[65] Such assets, it was alleged, existed in abundance: referring to West African palm oil production, Alfred Bigland, chairman of the ERDC, exclaimed, 'here is a proven success now yielding a handsome profit, and capable of great enhancement. Within the Empire there are many other such waiting, almost crying, to be taken over'.[66]

The machinery to be set up to enable the state to develop the empire profitably was outlined by Wilson Fox in 1917. An Empire Development Board was to be created by Act of Parliament; it was to have executive power and between fifteen and twenty members, 'all of whom would be selected for their personal, and especially their business, qualifications'.[67] The board would administer a fund, financed by a vote from Parliament, in the first instance of £10 million per annum for ten years. The board would also set up subsidiary authorities possessing statutory power and which would act as public corporations.

The ERDC was less explicit about how exactly the board was to make the large profits envisaged, but it seemed to be in four main ways. First, by the production and supply of electricity in the United Kingdom, for which it would have a monopoly. Second, by the gathering, distribution and sale of the empire's fish, chiefly those of Newfoundland, and whales in the Antarctic.[68] Third, by the state 'participating' in the trade of empire produce, especially West African palm produce.[69] Fourth, by opening up uncultivated areas, investing suitable amounts of capital for the production of wheat or sugar, etc., and then reaping the benefit of the incremental rise in the value of the land. It was envisaged that a profit of £50 million a year could be made by the state if it participated in the West African produce trade. As Bigland enthused to the members of the Royal Society of Arts in February 1917, 'Think what it would mean if all these products of West Africa, mineral and vegetable, were controlled for the benefit of the Empire as a whole! Think how huge is the potential profit which would be devoted to the service of the Empire's debt'.[70] And Wilson Fox outlined how this could be done:

> One of the methods by which the State can derive profits from its tropical estates is to keep in its own hands the power of producing, trading in, and exporting certain special products, especially products in which either a complete or partial monopoly can be established, such as jute or palm kernels.[71]

In February 1919 Wilson Fox called for a select committee of Parliament to consider the ERDC's proposals. Whilst supporting the ERDC's aims, Leopold Amery, the under-secretary of state for the colonies, issued a warning:

> I do not think that there is necessarily any conflict between the two conceptions of utilising the development of the vast resources of the Empire in order to help forward trade in this country, and at the same time help these people. But I do wish to put in a word of warning that in any particular methods which we apply and any particular measures taken we have to watch very carefully all the time to see that we should not be put, as an Imperial Government, in a false position as between our interests as representing the taxpayers of this country and our interests as trustees for million of people on a lower plane of political development, who look to us for their welfare and their elevation.[72]

In fact, the ERDC's proposals did call forth an outcry from the Aborigines Protection Society and others, such as Sir Frederick Lugard and E.D. Morel, particularly over the plans to monopolise West African palm exports.[73] When Cabinet debated the ERDC's proposal put forward in June 1919 for a joint committee of both Houses to examine whether, and, if so, how, the state could engage 'for profit' in the 'development of the overseas resources within the Empire', there was much dismay expressed at the 'deplorable failure to develop the Empire's tropical estates' in the past. Amery complained that the Crown colonies had been neglected and

> doubted very much whether we should be able to get along on our old methods of finance; and we should have to look round for some new sources of revenue. While it did not appear that our dependent Empire would bring in a great deal in the immediate future, he thought that a substantial return might be obtained at a later date for a small investment now[74]

Even a small amount, however, was not available according to Austen

Chamberlain, the Chancellor of the Exchequer, who 'was faced at present with the dearth of capital for our own urgent needs'. The ERDC's attempt to put its concept of empire development on a more official basis thus failed, and the committee remained solely a loose parliamentary lobby group and bête noir of the humanitarians. The significance of the ERDC lay in the way in which it perpetuated and encouraged the myth that the tropical colonies contained immense potential wealth which required only a small input of capital by the state to unlock. The persistence of this belief among the imperialists in the 1920s was partly the reason for such disillusion with colonial economic development in the 1930s, though indeed the myth never entirely disappeared.

No practical measures for economic development in the colonies were undertaken by the British government during the war. The Colonial Office established an advisory colonial development committee in December 1919, partly in response to ERDC propaganda and the support shown to it by the secretary of state for the colonies, Lord Milner. This committee met on a number of occasions in 1920 and discussed various problems connected with colonial development but no action directly flowed from its deliberations.[75] Tariff changes, on the other hand, were enacted to give greater preference to British goods in the colonial markets and in certain cases to divert raw materials to the British market. In June 1920 all colonies were invited to give greater preference to Britain in their tariff structures and some twenty-six colonial governments complied.[76] In October 1919 a differential export duty was imposed on British West Africa palm kernels in an attempt to divert exports to Britain to ensure the success of its infant kernel crushing industry. This action originated in the pre-war dependence of Britain on Germany for palm kernel oil and was the kind of development foreshadowed by the Paris Economic Conference in June 1916. Lord Balfour of Burleigh's committee also supported export controls for this purpose and recommended they be used for a range of commodities which were, or could become, raw materials for British industries.[77] In fact, differential export duties were not widely adopted in the Crown colonies – the only other example was that of Malayan and Nigerian tin ore – chiefly because the experience of the West African differential export tax on palm kernels showed that it was self-defeating: it stimulated output from non-British sources, substitution of other vegetable oils in the manufacture of margarine and it undermined the prosperity of the British export trade to West African palm products producers.[78]

The war had two effects on colonial economic development policy. On the one hand it raised expectations of rapid growth, in some minds at least, through such claims as those of the ERDC, whilst on the other hand it focussed attention on the rights of the colonial inhabitants to have their government conducted on the basis of the 'sacred trust'. The war created problems – debt and permanently high levels of unemployment in Britain – to which, it seemed to some, colonial economic development could help to provide solutions, if only such 'development' could be hurried along. Opposition to the ERDC, imperial preference, such measures as the differential export tax in West Africa, as well as the controversies arising from the colonial question at the Paris Peace Conference and the creation of the mandates system, strengthened the concept of 'trusteeship' as constituting the proper basis of British colonial rule. Conflict between 'development' and 'trusteeship' was inevitable in the ensuing decade: the Cabinet and political heads of the Colonial Office tended to support the idea of rapid economic development of the 'great estate' to assist British recovery, whilst the colonial administrators, including some, though not all, of the governors, and the permanent officials of the Colonial Office, tended to stress the 'welfare' arguments for slower development or even none at all. Undermining both sides was the Treasury view that colonies should be financially self-supporting and that public funds invested in the colonies were not generally very profitable investments from Britain's point of view. Native welfare was difficult to enhance if the colony in question was under Treasury control because it lacked sufficient funds to pay for even a rudimentary administration; 'developing the estate' became increasingly illusory without large injections of British public funds.

In the circumstances of the early post-war period, it was a somewhat modest announcement which Milner was able to make in a circular despatch addressed to all Crown colonies in June 1919 indicating the establishment of a Colonial Research Committee to assist colonies in scientific research. He referred to the problems of raw material shortages caused by the war and to the financial problems facing Britain, and asked the colonial governments

> to consider the position of any important industries in the Colony, on whose behalf no research work is at present carried on, and whether this state of affairs does not call for action on the part of the Colonial Government. I would particularly direct your attention to those raw materials required for Imperial trade or defence which are produced within the Empire either in inadequate quantities or not at all.[79]

However, despite the view that 'it is evidently more than ever necessary that the economic resources of the Empire in general should be developed to the uttermost', Treasury provided only £20,000 per annum for four years to fund the committee's work. Thus even in an area of colonial development where disagreement between the permanent and political heads of the Colonial Office was less evident – scientific research – the amount of money actually provided was spread very thinly indeed. This gap between aims and resources, illustrated by this measure, was to become a recurrent theme during the next two decades.

7

The economics of 'trusteeship'
Colonial development policy, 1921–9

British government funds for any kind of colonial economic development up to the early 1920s were meagre. Table 7.1 sets out the major loans and grants according to the Treasury's accounts. Over 90 per cent of the funds provided went to railway construction, nearly all of it in East and Central Africa. All but 2 per cent of the financial assistance was in the form of loans, the interest payments on which had to be met from the start of the loan period. This was not a satisfactory record in the view of the imperialists who took charge of colonial affairs during and after the First World War: Lord Milner, Leopold Amery, William Ormsby-Gore and J.H. Thomas.[1] Their aim was to provide more money, possibly on easier terms, in a more comprehensive programme of colonial development. As the unemployment situation in Britain deteriorated in the early 1920s the need for Britain to take measures to stimulate colonial economic development could be portrayed as being more urgent.[2]

COLONIAL DEVELOPMENT POLICY AND THE POLITICS OF UNEMPLOYMENT

By 1921 it was becoming clear that the industrial dislocation and high levels of unemployment of 1919 and 1920 were not temporary phenomena caused by the return to peacetime conditions, but a more fundamental problem requiring vigorous action. The unemployment crisis also brought the problems of colonial development to the Cabinet's attention, for it seemed clear to the government that one aspect of the problem was a lack of demand for British goods and that the colonial empire might become an important source of orders. The Colonial Office assured the Cabinet in October 1921 that 'everything possible is being done to enable the Colonies to make a substantial contribution towards the immediate problem of placing orders in this country'. In addition to immediate orders the colonial empire would be raising £25 million for schemes already contemplated, plus a further £20 million if the colonies in question could raise the necessary loans. Finally, a further

Table 7.1   Financial assistance to colonial development by the British
government, 1896–1923

| Purpose | Date(s) | Recipient | £000 | | |
			Loans	Grants	Total
Railway Construction	1896–1905	Uganda	5503		5503
	1910–13	Uganda	295		295
	1912–15	Nyasaland	180		180
	1921–3	Nyasaland	186		186
	1912–13	Kenya	375		375
	1921–2	Tanganyika	105		105
	1910–13	Nigeria	200		200
		Total	6844		6844
Public Works	1921–2	Uganda	400		400
	1921–2	Tanganyika	37		37
	1897–8	Dominica		15	15
	1897–8	St Vincent		15	15
		Total	437	30	467
Research	1906–23	Imperial Institute, etc.		127	127
		Grand Total	7281	157	7408

Source: Memorandum from Treasury to Colonial Office, June 1923, CO 323 905 20593.

£17,500,000 could be expended if 'a Treasury guarantee, a free grant or any other form of Treasury assistance was given'. The secretary of state, Winston Churchill, envisaged considerable benefits arising from imperial government assistance:

> A large amount of work would be provided in this country without delay, for it would, of course, be a condition of Imperial assistance that any plant or materials required should be ordered in this country. The works would benefit the colony, develop markets for British goods, and enhance the purchasing power of individual inhabitants in the Colonies, with future benefits to British trade.[3]

Others in the Cabinet were not convinced. The Treasury view was that Crown colonies did not in fact have any great difficulty in raising loans in the London market, and that making grants to colonies 'would be putting the colonies into a better position than the public utility undertakings at home'.[4]

This was as far as the demand for financial assistance to colonies which wanted to raise loans reached in 1921. The question continued to be pursued, notably by Leo Amery in 1922. In August he pointed out that since 1920 the colonial empire had raised loans amounting to £34 million and a further £10 million would be borrowed by the end of 1923. Much of this had been and was being spent in the United Kingdom.

This, however, was the limit of the colonies' unaided efforts. On the other hand, there were many development projects, especially for railway construction in East and West Africa and British Guiana, which might ultimately prove remunerative 'but for which none of the Governments concerned could venture to make themselves responsible, unless not only the interest, but also the capital – or at any rate as much of it as represented materials bought in this country – were found by the Imperial Treasury as a free gift'.[5]

In October 1922, he advanced the view to Cabinet that the empire was potentially highly valuable but that it had never been 'systematically developed'. What was needed was a flexible, continuous and long-term programme of development offering 'substantial inducements' to governments, public authorities or private companies to undertake at once schemes which would normally be started over the next decade, including those which might not prove remunerative for many years 'and which a poor and struggling Colonial Government could not venture to take up unless both the immediate cost and the future risk were reduced to a minimum'. To effect this he suggested an Empire Development Bill should be introduced authorising the expenditure of £10 million per annum for fifteen years for the promotion of development schemes. An 'Imperial Development Advisory Board' should be set up to administer the schemes. Assistance would consist of grants of interest, guarantees for loans raised by colonial governments, and direct subsidies up to 50 per cent of the value of orders placed in the United Kingdom. The kinds of schemes envisaged were those for transport facilities, irrigation, power supply and similar public utilities, and Amery made special note of the necessity to prevent the Treasury from exercising control over the schemes and subjecting them to criticism 'based solely on the desire to prevent expenditure'.[6]

No action was taken, but the question came up at the Imperial Economic Conference which took place in October and November 1923. Although discussion was related mainly to dominion problems rather than those of the colonial territories, they were included when the empire countries were invited to consider a proposal whereby they would submit schemes of economic development which the imperial government would facilitate by grants of interest on the necessary loans, up to a maximum of three-quarters of the interest for five years. On behalf of the colonial empire, William Ormsby-Gore, parliamentary under-secretary of state, welcomed the proposals, but warned that their success would depend entirely on the conditions imposed: 'if it means Treasury control I am afraid it does not mean Colonial development. That has been our experience in the past'.[7]

In November, however, the Cabinet Committee on Unemployment recorded the view that in present circumstances the arrangements adopted by the Imperial Economic Conference would not result in any appreciable development in the Colonies and Protectorates . . . and it was suggested that Colonial development on a substantial scale could best be obtained by setting aside a capital sum of £20,000,000 for the purpose.[8]

This suggestion was vigorously resisted by the Chancellor of the Exchequer, Neville Chamberlain, who wrote to the committee:

It seems to me premature to assume without further evidence or argument that the extremely generous proposals which we submitted to the Imperial Economic Conference will be quite ineffective in stimulating the development of the Colonies . . . and to embark upon an inquiry of which the object is presumably to formulate even more generous terms of assistance – which I should have the greatest difficulty in accepting.[9]

By December it was apparent that the only replies to the economic conference's proposals had been from the small colonies, and all of them were negative. The Colonial Office then suggested a scheme for railway building in Kenya and Uganda to cost about £6 million, which the Committee on Unemployment regarded as 'promising'.[10] In January 1924 the Labour government, which had won the general election in December 1923, took office, and the new Cabinet Committee on Unemployment took stock of the situation. Legislation was drafted to implement the conference's proposals for an extension of the Trade Facilities Act to include grants of up to three-quarters of interest for a maximum of five years. The previous Unemployment Committee's approval of the Kenya–Uganda railway scheme was accepted and the committee recommended a loan of £3,500,000 interest free for five years and repayable over thirty-seven years. The committee felt that the scheme would not only relieve unemployment but also 'contribute materially towards the solution of the British cotton shortage problem'.[11] Arrangements for the loan were introduced in the Colonial Office estimates presented to Parliament on 25 February 1924.[12]

The new government also had before them the report of a committee set up in July 1923 under the chairmanship of Lord Ronaldshay, to consider what role private enterprise had to play in the existing and future transportation services of East and West Africa.[13] This report concluded that there was no further scope at present for railway building in West Africa, but that a number of desirable projects in East Africa – especially the extension of the Nyasaland railway from the Shire Highlands to Lake Nyasa – were being held up for want of funds. None of these projects, however, was within the capabilities of private enterprise. The report stated:

> There is, indeed, little reason to suppose that private firms will be found willing to finance, construct and operate railways unaided by Government in the present stage of development of Tropical Africa.[14]

The terms of reference of the committee did not include discussion of which railways should be built and how they should be financed, and in a minority report, Sir Edwin Stockton MP, called for another inquiry, 'to consider ways of developing our Tropical African Dependencies other than those with which we were called on to deal'.[15]

It was partly in response to the Ronaldshay Report and Stockton's comments that one of the terms of reference of another commission of inquiry into East Africa, the establishment of which was announced by the secretary of state for the colonies, J.H. Thomas, in April 1924, included a consideration of the measures to be taken to promote the general economic development of the British East African dependencies.[16]

Meanwhile the process of bringing forward schemes of colonial development involving large orders in the United Kingdom continued, and in March 1924 the colonies were asked to furnish details of general utility works which might be started.[17] Once again, railway works – to the value of £710,000 in Tanganyika and £1 million to £1.2 million in Nyasaland – were put forward: again a loan free of interest 'for a considerable period' was regarded as essential. In addition, the construction of a bridge over the Zambesi (estimated to cost £500,000) was put forward as a possible project.

These proposals remained in abeyance while the East Africa Commission was sitting. In October 1924 the Labour government was defeated in the general election. In the following year there was another call for a substantial loan for Crown colony development, somewhat similar to that of Amery's of October 1922, this time from the President of the Board of Trade, Sir Philip Cunliffe-Lister:

> We should speed up, as much as possible, railway construction and other development in the Empire, particularly in Africa. I am convinced that nationally the most remunerative expenditure we can incur is in the development of markets which will be complementary and not competitive. Africa fulfils this condition to a peculiar degree, and is at the same time the great potential supply of raw cotton.[18]

The report of the East Africa Commission, was published in May 1925. It concluded that the further economic development of both native and non-native production in East Africa was dependent upon increased transport facilities, in particular new railways. However, the report continued, 'The outstanding problem is the finance of such undertakings. It is clear to us that, unless the Imperial Government is prepared to assist liberally in this matter, little or nothing can be done'.[19] Accordingly, the commission recommended the introduction of an East Africa Transport Loan Bill to provide a guaranteed loan of £10 million to be used for transport development in East Africa, with the proviso that the loan should be interest free for the first five years. The commission felt that the burden which this placed on the British taxpayer could be justified on the grounds of the moral obligation Britain had to develop her possessions; but also 'we maintain that the indirect benefits of increased trade and production within the Empire will more than counterbalance any initial sacrifice'. Approximately half of the sum advanced would be spent in the United Kingdom, much of it on railway and engineering equipment. One of the commission's members suggested the establishment of a 'National or Imperial Development Board', into which a fixed sum would be paid annually and from which schemes of imperial development would be financed. These schemes would be submitted by the Colonial Office. The board would advance money to colonial government, public utility companies, etc. as loans, at low rates of interest or free of interest for a number of years.[20]

The commission's recommendations were strongly supported by cotton, iron and steel and engineering lobby groups in Britain.[21] In October it was discussed in Cabinet. Amery argued that the Central and East African colonies were among the safest and most profitable areas for investment in the empire, for 'their development lies entirely in the field of the production of raw materials, notably cotton, which are urgently needed by British manufacturers, while every pound of tropical produce grown in these territories increases the purchasing power of their inhabitants for British manufactured goods in return'.[22]

Cabinet agreed to a £10 million guaranteed loan for East African and a £4.5 million one for Palestine, but did not agree to the suggestion that the loan should be interest free for five years.[23] Amery wrote in a memorandum in March 1926: 'I think we are all agreed that such a course would not be justifiable, and that were this to be provided for in the Bill to be laid before Parliament it would be difficult to get it accepted by the House of Commons.'[24] Presumably the reasoning behind this decision was that unemployment in 1926 was not such a serious issue as in 1924 because the levels were lower and the government had no need to face the electorate for another three years. The Bill became law on 15 December 1926 as the Palestine and East Africa Guaranteed Loan Act.

From 1921, then, the continuing crisis of high unemployment levels in Britain stimulated interest in schemes for colonial economic development, particularly railway construction in tropical Africa. This, it was soon discovered, could not be provided by private enterprise, and required grants of interest during the construction period, as happened in the case of the Kenya-Uganda railway loan of 1924. Finally, in 1926, £10 million was provided by Britain for development loans to East Africa, although without provision for periods free of interest, partly as a result of pressure from British manufacturing interests and partly in response to the consequence of the high level of unemployment. By 1926 several proposals for a more comprehensive system of colonial development by means of imperial money paid into a development fund had been suggested, but not yet taken up.

Early in 1929, as a general election approached, Cabinet again turned to colonial economic development as a response to the unemployment crisis.[25] Proposals for development of the colonies (among other measures) to help solve the unemployment problem, however, received little encouragement from the Treasury which asserted that the effects of colonial development 'in stimulating British industry, even assuming that it is not merely a diversion of resources, is less than is often supposed'.[26] The expenditure of £10 million over five years on railway development in the colonies, for instance, would increase iron and steel exports by only 1 per cent per annum, and those of rolling stock by 3 per cent. Moreover, the adoption of the proposal that the imperial government should pay the interest on loans raised for colonial development would result in 'the premature adoption of uneconomic schemes' which would only make matters worse.

In March Amery returned to the idea of a 'permanent Empire development policy' to be implemented by establishing an annual fund of £1 million, administered by a board of technical advisers, from which interest in whole or part could be paid on loans for colonial development. The Treasury reiterated its view: 'Attempts to accelerate colonial development by easy borrowing terms are apt to lead to wasteful and ill-advised expenditure', and 'orders immediately placed in this country for materials are often disappointingly small'.[27]

On 10 April 1929 Amery submitted another memorandum to the Cabinet on 'Colonial Development in relation to the problem of unemployment'. He felt that colonial development so far had been unbalanced: 'We have asked too much of the colonies and have offered too little ourselves for what is, after all, our problem, and unless we change these lines we shall continue to arrive at the same negative results when the Colonies are asked to do more than they are already doing.'[28] He proposed, therefore, a Colonial Development Fund of between £750,000 and £1,000,000 per annum, from which interest charges on loans for development projects involving orders in Britain could be met for a number of years. Schemes similar to those undertaken with the help of the East Africa Guaranteed Loan were envisaged, but it was now recognised that the rejection of the East Africa Commission's proposal that loans should be interest free for five years 'has made it impossible to proceed with any long-term development projects under this Act'. Only £3.5 million of the £10 million provided had been lent.[29]

These proposals were agreed to by Cabinet and on 30 April Amery announced to the Commons that a Colonial Development Fund would be set up to provide imperial assistance for colonial development.[30]

The Conservatives lost the election and a new Labour government took office at the beginning of July. Treasury warned against expecting too much from the Colonial Development Bill:

> It is not of course to be expected that employment at home will be immediately and directly affected by the Bill to a very large extent, though schemes for construction in the Colonies bring orders here. The Bill is primarily based on a far-sighted policy of Imperial development as one of the surest foundations of prosperity at home; the full fruits of this policy will be increasingly reaped in the years to come.[31]

The Bill was presented both as a method of promoting colonial economic development and of relieving unemployment in Britain. Its urgency was stressed by the parliamentary under-secretary of state:

> I hope that the House will agree to this Bill and that we shall not be delayed too long, as we are anxious to see the schemes of development begun and useful work provided for many of our people as we believe it will be – useful work for those who are unemployed or partially employed today.[32]

The Bill became law at the end of July 1929.

It seems clear that the proposal in 1929 for a Colonial Development Fund arose out of persistently high levels of unemployment combined with the need to fight a general election. As Amery himself pointed out, another measure like the East Africa Guaranteed Loan Act was not going to work, and a more comprehensive approach was required. The essential idea, however, was not a new one and had been put forward on a number of occasions since Amery's original proposal for an 'Empire Development Bill' in 1922. As an unemployment measure, it may be doubted whether the Colonial Development Act would have helped reduce unemployment even if the early 1929 position had persisted. As it was, as the world depression of 1930-3 deepened, the Act quickly became irrelevant to the problem of reducing Britain's unemployment.[33]

In May 1930, with unemployment standing officially at 1,750,000 persons, the Cabinet Committee on Unemployment Policy reported to the Cabinet 'the broad and undisputed fact that so far the schemes we have sanctioned do not appear to have made any substantial impression upon the volume of employment'. It was estimated that by 28 February 1930, the Colonial Development Advisory Committee (see Chapter 8) had approved schemes the expenditure on which would provide employment for only 8,000 workers. By the beginning of 1931, according to Skidelsky, 13,000 men were being employed directly through the Colonial Development Act, at which date 2,671,000 were without work.[34]

In March 1931, the National Committee on Expenditure, found that the 'element of benefit to the trade and industry of this country which is an essential condition of advances under the [Colonial Development] Act, is somewhat remote'.[35] It felt that Britain could afford neither to subsidise local colonial governments nor to finance 'a policy of development which will bring no appreciable benefit to this country for a long time ahead'. Consequently they recommended that only £750,000 per annum should be spent in future, and greater regard given to the effects of advances from the Fund in the United Kingdom.[36]

Measures introduced to promote colonial economic development in the 1920s were characterised by their *ad hoc* and expedient nature. Despite a realisation and acknowledgement that the process of colonial economic development was inevitably a long-term one, the measures were brought in hastily and often in immediate reaction to changes in the level of British unemployment. Moreover, the size and effectiveness of these measures were undermined by the preponderance of the 'Treasury view' which was at best sceptical of the benefits to Britain of expenditure on capital works in the tropical colonies and which ensured that the amount of money actually provided remained very small and not on easy terms. The inappropriate nature of the kind of assistance being proffered was emphasised by the fact that the sums actually spent fell far short of the amounts (themselves small) nominally provided: offers of financial assistance which consisted, for the most part, of loans on more or less commercial terms, were not ones the colonial governments, or their advisers in the Colonial Office, could readily take up. As we shall see in Chapter 8, by the end of the 1920s many of Britain's tropical colonies were over-burdened with external debt; if they had added to this burden by accepting further loans under the various schemes of colonial assistance which were suggested (though not all were enacted) their vulnerability by 1930 would have been even more serious.

IMPERIAL PREFERENCE AND THE EMPIRE MARKETING BOARD

Prior to 1929 the actual amounts of money spent by the British government for developing the 'great estate' were insignificant and provided in an unsystematic manner. There were other – equally *ad hoc* – initiatives resulting from the post-war economic crisis: the reorganisation of the Imperial Institute, the establishment of the Empire Cotton Growing Corporation, the establishment of the Imperial College of Tropical Agriculture and the Empire Settlement Act 1922.[37] Tariff reform and Imperial preference – the concomitant to economic development in the Joseph Chamberlain programme – was also given emphasis by the economic consequences of the First World War. As seen in Chapter 6, the 1917 Imperial War Conference endorsed preference in principle, but it became clear that taxes on imported foodstuffs and raw materials were not politically possible, and all the British government promised, in 1918, was that 'a preference will be given to our colonies on existing duties and upon any duties which for our purposes may be subsequently imposed'.[38] Imperial preference on existing import duties came into force in September 1919. In most cases imports originating in the empire paid two-thirds or five-sixths of the full import duty and covered tea, cocoa, coffee, chicory, currants, dried and preserved fruits, sugar, glucose, molasses, saccharin, motor spirit, tobacco, articles included under the Safeguarding of Industries Act 1916, wine, beer and spirits.[39]

At the Imperial Economic Conference in October 1923 the British delegation promised to give greater preference to certain imports which were already taxed and to extend tariffs to several new commodities.[40] They also agreed to establish an Imperial Economic Committee on a permanent basis to advise empire governments on economic and commercial matters.[41] Sir Philip Lloyd-Graeme, chairman of the conference and President of the Board of Trade, concluded 'We have all been saying here: we have got this great undeveloped Estate; and the whole job of this Conference is to push on with its development.'[42]

At the end of October Stanley Baldwin announced that the government could not fight unemployment effectively without a general policy of protection. However, he was careful to make it clear there would be no tax on wheat, flour, meat, bacon, cheese, butter or eggs, so the degree of imperial preference involved was small. The Conservative government was defeated in the December general election, and the new Labour government declined to implement the promises of wider and higher preference made at the Imperial Economic Conference or set up an Imperial Economic Committee.[43]

The Labour government fell in September 1924 and the Conservatives – Baldwin having renounced protection in June – won the ensuing election. The new Conservative government reversed Labour's decision on establishing a permanent Imperial Economic Committee (IEC), though the terms of reference were narrowed: instead of being empowered to give advice on all economic and commercial matters affecting the empire, the IEC was

> To consider the possibility of improving the methods of preparing for market and marketing within the United Kingdom the food products of the overseas parts of the Empire with a view to increasing the consumption of such products in the United Kingdom in preference to imports from foreign countries and to promote the interests both of producers and consumers.[44]

As regards the extension of tariffs and imperial preference, the government accepted that it had no mandate to tax foodstuffs and that a 'complete system of Preference' was therefore impossible. The government decided to compensate the empire for the tariff changes promised in 1923, and now not to be implemented, by a grant of £1 million per annum, which was the estimated value to the overseas empire of the lost preferences. This grant was to be spent by the IEC in 'finding entirely new and untried ways of developing trade with the Empire, trade which will bring in Empire stuff in lieu of foreign stuff'.[45]

In 1925 the IEC recommended that the grant of £1 million per annum should be spent by an 'Executive Commission' which would undertake a 'National Movement' to increase empire buying by the British public. There should be

> continuous publicity on a national scale with a view to spreading and fostering [the idea] that Empire purchasing creates an increased demand for the manufactured products of the United Kingdom and therefore stimulates employment at home.[46]

The executive commission to carry out this task was established in May 1926 as the Empire Marketing Board (EMB).

In the course of its seven years' existence the EMB developed four main areas of activity designed to promote the consumption of empire foodstuffs and raw materials in the United Kingdom: research, market intelligence, economic investigations and publicity.[47] It was discovered at the outset that one of the reasons why some empire produce could not compete with foreign produce on the United Kingdom market was that the empire goods were of an inferior quality in relation to price. The EMB concluded that there was no point in trying to use advertising to persuade the British consumer to buy inferior empire articles, and decided to use approximately half of its grant to support research projects in the United Kingdom and the overseas empire which were designed to raise the standard of empire primary exports.[48] The EMB did not initiate research but simply responded to applications for financial assistance from various research establishments and government departments. This resulted in it supporting a varied collection of projects with no provision for coordination between them. Moreover, the EMB made commitments to research bodies for a number of years in

150

advance, which tied up its funds and made it difficult to vary funding in the light of changed circumstances.[49]

The EMB's market intelligence activity took the form of publishing weekly 'intelligence notes' on various empire products sold in Britain such as dairy produce, fresh fruit, dried and canned fruit. These notes contained details of imports and prices and were distributed free to the appropriate trade bodies. Economic investigations were carried out into the production and marketing of the major primary products entering world trade from the overseas empire as well as into general questions such as agricultural research, geophysical surveying and the importance of empire markets for British manufactures. These reports were published either as EMB or IEC publications.

Publicity work was the most controversial part of the EMB's activities. It took a number of forms: newspaper advertisements, shop window display material, the organisation of 'Empire Shopping Weeks', documentary films, leaflets, radio broadcasts, exhibitions, distribution of material to schools in Britain and overseas and to overseas empire newspapers, lecture programmes and tours and posters on specially constructed hoardings.

The results were not convincing: after seven years, during which time hundreds of posters were displayed on some 2,000 hoardings throughout Britain, extensive press advertising undertaken, Empire Shopping Weeks organised by the score, and one million people (many of whom were children in organised school parties) visited the EMB cinema in the Imperial Institute at South Kensington, criticisms of the EMB remained unabated. There were three main areas of concern: first, that the EMB could not show whether, and if so, to what extent, its campaigns had increased empire trade; second, that its posters and press advertisements were ineffective because they were insufficiently aggressive, too subtle and too intellectual; and third, that the British agricultural industry was being adversely affected by the advertising of empire imports.[50]

As defenders of the EMB pointed out, it was engaged in selling an idea rather than specific commodities. The idea it sold was the Joseph Chamberlain concept of 'developing the great estate'. That is, that the empire could produce everything Britain needed in the way of foodstuffs and raw materials and that the empire represented Britain's best market for manufactured goods. Buying empire produce created work at home and opportunities for increased migration to the empire. Unlike the dominions, and to a lesser extent India, the tropical colonies were not expected to develop industries which competed with British imports and so, by the 1920s, these colonies fulfilled the role of 'complementary economies' to a greater extent. The task of the EMB, and especially of its poster artists, was to illustrate this economic relationship in picture form. Their attempts indicated that the racial division of labour, inherent in Chamberlain's programme, was still very much alive.[51] In 1932, in the wake of Britain's decision to abandon free trade and adopt a policy of imperial tariff preference, the EMB was abolished.

THE ECONOMICS OF TRUSTEESHIP

The measures taken between 1900 and 1929 by the British government represented an attempt to 'develop the estate' by the use of public funds in various forms. The loans and grants were intended to benefit the British economy by making the colonies better customers and suppliers. Although they involved the use of public capital, the philosophy was firmly that of assisting British private enterprise, rather than of supplanting it. However, when looked at from the colonial viewpoint, there were serious problems for the success of this development strategy. These problems were to do with the structure of the colonial economies, the role of expatriate private enterprise and the philosophy of the local British administrators.

References to the wealth of colonial territories, especially in Africa, was often qualified by the word 'potential' when reports were being drawn up in the early twentieth century. The circumstances of British colonies, like other underdeveloped societies, was that of extreme poverty. Rising real per capita incomes and living standards through sustained economic growth might be attainable but colonial economic development required large amounts of investment in social overhead capital as well as in productive enterprise. In most cases sufficient capital was not available on terms the colonies could afford. Moreover, structural changes in the colonial economy leading towards the growth of the domestic sector were essential if the earnings generated by the export sector were to flow on to the benefit of the colony as a whole. Increased production of goods and services for the domestic market might be expected to lead to a more diversified and stronger economy but usually required measures by government designed to facilitate and encourage the growth of the indigenous investor and business community. Colonial rule was not a form of government which could easily accomplish this. An overwhelming emphasis on exports, on the other hand, could lead to unbalanced development, with disastrous consequences if the world's demand for such exports declined and with the added problem of a drain of export earnings to foreign investors. The colonies were not only poor but caught in a relationship of dependence with the industrialised countries who bought their exports. They exported only primary produce, almost always in an unprocessed state. As demand for their exports grew, and as the colonial government and expatriate private enterprise developed export production, so dependence on one or several products increased. Almost without exception, British colonies became more dependent on a narrower range of export commodities between the wars and in most cases secondary industry based on processing did not develop. The colonies were therefore in no stronger a position to withstand the contraction of the international economy in the 1930s than they had been at the beginning of the 1920s. Indeed, to the extent that their economies were more integrated with the world economy by the end of the decade, they were in a more vulnerable position.

Many British tropical colonies were in a highly vulnerable position because of their extreme reliance on export cash crops and minerals. Table 7.2 shows the way in which the external trade of the tropical colonies virtually stagnated in the second half of the 1920s. Insofar as the trade balance indicates the direction of capital flows, the large export surpluses earned in some territories suggests that they may have experienced a net capital outflow. Yet physical production continued to rise, as illustrated by Table 7.3. With certain exceptions, the export drive inherent in the philosophy of 'developing the estate' resulted in dramatic increases in the volume of commodities entering world markets from Britain's tropical colonies between 1912–14 and 1927–9, from both plantation and peasant modes of production.[52] This occurred despite falling or weak commodity prices following the end of the 1919–20 boom. Table 7.4 indicates the extent of the price decline in the early 1920s, followed by patchy recovery in the middle years and further falls in 1929. Import prices fell also so that the terms of trade rose in most cases from 1922, following their collapse in 1921, to a peak around 1926 or 1927. Thereafter the terms of trade were static or falling prior to the major decline caused by the onset of the Great Depression. Public works expenditure to support the export sector had led to very high levels of external debt, shown in Table 7.5, the servicing of which was becoming an increasing burden for the colonial economies by the beginning of the 1930s.

The failure of the British development measures to work was partly due to the role played by expatriate private enterprise. Their investments extended to mining, agricultural production, and trading, but with a few notable exceptions – of which rubber in Malaya was one – interest concentrated on the first and third of these areas. Mining ventures could usually attract British capital, though direct and indirect government assistance was also a factor.[53] Foreign trading enterprises were often the oldest form of commercial contact between the colonial people and Europe, and they continued to dominate the import and export trades. In both trades profits were expatriated and local enterprise discouraged or ignored. Agricultural ventures were less popular. Even in the rubber industry in Malaya expatriate enterprise found itself in difficulties after 1921 and had to be assisted by the British govern-

Table 7.2   Imports, exports and balance of trade, selected colonies, 1920–30 (£000)

Colonies	1920	1921	1922	1923	1924	1925	1926	1927	1928	1929	1930
Imports											
West Africa	42574	20914	21005	22808	20458	26155	23476	28879	29858	25106	22987
East Africa	13847	6587	6979	8717	11214	14408	13640	14025	15499	15610	13380
Central Africa	1173	1372	1020	1015	1233	1914	2509	2952	3304	4398	5717
Eastern	165460	84958	77005	91743	105337	144830	152060	151861	135100	137562	109102
Caribbean	29794	18877	14851	15819	15447	16103	15769	16741	17349	18248	16143
Pacific	1652	1484	843	988	1066	1263	1464	1215	1455	1454	1219
Total	254500	134192	121803	141090	154755	204673	208918	215673	202565	202978	168548
Exports											
West Africa	33795	15852	17801	20908	25646	29156	30215	31774	32945	31653	26034
East Africa	9761	5931	6874	9032	12175	14375	12425	12017	14012	14471	11101
Central Africa	1205	976	1031	882	1031	991	1153	1715	1552	1522	1550
Eastern	143027	83789	82991	106451	117187	190175	188484	162285	131972	141728	101945
Caribbean	25890	12804	12755	15409	13705	11101	14256	16219	15716	15824	13381
Pacific	2876	2538	1843	1550	1491	2147	1696	1980	2692	1708	1452
Total	216554	121890	121395	154232	171235	247945	248229	225990	198889	206906	155463
Balance											
West Africa	-8779	-5062	-3204	-1900	5188	3001	6739	2895	3087	6547	3047
East Africa	-4086	-656	-105	315	961	-33	-1215	-2008	-1487	-1139	-2279
Central Africa	32	-396	11	-133	-202	-923	-1356	-1237	-1752	-2876	-4167
Eastern	-22433	-1169	5986	14708	11850	45345	36424	10424	-3128	4166	-7157
Caribbean	-3904	-6073	-2096	-410	-742	-5002	-1513	-522	-1633	-2424	-2762
Pacific	1224	1054	900	562	425	884	232	765	1237	254	233
Total	-37946	-12302	1492	13142	16480	43272	29311	10317	-3676	4528	-13085

Total imports and exports of merchandise (including re-exports), excluding bullion and coin.
West Africa: Gambia, Gold Coast, Nigeria, Sierra Leone;
East Africa: Kenya–Uganda, Tanganyika, Zanzibar;
Central Africa: Northern Rhodesia, Nyasaland;
Eastern: Ceylon, Malaya (Straits Settlements only in 1920, 1921), Mauritius;
Caribbean: Barbados, British Guiana, British Honduras, Jamaica, Trinidad.
Source: Statistical Abstract for the British Empire, Nos. 58, 63 (1911–13, 1922–4, 1924–33).

Table 7.3   Selected commodity exports, annual averages,
1912–14 to 1937–9

Commodity	Colony	1912–14	1917–19	1922–4	1927–9	1932–4	1937–9
Cocoa	Trinidad	456	564	520	512	357	254
cwt,000	Gold Coast	947	2223	3869	4487	4667	5203
	Nigeria	80	343	675	957	1399	2094
Coffee	Jamaica	76	72	64	73	77	76
cwt,000	Kenya-Uganda	22[f]	107[e]	171	226	354	612
Sugar	Mauritius	4486	4444	4586	4758	4003	5908
cwt,000	Trinidad	759	1081	854	1316	1920	2516
	Br. Guiana	1816	1940	1731	2165	2627	3628
Tea	Ceylon	192	195	1866	238	229	226
lb,mill							
Bananas	Jamaica	14	5	12	20	16	23
stems,mill							
Copra	Malaya[a]	11	24	161	175	199	181
tons,000	Ceylon	52	69	75	100	72	66
Palm Kernels	Nigeria	174	203	218	252	286	317
tons,000	Sierra Leone	45	50	57	64	70	70
Palm Oil	Nigeria	76	87	105	124	119	127
tons,000							
Groundnuts	Nigeria	13	49	42	114	213	218
tons,000							
Rubber	Malaya[b]	27	286	567	2425	1290	1315
lb,mill	Ceylon	25	73	91	145	144	135
Cotton	Nigeria	5461	4501	8005	10894	8547	14710
lb,000	Kenya-Uganda	11654[d]	13041[e]	38417	63366	105937	148741
Sisal	Kenya-Uganda	979d	4771[e]	9735	16001	19750	30382
tons	Tanganyika	n.a.	n.a.	13832	38309	67555	95047
Tobacco	Nyasaland	3112[d]	4058[e]	6178	12479	12673	13496
lb,000							
Copper	N. Rhodesia[c]	1426	991	256	5184	101771	208329
tons							
Bauxite	Br. Guiana	n.a.	n.a.	85	171	51	384
tons,000							
Manganese	Gold Coast	nil	31	143	371	219	396
tons,000							
Tin	Malaya[b]	64527	59473	72268	94951	50675	78794
tons	Nigeria	4391	8648	8483	13042	6237	13358
Petroleum	Trinidad	10	14	85	168	203	385
crude, gall, mill							

[a] Federated Malay States only 1912–14 and 1917–19; [b] Straits Settlements only 1912–14
and 1917–19; [c] Copper ore, concentrate, bar and ingot 1912–14, 1917–19 and 1922–24;
copper ore, concentrate and blister 1932–1934; copper blister and electrolytic, 1937–1939;
[d] 1 Apr. 1912–31 Mar. 1915; [e] 1 Apr. 1917–31 Mar. 1920; [f] 1 Apr. 1913–31 Mar. 1915.
Source: *Statistical Abstract for the British Empire*, Nos. 57, 58, 63, 68, 69 (1909–45).

Table 7.4 Terms of trade, selected colonies 1920–30 (1927–9 = 100)

Colony		1920	1921	1922	1923	1924	1925	1926	1927	1928	1929	1930
Gold Coast	E	160.6	74.7	76.3	72.0	69.7	79.2	83.7	113.2	102.0	84.9	77.0
	I	235.4	198.3	123.1	105.7	109.2	111.3	109.0	102.0	101.4	96.2	87.6
	T	68	38	62	68	64	71	77	111	101	88	88
Nigeria	E	160.7	94.6	88.8	91.4	98.4	102.8	104.7	104.4	102.0	95.0	78.8
	I	202.1	168.4	118.7	110.0	118.1	117.9	101.1	108.0	107.9	105.2	94.2
	T	80	56	75	83	83	87	104	97	95	90	84
Kenya–Uganda	E	241.9	89.1	96.4	105.1	126.2	125.6	99.6	88.5	107.2	104.0	78.3
	I	249.3	199.1	133.7	118.2	121.9	117.7	112.3	105.4	96.8	99.4	94.4
	T	97	45	72	89	104	107	89	84	111	105	83
Mauritius	E	444.9	292.3	130.8	130.8	117.9	105.1	102.6	115.4	98.7	87.2	65.4
	I	232.6	127.3	114.4	106.6	105.3	116.5	113.3	102.6	102.1	95.4	83.6
	T	191	230	114	123	112	90	91	112	97	91	78
Ceylon	E	126.0	80.4	86.0	108.1	105.3	145.6	133.0	116.5	88.1	86.3	71.3
	I	201.1	117.8	106.9	98.6	93.6	105.8	103.3	102.7	99.2	97.4	80.5
	T	63	68	80	110	113	138	129	113	89	89	89
Malaya	E	192.2	84.6	77.4	121.6	119.7	232.0	189.1	155.4	99.2	45.9	58.0
	I	243.7	95.7	158.7	169.3	106.6	112.5	116.0	105.7	96.8	96.6	92.6
	T	79	88	49	72	112	206	163	147	103	48	63
Jamaica	E	206.5	107.4	110.0	141.2	99.4	93.5	97.5	101.9	97.8	101.0	80.6
	I	266.5	141.7	103.4	111.1	120.6	116.6	110.1	102.7	97.8	99.0	92.4
	T	77	76	106	127	82	80	89	99	100	102	87
Trinidad	E	168.6	106.7	93.1	97.5	89.6	97.6	97.9	117.6	97.6	84.3	79.6
	I	177.6	153.1	112.4	102.5	105.8	114.1	108.8	101.9	100.0	98.3	94.2
	T	95	70	83	95	85	86	90	115	98	86	85

E, weighted index of the unit value of principal exports;
I, weighted index of the unit value of principal imports;
T, terms of trade: E divided by I x 100.
Source: Statistical Abstract for British Empire, Nos. 58–64.

Table 7.5 Public debt, selected colonies, 1913 and 1919–30 (£ m)

Colony	1913	1919	1920	1921	1922	1923	1924	1925	1926	1927	1928	1929	1930
Kenya	0.4	1.1	1.2	5.0	5.0	5.0	8.5	8.5	8.5	10.0	13.5	13.5	16.9
Uganda	0.3	0.4	0.4	0.7	0.9	0.9	1.1	1.1	1.1	1.1	1.1	1.1	1.1
Tanganyika	n.a.	n.a.	<0.1	0.8	1.6	2.4	3.1	3.1	3.1	3.1	5.2	5.2	5.2
Nyasaland	0.1	0.2	0.2	0.3	0.4	0.4	0.5	0.6	0.7	0.8	0.8	0.8	0.9
Gold Coast	2.5	3.4	7.4	7.3	7.3	7.3	11.8	11.1	11.8	11.8	11.8	11.8	13.0
Nigeria	8.3	12.0	10.3	13.6	13.6	19.3	19.3	19.3	23.6	23.6	23.6	23.6	28.4
Ceylon	6.1	7.0	7.0	10.0	13.0	13.0	12.9	12.9	12.9	12.9	12.9	12.9	15.9
Mauritius	1.3	1.3	1.2	1.3	1.3	1.3	1.6	1.7	1.8	1.8	1.9	1.9	2.8
West Indies	6.4	6.8	7.0	8.0	8.8	9.3	9.3	9.6	9.8	10.0	10.3	10.3	10.2
British Guiana	0.9	1.2	1.2	1.2	2.4	2.6	2.6	2.7	2.7	2.7	2.6	2.6	4.8
Total	26.3	33.4	35.9	48.3	54.3	61.5	66.2	71.3	76.0	77.8	83.7	86.1	99.1

Source: Statistical Abstract of the British Empire Nos. 57, 58; Colonial Annual Reports.

ment for much of the inter-war period.[54] This produced a situation where – except for mining – capital was in short supply in Britain's colonies, and inevitably this placed a brake on the speed at which growth could take place. Poverty and a narrow export base made local capital accumulation difficult.

The slow growth of a capitalist class in most colonies was not, however, simply a result of the economic circumstances. The colonial authorities followed policies which were directly and indirectly inimical to the development of colonial capitalism. In West Africa, for example, a conflict occurred between the metropolitan desire to develop the estate and the local authorities' determination to protect the native from such development. Soon after Joseph Chamberlain's call to British business-men to invest in the newly won tropical lands, William Lever was refused permission to establish oil-palm plantations in West Africa. After several attempts, he went elsewhere, to the Congo. Later he was asked to set up oil-crushing mills in Nigeria, since this was considered by the local authorities to be a legitimate role for expatriate enterprise. This time it was Lever's turn to refuse. The palm oil industry of Nigeria – accounting for up to one half of the colony's export earnings – stagnated, for the locally owned plantations which were established were negligible.[55]

The policy of the local colonial governments was not to oppose all forms of economic development. Some African colonial administrations – such as that of Sir Gordon Guggisberg in the Gold Coast in the 1920s – energetically built roads, harbours and railways, borrowing heavily on the London market to do so.[56] The export industries of Malaya were excellently served with infrastructure by the government. But where development seemed to lead away from a peasant-based society, local officials were far more cautious. Traditional ways of life were to be preserved as part of the policy of trusteeship. In West Africa natives were not to be allowed to drift to towns or work on European plantations and become wage-workers. In Malaya there was a racial segmentation of the economy, and the role assigned to the Malays was that of subsistence rice farmers who should remain in their villages.[57] Only in colonies where there were white settlers, as in East and Central Africa, was widespread rural wage employment for natives considered desirable, indeed essential, to provide the settlers with a labour force, but they were often discouraged from competing with the settlers in producing cash crops for export themselves, with varying degrees of success.[58] The image of the native which colonial administrators held was sometimes highly romantic, seeing them as 'sturdy peasants' of the kind long-disappeared in England, who were too backward to cope with modern capitalism.[59] Even where a vigorous export industry, such as cocoa in the Gold Coast, was in native hands, officials persisted in regarding the cocoa farmer as basically a subsistence peasant who grew cocoa as a cash crop sideline, who lacked the long-term perspective of a capitalist and who was unresponsive to market forces.[60] Indigenous capitalism undoubtedly emerged and grew – even flourished from time to time – in some of Britain's tropical colonies during the inter-war period, but it seemed to do so despite the policies of the colonial regime rather than because of them.[61]

To this antipathy towards local nascent capitalists was added the hostility of British firms. Trading companies were undercut by local traders and British manufacturers objected to import-substituting industries in the colonies. Even local governments found their railways losing money because of competition from motor transport companies owned by natives.[62] There was much opposition locally to the establishment of secondary industry, and in London the protective instincts of Colonial Office officials were encouraged by interested sections of Britain's trade and industry to produce a strong resistance to secondary industry in the colonial empire, as we shall see in the next chapter.

The twin pillars of British colonial economic policy were reinforced during the 1920s. Private enterprise remained predominantly British and the rise of native capitalism was resisted. The colonial economies remained complementary to the British economy, providing foodstuffs, raw materials and absorbing manufactured goods. The degree of dependence on a narrow range of primary exports increased in most cases, and tendencies towards the colonial economies becoming less complementary were successfully resisted. The general economic experience of colonies under British rule from 1900 to 1929 was one of bursts of growth in the export sector, but not development towards the creation of a strong diversified economy which might be regarded as a more appropriate fulfilment of 'trusteeship'.

8

Depression and disillusion
The colonial economies in the 1930s

THE WORK OF THE COLONIAL DEVELOPMENT
ADVISORY COMMITTEE[1]

As a result of the 1929 Colonial Development Act, British colonial aid
was intended to be more systematic in the 1930s. In August 1929, the
Colonial Development Advisory Committee (CDAC), established under
the Act to administer the Colonial Development Fund, determined the
procedure to be followed for applications for assistance. It decided that a
colonial government must first submit the project to the Colonial Office
which would then either pass it on to the committee (with or without a
recommendation that it be assisted), or return it to the colony for
revision. If revised and resubmitted by the colony, the Colonial Office
would pass the scheme to the CDAC, though an application without the
secretary of state's recommendation stood little chance of success. From
January 1930 the financial adviser to the secretary of state, Sir John
Campbell, attended the CDAC meetings and presented the Colonial
Office view. If the governor, or another senior official of the colony
making the application was in London at the time it came before the
committee, he generally appeared and explained the case, but there was
no formal provision for a direct submission from the colony to the
committee and the CDAC had no power to initiate schemes itself.

The number of applications, the cost of schemes accepted for assistance, the amounts of assistance recommended by the CDAC and the
actual amounts paid out of the fund in each of the financial years of the
committee's operations between 1929 and 1939 are shown in Table 8.1.
Between 1929 and 1939 the committee received 822 applications and
accepted 641 of them (78 per cent) as suitable for assistance. Of these, 24
were later abandoned and so 617 schemes assisted by the committee
were actually completed or were still in operation by 31 March 1939.
The total cost of these 617 was £17,287,000 and the CDAC recommended a total of £7,910,000 to assist them. That is, it found on average
45.8 per cent of the cost of each scheme, though such an average does
not mean very much with so varied a group of projects. The remainder

160

Table 8.1 Assistance from the Colonial Development Advisory Committee, 1929–39

Period[a]	No. of applications	No. of applications accepted	No. accepted excluding those later abandoned	Cost of Schemes in col. 3 (£)	Assistance by way of grant to schemes shown in col. 3 (£)	Assistance by way of loan to schemes shown in col. 3 (£)	Total assistance recommended (£)	Actual grants paid out (£000)	Actual loans paid out (£000)	Total assistance actually paid out (£000)
1929–30	62	50	46	5379327	756580	580200	1336780	222.3	119.5	341.8
1930–31	177	118	110	2996683	856766	329119	1185885	407.5	438.8	846.3
1931–32	86	48	43	423796	205466	15225	220691	400.1	207.8	607.9
1932–33	48	38	38	347763	144911	118444	263355	257.9	113.4	371.3
1933–34	55	43	40	2136631	421669	320732	733401	299.0	506.9	805.9
1934–35	96	83	82	1691133	435214	649187	1084401	409.9	329.9	739.8
1935–36	91	75	73	1016245	447778	421066	868844	321.2	365.4	686.6
1936–37	69	60	60	1258668	505987	304058	810045	430.6	269.0	699.6
1937–38	61	55	54	930475	492571	288317	780888	478.6	256.0	734.6
1938–39	77	71	71	1178052	565973	59905	625878	415.2	129.5	544.7
Total	822	641	617	17286773	4823915	3086253	7910168	3642.4	2736.1	6378.5

[a] 1 April to 31 March in each period except for 1929–30 (1 August to 28 February) and 1930–31 (1 March to 31 March 1931)
Source: *Reports of the Colonial Development Advisory Committee*, Nos. 1 to 10; *Abstract accounts of the Colonial Development Fund*, 1931 to 1941.

had to be found by the colonial governments themselves from public loans or surplus revenue. Assistance took three forms: a free capital grant, a loan (generally interest free for three to five years) and a free grant of interest on a loan raised elsewhere. Free capital grants accounted for 48.3 per cent of all assistance, or, if free grants of interest are included (as is shown in Table 8.1), 61 per cent, and thus were more important than loans. The actual amounts paid out from the Colonial Development Fund fell short of the committee's recommendations as schemes required the money gradually and some were still in operation in 1939, though in three years the amount paid out exceeded the amount recommended. Overall, by 1939, £6,378,000 had been spent in the colonial empire under the Act, 57.1 per cent of it in the form of grants.

The number of applications submitted was fairly low during the first seven months (sixty-two) but then increased to an average of 13.6 per month in the thirteen months March 1930 to March 1931. Thereafter the number fluctuated between four per month in 1932–3 and eight in 1934–5. Once the initial backlog of schemes which had been previously shelved for lack of funds had been submitted the number of applications tended to fall gradually. More than three-quarters of the applications were successful in obtaining some funds (though sometimes less than the amount asked for) and the 'success rate' was somewhat higher from 1934 onwards, reaching 92 per cent in 1938–9. The committee went through a more strict phase, from 1930 to 1932, when, largely under pressure from the Treasury, schemes which appeared not to have any immediate benefit to the colony or the United Kingdom, or were on the borderline between what was seen as 'economic development' and 'social develop- ment' were regarded less favourably. From 1933 there was a steady relaxation in the CDAC's attitude. Twenty-four schemes were aban- doned – 3.8 per cent of the total assisted – usually because the local government could not afford to pay its share of the cost.

The most expensive scheme, the Zambesi Bridge project in Nyasaland cost £3 million; the cheapest was for the visit of a medical expert to Barbados costing £78. With such a wide range, calculating the 'average cost' is not a very useful exercise. However, only thirteen schemes cost more than £200,000 and relatively low-cost schemes predominated. In fact, few large-scale schemes were submitted to the committee after 1931, the only major exception being one for a deep-water harbour at Port of Spain, Trinidad, to cost £1 million, recommended for assistance in 1933.

Briefly then, the majority of applications were successful, relatively few were abandoned and grants were rather more important than loans. Perhaps the most striking aspect was that most activity was in the early years: 30 per cent of all applications were received before 1931 and

schemes recommended for assistance by March 1931 cost £8.4 million –
slightly under half the total for the whole period. After this initial burst
of enthusiasm, applications tended to fall, and from 1931 applications
never exceeded eight per month, compared to an average of twelve per
month up to March 1931.

The kind of schemes assisted were not the large-scale schemes of
transportation and communications which the designers of the Act had
envisaged; indeed, most were not large-scale schemes at all. According to
J.H. Thomas, the typical project which he had in mind when introduc-
ing the money resolution for the Bill, was the construction of Takoradi
harbour in the Gold Coast, which had cost about £3.5 million. He also
mentioned the Zambesi Bridge project – estimated to cost £3 million – as
a suitable object.[2] In fact, very few large-scale projects were undertaken
with money from the fund.

The kind of development which was seen as necessary in the 1930s
was not the high-cost transport and communications schemes of the
1900–30 period. In the depressed trade conditions of the 1930s there
seemed to be little scope for further large-scale transportation projects.
Rather colonial governments focussed their attention on smaller-scale
projects, for example, for urban water supply, housing, provision of
electrical light and power, public health and sanitation and secondary
roads.

The Colonial Development Act set out thirteen categories of scheme,
shown in Table 8.2. The two most important categories were 'internal
transport and communications' and 'public health'. Over the period
1929–40 these two accounted for 30 and 16 per cent of the assistance
respectively. The most neglected categories were fisheries, forestry and
electricity; the first two of these indicated a failure to develop the natural
resources of the tropical colonial empire with money from the fund (as
did the fairly low proportion given to mineral development), and the last
the dislike of the committee for schemes which they regarded as not
particularly developmental. More importantly, agricultural development schemes accounted for only 13 per cent of the total number and 5
per cent of the assistance, a remarkable fact when it is remembered to
what extent all colonies relied on the production and export of agricultural produce, and that the need for a greater degree of export diversification in most colonies was an important problem in the 1930s. Since the
committee did not initiate schemes, the lack of attention to agriculture,
fishery and forestry schemes was an indication of the attitude of the local
governments towards developing these resources.

Well over half of the transport and communication schemes were for
roads and bridges and this category also accounted for over half the
assistance given to transport and communications. All but one of the
railway schemes were submitted before April 1931, whereas only fifteen

Table 8.2 Types of development schemes assisted by the Colonial Development
Act, 1929–39

Category	No. of schemes assisted	%	Assistance granted (£000)	%
Agriculture & veterinary	85	13.3	387.6	4.9
Fisheries	8	1.2	166.1	2.1
Forestry	15	2.3	79.1	1.0
Land reclamation, drainage and irrigation	21	3.3	356.0	4.5
Transport & communications	118	18.4	2626.2	33.2
Harbours	17	2.7	450.9	5.7
Medical & public health	114	17.8	1036.2	13.1
Water supply & sanitation	69	10.8	893.9	11.3
Electricity supply	5	0.8	63.3	0.8
Mineral resources	3	0.5	704.0	8.9
Geological surveys	32	5.0	245.2	3.1
Research	115	17.9	553.7	7.0
Miscellaneous	39	6.0	348.0	4.4
Total	641	100.0	7910.2	100.0

Source: *Reports of the CDAC*, 1929–39.

schemes for roads and bridges were submitted before that date.
Moreover, few of the railway schemes involved the construction of new
line, but were rather for the relaying and realignment of existing track,
much of which had seemingly been poorly built. Railway schemes were
also more geographically concentrated than road schemes: eight of the
eleven railway schemes were in African colonies south of the Sahara.
Clearly, new developments in transport in the 1930s involved road and
air rather than railways. These projects were much less costly than the
railway schemes: the eleven air transport schemes cost on average
£41,527 each (though they ranged from £118,000 to £342), the seventy-
one road schemes, £32,745 (with a range of £300,000 to £550), whilst
eleven railway schemes cost on average £431,365 (ranging from £3
million to £6,000). Thus there is little doubt that as far as transport
schemes financed by the CDAC were concerned, the pattern in the
1930s was for colonies to favour cheaper projects, usually for road
transport, filling-in some of the gaps left by the earlier railway development and acting as 'feeders' for the railways. This minor transport
revolution was, of course, closely linked to the growth of motor traffic in
the colonial empire in the inter-war period.

As the 1930s progressed, transport and communications schemes tended to become relatively less important and public health ones relatively more important. In 1929–30, 33 per cent of assistance went to transport and communications, while public health received only 7 per cent, and in 1933–4 the proportions were 10 and 7 per cent respectively. However, by 1936–37 transport and communications accounted for 3 per cent while public health received 25 per cent; and in 1937–38 the proportion of assistance given to public health again exceeded that granted to transport and communications schemes. In the last year of the committee's operation, 1939–40, public health received over 40 per cent of the total assistance.

The CDAC's policy towards public health and medical schemes illustrated very well attitudes current in the 1930s towards financing economic development. On the one hand, there was an older school of thought which stressed the need to spend money on infrastructure and 'practical research' – i.e., research which yielded useful results quickly. On the other hand, there was evidence of a growing feeling that the problems of the low standard of living in the colonies and their inability to increase prosperity (indeed the very opposite in many cases) was not going to be cured merely by more roads, railways, harbours, etc., but by tackling the 'social problems' of bad housing, disease, high infant mortality rates, malnutrition and so forth, more directly. These two views produced a conflict within the committee (and probably within individual committee members) because they were responsible for the expenditure of public money which was supposed to benefit the United Kingdom taxpayers who were providing it, as well as the colonial population. Yet they were aware of growing social problems in the colonies, the severity of which became increasingly clear with the publication of such reports as the *Report on Labour Conditions in the West Indies* (1938), the *Report of the Advisory Council on Nutrition in the Colonial Empire* (1939)[3] and Lord Hailey's influential *An African Survey* (1938). However, even, with such evidence of the appalling living standards in the colonial empire, the committee always had the Treasury looking over its collective shoulder, as well as differing opinions among its members.

It is not surprising, then, that the majority of schemes rejected by the committee because they were 'not of a development nature' were public health and medical schemes. The CDAC gave as many as thirty-three different reasons for rejecting schemes over the course of its operations, but in approximately half the cases the reason amounted to the judgement that the project was not developmental. This affected schemes other than public health, of course, but public health ones were the most vulnerable, and their 'success rate' was less than average – 67.5 per cent compared with 78.0 per cent for all applications.

In 1930 the committee expressed a willingness to devote 10 per cent of the fund to public health schemes each year, and in a circular letter to the colonies the secretary of state wrote:

> It may not . . . be so widely realised that the Committee are also prepared to give liberal assistance towards schemes of public health and research, which are not the less important because they involve a smaller outlay. You may rest assured that the economic import-ance of measures to safeguard the health of all classes of the community is fully appreciated in this country. Grants have been made towards works of drainage and water supply, and the erec-tion of hospital buildings and labourers' dwellings.[4]

Up to 31 March 1931, 25 per cent of the committee's assistance was to public health schemes, and between 1 April 1931 and 31 March 1937, 44 per cent.[5] This high level was drastically reduced in the next year to 5 per cent of total assistance, and in 1933–4 to 7 per cent. By March 1934, £496,981 had been allocated to assist public health in four and a half years, which was slightly above the target set in 1930 of 10 per cent.[6]

Increasingly, however, the committee saw medical and health schemes as 'less developmental' than others submitted, and from 1934 they hardened their attitude towards them. This was made easier when Sir Alan Rae Smith took over from Sir Basil Blackett as chairman in September 1935.[7] Assistance did not dry up completely – aid was given to a tuberculosis hospital and clinic in Jamaica in 1935 and to a tuberculosis sanitarium in Cyprus in 1936, but only because in both cases the Rockefeller Foundation was involved in medical research in the island and the proposed scheme would facilitate this.[8] An application from Trinidad for a tuberculosis sanitarium in 1935 was turned down on the grounds that it was a service which should be provided by the govern-ment of Trinidad in the normal way. There was no element of inter-national research in Trinidad's case.[9] In 1937 an application from Trans-Jordan for assistance in building a hospital at Amman was rejected on the argument that the hospital would engage in purely curative work rather than 'the attacking of causes leading to the spread of disease and the effecting of improvements in the health of the community generally'.[10]

This change of attitude – or more strict interpretation of their policy – was reflected in the proportion of assistance given to public health: 7 per cent in 1933–4, 4 per cent in 1934–5 and 8 per cent in 1935–6. In 1936–7, however, the proportion was 25 per cent and the next year, 31 per cent despite the committee's attitude on 'purely curative' public health schemes, which indicated that health schemes which they did feel able to assist were being submitted in some numbers. In 1938–9 the proportion fell once more, to 10 per cent – the level set by Blackett in 1930.

In the final 16 months of the committee's existence it seemed to revert to the pre-1934 attitude, for no less than 40 per cent of its assistance went to schemes for the advancement of public health.[11] One of these was for a new hospital in Uganda for which the committee gave a free grant of £240,000, a quite unprecedented amount for a single public health scheme. In outlining their grant the committee reaffirmed the opinion – which had been put forward by Lord Passfield in 1929 and the Colonial Development Public Health Committee in 1930 – that

> If the productivity of the East African territories is to be fully developed, and with it, the potential capacity of those territories to absorb manufactured goods from the United Kingdom, it is essential that the standard of life of the native should be raised and to this end the eradication of disease is one of the most important measures.[12]

This was the CDAC's attitude towards colonial development in a nutshell: that virtually any development in the colonies – from railways to public health – would help both Britain and the colony itself. This emphasis on indirect benefits to Britain explains why the committee paid relatively little attention to the proportion of their grants to be spent in the United Kingdom.[13] In this way too the committee reached a compromise on schemes regarded as on the borderline between 'developmental' and 'non-developmental' whereby such schemes could still benefit the United Kingdom and increase the productiveness of the colony. Over the period from 1929 to 1940 the view that 'social development' was important gradually gained ground, and, perhaps as a result of the reports referred to above and Lord Hailey's *Survey*, in the last year of the committee's work possibly gained ascendancy.

COLONIAL ECONOMIC POLICY IN THE 1930S

The impact of the 1929 Colonial Development Act on the British colonial empire in the 1930s was not great. The problems faced by the colonial economies were deep-seated, while the resources of the CDAC were very limited. The amount of money regarded as suitable for developing the empire and reducing unemployment levels in Britain – £1 million per annum – was partly decided upon as a result of an exaggerated concept of the working of the multiplier. J.H. Thomas was under the impression that the money would all be used to pay half of the interest on loans raised elsewhere – an impossibility for most colonies – and would thus result in some £40 million of work being undertaken each year.[14] Leo Amery was of the opinion that money spent abroad would be three times as productive as money spent on public works at home.[15] In reality, a nominal amount of £1 million a year spread over some 45 underdeveloped countries and 55 million people disappeared almost without trace. For the colonial empire as a whole Colonial Development Fund money represented only 7 per cent of the £96 million spent on capital works in the colonies between 1929 and 1938.[16] Faced with the pointlessness of large transport and communications developments after 1931, the CDAC gradually – and for some members, reluctantly – fell back on attempting merely to ameliorate the shockingly low levels of health, housing and social conditions which were just beginning to be recognised.

The 1929 Act also failed because it had to work within a constricted framework of colonial economic policy. The complementary relationship between the colonies and Britain which had been built up by the dynamics of the international economy since the late nineteenth century effectively prevented the colonies from breaking out of the straitjacket of increasing dependence on a narrow group of export cash crops and mineral ores in the 1930s. Indeed, as the economic plight of Britain worsened so the constraints on the colonial economies were tightened. This can be seen in the reluctance of the British government, and many colonial governments, to encourage the diversification of colonies' economies by the establishment of processing and secondary manufacturing industry. There was a sharp contrast between the CDAC's aid to transport and communications in the earlier part of the decade and public health in the later part on the one hand, and their efforts in establishing new or extending existing local industries in the colonies on the other. Between 1929 and 1939 the committee granted assistance to twenty-seven schemes involving the setting up of new or the extension of existing industries, although four of these, including one for a paper pulp factory to cost £930,000 in Kenya, were withdrawn by the local government in the same or succeeding financial year. All but two of the schemes assisted were for processing of some kind, and two were for the promotion of tourism. That only 1.2 per cent of all assistance from the Colonial Development Fund was spent on local industry was hardly a true indication of the potential for the development of such industry in the colonies.

The initiative for colonial economic development lay with the local governments and the Colonial Office and neither, for differing reasons, was very interested in expanding secondary industry. In the case of many local governments, especially in Africa, this was a result of a clash between a 'Native Policy', such as indirect rule in Nigeria and Tanganyika, which sought to preserve indigenous political institutions and rule through them, on the one hand, and the social effects of industrialisation which were seen as undesirable, such as urbanisation, detribalisation, unemployment and so forth, on the other. 'Developing the African along his own lines', the catch-phrase of indirect rule in

Africa, tended to be interpreted solely in political terms, perhaps because it was the course of least resistance. Many of the governors in Africa in the inter-war years who were capable of instituting reform – Clifford, Guggisberg, Byrne, Cameron – concentrated on refining the political structure through which they ruled and resisting the claims of the so-called 'westernised Africans' living in the cities.[17] Often 'political development' as in the establishment of indirect rule became an end in itself: in 1936 for example, the anthropologist Lucy P. Mair published *Native policies in Africa*.[18] Her main purpose was to show that indirect rule was a socially and culturally less disruptive system of government than French assimilationism or Rhodesian segregationalism. It appeared to have no aims, however, beyond the preservation of 'native institutions' as viable units. As G.L.M. Clauson, assistant secretary of state at the Colonial Office, and head of the economic department, wrote in 1939, 'Every Colonial Government is a going concern, but I am not at all sure that most Colonial Governors have any clear conception of where it is going except perhaps in the immediate future'.[19]

Even if local governments did wish to establish new industries and extend existing ones, there were major obstacles. First, there was the fact that many colonies lacked the expertise, especially as in the depression government staff was often reduced. Second, and more importantly, the Colonial Office and the British government were opposed to the establishment of manufacturing industry in the colonial empire. The major export commodities from British colonies were foodstuffs, raw materials and minerals, and nearly all the foodstuffs were in their unprocessed state. The prices of these commodities tended to fluctuate severely throughout the inter-war period, generally in a downward direction. In many colonies the export base was narrower at the end of the 1930s than it was before the First World War.

The traditional attitude of the British government was that the metropolitan and the colonial economies were complementary not competitive. At the Imperial Economic Conference of 1926 Leo Amery, secretary of state for the colonies, said

> one of the most striking features of modern industrial development is the marriage of tropical production to the industrial production of the temperate zone. They are essentially complementary regions, and owing to their character and the character of their inhabitants they are likely to remain so.[20]

In the House of Commons in 1929 Amery referred again to the complementary nature of colonial trade and pointed out that

> the Colonies are essentially agricultural and producers of primary commodities. It is not very probable, or indeed, very desirable in

the interests of the populations themselves, that industrial development should be unduly accelerated in their case.[21]

The situation changed, however, with the abandonment of free trade in 1931 and the conclusion of the Ottawa Agreements in 1932. These developments raised a number of issues which had not been foreseen at the time. First, there was the problem of colonial countries replacing the Japanese as producers of cheap goods. This was most important with regard to rubber and canvas footwear manufactured in Hong Kong and, to a lesser extent, Singapore, and imported into Britain under a preferential duty. On two occasions in the 1930s the Canadian and British footwear producers attempted to come to an agreement with Hong Kong over quotas, but were unable to agree among themselves sufficiently to present a united front.

Since the Canadian and British producers could not agree, the Far Eastern manufacturers were able to continue, but the conflict served as a warning to British business that there were great dangers in imperial preference, as well as benefits, if the colonies became industrialised. This was recognised too by the British government. Neville Chamberlain, Chancellor of the Exchequer in 1934, stated that

> While it was improbable that West Africa would set up factories to compete with those at home, there was a real and serious danger of such factories being established in Malaya and possibly other parts of the Colonial Empire, and we might well be faced with very serious developments of a problem of industrial competition of which we had already had some experience in the case of India.[22]

The response to this was to set up an inter-departmental committee in 1934 to consider industrial development in the colonies. The committee recommended that in the first place colonial industries should not be 'artificially' encouraged, and second, that where local workshops and factories already existed the government should seek to impose restrictions on conditions and working hours to bring them more into line with those of the United Kingdom – the constant complaint of the British manufacturer being that colonial producers benefited from low costs through 'sweated labour'.[23]

The report was considered by Cabinet in February 1936 but was sent back for reconsideration with little discussion. Chamberlain thought that there should be a different policy for each of the three types of colony – the eastern ones which were already industrialised such as Hong Kong, relatively prosperous colonies like Jamaica and lastly the African and other colonies where little industry existed.[24] Meanwhile a third problem of protectionism had arisen, that of colonies creating a differential between excise duty and import duty so as to favour locally produced import substitutes, particularly in beer, matches, soap, edible oils and fats and cement. Among the most persistent complainants to the Colonial Office were Ind Coope and Allsopp Ltd, two brewers, and Unilever. Clement Davies, managing director of Unilever, for example, wrote personally to Malcolm MacDonald, secretary of state for the colonies, in July 1935,

> It does seem extraordinary that these colonies, without improving the lot of their own people . . . should in effect stop imports from this country, especially imports of goods manufactured by a company which purchases from those colonies raw materials which are grown in those colonies and upon which the colonies exist.[25]

These complaints, in addition to the Hong Kong dispute and the passing of legislation such as Malta's Encouragement of New Industries Act and Jamaica's Safeguarding of Local Industries Law – which enabled the local governments to grant monopolies for the production of scheduled commodities – led to a new inter-departmental committee being set up in 1937. This was 'to consider and report how far it is desirable to frame and pursue a policy either to encourage or to discourage the establishment of industrial enterprises in the Colonial Empire', as the question was 'constantly turning up in one form or another'.[26]

The problem proved so difficult, however, that even by December 1938 only the second draft of the committee's report had been written. The committee came to the broad conclusion that industries in the colonies which could only exist with government assistance, usually in the form of an excise duty-import duty differential, 'Will place a permanent burden on the local community and are more likely to impoverish that community than enrich it.'[27] Therefore where the Colonial Office had the power – and effectively it did not in colonies such as Malaya, Malta, Ceylon and Jamaica – local governments should not be allowed to assist local industries by means of licencing or tariff policy. This was as far as the committee reached by the end of 1938 and its report was considered far too revealing and contentious to circulate to the colonies, and it was put aside. Sir John Campbell remarked of the report, 'It is altogether too dangerous, too full of explosive possibilities, too little susceptible of reduction to clear formulae, for a report which will presumably be circulated generally and will doubtless be published eventually, or leak out eventually.'[28]

The policy reached by the committee, however, was essentially the same as that exercised by the Colonial Office in a piecemeal fashion in dealing with individual cases. In nearly every case of a new industry being established some form of protection was regarded by the promoter and/or the local government as necessary, and if the colony was one over which the Colonial Office had sufficient influence, the granting of protection was refused.

The belief that industries established behind tariff protection were uneconomic in the long run, that infant industries never grow up and that the colonies should remain primary producers, was widely held in the Colonial Office. J.A. Calder, assistant secretary at the Colonial Office argued in June 1939 that the order of priority for colonial development should be firstly agriculture for food and export, secondly – 'and a long way behind' – the development of mineral resources, and lastly secondary industry:

> an important matter in itself but one for which there can be, comparatively speaking, little scope until the standards of living of the agricultural primary producers have been raised to much higher levels than exist at present in the Colonial Empire. The manufacturing industry, which can be established in a colony only at the price of a monopoly protected by a high tariff, ends in producing a locally manufactured article which is too expensive for the primary agricultural producers to buy.[29]

The Colonial Office advocated strict free trade for the colonies at a time when all other countries, including Britain, had abandoned the principle.

At the same time there was a strong element of protecting the United Kingdom manufacturer and exporter involved in the Colonial Office's policy towards colonial industrial development. In 1936 J. Melville, an assistant principal, wrote, in connection with a scheme for sugar refining in Palestine, that the Colonial Office policy towards industrialisation in the colonies 'is to oppose the establishment in the Colonial Empire of a new industry which is likely to affect adversely the interests of established United Kingdom industries'.[30] Sir Henry Moore, assistant secretary, noted that the recommendations of the 1937 inter-departmental committee on colonial industry went as far as they could for, 'No doubt a more forward policy would alarm the home manufacturers';[31] and in 1939 he wrote:

> at present any proposals for the creation of secondary industry in the Colonial Empire are received with a marked lack of enthusiasm, if not with suspicion. The reason for this, I suggest, appears to me to be found in the more or less unwritten rule that any proposals, whether in the field of industry or tariffs, which give rise to any conflict of economic interest, should be approached from the standpoint that United Kingdom trade interests must rank first, Dominion trade interests second, and those of the Colonial Empire last.[32]

Sir Henry Moore, unlike the other administrative officials in the

Colonial Office had been a colonial governor (of Sierra Leone); most of his colleagues had never visited the colonies they dealt with. The Colonial Office was always anxious to avoid giving the impression that they were holding a brief for the United Kingdom manufacturer, but the Board of Trade and the Treasury were quite clear whose interests came first. It is doubtful whether the Cabinet would have allowed a secretary of state for the colonies to promote industrial development behind tariff walls even if he had wanted to do so; the most Sir Phillip Cunliffe-Lister, for example, when he was colonial secretary in 1934 had asked for was that Cabinet would 'approve the principle that we should endeavour to get all the advantages we possibly could for the Colonial Empire [in tariff negotiations] provided this involved no prejudice or damage to the United Kingdom'.[33] In the 1920s the Colonial Office was petitioned by cotton and engineering manufacturers, not to mention the Board of Trade, for transport development to open up East Africa; in the 1930s footwear, margarine and beer manufacturers wrote angry letters demanding protection from 'unfair' competition.

The failure of the 1929 Colonial Development Act and the lack of any real power of the CDAC suggests that it was the colonial and imperial governments rather than the committee itself which were responsible for the failure to promote economic development in the 1930s. The local governments, on whom the responsibility for initiating schemes rested, tended to be limited in outlook, both through natural conservatism and the belief in a form of political rule which implied an unchanging social and economic structure. Local governments were, however, very much influenced by the Colonial Office which regarded the establishment of secondary industry in the colonies as undesirable for social and economic reasons, and by the British government who saw in colonial industrialisation the spectre of 'unfair competition', and indeed in the case of Hong Kong felt that this had already arrived. Although Britain abandoned free trade in 1931 and most industrialised countries had done so already, the colonies were expected to give a tariff preference to British manufactures and to refrain from encouraging local manufacturing enterprise.

Reviewing the measures taken to promote colonial development in the 1920s and 1930s it seems clear that the provision of British colonial aid in the inter-war period was closely linked to problems at home and tended at best to take the form of piecemeal treatment of symptoms rather than causes, and at worst hurried reaction to crises. The Colonial Office had no clear strategy for the long-term economic crises and no clear strategy for the long-term economic development of the colonial empire, and for most colonies could see no alternative to a total reliance on primary produce for export. As the governor of Nigeria wrote in 1939 to the secretary of state,

Table 8.3 Public debt, selected colonies, 1928 to 1938 (£m)

Colony	1928	1929	1930	1931	1932	1933	1934	1935	1936	1937	1938
Kenya	13.5	13.5	16.9	16.9	16.9	17.2	17.2	17.2	17.6	17.6	17.6
Uganda	1.1	1.1	1.1	1.1	2.0	2.2	2.2	2.2	2.2	2.2	2.2
Tanganyika	5.2	5.2	5.2	8.2	8.2	8.2	8.2	8.2	8.2	8.2	8.2
Nyasaland	0.8	0.8	0.9	1.1	3.2	3.3	5.0	5.1	5.2	5.3	5.4
Gold Goast	11.8	11.8	13.0	13.0	13.0	13.0	11.9	11.4	11.4	11.4	11.4
Nigeria	23.6	23.6	28.4	28.4	27.8	27.8	28.0	28.0	24.8	24.8	24.8
Ceylon	12.9	12.9	15.9	15.9	16.0	16.0	14.9	14.0	12.5	14.6	12.2
Mauritius	1.9	1.9	2.8	2.8	3.4	3.4	3.3	2.9.	2.9	2.9	3.1
West Indies	10.3	10.3	10.2	10.4	10.4	11.0	9.1	8.4	9.7	10.3	10.3
British Guiana	2.6	2.6	4.7	4.6	4.7	4.7	4.5	4.6	4.9	4.5	4.5
Total	83.7	86.1	99.1	102.4	105.6	106.8	104.3	102.0	99.4	101.8	99.7

Source: *Statistical Abstract of the British Empire*, Nos. 57, 58, 65 & 67; Colonial *Annual Reports*.

the plain fact is that no British Government has yet laid down a clear cut policy in this important matter of colonial development. . . . All that the Government of 1929 did was to recognise the propriety of granting casual assistance, strictly limited in amount, towards development. . . . The 'doctrine of individual self-sufficiency' has never been abandoned.[34]

Some degree of aid was channelled through the CDAC, but responsibility for initiating schemes rested with the local governments whose low level of applications for funds led to the Colonial Development Fund being underspent in most years. And yet when, in 1938 and 1939, the reorganisation of the CDAC was under discussion and it was suggested that the new development committee should be able to initiate schemes, this was firmly rejected on the grounds that such powers would undermine the authority of the secretary of state.[35]

THE IMPACT OF THE GREAT DEPRESSION

The various official loans, culminating in those under the Colonial Development Act, made to the tropical colonies as part of Britain's anti-unemployment policies were only a small part of public investment in the colonies in the 1920s and 1930s. Public debt in the nine colonies shown in Table 8.3 increased by over £70 million between 1919 and 1930 and peaked at about £125 million in the mid-1930s. Very little of this debt was locally subscribed after the British capital market reopened at the end of the First World War. Thus the colonies' public debt was also largely their public foreign debt and had to be serviced as to interest and repayments from export earnings. Indeed, the high prices paid for export commodities in the early 1920s convinced colonial governments that they should borrow heavily through the London money market in order to press on with the transport and communications projects regarded as vital to expand export volumes and hence overall export revenue. Implicitly they held the view that export growth and economic growth were positively correlated. The war showed up the inadequacies of colonial infrastructure; the post-war boom appeared to provide the means to finance more rapid economic development from the public purse. Most of these loans contracted in the 1920s were for railways, roads and harbours; typically they were spread over twenty-five to thirty-five years and carried a rate of interest of between 4 and 6 per cent. The projects on which these borrowed funds were expended were generally ones which took a considerable time to complete and where the economic returns were not usually dramatic. Their potential contribution to export earnings was through reduction of transport costs and easing of handling bottlenecks, but this would only augment export earnings if export prices remained reasonably high. In the 1930s export prices collapsed and, as a result, a substantial gap opened up between total public debt and gross export values. Since debts were not permitted to be written off or modified as to servicing, a serious foreign debt burden developed in many tropical colonies by the later 1930s.

The impact of the world depression on colonial indebtedness varied. Least troubled was Malaya where good export earnings from rubber and tin had enabled the public debt/export ratio to be kept relatively low and where the government-owned railways were profitable even in the early 1930s. Table 8.4 shows the debt burden for a number of tropical colonies in the mid-1930s. The burden was greatest on the more recent additions to the British Empire – East, Central and West Africa. In these colonies public debt charges absorbed over one-quarter of public expenditure in most cases. The colonies in Asia were less affected by debt servicing problems because they had been borrowing for longer and had not expanded their public debt so readily as the African ones in the post-war boom.

The debt crisis in Britain's tropical colonies in the 1930s should be kept in perspective. These funds were lent for a long period which permitted sinking fund payments to be low (generally 1 to 1.25 per cent), and the average rate of interest, although about one-third higher than before the First World War, was less than 5 per cent.[36] A few colonies were able to take advantage of the lower rates of interest prevailing by the mid-1930s to refinance earlier loans. Others received grants from the Colonial Development Fund (CDF) to pay interest for a number of years. Prior to 1936, for example, a CDF grant of £500,000 paid most of Nyasaland's interest costs, though when it expired the

Table 8.4 Public debt burden, selected colonies, 1936

Colony	Year	Public debt (£000)	Public debt charges (£000)	Public debt charges as a % of public debt	Public debt charges as a % of gross government expenditure	Public debt charges as a % of exports of domestic produce
Kenya	1936	17581	1043	5.9	31.8	29.1
Uganda	1936	2236	135	6.0	8.4	3.1
Tanganyika	1936	8191	436	5.3	24.5	10.9
N. Rhodesia	1936	2347	120	5.1	16.3	2.1
Nyasaland	1937	5264	278	5.3	42.1	31.4
Gold Coast	1936–7	11435	660	5.8	23.5	7.2[a]
Nigeria	1935–6	27965	1609	5.8	28.0	14.4[b]
Ceylon	1935–6	14082	632	4.5	7.8	3.5[a]
Mauritius	1936–7	2879	174	6.0	16.5	6.5[c]
Malaya	1936	7617	758	9.8	12.5	15.8
Jamaica	1936–7	3974	233	5.9	11.9	4.9[c]
Trinidad	1936	4223	240	5.7	12.9	4.8
Brit. Guiana	1936	4857	242	5.0	23.3	10.8

[a] 1936; [b] 1935; [c] 1937.

Source: *Economic Survey of the Colonial Empire*; *Statistical Abstract of the British Empire*, Nos. 66,67,68.

Nyasaland government had to devote over 40 per cent of its annual expenditure to servicing its public debt (see Table 8.4). Nevertheless, the colonial debt problem in the 1930s highlighted the development strategy of the previous decades and brought into question the appropriateness of financing large-scale transport and communication projects by long-term loans which could become a serious burden to the borrowing colonies. Since the immediate motivation of the British government for encouraging colonial governments to borrow development capital was to stimulate orders for British industry, it was sometimes suggested in the later 1930s that outright grants, especially for the least developed African colonies, would be a more effective policy.

At the same time as debt servicing became a more significant item in colonial public expenditure, the slump in export earnings also resulted in considerable reductions in total government outlays. With the exception of Northern Rhodesia, where an economic boom occurred in the second half of the 1930s based on the expansion of copper mining, colonial treasuries were reduced by up to 50 per cent at the depth of the depression. Most colonies relied heavily on customs revenue and it was inevitable that in the trade slump this would fall severely. Other sources of revenue, such as direct taxation, could not easily be developed and by the late 1930s customs revenue still accounted for about 45 per cent of total government revenue. Expenditure also declined, though at first not by so great a proportion as revenue as budget deficits continued to be run in nearly all colonies until 1933. Table 8.5 illustrates the change brought about by the depression: from the budget deficits of the late 1920s and early 1930s, financed by external borrowing, to the budget surpluses which were regarded as necessary in the second half of the 1930s to continue to finance the colonial debts. At the lowest point, public expenditure fell in most of the colonies shown in Table 8.5 by between 5 per cent (Jamaica) and 50 per cent (Federated Malay States) compared with the average for 1929.

The impact of the depression can be further illustrated by examination of the main items of colonial government expenditure shown in Table 8.6. Debt servicing, pensions paid to retired British officials and expenditure on law and order could account together for as much as 40 per cent of government expenditure in some colonies, and administration costs absorbed at least a further one-third, much of it in salaries of British colonial officials. This left relatively small amounts for social services and even less for economic development.

The mini-boom in world trade which occurred in 1937 lifted colonial government revenues. Public expenditure was generally above the pre-depression levels by 1938, except in the eastern colonies of Ceylon, Malaya and Mauritius. Some of the impact of reduced government outlays was offset by falls in the general price level (Britain's retail prices fell by 15 per cent between 1927–9 and 1933). Nevertheless the world trade collapse and financial crisis resulted in significant falls in real living standards for most of the 1930s in the tropical colonies, some of the social and political consequences of which were evident by the late 1930s and are discussed in Chapter 9. By the mid-1930s colonial government services were reduced in terms of staff and expenditure to a point not experienced since the end of the First World War.[37]

The Great Depression was transmitted to tropical primary producing and exporting countries by the collapse of prices paid for their exports. Britain's tropical colonies – like most indebted primary exporters – responded to falling prices by raising the volume of produce exported. Although in the short run this reaction could cushion the fall in export earnings, it added to the world economy's over-supply of foodstuffs and raw materials and eventually led to further price reductions. The pattern of price collapse varied between the main export commodities but generally the years of steepest descent were 1929 to 1934. Some price recovery occurred in the mid-1930s, usually peaking in 1937, but prices declined thereafter and were sluggish in 1938 and 1939. The capacity to increase output also varied: some export crops were newly established in the immediate pre-war or post-war period and production was expanding at the onset of the depression (e.g. cotton, sisal, and coffee); in other

Table 8.5 Balance of public revenue and expenditure, selected colonies, 1929–38 (£000)

Colony	1929	1930	1931	1932	1933	1934	1935	1936	1937	1938
Kenya	−171	−197	−149	−109	−46	+5	+56	+165	+80	+127
Uganda	+76	−228	−52	+66	+74	+166	+127	+89	+219	−156
Tanganyika	−92	−354	−299	+36	−86	−151	+224	+176	+171	−133
North Rhodesia	+117	+125	+36	−177	+10	−20	+27	−24	+73	+176
Nyasaland	−21	+14	−20	+25	+13	−11	+26	+44	+27	+32
Gold Coast	−464	−222	−540	−2	+372	+82	+41	−27	+175	+291
Nigeria	−245	−708	−1330	+1	−149	+124	+239	+1716	+1592	−655
Ceylon[a]	−1356	+49	+126	−902	+1005	+800	−621	−523	+780	−149
Mauritius[b]	−271	−82	−341	−416	+1229	+145	+173	+49	+31	+406
Malaya[c]	−334	−1973	−1145	−1158	−357	+1367	+1312	+1795	+1134	−128
Jamaica	−17	−125	−50	+87	−149	+4	−57	+6	+205	+74
Trinidad	+257	+57	−451	−4	+4	+4	+2	+706	+393	+253
British Guiana	+126	−80	−159	−16	+19	+66	−39	+10	−30	−10

[a] Year ended 30 September; [b] Year ended 30 June; [c] Federated Malay States. Excess of ordinary revenue over ordinary recurrent expenditure shown +.
Source: Statistical Abstract for the British Empire, Nos. 68, 69.

Table 8.6 Analysis of recurrent public expenditure, selected colonies, 1934.

Colony	Object of expenditure (% of total)					
	Public debt charges	Pensions	Law & order[a]	Social services[b]	Economic services[c]	Administration[d]
Kenya	9.2	8.6	4.4	21.9	20.7	35.2
Uganda	8.3	6.2	4.0	25.5	16.8	39.2
Tanganyika	6.2	3.9	4.9	16.9	10.8	57.3
N. Rhodesia	12.8	10.2	3.5	20.8	10.2	42.5
Nyasaland	15.2	8.6	4.7	16.8	14.5	40.2
Nigeria	16.8	9.9	6.8	16.6	16.4	33.5
Gold Coast	4.3	10.4	3.9	25.8	11.6	44.0
Sierra Leone	7.6	9.6	6.6	19.9	7.2	49.1
Ceylon	13.4	11.4	2.4	32.2	12.4	28.2
Fed. Malay States	15.4	16.0	2.7	18.4	11.6	35.9
Straits Settlements	0.1	7.6	13.4	28.5	13.7	36.7
Hong Kong	4.8	6.9	17.0	25.5	8.7	37.1
Barbados	3.9	7.9	1.0	32.3	8.4	46.5
Br. Guiana	26.6	9.9	0.5	28.8	1.3	32.9
Br. Honduras	23.1	6.9	0.5	19.8	5.8	43.9
Jamaica	5.1	4.8	0.9	32.5	4.9	51.8
Trinidad	10.7	7.8	0.3	37.8	14.3	29.1
Antigua	4.8	9.9	0.5	45.6	9.7	29.5
St Kitts	3.7	9.7	0.7	47.2	8.7	30.4
Fiji	13.6	5.7	0.7	27.7	12.7	39.6

[a] Defence, police, prisons, judiciary; [b] medical, public health, education, labour, food subsidies, housing; [c] agriculture, veterinary, forestry, transport and communications, public works, mines, water supply and irrigation, electricity; [d] includes self-balancing departments and miscellaneous.
Source: An Economic Survey of the Colonial Empire, 1933 (Col. No. 109, 1935).

cases, the industry was a long-established one which was operating at near to full capacity by the late 1920s (e.g. sugar, tea, palm oil and copra).

Export earnings, shown in Table 8.7, plummeted from over £207 million (for the tropical colonial empire as a whole) in 1929 to £155 million in 1930, £104 million in 1931 and to a low point of £93 million in 1932. Recovery to a pre-1929 level of export earnings took until 1937 to achieve and was followed by a further fall in 1938. The impact of the depression on the direction of exports from the colonial empire was fairly slight: the average proportion consigned to the UK in 1927–9 was 25 per cent, in 1937–9 it was 29.6 per cent. This shift was presumably the result of tariff preferences given in the British market to empire produce after the Ottawa Conference in 1932, together with the break-down of the international monetary system and emergence of the Sterling Area of which the colonial empire was part. However, the level of tariff preference for most tropical products was small and in some cases (e.g. cocoa) the UK market could not absorb all of the colonial empire's exports and in such instances the effect of the preference was negligible.

An important consequence of the drive to expand exports in the tropical colonies from the late nineteenth century was the rising volume of imports. By 1929 the tropical colonial economies were far more dependent upon imported goods (about one quarter of which came from Britain) than at the beginning of the century. Total imports were valued at over £200 million a year from 1925 to 1929. As can be seen from Table 8.7, with the decline of export earnings after 1929, most colonies experienced balance of trade deficits until imports could be curtailed and export earnings increased to produce export surpluses again from 1933. For the rest of the decade colonies required large export surpluses in order to service their foreign debt to Britain and imports continued to be low compared with the mid-1920s.[38] To the extent that colonial imports consisted of mass consumer goods, which predominately they did, constriction of imports resulted in a decline in living standards. Imported capital goods were also limited, which made it more difficult in the later 1930s to develop new areas of economic growth (in particular import-substituting industry) which required such imports to set up or expand. Thus the burden of external debt which forced colonies to try to earn large export surpluses in a world economy which was virtually static was felt not only through its depressive effects on material living standards, but also by the constraints it imposed on structural diversification.

The price collapse in the international economy in the early 1930s affected primary products to a greater degree than manufactured and capital goods. As the tropical colonies were entirely reliant on primary

179

Table 8.7 Imports, exports and balance of trade, selected colonies, 1929–39 (£000)

Colonies	1929	1930	1931	1932	1933	1934	1935	1936	1937	1938	1939
Imports											
West Africa	25106	22987	12184	14057	12688	10857	16790	21240	29928	17933	15658
East Africa	15610	13380	9235	7610	7576	8633	10427	11292	14879	13221	12532
Central Africa	4398	5717	6138	2669	2602	3445	3589	3009	4798	6001	5406
Eastern	137562	109102	72295	61222	56870	72786	74209	77646	100876	84551	93563
Caribbean	18248	16143	12901	12422	12280	13287	13599	15400	19064	18898	19189
Pacific	1454	1219	926	855	929	887	1121	1347	1576	1504	1464
Total	202378	168548	113679	98835	92945	109895	119735	129934	170034	142108	147812
Exports											
West Africa	31653	26034	16535	17123	15868	15274	19756	26553	34734	18403	19251
East Africa	14471	11101	8334	8625	10135	10143	12319	14966	16602	13958	14120
Central Africa	1522	1550	1686	3313	4245	5167	5524	6821	12895	11092	11044
Eastern	141728	101945	65135	52967	59996	84030	86563	94712	131352	89255	112130
Caribbean	15824	13381	10983	11056	9820	11038	11705	13657	15877	16057	16005
Pacific	1708	1452	997	1662	1438	1270	1549	1757	1822	1645	1620
Total	206906	155463	103670	94746	101502	126922	137416	158466	213282	150410	174170
Balance											
West Africa	6547	3047	4351	3066	3180	4417	2966	5313	5406	470	3793
East Africa	−1139	−2279	−901	1015	2559	1510	1892	3674	1723	737	1588
Central Africa	−2876	−4167	−4452	644	1643	1722	1935	3812	8097	5091	5638
Eastern	4166	−7157	−7160	−8255	3126	11244	12354	17066	30476	4704	18567
Caribbean	−2424	−2762	−1918	−1366	−2460	−2249	−1894	−1743	−3187	−2841	−3184
Pacific	254	233	71	807	509	383	428	410	246	141	156
Total	4528	−13085	−10009	−4089	8557	17027	17681	28532	42761	8302	26358

Total imports and exports of merchandise (including re-exports), excluding bullion and coin.
West Africa: Gambia, Gold Coast, Nigeria, Sierra Leone;
East Africa: Kenya–Uganda, Tanganyika, Zanzibar;
Central Africa: North Rhodesia, Nyasaland;
Eastern: Ceylon, Malaya, Mauritius;
Caribbean: Barbados, British Guiana, British Honduras, Jamaica, Trinidad;
Pacific: Fiji
Source: As for Table 8.5.

produce exports and generally their imports consisted largely of second-ary goods (but not wholly, for some colonies imported large quantities of basic foodstuffs, especially rice), a deterioration in their terms of trade was unavoidable. Table 8.8 presents an estimate of the terms of trade of eight colonies which between them accounted for about 90 per cent of the trade of the tropical colonial empire. The experience of each colony was different and since the import mix was diverse while the range of exports quite small (and statistics relating to the former were less com-prehensive than those for exports), these 'terms of trade' calculations must be regarded only as an indication of the relative price move-ments.[39] Generally the price fall for primary products preceded that of manufactures so that terms of trade moved swiftly down in 1930 to 1933 in most cases. Once primary prices levelled out an improvement in the terms of trade was experienced as cheaper imports began to arrive. Import prices also levelled out in the mid-1930s and as export prices rose in the brief boom of 1936–7, the terms of trade continued to rise; this improvement was ended in 1938, while in 1939 some export prices were stimulated by the onset of the war in Europe.

Import volumes also declined in the depression, particularly of manu-factured goods such as cotton textiles, but also of basic foodstuffs. There was a tendency for cheaper, lower quality imports to be substituted for the more expensive, higher quality ones: dried and salted food replaced canned food, rubber and canvas footwear replaced leather footwear, rice replaced flour and so on. Colonies which normally imported large quantities of basic foodstuffs found their import bill declined dramati-cally as both prices and volumes fell: this largely explains the less adverse terms of trade movements in the cases of Mauritius, Ceylon and the West Indies. Malaya experienced very volatile export prices as rubber and, (to a lesser extent), tin prices crashed in the early 1930s before recovering under the influence of government price-support schemes.[40] Malaya benefited too from cheaper rice imports from 1931 on. The tropical African colonies were probably the most adversely affected in international trade by the 1930s depression. Coffee, cotton, cocoa, sisal, palm oil and palm kernels and groundnuts generally fell in price by over 50 per cent in the first half of the decade and were not 'strategic' to the rearmament programmes to enjoy rising demand in the late 1930s. Some of these export crops were ones which had expanded rapidly in the 1920s and in which indigenous and expatriate capital and enterprise had been heavily invested. Their anticipated expansion also under-pinned much of the public expenditure on railways, roads and harbours after the First World War. In contrast to the Eastern and West Indian colonies, the tropical African ones imported a relatively high proportion of manufactures and did not benefit to the same extent therefore from cheaper basic foodstuffs. Attempts by Britain to exclude Japanese com-

Table 8.8 Terms of trade, selected colonies, 1929–39 (1927–9 = 100)

Colony		1929	1930	1931	1932	1933	1934	1935	1936	1937	1938	1939
Gold Coast	E	84.9	77.0	48.4	53.0	44.8	37.7	42.6	51.9	87.0	42.0	42.3
	I	96.2	87.6	79.0	76.2	72.8	70.9	73.5	69.8	79.6	78.9	81.0
	T	88	88	61	70	62	53	58	74	109	53	52
Nigeria	E	95.0	78.8	48.0	50.0	47.9	43.2	52.7	59.4	69.5	43.6	43.0
	I	105.2	94.2	80.7	76.2	73.8	67.8	71.3	71.6	80.0	80.3	78.6
	T	90	84	60	66	65	64	74	83	87	54	55
Kenya-Uganda	E	104.0	78.3	57.9	57.2	55.8	57.5	58.9	58.9	70.2	51.6	50.9
	I	99.4	94.4	76.1	72.8	67.8	67.5	69.4	67.7	81.3	82.8	81.3
	T	105	83	76	79	82	86	85	87	86	62	63
Mauritius	E	87.2	65.4	60.3	65.4	66.7	64.1	56.4	55.1	55.1	55.1	61.5
	I	95.4	83.6	62.1	59.9	52.2	52.8	54.0	54.9	57.2	61.6	58.7
	T	91	78	97	109	128	121	104	100	96	89	105
Ceylon	E	86.3	71.3	50.8	42.8	48.7	60.4	66.4	72.8	81.5	69.4	81.1
	I	97.4	80.5	65.8	59.8	55.3	57.7	58.9	55.6	55.8	57.8	56.6
	T	91	78	97	109	128	121	104	100	96	89	105
Malaya	E	45.9	58.0	35.6	32.2	43.1	63.4	84.0	74.8	91.4	66.9	85.4
	I	96.6	92.6	76.4	72.2	61.8	58.0	60.7	60.8	60.9	60.5	58.4
	T	48	63	47	45	70	109	138	123	150	111	146
Jamaica	E	101.0	80.6	68.7	72.4	73.9	80.3	81.6	79.6	82.9	91.3	98.2
	I	99.0	92.4	79.2	75.7	67.2	64.6	67.5	67.2	73.1	72.7	70.1
	T	102	97	87	96	110	124	121	118	113	126	140
Trinidad	E	84.3	79.6	55.8	58.4	55.8	61.5	53.7	61.8	72.3	57.2	65.4
	I	98.3	94.3	77.1	74.5	67.0	63.8	65.4	66.5	75.8	73.0	73.1
	T	86	85	72	78	83	96	82	93	95	78	90

E, weighted index of the unit value of principal exports;
I, weighted index of the unit value of principal imports;
T, terms of trade: E divided by I x 100.
Source: Statistical Abstract for the British Empire, 1925–39.

petition in manufactures from these colonies also had the effect of keeping manufactures import prices higher than elsewhere.[41] The African colonies revealed most acutely the problems which arose from the international division of labour at a time of widespread trade contraction.

The depression also highlighted the narrow range of exports of the tropical colonies. In many cases the range was narrower by the end of the 1930s than in the pre-war or 1920s periods, as shown in Table 8.9: this was true of Kenya–Uganda, Tanganyika, Northern Rhodesia, Nyasaland, the Gold Coast, Ceylon, Malaya, Mauritius, Barbados, Jamaica, British Guiana and British Honduras. Despite the development of new cash crops and mineral exports, the export base remained narrow: the first three export commodities by value accounted for over 70 per cent of total export earnings in all the colonies included in Table 8.9 (except Nigeria) and as much as 98 per cent in several instances. This represented a degree of vulnerability to the vagaries of the international economy which had become a structural feature of tropical colonial economies by the Second World War and was one which would prove difficult to alter substantially.

By the end of the 1930s, then, a severe economic crisis had developed in Britain's tropical colonies. Some attempt had been made to follow the philosophy of the Joseph Chamberlain model of developing the 'Great Estate' but it was predicated on a continuing expansion of the world economy and of Britain's place within it. When the international economy faltered in the mid-1920s and collapsed altogether in the Great Depression in the 1930s it left the very open colonial economies to varying degrees depressed, debt-ridden and disillusioned. The Great Depression weakened Britain's relationship with its tropical colonies and created a growing recognition of a specific 'colonial problem' and of a need for colonial reform. It is to these aspects that we turn now.

Table 8.9 The three principal exports of selected colonies as a percentage of all exports of domestic produce, 1899–1901, 1909–11, 1921–3 and 1934–8

Colony	1899–1901[a]		1909–11		1921–3		1934–8	
Gold Coast	Rubber	39.6	Cocoa	37.9	Cocoa	77.5	Cocoa	55.8
	Palm oil	28.0	Gold	33.2	Gold	11.6	Gold	29.9
	Palm kernels	11.8	Rubber	9.8	Kola	4.9	Manganese	6.4
	Total	79.4	Total	80.9	Total	77.5	Total	92.1
Nigeria[b]	Palm kernels	51.7	Palm kernels	49.2	Palm kernels	33.9	Palm kernels	21.9
	Palm oil	23.8	Palm oil	35.2	Palm oil	26.5	Groundnuts	19.4
	Rubber	9.4	Rubber	4.3	Tin ore	10.9	Cocoa	16.1
	Total	84.9	Total	88.7	Total	71.3	Total	57.4
Sierra Leone	Palm kernels	55.8	Palm kernels	65.3	Palm kernels	68.6	Diamonds	36.9
	Kola	21.5	Kola	19.8	Kola	20.2	Palm kernels	35.6
	Rubber	8.9	Palm oil	7.2	Palm oil	5.0	Iron ore	20.3
	Total	86.2	Total	92.3	Total	93.8	Total	92.8
Kenya-Uganda[c]	Ivory	59.8	Cotton	33.2	Cotton	41.6	Cotton	47.1
	Rubber	11.8	Hides	17.3	Coffee	11.6	Coffee	15.1
	Hides	7.6	Ivory	8.9	Sisal	5.8	Sisal	7.0
	Total	78.6	Total	59.4	Total	59.0	Total	69.2
Tanganyika	n.a.		n.a.		Hemp	22.1	Sisal	43.2
	n.a.		n.a.		Groundnuts	14.7	Cotton	14.8
	n.a.		n.a.		Coffee	14.2	Coffee	12.6
	n.a.		n.a.		Total	51.0	Total	70.6
Nyasaland	Coffee	76.9	Cotton	29.0	Tobacco	71.9	Tobacco	47.8
	Rubber	17.5	Tobacco	21.6	Cotton	18.6	Tea	34.4
	Ivory	2.9	Coffee	11.1	Tea	5.2	Cotton	15.6
	Total	97.3	Total	61.7	Total	96.2	Total	97.8
N. Rhodesia[d]	n.a.		Copper	43.6	Lead	57.8	Copper	87.3
	n.a.		Cattle	23.3	Cattle	13.3	Zinc	3.9
	n.a.		Maize	5.1	Tobacco	9.2	Cobalt	3.4
	n.a.		Total	72.0	Total	80.3	Total	94.6

Table 8.9 (continued)

Colony	1899–1901[a]		1909–11		1921–3		1934–8	
Mauritius	Sugar	92.1	Sugar	96.1	Sugar	99.1	Sugar	97.6
	Aloe fibre	2.2	Aloe fibre	0.2	Aloe fibre	0.2	Aloe fibre	0.5
	Molasses	1.0	n.a.	n.a.	n.a.	n.a.	Rum	0.1
	Total	95.3	Total	97.7	Total	99.3	Total	98.2
Ceylon	Tea	54.6	Tea	51.6	Tea	50.8	Tea	61.6
	Plumbago	14.8	Rubber	11.6	Rubber	20.9	Rubber	20.5
	Copra	4.2	Coconut oil	9.2	Coconut oil	8.6	Coconut oil	5.3
	Total	73.6	Total	72.4	Total	80.3	Total	86.9
Malaya[e]	n.a.	n.a.	Tin	62.3	Rubber	56.0	Rubber	48.1
	n.a.	n.a.	Rubber	31.8	Tin	45.4	Tin	28.1
	n.a.	n.a.	Copra	1.1	Copra	5.4	Copra	3.6
	n.a.	n.a.	Total	95.2	Total	96.8	Total	79.8
Fiji	n.a.	n.a.	Sugar	64.5	Sugar	75.2	Sugar	73.9
	n.a.	n.a.	Copra	23.6	Copra	18.8	Copra	16.4
	n.a.	n.a.	Bananas	9.2	Bananas	3.7	Bananas	4.3
	n.a.	n.a.	Total	97.3	Total	97.7	Total	94.6
Barbardos	Sugar	59.6	Molasses	48.9	Sugar	58.5	Sugar	54.1
	Molasses	15.5	Sugar	40.5	Molasses	36.4	Molasses	43.4
	Fish	2.5	Cotton	5.8	Cotton	1.6	Rum	0.6
	Total	77.6	Total	95.2	Total	96.5	Total	98.1
Jamaica[f]	Bananas	37.4	Bananas	38.9	Bananas	47.7	Bananas	56.1
	Sugar	9.1	Sugar	8.1	Sugar	18.7	Sugar	17.1
	Coffee	8.3	Rum	5.9	Coffee	5.3	Rum	4.9
	Total	54.8	Total	52.9	Total	71.7	Total	78.1
Trinidad	Cocoa	38.9	Cocoa	54.2	Cocoa	29.9	Petroleum	57.3
	Sugar	23.7	Sugar	28.3	Sugar	31.7	Sugar	21.8
	Asphalt	6.7	Asphalt	8.2	Petroleum	12.5	Cocoa	10.0
	Total	69.3	Total	90.7	Total	74.1	Total	89.1

Table 8.9 (continued)

Colony	1899–1901[a]		1909–11		1921–3		1934–8	
British Guiana	Sugar	72.9	Sugar	66.9	Sugar	59.4	Sugar	65.2
	Rum	14.8	Gold	11.4	Diamonds	22.7	Bauxite	10.8
	Cocoa	2.1	Gum	6.9	Gum	4.8	Rice	6.1
	Total	87.8	Total	75.2	Total	86.9	Total	82.1
British Honduras	Lumber	59.6	Lumber	39.2	Lumber	54.6	Lumber	51.8
	Bananas	9.1	Chicle Gum	22.1	Chicle Gum	12.8	Bananas	16.8
	Coconuts	3.0	Coconuts	10.7	Bananas	9.4	Chicle Gum	16.3
	Total	71.7	Total	72.0	Total	76.8	Total	84.9

[a] Total exports including bullion and coin; [b] Southern Nigeria only, 1900–1 and 1909–11; [c] 1899–1901 East Africa Protectorate; 1910, 1911 only; [d] 1910, 1911 only; [e] 1909–11 and 1921–3 Federated Malay States; 1934–8 British Malaya, estimated total exports of domestic produce; [f] 1900–2.

Source: Statistical Abstract for the British Empire, No. 51, (1899–1913), No. 58 (1922–5), No. 68 (1929–38).

9

The 'colonial question' and towards colonial reform, 1930–40

OTTAWA AND ITS AFTERMATH

The commercial and financial collapse which overwhelmed the British economy in 1930 and 1931 led to two major breaks with past economic policy. In September 1931 a massive haemorrhage of the Bank of England's gold and foreign exchange reserves caused the gold standard to be jettisoned and the pound to float: within three months it had lost 31 per cent of its gold value. In February 1932, the policy of free trade, which had been the cornerstone of British international commercial practice for at least 70 years, was abandoned as the new National government introduced a general 10 per cent import levy. The end of free trade meant that the government was at long last in a position to introduce a system of imperial tariff preference. The imperial economic conference, scheduled for Ottawa in July, was the venue for implementation of the long-held dream of the 'imperial visionaries' of an empire trade bloc.[1]

For the tropical colonies, the Ottawa Agreement meant a greater access to the British market in return for greater penetration of British exports of manufactured goods in their markets. Britain was able to give preference to imports from its colonies by allowing them in free of duty while imposing an import duty on the same commodities from non-empire sources. In practice, the benefits to the colonies were insubstantial: the foreign product was usually subject to only a 10 per cent impost which in the international conditions of rapidly declining commodity prices in the early 1930s and world over-supply of these commodities, amounted to very little advantage for colonial producers at all. Moreover, in some commodities the colonies produced more than Britain consumed (even in normal times) and thus the preference had virtually no effect on the world price. For certain commodities Britain was not an important market, or not a market at all. In other cases, Britain did not give any preference because it would not impose an import duty on foreign raw materials such as cotton and petroleum oil. In any event, Britain's demand for imports fell considerably in the depression (by 45 per cent in value and 13 per cent in volume between 1929 and 1933), so that even if the colonies' share of the British market increased as a result of Ottawa (perhaps a doubtful proposition) it represented a slightly greater share of a smaller total. The main problem, as outlined in the previous chapter, was steeply declining world prices for tropical exports and the consequent severe deterioration in their terms of trade. The agreements made at Ottawa, however, did nothing to arrest the downward slide in prices and worsening terms of trade.

The British government hoped to offset to some extent the decline in its export trade by expanding the share of British imports to the empire market, including the tropical colonies. Prior to the Ottawa Agreement most of Britain's colonies did not include any large degree of imperial preference in their import tariff schedules. Only in the West Indies, Cyprus, Mauritius and Fiji was a significant degree of preference granted. As a result of Ottawa, the colonies were expected to introduce imperial preference on a wider range of imports and to increase the level of existing preferences. Some colonies did so, but the general application of preference in colonial tariff regimes was hindered by the fact that some colonies had few dutiable items (particularly the Straits Settlements and Malay States) and a number were prevented from implementing imperial preference by international treaties which forbade discrimination in their customs duties and which had been signed on their behalf by Britain during the heyday of free trade. Now such treaties were regarded as a nuisance. Nevertheless they prevented Nigeria, the Gold Coast, Kenya, Uganda, Nyasaland, Tanganyika and Zanzibar from reciprocating Britain's concessions at Ottawa. Where preference was created it was usually achieved by increasing the level of duty on foreign imports rather than by reducing the tariff on British or empire products, which therefore did not make British goods any cheaper in the colonial markets. Following Ottawa, the degree of preference granted by those tropical colonies which were free to do so varied between 25 per cent and 50 per cent.

The chief beneficiary of colonial preference was intended to be British textile exports which had lost much ground to Japan, but there were considerable obstacles to the adoption of discriminatory measures in the colonies against Japanese textile imports. Indeed, although Japan was the target of Britain's efforts to secure a greater share of the colonial imported textile market for Lancashire, it was Indian textile exports which were the more effective competitor in the colonial empire, and India's position was protected by the Ottawa Agreement.[2] To reinforce tariff preference, which was unlikely to be of much assistance to the British exporter, quotas on foreign textile imports to Britain's colonies were introduced, except in those colonies which were prevented by international treaty from engaging in trade discrimination. In 1933 the possibility of denouncing the 1911 Anglo-Japanese Trade Treaty so as to be able to discriminate against Japan in colonial markets was canvassed among the colonial governors. Their replies were not at all encouraging from Lancashire's point of view. Only in West Africa – where Japanese imports had only recently begun to penetrate and where Lancashire still dominated – was there any enthusiasm for anti-Japanese action: Sir Donald Cameron, governor of Nigeria, recommended that all Japanese goods should be prohibited from West Africa – 'in the past the native of Nigeria has done quite well without cheap Japanese goods and can continue to do so'.[3]

Other governors, however, were more concerned with the likely social and political consequences of denying the mass of the population access to low priced Japanese manufactures. The East African governors objected that discrimination against Japanese goods would increase the cost of living to ordinary people and lead to retaliation by Japan. In any case, they pointed out, it would be India rather than Britain which would be the major beneficiary of any reduction in Japanese imports.[4] The view from Singapore was similar: the governor of the Straits Settlements argued that anti-Japanese measures would hurt the poorer classes who could not afford the high priced British products and might provoke Japan to military reaction which in 'the present desperate weakness of Singapore' would be 'extremely hazardous'. He concluded that 'the fortunes of the Lancashire cotton industry, great though they are, should not be allowed to jeopardise the future of this Colony'.[5]

The Manchester cotton manufacturers were not impressed:

> we can only view with dismay and despair the spectacle of our trade in our own Empire markets being allowed by our Government to pass to Japan whilst we are faced with the prospect of more mills being closed and the calamitous effects of still further unemployment. Other countries such as France use their possessions to keep their own industries alive.[6]

By March 1934 it was recognised that an agreement with Japan was not possible and negotiations were formally ended. The Board of Trade then moved to introduce a quota system in the colonial empire to limit the volume of Japanese textile imports. East Africa was omitted because of the Congo Basin treaties, but all other colonies were instructed to prepare a quota system which would limit all foreign imports though 'the system would in fact only operate to restrict Japanese imports'.[7] Some colonial governments objected: Malta, Cyprus, the Seychelles, Grenada, Barbados, Sierra Leone, the Federated Malay States, the Straits Settlements, Hong Kong, Mauritius and Ceylon. Only Hong Kong's objection was sustained on account of its free-port status; the others were told to force the legislation through using the official majority in the legislative assembly or, where such a majority did not exist, as in Ceylon, orders-in-council of the British government. Ceylon was the most intransigent but, Cabinet noted,

> to acquiesce in refusal of Ceylon to pass effective legislation would mean that an impossible situation would be created both in this country and in all colonies where the same legislation has been passed and where the same arguments that Ministers have advanced can be used from the consumers' point of view. Moreover, quota legislation has been carried by exercise of official majority in some colonies, e.g. Straits Settlements.[8]

In the end, Britain agreed to impose a 10 per cent duty on imports into Britain of foreign soya beans, which competed with Ceylonese copra, in return for compliance with the quota regulations. The Colonial Office was aware that since empire oilseeds production exceeded British import requirements this would not actually assist Ceylon, but assumed the Ceylonese politicians would think it would.[9]

The quota system continued in all colonies except those in East Africa and Hong Kong until the Second World War. By making the base period for calculation of the quota the years 1927–9, Japanese imports were curtailed. The shortage of Japanese goods, however, caused their price to the consumer to rise to close to that charged for the better quality British product, and colonial government revenue from import duties to be constricted. The main beneficiary of the quota system was not Lancashire since Indian competition proved to be far more damaging than Japanese, but those individuals or companies in the colonies fortunate enough to obtain an import licence for Japanese goods, and such importers were frequently British firms such as the United Africa Company or Jardine and Company. The Colonial Office conceded some time later that it had acted in a haphazard way and in panic. It was pointed out by the Colonial Office that the quotas

> have undoubtedly caused certain hardship to the poorer classes – and the poorer classes in some Dependencies are extremely poor – [and] in many places, not only in Ceylon but also, for example, in Malaya and Grenada, there has been considerable opposition to the scheme, which has only been carried through by the use of official majorities. . . . The Colonies have definitely made certain sacrifices for Lancashire and Lancashire has . . . reason to be grateful to them.[10]

For the meagre gains Britain obtained from discriminatory duties and textile quotas there was a high price to pay in colonial resentment and opposition. *The Economist* commented in May 1934 the cheapness of Japanese cotton exports has been doing the world a considerable service by helping the consumer in tropical countries to maintain his purchases. But for the future it appears that among the benefits of British rule the doubtful privilege of buying expensively from Lancashire is to be forced upon the 'native' in many corners of the globe.[11]

Thus whilst the Joseph Chamberlain concept of colonial economic development fell largely into abeyance during the 1930s depression, his aim of imperial tariff preference was achieved. However, it raised the question of whether the benefits were worth the cost. The share of Britain in the imports of the colonial empire increased during the 1930s from 26.1 per cent in 1927–9 to 28.1 per cent in 1936–8; similarly, the colonies sent a greater proportion of their exports to Britain: 24.9 per cent in 1927–9 rising to 28.5 per cent in 1936–8. The tropical colonies became a better market for British goods: they took 7.6 per cent at the earlier date, 8.6 per cent at the later; and as suppliers to Britain, the colonies improved their share from 4.9 per cent to 5.6 per cent.[12] Against these modest gains – if gains they really were and not simply a diversion of trade – had to be weighed not only the political implications of colonial opposition, but the reaction of some of the other major trading nations. Certainly Britain's Ottawa system – together with restriction schemes for colonial production of rubber, tin and tea – was regarded with hostility by the United States and as a direct attack on their economic security by Germany and Japan. Britain was to a limited extent able to mollify American official opinion by signing the Anglo-American Trade Treaty in 1937 and modifying some of the more objectionable aspects of the Ottawa system. But the perceived threat which the system posed to Germany and Japan was not overcome.

IMPERIAL AGGRESSION

Access to colonial raw materials and colonial markets by non-colonial countries appeared to be made more difficult in the 1930s as Britain and other imperial nations tightened the economic ties between the metropolitan centre and their tropical possessions. Germany, Italy and Japan took action which ostensibly at least was designed to redress these apparent disadvantages. In doing so, the 'Colonial Problem' of these years can be regarded as a contributory factor to the political instability which ultimately deteriorated into all-out war.

Germany's claims for the return of its colonies lost at the Versailles Peace Conference in 1919 were first raised by Hitler in March 1935.[13] Despite the emphasis given to the prestige value of colonies, Britain's reaction was to try to diffuse the economic arguments surrounding the question of access to colonial raw materials. In September 1935, British Foreign Secretary Sir Samuel Hoare called on the League of Nations to establish an inquiry into the whole problem of raw materials in colonies. The League agreed to the appointment of a Committee for the Study of the Problem of Raw Materials which reported in September 1937.[14] Meanwhile, in March 1936, the colonial question was again brought up by Germany following its successful re-occupation of the Rhineland.[15] The British Foreign Office view was that concessions would have to be made to Germany somewhere, either in Europe or Africa, and of the two, commented Sir Robert Vansittart (permanent head of the Foreign Office), 'I would prefer it to be in Africa, in regions with which we were well able to dispense.'[16] To determine which, if any, these regions might be, Cabinet set up a sub-committee of the Committee of Imperial Defence to consider the 'Transfer of a Colonial Mandate or Mandates to Germany'. In a lengthy report the sub-committee discussed the question from every angle, but concluded that there was no British territory in Africa which could be given up and that asking the dominions to transfer their mandates to Germany was out of the question. Reflecting the Foreign Office view, however, the sub-committee also conceded that

> If, however, wider considerations are held to outweight these grave objections, and if the transfer of territory has to be considered, the least objectionable course would be for France to join with us in the surrender of the whole or part of Togoland or the Cameroons, or both.[17]

The Colonial Office opposed any transfer of territory – it 'would open the door to measures compelling the natives to produce which no decent person could contemplate without a shudder'[18] – but the Cabinet Committee on Foreign Policy remained divided.

In November 1937 Lord Halifax (Lord President of the Council), following a meeting with Hilter at Berchtesgaden reported that the 'colonial issue' was now the only one which undermined Anglo-German relations.[19] Chamberlain seized on Halifax's report to urge the idea of a repartition of tropical Africa whereby

> two lines should be drawn across Africa, the northern line running roughly to the south of the Sahara, the Anglo-Egyptian Sudan, Abyssinia and Italian Somaliland, and the southern line running roughly to the south of Portuguese West Africa, the Belgian Congo, Tanganyika and Portuguese East Africa. There should be general agreement among the Powers concerned that all the territories between the two lines should be subjected to the proposed new rules and regulations covering the administration of the territories . . . those Powers which now held the territory, together with

Germany who would be given a territory of her own, would each administer their own territories subject to the over-riding rules and regulations laid down.[20]

Chamberlain could see no reason why Germany should reject this offer: 'In essential matters it met the German desiderata and gave them what they so strongly insisted upon, namely equality of opportunity and treatment.'[21]

Chamberlain's plan was put to the German government on 3 March 1938. By this time, however, the Austrian crisis was 'boiling hard and on the point of boiling over'.[22] Hitler was not in the least interested in the colonial question and though he promised a reply to Chamberlain's Africa plan, it never came.[23] Despite the Munich crisis in October 1938 and the German invasion of Czechoslovakia in March 1939, colonial revision was pursued by British proponents of appeasement up to July 1939.[24] According to Wolfe Schmokel, late in July 1939 Germany was offered a 25-year defence pact, 'junior partnership' in the Ottawa Agreements and the return of its colonies in stages. None of these later offers were taken up by Germany.[25]

For four years the question of German colonial restitution was in the news in Britain and in the colonies. The fact that colonial revision did not occur was due not so much to considerations of trusteeship on Britain's part (though moral repugnance was expressed in 1936 and 1937, it was noticeably muted in Cabinet committee in 1938 and 1939) but to the unwillingness of Germany to enter into negotiations for a general settlement in Europe. The prospect of a repartition of Africa or handing colonial territory to Germany did British prestige tremendous damage in Britain and in the colonies among those who looked to British rule for economic and social and eventually political progress. It may be that there was an element of bluff in both countries' posturing on the 'colonial question', but this only served to keep the issue in the limelight and to tarnish Britain's reputation in Africa and elsewhere.[26]

In this atmosphere of uncertainty it was hardly surprising that confidence in British rule in the colonies was threatened, as the governor of Nigeria wrote to the secretary of state in April 1939:

> there are clear signs that a considerable section of the British public is rapidly awakening from the complacency, indeed the apathy, with which it has been accustomed to regard colonial problems, and is beginning to have an uneasy feeling that all is not as it should be and, in particular, that certain other powers have some justification for suggesting that they would have succeeded in doing more than we have done for the development of tropical Africa, had they been in a position to make the attempt.[27]

One country which did make an attempt to become a major imperial power in tropical Africa was Italy, which invaded Ethiopia in 1935.[28] In May 1936 – two months after Germany re-occupied the Rhineland – Addis Abbaba fell to Italian forces which had used air bombing and poison gas against a virtually unarmed population. In July the League of Nations dropped all sanctions against Italy as Britain and France acknowledged *de facto* recognition of Italy's conquest.[29] Britain formally recognised Italian possession and Mussolini as 'Emperor of Abyssinia' in November 1938.[30]

There was little emphasis placed by Britain during the crisis on the impact the Italian conquest was likely to have on colonial opinion and even when this aspect was raised it was played down. Essentially the Abyssinian crisis was viewed from the perspective of European power politics.[31] Yet the invasion and violent conquest of Africa's last independent state (as it was widely viewed) by Italy produced a rising tide of anger, resentment and disillusion throughout the non-white world. The historian of non-white reaction to the invasion, Monique Rubens, wrote:

> From the United States to Japan non-whites bitterly condemned Mussolini's aggressions, writing letters of protest, forming ad hoc pro-Ethiopian committees, organizing mass demonstrations, collecting funds on Ethiopia's behalf and offering her their military services.[32]

The crisis had an impact on nationalist sentiment and anti-colonialism in East and West Africa, in Egypt, among colonial activists in London, and, perhaps most importantly, in the West Indies. In places where colonial nationalism was already well established – Egypt, the West Indies – the reaction was most visible, but, as Asante showed in the case of West Africa, even where an anti-colonial movement was only in its infancy, the crisis had the effect of raising political consciousness and undermining British (and Western) prestige.[33] Some people, previously supportive of British rule, found it incomprehensible that Britain would desert Ethiopia and do nothing effective to prevent its destruction.[34] In the West Indies the events of 1935–6 sparked off demonstrations and rallies which built up a momentum of their own during 1937, fuelled by the continuing depressed conditions in the West Indies, and exploded into the widespread labour riots of 1937 (Trinidad) and 1938 (Jamaica).[35] Even if the British government appreciated the far-reaching consequences in its tropical empire of letting such a symbol of African resistance to colonial aggrandisement as Ethiopia be overrun in an onslaught of nineteenth-century style militaristic imperialism, it is doubtful whether it would have acted any differently. But the full extent of colonial revulsion was not apparent until the disturbances of 1938 brought them to the fore, and by then the impetus given to colonial nationalism could not be rolled back.

Japan's launching of a full-scale war against China in July 1937 threatened the European colonial possessions in Southeast Asia. Alarm bells may have sounded in the various capitals, especially as Japan and Germany had signed the Anti-Comitern Pact in November 1936, but the policy of appeasement prevented any forceful action against Japan. Britain's defence strategy rested on the concept of 'Fortress Singapore' and the fortification programme was considerably expanded in 1938 as the Japanese threat loomed. Singapore could be defended from the sea but not from the land. British Malaya was not capable of supporting Singapore: it lacked any secondary industry and was dependent on imported food (mainly rice from Burma) for two-thirds of its needs. The absence of secondary industry was partly a result of British imperial policy which sought to restrain the spread of manufacturing in the tropical colonies; the dependence on overseas food supplies was directly a result of the plantation, mining and cash-crop development policy of the previous decades. British capital had created a valuable prize for Japanese aggression but had not provided it with the means for defending itself. The only notable strategic assets of the Malay peninsula were its roads and railways, all of which led south to Singapore.

The real blow to British prestige came, of course, with the retreat from the Japanese and the surrender of Singapore in February 1942, but the threat to Britain's colonies in Southeast Asia from Japan in the 1930s created some feelings of unease about Britain's ultimate ability to halt the Japanese expansion. Certainly it was clear that Britain had lost the economic and commercial war against Japanese goods and shipping companies and this inevitably led to some questioning, however hesitant, of Britain's military strength. Malay nationalists felt that it was wise to be more active in the late 1930s, to counter Chinese nationalism in Malaya and to ensure that the British authorities did not forget their commitment to the Malay population. The small Indian community in Malaya was also more vocal now, since for some at least, Japanese imperialism might be a means to removing Britain's grip from India itself.[36]

TOWARDS REFORM OF COLONIAL POLICY

Taken together, the German demands for colonial restitution, Italy's conquest of Ethiopia and Japanese expansion in East Asia, posed a challenge to British imperialism which undermined confidence in Britain's ability and willingness to protect its colonies. These events damaged the prestige upon which British rule in the colonies largely depended and in many of the tropical territories was a direct stimulus to nationalist sentiments and forces. If the apparent weakness of Britain in the face of imperial aggression provided the context for the development of the 'colonial problem', specific manifestations occurred in a series of outbreaks of discontent in the tropical colonies which revealed the extent to which the Great Depression had undermined standards of living amongst the mass of colonial inhabitants. The main outbreaks were in Northern Rhodesia, Mauritius, West Africa and the West Indies, and the reports of the commissions of inquiry which generally followed produced a mass of published evidence of the economic and social problems (including labour problems) which beset the tropical colonies in the 1930s.

Strikes and rioting took place at three mines on the copperbelt in Northern Rhodesia in May 1935 following the Northern Rhodesian government's decision to alter the method of assessing poll tax. As a result mine workers found their tax liability raised by between 20 per cent and 50 per cent without any commensurate increase in wage rates. Although this was the immediate cause of the strikes, a great many complaints were put to the commission of inquiry by workers concerning pay and conditions. At one of the mines, Luanshya, Northern Rhodesia police – some of whom 'seemed to have lost their heads' – opened fire on crowds of demonstrators, killing six miners and wounding 22 others.[37] The secretary of state's adviser on labour affairs, Major Orde-Brown, also reported on labour conditions in Northern Rhodesia in 1938 and recommended further improvements be made to the migratory labour system.[38]

In Mauritius in September 1938 there occurred a series of strikes in the sugar industry and in the docks which led to a state of emergency being declared and labour leaders deported.[39] In the West African colonies of the Gold Coast and Nigeria cocoa farmers protested the creation of a buying cartel by the leading European merchant firms by holding-up supplies of cocoa for six months. In its early stages the stoppage was accompanied by sporadic strikes by dock workers and transport workers.[40] The report of the commission of inquiry highlighted the marketing problems of small capitalist farmers who were engaged in supplying a cash crop to the international market which exhibited highly volatile price fluctuations.[41]

In addition, the League of Nations instituted a number of investigations which were relevant to conditions in the British colonies: one on international access to colonial raw materials (already referred to) focussed attention on the exploitation of colonial economies by the industrial countries and raised doubts about the effectiveness of colonial trusteeship. In 1935 it published a report on nutrition and public health which was discussed in the General Assembly in September.[42] As a consequence of the publicity which this gave to the question of nutritional standards, the Colonial Office established its own inquiry in 1936 into 'Nutrition in the Colonial Empire', the results of which were published in 1939. This survey indicated serious deficiencies in the diets of tropical inhabitants:

> there are few of the constituents considered necessary in Europe for a nutritionally adequate diet which are generally available in sufficient quantities in the Colonial Empire . . . there are few parts of the Colonial Empire (or indeed of any tropical country) where the diet of the majority of the population is at present anything like sufficient for optimum nutrition. . . . Colonial diets are very often far below what is necessary for optimum nutrition. This must rest not only in the prevalence of specific deficiency diseases but in a great deal of ill-health, lowered resistance to other diseases, and a general impairment of well-being and efficiency. There is in our minds no doubt whatever that these conclusions are correct.[43]

By the late 1930s the Permanent Mandates Commission of the League of Nations had recorded too many violations of the terms of the mandates (not to say the spirit) without having developed any effective means of countering such violations, for there to be any great confidence in the mandates system in its current form as a mechanism for protecting colonial indigenes from the ravages of the international economy.[44] By the end of the 1930s there was in Britain an outpouring of publications on the 'colonial question' in its various forms, not only from left-wing critics of imperialism, ranging from the Marxists George Padmore (*How Britain Rules Africa*, 1936) and Leonard Barnes (*Empire or Democracy?*, 1939) to the Fabians Arthur Creech Jones and Rita Hinden (*Plan for Africa*, 1941), but also from the Royal Institute of International Affairs (*Raw Materials and Colonies*, 1936, *The Colonial Problem*, 1937, *Germany's Claims to Colonies*, 1938, 1939), under whose auspices Lord Hailey published *An African Survey* in 1938. There were also a number of popular tracts of which the most influential was W.M. Macmillan, *Warning from the West Indies*, 1938.[45]

It was undoubtedly the West Indian riots in 1937 and 1938 which received the greatest publicity and which were most significant in fostering reform of colonial policy.[46] The extent of the violence and loss of life took the British press by surprise and led to a reaction which brought into question conditions throughout the colonial territories. *The Times* commented on 25 May and 11 June 1938:

> Long years of neglect by the Colonial Office, by local Governments and by employers have resulted in a state of things which is as dangerous as it is deplorable. . . . Everyone recognises that things cannot be allowed to remain as they are. . . . [11 June] Recent events in the West Indies have shaken the complacency with which

most people in this country have been accustomed to regard the Colonial Empire . . . they have created an uneasy suspicion that economic and social improvements may be just as badly needed in other parts as well.

For once there was a lively debate on a colonial issue in the House of Commons when the question of the West Indian rioting was aired on 14 June.[47] The government responded by establishing a Royal Commission to investigate economic, social, labour and political conditions in the West Indies. The commission's findings were presented to the government in February 1940 but at that time were suppressed as being too critical of British colonial policies to be released in wartime. Part of its conclusions ran:

> The social services in the West Indies are all far from adequate for the needs of the population, partly as a result of defects of policy, and largely through the paucity of the funds at the disposal of the Colonial Governments which are in the main necessarily responsible for these services . . . The diets of the poorer people are often insufficient and usually ill-balanced, although nutritious foods of all kinds necessary for health can be produced without much difficulty in almost every West Indian Colony. . . . The reason for this appears to lie fundamentally in the divorce of the people from the land without the provision of compensatory arrangements which would help to ensure adequate food supplies for the displaced population. . . . Housing is generally deplorable, and sanitation primitive in the extreme.[48]

It was hardly surprising that the full report was not published until 1945.

Efforts to improve the economic and social aspects of British colonial policy were evident from 1934 when the Colonial Office undertook an internal reorganisation and created an economic department for the first time. Social problems became more evident later in the decade and in 1937 a social department was also established and a labour adviser appointed.[49] There was more emphasis placed on the need to tackle economic problems by the use of scientific research and on the need for personnel with technical expertise. The colonial Civil Service was overhauled in the later 1930s, a process which culminated in the establishment of a unified service in 1938. The need for better training of administrative staff was acknowledged, as was the requirement for more technical experts to be appointed, but financial constraints made implementation of these aims difficult.[50] The permanent heads and the deputy heads of the various departments in the Colonial Office in

Whitehall were even encouraged to make visits to colonies by the end of the 1930s, though few actually did so prior to the war.

The main target for reform in the later 1930s, however, was the Colonial Development Act 1929. By 1937 the Act was recognised as a failure, both in terms of its impact on British levels of unemployment and on colonial development. Many regarded the Act as too narrow in scope, insufficiently funded and as too amateur in its approach to the selection of development projects to be assisted. The inability of the Colonial Development Advisory Committee or the Colonial Office to initiate development proposals was viewed by some in the Colonial Office as a major obstacle to its effectiveness.

At the end of June 1938, shortly after the dramatic events in the West Indies, the Colonial Office set up a departmental committee to examine the question of reform of the Colonial Development Act. The newly appointed secretary of state for the colonies, Malcolm MacDonald, intended to submit a proposal to Cabinet in the autumn for an enlargement of the Act. MacDonald's view was that much more money must be spent on social services, the inadequacy of which had been exposed by the crisis in the West Indies. In addition:

> Colonial affairs had come into particular prominence lately and the eyes of the world were upon us. We had, he thought, reached a critical stage when we must either decide whether to carry on the present hand to mouth basis or to deal with the problem of colonial development in a much bigger way than heretofore. In his view the latter course was essential if our reputation as a Colonial power was not to suffer irretrievable damage. Apart from the question of political expediency there was moreover our responsibility as trustees for peoples of the Colonial Empire.[51]

He envisaged an increase in the Colonial Development Fund from £1 million to £7 or £8 million per annum. The CDAC could remain, but its scope would have to be broadened to include social services, especially the provision of educational services. Since the colonial governments obviously required assistance in drawing up development schemes to submit to the CDAC, he suggested that a team of three or four officials could travel around the colonial empire helping colonial governments prepare development projects. There should be greater coordination between the Colonial Office, CDAC, and CEMB (Colonial Empire Marketing Board, established in 1937). Finally, 'It was important that the taxpayer in this country should be assured that the Colonies were at any rate doing their best to stand on their own two feet.'[52]

What of the 1929 Act's aim of assisting the British economy? It was pointed out by Sir John Campbell, the secretary of state's financial adviser who had attended many of the CDAC's meetings over the previous eight years, that the committee had gradually watered down the principle that schemes it assisted should benefit the United Kingdom; nevertheless, it was a stipulation which had inhibited colonial governments in submitting proposals and this was one reason why actual expenditure from the Colonial Development Fund had tended to fall short of the annual grant to it from Parliament. MacDonald thought that the House of Commons would accept now that colonial development had its own merits, but that this principle would not entirely disappear: 'and the House would want some economic justification for the schemes, in terms of benefits to the United Kingdom'.[53]

In December 1938 the Colonial Office prepared an internal report on colonial development. In the aftermath of the Munich crisis it was recognised that there would be less money available for colonial aid as Britain would have to devote more of its national resources to rearmament. However, the Munich crisis also made Britain more vulnerable to international criticism as MacDonald pointed out:

> In future, criticism of Great Britain would be directed more and more against her management of the Colonial Empire, and it was essential to provide as little basis as possible for such criticism. It was an essential part of her defence policy that her reputation as a Colonial power should be unassailable.[54]

The report prepared early in 1939 recommended an enlargement of CDAC to eight members (from its current five) and the establishment of an *ad hoc* committee within the Colonial Office to report on specialised topics. Senior Colonial Office staff would receive sabbatical leave of six or twelve months to visit colonies and colonial governments would be expected to draw up five-year plans of economic and social development. The CDAC would not be able to initiate schemes, but would be encouraged to submit proposals directly to the secretary of state. There should be greater provision of funds for recurrent costs of development projects (the heavy burden of which, it was suggested, was another reason colonial governments had been hesitant to make full use of the 1929 Act) and for social services. Those colonies receiving assistance from the Treasury would have the level of funding increased and its scope widened to include economic development and social services. Less poor colonies would receive assistance from the CDF for both capital and recurrent costs of development schemes, whilst the least poor colonies would be expected to find all their recurrent costs and meet some of the capital requirements: these colonies would examine their taxation systems to see if they could enhance their revenues. The new CDF would total £3 million per annum. The Colonial Development Act would be replaced by a new Act which would place much less emphasis on the benefits to British trade and industry (without omitting these altogether) and more emphasis on social services.[55] As a separate issue, Lord Hailey was asked to report on the provision of funds for scientific research into problems affecting the colonies, a problem which he highlighted in *An African Survey*. Hailey reported in May 1939 and recommended the establishment of a colonial research fund of £500,000 per annum to be administered by the Colonial Office.

MacDonald preferred to put both requests to the Treasury as a single package but delayed doing so pending receipt of the recommendations of the West India Royal Commission expected in August or September. He had already told the Cabinet when it had set up the Royal Commission that the British government would be obliged to spend whatever amounts Lord Moyne recommended on rehabilitation and development in the West Indies, so Treasury would not be willing to consider a new CDF and Research Fund until it knew what the bill for the West Indies crisis was likely to be.[56]

Meanwhile the Second World War broke out. The Treasury reaction to the onset of war as regards colonial aid was to suspend the CDF and cancel all grants-in-aid.[57] The Colonial Office took a more positive line. MacDonald met with his chief advisers on 4 September 1939, the day after Britain declared war. He argued that the war made it more vital, not less, that a reform of colonial development policy be pursued. Britain must be able to retain its reputation as a colonial power in case after the war there were moves for all colonies to be placed under international mandate. In his view,

> It was very important too that we should keep the colonies con-
> tented during the war, and he felt that a big scheme of colonial
> development, announced quite soon, would impress people here
> and abroad.[58]

The recommendation of the Colonial Office Committee on Colonial Development had been that the CDF should be increased from £1 million to £3 million a year, but prior to the outbreak of the war MacDonald had contemplated asking for £10 million per annum, and he felt that this should be pursued in the new circumstances.

The Colonial Office set about drafting a memorandum for the secretary of state to take to Cabinet. The draft put forward three reasons why a more forward colonial policy should now be undertaken:

> (1) A series of strikes and disturbances in the West Indies, Mauritius and elsewhere had brought home to people that all was not well in the economic or social field in these Colonies. This impression was confirmed by such reports as that of Major Orde Browne, my Labour Adviser, on his visit to the West Indies. Also, the Report of the Committee on Nutrition in the Colonial Empire

brought home to people how low is the standard of living in almost every part of the Colonial Empire and how great the volume of preventable ill health and inefficiency.

(2) Lord Hailey in his great 'Survey of Africa' published at the beginning of this year emphasised that 'the present is possibly the most formative and therefore the most critical period of African history'. He brought home to the public the fact that the lines our policy took now might mould the future of the whole continent.

(3) The 'Colonial question' as an international problem has focussed attention on Colonial matters. Foreign Governments have been quick to take note of talk about our 'slum Empire'. They have alleged that we are neglecting our vast possessions, that they impose a strain on our resources that we are unable to stand and that there should be some redistribution of Colonial territories. These arguments, it may be noted, are not confined to our present enemy but were heard also from Italy and from Poland. In the face of the evidence which I have mentioned above, public opinion here and in the world generally, particularly perhaps in America, has felt that there was at least some justification for these suggestions.[59]

With the outbreak of war it was important to press ahead with measures for colonial development in order to 'keep the Colonial Empire contented', to impress public opinion in Britain and in the United States and counter Nazi propaganda 'that we neglect our Colonial Empire'. To guard against the possibility of internationalisation of colonies after the war ended, 'we must be able to show that our record as a Colonial Power is so good that there can be no question of our being asked to surrender our colonies to anyone else'. A new fund, to be termed the Colonial Development and Welfare Fund, would be established with £10 million per annum for ten years, together with a Colonial Research Fund of £1 million per annum also for ten years. Advisory committees would be set up to advise the secretary of state on expenditure from both funds. In practice it was not expected that the full amounts of these funds would be spent in the first two or three years.

The draft memorandum then outlined the chief problems encountered by the colonies in financing economic development projects. The principle that colonies should pay their own way had continued to be applied and had starved most colonies of sufficient development funds, despite the Colonial Development Act of 1929. The West Indies was the 'depressed area' of the colonial empire and presented particular problems which the Royal Commission would consider and which would inevitably involve additional expenditure by the British government. African colonies remained undeveloped and were unable to provide even basic social services to most of their inhabitants: Nigeria alone could easily absorb the £1 million per annum provided under the 1929 Act 'if we are to do our duty by her'. In order to ensure that money provided by Britain was properly spent colonies would draw up 'comprehensive plans' for their economic and social development.[60]

This memorandum was sent to the Chancellor of the Exchequer, Sir John Simon, with an additional warning

> I think that in the present critical state of much colonial opinion trouble in some places is almost a certainty if we do not proceed with a policy of reasonable development of schemes for employment and social services. . . . I can think of few things what would have a more reassuring effect in the neutral world (and particularly in the United States), or that would add more to our moral prestige, than an announcement that despite the burdens that are put upon us by the necessity of fighting the war, we are going as far as conditions permit to find some additional money for promoting the welfare of the many million of peoples in the Colonial Empire for whom we are the trustees.[61]

Despite these sentiments, the Treasury remained unimpressed: it complained about 'welfare expenditure apparently without any end in view' and thought the draft memorandum was 'not very far short of amounting to saying that the only thing to do is to put the Colonies on the dole from henceforth and forever'.[62] Sir Henry Moore felt the Treasury officials had not grasped the essential point:

> Politically the whole point is that we should be able to make a big thing out of the 'welfare' side. If it is just going to be 'development' on the old lines it will look merely as if we are going to exploit the Colonies in order to get money to pay for the war![63]

Meetings took place in January and February 1940 between the Colonial Office and the Treasury in which the political arguments were accepted and a compromise was reached: the Colonial Development and Welfare Fund to be set up would be reduced from the proposed £10 million per annum to £5 million per annum, and the Research Fund from £1 million to £500,000 and in return the Treasury would somewhat expand the writing-off of colonial debt: as well as cancelling loans-in-aid and some CDF loans, the Treasury agreed to cancel railway loans made to Kenya, Uganda and Nyasaland and other loans made to Tanganyika.[64]

The Colonial Office proposal was put to Cabinet in February 1940 with these terms and including a commitment of £1.4 million to fund the recommendations of the Moyne Royal Commission on the West Indies which were now to be published (though the report itself was not) 'as an earnest of our good intentions'.[65] A central organisation for developing welfare services in the West Indies would be established under a comptroller with suitable staff, and an inspector general of agriculture for the West Indies would be appointed. In his statement to Cabinet, MacDonald argued that

> There was a widespread feeling that all was not well with the Colonial Empire. Some unfavourable comparisons were made between our own administration and that of other powers, and it was urged on all sides that bold measures of amelioration and reform were required.[66]

The Colonial Development Act, he continued, had been much appreciated in the colonies and had made constructive progress, but it had been limited by the total amount it was able to spend and its somewhat confined scope, especially as regards education and general (as opposed to specific) public health schemes. The secretary of state could not help concluding that the standard of health services were 'still such as to justify much of the criticism which has been made'. He did not think that the proposals should be suspended because of the war, on the contrary, there were additional reasons for going ahead. The expenditure of funds in the colonies would not involve the use of reserves of foreign exchange, and in the narrow sense such expenditure could be justified on its own merits. In addition, the social conditions in the colonies provided ammunition for Britain's enemies, including those in neutral countries. Nor, he continued,

> although there is a ferment of loyalty in the Colonial Empire at present, can we overlook the possibility of trouble there later on . . . in particular there is serious danger of trouble in the West Indies if no action is taken to implement the recommendations of the Royal Commission.[67]

Finally, MacDonald felt that when the war ended Britain must ensure that it was in a position to face any criticism which might be levelled at the administration of its colonial empire. Cabinet approved the proposal and a statement on colonial development and welfare was released in March 1940.[68]

The Colonial Office achieved in wartime what was probably beyond its reach in peace time, that is, a greatly enlarged measure for colonial development and social services. Certainly more trenchant opposition by the Treasury could have been expected if the proposal had been put up in peacetime, outbursts of unrest and discontent in the colonies notwithstanding. By the outbreak of the war British colonial policy was in crisis and it was hardly to be expected that the mere passing of the Colonial Development and Welfare Bill in 1940 would of itself — whatever its propaganda merits — provide a lasting solution to the 'colonial problem'. Lord Hailey argued in connection with the African colonies in 1938 that

History will doubtless look back on this period as being the most critical stage of African development; errors that are made now for lack of the knowledge which well-considered scheme of special study might supply may well create situations which the future can rectify only at the cost of great effort and much human distress.[69]

His recommendation for research funds was included in the 1940 Act and, as we shall see in the next chapter, Lord Hailey was now brought more directly into the process of planning for post-war colonial reconstruction. The reality of the tropical colonies in 1938 and 1939, however, was low and declining material standards of living, widespread abject poverty, stunted and distorted economic development and a serious burden of foreign debt. If 1938 had proved to be the final peacetime year of British rule over its tropical colonies (a not altogether inconceivable outcome during the war), its record as a colonial power would have been regarded as deplorable. History might then well have judged the more vociferous critics of British imperialism – such as Leonard Barnes, Alfred Viton, W.E. du Bois, George Padmore and Nnamdi Azikwe – to have been not far from the mark.[70] There was a noticeable air of failure in the contemporary assessments of the achievements of British colonial rule in the economic and social spheres by the end of the 1930s. It was this feeling of failure which was the real legacy of the 'colonial question' in the 1930s, and which also provided the context in which wartime aspirations for postwar colonial reconstruction and rehabilitation were made.

10

A new sense of urgency

Planning for colonial development during and after the Second World War, 1940–8

EXTERNAL TRADE DURING THE WAR

Colonial external trade was generally depressed as the British Empire entered the war, having declined in value from the brief rearmament boom of 1937 by over 20 per cent by 1939 (Table 10.1). The African and Caribbean colonies experienced subdued trade conditions until 1943, although export earnings rose faster in Ceylon and Mauritius. In the last two years of the war trade values increased more rapidly, by 19 per cent overall and in the first full year of peace trade values rose by 25 per cent, as the post-war boom got under way. The volume of trade declined during the war in many cases. Tables 10.2 and 10.3 present details of the movement in volumes of major export and import commodities. West African exports of cocoa, palm kernels, palm oil and groundnuts were all below their 1938 volume levels in 1945, although there was some increase in tin ore and manganese (and iron ore from Sierra Leone). A similar situation obtained in the Caribbean where sugar, cocoa and bananas were below 1938 volume levels by 1945, but bauxite from British Guiana expanded rapidly. In East and Central Africa the volume of cotton and coffee exports declined though sisal increased slightly. Copper and zinc output from Northern Rhodesia, however, doubled. As regards the the eastern colonies not overrun by the Japanese, tea and sugar export volumes from Ceylon and Mauritius were lower in 1945 than in 1938 though were higher in some of the intervening years. With the fall of Malaya in 1942, Ceylon became Britain's main source of rubber and the volume exported virtually doubled. Thus, except for strategic minerals and raw materials, for which special efforts were made, the physical quantities of commodities exported from the tropical colonies declined during the war. This was caused by low prices, diversion of labour, shortages of inputs such as fertilisers and machinery and inadequate shipping. Many colonial exports were subject to bulk purchase by Britain at rock bottom prices, which had a disincentive effect on producers. Where export volumes were increased in response to the war effort higher prices were paid and a higher priority for shipping given.

Table 10.1   Exports, imports and balance of trade, selected colonies
1937–47, (£m)

Colonies	1937	1938	1939	1940	1941	1942	1943	1945	1945	1946	1947
Imports											
West Africa	29.3	17.9	15.7	16.9	16.3	23.9	27.8	30.7	28.4	38.2	60.6
East & Central											
Africa	19.7	19.2	17.9	20.7	25.2	24.6	27.0	30.5	30.6	42.0	61.1
Eastern	20.8	20.3	20.7	24.2	24.7	23.6	35.4	42.5	48.7	50.2	80.7
Caribbean	19.1	19.0	19.2	21.6	25.3	23.7	29.1	33.3	33.0	40.4	61.6
Pacific	1.7	1.6	1.5	1.7	2.0	2.1	2.7	2.4	2.5	3.4	4.9
Total	90.6	78.0	75.0	85.1	93.5	97.9	122.0	139.4	143.2	174.2	268.9
Exports											
West Africa	34.3	17.9	18.7	19.5	20.4	20.6	23.5	25.7	32.8	41.2	58.5
East & Central											
Africa	27.0	22.6	22.6	27.3	27.4	30.2	30.8	33.2	37.3	41.7	56.1
Eastern	25.9	22.2	25.6	29.3	33.7	41.2	44.0	49.6	46.1	58.9	69.6
Caribbean	14.9	15.2	15.2	12.6	12.8	11.3	13.3	14.3	16.2	27.5	35.1
Pacific	1.9	1.7	1.6	1.5	1.1	2.0	1.7	1.6	1.4	2.7	4.7
Total	104.0	79.6	83.7	90.2	95.4	105.3	113.3	124.4	133.8	172.0	224.1
Balance of trade											
West Africa	5.0	0.0	3.0	2.6	4.1	–3.3	–4.3	–5.0	4.4	3.0	–2.1
East & Central											
Africa	7.3	3.4	4.7	6.6	2.2	5.6	3.8	2.7	6.7	–0.3	–4.9
Eastern	5.1	1.9	4.9	5.1	9.0	17.6	8.6	7.1	–2.6	8.7	–11.1
Caribbean	–4.2	–3.8	–4.0	–9.0	–12.5	–12.4	–15.8	–19.0	–16.8	–12.9	–26.5
Pacific	0.2	0.1	0.1	–0.2	–0.9	–0.1	–1.0	–0.8	–1.1	–0.7	–0.2
Total	13.4	1.6	8.7	5.1	1.9	7.4	–8.7	–15.0	–9.4	–2.2	–44.8

West Africa: Gambia, Sierra Leone, Gold Coast, Nigeria;
East & Central Africa: Northern Rhodesia, Tanganyika, Zanzibar, Kenya–Uganda,
Nyasaland;
Eastern: Mauritius, Ceylon;
Caribbean: Barbados, Jamaica, Trinidad, British Guiana, British Honduras Pacific Fiji.
Source: Statistical Abstract for the British Commonwealth, 1936–1945 (No. 69); *The
Commonwealth and Sterling Area Statistical Abstract, 1947–1950* (No. 71).

Compulsory labour was resorted to in Northern Rhodesia, Tanganyika,
Kenya and Nigeria to lift output of copper, sisal and tin.[1]

Not surprisingly, import volumes also declined during the war in
many colonies (Table 10.3). This was true of cotton piece goods imports
to East Africa and Ceylon, cement imports to the Gold Coast, Northern
Rhodesia and Tanganyika, iron and steel, footwear, motor vehicles and
amongst imported foodstuffs, fish and rice. Imports were in short
supply because of lack of shipping as well as because of shifts to war
production in Britain. Imports rose in price between 1939 and 1945
(Table 10.4): cotton piece goods by 178 per cent in Nigeria and 664 per
cent in Ceylon; cement by 78 per cent in the Gold Coast; iron and steel
by 45 per cent in Trinidad; footwear by 373 per cent in Jamaica; motor
vehicles by 104 per cent in Kenya; flour by 119 per cent in Jamaica; and
fish by 41 per cent and rice by 232 per cent in Ceylon. Exports, on the

Table 10.2   Export volumes, selected commodities 1938–46

Commodity	1938	1939	1940	1941	1942	1943	1944	1945	1946
FOODSTUFFS									
Sugar									
(000 cwt)									
Mauritius	5770	5806	4069	7156	5188	5907	5114	2639	3601
British Guiana	3670	3582	2854	3087	2691	2624	3560	2652	2956
Trinidad	2405	2287	1546	2166	1687	1088	1102	1187	1739
Jamaica	2101	2076	1629	2747	2568	2811	2629	2366	2974
Cocoa									
(000 cwt)									
Gold Coast	5265	5614	4478	4379	2478	3747	4057	4645	4726
Nigeria	1942	2277	1795	2094	1199	1750	1401	1540	2004
Trinidad	379	150	222	168	90	72	95	69	59
Jamaica	47	46	18	44	42	43	41	18	29
Bananas									
(000 stems)									
Jamaica	23811	18772	6849	5589	1347	289	1117	1797	5813
Groundnuts									
(000 tons)									
Nigeria	180	147	169	247	194	143	156	176	286
Gambia	47	49	39	40	16	18	28	40	38
Palm Kernels									
(000 tons)									
Nigeria	312	300	236	378	345	331	314	293	277
Palm Oil									
(000 tons)									
Nigeria	110	126	133	128	151	135	125	114	101
Coffee									
(000 cwt)									
Kenya	342	338	172	248	247	156	149	149	192
Uganda	280	343	359	406	344	403	383	405	628
Tea									
(mill lb)									
Ceylon	236	228	246	237	265	263	276	232	291
RAW MATERIALS & MINERALS									
Rubber									
(mill lb)									
Ceylon	115	135	197	202	251	220	224	215	228
Sisal									
(000 tons)									
Kenya	28.0	29.2	25.4	21.6	32.5	25.9	27.2	28.5	24.6
Tanganyika	101	93	79	75	136	97	119	111	112
Cotton									
(mill lb)									
Uganda	161	132	121	146	94	49	76	106	88
Hides									
(000 tons)									
Kenya	49.5	41.0	59.7	63.8	49.1	59.9	45.5	35.0	34.2
Tin ore									
(00 tons)									
Nigeria	10.5	14.6	14.8	18.4	16.6	17.5	18.2	15.2	13.9
Copper									
(000 tons)									
Northern Rhodesia	220	208	272	216	246	266	227	175	180

Table 10.2 (continued)

Commodity	1938	1939	1940	1941	1942	1943	1944	1945	1946
Zinc ore (tons) Northern Rhodesia	6683	13708	13369	13587	13665	11942	13593	13995	17217
Manganese (000 tons) Gold Coast	324	336	477	429	484	432	504	702	765
Bauxite (000 tons) British Guiana	376	476	624	1073	1116	1901	874	739	1120

Source: as for Table 10.1.

other hand, advanced in price less noticeably – most of those shown in Table 10.4 by between 75 and 100 per cent. As a result, many of the tropical colonies found export price increases did not keep up with import price rises and so their terms of trade deteriorated (Table 10.5). If 1945 is compared with 1939, the movement was adverse in all of the eleven colonies shown in Table 10.5 (and these colonies accounted for over 95 per cent of the external trade of the colonial empire excluding enemy occupied territories).

These trends in wartime trade led colonial government revenues, heavily dependent on external trade, to rise substantially, by 120 per cent between 1939 and 1945 (Table 10.6). Public expenditure rose also, but more slowly as wartime conditions curtailed services and development projects, with the result that most colonial governments accumulated larger surplus revenues – almost £21m for all colonies between 1939 and 1945 – a large proportion of which was lent to the British government as interest free loans.[2] The direct control of both colonial governments and of Britain over the colonial economies increased dramatically during the course of the war principally as a result of the drive to acquire resources for the war effort and to combat outbreaks of inflation caused by shortages. Table 10.7 presents some information on wartime inflation in a number of colonies. Unfortunately the data are patchy and not many colonies outside of the Caribbean made cost of living estimates. By 1943 consumer prices had risen by about 65 per cent over their 1939 level in the Caribbean colonies with annual average inflation rates which varied from 13.2 per cent in Trinidad to 16.7 per cent in British Guiana. The cost of living in Lagos, Nigeria, increased by a similar degree, though the greater rise in the prices of imported consumer goods is evident. Inflation appears to have abated somewhat in 1944 and 1945, probably as a result of government price and wage controls. In 1946 and 1947, however, some colonies experienced increased levels of inflation (though prices fell in Fiji) as pent-up war

Table 10.3   Import volumes, selected commodities, 1938–46

Commodity	1938	1939	1940	1941	1942	1943	1944	1945	1946
MANUFACTURES									
Cotton piece goods									
(myd^2)									
Gold Coast	30.9	38.4	29.3	27.4	42.0	37.5	36.3	36.4	37.0
Nigeria	68.8	60.1	80.0	59.9	84.9	84.8	107.4	83.3	82.6
Kenya–Uganda	61.1	62.2	53.9	80.6	38.4	33.8	36.1	40.6	49.9
Tanganyika	41.8	50.7	35.3	58.2	37.5	27.1	27.0	34.6	28.6
Ceylon	63.5	65.8	76.6	61.3	32.7	54.8	40.9	49.0	34.2
Cement									
(000 tons)									
Gold Coast	54.0	63.8	35.1	37.6	18.9	19.2	25.6	52.9	65.2
Nigeria	50.0	51.1	21.2	32.2	35.0	33.4	45.8	564.1	96.0
Northern Rhodesia	19.7	19.2	17.1	21.1	18.2	18.1	11.4	13.1	10.7
Tanganyika	23.3	15.9	7.6	7.8	7.4	5.1	6.8	17.8	16.1
Trinidad	48.1	43.1	46.9	50.0	22.7	22.7	26.9	33.4	38.6
Iron & Steel									
(000 tons)									
Trinidad	38.8	27.9	41.2	33.3	18.2	14.7	12.7	11.1	17.1
Tanganyika	8.3	7.0	4.3	2.3	1.6	2.3	3.0	7.6	6.2
Kenya–Uganda	30.8	25.9	25.3	23.1	20.6	15.0	15.0	17.2	28.8
Footwear									
(000 doz pairs)									
Trinidad	56.9	71.1	70.5	63.8	49.8	59.4	61.3	59.1	81.6
Jamaica	113.8	178.5	132.8	132.2	43.7	47.9	82.9	22.6	51.0
Northern Rhodesia	19.5	17.3	22.0	21.4	12.4	18.3	18.9	13.5	19.3
Nigeria	38.0	25.0	16.0	13.0	14.0	11.0	20.0	5.0	35.0
Motor Vehicles									
(No.)									
Jamaica	1436	1358	535	495	62	18	81	155	922
Ceylon	2030	1883	1481	471	193	153	711	1145	2369
Tanganyika	1147	861	563	513	223	194	134	500	757
Kenya–Uganda	3407	2618	3593	1565	767	874	913	371	1716
FOODSTUFFS									
Flour									
(000 cwt)									
British Guiana	326	354	333	325	334	378	408	407	283
Trinidad	614	678	647	773	597	711	919	839	897
Jamaica	742	858	810	647	768	853	1272	1522	1125
Mauritius	182	276	208	179	320	683	1120	751	421
Gold Coast	137	195	116	115	100	96	99	95	101
Fish									
(000 cwt)									
Gold Coast	68	66	21	7	22	12	11	8	4
Ceylon	381	320	322	360	310	419	477	413	496
Jamaica	264	259	207	210	139	169	222	237	208
Trinidad	72	74	64	68	70	57	89	73	66
Mauritius	23	23	19	20	17	24	29	3	6
Rice									
(000 cwt)									
Trinidad	389	421	336	397	297	253	274	264	216
Jamaica	376	335	437	317	78	1	132	44	133
Ceylon	10449	11675	10996	10937	4710	2772	2239	4577	5074
Mauritius	749	1147	1194	1078	444	100	29	97	367
Gold Coast	228	207	110	36	51	16	6	1	14

Source: as for Table 10.1.

Table 10.4 Indices of unit values, main commodities, 1937–47 1947–9 = 100

Commodity	1937	1938	1939	1940	1941	1942	1943	1944	1945	1946	1947
Exports											
Cocoa (Gold Coast)	30	12	13	14	13	14	13	14	22	29	66
Palm kernels (Nigeria)	32	21	19	19	18	21	28	35	36	45	59
Groundnuts (Nigeria)	33	19	19	23	23	23	27	34	40	52	64
Sugar (Mauritius)	33	33	37	44	45	48	48	51	55	85	88
Bananas (Jamaica)	27	33	35	42	44	55	44	48	55	77	101
Coffee (Kenya)	30	31	31	30	37	47	46	57	65	81	92
Tea (Ceylon)	39	36	40	41	46	47	50	55	58	64	96
Sisal (Tanganyika)	32	20	18	26	27	27	30	37	38	49	79
Cotton (Uganda)	33	22	21	32	30	32	69	69	69	66	73
Rubber (Ceylon)	72	57	73	83	85	99	112	144	147	144	109
Copper (Northern Rhodesia)[a]	55	42	44	45	47	47	47	47	53	56	94
Imports											
C.P.G. (Nigeria)	25	25	23	28	32	41	58	63	64	74	99
C.P.G. (Ceylon)	18	16	14	15	21	28	74	133	107	104	116
Cement (Gold Coast)	39	45	50	59	78	91	93	76	89	96	98
Iron & Steel (Trinidad)	48	54	53	63	68	68	75	75	77	84	74
Footwear (Jamaica)	20	28	22	27	25	81	95	91	104	95	111
Motor Vehicles (Kenya)	43	46	47	63	61	64	131	104	96	85	94
Flour (Jamaica)	33	33	27	29	34	38	41	57	59	72	103
Fish (Ceylon)	55	54	54	50	53	63	76	76	76	76	81
Rice (Ceylon)	18	19	19	22	29	34	50	56	63	46	94

C.P.G. = Cotton piece goods
[a] Copper exports from Northern Rhodesia relate to electrolytic copper
Source: as for Table 10.1.

Table 10.5 Terms of trade, selected colonies, 1937–47 (1947–9 = 100)

Colony		1937	1938	1939	1940	1941	1942	1943	1944	1945	1946	1947
Gold Coast	E	31.3	17.1	17.1	18.0	17.4	18.4	18.2	19.1	26.9	33.8	68.5
	I	38.6	33.4	32.9	42.4	49.6	57.4	66.6	68.1	70.5	75.2	97.9
	T	81	51	52	43	35	32	27	28	38	45	70
Nigeria	E	31.2	18.7	18.4	20.3	20.3	21.5	24.6	29.9	33.5	41.5	62.9
	I	31.7	32.0	30.7	39.1	45.1	54.4	71.2	73.0	73.1	83.7	99.5
	T	98	58	60	52	45	40	35	41	46	50	63
Northern Rhodesia	E	50.3	37.7	39.7	41.4	43.0	43.8	44.3	44.9	52.7	55.7	89.0
	I	60.5	54.6	53.3	59.9	64.0	72.7	78.0	85.5	81.9	88.7	97.0
	T	83	69	74	69	67	60	57	53	64	63	92
Tanganyika	E	32.2	22.5	24.2	28.5	30.6	34.2	38.5	44.6	49.5	59.6	97.7
	I	35.5	37.0	33.8	42.9	50.3	59.5	76.7	85.2	69.3	77.2	86.9
	T	91	61	72	66	61	57	50	52	71	77	92
Kenya	E	40.9	35.3	36.2	38.9	38.2	40.0	45.6	48.5	52.7	61.9	82.5
	I	35.5	35.3	33.3	49.4	53.5	68.3	92.4	84.2	72.6	76.2	93.1
	T	115	100	109	79	71	59	49	58	57	81	89
Mauritius	E	33.0	32.8	36.5	44.3	45.0	47.6	47.9	50.9	55.4	85.4	88.2
	I	26.4	25.6	23.1	32.1	39.5	49.2	63.9	61.0	64.1	62.7	94.0
	T	125	129	160	137	114	98	75	84	86	136	93
Ceylon	E	42.2	36.5	42.1	43.6	48.9	53.7	57.7	66.6	70.3	75.4	97.6
	I	26.5	26.0	26.2	30.9	36.8	45.2	66.4	82.4	80.7	70.2	99.5
	T	159	140	161	141	133	119	87	81	87	107	98
Jamaica	E	33.4	32.8	36.2	40.6	50.8	63.9	65.8	69.0	72.5	83.9	96.1
	I	31.6	32.9	31.6	33.8	41.5	51.5	63.4	69.6	77.5	81.5	99.8
	T	106	100	115	120	122	124	104	99	94	103	96
Trinidad	E	39.9	38.9	42.9	56.9	54.9	77.8	72.0	69.6	60.0	66.1	88.0
	I	34.4	34.7	34.0	44.3	49.2	62.9	72.1	74.3	72.2	82.3	83.2
	T	116	112	126	128	112	124	100	94	83	79	106
British Guiana	E	56.1	54.0	59.5	65.7	68.2	69.0	68.1	73.6	732.2	81.3	91.4
	I	28.5	26.0	24.2	34.5	37.2	51.6	61.7	65.7	66.6	72.4	99.0
	T	197	208	246	190	183	134	110	112	110	112	92

E, Weighted index of the unit value of principal exports;
I, Weighted index of the unit value of principal imports;
T, Terms of Trade: E divided by I = 100.
Source: as for Table 10.1.

Table 10.6 Public revenue and expenditure 1939–46 (£000)

Col. Group	1939	1940	1941	1942	1943	1944	1945	1946	Total
Revenue									
East & Central Africa	10653	11911	14650	15466	17799	19606	22147	23701	135933
West Africa	11130	12485	13645	15252	17857	19721	22801	25211	138102
Caribbean	8987	10222	11963	13643	17038	20354	21095	24919	128221
Other	5578	6627	7934	10093	12253	12737	13785	17309	86316
Total	36348	41245	48192	54454	64947	72418	79828	91140	488572
% change		13.5	16.8	13.0	19.3	11.5	10.2	14.2	
Expenditure									
East & Central Africa	10969	11589	12521	13628	16476	18370	20761	22297	126611
West Africa	11501	12277	11943	14788	16551	16878	19076	23061	126075
Caribbean	9115	11457	10609	12192	16572	19797	21722	21593	123057
Other	5749	6681	7898	9977	10897	12928	13575	16406	84111
Total	37334	42004	42971	50585	60496	67973	75134	83357	459854
% change		12.5	2.3	17.7	19.6	12.4	10.5	10.9	
Balance									
East & Central Africa	-316	322	2139	1838	1323	1236	1386	1404	9322
West Africa	-371	208	1702	464	1306	2843	3725	2150	12027
Caribbean	-128	-1235	1354	1451	466	557	-627	3326	5164
Other	-171	-54	36	116	1356	-191	210	903	2205
Total	-986	-759	5221	3869	4451	4445	4694	7783	28718

Figures include colonial development and welfare receipts and expenditure and grants-in-aid receipts. Loan expenditure and receipts from loans are excluded: East and Central Africa: Kenya, North Rhodesia, Nyasaland, Tanganyika, Uganda, Zanzibar; West Africa: Gambia, Gold Coast, Nigeria, Sierra Leone; Caribbean: Barbados, Br. Guiana, Br. Honduras, Jamaica, Antigua, St Kitts, Trinidad, Dominica, Grenada, St Lucia, St Vincent; Others: Cyprus, Malta, Fiji, Br. Solomon Is., Bahamas, Bermuda, Mauritius.
Source: The Colonial Empire (1939–1947) (Cmd. 7167, 1947).

Table 10.7 Cost of living indices, selected colonies, 1940–47 (1939 = 100)

Colony		1940	1941	1942	1943	1944	1945	1945	1947
Barbados		120	130	151	165	179	187	207	226
Jamaica		125	145	157	158	160	159	175	206
Trinidad		113	123	148	164	163	170	183	191
St Lucia		111	127	150	176	182	170	185	222
St Kitts		n.a.	n.a.	n.a.	n.a.	n.a.	173	180	186
Antigua		n.a.	n.a.	n.a.	n.a.	n.a.	162	166	176
Grenada		n.a.	n.a.	173	172	175	181	185	202
Dominica		n.a.	n.a.	n.a.	174	165	170	211	218
British Guiana		118	131	158	185	181	181	198	210
British Honduras		n.a.	n.a.	133	152	156	163	180	205
Sierra Leone		n.a.	n.a.	n.a.	n.a.	252	234	237	233
Nigeria	(Lagos)	n.a.	n.a.	147	158	159	176	200	n.a.
	(Imports)	131	143	166	221	241	226	n.a.	n.a.
Fiji	(Suva)	n.a.	n.a.	n.a.	n.a.	173	173	164	189
	(Country)	n.a.	n.a.	n.a.	n.a.	215	198	183	206
	(Europeans)	n.a.	n.a.	n.a.	n.a.	145	141	144	163

Indices are annual averages unless otherwise indicated
Barbados: January-August 1939 = 100; index in January of each year
Jamaica: August 1939 = 100; index in December of each year
Trinidad: December 1939 = 100; index in December of each year
St Lucia: September 1939 = 100; annual average of monthly index except 1947 which is for September only
St Kitts: September 1946; September 1946; June 1947
Antigua: September 1945; September 1946; June 1947
Grenada: August 1939 = 100; December 1942; annual average of quarterly index 1943–1947
Dominica: September 1939 = 100; annual averages except 1947 which is for June only
British Guiana: Index relates to East Indian sugar workers only
British Honduras: Annual average of quarterly index
Fiji: August 1939 = 100; Suva and Country indexes refer to Indian workmen and are for January in year states; European index refers to European families and are for July in year stated.
Sources: Colonial Office, *An Economic Survey of the Colonial Territories*, vols. 1–VII (1952–1955); *Colonial Annual Reports, 1947*; Colonial Office, *Enquiry into the Cost of Living and Control of the Cost of Living in the Colony and Protectorate of Nigeria* (1946, Colonial No. 204).

demand was released. These statistics can be considered only as a rough guide to changes in consumer prices in a handful of territories during the war, but from them it can be concluded that annual inflation rates of 10 to 15 per cent were generally experienced. Without government controls it is likely that inflationary forces would have been stronger and the considerable extension of government economic controls raised the question of whether such controls would be dismantled once peace was restored.[3]

WARTIME PLANNING FOR COLONIAL DEVELOPMENT AND LORD HAILEY'S COMMITTEE

The war caused far more destruction and distress in the colonies than is evident merely from a brief examination of trade and public finance statistics. From the point of view of economic development it continued or exacerbated the economic stagnation of the 1930s: disinvestment, damage from fighting, loss of life, diversion of labour, strikes and labour unrest, reduced flows of aid from Britain as well as physical and personnel shortages left the colonial economies in a weaker state in 1946 than in 1938 and with a huge backlog of development needs to tackle. The war produced a more encouraging atmosphere for constitutional change, a 'more constructive approach to trusteeship' and a pledge by Britain in 1942 'to guide Colonial people along the road to self-government within the British Empire'.[4] It provided an opportunity for colonial officials and others to review the lack of progress in colonial economic development during the previous decade and to re-examine the basis on which Britain would pursue its colonial economic policy when the war ended. This task began in 1940 when it became clear that the recently passed Colonial Development and Welfare Act could not be fully implemented.[5]

Although unable to contemplate extensive colonial development in wartime, the Colonial Office turned its attention to the need to plan for colonial reconstruction after the end of hostilities. A committee on post-war reconstruction in the colonies was established with Lord Hailey, author of the highly influential *African Survey*, as its chairman. The committee began its work in April 1941. It adopted a wide-ranging approach both to immediate post-war problems and to those with longer-term implications. It commissioned research papers on a variety of subjects, chiefly from bureaucrats within the Colonial Office, but some from outside experts including W. Arthur Lewis, Charlotte Leubuscher, Sir William Beveridge and C. K. Meek, as well as from Lord Hailey himself. In all 160 submissions were considered by the committee.[6]

Not surprisingly, most of the material dealt with by the committee looked back over the 1930s and formulated future directions in response to whether pre-war practices were regarded as beneficial or not. It was difficult at that stage of the war to envisage the condition of the post-war world economy, and it was generally assumed that many of the problems faced by Britain's tropical colonies in the 1930s – low prices for their exports, external debt burden, lack of capital and enterprise, inadequate colonial administrations and so forth – would continue to restrict their economic and social progress after the war. Some of the major economic studies concerned questions which had been controversial before the war. One was the question of whether manufacturing industry should be encouraged in the post-war era in the colonies and, if so, by what means and in regard to which sectors of secondary industry. This raised the point that if manufacturing industry was to be encouraged by tariff protection, such a policy might undermine imperial preference and the value of the colonies as markets for British manufactured exports, a consideration which had been given some weight before the war. It was felt that the United States' concerns about preferential tariffs would have to be taken into account to a greater extent than before, though it was not clear how influential the United States would be in practice. Discussion of possible post-war tariff policy turned attention to the contentious question of the League of Nations mandates system and the 'Open Door'. In the 1930s the Colonial Office would have liked to have escaped from the open door clauses of the class 'A' and 'B' mandates, and the war seemed to offer the opportunity to sweep away these international impediments to imperial preference. But again, the post-war role of the League of Nations (or its successor) was far from clear and there were doubts as to whether the mandates system would continue to operate at all. Consideration of this problem led to a discussion of the possibility of 'internationalisation' of all colonial empires after the war with some kind of shared responsibility between the major allies and the United States for colonial economic development and progress towards self-government. Some found this prospect alarming, but there was no doubt that the effects of the war on Britain's capacity to rule its empire might render 'internationalisation' a serious challenge.[7]

More strictly economic problems were canvassed. A number of papers were written on the difficulties colonial governments faced in finding adequate funds to provide basic services and promote economic development. The West Indian economist, W. Arthur Lewis submitted a long memorandum on the provision of capital to the colonies up to the war and his conclusions are worth citing:

> The supply of private capital is related to the rate at which public capital is spent. If the state waits for private capitalists to come, in the hope that out of the taxes on the profits of their enterprise it may begin to fulfil its functions, development may well be slow. But if in the absence of tax revenue it borrows or begs and spends judiciously it will have no dearth of private investment. Hardly any colonial government in the past has consciously planned the development of its territory. Law and administration have been the favourite sons, education and public health the not so favoured daughters. There has been no economic staff to look ahead and direct; prosperity and depression have been gifts from God or Satan, unforeseen, if not as often uncomprehended. This

approach to colonial administration belongs to an era that is passed. The economic development of the colonies deserves to be carefully planned and as carefully controlled. Unless British colonial administration takes this to heart, it will not attain those new standards of trusteeship which the modern world demands.[8]

Questions of marketing of colonial exports, of labour conditions and regulation were also raised and researched. Social conditions, particularly health among women and children, were considered, as well as future constitutional changes and the role of the British Parliament (as opposed to the Colonial Office) in shaping colonial policy.

The Hailey Committee did not come to detailed conclusions. Pressure of other work and the march of events left the committee insufficient time to digest all the information submitted to it, though it was a useful exercise for the Colonial Office in airing various broad problems and marshalling many of the facts and opinions. Some of Lord Hailey's comments hit home to the senior Colonial Office officials on the committee; for example, his observation at the committee's fourth meeting that

> few, if any, Colonies at present had proper machinery for dealing with economic questions and relations with business interests. . . .
> The ability to deal with economic matters was not a matter of specialized training, like the Colonial health or agriculture services, but should be part of the equipment and outlook of the administrative staff. Men with this ability should be attracted into the administrative service, and the Administration should regard economic production as part of its normal activities just as much as political management, on which the chief and almost exclusive emphasis is laid at present. As a necessary corollary, the training of Colonial probationers at the universities should gradually lay less emphasis on producing the ideal 'bush' officer, reflecting the present transition of administration in the Colonies out of the 'patriarchal' stage.[9]

The deliberations of the Hailey Committee and the Colonial Office's thoughts on post-war reconstruction were not of immediate relevance as German military dominance reached its zenith in 1941. They did, however, form a basis for future policy when it was reconsidered more urgently in 1943 and 1944 and the comments of Lewis and others on the need for planning in colonial economic development were revived and the colonial civil service overhauled.[10]

THE WORKING OF THE 1940 COLONIAL DEVELOPMENT AND WELFARE ACT

As was outlined in the previous chapter, in March 1940 the Cabinet agreed to a new measure for promoting economic development in the colonial empire, the Colonial Development and Welfare Act. The addition of the term 'welfare' was both a recognition of the extent of poverty in the tropical colonies revealed at the end of the 1930s and an acceptance of the large 'welfare' element in expenditure under the 1929 Colonial Development Act. The 1940 Act permitted expenditure of £5 million per year for ten years on development and welfare projects plus £500,000 per year with no time limit on research schemes. On its inception in July 1940 there were a number of schemes being financed under the previous (1929) Act, and these were transferred to the new measure. Expenditure under the Act was slow in the first two years because colonial governments were told in September 1940 that Britain could not afford development schemes which did not bear a direct relation to the war effort unless 'the scheme was of such urgency and importance as to justify the expenditure of United Kingdom funds in present circumstances'.[11] Applications from the colonies for development funds dried up to such an extent that in June 1941 the policy was eased somewhat.[12] Wartime shortages of trained personnel and essential capital equipment also discouraged applications. In the period July 1940 to October 1942 approval was given for expenditure under the Act of approximately £2 million (of which £88,000 was from the previous Colonial Development Fund), an annual average of £833,000, which was about the same as the level of expenditure on colonial development in the 1930s. Schemes for agriculture, forestry and veterinary services accounted for 45 per cent of approvals, social amenities (education, health, sanitation, water supply, housing, etc.) for 36 per cent and transport and communications for 19 per cent. Among the 37 agricultural schemes approved few involved large expenditure: one for agricultural development in Dominica cost £25,000, but most involved sums of less than £7,000. Forty per cent of the cost of agricultural schemes were for projects left over from the 1929 Colonial Development Fund. Support for education projects was not given under the 1929 Act so it was to be expected that with the wider scope of the new Act there would be more grants to education. Fifteen schemes were funded at a total cost of £145,000. Medical, public health and sanitation schemes were funded by grants totalling £317,000, at an average cost of £9,600. The more costly ones were for yaws control (£38,750) and malaria control (£38,235) in Jamaica, and an anti-yaws campaign in Dominica (£29,935). Only four housing and land reclamation schemes were supported, but one, in Jamaica, took £99,200 out of the £103,410 allocated to schemes in this category. Water supply, drainage and irrigation projects were fairly numerous (sixteen), but small in scale and cost in total only £147,000. Seventeen transport and communication projects were supported during this period at a total cost of £356,000. These included several large-scale schemes, for example landing facilities for aircraft in the West Indies and a road in British Honduras from Belize to Cayo costing £187,500. A grant of £35,700 was also made to Dominica for road development.[13]

Approved colonial development and welfare expenditure increased to £1,600,000 for the period 1 November 1942 to 31 March 1943. Social amenities absorbed 79 per cent of these funds, with over 40 per cent being used in schemes for water supply: one project alone for a reservoir in Jamaica was allocated an interest free loan of £382,000. Two water supply, drainage and irrigation schemes in British Guiana and Cyprus cost £96,000 and £129,600 respectively. Housing and land improvement schemes also tended to be relatively expensive: one for housing of colliery workers at Enugu, Nigeria, cost £104,000 and a native land settlement scheme in Swaziland cost £150,000. Education schemes were the most numerous (thirteen allocations) but all were low cost except for a grant of £127,000 to the Institute of West African Arts, Industries and Social Services, Achimota, in the Gold Coast. Agricultural expenditure accounted for 12 per cent of the total and involved only one large grant – of £100,000 for agricultural and veterinary scholarships to be disbursed by the secretary of state to all colonies. Transport and communications schemes were particularly hampered by wartime shortages and the emphasis placed on the use of local inputs; they accounted for 9 per cent of the total funds allocated in this period and contained one grant of £100,000 for enlargement of the airfield at Belize, British Honduras, and another of £30,000 for reconstruction of main roads in Montserrat.[14]

Altogether, funds totalling £3.6 million were allocated under the colonial development and welfare provisions of the 1940 Act in the thirty-three months from July 1940 to March 1943, out of a total permitted by the Act of £13,750,000 for this period. Spending under the research provisions of the Act came to a mere £72,498 out of a possible £1,375,000. The system of aiding colonial development and welfare, like the earlier system, still relied heavily on initiatives from the colonies and in their straitened circumstances in the war, especially with regard to personnel who could draw up development projects, it was not surprising that greater use of the 1940 Act was not made.

In the following financial year, 1943–4, allocation increased substantially to total £4.1 million. This was achieved by funding a number of quite expensive schemes rather than as a result of an increase in the number of applications. Fifteen projects accounted for two-thirds of the

219

total money allocated; of these, seven agricultural development projects in Jamaica, Barbados, Kenya, Sierra Leone and Bechuanaland amounted to £1,428,000; four water supply, drainage and irrigation schemes in Kenya, the Gold Coast, Sierra Leone and British Guiana totalled £728,000; Nigeria was allotted £230,000 to replace a dredger lost in Lagos harbour through enemy action; Fiji obtained £65,000 for malaria control and two land settlement and housing projects in Jamaica and Antigua received £232,100.[15]

By 31 March 1944, almost four years from the inception of the 1940 Act, agricultural projects had absorbed 28 per cent of total allocated funds, water supplies and irrigation 22 per cent, transport and communications 12 per cent, medical, public health and sanitation 9 per cent, housing and land settlement and education 7 per cent each and social services 6 per cent. (See Table 10.8.) Almost all of the funds went to colonies in Africa, the Mediterranean and the West Indies: 17 per cent to West Africa, 7 per cent to East Africa, 6 per cent to the South African High Commission Territories, 7 per cent to Malta and Cyprus and 60 per cent to the West Indies. (See Table 10.9.) On a per capita basis the West Indies received grants of more than £1.50 per head, whereas the African colonies received less than £0.05 per head. That such a high proportion of the available colonial development and welfare money should have gone to the West Indies was not surprising as their need for assistance had been emphasised by the West India Royal Commission appointed in 1939. Moreover, a comptroller for the West Indies was appointed in 1940 as a result of the Royal Commission's recommendations, and his secretariat assisted these colonies to draw up applications.

Almost twice as much colonial development and welfare money was allocated in the next financial year (1 April 1944 to 31 March 1945) as had been granted in the first four years of the Act. The total allocated to development and welfare projects was £15.9 million with a further £117,000 to research. Although 210 schemes were assisted in this period, the ten most expensive ones accounted for 50 per cent of the value of the allocations, the top twenty-eight schemes in order of cost for three-quarters of the total, and the sixty highest cost ones for 90 per cent. The geographical distribution of funds was concentrated on West Africa, which had become an important supply area for the Allied forces in the Middle East by 1944. Nigeria alone absorbed 44 per cent of all colonial development and welfare allocations in 1944–5. The West Indies took 26 per cent and East Africa 18 per cent.[16]

In the last year of the 1940 Act's operation, 1 April 1945 to 31 March 1946, the allocations were reduced as the new Colonial Development and Welfare Act was poised to take over from 1 April 1946 and the previous surge of activity had depleted the volume of new applications

Table 10.8 Allocations of funds under the 1940 Colonial Development and Welfare Act to development and welfare schemes, 1940–6

Class of Schemes	1940–4		1944–6		1940–6	
	£	%	£	%	£	%
Administration	46434	0.6	714975	3.4	761409	2.6
Agriculture & veterinary	2121428	27.5	2201605	10.4	4323033	15.0
Communications & transport	915991	11.8	3257075	15.4	4173066	14.4
Education	546114	7.0	3306685	15.6	3852799	13.4
Fisheries	4965	0.1	14876	0.1	19841	0.1
Forestry	437355	5.6	86150	0.4	523505	1.8
Housing	501835	6.5	2185499	10.3	2687334	9.3
Industrial development & public utilities	12995	0.1	451788	2.1	464783	1.6
Labour	3450	0.4	3800	0.0	7250	0.0
Medical, public health & sanitation	709921	9.2	3170820	15.0	3880741	13.4
Miscellaneous	23200	0.3	101050	0.5	124250	0.4
Nutrition	169353	2.2	90800	0.4	260153	0.9
Social Services	499947	6.4	490812	2.3	990759	3.4
Surveys	9800	0.1	101982	0.5	111782	0.4
Telegrams, telephones & wireless	35355	0.4	267500	1.3	302855	1.0
Water supply & irrigation	1684373	21.8	4721244	22.3	6405617	22.3
Total	7722516	100.0	21166661	100.0	28889177	100.0

Source: Colonial Development and Welfare Act 1940, Report on the Act and Return of Schemes, to 31 Oct. 1942 (Cmd 6422), 1942–3 (Cmd 6457), 1943–4 (Cmd 6532), 1944–5 (H of C Paper 106), 1945–6 (H of C Paper 150).

Table 10.9 Allocations of funds under the 1940 Colonial Development and Welfare Act to development and welfare schemes, by region, 1940–6

Region	1940–4 £	1940–4 %	1944–6 £	1944–6 %	1940–6 £	1940–6 %
General	76800	1.0	373834	1.8	450634	1.6
East Africa[a]	560620	7.3	3965424	18.7	4526044	15.7
West Africa[b]	1294304	16.8	8673151	41.0	9967455	34.5
South Africa H.C.T.[c]	481974	6.2	699082	3.3	1181056	4.0
Atlantic[d]	23900	0.3	60239	0.3	84139	0.3
Mediterranean[e]	518581	6.7	959073	4.5	1477654	5.1
Middle East[f]	33600	0.4	25000	0.1	58600	0.2
Eastern[g]	19150	0.2	47215	0.2	66365	0.2
West Pacific[h]	95400	1.3	18200	0.1	113600	0.4
West Indies[i]	4618187	59.8	6345443	30.0	10963630	38.0
Total	7722516	100.0	21166661	100.0	28889177	100.0

[a] Kenya, Northern Rhodesia, Nyasaland, Somaliland, Tanganyika, Uganda, Zanzibar.
[b] Gambia, Gold Coast, Nigeria, Sierra Leone.
[c] Basutoland, Bechuanaland, Swaziland.
[d] Falkland Is., St Helena.
[e] Cyprus, Malta, Palestine.
[f] Aden, Transjordan.
[g] Mauritius, Seychelles.
[h] Fiji, Gilbert & Ellice Is., Solomon Is.
[i] Bahamas, Barbados, British Guiana, British Honduras, Jamaica, Trinidad, Antigua, Montserrat, St Christopher, Nevis, Virgin Is., Dominica, Grenada, St Lucia, St Vincent.
Source: As for Table 10.8.

in the pipeline. A total sum of £5.5 million was allocated to 166 projects (an average of £33,000 compared to £75,000 in the previous year). As in 1944–5, the ten most expensive schemes accounted for almost half of the funds granted. Again, the three regions of East and West Africa and the West Indies took most of the money: 22 per cent, 27 per cent and 43 per cent respectively.[17]

Taking the final two periods together, 22 per cent of funds allocated went to water supply and irrigation schemes, 16 per cent to education, 15 per cent each to transport and communications and medical, public health and sanitation and 10 per cent each to housing and land settlement and agriculture and veterinary. These six classes of schemes, then, accounted for 88 per cent of all the funds allocated, and together represented a continuity with the types of schemes assisted in the 1930s, with the exception of education. Classes which received very small shares were administration, industrial development and public utilities, social services, telegrams, telephones and wireless, surveys, nutrition, forestry and fisheries and labour. Compared with the first four years of the 1940 Act, the final two years saw an emphasis placed on transport and communication, housing and land settlement and medical, public health and sanitation, but even in these years the 1940 Act did not really break any new ground. Overall, 'Welfare' received more attention than 'Development': water supply, housing, medical, public health and education took 58 per cent of funds allocated, while agriculture, veterinary, forestry, fishing, transport and communications (including telecommunications) and industrial development and public utilities accounted for 34 per cent. This reflected the way in which the allocations under the previous (1929) Act had been developing in the later 1930s, the publicity given to poor social conditions existing in the tropical colonies by the pre-war disturbances and wartime propaganda and the fact that funding was directed towards schemes which could utilise local resources (including labour) to the greatest possible extent and which did not make excessive demands on Britain for supplies of machinery, equipment and materials.

With the spurt in activity in 1944–5 the average annual amounts allocated to expenditure on development and welfare reached the total available under the 1940 Act of £5 million per annum. Research spending, however, remained low: out of a nominal amount available of £2.8 million only £1.1 million was allocated by March 1946. (See Table 10.10.) Over half of the research funds were allocated in the final period, 1945–6, £629,753. Unlike the colonial development and welfare schemes, research projects were initiated by the Colonial Office itself which showed much more interest in agricultural research than in research into social welfare problems. Of the amounts allocated in the period July 1940 to March 1944 (£297,333), half were for agricultural,

Table 10.10 Allocations of funds under the 1940 Colonial Development and Welfare Act to research schemes, 1940–6

Class of schemes	1940–4		1944–6		1940–6	
	£	%	£	%	£	%
Administration	–	–	32800	3.9	32800	2.9
Agriculture & veterinary	1284790	43.2	343101	41.0	471571	41.6
Communications & transport	–	–	–	–	–	–
Education	–	–	–	–	–	–
Fisheries	18820	6.3	168491	20.1	187311	16.5
Forestry	150	0.1	300	0.1	450	0.1
Housing	–	–	5897	0.6	5897	0.5
Industrial development & public utilities	–	–	3750	0.5	3750	0.3
Labour	–	–	–	–	–	–
Medical, public health & sanitation	11218	3.8	63293	7.5	74511	6.6
Miscellaneous	35000	11.7	90426	10.9	125426	11.1
Nutrition	–	–	1660	0.2	1660	0.1
Social services	18975	6.4	124640	15.0	143615	12.7
Surveys	39700	13.4	–	–	39700	3.5
Telegrams, telephones & wireless	–	–	–	–	–	–
Water supply & irrigation	45000	15.1	1500	0.2	46500	4.1
Total	297333	100.0	835858	100.0	1133191	100.0

Source: as for Table 10.8

veterinary and fisheries research carried out at research stations in Uganda, Tanganyika, the Gold Coast and Trinidad as well as in the United Kingdom. In the final two years of operation of the 1940 Act, agriculture, veterinary and fisheries research projects represented over 60 per cent of the funds allocated, with social services (15 per cent), miscellaneous (11 per cent) and medical, public health and sanitation (8 per cent) taking most of the remainder. Research schemes were inexpensive – the average cost over the whole period of the Act was only £11,220. Over 40 per cent of the expenditure was for research undertaken in the United Kingdom, 37 per cent in East Africa, 8 per cent in the West Indies and 7 per cent in West Africa. Undoubtedly the major cause of the low level of research expenditure was a shortage of skilled personnel and the need to devote as much as possible of Britain's scientific research effort to the war.[18]

ORIGINS OF THE 1945 COLONIAL DEVELOPMENT AND WELFARE ACT

As discussed above, subventions made for 1943–4 lifted the total allocated under the 1940 Act to £8 million, out of a nominal total available of £18,750,000. This was regarded by the Colonial Office as a disappointing performance and one which ill-fitted wartime propaganda in Britain and the United States as well as in the colonies themselves about the immense task of economic and social development which Britain had taken on, especially as allocations of funds always exceeded actual expenditure at any particular time. During the summer of 1944 the Colonial Office held discussions on the possibilities for raising the level of expenditure on colonial development both during the remainder of the war and, more importantly, in the post-war era. In a submission to Cabinet in November 1944, Oliver Stanley, the secretary of state, argued for a substantial increase in funding to meet the ever-growing needs for economic and social development in the colonies.[19]

Stanley began his appeal to his Cabinet colleagues with the assertion that 'The next few years may well determine the future course of the Colonial Empire'. The war was having two effects on colonial policy: on the one hand it 'increased our awareness of past deficiencies in our administration', whilst on the other hand it greatly raised the aspirations of the colonial populations for improved conditions, especially amongst those who,' in one branch or another of the Armed Services, have been enjoying a standard of living to which they have never been accustomed before [and] have travelled thousands of miles from their native villages'. The 1940 Colonial Development and Welfare Act 'was a magnificent gesture, but . . . for reasons outside our control, it has remained little but a gesture'. Although there were sound reasons why actual expenditure under the Act had fallen well short of its maximum (actual expenditure was estimated to be only £3.8 million by March 1945), this shortfall, 'has undoubtedly produced in many of the Colonies and even within the Colonial Service a cynical belief that the gesture was never meant to be more than a gesture'. In these circumstances Stanley felt justified to ask for an extension of the Act for ten years from 1946 and an increase in funding to £10 million per year in 1946–7 to 1948–9, £15 million per annum in 1949–50 to 1952–3 and £20 million per annum from 1953–4 to 1955–6, a total cost of £150 million, which would include research and higher education expenditure. Only with such an increase could colonial development be based on proper planning and avoid ending up with 'a collection of individual projects instead of integrated plans, a practice which has been properly criticised in the past'. From discussion already held with Sir John Anderson, Chancellor of the Exchequer, it was clear that the stumbling block was not the Colonial Office's concept of 'planned development', but Britain's ability to pay. Anderson would agree to only £10 million a year for ten years for development and £1 million a year for research. Stanley's response was that 'the Colonial Empire means so much to us that we should be prepared to assume some burden for its future. If we are unable or unwilling to do so, are we justified in retaining, or shall we be able to retain, a Colonial Empire?' In fact, Stanley argued, the amounts involved were really very small and Britain would undoubtedly benefit directly and indirectly from colonial development 'in the form of increased exports to us of commodities which otherwise we should have to obtain from hard currency countries, or in the form of increased exports from the Colonies as part of the sterling area to the hard currency countries outside'. Above all:

> without the Commonwealth and Empire, this country will play a small role in world affairs, and . . . here we have an opportunity which may never recur, at a cost which is not extravagant, of setting the Colonial Empire on lines of development which will keep it in close and loyal contact with us. To say now in 1945 that with these great stakes at issue we shall not be able to afford £15m in 1949 or £20m in 1953, is a confession of our national impotence in the future.

Stanley's memorandum was considered by the War Cabinet on 21 November 1944.[20] The chancellor objected to the overall sum of £150 million and the rising scale of funding which he thought implied that Britain would become increasingly better off after the war, which was not at all certain. Therefore he could not agree to more than a doubling of the sums provided under the 1940 Act. Winston Churchill, the prime minister, supported Anderson and Cabinet agreed that he and Stanley should work out a compromise and report back. The compromise they reached in December 1944 was for a total sum of £120 million over ten years with a maximum of £17.5 million to be used in any one year.[21] Stanley expressed satisfaction with the flexibility of this arrangement which would allow him' to proceed with comprehensive and intelligent planning of development programmes for the Colonial territories'.

Whether Stanley's expectations of comprehensive and intelligent planning of colonial development were justified will be considered in the next chapter. Suffice it to say here that there seemed to be no rationale on the part of the Colonial Office for an overall figure of £150 million or for acceptance of £120 million. It appeared to be an ambit claim based more on what Cabinet might be expected to accept in the circumstances rather than on any detailed costing of development plans for individual colonies. Perhaps in war time this was all that could be achieved, though the submission to Cabinet laid claim to a more sophisticated approach of 'planned development'. It was also the case that by 1944 the value of the 1940 Act had been eroded by inflation by one fifth, which indicated that a figure of about £6.25 million per annum was required just to maintain the level of real expenditure regarded as essential in September 1939. By the time the 1945 Act came into operation, in 1946–7, continued inflation had further reduced the real value of the 1940 Act, so that the new figure of £12 million per annum was only about 65 per cent higher in real terms than that provided by the measure it replaced, which was a far cry from the Colonial Office's intention to triple the value of the 1940 Act.

THE POST-WAR ECONOMIC CRISIS

In a sense the Colonial Office was only just in time in obtaining Cabinet approval for a new Act in December 1944 as Britain's economic problems became more severe as the war in Europe came to an end in May 1945 and against Japan in August. The United States announced the end of Lend-Lease aid to its allies in August and Britain faced its worst balance of payments crisis since the Great Depression.[22] The colonies were warned that they should not think of the British Exchequer as a 'fairly godmother', and that although the £120 million pledged under the 1945 Colonial Development and Welfare Act was safe, it would 'be misleading to hold out hopes for any increased generosity in assistance from HMG to the colonies'.[23] Gerard Creasy, an assistant under-secretary in the Colonial Office offered the observation that

unfortunately there is still the feeling in many quarters in the Colonies that the new development policy is not meant too seriously, and it is very difficult to eradicate such suspicion . . . the much advertised policy of pushing ahead with development had been, after all, very largely a wartime stunt.[24]

It was felt that public opinion in the colonies did not fully appreciate the difficult economic condition Britain now found itself in. Consequently a despatch was sent to all governors in September 1945 which outlined Britain's economic position. The colonies were advised that in the following few years Britain would be engaged in the process of rebuilding its capital stock which 'will certainly make heavy calls upon available resources and will leave little margin for anything but essentials'. The colonial empire could expect its sterling balances in London to rise and for there to be a shortage of 'imports involving payment in difficult currencies' (i.e. US or Canadian dollars).[25]

Colonial economic development became an important part of the British government's overall strategy to alleviate its chronic balance of payments deficit with the dollar area and tackle the 'dollar gap'. The colonies were regarded as potentially considerable dollar-earners. Colonial economic policy was drawn into this strategy and the economic crisis shaped the way in which policies of colonial development were implemented in the immediate post-war years and led directly to the creation of two new organisations which became heavily involved in project development – the Colonial Development Corporation and the Overseas Food Corporation.[26]

In June 1947 the Colonial Office submitted two memoranda to Cabinet on the production of foodstuffs and raw materials in the colonies.[27] These outlined the steps which had already been taken to increase production of these commodities. To begin with, 'Colonial Governments have been repeatedly urged to do everything possible to increase food supplies both for local consumption and for export. Explicit instructions were sent out to them in the early part of 1946, when the gravity of the post-war food crisis was appreciated and these have been repeatedly followed up'.[28] However, there were considerable obstacles to achieving substantial increases in production in the short run for most of the Colonial Office's initiatives were effective only in the medium to long term. Increases in output had occurred in some commodities in some colonies – examples given included timber, groundnuts, palm kernels, sugar, tobacco and tea – over the depressed levels of production of the late 1930s, but colonial economic development was – as the Colonial Office was always at pains to point out to the Cabinet – inevitably a long-term process.

To cut through this problem and achieve more rapid results, argued the Colonial Office, a new organization was needed. The Colonial development and welfare funds were tied up in schemes for basic social services and public works and utilities, so 'What is now urgently necessary is provision for the undertaking of *ad hoc* schemes for the development of individual agricultural and other industries.'[29] The body to do this would be a Colonial Development Corporation to be established' with adequate powers to promote and undertake the expansion of supplies of colonial foodstuffs, raw materials and other commodities'. The functions of the Colonial Development Corporation would be to conduct and pay for investigations of promising schemes for primary produce production, to operate such schemes and to set up *ad hoc* subsidiaries in partnership with colonial or other Commonwealth governments. It would be financed by a direct grant from the Treasury initially and then raise capital from the public, both in Britain and in the colonies themselves. As with public utility companies, the corporation would not aim to make large profits, but would be expected to break even over a number of years. It would be necessary for the corporation to take 'full account . . . of the needs of this country for physical supplies and of the possibilities of improving the balance of payments position of the sterling area as a whole'.

The proposal for the Colonial Development Corporation was put forward in conjunction with plans to establish a body to operate a large-scale groundnut-growing scheme in East Africa.[30] This project was based on the report of an oilseeds mission sent to East Africa in 1946 and had been approved by Cabinet in January 1947. It was then necessary to set up a corporation to manage this scheme. (See Chapter 12.) Since it was believed that there were other areas in the colonial empire where similar projects of mechanised land clearance and production of food-stuffs could take place, the minister of food, John Strachey, wanted to broaden the terms of reference of the corporation to allow it to promote 'similar schemes for Colonial development'. He proposed an Overseas Food Corporation which could grow groundnuts and other foodstuffs wherever suitable areas existed. The corporation could assist colonial governments 'who may be greatly in need of managerial skill and technical knowledge for the development of their resources to expand their food production for export to the United Kingdom. If schemes of this sort materialise they might lead to further benefits to the United Kingdom in the way of providing markets for our own manufactures of agricultural machinery and equipment'. A clear distinction would be necessary between the functions of the Colonial Development Corporation and the Overseas Food Corporation:

> the Colonial Development Corporation would have wider powers to develop mineral resources, improve communications, develop water power, etc., as well as to produce food and other agricultural products such as rubber, cotton, fibres and so forth; in so far as it produces food in the Colonies it would normally do so as part of its

plans for the general development of the Colonial Empire, whereas the Overseas Food Corporation would be concerned primarily with production of food for export to the United Kingdom, a part of the Ministry of Food's overseas procurement programme.[31]

To finance the activities of the Overseas Food Corporation direct funding from Treasury would be required together with guarantees for any loans or stocks issued up to £50 million, of which £25.5 million was required for the East African groundnuts scheme. These proposals were agreed to by Cabinet and legislation to create the corporations was prepared as the Overseas Resources Bill which was passed by Parliament in December 1947.

In August the secretary of state for the colonies was requested to prepare a memorandum on the degree to which the colonial empire could increase its exports to the United States so as to earn more dollars for the Sterling Area. In response, Creech Jones submitted a memorandum which pointed out that before the war the colonial empire had a large trade surplus with the United States the proceeds of which were spent chiefly on British goods and services. Thus the colonies had been 'among our principal earners of dollars' and the question now was how to restore that position.[32] Apart from rubber and a number of commodities which could be sold in greater quantities to the United States if Britain took less itself (cocoa, sisal, hides and skins and tin), the prospects for increasing dollar earnings from the colonies generally depended on longer-term schemes for development reaching fruition. Action which the Colonial Office was already taking included exhortations to the colonial governments and peoples to cut their imports of dollar-goods and increase output of dollar-earning products. It was admitted, however, that 'A number of such appeals have been made to Colonial Governments and peoples in the two years since the war ended, and it would be a mistake to expect too much from any further appeals of this kind'. In most cases rehabilitation and expansion of colonial industries required provision of capital equipment (in particular railway stock) and technical staff which were in severe shortage. The Malayan tin industry, for example, was seriously short of dredgers. Until such shortages could be overcome the role of the colonies in earning dollars would be restricted.

These problems continued to be discussed during the remainder of 1947 and into 1948. At a conference of African governors in London in November 1947 the minister for economic affairs, Sir Stafford Cripps, made the observation that, 'The whole future of the sterling group and its ability to survive, depends, in my view, on a quick and extensive development of our African resources.'[33] An analogy between colonial economic development and a military campaign had been made a few days earlier by the minister of food when describing to the House of Commons the East African groundnuts scheme which he liked to call 'Operation Groundnuts':

> this is also in one sense an expedition of war, but the enemy in this case is not other human beings. The enemy is the tsetse fly, the climate, the stubborn African bush, the ignorance of the cultivator and the lack of communications. . . . These are enemies who will give us difficulties or setbacks and even moments of heartbreak, just as the Afrika Korps did six years ago, but they are enemies, again like the Afrika Korps, which will be overcome.[34]

It was, perhaps, rather appropriate, therefore, that the Chief of the Imperial General Staff, Field Marshal Viscount Montgomery, should have been despatched by Cabinet to Africa in November 1947 to report on, amongst other matters, the potential for economic development there. He found it

> impossible to tour Africa without being impressed with the enormous possibilities that exist for development in British Africa, and the use to which such development could be put to enable Great Britain to maintain her standard of living and compete successfully in an increasingly competitive world.[35]

British Africa, he claimed, contained minerals, raw materials and labour in 'unlimited quantities', food there 'could be grown to any extent desired' and 'coal seemed to be unlimited and could be obtained cheaply'. To achieve the 'quick and vigorous' development of these resources properly a 'grand design' was required: it seemed to Montgomery that there was no overall plan for colonial development and the colonial civil service was suffering from a 'lack of brains and lack of vigour'. The secretary of state for the colonies, Arthur Creech Jones, refuted much of Montgomery's report when it was discussed in London (see below), but he wholeheartedly endorsed the field marshal's emphasis on the need for a 'quick and vigorous' development of Britain's African colonies:

> This was essential not only to this country but to Western Europe as a whole; it is necessary not only on strategic, but also on economic and political grounds. The effective economic development of the African Territories is needed both to secure their smooth progress in the social and political fields, and also to help in the supply to this country and the rest of the world of food and raw materials. Our departure from India and the reduction in our overseas investments generally will further increase the economic importance of the African Territories. Politically, our long-term aim must be to

231

secure that when the African Territories attain self-government they do so as part of the Western world.[36]

Sir Norman Brook, Secretary to the Cabinet, made it clear to the Colonial Office early in 1948 that although his approach was considered somewhat over-simplified, the thrust of Viscount Montgomery's report was considered correct. The Cabinet's study of the future course of the United Kingdom's economy, explained Brook, 'led them to the view that, when the period of Marshall Aid was over, this country would have to rely far more than ever before on the dollar-earning capacity of the Commonwealth and Empire'.[37] The Colonial Office had been criticised by Cabinet for inactivity and so it was essential that the Colonial Office should 'do everything possible to press forward with promising schemes for economic development'.

Creech Jones defended his department in January 1948 by arguing that the Colonial Office had done much to promote a 'quick and vigorous' development of Africa and cited the ten-year development programmes each colony had to submit to the Colonial Office's Colonial Economic Development Council under the terms of the 1945 Colonial Development and Welfare Act, as well as measures taken to improve the technical expertise of senior members of the Colonial Office.[38] Local development boards had been established in a number of colonies and a large recruitment drive was under way to provide the colonies with adequate numbers of trained personnel. Jones's colleagues recognised the importance of these initiatives, but remained dissatisfied with results so far.

Jones pointed out the present difficulties lay not in the realm of adequate planning as such but in execution – in particular bottlenecks created by severe shortages of equipment, materials (especially steel) and technical staff. Montgomery, suggested Creech Jones, 'greatly exaggerated' the material resources – minerals, raw materials, labour, food, coal, etc. – available: 'Africa is not an undiscovered Eldorado. It is a poor continent which can only be developed at great expense of effort and money'. This was the nub of the matter:

> To develop Africa on the scale which the Chief of the Imperial General Staff envisages we must be prepared to invest very large sums of money; we must supply capital goods, and above all, steel; we need to expand all our government services, which in itself involves the increased provision of supervisory personnel from this country. . . . The policy of successive Governments here was to make Colonies pay their way and the retrenchment which took place as a result of the 1931 economic crisis had a disastrous and lasting effect on all plans for development. . . . Matters have been rectified by the Colonial Development and Welfare Acts and the

Overseas Resources Development Bill. The sums provided under this legislation, large as they are, are yet not big enough to produce the development we all want and they will have to be supplemented by private investment under conditions of proper public control.[39]

In March 1948 Jones called on the British government to give a clear indication that it would give at least equal priority to the colonies as that given to the United Kingdom itself in the provision of capital goods and other resources, to allocate more staff to strengthen the Colonial Office and the Colonial Civil Service and to press on with the work of the Colonial Development Corporation and the Overseas Food Corporation as rapidly as possible. If the British government would do this – and be clearly seen to be doing so – then he thought Britain would obtain great benefits from colonial development:

> we shall be definitely on the path to development which, not quite immediately, but in a few years time, will bear fruit of inestimable value both to Colonial peoples and to the UK. Our position today is that prospective American aid gives us hope of surmounting the difficulties of the next few years, but we must prepare now for the time after that when we must again live of our own. Prompt action now will mean that we shall by that time be enjoying the first fruits of this new form of Colonial investment.[40]

Thus the Colonial Office view was that more rapid progress could be made in colonial economic development but only if Britain was prepared to provide more scarce resources. How Britain's initiatives in promoting colonial development would be regarded in the colonies themselves was altogether more problematic. Sir Norman Brook raised the question of whether the commitment to push ahead with the development of colonial resources 'might be represented as a policy of exploiting native peoples in order to support the standards of living of the workers in this country', and he advised 'that some care and preparation would be needed' in order to argue convincingly that 'colonial development' was as good for the colonies as it was anticipated it would be for Britain.[41] Creech Jones agreed that there indeed was a confidence factor involved in Britain's relations with the colonies which it was vital to sustain:

> I cannot stress too much how important it is to ensure that Colonial opinion is convinced that we have the benefit of the Colonial peoples at heart and are not out simply to get more supplies for United Kingdom use. The creation of the new C.D.C. and O.F.C. evoked almost as much criticism as a new form of exploitation as it evoked praise and any new initiative must be most carefully presented.[42]

To this end there should be a 'clear and public declaration' of Britain's commitment to the colonies, particularly to supplying essential equipment and other goods, in order 'to gain the confidence of the Colonial Governors and people'. If Britain intended to use economic and social development programmes as a counter to militant nationalism and demands for political independence, the way in which such programmes were presented publicly would be as important as their ultimate results. But however presented, it was difficult to avoid the fact that the driving force behind a greater commitment to colonial development was Britain's own economic crisis.

This inherent conflict in British policy-making in regard to colonial development between the relative benefits to the colonial and British economies was not a new concern, but it was heightened by the scale of the new colonial development proposals, the severity of the post-war plight of Britain and, above all, by the growing voice of colonial nationalism. Undoubtedly the initiatives of the period from 1944 to 1948 in planning for colonial economic development were the most far-reaching undertaken by the imperial government. What kind of impact and success they had in the subsequent decade and the experience of the colonial economies themselves in the years prior to self-government and independence are the subject of the following two chapters.

11

An impossible task?

Problems of financing colonial economic and social development, 1946–60

EXTERNAL TRADE, 1946–60

One of the most striking aspects of colonial international trade immediately after the Second World War was its rapid growth. Between 1946 and the end of the Korean War boom in 1951 trade values increased at an average rate of 73 per cent per annum (Table 11.1(a) and (b)). Export values increased faster than imports reflecting the colonies' rising trade surpluses. After the Korean War boom ended trade values generally fell and the remainder of the decade was one of much slower trade growth for these colonies. Their total trade increased by only an average of 2.2 per cent a year between 1951 and 1960. The eastern group experienced negative growth of external trade. In contrast to the 1946–51 period, in the 1950s imports grew slightly faster than exports as trade deficits became more common. Exports were sluggish in 1953 and 1954 and again in 1957 and 1958 followed by a sharp rise in 1960. In the first half of the 1960s trade was static in 1961 and sluggish in 1962, but then accelerated in response to the quickening tempo of world trade.

The surge in trade values between 1946 and 1951 was due more to price rises than increases in export volumes, though these often rose as well. Booming prices for the commodities which colonies exported were caused by increasing demand in Europe for tropical raw materials (rubber, cotton, sisal, minerals) as a result of post-war reconstruction and strong economic growth. Food shortages in Europe also translated into price rises for tropical foodstuffs, especially vegetable oils. Price controls and trade restrictions imposed during the war were gradually lifted and commodity markets re-opened, restoring 'world prices' for tropical produce and making prices more sensitive to demand forces. Political crises, notably the Berlin blockade (1948–9) and the start of the Korean War (1950), led to stockpiling of strategic supplies by the United States and its European allies which caused some colonial commodities (rubber, notably) to soar in price.

Export volumes also rose, but were subject to various constraints. In many cases there was a time lag before output could be increased in

235

COLONIALISM AND DEVELOPMENT

Table 11.1(a) Value of exports from the colonial empire, 1946–65 (£m)

Year	West Africa[a]	East Africa[b]	Central Africa[c]	Eastern[d]	Pacific[e]	Caribbean	Total
1946	43.1	30.5	32.0	191.4	2.6	29.0	328.6
1947	78.0	38.3	43.1	298.2	4.3	36.7	498.6
1948	119.3	47.2	51.3	382.0	6.0	46.5	652.3
1949	133.3	57.0	59.1	430.8	5.0	52.0	737.2
1950	167.6	75.7	86.4	819.6	5.6	63.8	1218.7
1951	215.5	118.3	104.1	1132.3	5.2	75.8	1651.2
1952	220.5	126.5	127.6	750.8	8.6	84.4	1318.4
1953	219.1	97.7	141.0	643.8	10.7	98.3	1210.6
1954	268.5	105.4	146.8	650.4	8.8	106.0	1285.9
1955	232.0	115.5	172.8	788.4	10.0	114.9	1433.6
1956	228.5	123.4	181.7	815.1	8.8	127.5	1485.0
1957	228.4	121.6	156.1	797.1	11.8	153.2	1468.2
1958	250.6	125.8	135.8	748.0	11.4	154.5	1426.1
1959	285.3	130.4	187.0	849.5	10.7	160.4	1623.3
1960	303.4	142.1	205.9	925.7	12.3	185.2	1774.6
1961	306.7	134.3	206.8	879.0	9.6	214.4	1750.8
1962	293.1	139.7	209.5	917.8	11.3	220.4	1791.8
1963	316.0	171.3	223.1	965.3	17.2	246.2	1939.1
1964	352.0	191.7	317.8	956.6	20.9	262.0	2101.0
1965	404.1	180.4	362.4	1053.9	16.1	261.6	2278.5

[a]Gambia, Sierra Leone, Gold Coast, Nigeria.
[b]Kenya, Uganda, Tanganyika, Zanzibar.
[c]Northern Rhodesia, Southern Rhodesia, Nyasaland. (Federation of Rhodesia and Nyasaland).
[d]Mauritius, Ceylon, Malaya, Singapore, Hong Kong.
[e]Fiji.
[f]Barbados, British Guiana, British Honduras, Jamaica, Trinidad.
Source: *Statistical Abstract for the British Commonwealth, 1946–65*

response to higher prices; transport bottlenecks frequently hampered attempts to raise production and exports quickly; some agricultural export industries had been adversely affected by low prices in the 1930s and during the Second World War and neglect had led to crop diseases, notably in West Africa and the Caribbean; in other cases capital and capital equipment was insufficient, especially in mining, to lift output levels in the short run: shortages of materials, equipment and trained personnel bedevilled the colonial export drive into the 1950s. Some export industries had been physically damaged by the war, particularly in Southeast Asia.[1] In addition, shortages of consumer goods acted as a disincentive to producers who found that high prices brought them much enlarged money incomes but insufficient goods to spend them on. Inflation in some colonies eroded the real gains from increased output. Marketing boards, which operated in West Africa and Uganda, exerted a different disincentive effect: by denying producers the full value of

Table 11.1(b) Value of Imports into the Colonial Empire, 1946–65 (£m)

Year	West Africa[a]	East Africa[b]	Central Africa[c]	Eastern[d]	Pacific[e]	Caribbean[f]	Total
1946	38.3	31.9	30.5	201.0	3.2	40.5	345.4
1947	60.6	46.8	47.7	336.3	4.6	61.8	557.8
1948	78.2	67.2	56.5	421.6	5.4	65.7	694.6
1949	109.9	94.2	7.32	477.7	6.3	70.9	832.2
1950	119.5	75.0	82.6	677.8	6.3	80.0	1041.2
1951	160.1	109.1	113.7	991.7	8.4	104.4	1487.4
1952	193.9	126.1	124.1	833.4	10.8	119.2	1407.5
1953	195.4	111.6	117.2	759.3	9.5	112.5	1305.5
1954	200.8	122.9	125.3	701.9	10.5	119.5	1280.9
1955	245.2	154.7	138.6	806.7	12.9	142.4	1500.5
1956	268.2	139.9	159.3	909.2	14.8	159.2	1650.6
1957	282.3	146.5	177.5	991.3	13.7	183.7	1795.0
1958	278.7	126.6	157.6	916.0	15.8	194.7	1689.4
1959	318.0	126.8	150.2	962.5	15.2	205.7	1778.4
1960	375.0	141.3	156.8	1067.3	14.8	235.5	1990.7
1961	399.9	140.7	155.0	1059.8	15.5	248.2	2019.1
1962	357.0	140.9	143.0	1126.1	15.6	254.9	2037.5
1963	371.9	150.4	134.8	1189.2	18.2	260.1	2124.6
1964	415.0	156.4	202.2	1210.6	24.9	315.4	2324.5
1965	478.7	182.5	245.6	1234.2	26.1	343.8	2510.9

Notes and Sources: as for Table 11.1(a).

their exports through their policy of withholding a proportion of the realised price, producers were discouraged from making an effort to raise output. Bulk purchasing of colonial produce by Britain also had a similar outcome.[2] Finally, colonial populations increased as the impact of modern medicine on death rates began to be felt, a development which would eventually cause population explosions in the tropics, and therefore more produce, especially foodstuffs, was required for domestic consumption.[3] These varied factors impinged on many commodities exported from the tropical colonies and to varying degrees inhibited a rapid rise in export volumes, as shown in Table 11.2. Prices eased in the 1950s and in many cases were lower in 1960 than in 1951. On the other hand, export volumes generally rose to new heights as investments paid off and the lagged effect of high prices between 1946 and 1951 was felt. Increased volumes only partly offset falling or sluggish prices, and it was clear that the boom in colonial export values was over by 1952.

The value of imports also rose substantially during the 1946 to 1951 trade boom and in some cases was due more to increased volumes of imports than prices, though both rose (Table 11.3). Import volumes for some items in the years 1946 to 1951 were below pre-war levels which gave rise to complaints that the colonies suffered a shortage of imports, especially in 1946 and 1947, and particularly in relation to export

Table 11.2 Unit values and quantum of principal commodities exported from the colonial empire 1938 and 1946–64 (1947–9 = 100)

Year	Cocoa/Gold Coast		Sugar/ Mauritius		Coffee/ Uganda		Tea/ Ceylon		Bananas/ Jamaica	
	UV	Q	UV	Q	UV	Q	UV	Q	UV	Q
1938	12	120	33	84	25	51	36	81	33	393
1946	29	108	85	63	61	114	64	99	77	96
1947	66	82	88	80	79	76	96	98	101	91
1948	141	98	104	104	92	137	97	101	104	101
1949	93	120	108	117	130	87	107	101	95	108
1950	146	122	118	127	280	115	123	102	100	95
1951	189	105	127	137	335	158	128	104	106	61
1952	178	97	137	137	335	143	112	107	126	66
1953	170	108	138	151	346	129	120	114	151	157
1954	284	98	127	159	416	126	152	123	126	192
1955	228	94	133	142	290	270	161	124	126	180
1956	157	107	141	159	273	223	146	119	129	185
1957	140	119	139	177	275	305	135	126	130	188
1958	224	91	139	156	283	285	135	140	137	164
1959	191	117	141	154	227	320	134	131	131	170
1960	156	140	146	91	n.a.	n.a.	131	140	129	168
1961	123	184	140	153	145	374	129	145	123	171
1962	114	192	134	168	199	393	125	154	113	180
1963	121	185	176	184	200	526	123	156	n.a.	n.a.
1964	128	174	176	155	275	499	123	156	n.a.	n.a.
Base 1947–9 average	£6.97 per cwt	4.388m cwt	£1.30 per cwt	7.338m cwt	£4.67 per cwt	552000 cwt	£153.74 per 000 lb	293m lbs	£366.01 per 000 stems	6.059m stems

UV, unit value (export value divided by export volume).
Q, quantity exported.
[a]Blister copper; 1938, 1946–53 Northern Rhodesia; 1954 Federation of Rhodesia and Nyasaland; 1964 Zambia.
Source: *Statistical Abstract for the British Commonwealth, 1946–57*; *Yearbook of International Trade Statistics, 1958–64*.

earnings, population growth and development needs.[4] Many colonies relied on imports for both capital and consumer goods and staple foodstuffs such as rice, flour and fish. Prices of imports eased during the 1950s and quantities of most imports rose, some substantially. Import restrictions and exchange controls were relaxed in the later 1950s as sterling moved towards convertibility in 1958. Thus the picture which emerges is one of quite severe supply constraints in the late 1940s and early 1950s gradually becoming less of a problem during the mid- to late 1950s.

These movements in export and import prices produced a favourable

Table 11.2 (continued)

Year	Groundnuts/ Nigeria		Palm Oil/ Nigeria		Palm Kernels/ Nigeria		Copra/ Ceylon		Rubber/ Malaya	
	UV	Q	UV	Q	UV	Q	UV	Q	UV	Q
1938	19	61	17	80	21	92	14	203	62	56
1946	52	98	38	70	45	81	51	111	113	55
1947	64	87	48	87	59	93	86	86	98	101
1948	105	84	121	96	105	96	95	154	106	104
1949	131	129	131	117	135	111	119	63	96	95
1950	126	108	130	119	123	121	147	60	263	117
1951	188	48	175	103	190	102	173	54	407	122
1952	223	89	190	115	183	110	98	117	246	95
1953	200	112	120	139	166	119	132	60	177	88
1954	183	146	120	143	148	136	120	131	172	97
1955	153	135	134	126	133	127	102	194	278	106
1956	162	153	153	102	136	133	162	166	249	105
1957	175	103	155	114	133	119	116	100	231	107
1958	138	175	138	118	140	130	128	80	209	72
1959	145	170	140	127	181	127	147	123	264	81
1960	173	113	134	126	181	123	136	83	287	80
1961	171	169	149	114	146	121	106	157	219	82
1962	160	181	140	82	139	108	100	206	208	84
1963	156	210	138	87	158	117	112	123	196	89
1964	165	186	149	92	160	116	116	166	185	90
Base 1947–9 average	£38.18 per ton	293000 tons	£53.76 per ton	145000 tons	£33.21 per ton	340000 tons	£61.87 per ton	35000 tons	£43.73 per ton	2114m lb

trend in most colonies' terms of trade, shown for the ten colonies with the highest trade values (excluding Hong Kong) in Tables 11.4 and 11.5. As can be seen from Table 11.4, a peak in the favourable movement of terms of trade was reached in 1953 or 1954 before weaker export prices led to a decline. In some colonies the improvement between 1946 and 1954 was substantial. Table 11.5, compiled from United Nations data, shows the slow decline in terms of trade from the peaks of 1954 and 1955 (except for Mauritius where there was a surge in sugar prices in 1963) to the mid-1960s, by which point most colonies had gained independence. In theory, rising terms of trade should have enabled the colonial economies to increase substantially their import volumes. Some did so, but it was a problem of post-war colonial economic development that during the ten years of rising terms of trade there were shortages and restrictions on imports which led to large trade surpluses being built up. As the supply constraints eased in the mid-1950s, the terms of trade

Table 11.2 (continued)

Year	Sisal/ Tanganyika		Cotton/ Uganda		Tin/ Malaya		Copper/ N. Rhodesia		Manganese/ Gold Coast	
	UV	Q	UV	Q	UV	Q	UV	Q	UV	Q
1938	20	88	22	148	37	137	37	119	62	50
1946	49	97	66	81	66	17	53	80	66	117
1947	79	83	73	93	79	72	87	83	84	90
1948	106	102	111	64	105	106	105	101	95	96
1949	116	115	116	143	116	123	108	117	120	113
1950	138	103	125	128	134	183	137	140	157	109
1951	231	123	217	127	206	145	176	121	199	123
1952	190	137	206	139	186	144	201	148	244	122
1953	104	147	131	123	147	138	215	146	260	114
1954	90	145	138	144	137	157	183	148	249	70
1955	80	151	139	113	141	159	261	125	214	83
1956	81	161	133	139	151	164	246	110	247	97
1957	72	158	135	124	147	158	161	124	312	98
1958	73	172	122	142	144	86	148	94	375	79
1959	87	181	108	137	156	99	185	103	286	81
1960	n.a.	n.a.	n.a.	n.a.	155	171	195	97	260	84
1961	97	174	125	128	181	166	182	95	349	59
1962	99	190	119	66	177	182	184	77	257	73
1963	146	186	110	125	176	189	184	86	231	59
1963	145	181	116	131	237	159	194	97	194	76
Base 1947–9 average	£72.28 per ton	115316 tons	£96.07 per ton	109m tons	£503.07 per ton	44690 tons	£10644 per ton	155000 tons	£4.49 per ton	653000 tons

fell and moved unfavourably for at least a decade. Thus, just at the time when the colonial authorities were attempting to speed up the process of economic development – from the mid-1950s as independence approached – this effort was hampered in many colonies by adverse movements in the terms of trade.

Diversification of exports was a central problem in colonial economic development. It was often recognised that the colonies relied on a very narrow export base which made them highly vulnerable to price fluctuations in the world market. On the other hand, post-war colonial economic policy tended to emphasise the importance of producing more of the existing range of primary commodities. The extent to which this problem was successfully overcome in the post-war era can be judged from the evidence presented in Table 11.6. This shows for a number of colonies the three most valuable exports as a proportion of the value of all exports and it also indicates those cases where a single export commo-

Table 11.3 Unit Values and Quantum of Selected Imports to Colonial Empire, 1938 and 1946–57 (1947–9=100)

Year	Commodities/colonies							
	Cotton piece goods/ Nigeria		Cotton piece goods/ Ceylon		Cement/ Gold Coast		Cement/ Tanganyika	
	UV	Q	UV	Q	UV	Q	UV	Q
1938	25	50	16	85	45	46	35	42
1946	74	60	104	46	96	56	80	29
1947	99	76	116	76	98	63	90	59
1948	102	90	101	99	101	97	107	91
1949	99	134	82	125	101	139	103	151
1950	97	107	84	130	109	153	103	199
1951	126	87	113	108	167	191	147	205
1952	124	147	97	107	173	150	169	194
1953	107	123	83	112	144	210	138	230
1954	99	124	77	101	136	201	128	198
1955	91	148	70	91	148	254	123	284
1956	100	107	69	112	151	260	124	185
1957	100	107	75	99	153	236	132	173
Base 1947–9 average	£97.071 per 000 yds^2	38.675 msq yds	£113.21 per 000 yds	74.891 myds	£5.951 per ton	16000 tons	£7.84 per ton	55576 tons

UV, unit value (import value divided by import volume) Q, quantity imported.
Source: as for Table 11.1(a)

dity dominated. Some export diversification took place in five colonies: Gold Coast, Nigeria, Tanganyika, Nyasaland and British Honduras; in seven cases (including Ceylon which ceased being a colony in 1948) there was no significant change: Sierra Leone, Uganda, Mauritius, Barbados, Trinidad and the Federation of Rhodesia and Nyasaland or Northern Rhodesia; and in four colonies export concentration increased: Kenya, Malaya, Fiji and Jamaica. Taking a longer-term perspective, Table 11.6 can be compared with Table 8.10. The main conclusion to be drawn is that in only two cases was there a significant move towards export diversification between the 1920s and the 1950s: Nyasaland and Nigeria. For all of the other colonial economies the rise of export industries was very narrowly based and in a number of colonies, increasingly so.

As noted in Chapter 10, at the end of the Second World War Britain was a more important market for the tropical colonies than pre-war (Table 11.7): Britain absorbed 37 per cent of the colonies' exports in 1946 in contrast to 28 per cent in 1938. Largely this was the result of wartime shipping and marketing arrangements and it applied to all

Table 11.3 (continued)

Year	Iron and steel/ Malaya		Iron and steel/ Trinidad		Footwear/ Nigeria		Footwear/ Jamaica	
	UV	Q	UV	Q	UV	Q	UV	Q
1938	37	175	54	126	25	34	28	179
1946	84	22	84	55	106	31	95	80
1947	105	92	74	94	137	56	111	110
1948	97	79	110	80	82	103	104	101
1949	97	129	116	125	81	141	85	89
1950	92	159	126	104	101	105	97	143
1951	135	256	124	100	117	185	129	94
1952	148	432	154	156	128	167	137	81
1953	124	396	151	149	132	258	122	107
1954	109	432	143	143	112	349	121	100
1955	110	536	135	192	121	347	113	111
1956	122	579	160	168	121	458	132	101
1957	139	542	161	223	139	352	136	114
Base 1947–9 average	£49.95 per ton	36599 tons	£49.06 per ton	30801 tons	£4.36 per doz pairs	11300 doz pairs	£6.45 per doz pairs	63490 doz pairs

regions except the Pacific. During the price boom 1946–51 the United Kingdom declined in importance as a market for the colonies but increased again when the boom was over and North American demand for tropical products subsided. The second post-war peak in UK share of colonial exports was reached in the mid-1950s (1953 for all colonies taken together) but was lower than in 1946. From 1953 the share of the UK in colonial exports declined steadily reaching its 1938 level in 1959 and continuing to contract into the 1960s. UK demand for tropical produce was not growing strongly as its overall rate of growth was subdued, and its industries made greater use of synthetics. In the 1950s Britain declined to renew the marketing arrangements (long-term contracts, bulk purchases and so forth) which had operated after the war and might have attracted more colonial produce to Britain. In 1961 the British government applied to join the European Economic Community (EEC) which signalled a reorientation of trade policy away from the Commonwealth.

Immediately after the end of the war UK exports to the colonies were constrained by domestic production difficulties and higher priority given to home consumption. Gradually the UK share of colonial imports rose (to an all-time peak of 32.1 per cent in 1949) as dollar-saving import restrictions prevented the colonies expanding their imports from out-

Table 11.3 (continued)

Year	Commodities/colonies							
	Motor vehicles/ Jamaica		Motor vehicles/ Tanganyika		Flour/ Br. Guina		Flour/ Gold Coast	
	UV	Q	UV	Q	UV	Q	UV	Q
1938	42	70	42	37	28	90	34	61
1946	79	45	66	25	68	78	67	45
1947	108	113	68	95	104	95	100	59
1948	92	106	108	118	106	105	105	66
1949	99	82	124	87	89	99	95	176
1950	111	70	128	71	91	124	107	192
1951	117	60	134	93	96	107	120	225
1952	110	66	169	91	104	127	128	244
1953	115	83	174	53	106	121	132	259
1954	92	180	162	59	92	144	125	278
1955	117	192	151	159	84	142	126	300
1956	144	227	164	137	84	133	116	312
1957	129	253	163	122	86	147	114	447
Base 1947–49 average	£389.87 per vehicle	2056 veh.	£367.28 per vehicle	3065 veh.	£2.05 cwt	361000 cwt	£2.56 per cwt	223000 cwt

side of the sterling area. Dollar restrictions eased during the Korean War boom and the UK share fell; however, as the 'dollar gap' re-emerged in 1952, colonial imports were once again drawn increasingly from Britain. Only in the later 1950s and early 1960s when the dollar imbalance in world trade disappeared altogether and independence opened new horizons for ex-colonial economies, did the share of the UK drop significantly.

In the late 1930s the tropical colonies purchased about 10 per cent of Britain's exports and about the same proportion in 1946. Just as Britain became a more important supplier of imports for the colonies in the post-war boom so they took a greater share of UK exports, reaching a peak of 16.4 per cent in 1952 (Table 11.8). Perhaps the colonies were an easier market for British exporters than either North America or Continental Europe. There was a gradual decline during the 1950s but even in 1965 the colonies (or ex-colonies as most of them were by then) accounted for a slightly greater share of Britain's exports than they did in 1938 or earlier. At the peak in 1952 the colonies were as important a market to Britain in terms of share of total exports as Australia, New Zealand and South Africa together and more important than North America or the future EEC. By 1960, however, whilst the colonies were

Table 11.3 (continued)

Year	Rice/ Malaya		Rice/ Trinidad		Fish/ Gold Coast		Fish/ Jamaica	
	UV	Q	UV	Q	UV	Q	UV	Q
1938	19	204	35	163	21	221	27	118
1946	51	35	83	91	78	12	96	93
1947	69	60	91	82	106	72	96	100
1948	117	113	119	103	96	84	100	98
1949	115	127	90	115	97	144	104	101
1950	115	111	98	113	98	254	123	72
1951	125	137	104	123	102	306	128	81
1952	143	130	163	118	105	339	141	61
1953	159	135	173	165	103	484	156	75
1954	133	79	181	121	101	434	189	98
1955	98	135	174	155	92	741	149	107
1956	102	146	169	155	85	672	163	110
1957	108	130	169	223	93	666	162	128
Base 1947–59 average	£2.05 percwt	7971 000 cwt	£1.53 per cwt	238 000 cwt	£9.97 percwt	30632 cwt	£4.35 per cwt	224 000 cwt

still as important as the 'southern dominions' or North America, the EEC took 15.4 per cent of UK exports compared with the colonies' 14.5 per cent, and by 1965 the proportions were 20 per cent and 11.5 per cent respectively.

As a source of imports for the UK the colonies became much more important during the Second World War as other sources of supply were restricted, even despite the loss of Malaya and Hong Kong. In 1946, with the eastern colonies supplying nearly 5 per cent of Britain's imports alone, the colonies' share increased to 11.4 per cent compared with 6.8 per cent in 1938. The desire to purchase as much as possible from the sterling area for balance of payments reasons, combined with bulk purchasing (and other arrangements) of colonial food exports, raised the share of colonial sources in the United Kingdom's imports to a peak of 14.3 per cent in 1952. At this point the colonies were a more important source of supply to Britain than either the southern dominions or Western Europe (though less important than North America). There was a gradual decline in the colonial share during the 1950s as Britain's imports of manufactured goods increased more rapidly than its imports of tropical primary produce. Indeed, manufactured goods were the fastest growing sector in world trade in the 1950s but not one in

Table 11.4 Terms of Trade, 1947–57, selected colonies (1947–49=100)

Colony		1946	1947	1948	1949	1950	1951	1952	1953	1954	1955	1956	1957
Gold Coast	E	33.8	68.5	135.7	91.2	147.1	189.8	183.0	178.2	275.6	224.0	165.1	155.1
	I	75.2	97.9	103.5	99.3	100.1	125.7	130.1	112.7	108.2	105.0	106.6	105.5
	T	45	70	131	96	147	151	141	158	255	213	155	147
Nigeria	E	41.5	62.9	116.1	125.4	129.9	195.1	192.9	166.2	188.2	159.9	148.3	148.0
	I	83.7	99.5	100.5	100.8	89.5	130.0	131.4	114.8	106.4	99.5	106.8	108.1
	T	50	63	116	124	145	150	147	145	177	161	139	137
Tanganyika	E	59.6	79.7	100.8	120.2	159.2	236.9	225.0	176.6	186.8	153.0	161.0	160.2
	I	77.2	86.9	109.0	104.2	99.7	132.7	141.2	123.5	101.5	103.0	105.1	118.6
	T	77	92	92	115	160	179	159	143	184	149	153	135
Kenya	E	61.9	82.5	102.4	115.3	165.7	220.0	196.7	176.6	187.1	173.1	177.7	169.3
	I	76.2	93.1	110.1	96.7	100.8	125.5	134.0	111.0	98.5	104.2	105.6	106.9
	T	81	89	93	119	164	175	147	158	190	166	168	158
N. Rhodesia[a]	E	55.7	89.0	103.2	107.5	140.8	187.7	200.5	209.9	n.a.	n.a.	n.a.	n.a.
	I	88.7	97.0	103.3	100.2	105.7	131.1	133.1	128.2	n.a.	n.a.	n.a.	n.a.
	T	63	92	100	107	133	143	151	164	n.a.	n.a.	n.a.	n.a.
Mauritius	E	85.4	88.2	104.1	108.3	118.0	127.3	137.3	137.8	126.8	132.9	141.2	139.0
	I	62.7	94.2	108.2	97.7	111.0	132.3	138.7	145.3	126.6	111.7	98.5	99.1
	T	136	93	96	111	106	96	99	95	100	119	143	140
Ceylon	E	75.4	97.6	96.9	105.5	141.1	171.7	133.8	137.6	155.0	163.1	151.2	142.8
	I	70.2	99.5	104.4	95.5	99.5	115.0	134.3	127.9	117.1	106.8	103.5	103.4
	T	107	98	93	110	142	149	100	108	132	153	146	138
Malaya	E	100.0	91.8	107.1	100.9	226.1	345.6	222.7	165.6	160.0	235.8	216.6	203.3
	I	101.0	91.4	109.4	105.6	118.9	130.1	133.4	129.3	111.5	135.2	101.8	107.4
	T	99	100	98	96	190	266	167	128	143	174	213	189
Jamaica	E	83.9	96.1	106.7	96.3	104.8	119.3	136.7	151.1	141.2	153.0	138.0	154.2
	I	81.5	99.8	101.8	97.7	112.2	131.1	122.3	124.5	148.9	136.5	144.1	141.1
	T	103	96	105	99	93	91	112	121	95	112	96	109
Br.Guiana	E	81.3	91.4	99.7	109.5	121.5	135.0	164.3	173.8	167.5	166.1	181.8	206.7
	I	72.4	99.0	101.6	99.1	107.5	137.5	137.9	107.9	103.8	100.6	95.7	95.6
	T	112	92	98	110	113	98	119	161	161	165	190	216

E: Weighted index of the unit value of principal exports.
I: Weighted index of the unit value of principal imports.
T: Terms of trade – E divided I × 100.
[a] Northern Rhodesia joined with Southern Rhodesia and Nyasaland in the Federation of Rhodesia and Nyasaland, 1953–63
Source: as for Table 11.1.

Table 11.5 Terms of Trade, selected colonies[a] 1952–64, (1958=100)

Colony		1952	1953	1954	1955	1956	1957	1958	1959	1960	1961	1962	1963	1964
Gold Coast	E	82	79	111	94	76	72	100	89	78	63	58	59	63
	I	115	104	99	97	100	101	100	103	106	106	102	99	103
	T	71	76	112	97	76	71	100	86	74	59	57	60	61
Nigeria	E	121	106	118	104	98	99	100	105	106	99	94	99	101
	I	121	108	101	99	101	103	100	98	103	103	102	108	111
	T	100	98	117	105	97	96	100	107	103	96	92	92	91
Tanganyika	E	n.a.	n.a.	123	120	111	107	100	105	110	106	107	123	125
	I	n.a.	n.a.	105	101	102	100	100	99	104	100	95	104	114
	T	n.a.	n.a.	117	119	109	107	100	106	106	106	113	118	110
Kenya	E	n.a.	n.a.	118	121	112	108	100	104	104	99	96	100	101
	I	n.a.	n.a.	94	97	102	104	100	101	104	94	98	104	104
	T	n.a.	n.a.	126	125	110	104	100	103	100	105	98	96	97
Uganda	E	n.a.	n.a.	128	112	108	108	100	88	81	82	81	86	99
	I	n.a.	n.a.	103	101	104	101	100	101	106	104	99	115	112
	T	n.a.	n.a.	124	111	104	107	100	87	76	79	82	75	88
Federation of	E	118	123	118	152	142	113	100	111	112	108	106	109	n.a.
Rhodesia &	I	97	94	92	94	96	98	100	97	99	103	103	106	n.a.
Nyasaland	T	122	131	128	162	148	115	100	114	113	105	103	103	n.a.
Mauritius	E	96	102	97	96	101	102	100	102	110	102	103	131	112
	I	117	116	99	101	98	99	100	95	94	94	92	95	97
	T	82	88	98	95	103	103	100	107	117	109	112	138	116
Ceylon	E	96	98	109	114	107	102	100	104	104	95	91	93	93
	I	127	114	106	98	102	114	100	100	101	104	101	109	112
	T	76	86	103	116	105	90	100	104	103	91	90	85	83
Malaya	E	122	91	87	125	116	110	100	120	127	105	102	99	101
	I	123	120	107	98	101	105	100	98	101	99	97	101	107
	T	99	76	81	128	115	105	100	122	126	106	105	98	94
Jamaica	E	85	87	88	94	94	108	100	98	97	97	96	114	108
	I	88	82	81	89	95	98	100	102	102	107	116	116	119
	T	97	106	109	106	99	110	100	96	95	91	83	98	91

Notes: as for Table 11.4.
[a] Ceylon became independent in 1948 and Malaya and Ghana in 1957.
Source: United Nations, *Yearbook of International Trade Statistics, 1952–1964*.

Table 11.6 The three principal exports of selected colonies as a percentage of all exports of domestic produce, 1947–9 to 1962–4

Colony	1947–9		1955–7		1962–4	
Gold Coast	Cocoa	81.9	Cocoa	68.0	Cocoa	66.5
	Manganese ore	7.9	Lumber	11.1	Lumber	13.1
	Lumber	4.5	Diamonds	9.1	Diamonds	5.5
	Total	94.3	Total	88.2	Total	85.1
Nigeria	Cocoa	25.5	Cocoa	19.8	Cocoa	18.9
	Palm kernels	19.4	Groundnuts	18.4	Groundnuts	18.5
	Groundnuts	18.0	Palm kernels	15.0	Petroleum	12.3
	Total	62.9	Total	53.2	Total	49.7
Sierra Leone	Palm kernels	42.6	Iron ore	33.3	Diamonds	61.3
	Diamonds	27.5	Diamonds	31.1	Iron ore	19.9
	Iron ore	19.3	Palm kernels	20.0	Palm kernels	9.5
	Total	89.4	Total	84.4	Total	90.7
Uganda	Cotton	64.7	Coffee	44.8	Coffee	53.9
	Coffee	15.6	Cotton	41.5	Cotton	25.0
	Tobacco	3.3	Oil seed cake	3.3	Tea	4.1
	Total	83.6	Total	89.6	Total	83.0
Kenya	Sisal	21.3	Coffee	41.6	Coffee	28.8
	Coffee	15.5	Tea	10.3	Sisal	13.9
	Tea	7.3	Sisal	7.6	Tea	13.2
	Total	44.1	Total	59.5	Total	55.9
Tanganyika	Sisal	56.6	Sisal	25.6	Sisal	33.3
	Cotton	9.3	Coffee	18.2	Cotton	15.4
	Coffee	7.4	Cotton	16.6	Coffee	13.5
	Total	73.3	Total	60.4	Total	62.2

Table 11.6 (continued)

Colony	1947–9		1955–7		1962–4	
Nyasaland	Tobacco	59.9	n.a.		Tobacco[c]	36.7
	Tea	29.1			Tea[c]	29.0
	Cotton	6.7			Groundnuts[c]	9.7
	Total	95.7			Total[c]	75.4
Federation of Rhodesia & Nyasaland	n.a.		Copper	61.6	Copper[d]	55.6
			Tobacco	16.4	Tobacco[d]	20.8
			Asbestos	4.9	Asbestos[d]	3.4
			Total	82.9	Total[d]	79.8
North Rhodesia	Copper	85.0	n.a.		Copper[c]	90.8
	Zinc	5.5			Zinc[c]	3.0
	Tobacco	2.1			Tobacco[c]	1.7
	Total	92.6			Total	95.5
Mauritius	Sugar	96.3	Sugar	99.3	Sugar	95.2
	Rum	2.9	Other foodstuffs	0.5	Molasses	2.9
	Aloe fibre	0.1			Tea	1.3
	Total	99.3	Total	99.8	Total	99.4
Ceylon	Tea	65.0	Tea	63.8	Tea	64.5
	Rubber	14.4	Rubber	18.5	Rubber	15.8
	Coconut oil	9.1	Coconut oil	5.0	Coconut oil	6.6
	Total	88.5	Total	87.3	Total	86.9
Malaya[a]	Rubber	50.6	Rubber	52.8	Rubber	49.9
	Tin	12.7	Tin	11.3	Tin	24.4
	Coconut oil	2.8	Coconut oil	1.8	Iron ore	6.2
	Total	66.1	Total	65.9	Total	80.5

Table 11.6 (continued)

Colony	1947–9		1955–7		1962–4	
Fiji	Sugar	63.8	Sugar	63.0	Sugar	80.0
	Copra	16.6	Coconut oil	22.9	Coconut oil	11.0
	Bananas	1.7	Bananas	3.1	Copra	2.4
	Total	82.1	Total	89.0	Total	93.4
Barbados	Sugar	59.9	Sugar	76.5	Sugar	73.7
	Molasses	27.2	Molasses	11.8	Molasses	12.0
	Rum	9.1	Rum	5.6	Rum	4.5
	Total	96.2	Total	93.9	Total	90.2
Jamaica	Sugar	31.2	Bauxite[b]	34.4	Bauxite	44.9
	Bananas	20.2	Sugar	30.3	Sugar	26.6
	Rum	17.9	Bananas	13.3	Bananas	6.4
	Total	69.3	Total	78.0	Total	78.9
Trinidad	Petroleum	69.0	Petroleum	77.4	Petroleum	84.2
	Sugar	13.4	Sugar	10.4	Sugar	7.1
	Cocoa	5.7	Cocoa	3.7	Cocoa	1.2
	Total	88.1	Total	91.5	Total	92.5
Br. Guiana	Sugar	49.1	Sugar	47.1	Sugar	37.8
	Bauxite	24.5	Bauxite	29.1	Bauxite	32.7
	Rice	6.5	Rice	11.0	Rice	12.6
	Total	80.1	Total	87.2	Total	83.1
Br. Honduras	Lumber	58.4	Lumber	55.9	Sugar	32.5
	Chicle gum	22.1	Fruit	23.1	Fruit	24.2
	Coconuts	3.1	Sugar	8.3	Lumber	17.1
	Total	83.6	Total	87.3	Total	73.8

[a] Total Exports.
[b] Including alumina.
[c] 1964 only.
[d] 1962, 1963 only.
Source: as for Table 11.1(a)

Table 11.7 Colonial empire: imports from and exports to the United Kingdom as a percentage of total colonial imports and exports, 1938 and 1946 to 1965

Year	Total colonial trade (£m)		West Africa (%)		East Africa (%)		Central Africa (%)		Eastern (%)		Pacific (%)		Caribbean (%)		All Colonies (%)	
	Imp	Exp	Imp	Exp	Imp	Exp	Imp	Exp	Imp	Exp	Imp	Exp	Imp	Exp	Imp	Exp
1938	222.1	182.6	55.9	47.5	35.6	24.1	48.1	43.7	16.2	19.8	32.8	47.2	36.3	49.2	22.4	27.6
1946	345.4	328.6	62.7	61.3	36.1	30.2	34.8	45.3	12.4	29.6	23.8	23.5	25.9	49.4	23.9	37.0
1947	528.8	498.6	50.0	61.4	36.8	26.9	30.0	52.7	18.2	17.2	22.2	30.8	22.5	52.6	25.1	30.6
1948	694.6	652.3	55.4	56.7	50.6	37.5	47.1	63.0	17.9	15.8	33.8	35.9	35.2	47.0	29.4	31.0
1949	832.2	737.2	54.9	63.7	51.3	33.7	52.9	57.4	18.6	15.6	32.6	31.6	40.9	43.2	32.1	31.1
1950	1041.2	1218.7	58.6	60.9	53.8	33.7	50.5	50.1	15.9	13.2	31.9	35.5	42.1	37.4	28.3	25.0
1951	1487.4	1651.2	52.8	60.4	42.5	32.2	46.7	55.2	16.5	18.5	32.8	45.0	39.3	39.5	26.3	28.3
1952	1407.5	1318.4	54.0	63.2	46.8	31.7	47.3	63.1	19.5	18.9	34.3	36.5	38.3	43.9	30.8	33.5
1953	1305.5	1210.6	55.3	63.2	50.4	29.9	50.9	57.9	18.6	16.4	34.5	57.3	40.7	51.6	31.7	34.0
1954	1280.9	1285.9	47.8	57.0	43.6	28.4	42.6	55.7	16.9	17.7	32.6	42.2	40.5	47.3	29.1	33.7
1955	1500.5	1433.6	47.8	55.9	43.0	25.1	43.0	54.0	17.2	19.4	36.8	43.2	40.1	44.1	29.6	32.1
1956	1650.6	1485.0	46.4	51.0	43.5	25.0	40.9	58.3	16.7	18.1	30.6	40.4	37.2	41.8	28.3	30.8
1957	1795.0	1486.2	43.1	50.4	37.6	23.4	37.8	47.1	16.8	17.3	31.6	48.9	38.2	39.5	27.0	28.4
1958	1689.4	1426.1	43.7	46.7	38.9	24.8	38.1	48.2	16.9	18.6	34.0	49.4	36.8	34.9	27.6	28.9
1959	1778.4	1623.3	44.6	41.6	38.7	25.7	37.3	46.0	15.6	16.1	26.5	50.6	35.3	38.2	26.6	27.2
1960	1990.7	1774.6	41.1	41.9	34.6	23.2	33.4	44.2	15.2	16.4	25.3	50.2	33.0	35.7	25.1	26.8
1961[a]	2013.4	1747.7	38.6	39.2	36.7	24.1	33.6	47.0	16.0	16.5	28.3	53.2	29.4	27.4	25.0	26.2
1962[b]	2007.0	1756.3	36.4	37.1	34.8	26.3	33.1	41.9	15.0	15.9	27.4	45.9	24.8	27.5	22.8	24.8
1963[b]	2099.8	190.9	35.1	36.6	33.4	24.3	32.5	38.8	14.7	16.1	23.4	48.7	23.2	28.2	21.8	24.5
1964[c]	2280.5	2058.8	30.9	34.7	32.9	20.7	24.9	25.6	13.8	17.1	21.8	42.5	21.5	26.6	20.2	23.5
1965[c]	2459.8	2236.0	29.7	34.1	32.4	22.0	25.5	30.2	14.6	14.4	22.6	49.1	20.4	22.5	20.7	22.2

West Africa: Gambia, Sierra Leone, Gold Coast, Nigeria.
East Africa: Kenya, Uganda, Tanganyika, Zanzibar.
Central Africa: Nyasaland, North Rhodesia, South Rhodesia; Federation of Rhodesia and Nyasaland.
Eastern: Mauritius, Ceylon, Malaya, Singapore, Hong Kong.
Pacific: Fiji.
Caribbean: Barbados, British Guiana, British Honduras, Jamaica, Trinidad.
[a] Excluding British Honduras.
[b] Excluding British Honduras and British Guiana.
[c] Excluding British Honduras, British Guiana and Gambia.
Source: Statistical Abstract Commonwealth and Sterling Area, Nos. 70, 86 (1950–1965).

Table 11.8 United Kingdom: imports from and exports to colonial territories as a percentage of total UK imports and exports, 1938 and 1946 to 1965

Year	West Africa (%)		East Africa (%)		Central Africa (%)		Mediterranean (%)		Eastern (%)		Pacific (%)		Caribbean (%)		All Colonies (%)	
	Imp	Exp	Imp	Exp	Imp	Exp	Imp	Exp	Imp	Exp	Imp	Exp	Imp	Exp	Imp	Exp
1938	1.0	2.0	0.4	0.8	0.8	1.1	0.1	0.6	3.2	4.2	0.1	0.1	1.2	1.6	6.8	10.0
1946	2.8	2.2	0.7	1.1	1.3	1.0	0.1	1.1	4.6	4.0	0.1	0.1	1.9	1.2	11.4	10.7
1947	3.0	2.3	0.6	1.2	1.4	1.1	0.1	1.0	3.2	5.0	0.1	0.1	1.7	1.3	10.1	12.0
1948	3.7	2.8	0.8	1.8	1.7	1.3	0.1	0.9	3.5	4.8	0.2	0.1	1.6	1.6	11.6	13.3
1949	4.1	3.5	0.9	1.9	1.6	1.7	0.1	0.8	3.3	5.1	0.1	0.1	1.5	1.7	11.6	14.9
1950	3.9	2.9	1.0	1.5	1.7	1.5	0.1	0.7	4.1	4.9	0.2	0.1	1.4	1.7	12.4	13.2
1951	3.4	2.9	1.0	1.6	1.6	1.5	0.1	0.7	5.7	6.0	0.1	0.1	1.1	1.7	13.1	14.5
1952	4.3	3.7	1.1	2.0	2.4	1.7	0.2	0.8	4.6	6.1	0.2	0.1	1.6	2.0	14.3	16.4
1953	4.4	3.7	0.9	2.0	2.5	1.8	0.2	0.8	3.5	5.6	0.2	0.1	2.0	2.0	13.8	16.1
1954	4.4	3.4	0.9	2.0	2.6	1.7	0.2	0.8	3.9	4.9	0.3	0.1	2.0	1.9	14.2	14.9
1955	3.6	3.6	0.7	2.2	2.6	1.8	0.2	0.8	4.6	4.7	0.2	0.1	1.9	2.1	13.8	15.3
1956	3.0	3.5	0.8	1.8	2.8	1.8	0.2	1.0	4.6	4.9	0.1	0.1	2.0	2.5	13.4	15.5
1957	2.8	3.4	0.7	1.5	2.0	1.7	0.2	1.0	4.4	4.7	0.2	0.1	2.2	2.5	12.6	14.8
1958	2.9	3.4	0.8	1.3	1.8	1.6	0.2	0.9	4.4	4.5	0.2	0.2	1.9	2.7	12.3	14.6
1959	2.9	3.7	0.8	1.3	2.3	1.4	0.2	0.8	4.1	4.4	0.2	0.1	2.0	2.7	12.5	14.5
1960	2.4	3.8	0.7	1.3	2.3	1.3	0.2	0.8	3.8	4.5	0.1	0.1	1.8	2.8	11.4	14.5
1961	2.5	3.7	0.7	1.2	2.3	1.2	0.2	0.8	3.8	4.5	0.1	0.1	1.8	2.4	11.5	14.0
1962	2.3	2.9	0.8	1.1	2.1	1.1	0.3	0.8	3.8	4.5	0.1	0.1	1.6	2.1	11.0	12.6
1963	2.2	2.8	0.8	0.9	2.0	1.0	0.3	0.8	4.2	4.4	0.3	0.1	2.4	1.8	12.1	11.6
1964	2.0	2.7	0.7	1.1	1.8	0.9	0.2	0.7	3.7	4.2	0.2	0.1	2.0	1.9	10.7	11.6
1965	2.8	2.6	0.8	1.1	2.0	1.0	0.2	0.7	3.4	4.1	0.2	0.1	1.6	1.8	10.9	11.5

Notes and Source: as for Table 11.7.

which the tropical colonies participated to any significant extent. By 1960 the colonies supplied 11.5 per cent of Britain's import needs compared with 20.7 per cent which came from North America and 14.6 per cent from the EEC. Five years later the colonial share had fallen to 10.9 per cent while that of the EEC had risen to 17.3 per cent.

Thus the last ten years of British colonial rule witnessed a gradual decline in the trading ties between the colonies and the UK. Britain edged closer to Western Europe and North America as international trade in secondary goods and services increased. The colonies became relatively less attractive to British exporters looking for markets with higher per capita incomes and the value of colonial preferential tariffs was eroded by inflation. There was also more competition for Britain in supplying the colonial and ex-colonial markets from other industrial countries, including Japan, by the early 1960s. Britain's decision to apply for membership of the EEC both reflected its rapidly expanding trade with nearby Europe compared with that with its far-flung imperial trading partners, and reinforced this trend, even though Britain's entry to Europe was in fact delayed until 1973.

COLONIAL DEVELOPMENT AND WELFARE

It is against this background of colonial external trade and trade relations with Britain that the renewed efforts towards economic development and welfare in the colonies must be examined. The novel feature of colonial development policy after the war was that all development expenditure whether from colonial development and welfare grants, colonial government surplus revenues or loans raised by colonial governments in the London money market was to be within the context of a ten year plan for economic and social development drawn up by each colony and approved by the Colonial Office. In contrast to earlier colonial development measures, under the 1945 Colonial Development and Welfare (CDW) Act each colony was given an allocation to be spent over the following ten years. Of the £120 million available, £23.5 million was kept back for centrally administered schemes and research and a further £11.5 million was retained by the Colonial Office for contingencies. The remaining £85.5 million was divided up between the colonies. Such factors as 'the size and population of the territory, its known economic resources and possibilities, the present state of development, the development schemes known to exist or to be under contemplation, and the financial resources likely to be available locally', were the criteria used in this exercise.[5] The resulting distribution corrected 'distortions' in CDW aid which had arisen during the war: the West Indies, which received almost 40 per cent of CDW funds between 1940 and 1946 (see Table 10.9) now was allocated only 18 per cent, while the share of the

East and Central African colonies rose from 16 per cent to 25 per cent and that of the eastern colonies (excluding Ceylon) occupied by Japan during the war from virtually nothing to 11 per cent.

The colonies set about drawing up and submitting their ten-year plans. A summary of the twenty plans approved by March 1949 is shown in Table 11.9. Each colonial administration was told what its allocation of funds from CDW was and it then had to estimate how much surplus from government revenues over the next ten years could be added and how much could be raised in loans in London. Many colonies had accumulated reserves during the war when public expenditure had been cut severely and high post-war export prices promised swollen public coffers in the immediate future; and although the London loans market was still closed, interest rates in Britain were low and none of the colonies had been able to borrow for at least twelve years (and some had their public debt written down in 1940) so that their exposure to foreign debt was not great in the immediate post-war period. For the entire coloniale empire total foreign debt fell from £87.5 million in April 1940 to £78.8 million in March 1947 and a number of loans were converted to lower rates of interest.[6] In the light of this, many colonial governments took an optimistic view and assumed (on average) that they could treble their CDW allocation by the use of surplus revenues and future borrowing. On the expenditure side, most colonies put more emphasis on social development, especially education, health, water supply and sanitation and housing. The Colonial Office criticised some colonies for this, arguing that it would be a mistake to build up social services which carried recurrent costs which could not be afforded in later years.[7] Only strong economic growth, it was urged, would ensure that living standards were permanently raised. Some plans were revised to reflect this view and a number were delayed while the 'correct' balance between economic and social claims on limited funds was struck.

Ten-year planning was a method of making colonial governments arrange their objectives for economic and social development in an order of priority and considering where funds could be acquired apart from the CDW fund. The process also forced administrators to look ahead and so reduce the tendency to use development funds as a short-term response to crisis as had happened in the past. Additionally, they provided an assurance of continuing British government financial support which had been lacking at times in the 1930s. Drawing up plans at a time when shortages of materials, equipment and technicians ensured that few schemes could actually go ahead also meant that the enforced delays were used fruitfully. Yet despite these potential benefits, the planning process remained superficial – plans consisted of 'shopping lists' of desirable projects which often were not integrated with each other or the total economy. Colonial governments lacked the statistical

Table 11.9 Ten-year development plans (1949)

Colony	Total plan £000	CDW £000	%	Loan £000	%	Local sources £000	%	Communications (%)	Economic (%)	Social (%)	Admin. & Misc. (%)
Gambia	1980	1300	65.7	250	12.6	430	21.7	4.7	14.0	80.6	0.7
Nigeria	55000	23000	41.8	16000	29.1	16000	29.1	23.7	12.4	57.3	6.6
Sierra Leone	5256	2900	55.2	1400	26.6	956	18.2	22.0	17.0	53.9	7.1
Kenya	22000	5100	23.2	7000	31.8	9900	45.0	12.0	48.0	29.3	10.7
Tanganyika	18005	7150	39.7	6879	38.2	3976	22.1	38.6	12.5	39.7	9.2
Uganda	13863	2500	18.0	2000	14.4	9363	67.5	11.7	18.0	41.9	29.4
Zanzibar	1436	750	52.2	250	17.4	436	30.4	1.6	10.1	87.3	1.0
Aden	2503	800	32.0	660	26.4	1043	41.7	20.4	28.6	44.3	6.7
N. Rhodesia	17000	2728	16.0	9000	52.9	52.72	31.0	17.6	17.6	36.4	28.4
Nyasaland	8258	2303	27.9	2500	30.3	3455	41.8	20.9	18.6	45.6	14.9
Mauritius	7698	1786	23.2	3750	48.7	2162	28.1	4.3	25.3	69.1	1.3
Seychelles	325	250	76.9	–	–	75	23.1	8.7	20.2	68.8	2.3
St Helena	200	200	100.0	–	–	–	–	4.7	40.0	54.2	1.1
Cyprus	6350	1750	27.6	3000	47.2	1600	25.2	8.3	40.1	45.5	6.1
Barbados	3411	800	23.5	1000	29.3	1611	47.2	3.5	24.0	63.2	9.3
Br. Guiana	6646	2500	37.6	2757	41.5	1389	20.9	26.5	45.7	15.0	12.8
Jamaica	23030	6350	27.6	5282	22.9	11398	49.5	8.8	29.6	56.6	5.0
Grenada	1732	382	22.1	500	28.9	850	49.1	15.0	33.2	42.7	9.1
St Vincent	1106	346	31.3	35.9	32.5	401	36.3	23.4	31.3	37.5	7.8
N. Borneo	3653	1150	31.5	1300	35.6	1203	32.9	28.9	10.7	21.5	38.9
Total	199452	64045	32.1	63887	32.0	71520	35.9	18.9	22.5	47.1	11.5

Source: The Colonial Territories 1948–49, (Cmd 7715), pp.129–31.

information for national accounting which was essential for development planning and the setting of targets at a more sophisticated level. Most importantly, the plans did not contain any indication of how their aims were to be achieved, what significant policies were to be followed to ensure the various objectives were met, and what structural changes to the economy were required over the planning period. They lacked strategy. The largest plan, that for Nigeria, was criticised by a parliamentary select committee in 1948:

> The Plan does not propound a complete strategy of development; it is merely an aggregate of proposals for spending money . . . there is a list of 'certain fundamentals' which must be put right before any policy of wide economic development can be considered. Beginning with water supply, the list goes on with education, agriculture, forestry and veterinary services – in fact, through the whole gamut of possible development. The Plan concludes with a series of appendices in which the heads of several Departments put forward their suggestions for spending their share of the money. This is not planning.[8]

These characteristics of the ten-year plans were evident in the allocation of CDW funds over the following years. Table 11.10 summarises the type of schemes on which CDW funds were spent between 1946 and 1970. The bulk of funds were allocated to projects for social development, though the percentage fell slightly in the later period. Communications received a higher proportion from the mid-1950s than earlier. Most of this went on road construction though there was an increase in expenditure on port and harbour development due to a large development in Malta in 1959. Much of the expenditure on economic development was accounted for by agriculture, forestry and land maintenance and improvement, reflecting the overwhelmingly agrarian nature of the colonial economies. There was a rise in the proportion accounted for by industrial development in the late 1950s, but this did not reflect a general increased interest in schemes promoting industrialisation, rather several large loans made to Malta to convert its naval dockyard to commercial use and establish an industrial estate. Apart from Malta, the colonies did not receive significant funds from CDW for industrial development and many of the schemes which were assisted were for very small food-processing and cottage industries in the smaller colonies. Social welfare schemes were dominated by educational development which had been almost entirely neglected by colonial authorities and the imperial government up to the post-war period. Education for all age-groups was clearly regarded as a major priority and the establishment of university colleges in the colonies was a startling new development in the 1950s vitally aided by CDW funds. Problems of health –

Table 11.10 Allocation of colonial development and welfare funds (% based on cumulative totals), 1946–70

Category	Period				
	After 5 yrs (to Mar '51) (%)	After 10 yrs (to Mar '56) (%)	After 15 yrs (to Mar '61) (%)	After 20 yrs (to Mar '66) (%)	After 24 yrs (to Mar '70) (%)
Communications	14.5	18.7	24.1	23.3	23.5
Economic	23.8	21.6	21.7	23.6	22.0
Social	49.7	48.4	43.8	42.7	43.8
Admin. & Misc.	12.0	11.3	10.4	10.5	10.7
Communications					
Civil Aviation	15.9	18.1	12.1	11.7	12.6
Ports etc	2.1	4.1	10.4	12.7	12.4
Railways	0.9	0.5	1.1	1.1	1.0
Roads	78.4	76.1	75.8	73.4	72.3
Telecommun.	2.6	1.2	0.6	1.0	1.6
Economic					
Agric. & Vet.	57.5	62.1	57.6	53.5	54.3
Fisheries	3.1	2.5	2.0	2.3	2.5
Forestry	9.7	8.8	8.0	7.6	7.8
Irrig. & Drainage	15.1	14.1	12.5	9.7	9.4
Land Settlement	3.6	3.3	3.3	8.2	7.6
Soil Conservation	6.8	6.2	5.2	5.7	5.5
Elec. Power	2.3	1.2	0.8	0.8	1.1
Industrial	1.8	1.7	10.4	12.2	11.8
Social					
Education					
Primary	20.5	18.8	22.8	24.7	24.7
Tech & Voc	8.6	9.3	8.6	8.2	8.0
Higher	13.3	13.0	17.5	17.4	16.3
Total Ed	42.2	41.1	49.0	50.3	49.0
Med & Health	24.4	26.1	20.2	20.7	20.2
Housing & Town Plan	5.8	7.9	7.0	7.3	10.7
Nutrition	0.4	0.2	0.2	0.2	0.2
Water & Sanitation	21.2	19.9	18.3	16.3	15.3
Broadcasting	2.7	2.4	2.9	3.0	2.7
Welfare	3.1	2.3	2.5	2.2	2.0
Admin. & Misc.					
Admin. & Org.	1.8	1.4	0.9	1.2	1.4
Planning	6.3	6.0	6.3	5.6	5.2
OCS training	2.2	2.4	1.7	1.5	1.5
Miscellaneous	1.7	1.5	1.4	2.1	2.5

[a] Overseas Colonial Service.
Source: *Return of Schemes Colonial Development and Welfare 1946–7 to 1969–70.*

including medical services, water supply and sanitation – absorbed most of the rest of the funds available. Nutrition, which might well have been regarded as one of the key elements in tropical health, was virtually ignored.

On the whole, CDW funds were used in much the same way as under previous Acts, with the important exception of expenditure on education. These were the major problem areas of colonial development as understood by the administrators in the colonies and in Whitehall and they directed their efforts to alleviating them. As most of these funds came to the colonies in the form of grants, colonies obtained economic and social amenities they probably could not otherwise have afforded and which remained as a more or less permanent improvement in the colonies' economies, though the maintenance and staffing of these amenities after the grants ran out did cause problems to the newly independent countries in some instances. As seen in the previous chapter, the Treasury and the Colonial Office eventually settled on a figure of £120 million over the ten-years life of the 1945 CDW Act. Expenditure fell below the £12.0 million per annum target in the first few years because of shortages of materials, equipment and staff, though there was a further £17.5 million expended in the late 1940s on schemes under the 1940 Act which had been postponed during the war. In 1950 the total amount available under the Act was raised from £120 million to £140 million. After five years allocation of funds under the 1945 Act reached a total of only £50.4 million, but the pace accelerated in the early 1950s so that by March 1956 the amount allocated (adjusted for revisions and cancellations) totalled £129.2 million. Actual expenditure was below these levels, reaching £41.6 million in 1951 (barely £8 million per year) and £107.5 million in 1956 on development and welfare schemes, to which should be added £10.4 million spent on research schemes.

In 1954, as the 1945 Act neared its expiry date of March 1956, the secretary of state for the colonies, Alan Lennox-Boyd, requested a further £150 million to extend the Act to March 1960. Although this appeared to be a significant increase over the £140 million provided during the ten years 1946–55, it did 'not in fact represent much expansion in the current rate of development' and 'anything appreciably less would involve a slowing down of development'.[9] Such factors as inflation, rising population in the colonies, lower export prices and the greater needs for development now apparent should be taken into account. Lennox-Boyd further warned that failure to fully fund colonial development and welfare 'could do much harm in the colonies themselves to the Imperial connections . . . would expose us to international criticism . . . and would undoubtedly provoke a reaction at home, not only amongst the supporters of a forward policy of Colonial development . . . but also from the firms and industries with commercial connections in the Colonies'. The Treasury view, however, was that Britain could not afford as much as £150 million: 'Admittedly costs have been rising . . . but when and how do the Colonial Office see the process of constantly increasing grants being arrested?' The relevant consideration was not Britain's national income but its balance of payments problem and the fact that only one-third of the colonies' imports were purchased from the UK. Moreover, as colonies approached independence they 'should be encouraged to become less, not more, dependent of the UK for development finance'. Treasury interpreted the tendency to underspend previous CDW allocations – caused by shortages following the end of the war – as evidence that the absorptive capacity of the colonies for capital investment was below that put forward by the Colonial Office. Finally, even on the assumption that a lower figure was more appropriate, 'We think the colonies could do more from local resources than the Colonial Office allows'.[10] The Treasury view prevailed and the Colonial Office's proposal was scaled-down. The Colonial Development and Welfare Act was renewed to March 1960 with the provision of a further £80 million, bringing the total for the fourteen years 1946–7 to 1959–60 to £220 million or £15.7 million annually. The Act was renewed in 1959 to run to March 1964 with a further injection of £95m which brought the total from 1946 to £315 million. A final renewal brought the Act to an end in March 1970 with a total allocation from 1946 of £390m. Actual expenditure increased in line with total allocations: by 1960 the annual average from 1946 reached £14.2m and by 1965 £15.6m, after which it fell away as more colonies became independent, with the result that for the whole twenty-four-year period 1946 to 1970, £343.9 million was actually spent at an average annual rate of £14.3 million.[11]

How important were CDW funds in relation to these colonial governments' total revenues? It has already been noted that colonies expected at least to treble their CDW allocation by the use of surplus revenue and external borrowing. In the second half of the 1950s, government revenues fell as export values declined or stagnated, and borrowing in London became more expensive as British interest rates increased and, at times, impossible. CDW funds had the advantage of being reliable and predictable even if relatively small compared to total public expenditure. In a few colonies – the smallest ones, not surprisingly – CDW funds represented 15 to 20 per cent of total public revenues between 1946 and 1958, and in many other small colonies these funds accounted between 6 and 10 per cent. In the most populous colonies, however, public revenues were so much larger that even their greater amount of CDW aid did not add significantly to their resources overall. In Nigeria these funds represented 3.6 per cent of public revenues and in East Africa and the Far East the proportion was 1 per cent or less.

OTHER SOURCES OF DEVELOPMENT FINANCE

When the first ten-year plans were drawn up it was assumed that CDW, surplus government revenues and loans would each supply approximately one-third of the finance required. As further plans were approved and the earlier ones revised upwards the share of CDW finance fell to 18 per cent. Nearly all of the additional funds were expected to be found from colonial government surplus revenues which were rapidly expanding as prices soared, particularly during the Korean War crisis. In the next planning period, 1955–60, planned expenditure again increased and the provision of CDW funds fell further behind the anticipated expenditure on development so that they accounted for less than 10 per cent of planned outlays. Again the share of loans remained at one-third and government revenues were expected now to provide 56 per cent of the total cost of development. Not only did this represent a major shift in the burden of development finance from the centre to the local economies, but it was also based on the assumption that the boom in colonial revenues and expenditure would continue.[12] The colonies were in a relatively strong position as regards public finance by the end of the war, with surpluses from 1941–6 amounting to £30.5 million. (see Table 10.6). In the next few years, government revenues and expenditure shot up: between 1948 and 1951 public revenue by 105 per cent and public expenditure by 62 per cent (Table 11.11). In the early to mid-1950s, however, the rate of increase in revenue and expenditure slowed and in some colonies deficits were recorded for the first time since the beginning of the Second World War. This was due mainly to falls in commodity export prices, particularly in 1956. In the second half of the 1950s, colonial public revenues grew only modestly, by 22 per cent between 1956 and 1960 while budget surpluses were restored by reducing the growth of public expenditures to less than 20 per cent over this period. (Table 11.12). As a result, the development plans in the third period, 1960–64, relied on colonial government surpluses to a much reduced extent and the contribution of CDW rose to 30 per cent while that of government surpluses fell to 32 per cent, roughly restoring the shares in the initial set of plans. Thus, although more of the responsibility for financing colonial development was put on local resources in the 1950s, these proved very vulnerable to fluctuations in export earnings upon which most colonial government revenues directly or indirectly rested. This resulted in a shift back towards CDW finance in the early 1960s, but it is clear that colonial government revenues were playing a much more important role in colonial development in the post-war than in the inter-war period.

As CDW funds did not keep up with the ambitions of the ten-five-year plans, and in the early 1950s even colonies' surplus revenues were

Table 11.11 Public revenue and expenditure, 1947–56 (£000)

Colony group	1947	1948	1949	1950	1951	1952	1953	1954	1955	1956	Total
Revenue											
E.&C. Africa	28719	35654	51979	54803	67732	87096	97630	103877	124139	110141	761770
W. Africa	31454	38966	52565	57923	86137	102114	120956	154990	151161	179185	975451
Eastern	53561	52681	73585	90754	141032	150581	145822	150166	168963	168908	1196053
Caribbean	26051	28600	31032	33104	39400	42926	45533	50057	55269	62199	414171
Other	19018	20575	21102	23588	27661	32061	35107	39052	42319	52264	312747
Total	158803	176476	230263	260172	361962	414778	445048	498142	541851	572697	3660192
Change (%)		11.1	30.5	13.0	39.1	14.6	7.3	11.9	8.8	5.7	
Expenditure											
E.&C. Africa	27056	34614	49551	48278	63341	81976	101408	109779	123667	124085	763755
W. Africa	30905	38572	46028	52263	81652	91552	103968	117137	153474	175837	891388
Eastern	50225	55812	66516	72178	76026	124585	133256	148224	151487	164591	1042900
Caribbean	24811	27909	29237	32596	37741	41142	45918	48759	50925	64575	403613
Other	17994	19481	20319	22388	26668	30179	33249	37280	40740	52232	300530
Total	150991	176388	211651	227703	285428	369434	417799	461179	520293	581320	3402186
Change (%)		16.8	20.0	7.6	25.4	29.4	13.1	10.4	12.8	11.7	
Balance											
E.&C. Africa	1663	1040	2428	6525	4391	5120	-3778	-5902	472	-13944	-1985
W. Africa	549	394	6537	5660	4485	10562	16988	37853	-2313	3348	84063
Eastern	3336	-3131	7069	18576	65006	25996	12566	1942	17476	4317	153153
Caribbean	1240	691	1795	508	1659	1784	-385	1298	4344	-2376	10558
Other	1024	1094	783	1200	993	1882	1858	1772	1579	32	12217
Total	7812	88	18612	32469	76534	45344	27249	36963	21558	-8623	258006

Figures include colonial development and Welfare receipts and expenditure and grants-in-aid receipts. Loan expenditure and receipts from loans are excluded. East and Central Africa: Kenya, N. Rhodesia, Nyasaland, Tanganyika, Uganda, Zanzibar; W. Africa: Gambia, Gold Coast, Nigeria, Sierra Leone; Eastern: Malaya, Singapore, Brunei, N. Borneo, Sarawak, Hong Kong; Caribbean: Barbados, Br. Guiana, Br. Honduras, Jamaica, Antigua, St Kitts, Trinidad, Dominica, Grenada, St Lucia, St Vincent; Others: Cyprus, Malta, Fiji, Br. Solomon Is., Bahamas, Bermuda, Mauritius.
Source: The Colonial Territories 1939–62.

Table 11.12 Public revenue and expenditure, 1956–60 (£000)

	1956	1957	1958	1959	1960	Total
Revenue						
Africa	119438	122394	111089	111477	111991	576389
Caribbean	62199	71268	81116	92788	100494	407915
Other	93307	101917	102019	107418	124091	528751
Total	274944	295579	294274	311683	336.576	1513056
% Change		7.5	−0.4	5.9	8.0	
Expenditure						
Africa	133862	127947	110563	112263	114954	599589
Caribbean	64575	65289	78810	87759	103533	399966
Other	80695	91677	85062	97254	115077	469765
Total	279132	284913	274435	297276	333564	1469320
% Change		2.1	−3.7	8.3	12.2	
Balance						
Africa	−14424	−5553	526	−786	−2963	−23200
Caribbean	−2376	5979	2356	5079	−3039	7949
Other	12612	10240	16957	10164	9014	58987
Total	−4188	10666	19839	14407	3012	43736

Africa: Kenya, Uganda, Tanganyika, Zanzibar, Northern Rhodesia, Nyasaland, Gambia, Sierra Leone.
Caribbean: Antigua, Barbados, Dominica, Grenada, Jamaica, St. Kitts, St. Lucia, St. Vincent, Trinidad, British Guiana, British Honduras.
Other: Brunei, North Borneo, Sarawak, Hong Kong, Malta, Fiji, British Solomon Islands, Bahamas, Bermuda, Mauritius.
Source: as for Table 11.11.

insufficient to cover all of the shortfall, other sources of finance were sought. The traditional place for colonies to turn was the London loan market where colonial stocks had enjoyed a guaranteed status since the beginning of the century. After the war the London capital market remained closed to all foreign borrowers including British colonies. However, by 1948 it was apparent that the colonies' plans would be further hindered if London loans were not made available and at the end of that year permission was granted to Trinidad to raise £3 million, which it did at 3 per cent.[13] Further loans followed, listed in Table 11.13. Five colonies borrowed £18.1 million in the summer of 1949 and the municipal council of Nairobi also borrowed £1 million, the first African municipal authority to raise money on its own credit in London. The international crisis at the end of 1949 interrupted the flow of loans though they resumed in April 1950, and in the thirty-six months following Trinidad's loan a further nineteen loans were made to twelve colonies, Nairobi and the East Africa High Commission, bringing the total lent by September 1951 to £72 million, a rate of just over £2 million per month.[14] In the next three years, to November 1954, twenty-three loans

Table 11.13 London loans, 1948–60

Colony	Date		Amount £m (nominal)	Interest rate (%)	Price	Redemption
Trinidad	Nov	1948	3.000	3	n.a.	1967–71
Malaya	May	1949	8.050	3	par	n.a.
N. Rhodesia	July	1949	3.540	3	97	1963–5
St Lucia	Oct	1949	0.408	3.25	98.5	1965–70
Nigeria	June	1949	3.000	3	par	1975–7
Nairobi Munic.[a]	June	1949	1.500	3.25	98	n.a.
Jamaica	Jan	1950	3.250	3.5	par	1968–73
E.A.H.C.	Mar	1950	3.500	3.5	97.5	1966–8
Uganda	Apr	1950	3.100	3.5	98	1966–9
EAHC[c]	May	1950	7.100	3.5	99.5	1966–68
Sierra Leone	Aug	1950	2.030	3.5	99.5	1968–70
E.A.H.C.	Aug	1950	2.000	3.5	par	1968–70
Cyprus	Aug	1950	2.540	3.5	par	1969–71
Tanganyika	Sept	1950	1.750	3.5	par	1970–3
Kenya	Jan	1951	6.070	3.5	par	1973–8
N. Rhodesia	Mar	1951	7.730	3.5	99	1970–2
Mauritius	June	1951	2.615	3.5	97	1965–8
Br. Guiana	Aug	1951	2.180	3.5	97	1966–8
Nigeria	Sept	1951	6.800	3.5	97	1964–6
Trinidad[b]	Dec	1951	2.500	3	83.5	1967–71
Uganda[b]	Feb	1952	5.983	3.5	89	1966–9
Nairobi[b]	June	1951	2.000	3.25	99	1968–70
Tanganyika[ab]	May	1952	1.780	3.5	88	1970–3
Kenya[a]	May	1952	5.115	4.5	99.5	1971–8
Nyasaland	Aug	1952	2.060	4.5	98.5	1971–8
Grenada	Aug	1952	0.321	4.5	97.5	1969–76
EAHC[abc]	Sept	1952	2.500	3.5	88.5	1968–70
EAHC[ac]	Sept	1952	6.135	4.5	99.5	1965–70
N. Rhodesia[a]	Dec	1952	2.040	4.5	99.5	1965–70
Cyprus[b]	Dec	1952	1.700	3.5	88.5	1969–71
Jamaica	Apr	1953	3.590	4.25	97.5	1973–8
Tang[a]	June	1953	3.660	4.25	97.5	1967–72
St Lucia[b]	June	1953	0.230	3.75	88	1965–70
EAHC[ac]	Aug	1953	5.459	4	95	1968–71
Sierra Leone[b]	Sept	1953	1.150	3.5	89.5	1968–70
Kenya[ab]	Dec	1953	5.885	4.5	par	1971–8
Aden[a]	Dec	1953	1.230	4.25	98	1972–4
EAHC[c]	Apr	1954	2.045	4	97.75	1972–4
Trinidad	May	1954	4.245	4	99.5	1973–6
Malaya[b]	June	1954	2.900	3	85	1960–70
Malaya[b]	June	1954	1.895	3	81.5	1974–6
EAHC[c]	Sept	1954	4.500	4	par	1973–6
Nairobi	May	1954	1.000	4.5	97.5	1964–6
Uganda[a]	Aug	1955	4.000	4.75	97	1968–73
Mauritius	Oct	1955	2.090	4.75	97	1972–7
Cyprus[b]	Nov	1955	3.608	3.5	83.25	1969–71
Kenya	Feb	1956	4.225	5	96	1978–82
Br. Guiana	Apr	1957	3.540	5	96.5	1980–5
EAHC[c]	Sept	1957	3.500	5.5	98.5	1980–4

Table 11.13 (continued)

Colony	Date		Amount £m (nominal)	Interest rate (%)	Price	Redemption
Tanganyika	Jan	1957	3.000	5.75	99.5	1978–82
Tanganyika[b]	Apr	1957	1.000	5.75	102.6	1978–82
EAHC[c]	May	1957	8.500	5.75	100	1977–83
E.A.H.C.	May	1957	3.000	5.75	100	1977–83
Jamaica	July	1958	4.212	6	96.5	1977–82
Grenada	Dec	1958	0.289	6	96	1976–8
Antigua	Dec	1958	0.470	6	97	1977–80
St Lucia	Jan	1959	0.418	6	98	-1967–8
Barbados	Jan	1959	2.584	6	98.5	1971–73
Jamaica	Apr	1960	3.380	6.25	99.5	1978–80
Sarawak	June	1960	2.399	6.25	97.25	1975–80

[a] part reserved for subscription by colonial residents.
[b] Further issues of previous loans.
[c] East Africa High Commission.
Source: as for Table 11.11.

totalling £68 million were made to twelve colonies, Nairobi municipality and the East African High Commission. From 1955, however, the raising of London loans became more difficult, and interest rates rose in response to Britain's worsening balance of payments situation. Only ten loans totalling £36.5 million were issued in the three years December 1954 to November 1957, and rates rose to 5¾ per cent. From the end of 1957 to June 1960, six colonies raised seven loans totalling £13.8 million at 6 or 6¼ per cent rates of interest. Thus whilst the London market did not dry up completely, the provision of loan capital to colonial governments in the later 1950s was much restricted. Over the twelve years from the re-opening of the market, nineteen colonies, together with Nairobi municipality (three times) and the East African High Commission (eleven times) borrowed £190.3 million – three-quarters of this sum in the first six years. Obviously London loans were again an important source of colonial development finance, but the restrictions of the later 1950s and higher interest charges made them inaccessible to many of the medium and small colonies. Almost two-thirds of the London loans were made to the East and Central African colonies which probably reflected the market's greater familiarity with, and confidence in, the settler colonies of East African and the mineral riches of Northern Rhodesia.

By 1959 it was evident that there was a 'serious shortage' of London loans and a slackening in the growth of colonial surplus revenues which together had 'adversely affected the pace of development' in the colonies, many of which were now 'in urgent need' of long-term finance.[15] Locally floated loans also had become more difficult to raise. In response, the British government introduced a scheme of Exchequer loans to be made available to colonies and colonial public utilities which were unable to raise funds on the London market. A maximum of £100 million would be provided over five years (1959–64) at a rate of interest one-quarter of one per cent above that charged by the British government to its own public corporations. These funds were not strictly 'tied' to purchases of British equipment, but it was anticipated by the British government that, 'The measure now proposed should . . . have a valuable effect on the orders coming forward for UK industry'.[16] The colonial governments responded positively to this offer of funds – £57.3 million was lent in the following three years to eighteen colonies and £80 million over the first five years of the scheme. It was extended for a further period in 1964, though as the number of colonies fell dramatically in the mid-1960s those remaining colonies tended to be too small and too poor to afford loans at market rates or higher, and only £11.1 million was lent between 1964 and 1970. Altogether, London loans plus Exchequer loans amounted to £282.5 million over the period 1948–9 to 1969–70, an annual average rate of £13.5 million, slightly less than the annual average amount provided under the CDW Acts over this period of £14.3 million.

An additional source of capital might be found in locally floated public loans. In nearly all colonies, however, the local money market was either non-existent or underdeveloped. The Colonial Office was anxious to encourage colonial governments and their statutory bodies to raise local loans but the major obstacle was finding local subscribers: some colonies might be more prosperous than at any other time in their recent history, but nevertheless did not possess a large investing class. Under the terms of some London loans a proportion was earmarked for local subscription (see note to Table 11.13). This provided an opportunity for colonial investors to lend to their local government, but it did nothing to strengthen the local capital market as these funds were loaned via the London finance houses. Institutional investment in local public loans was essential. Colonial currency authorities invested very large reserve funds in British, dominion and colonial securities but were not allowed to lend to the government of the colony where the currency circulated.[17] Such 'fiduciary issues' were permitted for small amounts from 1955 onwards and loans were made to the governments of Keyna, Uganda, Sierra Leone and Jamaica, but in the main the colonial currency authorities continued to invest the great bulk of their reserves in British securities.[18] Another potential source was colonial government savings banks which were permitted to invest up to one-third of their deposits in local government securities, but in fact they declined to do so.[19] In addition, the colonial branches of British banks continued to look to the London money market rather than the local colonial one to invest their surplus funds.[20] Institutional investment was obviously necessary for the growth of viable local capital markets, but in the colonial era these remained insignificant.

In West Africa and Uganda a more promising source of local loans and one more directly under the control of the local government were marketing boards and price assistance funds. These boards had grown out of wartime arrangements to market colonial exports and had been established as peacetime bodies initially to iron out the effects of fluctuations in world prices for colonial export commodities. To do this they required large reserves which they obtained by the compulsory purchase of export produce from producers at prices substantially below ruling world prices. As export prices in the late 1940s and early 1950s rose rapidly there was no need for the boards to use their surpluses to subsidise producers and in colonies starved of capital it seemed to many administrators preferable to use some of these funds as loans to the colonial government for development projects. This practice was enhanced by the gradual extension of internal self-government in West Africa which led to regional governments being established each with their own regional produce marketing board or boards. By the mid-1950s the function of marketing Boards had changed: their purpose now was to syphon off part of the colony's export revenue and place it in the hands of government for social and economic development projects. When commodity prices did fall in the second half of the decade the boards' funds were considered too useful to government to be used to support producers incomes and the boards generally continued to purchase at below the (now falling) world price. Marketing boards in the Gold Coast and Nigeria made loans to their respective governments in 1950–1 and in subsequent years it became more common for locally floated public loans to be subscribed to by marketing boards or price assistance funds, specifically in Sierra Leone, Western Nigeria, Northern Nigeria, and Uganda.[21] The overall extent of this practice, however, was circumscribed by the British government's policy on colonial sterling balances, discussed below.

Locally floated loans in the larger colonies during the mid-1950s totalled above £40 million, at an average of £8 million per annum between 1954–5 and 1958–9. These colonies were Malaya, Kenya, Jamaica, British Honduras, Uganda, Northern Rhodesia, Sierra Leone, Mauritius, Tanganyika, Fiji, Barbados and Trinidad. At the end of the decade, however, local loans became much more difficult to raise, even with the help of marketing boards and currency boards, partly because the export-led prosperity of the early 1950s waned and partly because the transition to independence produced political uncertainty. As noted already, the introduction of Exchequer loans in 1959 was partly a response to the difficulties associated with local capital markets.

The problem of financing colonial development in the post-war period was not satisfactorily solved before independence in the 1960s: the British government felt it could not ask Parliament for more than it did under CDW and (from 1960) Exchequer loans, the London market dried up, and local financial resources, consisting mainly of surplus government revenues, were hard pressed in the less prosperous conditions of the late 1950s. In 1962 the Colonial Office, in its final edition of *The Colonial Territories*, offered the comment: 'Whereas a decade ago the principal factors limiting the rate of development expenditure in the public sector in many territories were physical and administrative, now they are mainly financial: in particular, the lack of local financial resources.'[22]

There can be no doubt that there was far more money made available to the colonial economies for economic and social development from more diverse sources in the fifteen years following the end of the war. However, three main qualifications need to be made in respect of this effort: overall the amounts fell short of the aspirations for progress unleashed by the ten-year development plans; the distribution of funds left the smaller to medium colonies even worse off than the largest colonies; and the financing of development relied too heavily on local resources which were subject to pressures from fluctuating export earnings. In a sense the renewed emphasis on local financial sources – expected to fund from between half and two-thirds of the development programmes – raised an echo of the pre-1929 philosophy that colonies should live within their means and be financially self-sufficient. As Britain's economic condition deteriorated in the late 1950s many colonies approached independence with an array of economic and social development schemes whose effectiveness was undermined by inadequate finance.

COLONIAL STERLING BALANCES AND THE 'TRANSFER PROBLEM'

All of these manifestations of inadequate finance for colonial economic development came together in the question of the so-called 'colonial sterling balances'. These arose initially because Britain's indebtedness to overseas members of the sterling area increased dramatically during the Second World War, reaching more than £3 billion by the end of 1945. This sum was far in excess of what Britain could afford to repay, particularly as it continued to experience severe balance of payments deficits and was in urgent need of financial assistance from the United States and Canada. The 'sterling balances' were frozen. Over the next ten years some countries were permitted to run down their balances and use the funds for the purchase of sterling goods. The balances belonging to non-sterling area countries (for example, Argentina) were depleted quite rapidly; those of the 'white dominions' much more slowly; the balances belonging to newly independent sterling area countries – India, Pakistan, Ceylon – more slowly still. Countries which left the sterling area – Egypt, Palestine/Israel, Iraq – engaged in lengthy negotiations with Britain which also produced a gradual release.[23] However, as the Treasury had warned in 1945, the colonial sterling balances increased during the post-war decade to such an extent that by 1956 they accounted for more than half of the total, compared with less than 10 per cent in 1946.[24] Colonial sterling balances doubled in value during the war, from about £300 million to £600 million and then rose steadily to a peak of £1,444 million in 1955 and £1,454 million in 1956 (Table 11.14). Although they then declined to around £1000 million, this was due almost entirely to the reclassification of balances belonging to Ghana and Malaya when they attained independence in 1957.

The growth of the colonial sterling balances by about £850 million in the eight years between 1947 and 1955 represented the accumulation abroad of a considerable potential purchasing power for imports of goods and services. By building up these funds the colonies were forego-ing imports from Britain.[25] In a sense they were investing their 'surplus' funds in Britain as most of this money was held in British government securities. A situation in which some of the poorest and least-developed countries were effectively lending to one of the richest and most devel-oped did not escape critical comment, especially in view of the contrast between the size of the funds being accumulated by the colonies in London and the flow of capital from Britain to the colonies in the form of colonial development and welfare (£118 million). Colonial Development Corporation (£50 million) and Overseas Food Corporation (£35 million) and London loans (£150 million).[26] It did not seem rational for the colonies to hold reserve funds, even though most of them earned interest, in London, rather than to speed up the devel-opment process by spending some of these funds on a greater volume of imports and economic development projects in general, some of which might be expected to 'directly or indirectly contribute to the improve-ment of the [sterling] areas' balance of payments with the rest of the World'.[27]

The ways in which colonial sterling balances were held is indicated by the classes of funds shown in Table 11.14. The colonial currency system automatically transferred part of each colony's export surplus to sterling balances as increases in the circulation of colonial currency – which occurred if exports exceeded imports – had to be backed by the deposit of an equivalent amount in the sterling reserves of the currency authori-ties held in London. These currency board funds – partly invested in short-and long-term securities and partly held in liquid balances –

Table 11.14 Sterling assets of colonial territories, 1946–60 (end of year; £m)

Class of Funds	1946	1947	1948	1949	1950	1951	1952	1953	1954	1955	1956	1957	1958	1959	1960
Currency board	na	na	na	236	282	337	363	372	395	439	464	327	327	300	284
Govt: special reserves[a]	na	na	na	146	145	181	199	216	232	237	238	166	169	167	160
Govt: general reserves	na	na	na	70	120	180	245	288	322	347	384	254	251	245	253
Marketing boards[b]	na	na	na	55	86	137	144	144	139	143	118	74	62	52	51
On deposit, UK banks	na	na	na	163	219	255	271	305	299	278	250	184	194	241	235
Total	607	600	645	670	852	1090	1222	1324	1324	1444	1454	1005[ce]	1003	1005	983
Area															
West Africa[c]	115	125	180	200	256	333	362	400	488	507	481	296[c]	278	270	218
East Africa[d]	100	105	105	138	172	217	259[d]	288	217[d]	197	192	186	172	170	166
Malaya[e]	125	115	105	107	164	252	283	282	305	363	369	94[e]	104	119	140
Hong Kong	g	75	80	68	94	116	120	132	135	132	143	140	155	167	183
West Indies[f]	g	g	g	67	78	81	90	107	122	118	133	147	148	138	140
Other territories	267	180	175	90	88	91	107	110	120	127	136	142	146	141	136
Total	607	600	645	670	852	1090	1222	1324	1387	1444	1454	1005[ce]	1003	1005	983

Notes: [a] Comprised: Renewals fund, pension fund, sinking fund, miscellaneous funds and government savings bank deposits.
[b] Gambia, Gold Coast, Sierra Leone, Nigeria, Uganda.
[c] Excludes Ghana 1957–60.
[d] Excludes Northern Rhodesia and Nyasaland 1952–60; includes Kenya, Uganda, Tanganyika, Zanzibar, Somaliland and Aden throughout.
[e] Excludes Federation of Malaya and State of Singapore 1957–60; includes British Borneo Territories throughout.
[f] Includes Bahamas and Bermuda.
[g] Included with Other Territories.
Source: The Colonial Territories 1939–47 to 1960–1; Memorandum on the Sterling Assets of the British Colonies (Colonial No. 298, 1953).

formed around one-third of the colonial sterling assets and accounted for 29 per cent of their increase between 1949 and 1956.[28]

Second, in the export price boom of the post-war years, colonial governments found their revenues swollen by taxation receipts. They generally followed conservative fiscal policies and aimed to produce budget surpluses which were a vital element in funding their ten-year development plans. As Tables 11.11, and 11.12 show, there was only one year (1956) when the colonies taken together did not produce a budget surplus. Between 1947 and 1955 colonial government surpluses totalled £267 million, much of which was held as sterling balances in London. Together with unspent portions of London loans and miscellaneous government funds, these 'Government General Reserves' reached £384 million in 1956 by which time they represented 26 per cent of total colonial sterling balances compared with 10 per cent in 1949. Other colonial government funds held in London comprised pension funds (for colonial government employees), sinking funds (for the repayment of London and other loans) and renewal funds (kept by some colonies as depreciation funds for government-owned public utilities). The amounts paid into these accounts depended upon decisions made for various reasons by each colonial government, but they were all further ways of salting away part of the government's surplus revenues. Additionally, most of the deposits in colonial government savings banks were invested in London even though legally such banks were permitted to invest up to one-third of their deposits locally. Details published for the period 1949–52 show that savings banks were the most important of this group of government funds (39 per cent), followed by miscellaneous (26 per cent), sinking (18 per cent), renewal (11 per cent) and pensions (5 per cent). Total colonial government funds held in London contributed just over half of the increase in the colonial sterling balances between 1949 and 1956.[29]

Third, the four West African colonies plus Uganda in East Africa diverted a proportion of export earnings to government owned produce marketing boards or, in the case of Uganda, price assistance boards. As discussed above, the marketing boards' strategy was to accumulate as large reserves as possible against the day when colonial agricultural export prices would fall. As West African and Ugandan export prices soared from the late 1940s, boosted by the Korean War in 1950, these boards' funds increased rapidly – from £55 million in 1949 to £137 million two years later. They then stabilised at this level until 1956 when a portion was transferred to the Gold Coast and Nigeria for local development projects. Marketing board funds accounted for 8 per cent of total colonial sterling balances in 1949 and 10 per cent in 1955.

Finally, colonial branches of United Kingdom banks kept surplus liquid reserves on deposit at head office in London. Their colonial business was almost entirely concerned with the import-export trade of the colonies. Branches were not treated as autonomous units and surplus funds – which naturally arose when export receipts exceeded import expenditures – were more profitably employed in the London market. These funds also included deposits with London banks of residents in the colonies. They represented between one-fifth and one-quarter of the colonial sterling balances.[30]

The 'colonial sterling balances' thus comprised a number of diverse elements. The Colonial Office view of the colonial sterling assets was that their growth was largely a temporary phenomenon caused by unusually high export prices together with shortages of imports and that their existence constituted a reserve against instability in the future:

> There can . . . be little doubt that the building up of Government reserves has enabled some Colonies to plan long-term development with confidence and that those Colonies which have accumulated large sterling assets will be in a stronger position to meet any serious recession in raw material prices than those which have been unable to do so.[31]

This was a succinct statement of the Colonial Office view that a collapse of world prices for primary produce was a serious possibility. Yet, as Hazlewood observed, 'It is not the existence of sterling balances, which play a necessary part in the economies of the colonial territories, but their magnitude and their continuous increase which merit comment'.[32]

A faster rate of economic growth in the colonies in the 15 years following the end of the Second World War would have raised the level of colonial imports – on capital and consumer goods and payments to outside contractors, engineering consultants and so forth – which would have slowed the growth of the balances and have led eventually to their decline. This was not a desirable development, however, from the point of view of Britain's balance of payments since a rundown of sterling assets would have undermined confidence in the pound and might well have caused a 'sterling crisis'. Indeed, such crises did occur regularly even after Britain's 30 per cent devaluation of the pound in 1949. Moreover, the colonial sterling balances were the only component of Britain's external sterling liabilities over which the British Treasury and the Bank of England had firm control. The independent members of the sterling area could not, in the end, be prevented from drawing down some part of their sterling reserves and, indeed, moving away from sterling as a reserve asset altogether. The colonies, however, were obliged to maintain stringent import controls, especially against dollar goods, and the slow pace of public development work meant that the colonies invested their surplus funds in British government securities to a far greater extent than the British government invested funds in the colonies.[33]

Some colonies might be said to have suffered a 'transfer problem' in these years in that they had funds invested in London which they could not translate into imports of goods and services. This was a result of three factors: shortages of materials and equipment (and shipping space); import restrictions, especially on dollar goods, imposed by the colonies at the behest of the British government; and the control over the colonial sterling balances exercised by the Bank of England and the Treasury. The extent of the 'transfer problem' varied between colonies, mainly as a result of their different capacities to attract private and public capital inflows which could be used to finance a current account deficit and it was more apparent for the African colonies, less so in Malaysia and the West Indies. Only in the second half of the decade did trade and current account deficits and the flow of private and public capital indicate an increased tempo of economic development, that is, during the main period of decolonisation.

The important contribution which the colonies made to Britain's balance of payments was particularly clear in the case of relations with the dollar area. Philip Bell calculated that between 1946 and 1952 – the worst years of the 'dollar gap' – the colonies made a net contribution to the sterling area's dollar pool (held in the Bank of England's exchange equalisation account) of US $1,830 million (plus net gold sales of $160 million, Table 11.15). Their contribution was particularly large in 1950 and 1951, totalling £870 million. In contrast, the independent members of the overseas sterling area ran a deficit with the dollar area which amounted to $3,318 million (although South Africa and Ceylon were net dollar earners) and Britain's own deficit with the dollar area was $7,743 million. Gold sales to Britain from the independent members (mainly South Africa), together with United States and Canadian credits and loans and International Monetary Fund (IMF) drawings, reduced the gold and dollar deficit of Britain and the independent sterling area members to $870 million. Since the sterling area also had a large dollar deficit ($1,748 million) with South America and Western Europe, the overall fall in the area's central dollar reserves over this period was $628 million – but without the net dollars contributed by the colonies it would have been $2,618 million, over four times higher.

Not all of the colonies earned dollars: 70 per cent of the net colonial gold and dollar contribution was attributable to Malaya and 29 per cent to West Africa, arising from exports to the United States of rubber, tin, cocoa and vegetable oils and gold sales from the Gold Coast.[34] East Africa made a small net contribution, but the West Indies and the Mediterranean colonies were net dollar spenders. However, as revealed by Table 11.16, all colonies contributed by holding down dollar imports

Table 11.15 Contributions to and drawings from the sterling area gold and dollar pool by member countries, 1946–52

	1946	1947	1948	1949	1950	1951	1952	1946–52
On UK account								
Surplus (+) or deficit (–) with dollar area	–1128	–2237	–1265	–1058	+147	–1480	–722	–7743
Subscriptions to IMF[c] & IBRD[d]	–30	–206	–	–	–	–	–	–236
Special dollar receipts[a]	+1123	+3513	+1076	+1209	+725	+177	+337	+8160
Net contributions to (+) or drawings from (–) gold & dollar pool	–35	+1070	–189	+151	+872	–1303	–385	+181
On dominion and independent sterling area member account								
Surplus (+) or Deficit (–) with dollar area	–427	–1272	–545	–577	+8	–198	–307	–3318
Subscriptions to IMF[c] & IBRD[d]	–	–28	–	–	–7	–	–	–35
Special dollar receipts[b]	+130	+320	+596	+323	+310	+217	+226	+2302
Net contribution to (+) or drawings from (–) gold & dollar pool	–117	–980	+51	–254	+311	+19	–81	–1051
On colonial dependency account								
Surplus (+) or Deficit (–) with dollar area	+134	+40	+206	+202	+408	+462	+378	+1830
Gold sales to UK	+24	+22	+27	+27	+28	+25	+7	+160
Net contributions to (+) or drawings from (–) gold & dollar pool	+158	+62	+233	+229	+436	+487	+385	+1990
On whole sterling area account								
Net dollar receipts from (+) or payments to (–) non-sterling & non-dollar countries	+213	–770	–317	–293	–7	–167	–407	–1748
Total Change in central reserves	+219	–618	–222	–167	+1612	–964	–488	–628

[a] Comprises, 1946–52:

US credits	+3750
Canadian credits	+1159
IMF drawings	+300
Marshall aid	+2951

[b] Comprises, 1946–52:

IMF drawings	+159
Gold sales to UK	+1672
South African gold loan	+325
Marshall aid to Ireland	+146

[c] International Monetary Fund
[d] International Bank for Reconstruction of Development (World Bank)
Source: Philip W. Bell, *The Sterling Area in the Post-War World* (Oxford, 1956), p.56.

Table 11.16 Balance of trade with the dollar area[a], selected colonies, 1947–57 (£000)

	West Africa			East Africa			Central Africa			Malaya			Total above colonies		
	I	E	B	I	E	B	I	E	B	I	E	B	I	E	B
1947	11316	21398	10037	8571	1847	−6724	10253	1320	−8933	18775	57295	39520	121218	107170	−14093
1948	8644	28698	20054	7371	4548	−2823	8433	3687	−4746	28348	60243	31895	122651	130920	8269
1949	6443	21596	15153	7708	5371	−2337	8461	7267	−1194	15856	56276	40420	118314	107575	−10739
1950	6057	39199	33142	4169	8958	4789	6767	13630	6863	12647	137533	124886	113123	253608	140485
1951	8550	46938	38388	3772	15081	11309	8170	9212	1042	30160	164082	133922	133073	278245	145172
1952	12051	41816	29765	6445	15934	9489	8900	8235	−665	26215	89196	62981	124529	194621	70092
1953	9782	41239	31457	5664	10827	5163	7845	23839	15994	18377	68835	50458	116638	186755	70117
1954	11328	36882	25554	3680	12266	8586	7249	15876	8627	20358	68294	47936	123620	180483	56863
1955	13206	30847	17641	5117	14431	9314	8896	22557	13661	20139	101155	81016	142543	221698	79155
1956	12580	30420	17840	4171	14434	10163	11903	13519	1616	25964	92164	66200	170218	215756	45538
1957	19869	25231	5626	4366	16591	12225	13093	16663	3570	22227	83441	61214	182325	225097	42772

	Hong Kong			Caribbean			Other colonies		
	I	E	B	I	E	B	I	E	B
1947	20740	13528	−7212	48173	10997	−37176	3390	785	−2605
1948	26906	18630	−8276	40075	13391	−26684	2874	1723	−1151
1949	40231	22401	−17830	35851	14375	−21476	3764	2690	−1074
1950	45759	26114	−19645	33981	22911	−11070	3743	5263	1520
1951	29871	16091	−13780	47911	24187	−23724	4639	2654	−1985
1952	19507	11925	−7582	45925	22928	−22997	5486	4587	−899
1953	18560	11084	−7476	51713	25014	−26699	4997	5917	920
1954	22237	11784	−10543	54717	29386	−25331	3961	5995	2034
1955	24619	13871	−10748	65902	32551	−33351	4664	6286	1622
1956	31703	16005	−15698	77381	40448	−36933	6416	8766	2350
1957	38077	24765	−13312	79112	50798	−28314	5581	7608	2027

[a] USA, Canada, Central and South America (except Argentina, Brazil, Chile, Paraguay, Peru, Uruguay)

West Africa: Gambia, Sierra Leone, Gold Coast, Nigeria.
East Africa: Kenya, Uganda, Tanganyika, Zanzibar.
Central Africa: Northern Rhodesia, Southern Rhodesia, Nyasaland.
Caribbean: Bermuda, Bahamas, Barbados, Jamaica, Trinidad, British Guiana, British Honduras.
Other Colonies: Malta, Cyprus, Mauritius, Fiji.
I = Imports (carriage insurance freight).
E = Exports (free on board).
B = Balance (E minus I).
Source: as for Table 11.1(a).

and maximising dollar exports, so that even those which had a dollar deficit reduced its size. Between 1947 and 1950 dollar imports contracted in value in the African colonies by 46 per cent, and by about one-third in Malaya and the Caribbean. This was achieved by import licensing and exchange controls and reinforced by the 30 per cent increase in the cost of dollar goods following sterling's devaluation in September 1949. Only in Hong Kong and the Mediterranean did dollar imports rise, and substantially in the former owing to the practical difficulties encountered in enforcing import controls. The very high dollar earnings of the colonies in 1950 and 1951 led to a slight rise in dollar imports, but these fell again between 1952 and 1954 except in the Caribbean and Hong Kong. Even by 1957, when the dollar shortage was over, dollar imports were subdued in a number of colonies, although the high point of dollar surpluses had passed. Judd Polk aptly described the colonies as being 'the dollar bulwark of the system' alongside United States and Canadian aid to Britain.[35]

The significance of dollar earning and saving by the colonies for their economic development was that it restricted their access to United States and Canadian goods, which was especially important for capital goods and equipment because the dollar area was often the only source of supply. Severe restrictions on dollar imports shifted colonial trade patterns towards a greater reliance on the United Kingdom (see Table 11.7) although colonies were not always able to run a trade deficit with Britain despite being encouraged to maximise export sales to and minimise imports from the dollar area. Import restrictions and exchange controls thus produced a double burden on many colonies: first, they were unable to convert their dollar earnings into dollar merchandise, while, second, their overall trade surpluses built up as sterling balances and investments in London which could not (or were not) used to purchase imports from the sterling area.[36] In a situation where construction projects were frequently held back because of shortages of even basic inputs, such as cement, which had to be imported, the import component of economic development whether carried out by private or public enterprise was in reality extremely high. Import volumes did increase, but limitations on the ability of colonies to finance a greater volume of imports were a major constraint on economic development in the 1940s and 1950s.

CONCLUSION

During the six years following the end of the Second World War most colonies experienced the strongest growth of export earnings in their history. Although there was a renewal of capital inflows to the colonies – after fifteen years of the Great Depression and the war when there was a dearth of fresh investment – the full benefits of the export boom were lost in the post-war shortages and Britain's chronic balance of payments condition. In particular, imports from the dollar area were severely restricted as far as the colonies were concerned. Hence the colonies tended to build up reserves in London rather than raise the level of expenditure in their economies. Colonial aid reached new levels but had to be augmented by loans at market rates and colonial surplus revenues, both of which suffered from uncertainty. Under the ten-year plans many colonial governments chose to emphasise social welfare projects rather than ones which might have added more directly to production of goods and services and export earnings, a choice which would not have been so difficult to make had development and welfare been adequately funded. Above all, Britain could not afford as high a level of investment in colonial development as was required to tackle the fundamental economic and social problems in the limited time available. Indeed, colonial development and welfare aid in the fifteen years following the end of the Second World War represented on average barely 0.1 per cent of Britain's gross domestic product. Colonial trade showed little sign of diversification during the latter phases of colonial rule either in terms of the breadth of export commodities or markets. The world economy was fairly buoyant in these years (especially when compared with the 1930s) but it did not seem to be the case that structural adjustments towards more self-sustaining kinds of economic growth were taking place very quickly, if at all, in many of the colonial territories. Britain tended to struggle in its relations with the world economy in the 1950s and its tropical colonies suffered as a consequence. Insofar as structural economic problems were tackled it was after the end of the colonial era. The concept of colonial economic development and the role of government in it also underwent some important changes during these years, and it is to some of these innovations that we now turn.

12

The triumph of the Chamberlain view

New directions in colonial economic development after the Second World War

With the establishment of the Overseas Food Corporation and the Colonial Development Corporation in 1947 (Chapter 10), the British government for the first time moved into direct production of commodities in the tropical colonies. Faced with a severe shortage of primary products, the long-term nature of colonial development and welfare schemes and an apparent failure of private enterprise – whether expatriate or indigenous – to lift output quickly, the state became a producer in addition to carrying out its more traditional tasks of building infrastructure and providing economic and social services.

THE TANGANYIKA GROUNDNUT SCHEME, 1946–54

Tanganyika bore the brunt of the 'new colonialism'.[1] The Tanganyika Groundnut Scheme was a large-scale project which was intended to demonstrate what the state was capable of in tropical Africa when it harnessed modern Western technology and expertise. The scheme was designed not only to provide 'the largest possible production of groundnuts in the shortest practicable period of time', but also to be a pioneer in new ways of organising and managing production and to amount, indeed, to a revolution in economic development under tropical conditions.[2] The idea that groundnuts could be grown on a large scale in East Africa using mechanised methods of clearing and cultivation came initially from the managing director of the United Africa Co. (UAC), Frank Samuel. The UAC, a subsidiary of Unilever Ltd, was a British firm mainly concerned in the import and export trade of Britain's West African colonies, although Unilever itself owned extensive oil-palm plantations in the Belgian Congo.[3] A proposal was drawn up with the Tanganyika Department of Agriculture and submitted to the Ministry of Food in March 1946. Cabinet authorised the despatch of a mission of three experts led by A.J. Wakefield, a former director of agriculture in Tanganyika, to East Africa to report on the feasibility of Samuel's plan. They arrived in June and spent nine weeks touring in Tanganyika,

Kenya and Northern Rhodesia examining possible sites suitable for mechanised groundnut growing.

The Wakefield plan, presented to the Ministry of Food in September 1946, was an ambitious one. It entailed clearing and planting 107 farming units of 30,000 acres each (totalling 3.21 million acres) in three colonies over a five-year period, to produce 600,000 tons of groundnuts per year by the fifth year and with an eventual annual output of 800,000 tons. The cost was estimated at £24 million, and the annual saving to Britain on its food import bill at £10 million. In October 1946, the Wakefield Plan was accepted in principle by the Ministry of Food and in December the plan was adopted in full (with minor revisions) and published as a government white paper. It was recommended that work should begin at once on sites in Tanganyika with a view to clearing and planting 150,000 acres by the end of 1947 so that the first harvest would be available early in 1948: 'Time . . . is of the essence and a delay of even a week or two in establishing new areas of oil seed production may mean missing the 1947 planting season.'[4]

Both the Samuel and Wakefield proposals were based on the use of mechanised methods of clearing virgin bush, preparing the soil, planting and harvesting the groundnuts. As much machinery as possible – and as little labour – was to be used in all phases of production: heavy bulldozers, tractors, rooters, sowing machines and combine harvesters. Only mechanised production, it was argued, could produce the volume of groundnuts required to alleviate Britain's severe oil and fat shortages. Peasant production was dismissed as being quite inadequate.[5] Indeed, argued Wakefield, one of the major benefits which would result from the scheme, apart from producing large quantities of groundnuts, would be to provide an alternative form of agricultural production which in time could be emulated by African farmers organised in large-scale cooperatives. The government agreed:

> By far the most important long-term advantage of the scheme from the African point of view, is . . . the revolution in agricultural technique which it represents. . . . The scheme is an example of the bold economic planning which is necessary to raise the standard of living of the African peasant, dependent as this must be for many years to come on agriculture, and based as it is on primitive methods of cultivation.

It was true that the African inhabitants of Tanganyika would not consume any of the groundnuts (malnourished though they might be compared with those in Britain who were destined to consume them) but they needed to be given an 'ocular demonstration' of the superiority of large-scale mechanised agriculture: 'It is the hope of His Majesty's

Government that the Groundnut Scheme will provide that ocular demonstration.'[6]

The Wakefield mission recommended that the scheme be run by a government-owned corporation which would have considerable freedom of action in day-to-day operations. It also suggested that work begin in the southern province of Tanganyika, one of three areas in the colony identified as suitable for mechanised groundnut production. The reason for preferring the southern province was that it had better soil and more rainfall than the other two areas. The government agreed to establish a corporation to operate the scheme; in the meantime, to avoid delays, it asked the UAC to start the project acting as managing agents for the ministry of food. Although the scheme was one of far-reaching economic – and possibly social – development located in a trusteeship territory held by Britain under the auspices of the United Nations, the Colonial Office was excluded at the outset from responsibility for it. This decision emphasised the prime purpose of the scheme as winning food for Britain – as John Strachey, the new minister for Food, said to the men starting up the project – 'On your success depends, more than on any other single factor, whether the harassed housewives of Britain get more margarine, cooking fat and soap, in the reasonably near future.' Moreover, its 'revolutionary' approach to agriculture in Africa was one which it was felt the Colonial Office might regard as diametrically opposed to its traditional policy of building up peasant farming.[7]

Strachey recognised that this scheme was risky, but, he asked his Cabinet colleagues in January 1947:

> What . . . are the risks of not undertaking this project? First: in 1950 we may have the same, or a lower, margarine ration than today. Or second: in 1950 we may have to spend so many dollars on buying fats from dollar sources that we shall have too few left to buy other indispensable dollar imports . . . a large enterprise of this type is the only way in which our Central African possessions can be rapidly developed, so that they may become an economic and strategic asset instead of a liability, as to a large extent they are now.[8]

The UAC took on the job of managing agency – albeit, as they claimed later 'most reluctantly' and at no profit to themselves[9] – and an advance party of personnel arrived in Dar-es-Salaam in February 1947. The first area to be developed was at Kongwa in the central province, about 200 miles inland from Dar-es-Salaam and about twenty miles north of the central province railway. Kongwa was chosen in preference to the southern province because of its access to the railway and because the bush appeared to be easier to clear, as there were no trees. However, Kongwa was the least favoured of the three areas in terms of soil quality and adequate rainfall, so this decision by the managing agency was a significant one.

Work at Kongwa was beset with difficulties from the outset. The equipment needed for clearing the bush and preparing the soil for planting was inadequate and nearly all of it was second-hand, purchased from military disposal dumps around the world. There were long delays in moving equipment through the congested lighterage port of Dar-es-Salaam and up to the Kongwa site. Once in operation frequent break-downs were experienced so that only a small number of the bulldozers and heavy tractors available were in working order at any one time. These problems had not been foreseen, so to begin with there were no repair workshops and few spare parts. Bulldozers could flatten the bush but roots proved almost intractable. The rooting equipment, although specialised, was not designed for such conditions. It cleared the ground very slowly and was subject to damage. Progress was slow and fell well behind schedule. By the end of the year only 7,500 acres were ready to plant, in contrast to the target of 150,000 acres, and 3,400 acres of this consisted of grasslands that did not require clearing. Planting was also retarded because the US-designed machines were not suitable for African conditions. Mechanical harvesting fared no better: after the rains, the denuded ground baked hard in the sun and proved too difficult for the harvesters, with the result that many groundnuts were left in the ground or had to be dug up by hand. Yields were disappointing: 850 lb per acre had been confidently predicted by Wakefield, 750 lb by the Ministry of Food, but the harvest in early 1948 yielded only 355 lb per acre.[10]

In March 1948 the Overseas Food Corporation, set up to administer the groundnut scheme, took over from the managing agents. Clearing continued at Kongwa and a start was made at the southern province site and at Urambo in the western province. Problems similar to those which dogged progress at Kongwa were experienced at the other two areas and by the end of 1948 only 2,800 acres had been cleared at Urambo and 560 in the southern province.[11]

It was clear that the Wakefield plan required re-examination. In December 1948 the Overseas Food Corporation produced a ten-year plan which envisaged bringing 2,355,000 acres under cultivation by 1958 but which would – by the substitution of sunflower for groundnuts to a considerable extent – produce as much vegetable oil as the 3.25 million acres of the Wakefield plan. However, this revision would require the corporation to borrow around £67 million and the Overseas Food Corporation's total borrowing limit was only £50 million. In January 1949 the British Treasury refused to sanction an increase in the corporation's borrowing powers, and the corporation had to devise a new plan.[12] Meanwhile, planting was completed early in 1949 for the second harvest of the scheme. At Kongwa, 25,000 acres of groundnuts were planted accompanied by 20,000 acres of sunflower (which could be cultivated on semi-cleared land) and 2,000 of maize for African labourers' rations. Another 2,000 acres were planted with sunflower at Urambo, together with 500 of groundnuts, bringing the total planted to 49,000 acres. The harvest at Kongwa was ruined by inadequate rainfall during the growing season – only 12 inches fell when a minimum of 20 inches was needed – and yields of groundnuts declined to 144 lb unshelled per acre.[13] At Urambo the groundnut crop failed, afflicted by the drought and an outbreak of disease. Sunflower proved even less susceptible to mechanised planting and harvesting than groundnuts and yields were poor.[14]

The Overseas Food Corporation's new plan in 1949 reduced the total area to be cultivated from 2,355,000 acres to 600,000. Most effort was to be made in the southern province where 420,000 acres would be cleared and planted by 1954. Kongwa and Urambo would now be limited to 90,000 acres each as opposed to the previous targets of 450,000 acres and 300,000 acres respectively. This plan was approved by the Ministry of Food in November 1949. Clearing at Urambo fell behind schedule as machinery continued to fail under African conditions and only 65,000 acres of the projected 90,000 were cleared. At Kongwa semi-drought conditions slowed progress.[15] In the southern province less than 1,000 acres were planted. The total for the 1949–50 season was 65,550 acres in contrast to 102,000 acres planned, and 48,100 acres of these were under sunflower. Results were again disappointing: groundnut yields were 244 lb per acre at Kongwa compared to 532 lb at Urambo, while sunflower was affected by disease in both areas. At Urambo mechanised harvesting was more or less abandoned.[16]

By 1950 it was evident to the Overseas Food Corporation that it would be unable to meet its financial commitments to the Exchequer to operate on a commercial basis and repay advances made to it. Clearing had fallen well behind even the reduced targets and the cost of clearing had proved to be at least ten times greater than originally estimated by the Wakefield mission. The three harvests so far had been very poor so that the contribution of the scheme to Britain's food needs were negligible.[17] The lesson of three years of effort in Tanganyika had shown the corporation that:

> The groundnut is not a plant which lends itself readily to mass methods over vast acreages. The attainment of economic yields demands intensive farming. The conception of 30,000 acre units with a thin spread of European supervision and machinery has proved unworkable[18]

The failure of mechanised clearing was acknowledged having proved impracticable within either the time or the cost envisaged in earlier plans. Mechanical clearing can be done, but it cannot be done at an economic cost in relation to the value of the arable land created. Simpler and slower methods must be substituted for a part of the mechanical technique so far employed in order to reduce these costs.[19]

A radical revision was proposed and accepted at the beginning of 1951. The corporation's losses to 31 March 1951 – £36.5 million – were written off and the corporation financed from annual votes by Parliament from then on. Responsibility for the corporation was transferred from the Ministry for Food to the Colonial Office. The area under cultivation was drastically reduced: to 12,000 acres at Kongwa, 45,000 at Urambo and a maximum of 60,000 in the southern province over the following three years. The objective of the scheme was changed: it was now to be 'a scheme of large-scale experimental development to establish the economics of clearing and mechanised or partially mechanised agriculture under tropical conditions', but one which 'cannot in itself contribute significantly towards Britain's food supplies'.[20]

Over the next four years the corporation's work was gradually wound down, large numbers of European and African employees were retrenched, surplus equipment sold and support facilities, such as a 120-mile oil pipeline in the southern province, closed. Non-productive assets – townships, hospitals, power generators, shops and police force – were transferred to the Tanganyika government. Agricultural experiments confirmed that groundnuts could not be grown at Kongwa or Urambo and experimental work was switched to raising cattle and growing tobacco respectively.[21] Hand labour continued to be substituted for mechanical methods in planting and harvesting operations in the southern province where experiments were carried on into growing food crops such as maize and sorghum as well as with African varieties of groundnuts.[22] At all three sites trials were conducted in the development of African tenant farms with rather inconclusive results and at Kongwa the trial was discontinued.[23] By 1953 there seemed little point in organising such experimental work from Britain and in the following year the scheme was converted into a colonial development and welfare project and its administration taken over by the Tanganyikan government.[24] The Overseas Food Corporation was then dissolved.

The Tanganyika Groundnut Scheme was a failure from every point of view. It did nothing to ease Britain's vegetable oil and fat shortages, it consumed more food locally than it produced and diverted labour from regional food production. It lost the British government over £36 million and yet it was of no benefit to Tanganyika. Even the facilities built by the corporation were of little value: Kongwa, for example, was left with a small modern hospital but this was far from the main centres of population. Naturally the comment was frequently made that the money could have been better spent elsewhere – particularly on improving Northern Nigeria's rundown railway system where frequent breakdowns and shortages of locomotives and rolling stock were preventing a stockpile of groundnuts far larger than the Tanganyika scheme ever produced from reaching the coast.[25]

Undoubtedly the scheme was undertaken at great speed driven on by the perceived urgency of the oil and fats shortages.[26] When the initial difficulties arose in 1947 the British government urged the scheme on as being more on the lines of a military operation which must go ahead at all cost than a commercial undertaking.[27] There were no pilot schemes to try out the equipment on smaller areas nor any experimentation prior to starting on a full-scale basis. This was deliberate policy.[28] Sir Leslie Plummer, the chairman of the corporation, commented, 'the way in which you discover snags attendant on large-scale mechanised agriculture is to proceed with large-scale mechanised agriculture', an opinion which was shared by the Wakefield mission.[29] In Plummer's view any results from small-scale experimental pilots as to yield, use of machinery, effect of variations in rainfall or the training of managers, drivers and machine operators, would not 'have been conclusive or of real value to the Corporation'.[30]

As the blueprint for the scheme, the Wakefield mission report was criticised when its estimates and assumptions proved 'seriously misleading'.[31] As members of the mission explained, there was 'a total lack of any experience of mechanised agriculture': no-one had ever attempted what was being proposed; the areas chosen lacked information regarding rainfall patterns and soil composition.[32] The estimates for the cost of clearing the bush by bulldozers were based on clearing for airstrips during the war.[33] Many of the problems were of a logistic and engineering nature but the three-man mission did not include an engineering expert. One of the mission's members (an accountant) summed up: 'It was all guesswork, and our guess was as good as anybody else's.'[34]

The novel feature of the Tanganyika Groundnut Scheme was its use of agricultural machinery on a large-scale – which was a complete failure. In other respects it did not represent a step forward in colonial development: its management was that of the plantation or estate already familiar in European agriculture in East and Central Africa. The role of the African in the scheme was that of a low-paid unskilled or semi-skilled labourer, working for a European manager. The corporation operated the scheme in a highly centralised fashion, with many of the key decisions being made in London, and with no attempt in practice to integrate the scheme into the Tanganyikan rural economy. There was no effective transfer of technology and its cost was equivalent to three year's worth of CDW funding for the whole colonial empire. Even if it had been successful, its cost was such that few other tropical colonies could have afforded to emulate it. As it was, its failure was a blow to British prestige in the colonies and elsewhere and perhaps made it more difficult in the later 1950s for imaginative schemes of economic development to be undertaken in the colonies. And this was compounded by the fact that in the early 1950s the Tanganyika scheme was not an isolated example, as shown by the operations of the Overseas Food Corporation's sister body, the Colonial Development Corporation.

COLONIAL DEVELOPMENT CORPORATION, 1948–62

The Colonial Development Corporation (CDC) also began its work with a great sense of urgency: as soon as the Overseas Resources Development Bill passed through Parliament in June 1947, and eight months before it received Royal Assent in February 1948, its chairman-designate, Lord Trefgarne, was appointed and by November he had a Board appointed and able to meet for first time. The corporation's first official meeting was in March 1948.

The CDC was set up with a complex organisational structure involving five regional corporations (West Indies, West Africa, Central Africa, East Africa and Far East) and nine commercial operating divisions, a total of fifteen managers/chairmen below the level of the two joint controllers, an executive council and the chairman. The commercial operations divisions consisted of equipment and supplies, animal products, agriculture (crops and forestry separately), fisheries, minerals, engineering and works, factories, marketing and hotels. Its headquarters staff in London numbered 216 by the end of 1949 and 340 by the end of 1950. Additionally there were over one hundred staff working in the regional offices or on particular schemes, not counting employees recruited locally in the colonies.[35]

The aims of CDC were two-fold: first, to increase colonial output, especially exports: 'It is . . . only by increased production and trade that these territories can earn the funds with which to purchase many of the commodities and supplies which they at present lack'.[36] Second, to save dollars. Although the colonial empire was a net dollar-earner, this was mainly so because of West African cocoa and Malayan rubber and tin. The perceived need was to reduce purchases from, and to increase sales of produce to, the United States. This aim also required lifting output. The problem faced by colonial agriculture was indentified as a 'low level of agricultural technique and mechanisation' which would have to be raised.[37]

The CDC intended to fulfil its mission to raise the physical output of the colonial economies by engaging directly in production itself – by owning and operating plantations, ranches, mines and factories. This attitude was part of the ethos of 'getting the job done' and it also reflected a belief in the ability of Western technology and management skills – especially mechanised methods in agriculture – to raise productivity in the colonies. The sense of urgency and predilection for hands-on methods was reinforced by a strong desire on the part of the CDC board to exercise its independence from close control by the Colonial Office or government.[38] However, the CDC's desire for quick results and to be free from having to check back with the Colonial Office over every proposal led to some unwise choices of development projects. The CDC's philosophy was to 'prefer venture to caution, launch the project and do their best to push it through every obstacle to success', which displayed perhaps an understandable enthusiasm after the many years of neglect of colonial development, inaction and excessive caution by the Colonial Office, colonial governments and the Treasury.[39] Like the OFC, the CDC saw itself as engaged on a crusade to bring about a new era in colonial development using methods not attempted before and tackling problems considered to be at the root of colonial economic stagnation head on and with full vigour. Yet the corporation swung too far in the opposite direction and this led to problems when the successes which it had pushed so hard for and so loudly heralded did not materialise, benefiting neither the British taxpayers nor the colonial inhabitants.

By the end of 1949, the CDC had approved twenty-nine projects of which nineteen were operational. These were selected from those submitted by colonial governments or private concerns operating in the colonies, using as criteria the likelihood of increasing exports on a long-term basis and 'subject to this condition, the corporation has naturally aimed at selecting the projects which show promise of either earning or saving dollars, in the interests of the territory itself and the sterling areas as a whole'.[40] The devaluation of sterling by 30 per cent in September 1949 intensified the need to find alternative sources of supply within the sterling area of commodities normally purchased from the United States and made the dollar area an even more attractive market. Colonial development could assist by production of such commodities as tobacco, cotton, sugar and softwoods, by increasing production of rice for colonial consumption and by stepping-up exports of cocoa, rubber and tin to the US market.

Whatever the prospects for colonial development helping to close the dollar gap, most of the projects established by the CDC were for the production of food for the UK market. Quite apart from the enormous problems encountered in raising the output of agricultural and animal products, there arose the question of marketing in Britain. The sole buyer in the UK for nearly all colonial food exports was the Ministry of Food, and the CDC therefore sought assurances and long-term contracts from the Ministry of Food for the foodstuffs it was proposing to produce in the tropical colonies, but without success: the Ministry of Food could buy from UK, dominion, colonial and foreign sources and was not willing to jeopardise its buying power and flexibility by offering a guaranteed market for colonial foodstuffs in the British market. This caused further uncertainty in the CDC's calculations as to the viability of projects – how much could be sold in the United Kingdom, and at what price.

By 1950 the CDC had lost £1.7 million with a loss of £1.3 million in 1950 alone.[41] Of the £1.7 million, trading losses on the schemes which were operational amounted to £296,000, a further £776,000 was for investments written off in failed projects and £618,000 represented the overhead costs of head office and regional offices, of which three-quarters was due to staff wages. The CDC's income consisted of the profits which could be made from its projects, but of the twenty schemes which were operating by the end of 1950, only eight registered a profit. It had not been anticipated that the CDC would show a net profit in its first five years, but the extent of its losses and the dramatic failure of a number of schemes caused considerable concern. In October 1950 the CDC's chairman, Lord Trefgarne, resigned following widespread criticism of one failed scheme, the Gambia Poultry Farm (see below for discussion of individual schemes), and was replaced by Lord Reith, a man whose control of the BBC in the 1920s and 1930s had given him a reputation for fearless efficiency.

The main problem seemed to be cost overruns resulting from initial underestimation and rising costs of materials and equipment during the Korean War. The rapid expansion of schemes – 'the pace set by urgent needs which the corporation was set up to meet' – exposed a lack of adequate investigatory work and pilot schemes: 'Where the Corporation has tried to avoid the expense and delay of adequate experiments and trials . . . the consequences have certainly been unfortunate.'[42] From now on, Reith warned, 'Schemes which show little or no prospect of paying their way are being radically overhauled, as with the Gambia Poultry Farm; they will be shut down if no sound alternative can be devised.'[43] Reith spent the next four years putting this policy into practice, jettisoning twenty-nine projects and writing off over £9 million in irretrievable losses in the process. As well as having to abandon schemes, the CDC continued to make operating losses. In 1951 its projects (including loans) made a net loss of £643,000, to which administration costs were added to bring the operating loss to £1,070,000.[44] In 1952 its projects lost £635,000 and administration costs brought the overall operating loss to £1,097,000. Only in 1953 did the net loss on projects decline – as some were abandoned and others increased their revenues – to £148,000 which with administration expenses brought the net operating loss of the CDC to £644,000. In 1954 a net profit on projects and loans to colonial governments was recorded for the first time – of £167,000 – but with administration expenses a net operating loss of £201,000 was made. However, this marked a turning point, the last year in which a net operating loss was made by the CDC.

The harrowing experience of the CDC in the early 1950s, when failed schemes outnumbered successful ones and the financial results were alarming, suggested a number of lessons of a general nature, not least of which was' that any suggestions for immediate large-scale development must be treated with particular caution'.[45] Other 'lessons' learned included not overstocking expensive heavy equipment, not over-using expensive European personnel and being aware of rising costs and over-capitalisation. CDC policy now emphasised the need for partners – governments and private enterprise – to share the risk and provide expertise. In Reith's view, the company suffered from 'inaccurate estimating, and from incompetence' which cooperation with outside investors might help alleviate.[46] However, attracting private capital proved almost impossible in the first half of the decade, though some colonial governments became willing partners. The CDC lacked 'financial discipline and sense of responsibility at head office and throughout the world', its projects were often 'misbegotten', 'mishandled' and 'prejudiced by extravagance and inefficiency'.[47] Looking back from 1954, Reith concluded 'too much was attempted too quickly in early years'.[48]

The failure of so many of the CDC's projects meant that 'preoccupation of senior staff with liquidations and riddances and reorganisation has been, in the last four years, a serious and sickening limitation on activity'.[49] It also brought to a head the CDC's financial relations with the British government, for as the CDC wrote off capital invested in failed schemes the question was raised as to whether it would have to continue paying interest to the government on this capital and whether it would have to be repaid. Negotiations dragged on for several years. In 1953 the government agreed to waive interest due from the CDC on approximately three-quarters of the capital advanced for schemes now abandoned, but insisted that the lost capital itself must be repaid. Suggestions that advances to the CDC should only be repayable if the project they were used for was profitable, made in 1952, fell on deaf ears in the Treasury. As a result, CDC projects veered away from agricultural schemes, which were the most risky, and towards loans to colonial governments and public utilities, even thought it was argued this prevented the corporation from fulfilling what it saw as its 'real function'.[50]

After seven very lean years, the CDC at last made a net profit of £409,000 in 1955 after all out-goings including interest paid to the British government. The special losses account was increased to £8 million, but this, claimed Reith, was the end of its rise: from now on all schemes either were viable or would become so and if any losses did occur it would be as a result of normal market forces rather than being 'rashly undertaken or badly managed'.[51] In Reith's view 'the past is passed'.

Certainly this was true financially as the CDC continued to make net operating profits from 1955 to its transformation into the Commonwealth Development Corporation in 1963. Continued disagreement between the CDC and the British government over the special losses account, which by 1958 had risen to £8.8 million, led to an independent inquiry being held in 1959 under the chairmanship of Lord Sinclair of Cleve.[52] This inquiry was sympathetic to the problems which the CDC now faced as a result of its earlier financial losses and project failures. The CDC's policy of shifting its activity away from risky direct projects and towards 'finance house' type business was regarded as both necessary and responsible. The Sinclair Committee recommended that CDC debts to the British government be converted into stock, current borrowing for 'finance house' type projects to pay interest immediately, funds borrowed for other projects to enjoy an interest free period of seven years and the special losses to bear no interest at all and be repaid if and when the CDC's other obligations to the British government had been met. The Sinclair Committee reported in September 1959 but it was not until April 1961 that the secretary of state for the colonies announced new financial arrangements for the CDC, by which time the special losses account had reached £9.9 million. The government declined to swap debt for equity and insisted that the CDC must repay all of the lost capital plus accumulated interest on the special losses account. This totalled £230 million. A formula was devised whereby the CDC kept £250,000 from each year's net operating profits, but gave 60 per cent of the remainder to the government to repay this debt. This was accepted by the CDC – under its new chairman, Lord Howick – as providing 'a sounder, stronger and more realistic basis for its future operations than has obtained hitherto', but it did not remove the burden of past debt from the CDC's balance sheets and thus made it difficult for the CDC either to attract more private capital in partnership in projects or alter its policy of seeking low-risk investments and 'finance house' type business.[53]

The extent to which loans to governments and statutory authorities and to commercial enterprises dominated CDC activity in the later 1950s is indicated by Table 12.1. There was a marked fall in the share of CDC income from direct projects and subsidiaries from 1955, the first year in which the CDC became profitable. By the end of the 1950s only one-quarter of CDC's total revenue came from these projects. Similarly, the importance of income from interest on loans can be seen in Table 12.2 from 1958 (the first year for which information on interest is shown

COLONIALISM AND DEVELOPMENT

Table 12.1 Sources of Colonial Development Corporation income, 1950–62

Year	Total income £'000	Direct projects (%)	Subsidiary companies (%)	Loans to govt & SAs (%)	Other investments (%)
1950	89.5	4.2	17.7	29.7	48.5
1951	202.7	3.9	21.1	51.6	23.4
1952	470.7	5.4	55.1	34.1	5.4
1953	639.0	3.6	52.7	35.6	8.1
1954	807.6	8.8	43.0	38.1	10.1
1955	1,123.6	14.9	13.8	37.1	34.1
1956	1,570.1	8.9	21.5	34.9	34.7
1957	1,857.6	3.1	25.6	41.6	29.7
1958	2,352.4	7.9	26.8	36.1	29.2
1959	2,367.9	10.8	17.4	40.4	31.4
1960	2,832.8	6.6	22.2	38.5	32.7
1961	3,900.0	5.7	20.3	39.2	34.8
1962	4,932.9	6.9	18.3	42.7	32.1

SAs, Statutory authorities
Source: Profit/Loss Accounts, CDC Annual Reports.

Table 12.2 Sources of Colonial Development Corporation income, 1958–1962

Year	Total income £000	% from profits	% from dividends	% from interest
1958	2,352.4	9.9	14.3	75.8
1959	2,367.9	10.8	15.2	74.0
1960	2,832.8	6.6	12.9	80.4
1961	3,900.0	5.7	19.7	74.6
1962	4,932.9	6.9	9.7	83.4

Source: as for Table 12.1.

separately from dividends). By the end of the 1950s the CDC received four-fifths of its earned income in the form of interest payments on loans which it had made. The chairman defended this policy on the grounds that the CDC must be able to cover its overheads before it could look to investing in riskier development schemes:

critics who complain that CDC is not venturesome enough – 'not doing the job it was set up to do' – should understand [that] ... CDC must pay its way ... profit and loss account must show a profit – taking one year with another. Each year some projects will contribute a plus and some a minus ... since an undue number of early projects showed minuses and had to be abandoned or

288

severely cut back, CDC must necessarily avoid riskier and less profitable schemes until balance is restored'.[54]

From 1956 a second source of conflict with the British government developed as the CDC was told to cease investment in colonies which were about to become independent – in this case, the Gold Coast and Malaya – as it ruled that the operations of the CDC must be confined to Britain's colonies. The CDC responded by adopting a strategy of establishing development agencies in colonies which were approaching independence which could act as vehicles for post-independence economic development under the guidance of the CDC, though it still could not invest its own money in any particular scheme. In 1961 the government set up a review into the question of the geographical constraints on CDC activities and as a result announced the creation of a new body to take over from the CDC: the Commonwealth Development Corporation, which from 1963 would operate throughout the Commonwealth.[55]

CDC PROJECTS

Although the CDC was not charged with production of any particular commodity in the colonies, foodstuffs and agricultural raw materials were its main concern in its early years of operations. This reflected a view that there was a world shortage of primary products in the immediate post-war years and of tropical foodstuffs in particular. Many foods were still rationed in Britain, including fats and vegetable oils, some of which could be produced in Britain's colonies. Local supplies of foodstuffs in the colonies were regarded as inadequate. They caused malnutrition and in some colonies a heavy reliance on food imports. The CDC recognised the problems of growing food in tropical conditions, especially that of soil erosion and soil exhaustion, and stressed the need for extensive preliminary investigation before going ahead with food production.[56] In practice, however, the CDC frequently did not heed its own advice, with disastrous consequences.

Over the fifteen years to 1962 the CDC was involved in forty-two schemes for producing foods, including animal products and fisheries, and thirty-five of these were started during the first five years of operation (1948–52 shown in Table 12.3). The CDC was not very successful at producing food, whether to alleviate hunger in the colonies, assist Britain's food shortages or earn export revenue: twenty-nine of the forty-two schemes started were failures and three-quarters of those begun in the first five years failed. Fisheries were regarded as an underdeveloped area of the colonies' economies, as one to which advanced Western technology could be successfully applied, and as an important element in the fight against 'the continuing shortage of oils and fats'.[57]

Table 12.3 Colonial Development Corporation projects for food production, 1948–52

Colony	Year	Project Name	Purpose	Result
Falkland Is.	1948	South Atlantic Sealing Co.	Seal oil for UK	Abandoned 1952
Gambia	1948	Poultry Scheme	Poultry products for UK	Abandoned 1951
Nyasaland	1948	Lake Nyasa Fishery	Dried fish, local market	Abandoned 1951
Gambia	1949	Gambia Rice Farm	Rice, local and export market	Abandoned 1952
Nigeria	1949	Niger Agricultural Project	Groundnuts, local and export	Abandoned 1953
Br. Honduras	1949	Sittee Cocoa Ltd	Cocoa & bananas for export	Abandoned 1952
Br. Honduras	1949	B.H. Fruit Co. Ltd	Bananas for export	Abandoned 1952
Malaya[a]	1949	Malayan Cocoa Ltd	Cocoa for export	Began trading 1961
Dominica[a]	1949	Melville Hall Estate	Bananas, citrus for export	Profitable most years
Dominica	1949	Castle Bruce Estate	Citrus, coconut for export	Abandoned 1853
Dominica	1949	Packing & Grading Station	Citrus for export	Abandoned 1952
Falkland Is.	1949	Abattoir & Freezer	Sheepmeat, beef for export	Abandoned 1955
Jamaica[a]	1949	Cool Store	Citrus for export	Profitable from 1952
Nigeria	1949	West African Fisheries	Fish for local market	Abandoned 1953
Gambia	1949	Atlantic Fisheries Ltd	Shark for vitamin A for UK	Abandoned 1952
Bahamas	1949	Eleuthera Is. Estate	Vegetables for local market	Abandoned 1954
Bechuanaland	1950	Bechuanaland Cattle Ranch	Fatten cattle	Abandoned 1960
Bechuanaland[a]	1950	Lobatsi Abattoir	Beef for S. African market	Profitable from 1955
Br. Honduras	1950	B.H. Stock Farms	Cattle & sheep, local market	Abandoned 1951
Jamaica	1950	Grand Cayman Turtle Cannery	Turtle soup for US market	Abandoned 1954
Malaya[a]	1950	Kulai Oil Palm Estate	Palm oil for export	Profitable from 1950
N. Borneo	1950	Rice Project	Rice for local market	Abandoned 1950
Nyasaland	1950	Kasunga Tobacco Estates	Tobacco for export	Made losses 1951–62
Nyasaland	1950	Limpassa Dambo Farm	Rice for local market	Abandoned 1951
Seychelles	1950	Seychelles Fishery	Dried fish, E. Africa market	Abandoned 1952
Swaziland[a]	1950	Swaziland Irrigation Scheme	Rice, sugar, local & export market	Profitable from 1958
Tristan da Cunha	1950	Tristan da Cunha Fishery	Crawfish, lobster, S. African market	Losses, sold 1961
Br. Honduras	1951	Cramer Estates	Cocoa for export	Abandoned 1956
Jamaica[a]	1951	Citrus Growers Ltd	Loan to company to expand	Loan repaid
Gambia	1951	Yundum Farm	Experimental farm	Abandoned 1954
N. Borneo	1951	Kasunga Cattle Ranch	Beef cattle (investigation)	Abandoned 1952
Br. Somaliland	1951	Abattoir	Camel & sheepmeat	Abandoned 1952
Bechuanaland[a]	1952	Molopo Holding Ranch	Fatten cattle for Lobatsi abattoir	Profitable from 1953
Kenya	1952	Kenya Fish Farms	Fish farming, local market	Abandoned 1953
Swaziland[a]	1952	Ubombo Ranches	Loan to ranching company	Loan repaid

[a] These projects were generally commercially viable.
Source: Annual Reports of the CDC.

All of the fishery projects were started in the first five years of operations and all failed. They involved sealing off the Falkland Islands, deep-sea fishing off Nigeria and Gambia, and in the Seychelles and at Tristan da Cuhna, as well as a scheme for developing fish products on Lake Nyasa and another one for fish farming in Kenya. Together they cost the CDC about £1 million in lost capital invested. The main causes of failure were the cost, delay in supplying and frequent breakdown of boats and equipment, high European salaries which added to overheads, far smaller catches than had been anticipated and, as far as selling in local markets was concerned, a great difficulty in competing with local fishers. Schemes were generally under-costed and poorly managed. Some were also overly ambitious.

The CDC made only six attempts to produce food using farming schemes as opposed to plantations, and two of these were investigations in Gambia (in 1951 and 1959) which yielded no positive results. The remaining four were started prior to 1951 and reached the production stage before being abandoned as commercially unviable. Each involved the use of mechanical methods for clearing, planting and/or harvesting. Three were for rice in the Gambia, Nyasaland and North Borneo, and one, the Niger Agricultural Project in Nigeria, produced groundnuts.[58] The lost capital was put at around £750,000. Reasons for their failure were the cost of mechanised cultivation, including costs associated with problems of breakdown and maintenance in tropical conditions of machines designed for European or North American farming; high overhead costs resulting from the employment of European technicians, mechanics, machinery operators and supervisors; inadequate time allotted for experimental work because the schemes were urged on to full production by the world food crisis; and the fact that both rice and groundnuts were crops which were produced by peasant farmers in many parts of the world and against which the produce of these kind of farms had to compete in open markets. The CDC did try to obtain long-term contracts for its food production from the Ministry of Food, but the latter interpreted its duty to buy as cheaply as possible in world markets rather than to provide a guaranteed market for colonial producers including the CDC. Consequently, when foodstuffs were grown, the prices they fetched were far from remunerative.

Animal products schemes suffered a deal of failure too, but two of the six projects the CDC started were successful. Of these six, five were for beef cattle and one for poultry; of the cattle schemes, two were short-lived experiments, one consisted of a small commercial loan to an existing South African cattle ranch operating in Swaziland which was successful in the sense that it was repaid on time; and there were two schemes in Bechuanaland where the CDC itself attempted to run beef cattle one of which was eventually profitable.

The Gambia Poultry Farm was the first of the CDC's large food-producing projects to fail and the first to bring serious parliamentary criticism down on the CDC. It was a scheme closely associated with the CDC chairman, Lord Trefgarne, who took personal responsibility for its success. When its collapse became inevitable in 1950 he resigned.[59] The concept was to develop a large-scale poultry farm growing its own supplies of feedstuffs and supplying the British market with chickens and eggs. It aimed at an output of 20 million eggs and 1,000,000 lb of dressed chicken per year. Begun at the end of 1948, it expected to have 90,000 hens in place by the end of 1950 and 10,000 acres of land mechanically cleared and cultivated for feedstuffs. Although Lord Trefgarne expressed 'every confidence in this soundly conceived and executed undertaking' in 1949, early in 1950 it became clear that the sixteen crawler tractors used to clear and plough the land were failing to do so – because they were inadequate for the job and kept breaking down – which meant the feedstuffs were insufficient for the chickens and half the flock died.[60] Moreover, the laying performance of the birds was below initial estimates, the flock succumbed to disease and most of the poultry and eggs shipped to Britain were declared unfit for consumption. The scheme was abandoned early in 1951 following a report that showed it could never be viable. The CDC lost over £800,000 in this scheme, £532,000 of which was written-off capital. The CDC had expressed the belief at the outset that

> Animal husbandry in the colonies holds out very large possibilities. . . . The Boards believe that the prospects are of an order which, if vigorously pursued, will make a material contribution to world meat supplies.[61]

As with other food production schemes, however, early failures accompanied by large financial losses and hostile public criticism, led the CDC to completely avoid this area of development in subsequent years.

The CDC was hardly more successful with its projects for food processing where five out of its eight schemes failed. These comprised three abattoirs, two schemes for storage, packing and grading of fruit, two canneries and a flour mill. Two of the abattoirs failed, the one on the Falkland Islands for the development of an export trade in frozen beef and mutton was a complete disaster which cost the CDC £525,000. The causes were rising costs of equipment and delays in its delivery, high turnover of managerial staff on site, insufficient supply of stock, substandard produce which led to one-quarter of exports being rejected by UK inspectors and the high cost of construction work carried out by the CDC's engineering branch.

In the West Indies a citrus packing and grading station in Dominica was built in 1949 but abandoned after three years of losses caused by an inadequate supply from the growers. This problem was avoided by a Jamaican cooling store operated by the CDC from 1952 as its supplies were guaranteed by the local citrus growers' association and it returned modest profits to the CDC throughout. Both of the cannery projects attempted by the CDC ended in failure. Investment in a Kenyan flour mill, however, in 1956 was viable and produced interest and dividends for the CDC, though it played no role in managing the mill.

The type of food production where the CDC experienced least failure was plantation schemes where fifteen projects were launched and seven failed. Seven schemes involved the purchase of moribund plantations in Dominica, the Bahamas, Malaya, Swaziland, British Honduras and Tanganyika growing bananas, citrus, coconuts, vegetables, palm oil, rice, sugar and cocoa. Of these, four were abandoned, while Melville Hall Estate on Dominica survived but operated at a loss. The outstanding success was Kulai Oil Palm Estate in Malaya purchased in 1950 and rehabilitated. Good management and high prices for plantation-quality palm oil were the main reasons for its making profits and an average return on the investment of £1 million of 2.3 per cent per annum. A further five plantation schemes were ones where the CDC started from scratch, though the results were not much better: three were abandoned and the two surviving schemes in 1962 were still making losses.

Food production in the colonies was the major activity of the CDC in its early years and the least successful. Three-quarters of the food-producing schemes in the first five years failed and some of the surviving schemes were not commercially viable. The CDC set itself the task of alleviating food shortages in the colonies and in Britain but could not be said to have done so as far as fisheries and rice and groundnut farms were concerned and only one of its animal products schemes (Molopo) was at all successful. Amongst the plantations Kulai Oil Palm Estate was definitely a success and possibly the Swaziland irrigation scheme and the investments in two sugar plantations could be counted as successes; two food processing plants were also successful. Of the thirty-five early schemes for producing more food for a hungry world, then, at least thirty were failures which produced little or nothing in increased supplies and contributed considerably to the CDC's growing problem of indebtedness.

Like foodstuffs, agricultural raw materials and forestry products were regarded as being in short supply after the war and the CDC was anxious to develop new and existing colonial sources to help alleviate the problem. It embarked on seven schemes for the production of agricultural raw materials and four forestry projects, all but two of these in its first five years (see Table 12.4). These endeavours proved somewhat less disaster-prone than those for foodstuffs, though were not outstanding commercial successes.

Table 12.4 Colonial Development Corporation projects for agricultural raw materials and minerals, 1948–52

Colony	Year	Project Name	Purpose	Result
Br. Guiana[a]	1948	British Guiana Timbers	Lumber exports to UK market	Profitable from 1956
Nyasaland[a]	1948	Vipya Tung Estates	Tung oil, UK market	Profitable from 1962
N. Borneo[a]	1948	N. Borneo Abaca Ltd	Rubber, hemp for export	Profitable from 1956
Tanganyika[a]	1949	Tanganyika Wattle Estate	Wattle bark extract for export	Began production 1959
Swaziland[a]	1949	Usutu Forests	Conifers for pulp mill, export market	Began production 1961
Br. Honduras	1950	Barton Ramie Estate	To grow ramie fibre, export	Abandoned 1955
Nigeria	1950	Omo Sawmills	Timber for local market	Losses, sold off 1961
Kenya	1951	East Africa Ramie	To grow ramie (investigation)	Abandoned 1956
Nyasaland	1952	Nyika Forestry Syndicate	Pine trees for pulp (investigation)	Abandoned 1956
Br. Guiana	1948	B.G. Goldfields Ltd	Gold mining, export	Abandoned 1958
Jamaica	1948	Turks and Caicos Salt	Salt production	Abandoned 1956
Kenya	1950	Macalder-Nyanza Mines Ltd	Copper for export	Abandoned 1960
Tanganyika	1950	Coalfields Investigation	Coal (investigation)	Abandoned 1953
Tanganyika[a]	1950	Tangold Mining Co Ltd	Loans to mining company	In default 1962
Tanganyika	1951	Murongo Mines	Tin, wolfram (investigation)	Abandoned 1955
Kenya	1952	Vitingini Lead Mine	Lead deposits (investigation)	Abandoned 1953
Tanganyika	1952	Liganga Iron Ore Mine	Iron-ore (investigation)	Moribund 1954

[a] Commercially viable scheme.
Source CDC Annual Reports.

The CDC undertook four forestry projects one of which, an investigation into the possibilities of growing pines in Nyasaland, which was not followed up. Two of the others were for sawmills using native forest but neither was successful: one at Omo in Nigeria was sold off in 1961 following a series of losses, and a scheme in British Guiana begun in 1948 only survived losses throughout the 1950s by writing off a large part of its capital in 1961. In both cases the CDC blamed poor local management and a fickle market for timber products. In the case of British Guiana Timbers Ltd, the CDC was influenced in its original decision to invest by the propect of sales to the US market for much needed hard currency. The chairman commented a few year later: '[The] Company earns dollars but it has been at monstrous cost in sterling.'[62] The most successful of the forestry projects was Usutu Forests in Swaziland. From 1949 the CDC spent ten years and £13 million growing a 95,000 acre pine forest which it then sold at a profit to Courtaulds Ltd, who erected a pulp mill in partnership with the CDC and first went into production in 1962. This scheme was much closer to the model developed in the later 1950s which saw the appropriate role of the CDC as a pioneer which broke new ground and then went into partnership with an established and successful private company once the production stage was reached. Usutu was, however, one of the few schemes which ultimately conformed to this plan; in the earlier years the CDC tended to go in for direct production which frequently failed, in the later years it veered toward safe commercial loans.

Mining was the one other area where the CDC addressed the post-war shortages of primary products head on and with a similarly distinct lack of success as experienced with food, agricultural raw materials and forestry. Five mines were brought into operation by the CDC and a further six schemes were investigated but not followed up. Only two of the five were successful and one of these was not viable commercially being in default of interest in 1961 and 1962. The one clear success was at Kilembe in Uganda where an existing copper and cobalt mine required a capital injection which CDC agreed to provide in 1953. The CDC invested £1 million in equity (20 per cent of the total) and made loans of £1.05 million. The project's profits fluctuated with variable copper prices in the later 1950s, but it paid its first dividend to CDC in 1961 of $6\frac{1}{4}$ per cent. The major shareholder was a Canadian-based international mining company. Part of the recipe of success here seemed to be control and management by an experienced private concern.

The failed mining ventures showed some of the same problems encountered in the agricultural projects: delays in equipment delivery, mechanical failure, poor management, cost-overruns and lower than expected mineral prices. The two major failures were in British Guiana and Kenya, British Guiana Consolidated Goldfields and Macalder-Nyaza

Mines Ltd. Mining was a notoriously risky business, the CDC did not have any particular expertise and was under pressure to achieve quick results. Inevitably it tended to fail and where it was successful it was in junior partnership with an experienced mining house.

The fifty-two schemes for production of foodstuffs, raw materials, forestry and minerals began during the first five years of the CDC's operations, represented three-quarters of all the projects started in that period. The remainder were mainly in service industries and were substantially more successful in commercial terms although two attempts at developing transport services failed and the CDC lost over £1 million on its engineering and works division alone. The CDC proved no more interested in schemes to promote industrialisation in the colonies than occurred under the Colonial Development and Welfare Act: it started only six industrial projects in its twelve years, one of which was abandoned. Its main novel contribution was in financing several building societies and constructing eight hotels.

The CDC was not established in order to make loans to colonial governments, which could apply for CDW funding, though it was not precluded from making such loans by its charter. Increasingly it did so, in order to provide a safe return on its funds as its more direct projects ran into difficulties. Loans to colonial governments and their statutory authorities accounted for 40 to 50 per cent of the CDC's advances, one-third of its committed capital and around 35 per cent of its income on average in the second half of the 1950s. These loans differed from commercial loans to private companies in that they were risk-free, though like commercial loans they usually involved the CDC in little or no management activity. The loans were put to varied uses: of the seventeen loans made between 1948 and 1962, five were for agricultural projects, four were for housing, two each were for electricity supply, air transport and water supply, one was for property development in Lagos and one was for a hotel in Freetown. The agricultural projects consisted of rice growing in British Guiana, an abattoir in Kenya, plantation rehabitation in the British Cameroons, tea-growing in Kenya and small-holder development in Malaya. A little over half its total lendings went to the two electricity supply projects in Malay and the Federation of Rhodesia and Nyasaland (Kariba). In these investments CDC money fulfilled a function similar to that of CDW funds, though there was no formal integration of the projects of the two sources of finance. In both types of colonial development the initiative really lay with the local government which conceived of the project and carried it through, often contributing its own funds as well.

That the CDC survived to 1962 and then formed the core of the Commonwealth Development Corporation was perhaps surprising in view of its failures during its first five years. As a Labour government creation involving the use of public money to invest in production in the colonies, and one which was in serious financial difficulties, it might well have been scrapped by the Conservative administration. The CDC was saved by the resistance and hard work of its chairman, Lord Reith, who managed to keep the government at bay on the one hand while shifting the CDC away from risky direct projects in primary production and towards safe loans and investments in the services sector and cutting administrative costs on the other.[63]

In breaking new ground in state-directed economic development in the colonies the CDC discovered why so little had been accomplished during the previous half-century or more of British rule and why private enterprise was so often unwilling to be adventurous and had so often failed. Agricultural development in the tropics was extremely hazardous and the experience of the CDC in its early years showed the problems of depending on European technology and expertise to obtain quick results. Under Reith the CDC too became much less adventurous but also much less unprofitable. The eventual financial success of the CDC from the British government's point of view tended to obscure the question of whether it made any worthwhile contributions to the problem of economic development in the tropical colonies from the viewpoint of the colonial inhabitants. The CDC felt that it had helped to increase production, earn more export revenue and raise living standards, though in the total context of colonial economics its contribution remained small. Insofar as it did assist even in a minor way to point to some new avenues for economic development during the final phases of colonial rule it could be concluded that the experiment of 1947 was worthwhile, although the results achieved were rather different by the early 1960s from those envisaged at that time.

The new directions in colonial economic development and the revolution in ways of producing in the tropics which the OFC and CDC pursued between 1946 and 1955 were fraught with difficulties. Not least of these was the conflict between the needs of Britain for quick results in the form of supplies of foodstuffs and other primary products and the needs of the colonies for schemes of economic development to raise the productivity and eventually the living standards of the mass of their inhabitants. Many of the projects begun by these two corporations, as we have seen, ended in disaster and failure because of inappropriate organisation and techniques, particularly the attempts to use mechanised agriculture. In most cases it could hardly be claimed that the activities of these corporations led to any significant transfer of Western technology to the colonial economies since much of it failed under tropical conditions. The imaginative projects undertaken by these corporations tended to steal the limelight in post-war colonial economic development which only increased their negative influence when they collapsed. The less spectacular but safer efforts of colonial development and welfare continued to be made, albeit at levels of expenditure which were quite inadequate in the time-frame of British colonial rule. If the British government had not been distracted by the allure of the 'big scheme' driven by a crash-through mentality it is possible that more attention and more resources (including the £45 million lost by the OFC and the CDC) would have been devoted to the work of the colonial governments assisted by CDW funds and with rather better results for the colonial economies.

13

Developing the 'great estate'
The legacies of colonialism and development

The British government was rather wary of making specific promises on colonial development. Its statements about its long-term aims in this regard were made mainly in the post-war years in response to Britain's economic crisis and international and colonial nationalist criticism that Britain was failing to fulfil its obligations as an imperial power. Emphasis was often placed on the role of export production:

> Against the background of national economic difficulties there are four features of economic development in the Colonies which can be readily appreciated and which are consistent with the indispensable objective of strengthening the colonial economies. First, the Colonies are already producing important quantities of many commodities in world demand, notably rubber, cocoa, fibres, vegetable oils, sugar and tropical fruits, and improvements and expansion in these established industries offer the greatest contribution to Europe's distress. . . . Second, there exist possibilities of production in new fields; but considerable practical and material difficulties have to be overcome if these possibilities are to be of medium or long-term significance. Third, if results are to be obtained the necessary priorities have to be given for plant and materials in short supply, and also for supplies of consumer goods. Fourth, machinery has to be devised to make available the necessary capital, and to undertake the tasks of investigation and supervision. [June 1948][1]

The Colonial Empire produces foodstuffs and raw materials which the Western nations need. The more of them they can export, the more money they will earn with which to purchase consumer goods, improve their social services, and further expand their production through the provision of better or more extensive basic services – roads and railways, water and power supplies, irrigation schemes, and so on. With the rise in Colonial living standards comes a further advantage to the Western countries, in the stimulus given to the colonial markets for their manufactured goods. [June 1949][2]

The problem of unbalanced development was also acknowledged:

I turn first to consider economic developments in the Colonial Territories. On the economic side, our aim is to seek to build, in every one of the Territories, a stable economy by developing its agricultural, mineral or industrial resources, by improving methods of production, by safeguarding the natural wealth of the country and by instilling 'good husbandry' in all economic activities, and, most important, by diversifying those activities so that development is not lop-sided, and, consequently, dependent upon a few basic products. [July 1950][3]

The United Kingdom's economic development policy for the Colonies may be summed up as aiming to build in every territory a stable economy that is not dependent on a few basic products. Much of the assistance the United Kingdom makes available to the Colonies is devoted to this end. [March 1951][4]

The importance of the colonies own financial and other resources and the primacy of private enterprise was also stressed:

Most Colonies have plans for long-term development financed primarily from their own resources but assisted by grants from Colonial Development and Welfare funds and from public loans raised on the London market. . . . The major role in the development of direct production is played by private enterprise, and it is the aim of Governments to create and maintain conditions favourable to it. [May 1954][5]

The theory of economic development which officials held in relation to the tropical colonies was one of export-led growth. Exports were regarded as essential to economic growth, first to service external loans and second to pay for the import of capital goods which were required. Imports were mainly financed by export earnings plus foreign borrowing because levels of domestic savings in the colonial economies were extremely low.[6] Imports of capital goods (and services such as those provided by engineering consultants) were needed to develop the infrastructure of the colonial economies which in turn was necessary in order to attract private investment, mainly foreign but possibly domestic as well. Developing the capacity of the colonies to import goods and services from Britain was an essential element in the colonial relationship of 'complementary economies'. The colonies were to complement

300

the British economy by exporting primary products and importing manufactured goods. In this sense the Chamberlain concept of development persisted in the minds of officials throughout the colonial era. However, two major modifications to the Chamberlain view were made. In the 1930s it was recognised that loans needed to be supplemented (or replaced) by free capital grants as the colonies were too poor to afford sufficient loan capital; additionally, it gradually came to be accepted that social welfare development could not wait until a higher level of economic development had been achieved, but must be provided in order to alleviate the worst manifestations of poverty and that this expenditure should be financed mainly by colonial governments assisted by external grants of aid. These were partial qualifications to the earlier attitude but, of course, their impact depended on how much aid Britain was willing or able to supply and the condition of colonial public finances. In the latter stages of the colonial era there was some reversion to the earlier position that colonies should be as self-sufficient as possible.

Export earnings were partly commandeered by the colonial governments via taxation to be used to pay for economic and social services and development projects, and to service the foreign loans they had raised. Loans were used mainly to finance development schemes, often for transport and communications. Export earnings also serviced foreign private investment, nearly all of which was in the export sector. Because exports were regarded as the 'engine of growth' the export industries received the bulk of the state's attention and resources and most of the private foreign investment (and domestic investment where this occurred), to the relative neglect of the subsistence sector and the non-export market sector (i.e. food and simple manufactures produced for the home market).[7]

As discussed at various points earlier in this book, there were a number of problems with this approach to economic development. First, despite the emphasis placed on their growth, exports did not always increase in real terms as fast as might have been expected from their initial surge prior to the First World War. The best decade for growth was the final one of the colonial era. Moreover, the export sector in some colonies was small in relation to the entire economy, especially where large subsistence or semi-subsistence sectors existed.[8] Exports may have been the 'engine of growth' but often were not a very powerful engine. Exports as an 'engine of growth' were rendered even less effective because of the high propensity for consumption which the colonies exhibited. A substantial part of export earnings were used to finance the import of consumer goods, including basic foodstuffs and even luxury goods in colonies with a large number of European settlers. A policy of encouraging import substitution would have had the effect of raising the proportion of capital goods in the total import mix.[9] Such 'leakages' occurred because the colonies lacked an import-substitution policy, the absence of which largely resulted from the persistence of the 'complementary economies' approach.

Second, linkages between the export sector and the rest of the colonial economy were quite weak. Such linkages are often characterised as backward, forward and final demand linkages.[10] The nature and power of these varied between the tropical colonies and differed between export industries which consisted predominately of plantations, or peasant producers or mining. Backward linkages referred to the supply by the non-export sector of inputs to the export industries; for example, plant and equipment, tools and machinery, fertiliser. However, in the colonial economies, most of these were imported. The most important backward linkage was transport, principally government-owned railways and harbours and privately owned trucking enterprises. Forward linkages were industries for which the export commodity was an input and chiefly consisted of processing. Since most primary produce was exported in an unprocessed state, however, this linkage was usually weak. Final demand linkages were those which connected the export industry to the domestic economy via the expenditures of workers employed in the export activity. The sale of food and consumer goods to plantation or mine workers was an obvious example. Overall, the purchasing power of the export workers depended on their wage levels which typically were extremely low. They did not, therefore, constitute a buoyant home market for other sectors of the economy. Some part of their demand, moreover, was satisfied by imported goods, including foodstuffs in many cases. Additionally, some part of the incomes of, say, plantation or mine managers was paid abroad. Peasant producers of exports, such as West African cocoa farmers, Ugandan cotton growers, Malayan rubber small-holders, might have higher disposable incomes than plantation and mine workers, but there was little sign of their demand stimulating the non-export sector to develop extensive trades and industries to satisfy them during the colonial period. In any case, the prices received by the grower for export commodities were generally low and the export trade itself was in the hand of expatriate trading firms for the most part. Peasant producers also spent a portion of their income on imported goods. Because colonialism favoured expatriate enterprise over indigenous and metropolitan processing industry over local, these various linkages were never able to develop strongly.

Although it is not possible to measure linkages in the colonial economies without reliable input : output data, it can be concluded that these linkages were weak and that therefore the export sectors, structurally speaking, remained enclaves. The problem was partly one of slow growth of exports, but mainly it was one of their ineffectiveness in stimulating activity in the rest of the economy. This meant that even when they did grow rapidly their impact on the development of the entire colonial economy was restricted. One of the functions of government, in these circumstances, was to tax the export sector and use the revenue for development projects elsewhere; the extent to which this was in fact done depended on the willingness of the government to impose fiscal burdens on the export sector, its willingness or ability to actually spend its revenues, and the appropriateness of the projects it financed with the proceeds. We have noted in earlier chapters the limitations which applied to this process. What was required was more than simply stimulation of a narrow range of unprocessed primary exports but, in addition to encouraging export earnings to rise, action to improve the linkages between the export sector and the rest of the economy and to obtain resources from the export industries which could be invested in raising productivity in the non-export area. As W.A. Lewis pointed out, the fundamental problem facing the tropical colonies was the very low levels of productivity (output per worker and output per acre) in traditional agriculture.[11] Because productivity was so low it was possible to effect quite dramatic increases by relatively small investments in tools, improved seed strains and animals, equipment, fertilisers, small-scale irrigation, marketing and distribution, scientific research and so forth, but instead the economic development effort of the colonial authorities was diverted to large-scale transportation and communications works to benefit chiefly the export sector, or grandiose and wasteful agricultural projects like those of the OFC and the CDC. The tropical colonies received the benefit of little effective scientific agricultural research even in the post-1945 era, but what was undertaken related almost entirely to peasants' cash crops or plantation crops for export. Typically colonial economies exhibited periods of export growth but this did not lead to a transformation of the economy as a whole. This remained the formidable task of the post-independence governments and development agencies.

Third, the colonial export sectors were dominated by foreign firms which produced directly, by foreign trading companies which purchased produce for export from settlers and peasant producers and by foreign banks which financed the export and import trades. This high level of foreign ownership in the export industries led to an outflow of profits which accumulated externally in the hands of these firms. If the outflow exceeded re-investment and new investment the colony suffered a net drain of private capital. When the state became a purchaser of export produce during and after the Second World War in some colonies, public capital accumulation also occured externally as the profits were largely retained in London as sterling balances. Some degree of foreign ownership in the colonial economies was inevitable and necessary if the level of investment was to be raised. For some colonies, at some times,

303

there was a net inflow of private capital and no doubt it was preferable for a colony to be attractive to foreign investors than to be completely neglected by them. The fact remained, however, that foreign investment imposed costs on the host economy. It was the role of government to minimise these costs, which related chiefly to the drain of profits and employment practices, by adopting policies which maximised the advantages of foreign investment to the host nation, for example through improved taxation measures. This was a difficult exercise for any government, but impossible for a colonial government where the bulk of foreign investment came from the citizens and firms of the imperial power. The purpose of colonial rule was to create conditions as favourable as possible for expatriate investment and British firms were often able to obtain more advantageous treatment from a British colonial government than they would have received from an independent one. These firms were also notoriously poor at effectively transferring the advanced knowledge, skills and technology at their disposal to the inhabitants of the colonies where they invested. They did not provide training facilities or employ indigenes at any but the most unskilled tasks. Any notion of the employment of natives in management positions, which would have required some period of work experience at head office in Britain, was completely out of the question until the imperatives of decolonisation forced a change of policy. The colonial governments sometimes criticised expatriate firms for this practice, but in reality were themselves no more willing to train and employ indigenes in responsible positions in colonial administration until the very end of colonial rule. Indeed, for most of the period they decried the emergence of the 'educated native'. Thus colonialism denied these countries one of the major potential benefits of direct foreign investment, the transfer of technology and skills and the stimulation which the activity of the foreign firm in the host economy can give to local capitalists.[12]

Finally, the tropical colonies faced unstable and usually declining terms of trade, the extent of which is shown in the relevant tables in the text (6.7, 7.4, 8.8, 10.5, 11.4, 11.5). There were several reasons why this happened. One factor was the narrow export base of the colonies. As we have seen, the three main exports in most cases accounted for 70 per cent or more of export earnings (Tables 8.9, 11.6). Despite lip service which was sometimes paid to the need to diversify exports (for example, in the quotations cited at the beginning of this chapter), the emphasis which colonialism placed on export growth inevitably led to over-investment in particular export commodities and therefore to a narrowing of the export base. Export diversification as a long-term goal was a chimera. In addition, when 'new' export commodities were promoted – to meet Britain's needs rather than those of the colonies – it frequently led to disastrous results, for instance, Tanganyikan groundnuts and

Gambian poultry. In the second place, declining terms of trade in the colonies reflected the global tendency for primary products to decline in price in relation to the prices of manufactured goods.[13] Of the export commodities of the colonies, tropical foodstuffs such as coffee, tea, cocoa, sugar and fruit, should have been less affected by this phenomenon as the temperate zone countries which were the main consumers of these foodstuffs could not (except in the case of sugar) produce their own supplies and nor were synthetics developed as substitutes for tropical foodstuffs. Even so, these commodities did suffer price collapses as well as periods of low static prices since the elasticity of demand in the industrial countries was low, and there were many tropical producers vying for the existing markets (even in cases where British colonies produced a large proportion of world output, as in cocoa) which lowered prices. Vegetable oils were one important group of tropical foods produced in British colonies which did suffer from competition from temperate zone production and the substitution of animal fats or mineral oils. Some foodstuffs were affected by the ability of the industrial countries to economise in their use in the manufacturing process (e.g. cocoa). Other tropical primary products (agricultural raw materials like rubber, cotton and sisal and minerals) entering world trade were even more vulnerable to competition from the temperate zone countries, to the substitution of synthetics and to economies in manufacturing. Third, the terms of trade declined because the primary products were exported in their raw state. Some degree of processing prior to export would have enhanced the value and therefore the relative price of primary commodities. Local processing, however, was not part of the colonial paradigm. It should also be pointed out that the cost of ocean transport (including insurance) increased substantially over the colonial period. External transport costs added to the price paid for imports while at the same time squeezed the price paid by the exporting firm to the producer, except where the producer could ship directly to the final market, which was not usually the case.

A broader base of exports would have created more stable export growth, although in periods of world trade depression or stagnation there was less scope for tropical countries to raise export earnings. Such periods, however, were ones in which import substitution could have been encouraged to save on imports and absorb resources (especially labour) released from the depressed export sector. Import substitution would also have lessened the burden on export earnings to pay for imported consumer goods, though in the circumstances it might not have been viable for import substitution to go much beyond fairly simply manufactured commodities. If these could also have been exported it would have widened the export base and shifted its structure away from commodities whose relative prices were falling. Additionally, for a number of tropical colonies, import substitution included producing more basic foodstuffs for domestic consumption which in turn required a greater proportion of the resources available for economic development to be devoted to raising the productivity of non-export agriculture. Improvements to the productiveness of domestic agriculture and the development of secondary industry were necessarily complementary, not competitive, activities.[14] The provision of external capital not tied to export earnings (i.e. greater amounts of economic aid) would have reduced the dependence on the external market and allowed a re-orientation of resources towards the non-export sectors. Domestic markets (and perhaps regional markets) could have had as much potential for growth – possibly more in foodstuffs and simple manufactures – as trade with the industrial countries, but the fundamental necessities of colonialism precluded a serious pursuit of alternatives to what amounted at times to a virtual 'export or die' mentality. The argument here is not that a more balanced approach to economic development was not considered – the Select Committee on Colonial Development in 1948 argued

A large-scale advance in agriculture means reaching into every village, forming farmers' groups and agricultural societies, demonstrating new techniques on farmers' holdings, promoting co-operatives and providing fertilisers, improved tools and cattle. Individual farmers must become links in a chain reaction that stirs the whole community.[15]

Rather, it is that the resources provided were not enlarged sufficiently to meet this goal and government priorities in practice were not re-ordered to give greater emphasis to the domestic economy.[16] The theory of economic development held by the colonial authorities thus remained at the rather superficial level of attempting to maximise production of primary products for export without any real investigation as to how export earnings could be used to achieve diversification and development in the economy as a whole. In short, a colonial economy.

From these generalisations we turn now to the specific questions raised in Chapter 1 concerning the obstacles to achievement of colonial economic development in practice: the widespread illusions about the richness of the colonies' resources; the problems of capital supply; the considerable political divisions and uncertainties in Britain; and the different views and perspectives about what type of colonial development was needed.[17]

It was not surprising that initially there should have been illusions about the economic potential of the tropical colonies, for they were largely unknown to the British, and in the case of Africa comprised a vast area. What was more surprising was that the myths should have persisted for so long, in fact to the closing years of the colonial epoch. The very luxuriance of tropical vegetation (the 'huge greenhouse with free heat and water' in Leverhulme's phrase) masked the thinness and instability of tropical soils, while the legends of the gold of ancient Ghana and the very real gold and diamonds which were beginning to pour out of South Africa in the 1880s encouraged the belief that the unexplored centre of Africa would turn out to be a mineral Eldorado. We have noted the easy assumption of unlimited wealth in the tropical colonies of Churchill and Chamberlain before the First World War, of Milner, Amery, Ormsby-Gore, Thomas and others in the 1920s and 1930s and of Cripps, Creech Jones and Strachey in the years after the Second World War. The persistence of this view led to the kind of thinking behind the Tanganyika Groundnut Scheme and many of the early projects of the Colonial Development Corporation. Colonialism, with its constant emphasis on alleged benefits to Britain, encouraged this kind of shallow analysis. Perhaps ignorance and self-delusion together with a desire for quick results go some way towards explaining the longevity of the tropical myth. The consequences of such illusions about the extent and speed with which the tropical colonies could be developed were particularly damaging when the resources which were available were in reality so meagre. The British tropical colonies were among the poorest societies on earth and yet the view that small amounts of capital would unlock the 'riches of the tropics' remained an underlying belief of many of those who had taken on the task of overseeing colonial economic development policy and made the success of such policy much more problematical.

Undoubtedly the low level of capital investment was the major obstacle to economic growth and development in the tropical colonies. As we have seen, the provision of public capital for basic services such as transport and communications, urban amenities, water supply and so forth was an essential part of the Chamberlain approach to colonial development which assumed that private investment would follow once such infrastructure was in place. Investment by colonial governments in the economic development of their countries was severely handicapped by their small public revenues and limited ability to borrow funds from London. Colonial public revenues were closely tied to taxes on trade and these were necessarily kept fairly low. Expatriate firms operating in colonies were taxed lightly or not at all so that the burden of colonial taxation fell mainly on the mass of the people – who were generally the least able to bear it. Since colonial governments had to provide a range of social services in addition to paying the costs of administration, defence and the pensions of retired British officials, their meagre resources were too stretched to finance expensive infrastructure as well.

Colonial governments could borrow from the London money market, and many of them did so at various times, but the amounts which they could afford to service were really quite small and a number ran into a foreign debt crisis. Borrowing internally depended on local capital markets which, as we have seen, were not regarded as necessary or desirable by the colonial regime and therefore remained very limited or non-existent in the colonial era.

A further source of public finance was British government aid. The main ways in which this was made available have been detailed throughout this book. The shortcomings of aid were obvious: far too little was given and up to the 1930s nearly all of it was in the form of loans. Even after the Second World War in the final years of colonial rule, the amounts provided were not large in relation to either the size of the colonial empire or Britain's national income. Partly this may have been because the amount of money required to provide adequate transportation systems and other public works was underestimated. More importantly, aid under conditions of colonial rule was viewed from the perspective of the centre. Its provision was regarded as a cost to the British taxpayer while its efficacy was measured in terms of its benefits to the British economy and to the prolongation of British authority. The Colonial Office bureaucrats sometimes laid stress on the benefits to the colonies, but it was the Treasury view which was the dominant one. In any case, just as frequently the Colonial Office advised the colonies that they should be grateful that anything at all was being done for them by the hard-pressed British economy. The Treasury both depreciated the effectiveness of public development expenditure and demanded that the British economy should benefit from such outlays of taxpayer's funds as were allowed and the power of the Treasury line explains why it was impossible during the colonial era to produce any significant transfers of funds from the 'centre' to the 'periphery'. The Colonial Development Corporation, too, was required in its operations to show an overall profit in the medium term and to engage (unsuccessfully as it turned out) in projects which were intended to help Britain. British colonial aid was given grudgingly and tied to the needs of the British economy as they were perceived from time to time and as a result was ineffective in promoting economic development.

Private British capital did not, on the whole, respond to the Chamberlain strategy as anticipated. Possibly less subject to the illusions of the bountiful tropics (Leverhulme notwithstanding), the British business community showed scant interest in investing in the tropical colonies. Some investment in mining occurred but the number of new mining ventures was small and most colonies did not possess significant deposits (or they were not known about in the colonial period). Mining companies proposing new projects often demanded and received government assistance of various kinds before they would go ahead. Plantation industries such as rubber, tea, cocoa, sugar, fruit, sisal, copra, tobacco and coffee also received private capital for production but were discouraged by low prices and relative over-supply in the inter-war period and also turned to the state for support. The European plantation as a mode of production of tropical produce was often not competitive with smallholders who farmed more intensively and without the burden of overheads the expatriate firms struggled with. Thus the profits from private investment in agriculture by British capitalists, even under the favourable regime of colonial rule, were far from assured and often did not amount to the bonanza expected. After the Second World War high primary produce prices attracted foreign private investment again and undoubtedly export volumes and profits increased. Investment was hampered, however, by Britain's balance of payments crisis and uncertainty caused by decolonisation. Disinvestment of British private capital was experienced by some colonies upon becoming independent.[18]

Other areas of the colonial economies received even less private British capital. The Ronaldshay Report in 1923 (Chapter 7) commented on the disinclination of British investors to develop transport and communications in the tropical colonies. Ocean shipping remained the only major activity of private expatriate investment for British colonies and these services frequently required government subsidy. Private investment in secondary industry was also minimal, particularly prior to the Second World War. Processing of primary export produce was the main sector where there was reasonable scope for local industry, but vested British interests ensured processing remained a metropolitan activity. Even when colonial governments did offer tax incentives to British investors in the 1950s these were nullified by the policy of the British taxation authorities.[19]

Thus it was merchant trade which remained the first and last stronghold of British capital's interest in the 'great estate'. Merchanting was a more attractive proposition than producing: investment was flexible, relatively little fixed capital was required, there were good opportunities for oligopoly profits and little opposition (which anyway could usually be crushed by the expatriate firms) from local traders. After the Second World War the continuation of statutory marketing in some colonies also opened opportunities to the large British trading firms to act as agents of the government. It was Britain as a nation of shopkeepers rather than as workshop or banker of the world which really responded to Chamberlain's appeal. Had he lived to see it, he might well have been very disappointed with the lack of dynamism and commitment of the British business community.

It was never part of the Chamberlain programme to strengthen the growth and development of a class of vigorous indigenous capitalists.

Indeed, quite the opposite. Indigenous capitalism did emerge, slowly and inevitably, but its impact on capital accumulation and investment was muted by limitations imposed by colonial rule, for example, in the support given by government to the entrenched position of British trading firms and banks, and in the post-1945 fashion for experiments in 'state capitalism' as manifested by marketing boards and other bodies. The British colonial authorities were usually hostile to indigenous capitalism also on social policy grounds, being unwilling to accept or even acknowledge the social changes being wrought by the integration of the colonial economies into the world economy and preferring to regard the indigenous entrepreneur as a parasite or a scoundrel or, at best, an aberration. When colonial rule ended there was often an upsurge of indigenous enterprise in reaction.[20]

Some of the reluctance which financiers felt about colonial investment may have arisen from continuing political uncertainty in the United Kingdom about the depth of commitment to imperial development, and this was so even before 1914. Despite the enthusiasm of Joseph Chamberlain, Alfred Milner, Lionel Curtis (and other members of 'Milner's kindergarten') and Leo Amery, the imperial cause never succeeded in capturing even its most promising potential political ally, the Conservative Party. Chamberlain's great campaign for imperial preference (1903–6) ended up by dividing the party and was a major contributor to its humiliating defeat in the 1906 general election. Stanley Baldwin's attempt to fight the same battle in 1923 led to a similar result. Ultimately imperialists of the Milner stamp were unable to make 'constructive imperialism' the centrepiece of Conservative Party political philosophy.

The other political parties were even more ambivalent towards imperial development. Though Herbert Asquith, Sir Edward Grey and Richard Haldane were counted as Liberal imperialists, the Little Englander tradition was by no means dead in the party, and people on its radical wing opposed imperialist involvement for a variety of reasons, the belief that it was all being done for the benefit of financial speculators being prominent amongst them.

Socialists and Labour politicians before the First World War were either hostile to the empire or else lukewarm supporters, like Ramsay MacDonald, whose two books, *Labour and Empire* (1907) and *The Awakening of India* (1910), while advocating colonial development also showed sympathy for nationalist aspirations. It must have been unclear to potential investors whether a future Labour government (admittedly something of a remote possibility in the years before 1914) would show much enthusiasm for the development or even the continuation of the empire.

As it turned out, most of the important measures for promoting colonial economic development after the First World War were taken by Conservative governments; or by Labour administrations carrying out previously formulated Tory programmes. The only genuinely Labour initiative in this field was the creation of the Colonial Development Corporation and the Overseas Food Corporation in 1947, which represented the application of the Labour philosophy of 'State Capitalism' to colonial development. And, despite the CDC's troubled early years it (like a number of Labour creations, though not, as we have seen, the OFC) was continued and supported by the Conservative governments of the 1950s. Developing the 'Great Estate' was not an area of significant conflict between the two main political parties in Britain, which no doubt contributed to the lack of general parliamentary and public interest in the matter.[21] Several important studies have shown that public opinion was aroused only by a few specific questions concerning the colonies, such as the future of white settlers in East and Central Africa, or the demand by Germany for the return of its former colonies in the 1930s, and by particular events such as the riots in the West Indies in 1938, the Malayan emergency (1948–60), rioting in the Gold Coast in 1949 and Mau Mau in Kenya in the 1950s.[22] Public ignorance of the colonial empire was deplored by Leo Amery in the 1920s, but there is no evidence that it was any less by the end of the colonial era, despite some attempts by the Colonial Office after the Second World War to publicise the colonies more.[23]

Parliamentary debates on the colonies were infrequent and poorly attended. The establishment of a parliamentary standing committee on colonial affairs was mooted in the 1930s, but not acted upon and only four select committees on colonial matters were ever appointed.[24] In addition, there were relatively few Royal Commissions or commissions of inquiry established on colonial questions. The colonies, it would seem, were largely taken for granted, and even the question of decolonisation in the early 1960s received scant attention compared, say, to the debates over Britain's entry into the European Community. The low profile of colonial development in British politics ensured that the 'Treasury view' prevailed and the flow of public funds to the colonies remained highly restricted. It also meant that important moves forward in colonial aid and development policy came only when either Britain faced particular economic crises (such as unemployment in the 1920s or shortages and balance of payments difficulties after the Second World War) or when resistance to colonial rule by nationalists reached a crescendo, or when British imperialism was the subject of foreign comment and criticism. This produced a pattern whereby assistance to colonial development was a hurriedly executed response to an immediate British problem or concern. Finally, the lack of interest in the tropical colonies reinforced the tendency for the political heads of the Colonial Office to remain for only short periods and for the colonial civil service to attract 'caretakers' rather than 'builders'.[25]

To what extent was the economic development of the colonies necessarily the central aim of British rule as far as the colonial administrators were concerned? There was a pronounced dichotomy of views on this question. On the one hand, there were those who believed that economic development was desirable, even if it disrupted the traditional societies over which they ruled, whilst on the other hand there were those who believed that their ultimate purpose should be to exercise a 'trusteeship' over the colonial peoples and that no development should be encouraged if it seemed likely to cause rapid disintegration of traditional society. Lord Lugard tried to integrate these two points of view in his work, *The Dual Mandate in Tropical Africa* (1922) which was widely read by colonial administrators and remained influential as a basis for British colonies policy into the 1950s.[26] He argued, as Benjamin Kidd had done twenty years before, that Britain had a responsibility to the other industrialised nations to ensure that valuable tropical resources were made available to them (and to Britain) in sufficient quantities and on equitable terms and that the inhabitants of the tropics had no right to prevent the exploitation of resources which the world market required.[27] At the same time, Britain had a duty to the indigenes to protect them from unfair practices and the social consequences of rapid economic growth. Thus British rule should 'open up' the colonies to expatriate enterprise while at the same time denying a major economic role to the indigenous population whose social position was to remain as unaltered as possible. Conveniently, this approach provided a justification for doing little in education or social welfare, since such initiatives might further exacerbate the adverse social effects of economic change. Colonial officials, whether in London or the colonies, often interpreted the 'Dual Mandate' in a way which placed preservation of the existing social structure ahead of more rapid economic change. In 1948 when Creech Jones assured the Cabinet that the Colonial Office and the colonial governments were indeed committed to a policy of 'quick and vigorous' economic development, he warned them:

The rapid transformation of agricultural methods or the introduction of new industries must upset the existing social organisation, especially in Africa. Agricultural reform generally means some change in the systems of land holding, on which the whole social structure depends. It is our deeply rooted policy to preserve the social organisations we have inherited and modify them only gradually. That point is not merely wise in the best interests of Colonial peoples; it is practically wise in the sense that any more revolutionary policy, especially one which appeared to touch the

312

African's rights in his land, would cause serious political trouble. We must work, therefore, within the limits set by the tolerable pace of social change.[28]

Of course, there was also a political dimension to the policy of preserving the existing social structure in the African and Asian colonies, for British rule depended on the active cooperation of traditional rulers to continue to be effective. If rapid economic change undermined the political power of these rulers, British control through 'Indirect Rule' would be threatened. These considerations may explain the marked lack of enthusiasm of British colonial officialdom towards the emergence of indigenous capitalism, especially if it competed with British enterprise and had nationalistic overtones. However applied, of course, trusteeship was never totally effective in suppressing indigenous enterprise: rural capitalism spread in West Africa; East Africans grew cash crops such as coffee and sisal; and Malays entered the forbidden world of smallholder rubber production. But the particular interpretation of 'colonial trusteeship' was undoubtedly part of the reason why the colonial regime did not press ahead with economic development as fast as it might have done.[29]

Even if there had been a sustained effort to stimulate colonial economic development there remained the problem of framing long-term plans or programmes to achieve this aim. This arose partly from the short-term nature of the colonial experience of so many British businessmen and colonial administrators. Senior businessmen involved in colonial trade or production were usually resident in Britain and made only brief trips to the colonies, so that even if they had a genuine interest it was difficult for them to see the perspectives of the development picture in the same light as local residents. The idea for a large-scale groundnut scheme, for example, came to Frank Samuel, managing director of the United Africa Company, while making a plane trip across Tanganyika; perhaps he would have been less enthusiastic if he had been travelling by land.[30] Colonial administrators sometimes spent quite long periods in particular colonies when they were young (Sir Hugh Clifford, for instance, was in Malaya for 20 years between 1883 and 1903) but once they became more senior, periods of service shortened. Colonial governors seldom served for more than four years in any one colony, and thus found it difficult to initiate any but the most temporary developments. They were often dogged by ill-health and even when they did propose specific projects they always had to overcome the suspicion of the Colonial Office. Even when it was not obsessed with short-term financial savings, the Colonial Office was always jealous of governors' pretensions. During the 1930s some of the problems of the Colonial Office and the colonial service were recognised and the office was reorganised to include an economic department in 1934 and the service overhauled and unified by 1938. The need for better training of administrative staff was acknowledged and for more technical experts to be appointed, although financial constraints made implementation difficult.[31]

The Second World War created a crisis in which long-term planning for colonial economic, political and social development was seen as vital. As discussed in Chapter 10 a more positive attitude towards economic questions was regarded by Lord Hailey as an essential area for reform in the training of colonial civil servants for the post-war period. And as shown in Chapter 11, planning became an essential part of the provision of British aid funds to the colonies under the 1945 Colonial Development and Welfare Act. The shortcomings of the ten-year plans drawn up by the colonies after the war have been noted. The Colonial Office in the post-war years was a much larger and more technically orientated body with a greater responsibility for the long-term development of the tropical colonies. There was more interchange between officials in London and in the field. There was even slightly greater continuity of its political heads.[32] By the end of the colonial epoch the administrative machinery for colonial development was undoubtedly far superior to that which had existed at earlier times, (although still lacking in economic expertise) and possibly this contributed to the more rapid economic change at the later stage; political independence from the late 1950s, however, cut short the full potential for long-term planning using this improved machinery and therefore it must be concluded that for much of the colonial period there was a marked absence of 'forward vision'.

Was economic development possible at all under British colonial rule or was the British colonial system inimical to economic progess? Perhaps the problem of colonial development was insoluble or at any rate too large for Britain to handle financially or in terms of the human resources it was prepared to devote to the task? It was sometimes suggested that one of the positive contributions which British colonial rule made was to provide political stability ('law and order') over much of the tropical world in contrast to the state of anarchy which allegedly preceded it.[33] This argument accepted without question the judgements of Europeans that what they witnessed was indeed 'instability' and also missed the point that much of what was taken to amount to inherent instability in the pre-colonial societies was itself the result of the invasion of European forces as they fought over the potential prizes available in the tropics. It implied that the various societies which came under European rule as a result of the 'Scramble for Colonies' were incapable of providing social stability themselves had they been allowed the opportunity to do so. That Britain was able to impose a *pax* on the tropics in the early twentieth century obscured consideration of the question as to what the sources of instability were, their real extent and whether these societies really required foreign invasion and conquest in order to achieve a peaceful existence.

It was also sometimes argued that British colonial rule benefited the colonial economies in the tropics by the provision of transport and communications: railways, roads, airports, telegraph and telephones, ports and harbours. This is a stronger argument insofar as these facilities were provided to a significant extent and paid for by the British authorities. However, there are qualifications to be made in this regard. Much of the transport and communications system was built mainly to facilitate the export industries of the colonies and while this was important in stimulating the development of exports it left the colonies with a system which was lopsided in that transport links which served to integrate the domestic economy were generally assigned a lower order of priority or simply ignored. Just as colonial rule tended to build up strong trading links between the colony and the metropolitan centre, but to inhibit regional integration, so the export-oriented transport systems concentrated on the movement of goods between the export sectors and the ports, while failing to provide a network of communications which would serve the entire country and encourage diversification.

Moreover, despite claims by the British to the contrary, the amount of investment in transport in the tropical colonies was extremely small compared with the size of the problem. Finally, much of it was financed in a way which placed the main burden for its construction and operation on the mass of the colonial inhabitants and on the export earnings of the colony in particular. Yet such investments usually exhibited a high capital equal output ratio and to be effective from the viewpoint of economic development in the interests of the colonial peoples should have been financed to a much greater extent by the British exchequer.

Another alleged economic advantage of British colonial rule was the access it gave the colonies to Britain's unsurpassed international trade and financial institutions. Britain was the world's major market for tropical produce; it was a major exporter of manufactured goods; its capital market and commercial services were unrivalled. At least until Britain turned away from the Commonwealth and towards Europe in the later 1950s, this connection gave the British colonies access to significant markets for their exports and to British finance capital. However, while demand by Britain for tropical colonial produce was important, reliance on the British market represented a narrowing, not a widening, of export opportunities, and the limitations of access to finance capital for underdeveloped economies which could hardly afford 'hard' loans have been discussed already. It should also be borne in mind that the colonial monetary system was a rigid one which did not allow the local government any influence over the domestic money supply. The gold standard (and sterling exchange standard which replaced it after the First World War) of the colonial era may have encouraged investment by persuading foreign investors that British colonies were safe places to invest, and that colonial governments would not be permitted to print money or alter the foreign exchange rate, but at the same time it was a monetary mechanism which was brutal in its transmission of major fluctuations in the international economy to the local colonial one.[34]

To return to our previous question. British colonial rule in the tropics was not so rapacious as to prevent any economic growth but, as we have pointed out, the major economic failing was structural imbalance which created colonial economies which were excessively dependent on the export of a narrow range of unprocessed primary commodities and which experienced deteriorating terms of trade as a result. British colonial rule was not able to do more to facilitate the development of secondary industries of various kinds because of its intertia, deference to British commercial interests and misguided ideas of 'trusteeship'.

At the more general level, British rule created nation states by redrawing the existing pre-colonial political boundaries. Whatever the economic benefits of this for economic growth, the new frontiers were drawn in a largely arbitrary manner, suiting the diplomatic imperatives of the European powers at the time but having little or no regard for ethnic, cultural or topographical factors and often cutting across existing regional economies. This process inhibited regional economic and political integration and left some small ex-colonies economically unviable as independent states.[35] This legacy of colonialism proved very difficult to reverse.

On the social side, living standards in the tropical colonies rose only slowly (if at all) as increases in national income hardly exceeded those of population, yet colonial rule, at least in its later phases, was delivering rudimentary medical, public health and sanitation, education and other welfare services and aiming to do so on a mass basis. Had these problems been addressed at a much earlier stage the contribution of colonial rule could have been far more significant. However, it is difficult to imagine the British State providing health and welfare services to the inhabitants of its 'tropical estate' superior to those which were available at home, (even though health problems were far worse in the tropics), and prior to the Second World War Britain itself did not enjoy the benefits of a welfare state. Such an outcome would have hardly have fitted the nature of the colonial relationship.

Economic development failed under colonial rule because the British government always wanted quick results from colonial economic expansion and expected to obtain these from unrealistically small financial outlays. Before the First World War the British government provided virtually no financial assistance to the tropical colonies and yet some at least expected the Chamberlain dream to become reality. In the 1920s the British government's efforts increased somewhat as the unemployment situation worsened (or at least did not improve), culminating in the passing of the 1929 Colonial Development Act. With the advent of the slump and much higher levels of unemployment, the government tightened imperial preference and exhorted the Colonial Development Advisory Committee to do more for Britain's economic plight yet cut its budget by 25 per cent. When these initiatives failed to alleviate unemployment, the government lost interest, and the colonial development fund drifted more and more into palliative welfare spending. The wartime measures of colonial development and welfare had a deal of political expediency about them – and nominally more money – but by 1943 the post-war shortages loomed and the colonial empire was now to be developed in order to feed a hungry world. Production of cash crops for export to Britain or the dollar area was given priority over production of foodstuffs for domestic consumption in the colonies. As the post-war crisis deepened, the colonies were once again urged to do more, and, since they were already doing all they could, new institutions to boost food and raw materials output were created in 1947, the Overseas Food Corporation and the Colonial Development Corporation. The quick results were not forthcoming: by the early 1950s expenditure under the ten-year plans was still going on but, owing to bottlenecks in supply of capital equipment and trained personnel, most plans were underspent. The OFC's Tanganyika Groundnut Scheme was a disaster, the CDC was administratively in a mess and suffering from heavy project failure. The Colonial Development and Welfare Acts were renewed and five-year plans replaced the earlier ones, but after the Suez Crisis in 1956 the rising tide of colonial nationalism made formal independence an immediate reality and threw the whole future of British expenditure on colonial development into jeopardy. By the end of the 1950s the problems of economic development in the tropical colonies seemed more intractable and the costs higher while the supposed benefits of colonial rule to Britain's economy appeared less tangible, especially as Britain moved closer to the economies of nearby Europe. Hanging on seemed less worthwhile and, the political initiative having been seized by the colonial nationalists, an increasingly unavailable option in any case. In the following five years nearly all of Britain's tropical colonies attained independence.[36]

Throughout this book we have shown that colonialism and development were largely contradictory and that this produced a gap between the dreams (or myths) of developing the 'great estate' and the economic realities. The structural imbalances in the economies of the British colonies which were apparent by the end of the colonial era were the direct result of the pursuit of the Chamberlain aim of buttressing the British economy with a 'great estate' in the tropics. In the end the Chamberlain dream was abandoned along with formal colonial rule but its persistence over the previous seventy years bequeathed the now ex-colonies a legacy which would continue to inhibit their economic development in the years to come.

Appendixes

APPENDIX 1: COLONIAL EXPORTS BY VALUE (£) 1852–4, 1882–4 AND 1910–12 (ANNUAL AVERAGES)

Colony	Dates	Yrs	Exports (less bullion)	Annual growth rate	Yrs	Exports to UK (incl. bullion)	Annual growth rate	% UK export
TROPICAL AMERICA								
Barbados	1852–4	3	890,131	*	3	702,015	*	78.9
	1882–4	3	1,217,666	1.2	3	475,666	−1.1	39.1
	1910–12	3	1,037,667	−0.5	3	110,000	−2.7	10.6
British Guiana	1852–4	3	1,132,857	*	3	1,059,450	*	93.5
	1882–4	3	2,901,000	5.2	3	1,776,333	2.3	61.2
	1910–12	3	1,653,668	−1.5	3	778,000	−2.0	47.0
British Honduras	1852–4	3	379,533	*	3	334,026	*	88.0
	1882–4	3	290,333	−0.8	3	172,000	−1.6	59.2
	1910–12	3	540,333	3.1	3	67,000	−2.2	12.4
Jamaica	1852–4	3	919,921	*	3	709,624	*	77.1
	1882–4	3	1,500,333	2.1	3	804,000	0.4	53.6
	1910–12	3	2,575,000	2.6	3	441,000	−1.6	17.1
Tobago	1852–4	3	54,252	*	3	53,782	*	99.1
	1882–4	3	45,666	−0.5	3	35,000	−1.2	76.6
	1910–12		included in Trinidad below					
Trinidad	1852–4	3	428,600	*	3	400,196	*	93.4
	1882–4	3	2,636,333	17.2	3	917,666	4.3	34.8
	1910–12	3	4,024,000	1.9	3	1,033,000	0.4	25.7
Turks & Caicos Islands	1852–4		no returns					
	1882–4	3	30,666	*	3	333	*	1.1
	1910–12	3	24,700	−0.7	2	250	−0.9	1.0
Leeward islands	1852–4		see below		*	367,786	*	*
	1882–4		see below		*	274,332	−0.8	*
	1910–12	3	562,766	*	3	215,766	−0.8	38.3
Antigua	1852–4	3	184,720	*	3	182,196	*	98.6
	1882–4	3	224,000	0.7	3	62,666	−2.2	28.0
	1910–12		included in Leeward Islands above					
Dominica	1852–4	3	63,053	*	3	52,198	*	82.8
	1882–4	3	58,333	−0.2	3	28,333	−1.5	48.6
	1910–12		included in Leeward Islands above					
Montserrat	1852–4	3	10,529	*	1	50	*	0.5
	1882–4	3	33,666	7.3	3	24,000	1596.7	71.3

Colony	Dates	Yrs	Exports (less bullion)	Annual growth rate	Yrs	Exports to UK (incl. bullion)	Annual growth rate	% UK export
	1910–12		included in Leeward Islands above					
Nevis	1852–4	3	32,183	*	3	24,653	*	76.6
	1882–4		included in St. Christopher below					
	1910–12		included in Leeward Islands above					
St. Christopher	1852–4	3	118,881	*	3	108,689	*	91.4
	1882–4	3	267,333	4.2	3	159,333	1.6	59.6
	1910–12		included in Leeward Islands above					
Virgin Islands	1852–4	3	4,556	*	3	*	*	*
	1882–4	3	4,333	–0.2	3	*	*	*
	1910–12		included in Leeward Islands above					
Windward Islands								
Grenada	1852–4	3	131,431	*	3	114,335	*	87.0
	1882–4	3	196,666	1.7	3	171,666	1.7	87.3
	1910–12	3	280,366	1.4	3	178,166	0.1	63.5
St. Lucia	1852–4	3	56,683	*	3	46,331	*	81.7
	1882–4	3	194,000	8.1	3	130,333	6.0	67.2
	1910–12	3	121,233	–1.3	3	72,633	–1.5	59.9
St. Vincent	1852–4	3	193,537	*	3	171,432	*	88.6
	1882–4	3	145,333	–0.8	3	98,000	–1.4	67.4
	1910–12	3	108,766	–0.8	3	71,333	–1.0	65.6
Total: Tropical America	1852–4	*	*	*	*	3,958,977	*	*
	1882–4	*	*	*	*	4,855,329	0.8	*
	1910–12	*	*	*	*	2,967,148	–1.4	*
ASIA & THE PACIFIC								
B. Solomon Is.	1910–12	3	78,513	*		n.a.		
Ceylon	1852–4	3	1,382,015	*	3	828,333	*	59.9
	1882–4	3	3,292,625	4.6	3	1,919,531	4.4	58.3
	1910–12	3	12,168,000	9.0	3	5,833,666	7.3	47.9
Fiji	1882–4	3	296,000	*		n.a		
	1910–12	3	1,114,900	9.9	1	45,700	*	4.1
Gilbert & Ellice Is.	1910–12	3	267,000	*		n.a		
Tonga	1910–12	3	234,166	*		n.a		
Malaysia								
Labuan	1852–4	3	16,470	*	*	*	*	*
	1882–4	3	100,333	17.0		incl. in Straits Settlements		
	1910–12		included in Straits Settlements below					
Malacca	1882–4	3	449,886	*		incl. in Straits Settlements		
	1910–12		included in Straits Settlements below					
Pahang	1882–4	3	4,159,639	*		incl. in Straits Settlements		
	1910–12		included in Straits Settlements below					
Singapore	1882–4	3	9,623,731	*		incl. in Straits Settlements		
	1910–12		included in Straits Settlements below					
Straits Settlements	1882–4		see above		3	3,543,333	*	*
	1910–12	3	40,491,333	*	3	10,059,000	6.6	24.8
Fed'd Malay States	1910–12	3	14,548,333	*	3	3,582,768	*	24.6
Prot'd. Malay States	1910–12	3	361,925	*		n.a		
Br. N. Borneo	1910–12	3	587,729	*		n.a		
TOTAL: Malaysia	1882–4	*	*	*	*	3,543,333	*	*
	1910–12	*	*	*	*	13,641,768	10.2	*

Colony	Dates	Yrs	Exports (less bullion)	Annual growth rate	Yrs	Exports to UK (incl. bullion)	Annual growth rate	% UK export
Mauritius	1852–4	3	1,256,624	*	3	766,000	*	61.0
	1882–4	3	3,942,333	7.1	3	472,000	–1.3	12.0
	1910–12	3	2,576,333	–1.2	3	580,666	0.8	22.5
TOTAL: Asia & The Pacific	1852–4	*	*	*	*	1,594,333	*	*
	1882–4	*	*	*	*	5,934,864	9.1	*
	1910–12	*	*	*	*	20,101,800	8.5	*
EAST AFRICA								
Kenya (E. Afr. Prot.)	1910–12	3	856,666	*	3	318,666	*	37.2
Nyasaland	1910–12	3	157,333	*	3	141,666	*	90.0
Rhodesia, North	1910–12	3	97,666	*	1	31,800	*	32.6
Rhodesia, South	1910–12	3	3,105,433	*	3	2,663,200	*	85.8
Seychelles	1910–12	3	130,900	*	3	22,400	*	17.1
Somaliland	1910–12	3	221,667	*	1	3,000	*	1.4
Uganda	1910–12	3	319,333	*	3	124,000	*	38.8
Zanzibar	1910–12	3	1,087,566	*		n.a		
Total: East Africa	1910–12	*	*	*	*	3,304,732		*
WEST AFRICA								
Gambia	1852–4	3	192,521	*	3	30,250	*	15.7
	1882–4	3	215,333	0.4	3	33,333	0.3	15.5
	1910–12	3	464,197	4.1	3	50,933	1.9	11.0
Gold Coast	1852–4	3	154,134	*	3	90,633	*	58.8
	1882–4	3	390,333	5.1	3	280,666	7.0	71.9
	1910–12	3	3,599,000[a]	29.4	3	2,324,333	26.0	64.6
Nigeria	1882–4[b]	3	616,000	*	3	258,333	*	41.9
	1910–12	3	5,171,000	26.4	2	3,095,250	39.2	59.9
Sierra Leone	1852–4	3	127,847	*	3	78,403	*	61.3
	1882–4	3	387,667	6.8	3	171,000	3.9	44.1
	1910–12	3	1,216,333	7.6	3	255,666	1.8	21.0
Total: West Africa	1852–4	*	*	*	*	199,286	*	*
	1882–4	*	*	*	*	743,332	9.1	*
	1910–12	*	*	*	*	5,726,182	23.9	*
Total: Tropical Colonies (including bullion)	1852–4	*	*	*	*	5,752,596	*	*
	1882–4	*	*	*	*	11,533,525	3.3	*
	1910–12	*	*	*	*	32,099,862	6.4	*
OTHER COLONIES Non-Tropical Africa								
St. Helena	1852–4	3	11,123	*	3	7,990	*	71.8
	1882–4	3	1,216	–3.0	3	1,000	–2.9	82.2
	1910–12		no returns					
Cape of Good Hope	1852–4	3	596,769	*	3	543,060[c]	*	91.0
	1882–4	3	4,542,333	22.0	3	4,105,000	21.9	90.4
	1910–12		included in South Africa below					
Natal	1852–4	3	33,577	*	3	3,337	*	9.9
	1882–4	3	840,000	80.1	3	673,666	669.6	80.2

321

Colony	Dates	Yrs	Exports (less bullion)	Annual growth rate	Yrs	Exports to UK (incl. bullion)	Annual growth rate	% UK export
	1910–12		included in South Africa below					
South Africa	1910–12	3	58,173,333[a]	*	3	51,472,000	*	88.5
TOTAL: *Non-Tropical*								
Africa	1852–4	*	*	*	*	554,387	*	*
	1882–4	*	*	*	*	4,778,666	25.4	*
	1910–12	*	*	*	*	51,472,000	34.9	*
Australasia								
New South Wales	1852–4	3	4,392,333	*	3	2,965,333	*	67.5
	1882–4	3	18,284,666	10.5	3	8,292,333	6.0	45.4
	1910–12		included in Australia below					
South Australia	1852–4	3	873,382	*	3	1,131,333	*	129.5
	1882–4	3	5,622,333	18.1	3	3,201,333	6.1	56.9
	1910–12		included in Australia below					
Tasmania	1852–4	3	1,566,833	*	3	601,127	*	38.4
	1882–4	3	1,598,000	0.1	3	378,333	−1.2	23.7
	1910–12		included in Australia below					
Victoria	1852–4	3	9,808,333[a]	*	3	8,783,333	*	89.5
	1882–4	3	16,214,333[a]	2.2	3	7,626,333	−0.4	47.0
	1910–12		included in Australia below					
Western Australia	1852–4	3	30,690	*	3	19,320	*	63.0
	1882–4	3	478,333	48.6	3	297,000	47.9	62.1
	1910–12		included in Australia below					
Queensland	1852–4		included in New South Wales above					
	1882–4	3	4,031,333	*	3	1,645,333	*	40.8
	1910–12		included in Australia below					
Australia	1852–4		see above		3	13,500,446	*	*
	1882–4		see above		3	21,440,665	2.0	*
	1910–12	3	77,689,666	*	3	34,822,333	2.2	44.8
New Zealand	1852–4	3	149,800	*	3	33,272	*	22.2
	1882–4	3	6,014,333	130.5	3	5,071,333	504.7	84.3
	1910–12	3	19,307,333	7.9	3	16,876,333	8.3	87.4
Total: *Australasia*	1852–4	*	*	*	*	13,533,718	*	*
	1882–4	*	*	*	*	26,511,998	3.2	*
	1910–12	*	*	*	*	51,698,666	3.4	*
Central & S. America								
Bahamas	1852–4	3	79,441	*	3	13,458	*	16.9
	1882–4	3	143,666	2.7	3	34,666	5.3	24.1
	1910–12	3	226,400	2.1	3	36,266	0.2	16.0
Bermuda	1852–4	3	23,819	*	3	6,752	*	28.3
	1882–4	3	95,666	10.1	3	1,666	−2.5	1.7
	1910–12	3	105,333	0.4	3	2,666	2.1	2.5
Falkland Islands	1852–4	3	13,809	*	3	*	*	0.0
	1882–4	3	88,333	18.0	3	86,666	*	98.1
	1910–12	3	468,033	15.4	3	307,600	9.1	65.7
TOTAL: *Central &*								
S. America	1852–4	*	*	*	*	20,210	*	*
	1882–4	*	*	*	*	122,998	17.0	*
	1910–12	*	*	*	*	346,532	6.5	*
India	1852–4	3	19,502,904	*	3	7,939,333	*	40.7
	1882–4	3	80,123,428	10.4	3	33,629,063	10.8	42.0
	1910–12	3	144,404,333	2.9	3	38,078,333	0.5	26.4
Europe								
Ionian Islands	1852–4	3	297,156	*	*	*	*	*

322

Colony	Dates	Yrs	Exports (less bullion)	Annual growth rate	Yrs	Exports to UK (incl. bullion)	Annual growth rate	% UK export
	1882–4		pt. of Greece		*	*	*	*
	1910–12		pt. of Greece		*	*	*	*
Cyprus	1882–4	3	329,333	*	3	48,666	*	14.8
	1910–12	3	622,667	3.2	3	183,333	9.9	29.4
Malta	1852–4		no	n.a				
	1882–4	3	85,333	*	3	27,666	*	32.4
	1910–12		n.a					
Total: Europe	1882–4	*	*	*	*	76,332	*	*
	1910–12	*	*	*	*	183,333	5.0	*
British North America								
Canada	1852–4[d]	3	5,177,333	*	3	1,946,538	*	37.6
	1882–4	3	19,353,220	9.1	3	9,217,898	12.5	47.6
	1910–12	3	59,315,334	7.4	3	30,042,000	8.1	50.6
New Brunswick	1852–4	3	991,013	*	3	737,596	*	74.4
	1882–4			included in Canada above				
	1910–12			included in Canada above				
Nova Scotia	1852–4	3	901,428	*	3	26,039	*	2.9
	1882–4			included in Canada above				
	1910–12			included in Canada above				
Prince Edward Island	1852–4	3	128,189	*	3.0	24,165	*	18.9
	1882–4			included in Canada above				
	1910–12			included in Canada above				
Total: Canada	1852–4	*	*	*	*	2,734,338	*	*
	1882–4	*	*	*	*	9,217,898	7.9	*
	1910–12	*	*	*	*	30,042,000	8.1	*
Newfoundland	1852–4	3	1,051,949	*	3	450,117	*	42.8
	1882–4	3	1,432,201	1.2	3	342,029	–0.8	23.9
	1910–12	3	2,581,666	2.9	3	484,000	1.5	18.7
Total: British N. America	1852–4	*	*	*	*	3,184,455	*	*
	1882–4	*	*	*	*	9,559,927	6.7	*
	1910–12	*	*	*	*	30,526,000	7.8	*
Total: Non-Tropical Colonies	1852–4	*	*	*	*	25,232,103	*	*
	1882–4	*	*	*	*	74,678,984	6.5	*
	1910–12	*	*	*	*	172,304,864	4.7	*

n.a., Figures not available.
[a] Includes gold bullion
[b] Lagos only.
[c] Estimate (see note below).
[d] Upper (Ontario) and Lower (Quebec) Canada only.
Note: The source from which the figures were taken (PRO, CO/442/27) did not give exports to UK, but these were shown in a parliamentary return of 1865 (Parl. Papers, Sess. 1865, Vol. LV, p. 459) which gave slightly larger total export figures. However, exports to UK were 91% of total exports, and this figure is 91% of the total exports recorded in CO/442/27.

APPENDIX 2: COLONIAL IMPORTS BY VALUE (£) 1852–4, 1882–4 AND 1910–12 (ANNUAL AVERAGES)

Colony	Dates	Yrs	Imports	Annual growth rate	Yrs	Imports from UK	Annual growth rate	% UK import
TROPICAL AMERICA								
Barbados	1851–4	4	681,027	*	3	449,328	*	66.0
	1882–4	3	1,158,000	2.3	3	452,666	0.0	39.1
	1910–12	3	1,450,000	0.9	3	584,000	1.0	40.3
British Guiana	1852–4	3	909,555	*	3	531,137	*	58.4
	1882–4	3	2,029,667	4.1	3	1,193,333	4.2	58.8
	1910–12	3	1,675,666	–0.6	3	833,000	–1.1	49.7
British Honduras	1852–4	3	213,994	*	3	146,666	*	68.5
	1882–4	3	246,666	0.5	3	131,666	–0.3	53.4
	1910–12	3	630,666	5.6	3	129,666	–0.1	20.6
Jamaica	1852–4	3	943,721	*	2	535,423	*	56.7
	1882–4	3	1,504,000	2.0	3	859,666	2.0	57.2
	1910–12	3	2,843,666	3.2	3	1,246,000	1.6	43.8
Tobago	1852–4	3	52,944	*	3	18,893	*	35.7
	1882–4	3	42,333	–0.7	3	20,333	0.3	48.0
	1910–12		included in Trinidad below					
Trinidad	1852–4	3	518,907	*	3	262,615	*	50.6
	1882–4	3	1,738,333	7.8	3	857,666	7.6	49.3
	1910–12	3	4,514,666	5.7	3	1,229,000	1.5	27.2
Turks & Caicos Islands	1852–4		no returns					
	1882–4	3	26,333	*	3	3,000	*	11.4
	1910–12	3	26,766	0.1	3	5,066	2.5	18.9
Leeward Islands	1852–4		see below		*	134,257		
	1882–4		see below		*	221,665	2.2	
	1910–12	3	640,366	*	3	272,066	0.8	42.5
Antigua	1852–4	3	154,084	*	3	60,425	*	39.2
	1882–4	3	178,000	0.5	3	81,333	1.2	45.7
	1910–12		included in Leeward Islands above					
Dominica	1852–4	3	52,256	*	3	19,937	*	38.2
	1882–4	3	68,000	1.0	3	28,666	1.5	42.2
	1910–12		included in Leeward Islands above					
Montserrat	1852–4	3	9,610	*	1	89	*	0.9
	1882–4	3	28,000	6.4	3	9,666	358.7	34.5
	1910–12		included in Leeward Islands above					
Nevis	1852–4	3	19,925	*	3	6,897	*	34.6
	1882–4		included in St. Christopher below					
	1910–12		included in Leeward Islands above					
St. Christopher	1852–4	3	92,193	*	3	46,909	*	50.9
	1882–4	2	218,667	4.6	2	102,000	3.9	46.6
	1910–12		included in Leeward Islands above					
Virgin Islands	1852–4	3	4,404	*		n.a.		
	1882–4	3	6,666	1.7	n.a.			
	1910–12		included in Leeward Islands above					
Windward Islands								
Grenada	1852–4	3	133,730	*	3	66,619	*	49.8
	1882–4	3	141,333	0.2	3	74,000	0.4	52.4
	1910–12	3	287,300	3.7	3	134,600	2.9	46.8
St. Lucia	1852–4	3	83,320	*	3	35,502	*	42.6
	1882–4	3	156,666	2.9	3	67,000	3.0	42.8
	1910–12	3	303,733	3.4	3	75,000	0.5	24.9

Colony	Dates	Yrs	Imports	Annual growth rate	Yrs	Imports from UK	Annual growth rate	% UK import
St. Vincent	1852–4	3	157,224	*	3	72,527	*	46.1
	1882–4	3	141,000	–0.3	3	73,333	0.0	52.0
	1910–12	3	109,500	–0.8	3	46,533	–1.3	42.5
Total: Tropical America	1852–4	*	*	*	*	2,252,967	*	*
	1882–4	*	*	*	*	3,954,328	2.5	*
	1910–12	*	*	*	*	4,555,597	0.5	*
ASIA AND THE PACIFIC								
Brit. Solomon Is.	1910–12	3	97,433	*		n.a.		
Ceylon	1852–4	3	746,857	*	3	343,000	*	45.9
	1882–4	3	4,011,239	14.6	3	1,264,219	9.0	31.5
	1910–12	3	10,703,667	6.0	3	3,035,333	5.0	28.4
Fiji	1882–4	3	416,666	*		n.a.		
	1910–12	3	922,400	4.3	3	162,833	*	17.7
Gilbert & Ellice Is.	1910–12	3	75,866	*		n.a		
Tonga	1910–12	3	209,800	*	3	4,166	*	2.0
Malaysia Labuan	1852–4	3	23,254	*	*	*	*	*
	1882–4	3	96,333	10.5	2	2,000	*	2.1
	1910–12		Included in Straits Settlements below					
Malacca	1882–4	3	423,745	*		incl. in Straits Settlements		
	1910–12		included in Straits Settlements below					
Pahang	1882–4	3	4,009,274	*	*	incl. in Straits Settlements		
	1910–12		included in Straits Settlements below					
Singapore	1882–4	3	11,531,876	*		incl. in Straits Settlements		
	1910–12		included in Straits Settlements below					
Straits Settlements	1882–4		see above		3	4,306,667	*	*
	1910–12	3	44,900,666	*	3	4,927,000	0.5	11.0
Fed. Malay States	1910–12	3	7,794,666	*	3	730,581	*	9.4
Prot'd Malay States	1910–12	3	343,759	*		n.a.		
Br. N. Borneo	1910–12	3	539,955	*		n.a.		
Total: Malaysia	1882–4	*	*	*	*	4,308,667	*	*
	1910–12	*	*	*	*	5,657,581	1.1	*
Mauritius	1852–4	3	1,025,312	*	3	406,333	*	39.6
	1882–4	3	2,875,666	6.0	3	769,666	3.0	26.8
	1910–12	3	2,407,333	–0.6	3	779,666	0.0	32.4
Total: Asia & The Pacific	1852–4	*	*	*	*	749,333	*	*
	1882–4	*	*	*	*	6,342,552	24.9	*
	1910–12	*	*	*	*	9,639,579	1.9	*
EAST AFRICA								
Kenya (E. Afr. Prot.)	1910–12	3	1,035,000	*	3	393,000	*	38.0
Nyasaland	1910–12	3	211,000	*	3	154,666	*	73.3
Rhodesia, North	1910–12	3	181,333	*	3	91,600	*	50.5
Rhodesia, South	1910–12	3	2,849,866	*	3	1,499,800	*	52.6
Seychelles Isles	1910–12	3	88,466	*	3	27,800	*	31.4
Somaliland	1910–12	3	262,333	*	1	1,000	*	0.4
Uganda	1910–12	3	442,333	*	3	182,333	*	41.2
Zanzibar	1910–12	3	1,067,900	*		n.a.		
Total: East Africa	1910–12	*	*	*	*	2,350,199	*	*

325

Colony	Dates	Yrs	Imports	Annual growth rate	Yrs	Imports from UK	Annual growth rate	% UK import
WEST AFRICA								
Gambia	1852–4	3	113,372	*	3	55,030	*	48.5
	1882–4	3	184,333	2.1	3	91,666	2.2	49.7
	1910–12	3	714,300	10.3	3	258,700	6.5	36.2
Gold Coast	1852–4	3	79,611	*	3	49,450	*	62.1
	1882–4	3	365,334	12.0	3	335,000	19.2	91.7
	1910–12	3	2,996,000	25.7	3	2,656,333	24.7	88.7
Nigeria	1882–4[a]	3	468,333	*	3	310,667	*	66.3
	1910–12	3	5,436,333	37.9	2	4,178,200	44.5	76.9
Sierra Leone	1852–4	3	99,041	*	3	78,928	*	79.7
	1882–4	3	417,333	10.7	3	301,333	9.4	72.2
	1910–12	3	1,080,333	5.7	3	912,666	7.2	84.5
Total: West Africa	1852–4	*	*	*	*	183,408	*	*
	1882–4	*	*	*	*	1,038,666	15.5	*
	1910–12	*	*	*	*	8,005,899	24.0	*
Total: Tropical Colonies (including bullion)	1852–4	*	*	*	*	3,185,708	*	*
	1882–4	*	*	*	*	11,335,546	8.5	*
	1910–12	*	*	*	*	24,551,274	4.2	*
OTHER COLONIES								
Non-tropical Africa								
St. Helena	1852–4	2	64,311	*	2	30,802	*	47.9
	1882–4	3	45,333	–1.0	3	29,666	–0.1	65.4
	1910–12		no returns		*			
Cape of Good Hope	1852–4	3	1,492,471	*	3	1,109,061	*	74.3
	1882–4	3	7,201,000	12.7	3	5,512,000	13.2	76.5
	1910–12		included in South Africa below					
Natal	1852–4	3	108,849	*	3	51,987	*	47.8
	1882–4	3	1,880,333	54.2	3	1,493,000	92.4	79.4
	1910–12		included in South Africa below					
South Africa	1910–12	3	38,940,333	*	3	23,167,000	*	59.5
Total: Non-Tropical Africa	1852–4	*	*	*	*	1,191,850	*	*
	1882–4	*	*	*	*	7,005,000	16.3	*
	1910–12	*	*	*	*	23,167,000	8.2	*
Australasia New South Wales	1852–4	3	4,741,000	*	3	3,476,000	*	73.3
	1882–4	3	20,675,000	11.2	3	11,067,666	7.3	53.5
	1910–12		included in Australia below					
South Australia	1852–4	3	1,442,194	*	3	1,294,000	*	89.7
	1882–4	3	6,077,333	10.7	3	3,313,666	5.2	54.5
	1910–12		included in Australia below					
Tasmania	1852–4	3	1,894,855	*	3	1,272,659	*	67.2
	1882–4	3	1,656,000	–0.4	3	550,666	–1.9	33.3
	1910–12		included in Australia below					
Victoria	1852–4	3	11,972,228	*	3	6,994,000	*	58.4
	1882–4	3	17,895,000	1.6	3	8,709,666	0.8	48.7
	1910–12		included in Australia below					
Western Australia	1852–4	3	117,433	*	3	80,742	*	68.8
	1882–4	3	504,666	11.0	3	209,666	5.3	41.5
	1910–12		included in Australia below					

Colony	Dates	Yrs	Imports	Annual growth rate	Yrs	Imports from UK	Annual growth rate	% UK import
Queensland	1852–4			included in New South Wales above				
	1882–4	3	5,479,334	*	3	2,448,666	*	44.7
	1910–12			included in Australia below				
Australia	1852–4		see New South Wales, etc. above		3	16,593,401	*	*
	1882–4	*	*	*	3	26,299,996	1.9	*
	1910–12	3	68,380,000	*	3	40,690,000	2.0	59.5
New Zealand	1852–4	3	463,794	*	3	194,421	*	41.9
	1882–4	3	7,843,000	53.0	3	5,243,000	86.6	66.8
	1910–12	3	19,191,666	5.2	3	11,595,333	4.3	60.4
Total: Australasia	1852–4	*	*	*	*	16,787,822	*	*
	1882–4	*	*	*	*	31,542,996	2.9	*
	1910–12	*	*	*	*	52,285,333	2.3	*
Central & S. America								
Bahamas	1852–4	3	134,114	*	3	29,640	*	22.1
	1882–4	3	205,667	1.8	3	45,000	1.7	21.9
	1910–12	3	332,737	2.2	3	82,733	3.0	24.9
Bermuda	1852–4	3	121,824	*	3	25,550	*	21.0
	1882–4	3	266,333	4.0	3	65,333	5.2	24.5
	1910–12	3	566,666	4.0	3	161,000	5.2	28.4
Falkland Islands	1852–4	3	18,846	*		n.a.		
	1882–4	3	52,333	5.9	3	46,666	*	89.2
	1910–12	3	93,500	2.8	3	83,666	2.8	89.5
Total: Central & S. America	1852–4	*	*	*	*	55,190	*	*
	1882–4	*	*	*	*	156,999	6.1	*
	1910–12	*	*	*	*	327,399	3.9	*
India	1852–4	3	11,313,184	*	3	9,558,263	*	84.5
	1882–4	3	46,781,240	10.5	3	43,533,750	11.8	93.1
	1910–12	3	89,032,333	3.2	3	72,897,666	2.4	81.9
Europe Ionian Islands	1852–4	3	683,075	*		n.a.		
	1882–4			pt. of Greece				
	1910–12			pt. of Greece				
Cyprus	1882–4	3	327,333	*	3	98,333	*	30.0
	1910–12	3	547,334	2.4	3	143,666	1.6	26.2
Malta	1852–4		n.a.					
	1882–4	3	744,000	*	3	122,333	*	16.4
	1910–12		n.a.					
Total: Europe	1852–4	*	*	*	*	*	*	*
	1882–4	*	*	*	*	220,666	*	*
	1910–12	*	*	*	*	143,666	−1.2	*
British North America Canada	1852–4[a]	3	6,959,820	*	3	4,343,666	*	62.4
	1882–4	3	24,832,666	8.6	3	9,503,824	4.0	38.3
	1910–12	3	94,916,666	10.1	3	22,076,333	4.7	23.3
New Brunswick	1852–4	3	1,631,827	*	3	751,990	*	46.1
	1882–4			included in Canada above				
	1910–12			included in Canada above				
Nova Scotia	1852–4	3	1,348,819		3	446,846	*	33.1
	1882–4			included in Canada above				
	1910–12			included in Canada above				
Prince Edward Island	1852–4	3	219,713	*	3	69,648	*	31.7

327

Colony	Dates	Yrs	Imports	Annual growth rate	Yrs	Imports from UK	Annual growth rate	% UK import
	1882–4			included in Canada above				
	1910–12			included in Canada above				
Total: Canada	1852–4	*	*	*	*	5,612,150	*	*
	1882–4	*	*	*	*	9,503,824	2.3	*
	1910–12	*	*	*	*	22,076,333	4.7	*
Newfoundland	1852–4	3	890,793	*	3	335,767	*	37.7
	1882–4	3	1,774,666	3.3	3	680,169	3.4	38.3
	1910–12	3	2,803,666	2.1	3	689,000	0.0	24.6
Total: British N. America	1852–4	*	*	*	*	5,947,917	*	*
	1882–4	*	*	*	*	10,183,993	2.4	*
	1910–12	*	*	*	*	22,765,333	4.4	*
Total: Non-tropical Colonies	1852–4	*	*	*	*	33,541,042	*	*
	1882–4	*	*	*	*	92,643,404	5.9	*
	1910–12	*	*	*	*	171,586,397	3.0	*

n.a., Figures not available
[a] Lagos only.
[b] Upper (Ontario) and Lower (Quebec) Canada only.

Appendix 3: LEADING EXPORTS FOR COLONIAL SETTLEMENTS, ANNUAL AVERAGES FOR SELECTED PERIODS (£)

TROPICAL AMERICA

	1852–4[a]				1882–4[a]				1910–12		
Commodity	Leading exports (£)	% Exports	Per cap (£)	Commodity	Leading exports (£)	% Exports	Per cap (£)	Commodity	Leading exports (£)	% Exports	Per cap (£)
Barbados											
Sugar muscavodo	649,597	72.97	4.78	Sugar muscavado	809,666	66.49	4.71	Molasses	347,333	33.47	1.89
Molasses	50,138	5.63	0.37	Molasses	157,666	12.94	0.92	Sugar of all kinds	333,666	32.15	1.82
Cotton	1,872	0.21	0.01	Petroleum	2,000	0.16	0.01	Coal, coke, etc.	84,333	8.12	0.46
	*	*	*	Tamarinds	1,000	0.08	0.01	Fish, dried, etc.	25,333	2.44	0.14
British Guiana											
Sugar (raw)	727,815	64.24	5.70	Sugar (raw)	2,333,333	80.43	9.05	Sugar of all kinds	1,208,666	73.09	4.21
Rum	271,417	23.95	2.13	Rum	271,000	9.34	1.05	Balata gum	126,000	7.61	0.44
Molasses	21,722	1.91	0.17	Molasses	73,333	2.52	0.28	Rum	113,333	6.85	0.40
Hardwood	11,839	1.04	0.09	Timber	20,333	0.70	0.08		*	*	*
Coffee	642	0.05	0.01	Charcoal	5,666	0.19	0.02		*	*	*
British Honduras											
	*	*	*	Mahogany	79,666	27.44	2.90	Gum, sapodilla, etc.	194,666	36.02	5.34
	*	*	*	Logwood	57,666	19.86	2.10	Mahogany	174,000	32.20	4.77
	*	*	*	Sugar (raw)	10,666	14.00	1.48	Coconuts	25,666	4.75	0.70
	*	*	*		*	*	*	Bananas	21,000	3.88	0.58
	*	*	*		*	*	*	Cedar	20,000	3.70	0.55
Jamaica											
Sugar	428,348	46.56	1.13	Sugar raw	531,333	35.41	0.91	Bananas	1,370,000	53.20	1.85
Spirits, rum	180,179	19.58	0.48	Rum	247,666	16.50	0.43	Sugar of all kinds	213,666	8.29	0.29
Pimento	84,919	9.23	0.22	Coffee	131,333	8.75	0.23	Coffee, raw	198,333	7.70	0.27
Coffee	74,172	8.06	0.20	Fruits, fresh bananas	125,000	8.33	0.22	Logwood extract	168,666	6.55	0.23
Logwood	8,222	0.89	0.02	Wood, logwood	105,333	7.02	0.18	Cocoa	101,333	3.93	0.14
	*	*	*	Pimento	103,000	6.86	0.18		*	*	*
Tobago											
	*	*	*	Sugar	35,333	77.37	1.96	Included with	*	*	*
	*	*	*	Molasses	3,333	7.29	0.18	Trinidad below	*	*	*
	*	*	*	Cocoa nuts	3,000	6.56	0.17		*	*	*
	*	*	*	Rum	2,000	4.38	0.11		*	*	*

	1852–4[a]				1882–4[a]				1910–12		
	Leading exports (£)	% Exports	Per cap (£)		Leading exports (£)	% Exports	Per cap (£)		Leading exports (£)	% Exports	Per cap (£)
Trinidad											
Sugar	332,113	77.48	4.84	Sugar muscavado	801,000	30.38	5.23	included with Tobago below	*	*	*
Cocoa	53,096	12.38	0.77	Cocoa	357,000	13.54	2.33		*	*	*
Molasses	19,159	4.47	0.28	Molasses	68,333	2.59	0.45		*	*	*
Rum	15,076	3.51	0.22	Asphalt	42,333	1.60	0.28		*	*	*
Coffee	2,924	0.68	0.04	Coconuts	36,000	1.36	0.23		*	*	*
	*	*	*	Bitters	32,000	1.21	0.21		*	*	*
Trinidad and Tobago											
	*	*	*		*	*	*	Cocoa	1,357,666	33.73	4.93
	*	*	*		*	*	*	Sugar of all kinds	611,666	15.20	2.22
	*	*	*		*	*	*	Balata gum	350,000	8.69	1.27
	*	*	*		*	*	*	Asphalt	193,333	4.80	0.70
Turks Islands											
	*	*	*	Salt	24,666	80.43	5.16	Included with Caicos Islands below	*	*	*
Turks and Caicos Islands											
	*	*	*	Cave earth	3,666	11.95	0.77	Salt	17,500	70.85	3.12
	*	*	*	Sponge	1,000	3.26	0.21				
Virgin Islands											
Cattle	2,581	56.65	0.39	Sisal grass	*	*	*	Included in Leeward Islands below	*	*	*
Sugar	589	12.92	0.09	Sponges	*	*	*		*	*	*
Antigua											
Sugar	*	*	*	Sugar	183,333	81.84	5.24	Included in Leeward Islands below	*	*	*
Molasses	*	*	*	Molasses	29,666	13.24	0.85		*	*	*
Dominica											
Sugar muscovado	45,031	71.41	2.03	Sugar	36,000	61.71	1.28	Included in Leeward Islands below	*	*	*
Rum	4,076	6.46	0.18	Cocoa	6,666	11.42	0.24		*	*	*

Region / Commodity	Value	%	%	Commodity	Value	%	%	Commodity / Note	Value	%	%			
Sugar, Molasses	2,872	4.55	0.13	Lime juice	4,333	7.42	0.15					*	*	*
Wheat, flour	2,035	3.22	0.09	Molasses	2,333	3.99	0.08					*	*	*
Cottons, linens, etc.	1,386	2.19	0.06	Fruit and vegetables	1,666	2.85	0.06					*	*	*
Coffee	1,311	2.07	0.06		*	*	*					*	*	*
Montserrat														
Sugar	8,251	78.36	1.17	Sugar	23,333	69.30	2.27	Included in Leeward Islands below				*	*	*
Molasses	660	6.26	0.09	Lime juice, raw	5,000	14.85	0.49					*	*	*
	*	*	*	Lime juice, conc.	2,333	6.93	0.23					*	*	*
Nevis														
Sugar	27,432	85.23	2.87	Sugar	72,000	85.71	6.07	Included in Leeward Islands below				*	*	*
Rum	1,961	6.09	0.20	Molasses	11,000	13.09	0.93					*	*	*
Molasses	1,952	6.06	0.20										*	*
St Christopher														
Sugar	92,154	77.51	4.44	Sugar muscavado	210,000	80.46	7.21	Included in Leeward Islands below				*	*	*
Rum	9,937	8.35	0.48	Molasses	25,000	9.57	0.86					*	*	*
Molasses	9,316	7.83	0.45	Rum	6,000	2.29	0.21					*	*	*
Potatoes	975	0.82	0.05		*	*	*					*	*	*
Arrowroot, etc	374	0.31	0.02		*	*	*					*	*	*
St Christopher Nevis														
Sugar	*	*	*	Sugar	190,500	83.37	4.48	Included in Leeward Islands below				*	*	*
Molasses	*	*	*	Molasses	16,500	7.22	0.39					*	*	*
Rum	*	*	*	Rum	6,000	2.62	0.14					*	*	*
Salt	*	*	*	Salt	1,000	0.43	0.02					*	*	*
Leeward Islands [b]	*	*	*		*	*	*	Sugar, muscovado	174,088	30.94	1.37			
								Cotton	110,655	19.67	0.87			
								Cane syrup	98,270	17.47	0.77			
Grenada														
Sugar	93,243	70.94	2.85	Cocoa	145,666	74.06	3.33	Cocoa	241,000	85.95	3.61			
Rum	28,351	15.48	0.62	Sugar	21,666	11.01	0.50	Nutmegs	12,500	4.45	0.19			
Cocoa	6,770	5.15	0.21	Animals, live	6,666	3.39	0.15	Cotton	6,500	2.31	0.10			

	1852–4[a]			1882–4[a]				1910–12			
	Leading exports (£)	% Exports	Per cap (£)	Leading exports (£)		% Exports	Per cap (£)	Leading exports (£)		% Exports	Per cap (£)
Molasses	406	0.30	0.01	Cotton	6,000	3.05	0.14	*	*	*	*
	*	*	*	Spices	4,666	2.37	0.11	*	*	*	*
St Lucia											
Sugar muscavado	42,981	75.82	1.78	Muscavado	129,333	66.66	3.22	Sugar	60,000	49.49	1.23
Molasses	3,631	6.40	0.15	Sugar crytallised	38,333	19.75	0.95	Cocoa	44,000	36.29	0.91
Cocoa	1,437	2.53	0.06	Cocoa	10,666	5.49	0.27	Logwood	7,300	6.02	0.15
*	*	*	*	Molasses	10,000	5.15	0.25	*	*	*	*
*	*	*	*	Logwood	2,133	1.09	0.05	*	*	*	*
St Vincent											
Sugar	133,737	69.10	4.44	Sugar muscavado	94,333	64.90	2.33	Cotton	40,000	36.77	0.95
Arrowroot	18,327	9.47	0.61	Arrowroot	26,000	17.89	0.64	Arrowroot	35,000	32.17	0.84
Rum	15,072	7.78	0.50	Rum	10,000	6.88	0.25	Cocoa	4,500	4.13	0.11
Molasses	8,275	4.27	0.27	Molasses	6,666	4.58	0.16	*	*	*	*
Wheat, flour	4,787	2.47	0.16	Cotton	1,000	0.68	0.02				
TROPICAL ASIA AND THE PACIFIC											
British Solomon Islands											
*	*	*	*	*	*	*	*	Copra	,333	76.84	0.00
*	*	*	*	*	*	*	*	Ivory nuts	3,233	23.22	0.00
Ceylon											
Coffee	738,929	53.46	0.43	Coffee (plantation)	1,304,531	39.62	0.47	Tea	5, 9,333	45.27	1.55
Oil, coconut	107,921	7.80	0.06	Chinchona bark	390,437	11.85	0.14	Rubber	2,595,666	21.33	0.73
Silk manufactures	82,972	6.00	0.05	Cocoa	367,437	11.15	0.13	Coconut oil	912,333	7.49	0.26
Cinnamon	46,330	3.35	0.03	Plumbago	220,437	6.69	0.08	Copra	799,000	6.56	0.22
*	*	*	*	Copperah	120,500	3.66	0.04	Plumbago	510,000	4.19	0.14
Federated Malay States											
*	*	*	*	*	*	*	*	Tins	8,204,000	56.39	11.53
*	*	*	*	*	*	*	*	Rubber	5,504,505	37.83	7.74
*	*	*	*	*	*	*	*	Copra	2,147,548	1.01	0.21
*	*	*	*	*	*	*	*	Rice	2,128,564	0.88	0.18
*	*	*	*	*	*	*	*	Sugar	741,584	0.28	0.06

Protected Malay States								Tin ore		166,998	46.14	0.23
Malacca	*	*	*	Tin	*	305,545	67.91	3.27	Included in Straits Settlements below	*	*	*
				Topioca	*	144,176	32,05	1.54		*	*	*
Pahang	*	*	*	Tin	*	1,337,519	32.15	7.02	Included in Straits Settlements below	*	*	*
				Tobacco	*	401,065	9.64	2.10		*	*	*
				Grain rice	*	388,408	9.33	2.04		*	*	*
				Pepper	*	367,394	8.83	1.93		*	*	*
Singapore	*	*	*	Grain	*	933,171	9.69	6.70	Included in Straits Settlements below	*	*	*
				Gambier	*	889,649	9.24	6.39		*	*	*
				Cotton piece goods	*	840,397	8.73	6.04		*	*	*
				Opium	*	776,040	8.06	5.57		*	*	*
Labuan Coal	7,173	43.55	6.24	Sago flour	*	13,333	13.28	2.29	Included in Straits Settlements below	*	*	*
Sago	2,822	17.13	2.45	Coals	*	1,000	0.99	0.17		*	*	*
Birds nests	1,822	11.06	1.58		*	*	*	*		*	*	*
Camphor	1,499	9.10	1.30		*	*	*	*		*	*	*
Straits Settlements	*	*	*		*	*	*	*	Tin	*	5,678,000	26.37	17.57
									Rice and paddy	*	4,715,000	11.64	7.76
									Rubber	*	2,921,666	7.21	4.81
									Copra	*	1,949,666	4.81	3.21
									Opium	*	1,353,333	3.34	2.23

	1852–4[a]				1882–4[a]				1910–12		
Commodity	Leading exports (£)	% Exports	Per cap (£)	Commodity	Leading exports (£)	% Exports	Per cap (£)	Commodity	Leading exports (£)	% Exports	Per cap (£)
Fiji											
	*	*	*	Sugar	151,000	51.01	1.16	Sugar	669,432	60.05	4.80
	*	*	*	Copra	71,000	23.98	0.55	Copra	258,841	23.22	1.86
	*	*	*	Cotton	24,000	8.10	0.18	Fruit, green	47,302	4.25	0.34
	*	*	*	Fruit, green	14,666	4.95	0.11		*	*	*
Gilbert and Ellice Islands											
	*	*	*		*	*	*	Phosphates	231,500	86.70	7.44
	*	*	*		*	*	*	Copra	25,500	9.55	0.82
Mauritius											
Sugar	1,185,384	94.33	6.16	Sugar, raw	3,496,333	88.68	9.43	Sugar, raw	2,414,666	93.72	6.52
Copper sheets, nails	6,169	0.49	0.03	Spirits, rum	58,666	1.48	0.16	Aloe fibre	42,333	1.64	0.11
Rum	5,622	0.44	0.03	Vanilla	37,000	0.93	0.10		*	*	*
Rice	4,457	0.35	0.02	Fibre, aloe	30,000	0.76	0.08		*	*	*
	*	*	*	Oil, coconut	5,333	0.13	0.01		*	*	*
	*	*	*	Molasses	2,333	0.05	0.01		*	*	*
BRITISH NORTH BORNEO											
	*	*	*		*	*	*	Tobacco	261,675	44.52	1.26
	*	*	*		*	*	*	Timber	78,583	13.37	0.38
	*	*	*		*	*	*	Rubber	65,787	11.19	0.32
Tonga											
	*	*	*		*	*	*	Copra	209,600	89.50	9.65
TROPICAL EAST AFRICA East Africa (Kenya)											
	*	*	*		*	*	*	Cotton, raw	179,333	20.93	0.06
	*	*	*		*	*	*	Hides, etc. (from Uganda)	160,333	18.71	0.05
	*	*	*		*	*	*	Grain and pulse	80,666	9.41	0.03
	*	*	*		*	*	*	Ivory (from Uganda)	69,666	8.13	0.02

	Commodity	Value	%	%
	Hides, etc. (from Kenya)	61,666	7.19	0.02
Northern Rhodesia	Copper	25,000	25.59	0.03
	Cattle	13,500	13.82	0.02
	Maize	6,000	6.14	0.01
Nyasaland	Cotton raw	44,000	27.96	0.05
	Tobacco	41,333	26.27	0.05
	Coffee	13,000	8.26	0.02
	Rubber	12,000	7.62	0.01
Somaliland	Skins	144,666	65.26	0.58
	Sheep and goats	24,666	11.12	0.10
	Ghee	12,666	5.71	0.05
	Gum and resins	7,333	3.30	0.03
Southern Rhodesia	Gold	2,537,500	81.71	3.29
	Chrome	109,500	3.52	0.14
	Tobacco	47,500	1.53	0.06
Uganda	Cotton, raw (ginned)	114,333	35.80	0.04
	Cotton, raw (unginned)	37,666	11.79	0.01
	Skins, sheep and goat	26,666	8.35	0.01
	Hides	21,666	6.78	0.01
	Chillies	14,666	4.59	0.00
Zanzibar	Cloves	344,233	31.65	1.75
	Copra	204,733	18.82	1.04
	Piece goods, clothing	124,466	11.44	0.63

TROPICAL WEST AFRICA

	1852–4[a]				1882–4[a]				1910–12		
	Leading exports (£)	% Exports	Per cap (£)		Leading exports (£)	% Exports	Per cap (£)		Leading exports (£)	% Exports	Per cap (£)
Gambia											
Groundnuts	132,709	68.93	24.12	Groundnuts	180,333	83.74	12.74	Groundnuts	425,666	91.69	2.92
Wax, clean	23,959	12.44	4.35	Rubber	14,500	6.73	1.02	Hides	11,222	2.44	0.08
Hides	16,011	8.31	2.91	Hides	5,000	2.32	0.35		*	*	*
Cotton goods	4,684	2.43	0.85	Cotton goods	4,000	1.85	0.28		*	*	*
Tobacco	2,997	1.55	0.54		*	*	*		*	*	*
Gold Coast											
Gold dust	82,596	53.58	61.96	Palm oil	223,333	57.21	0.34	Cocoa	1,374,333	40.85	0.92
Palm oil	69,333	44.98	52.01	Palm nut kernels	63,000	16.14	0.10	Gold bullion	1,095,666	32.57	0.74
Ivory	3,333	2.16	2.50	Gold bullion	60,000	15.37	0.09	Palm kernels	188,666	5.60	0.13
Gum	1,370	0.88	1.03	India rubber	8,000	2.05	0.01	Lumber	172,000	5.11	0.12
Lagos											
	*	*	*	Palm kernels	288,666	46.88	3.84	Included in Nigeria below	*	*	*
	*	*	*	Palm oil	210,333	34.16	2.79		*	*	*
	*	*	*	Cotton goods	27,000	4.38	0.36		*	*	*
	*	*	*	Spirits (gin)	22,000	3.57	0.29		*	*	*
	*	*	*	Tobacco	11,000	1.78	0.15		*	*	*
Nigeria											
	*	*	*	Palm kernels	*	*	*	Palm kernels	2,607,333	50.42	0.17
	*	*	*	Palm oil	*	*	*	Palm oil	1,698,000	32.83	0.11
	*	*	*	Rubber	*	*	*	Rubber	205,333	3.97	0.01
	*	*	*	Tin, ore or metal	*	*	*	Tin, ore or metal	198,333	3.83	0.01
	*	*	*	Cocoa	*	*	*	Cocoa	132,333	2.55	0.01
Sierra Leone											
Timber	32,759	25.62	0.74	Palm kernels	84,000	21.66	1.39	Palm kernels	1,793,000	65.19	0.95
Palm oil	22,761	17.80	0.51	Rubber	79,333	20.46	1.31	Kola nuts	277,000	22.77	0.35
Hides	14,299	11.18	0.32	Cotton goods	45,000	11.60	0.74	Coal and patent fuel	91,000	7.48	0.11
Groundnuts	12,186	9.53	0.27	Cola nuts	32,666	8.42	0.54	Palm oil	67,000	5.50	0.08
Ginger	10,660	8.33	0.24		*	*	*		*	*	*

[a] Occasionally data from earlier or later years have been used when there were no data 1852–4 or 1882–4

[b] 1911 figures only

	1852–4[a]				1882–4[a]				1910–12		
	Leading imports (£)	% Imports	Per cap (£)		Leading imports (£)	% Imports	Per cap (£)		Leading imports (£)	% Imports	Per cap (£)
TROPICAL AMERICA											
Barbados											
Goods, unenumerated	423,332	62.16	3.11	Linens and cottons	153,666	13.27	10.89	Flour, wheat or rye	93,666	6.46	0.51
Wood and lumber	38,053	5.58	0.28	Flour wheat or rye	106,000	9.15	0.62	Grain, rice	87,333	6.02	0.48
Dried fish	34,202	5.02	0.25	Rice	74,000	6.39	0.43	Cool,coke etc.	81,000	5.58	0.44
Wheal, flour	33,848	4.97	0.25	Meat, salted	58,000	5.00	0.34	Machinery	62,333	4.29	0.34
Meal	30,464	4.47	0.22	Fish	49,000	4.23	0.29	Sulphate of ammonia	52,000	3.58	0.28
Rice	17,091	2.51	0.13		*	*	*		*	*	*
Manure	16,116	2.36	0.12		*	*	*		*	*	*
Horses	13,018	1.91	0.10		*	*	*		*	*	*
British Guiana											
	*	*	*	Rice	211,333	10.41	0.82	Flour	187,333	11.18	0.65
	*	*	*	Machinery	162,000	7.98	0.63	Cotton, linen, etc.	186,000	11.10	0.65
	*	*	*	Linens, cottons, etc	143,00	7.07	0.56	Manures	144,666	8.63	0.50
	*	*	*	Corn and flour	120,333	5.92	0.47	Machinery	66,333	3.95	0.23
	*	*	*		*	*	*	Haberdashery, etc.	58,333	3.48	0.20
British Honduras											
	*	*	*	Cotton goods	43,333	17.56	1.58	Gum, chick, etc.	88,000	13.95	2.41
	*	*	*	Drapery	18,666	7.56	0.68	Cotton goods	43,333	6.87	1.19
	*	*	*	Flour	12,333	5.00	0.45	Unenumeraled foods	30,333	4.81	0.83
	*	*	*	Beef and pork	11,666	4.72	0.42	Flour	23,666	3.75	0.65

	1852–4[a]				1882–4[a]				1910–12		
	Leading imports (£)	% Imports	Per cap (£)		Leading imports (£)	% Imports	Per cap (£)		Leading imports (£)	% Imports	Per cap (£)
Jamaica											
	*	*	*	Preserved provisions	6,000	2.43	0.22	Boots and shoes	21,000	3.33	0.58
Cotton manufactures	110,790	11.74	0.29	Cotton manufactures	301,000	20.01	0.52	Cotton manufactures	361,000	12.69	0.49
Flour, wheat, meal	98,704	10.45	0.26	Flour	143,000	9.50	0.25	Flour wheat	282,333	9.92	0.38
Fish, cod	57,803	6.12	0.15	Fish	107,000	7.11	0.18	Fish, dried or salted	148,333	5.21	0.20
Linen	45,475	4.81	0.12	Haberdashery	85,666	5.69	0.15	Lumber	103,000	3.62	0.14
Beef and pork	42,937	4.55	0.11	Rice	58,666	3.90	0.10	Rice	78,000	2.74	0.11
Tobago											
	*	*	*	Linens and cottons	8,666	20.47	0.48	Included with Trinidad below	*		*
	*	*	*	Flour wheat	4,333	10.23	0.24		*	*	*
	*	*	*	Fish dried	3,666	8.66	0.20		*	*	*
	*	*	*	Beef and pork, salted	2,000	4.72	0.11				
	*	*	*	Hardware	1,666	3.93	0.09		*	*	*
Trinidad											
Cottons, linens, etc.	105,657	20.36	1.54	Textile manuf., apparel	324,666	18.67	2.12	Included with Tobago below	*	*	*
Flour	38,193	7.36	0.56	Flour and meal	133,333	7.67	0.87		*	*	*
Hardware	27,316	5.26	0.40	Rice	108,000	6.21	0.70		*	*	*
Dried fish	24,965	4.81	0.36	Hardware	102,666	5.90	0.67		*	*	*
Leather	20,308	3.91	0.30		*	*	*		*	*	*
Rice	19,018	3.66	0.28		*	*	*		*	*	*
Trinidad and Tobago											
	*	*	*		*	*	*	Apparel, haberdashery	493,666	10.93	1.79
	*	*	*		*	*	*	Balata gum	348,666	7.72	1.27
	*	*	*		*	*	*	Flour	238,000	5.27	0.86

Commodity				Commodity				Commodity			
Turks Islands	*	*	*	Cotton, linen etc.	4,666	17.71	0.98	Cocoa, raw	207,666	4.60	0.75
	*	*	*	Flour, wheat	3,000	11.39	0.63	Rice	156,000	3.45	0.57
				Meat, salted	1,000	3.79	0.21				
				Boots and shoes	1,000	3.79	0.21				
Virgin Islands											
Wheat flour	1,841	41.80	0.28	Flour and	2,666	39.99	0.50	Included in	*	*	*
Meal corn	275	6.24	0.04	Linens and cottons	1,000	15.00	0.19	Leeward	*	*	*
Cotton manufactures	268	6.08	0.04		*	*	*	Islands below	*	*	*
Antigua											
	*	*	*	Flour wheaton	21,000	11.79	0.60	Included in	*	*	*
	*	*	*	Cottons woollens, etc.	21,000	11.79	0.60	Leeward	*	*	*
	*	*	*	Wood, various	14,666	8.23	0.42	Islands below	*	*	*
				Fish dried	10,333	5.80	0.30		*	*	*
				Haberdashery, etc.	10,333	5.80	0.30		*	*	*
Dominica											
Cottons, linens etc.	8,875	16.98	0.40	Linens, cottons, etc.	13,333	19.60	0.47	Included in	*	*	*
Wheat, flour	7,436	14.23	0.33	Flour, wheat	8,666	12.74	0.31	Leeward	*	*	*
Fish dried salted	4,740	9.07	0.21	Fish, dried	4,333	6.37	0.15	Islands below	*	*	*
Manure	2,840	5.43	0.13	Manure	4,333	6.37	0.15		*	*	*
Meat, salted, etc.	2,225	4.25	0.10	Haberdashery, etc.	2,333	3.43	0.08		*	*	*
Montserrat											
Flour	1,241	12.91	0.18	Cotton, woollens, etc	5,666	20.23	0.55	Included in	*	*	*
Fish	889	9.25	0.13	Flour	3,333	11.90	0.32	Leeward	*	*	*
	*	*	*	Fish dried	2,000	7.14	0.19	Islands below	*	*	*

	1852–4[a]				1882–4[a]				1910–12		
	Leading imports (£) Imports	% Imports	Per cap (£)		Leading imports (£) Imports	% Imports	Per cap (£)		Leading imports (£) Imports	% Imports	Per cap (£)
Nevis											
	*	*	*	Lumber	1,333	4.76	0.13		*	*	*
	*	*	*	Hardware	1,000	3.57	0.10		*	*	*
Flour	2,995	15.03	0.31	Cotton and woollens	9,000	18.75	0.76	Included in Leeward Islands below	*	*	*
Corn meal	2,599	13.04	0.27	Flour, wheat	9,000	18.75	0.76		*	*	*
Cotton, linen	2,128	10.68	0.22	Fancy goods, haberd'y	3,000	6.25	0.25				
Corn	536	2.69	0.06	Corn meal	3,000	6.25	0.25		*	*	*
	*	*	*	Rice	2,000	4.16	0.17		*	*	*
St Christopher											
Flour	15,639	16.96	0.75	Cottons and linens	29,000	15.42	1.00	Included in Leeward Islands below	*	*	*
Beef, pork, hams, etc.	4,051	4.39	0.20	Flour and wheat	27,000	14.36	0.93		*	*	*
Butter	2,118	2.29	0.10	Timber of all kinds	11,000	5.85	0.38		*	*	*
Corn meal	1,828	1.98	0.09	Haberdashery, etc.	8,000	4.25	0.27		*	*	*
Cattle	1,495	1.62	0.07	Oil meal	6,000	3.19	0.21		*	*	*
Leeward Islands[b]											
	*	*	*		*	*	*	Machinery for sugar, etc.	107,408	16.78	0.84
	*	*	*		*	*	*	Cotton, woollens, etc.	77,696	12.14	0.61
	*	*	*		*	*	*	Flour and wheat	71,608	11.19	0.56
Grenada											
Flour	11,166	8.35	0.34	Flour, wheat	15,666	11.08	0.36	Cotton goods	44,017	15.32	0.66
Dried fish	8,261	6.17	0.25	Fish, dried	10,666	7.54	0.24	Wheaten flour	34,227	11.92	0.51
Salt meat	4,816	3.60	0.15	Meat, dried, etc.	6,666	4.71	0.15	Fish	17,036	5.93	0.26
Lumber	3,411	2.55	0.10	Lumber, white, yellow	6,000	4.24	0.14		*	*	*

Commodity	Value	%	%	Commodity	Value	%	%	Commodity	Value	%	%
Manures	3,270	2.44	0.10	Rice	4,000	2.83	0.09		*	*	*
wine	2,854	2.13	0.09		*	*	*		*	*	*
Butter	2,588	1.93	0.08		*	*	*		*	*	*
St Lucia											
Goods, British manuf.	43,096	51.72	1.79	Cottons, linens, etc.	27,000	17.23	0.67	Raw materials	108,264	35.65	2.23
Wheat, flour	6,363	7.63	0.26	Machinery	17,000	10.85	0.42	Manufactures	88,062	29.00	1.81
Dry fish	5,988	7.18	0.25	Fish	11,333	7.23	0.28	Food, drink & tobacco	74,110	24.40	1.52
Livestock	3,866	4.64	0.16	Flour, wheat	11,000	7.02	0.27		*	*	*
Lumber	2,852	3.42	0.12	Haberdashery	5,500	3.51	0.14		*	*	*
Cotton, woollens, etc.	2,010	2.41	0.08		*	*	*		*	*	*
St Vincent											
Linens, cottons	48,748	31.00	1.62	Hardware, leather, etc.	49,000	34.75	1.21	Textiles	20,832	19.03	0.50
Wheat, flour	15,268	9.71	0.51	Manures	13,333	9.45	0.33	Wheaten flour	8,934	8.16	0.21
Dried fish	11,293	7.18	0.37	Fish dried or salted	10,666	7.56	0.26	Timber and shingles	4,992	4.56	0.12
Guano	9,815	6.24	0.33	Flour wheat	10,333	7.32	0.25		*	*	*
Salt meats	8,074	5.13	0.27	Rice	4,000	2.83	0.10		*	*	*

TROPICAL ASIA AND THE PACIFIC

Commodity	Value	%	%	Commodity	Value	%	%	Commodity	Value	%	%
British Solomon Islands											
	*	*	*		*	*	*	Drapery	14,650	15.03	0.00
	*	*	*		*	*	*	Rice	9,950	10.21	0.00
	*	*	*		*	*	*	Tobacco	9,350	9.59	0.00
Ceylon											
Rice	416,976	55.83	0.25	Rice	1,725,938	43.02	0.62	Rice	3,228,333	30.16	0.91
Cotton manufactures	246,457	33.00	0.15	Cotton goods	469,125	11.69	0.17	Coal and coke	926,666	8.65	0.26
Coal and coke	83,424	11.17	0.05	Coal and coke	362,719	9.04	0.13	Cotton manufactures	773,000	7.22	0.22
	*	*	*	Fish	98,375	2.45	0.04	Manures	429,000	4.00	0.12
	*	*	*	Paddy rice	95,344	2.37	0.03	Sugar	308,000	2.87	0.09

1852–4[a] Leading imports	Imports (£)	%	Per cap (£)	1882–4[a] Leading imports	Imports (£)	%	Per cap (£)	1910–12 Leading imports	Imports (£)	%	Per cap (£)
Fiji											
	*	*	*	Machinery	66,000	15.84	0.51	Drapery	141,818	15.34	1.02
	*	*	*	Drapery	61,666	14.80	0.47	Bread and biscuits	57,638	6.25	0.41
	*	*	*	Iron (bar rod rails)	54,666	13.12	0.42	Hardware	45,145	4.90	0.32
	*	*	*	Timber	23,000	5.52	0.18		*	*	*
	*	*	*	Meats	16,333	3.92	0.13		*	*	*
Hong Kong											
Opium chests	41,632	0.87	0.95		*	*	*		*	*	*
Mauritius											
Rice	279,283	27.23	1.45	Rice	434,666	15.11	1.17	Rice	516,666	21.46	1.40
Wine	41,933	4.67	0.25	Cotton manufactures	193,999	6.74	0.52	Coal	168,000	6.97	0.45
Machinery, etc.	44,448	4.33	0.23	Coals	119,666	4.16	0.32	Sulphate of ammonia	104,000	4.32	0.28
Wheat	35,917	3.50	0.19	Hardware and cutlery	103,666	3.60	0.28	Grain and pulse	102,666	4.26	0.28
	*	*	*	Wheat flour	65,000	2.26	0.18	Bags, incl. pockets	67,666	2.81	0.18
North Borneo											
	*	*	*		*	*	*	Rice, grain	133,608	24.74	0.64
	*	*	*		*	*	*	Cloth	64,124	11.87	0.31
	*	*	*		*	*	*	Provisions	43,981	8.14	0.21
Tonga											
	*	*	*		*	*	*	Drapery	31,700	15.11	1.46
	*	*	*		*	*	*	Meats	15,000	7.15	0.69
	*	*	*		*	*	*	Timber	11,900	5.67	0.55
Federated Malay States											
	*	*	*		*	*	*	Rice, paddy	1,787,183	22.92	2.51
	*	*	*		*	*	*	Opium	685,029	8.78	0.96
	*	*	*		*	*	*	Hardware cutlery	539,310	6.91	0.76

	Value	%	%	Article	Article	Value	%	%
Malacca	*	*	*		Tobacco and cigars	331,856	4.25	0.47
	*	*	*		Cottons	274,945	3.52	0.39
Penang	*	*	*	Included in Straits Settlements below	Tin	287,635	66.47	3.07
	*	*	*		Grain rice	119,340	27.58	1.28
	*	*	*		Opium	25,611	5.92	0.27
	*	*	*	Included in Straits Settlements below	Tin	1,074,003	26.78	5.63
	*	*	*		Grain rice	511,510	12.75	2.68
	*	*	*		Pepper	310,679	7.74	1.63
	*	*	*		Tobacco	274,262	6.84	1.44
Singapore	*	*	*	Included in Straits Settlements below	Grain rice	1,149,523	9.96	8.26
	*	*	*		Cotton piece goods	1,071,914	9.29	7.70
	*	*	*		Opium	913,589	7.92	6.56
	*	*	*		Metals, tin	788,338	6.83	5.66
Labuan	6,836	29.39	5.94	Cottons	Sago and sago flour	15,666	16.26	2.69
	1,259	5.41	1.09	Rice	Cloth piece goods	15,000	15.57	2.57
	963	4.14	0.84	Brasse and copper	Rattans	9,666	10.03	1.66
	817	3.51	0.71	Bees Wax	Rice	8,000	8.30	1.37
	*	*	*		Coal	4,666	4.84	0.80
Straits Settlements	*	*	*		Tins	9,928,000	22.11	16.34
	*	*	*		Rice paddy	5,972,333	13.30	9.83
	*	*	*		Cotton manufactures	2,979,666	6.63	4.90
	*	*	*		Rubber	1,797,000	4.00	2.96
	*	*	*		Copra	1,711,000	3.81	2.82

TROPICAL EAST AFRICA

	1852–4[a]			1882–4[a]				1910–12		
	Leading imports (£)	% Imports	Per cap (£)	Leading imports (£)	% Imports	Per cap (£)		Leading imports (£)	% Imports	Per cap (£)
East Africa (kenya)										
Cotton piece goods	*	*	*	*	*	*	Cotton piece goods	274,000	26.47	0.09
	*	*	*	*	*	*	Grain and flour	85,666	8.27	0.03
	*	*	*	*	*	*	Provisions	73,000	7.05	0.02
	*	*	*	*	*	*	Hardware, cutlery, etc	41,000	3.96	0.01
	*	*	*	*	*	*	Building materials	31,666	3.06	0.01
Northern Rhodesia										
	*	*	*	*	*	*	Cotton piece goods	18,120	10.00	0.02
	*	*	*	*	*	*	Blankets, rugs & sheets	6,665	3.68	less than 1p
	*	*	*	*	*	*	Apparel, etc	6,623	3.66	
	*	*	*	*	*	*	Mining machinery	4,137	2.29	
Nyasaland										
	*	*	*	*	*	*	Soft goods	116,666	55.29	0.14
	*	*	*	*	*	*	Provisions	21,666	10.26	0.03
	*	*	*	*	*	*	Hardware	17,000	8.05	0.02
	*	*	*	*	*	*	Arms and ammunition	2,666	1.26	0.00
Somaliland										
	*	*	*	*	*	*	Rice	102,666	39.13	0.41
	*	*	*	*	*	*	Texliles, grey	48,666	18.55	0.20
	*	*	*	*	*	*	Dates	19,000	7.24	0.08
	*	*	*	*	*	*	Grain jowaree	127,000	4.57	0.05
Southern Rhodesia										
	*	*	*	*	*	*	Iron & manufactures	179,757	6.31	0.23

Commodity	Value	%	%
Apparel etc.	164,965	5.79	0.21
Railway materials, etc.	151,839	5.33	0.20
Cotton manufactures	141,092	4.95	0.18
Machinery, mis. & parts	94,454	3.32	0.12

Uganda

Commodity	Value	%	%
Textilea (not American)	84,000	18.99	0.03
Textiles (American)	64,333	14.54	0.02
Provisions	23,333	5.27	0.01
Hardware	15,666	3.54	0.00

Zanzibar

Commodity	Value	%	%
Clothing	210,466	19.70	1.07
Rice	181,600	17.00	0.92
Ivory	55,500M	5.19	0.28

TROPICAL WEST AFRICA

Gambia

Commodity	Value	%	%	Commodity	Value	%	%	Commodity	Value	%	%
Cotton goods	28,927	25.51	5.26	Cotton goods	51,333	27.84	3.63	Cotton goods	128,400	17.97	0.88
Tobacco	11,621	10.25	2.11	Cola nuts	27,666	15.00	1.96	Kola nuts	74,733	10.46	0.51
Guns and pistols	6,971	6.14	1.27	Rice	15,666	8.49	0.71	Rice	64,800	9.07	0.44
Hides	6,220	5.48	1.13	Rubber	10,000	5.42	*	*	*	*	*
Wax, clean	5,617	4.95	1.02	*	*	*	*	*	*	*	*

Gold Coast

Commodity	Value	%	%	Commodity	Value	%	%	Commodity	Value	%	%
Manchester goods	22,666	28.47	17.00	Cotton goods	140,666	38.50	0.22	Provisions	171,333	5.71	0.12
Spirits and wine	18,260	22.93	13.70	Rum	65,333	17.88	0.10	Apparel, wearing	100,666	3.36	0.07
Gunpowder	9,780	12.28	7.34	Hardware and cutlery	19,666	5.38	0.03	Rum	89,000	2.97	0.06
Tobacco and cigars	8,383	10.53	6.29	Coopers stores	12,000	3.28	0.02	Rice	79,666	2.65	0.05
Hardware	6,086	7.64	4.57	*	*	*	*	*	*	*	*

Lagos / Nigeria / Sierra Leone — Leading imports

Category	1852–4 Leading imports (£)	% Imports	Per cap (£)	1882–4 Leading import	Leading imports (£)	% Imports	Per cap (£)	1910–12 Leading import	Leading imports (£)	% Imports	Per cap (£)
Lagos	*	*	*	Cotton goods	214,666	43.45	2.85	Included in Nigeria below	*	*	*
	*	*	*	Spirits (gin)	76,000	15.38	1.01		*	*	*
	*	*	*	Tobacco	26,333	5.33	0.35		*	*	*
	*	*	*	Rum	25,333	5.12	0.34		*	*	*
Nigeria					*	*	*	Cotton piece goods	922,100	16.96	0.06
					*	*	*	Spirits	414,300	7.62	0.03
					*	*	*	Iron, steel and manuf.	346,533	6.37	0.02
					*	*	*	Tobacco	181,533	3.33	0.01
					*	*	*	Grain and flour	149,300	2.74	0.01
					*	*	*	Kola nuts	95,800	1.76	0.01
					*	*	*	Machinery	87,500	1.61	0.01
Sierra Leone Cotton goods	37,216	37.57	0.84	Cotton goods	177,000	42.41	2.92	Cotton piece goods	219,000	20.27	0.26
Miscellaneous goods	26,801	27.06	0.60	Tobacco (unmanu-factured)	35,666	8.54	0.59	Cotton manu-factures	74,666	6.91	0.09
Rum	4,978	5.02	0.11	Rum	30,333	7.26	0.50	Tobacco (unmanu-factured)	56,000	5.18	0.07
Tobacco	4,880	4.92	0.11	Haberdashery	19,666	4.71	0.32	Coal, coke etc.	52,666	4.87	0.06
Hardware	4,443	4.48	0.10		*	*	*		*	*	*

[a] Occasionally data from earlier or later years have been used when there was no data for 1852–4 or 1882–4.
[b] 1911 figures only.

Notes

1 INTRODUCTION AND FRAMEWORK

1 See Chapter 12 for details.

2 See W.A. Sinclair, *The Process of Economic Development in Australia* (Melbourne, 1976), pp.1–18. For a recent discussion of the role of staples in economic development, see C.B. Schedvin, 'Staples and Regions of Pax Britannica', *Economic History Review*, 2nd ser., XLIII, 4 (1990) 533–50.

3 See Bibliography for details.

4 Lance E. Davis and Robert A. Huttenback, *Mammon and the Pursuit of Empire: The Political Economy of British Imperialism, 1860–1912* (Cambridge, 1986), pp.1–2.

5 Andrew Porter, 'The Balance Sheet of Empire, 1850–1914', *The Historical Journal*, 31, 3 (1988), p.692.

6 ibid., pp.689–90. See also S.D. Chapman, 'British-based Investment Groups Before 1914', *Economic History Review*, XXXVIII, 2 (1985), 230–51; R.V. Turrell and J.J. Van-Helten, 'The Investment Group: the Missing Link in British Overseas Expansion Before 1914', ibid., XL, 2 (1987), 267–74; and J. Forbes Munro, 'Shipping Subsidies and Railway Guarantees: William McKinnon, East Africa and the Indian Ocean', *Journal of African History* XXVIII, 2 (1987), 209–30.

7 See for instance D.K. Fieldhouse, *Black Africa, 1945–80: Economic Decolonization and Arrested Development* (London, 1986); John Darwin, *Britain and Decolonisation: The Retreat from Empire in the Post-War World* (London, 1988); A.N. Porter and A.J. Stockwell, *British Imperial Policy and Decolonisation, 1938–64*, vol. 1, *1938–51* (London, 1987), vol. 2, *1951–64* (London, 1989).

8 See Gerald K. Helleiner, *Peasant Agriculture, Government and Economic Growth in Nigeria* (Homewood, Illinois, 1966); Vincent Harlow, E.M. Chilver and Alison Smith (eds), *History of East Africa* (Oxford, 1965); R. Van Zwanenberg and Anne King, *An Economic History of Kenya and Uganda, 1800–1970* (London, 1975); Chai Hon-Chan, *The Development of British Malaya, 1896–1909* (London, 1967); Tek Ghee Lim, *Peasants and Their Agricultural Economy in Colonial Malaya, 1874–1941* (London, 1977).

9 P.J. Cain, and A.G. Hopkins, 'Gentlemanly Capitalism and British Expansion Overseas II: New Imperialism 1850–1945', *Economic History Review*, 2nd ser., XL, 1 (1989) (1987), 1–26. For a critique urging that more stress should have been put on the autonomous power of peripheral change, see Andrew Porter, '"Gentlemanly Capitalism" and Empire: The British Experience Since 1750', *Journal of Imperial and Commonwealth History*, XVIII, 3 (1990),

265–95.

10 See Andrew Porter (ed.), *Atlas of British Overseas Expansion* (London, 1991).

11 Sir Arthur Grimble, *A Pattern of Islands* (London, 1952).

12 Pierre Gourou, *The Tropical World* (4th edn, London, 1966), p.6.

13 See Sinclair, op.cit., pp.15–18, for a discussion of its evolution in a Canadian and Australian context.

14 See R. Szereszewski, *Structural Change in the Economy of Ghana, 1891–1911* (London, 1965), and Polly Hill, *Migrant Cocoa Farmers of Southern Ghana, A Study in Rural Capitalism* (Cambridge, 1963).

15 See Daniel R. Headrick, *The Tools of Imperialism* (Oxford, 1982).

16 W. Arthur Lewis (ed.), *Tropical Development 1880–1913* (London, 1970), pp.13–45.

17 See W.K. Hancock, *Survey of British Commonwealth Affairs*, vol. II, part 2 (London, 1942), pp.154–346 for the economic problems of West Africa.

18 Sir Hugh Clifford (1866–1941) developed his paternalistic ideas during his service in Malaya (1883–1903) which was spent mainly as British resident in Pahang. His short stories show great sympathy for Malayan ways of life. (See William R. Roff (ed.), Stories by Sir Hugh Clifford, London, 1966). Clifford was an aristocratic Roman Catholic and Roff comments that he had 'a strong bent for benevolent paternalism and mistrust of material progress' (p.x). Clifford later became Colonial Secretary in Trinidad and Tobago (1903–7) in Ceylon (1907–12), Governor of the Gold Coast (1912–19) and Nigeria (1919–24) and Governor of the Straits Settlements and High Commissioner for the Malay States and Borneo (1927–9). Sir Donald Cameron (1872–1948) made his name resisting the attempts of Kenya to absorb Tanganyika and to open it up for European settlement, when he was Governor of Tanganyika in the 1920s. He commenced his career in the colonial service in British Guiana in 1890 and served in Mauritius and Nigeria before becoming Governor of Tanganyika (1924–31) and of Nigeria (1931–5).

19 Cited by Allan McPhee, *The Economic Revolution in British West Africa* (London, 1926), p.172.

20 See William Allan, *The African Husbandman* (London, 1965) and Daniel Biebuyck (ed.), *African Agrarian Systems* (Oxford, 1963).

21 Cited in William G. Hynes, *The Economics of Empire, Britain, Africa, and the New Imperialism* (London, 1979), pp.110–11.

22 Cited in Ronald Hyam, *Elgin and Churchill at the Colonial Office, 1905–8, The Watershed of Empire – Commonwealth* (London, 1968), p.350.

2 THE TROPICAL COLONIES IN THE MID-VICTORIAN AGE (1850–70)

1 W.F. Moneypenny and G.E. Buckle, *The Life of Bejamin Disraeli, Earl of Beaconsfield*, vol. III, 1846–1855 (London, 1914), p.385. The remark was actually made in a private letter to Lord Malmesbury, the Foreign Secretary, when Britain had become involved in a dispute between the USA and the Canadian colonies over fishing rights. It thus referred to the colonies of settlement which Disraeli thought would be 'independent in a few years', but many people thought that the retention of tropical colonies, where British settlers could not remain permanently, was even more undesirable than the retention of the settlement colonies like Canada, Australia and New Zealand. Disraeli soon reverted to his customary pro-imperial position.

2 There is an immense literature on the reasons behind Britain's expansion of its Empire after 1850. Some authorities believe that the need to protect Britain's ever-growing foreign trade made colonial expansion inevitable: others argue that chance political factors, and the need to respond to challenges from rival colonial powers, were paramount. Perhaps the reasons are less important than the fact of expansion. Good summaries of the literature may be found in Bernard Porter, *The Lion's Share. A Short History of British Imperialism, 1850–1970* (London, 1975), pp.1–27, Ronald Robninson and John Gallagher with Alice Denny, *Africa and the Victorians. The Official Mind of Imperialism* (London, 1961), pp.1–52; and P.J. Cain and A.G. Hopkins, 'Gentlemanly Capitalism and British Expansion Overseas II: New Imperialism, 1850–1945', *Economic History Review*, 2nd ser. XL, 1, 40 (1987), 1–26. For a rather different view, see Ronald Hyam, 'Empire and Sexual Opportunity', *Journal of Imperial and Commonwealth History*, XIV, 2 (1986), 34–90.

3 See Philip Curtin, *The Atlantic Slave Trade: A Census* (Madison, Wisconsin, 1969), pp.231–51.

4 *Report of the Select Committee appointed to consider the state of the British Settlements on the western coast of Africa*, PP 1865, 1 (412), p.3.

5 ibid., p.101.

6 ibid.

7 Fawn M. Brodie, *The Devil Drives: A Life of Sir Richard Burton* (London, 1967), p.209.

8 For a discussion of colonial expansion in West Africa, see A.G. Hopkins, *An Economic History of West Africa* (London, 1973), esp. pp.124–67; Michael Crowder, *The Story of Nigeria* (2nd edn, London, 1966), pp.150–87; Edward Reynolds, *Trade and Economic Change on the Gold Coast, 1807–1874* (London, 1974), pp.139–81; and J.D. Hargreaves, *Prelude to the Partition of West Africa* (London, 1963), passim.

9 Eric Williams, *Capitalism and Slavery* (London, 1944), pp.150–3; J. Holland Rose, A.P. Newton, E.A. Benians (eds), *The Cambridge History of the British Empire* [hereafter *C.H.B.E.*], vol. II, *The Growth of the New Empire* (Cambridge, 1940), p.410; E.A. Benians, J. Butler, C.E. Carrington (eds), *The Cambridge History of the British Empire*, vol. III, *The Empire-Commonwealth 1870–1919* (Cambridge, 1959), pp.705–7. See also J.R. Ward, *Poverty and Progress in the Caribbean, 1800–1960* (London, 1985).

10 Anthony Trollope, *The West Indies and the Spanish Main* (1859, reprinted Gloucester, 1985), pp.21–2.

11 ibid., pp.32–3.

12 ibid., pp.81–2.

13 'Despatch from the Governor of Jamaica, December 31, 1851', *Reports of Her Majesty's Colonial Possessions, 1851*, PP 1852, XXXI (1539), pp.38–9.

14 ibid., p.36.

15 'Despatch from the Governor of British Guiana, May 1851', *Reports of Her Majesty's Colonial Possessions, 1850*, PP 1851, XXXIV (1421), p.143.

16 Trollope, *The West Indies*, p.171.

17 ibid., p.176.

18 *Reports, 1850* (1421), p.142.

19 ibid.

20 ibid.

21 Trollope, *The West Indies*, p.128.

22 ibid., pp.128 and 130–1.

23 ibid., p.134.

24 ibid., p.140.
25 Reports, 1850 (1421), pp.124–5.
26 Trollope, *The West Indies*, pp.153–7.
27 V.T. Harlow, *A History of Barbados, 1625–1685* (Oxford, 1926) passim, and Williams, *Capitalism and Slavery*, pp.23–9.
28 Trollope, *The West Indies*, p.154.
29 ibid., p.154.
30 ibid., pp.154–5.
31 ibid., pp.160–2.
32 'Despatch from the Governor of Barbados, August 27, 1851', Reports 1850 (1421), p.55.
33 ibid., Despatch of 12 May 1851, p.50.
34 ibid., Despatch of 27 August 1851, p.55.
35 ibid., Despatch of 12 May 1851, p.51.
36 Trollope, *The West Indies*, p.119.
37 ibid., pp.123–4.
38 James Williamson, *A Short History of British Expansion, The Modern Empire and Commonwealth* (2nd edn, London, 1934), pp.158–61.
39 Trollope, *The West Indies*, pp.124–5.
40 See Harry Williams, *Ceylon, Pearl of the East* (2nd edn, London, 1963), for a good general description, albeit written from a retired tea planter's point of view.
41 *C.H.B.E.*, vol. II, pp.165–72. See also C.D. Cowan, *Nineteenth Century Malaya* (Oxford, 1961), pp.1–6.
42 See Tilak Hettiarachchy, *The Sinhala Peasant* (Lake House Investments Ltd, Colombo, 1982), esp. pp.42–71, for a detailed account of the effects of the introduction of British legal and financial regulations on traditional Sinhala peasant society.
43 *C.H.B.E.*, vol. II, pp.517–24 and 543–50.
44 C 1421, pp.296–301.
45 Hettiarachchy, *The Sinhala Peasant*, pp.132–3.
46 James C. Jackson, *Planters and Speculators, Chinese and European Agricultural Enterprise in Malaya, 1786–1921* (Kuala Lumpur and Singapore, 1968), p.xiii.
47 Cowan, *Nineteenth Century Malaya*, pp.1–13; *C.H.B.E.*, vol. II, pp.598–614.
48 *C.H.B.E.*, vol. II, p.614; *A Return of the Area and Population of each Division of each Presidency of India from the latest inquiries*, PP 1857, XXIX (215. Ser. 2), 83. See also C.M. Turnbull, *A History of Singapore 1819–1988* (2nd ser., Oxford, 1989).
49 The 1833 trade was valued at 14.5 million Spanish dollars, worth about 5 shillings each, and the 1860 trade at 58 million Mexican or Hong Kong dollars worth about 4 shillings each. See Cowan, *Nineteenth Century Malaya*, p.21, and Jackson, *Planters and Speculators*, p.xi for the exchange rates.
50 Jackson, *Planters and Speculators*, pp.128–33.
51 Cowan, *Nineteenth Century Malaya*, pp.13, 213–71; W.D. McIntyre, *The Imperial Frontier in the Tropics, 1865–1875* (London, 1967), passim.
52 Jackson, *Planters and Speculators*, pp.52–61.
53 *C.H.B.E.*, vol. II, pp.315–16, 510–11 and 716–18.
54 ibid., p.506.
55 ibid., pp.510, 731.
56 *Despatch from Governor John Higginson to Colonial Secretary*, 16 May 1851, C 1421, p.271.
57 ibid., pp.269, 268, 274. The dangerous dependence on sugar however

continued. See Richard B. Allen, 'The Slender, Sweet Thread: Sugar, Capital and Dependency in Mauritius, 1860–1936', *Journal of Imperial and Commonwealth History* XVI (2) (1988), 177–200.

58 *C.B.H.E.*, vol. II, pp.400–1.
59 ibid., p.400; Porter, *Lion's Share*, pp.10–11.
60 *C.H.B.E.*, vol. II, p.778; Porter, *Lion's Share*, p.341.
61 *Information Malaysia* (Kuala Lumpur, 1981), p.382; Colin N. Crisswell, *Rajah Charles Brooke. Monarch of all he surveyed* (Kuala Lumpur, 1978), pp.1–17.

3 EARLY DEVELOPMENT THEORY AND THE SPREAD OF THE EMPIRE, 1870–85

1 John Gallagher and Ronald Robinson, 'The Imperialism of Free Trade', *Economic History Review*, 2nd ser. VI, 1 (1953), 1–15. Bernard Porter, *The Lion's Share: A Short History of British Imperialism, 1850–1970* (London, 1975), pp.1–28, 49–73; Ronald Robinson and John Gallagher with Alice Denny, *Africa and the Victorians, The Official Mind of Imperialism* (London, 1961), pp.1–52; C.A. Bodelsen, *Studies in Mid-Victorian Imperialism* (Copenhagen, 1924), pp.32–147; W. David McIntyre, *The Imperial Frontier in the Tropics 1865–75* (London, 1967) passim.
2 Cited by Robinson and Gallagher, in *Africa and the Victorians*, p.2.
3 ibid., pp.3–4.
4 McIntyre, *The Imperial Frontier in the Tropics*, pp.372–85. On the need for formal colonial rule, see also Martin Lynn, 'The "Imperialism of Free Trade" and the Case of West Africa, c.1830–c.1870', *Journal of Imperial and Commonwealth History* XV, 1 (1986), 22–40.
5 W.F. Moneypenny and G.E. Buckle, *The Life of Benjamin Disraeli*, vol. 4 (London, 1914), p.476, cited by Bodelsen, *Studies in Mid-Victorian Imperialism*, p.122.
6 McIntyre, *The Imperial Frontier in the Tropics*, pp.20–5.
7 ibid., pp.19 and 63.
8 Brian L. Blakeley, *The Colonial Office, 1868–1892* (Durham, N.C., 1972), pp.41 and 127 (footnote).
9 ibid., pp.42 and 128 (footnote); McIntyre, *The Imperial Frontier in the Tropics*, pp.73–4.
10 Blakeley, *The Colonial Office*, p.43.
11 McIntyre, *The Imperial Frontier in the Tropics*, p.65.
12 ibid., pp.67–9; Blakeley, *The Colonial Office*, pp.32–40.
13 See Paul Kennedy, *The Realities Behind Diplomacy: Background Influences on British External Policy, 1865–1980* (London, 1981), pp.1–82.
14 See Matthew Simon, 'The Pattern of New British Portfolio Foreign Investment, 1865–1914', in A.R. Hall, ed. *The Export of Capital from Britain 1870–1914* (London, 1968), pp.15–44; E.J. Hobsbawn, *The Age of Empire, 1875–1914* (London, 1987), pp.73–6 and 348; John A. Hobson, *Imperialism, A Study* (3rd edn, London, 1988), pp.51–4. For more recent comments on these earlier works see: Lance E. Davis and Robert A. Huttenback, *Mammon and the Pursuit of Empire: The Economics of Imperialism, 1869–1912.* (Cambridge, 1986); 'The Export of British Finance, 1865–1914', in A.N. Porter and R.F. Holland (eds), *Money, Finance and Empire, 1790–1960* (London, 1985); Philip L. Cottrell, *British Overseas Investment in the Nineteenth Century* (London, 1975); Michael Edelstein, *Overseas Investment in the Age of High*

Imperialism: The United Kingdom, 1850–1914 (New York. 1982); A.G. Hopkins' review article of Davis and Huttenback, 'Accounting for the British Empire', *Journal of Imperial and Commonwealth History*, XVI, 2 (1988), 234–47. For a defence of an earlier view concerning the importance of capital exports for imperialism, see A.M. Eckstein, 'Is There a "Hobson-Lenin Thesis" on Late Nineteenth Century Colonial Expansion?', *Economic History Review*, XLIV, 2 (1991), 297–318.

15 A.E. Musson, *The Growth of British Industry* (London, 1978), pp.221 and 235; B.E. Supple, 'Income and Demand, 1860–1914', in Roderick Floud and Donald McCloskey, eds, *The Economic History of Britain Since 1700* vol. 2, *1860 to the 1970s* (Cambridge, 1981), pp.134–5; and D.K. Fieldhouse, *Unilever Overseas. The Anatomy of a Multinational, 1895–1965* (London and Stanford, USA) pp.10–23, 317–18, 340–4, 448–67 and 494–507. See also William H. Lever, *Viscount Leverhulme by his Son* (London, 1927).

16 See The Royal Institute of International Affairs, *The Colonial Problem* (London, 1937), pp.1–27; and William G. Hynes, *The Economics of Empire Britain, Africa and the New Imperialism* (London, 1979), passim and esp. pp.57–105.

17 Cited by H.J. Habakkuk in J. Holland Rose, A.P. Newton, E.A. Benians (eds), *The Cambridge History of the British Empire*, vol. II, *The Growth of the New Empires* (Cambridge, 1940), p.780.

18 Kennedy, *Realities Behind Diplomacy*, pp.20–5.

19 Sir Charles Dilke, *Greater Britain* (London, 1868), vol. II, p.394; cited in Bodelsen, *Mid-Victorian Imperialism*, p.67.

20 Cited in E.A. Benians, J. Butler, C.E. Carrington (eds), *The Cambridge History of the British Empire*, vol. III, *The Empire-Commonwealth 1870–1919*, p.159.

21 Cited in ibid, pp.125–8.

22 Minute of 3 Oct. 1872, cited by McIntyre, *The Imperial Frontier in the Tropics*, p.370.

23 Christopher Fyfe, *A Short History of Sierra Leone* (London, 1962), pp.26–141; J.J. Crooks, *A History of the Colony of Sierra Leone, West Africa* (Dublin, 1903), pp.1–46, 164–86; J.I. Clarke (ed.), *Sierra Leone in Maps* (London, 1966) passim; John Peterson, *Province of Freedom, A History of Sierra Leone, 1787–1870* (London, 1969) passim. Another important factor affecting expansion in West Africa was the development of the steamship. See Martin Lynn, 'From Sail to Steam: The Impact of Steamship Services on the British Palm Oil Trade with West Africa, 1850–90', *Journal of African History*, 30, 2 (1989), 227–45; Robert V. Kubicek, 'The Colonial Steamer and the Occupation of West Africa by the Victorian State, 1840–1900', *Journal of Imperial and Commonwealth History*, XVIII, 1 (1990), 9–32; and Peter N. Davies, *Trading in West Africa, 1840–1920* (London, 1976).

24 Clarke, *Sierra Leone in Maps*, pp.9–27.

25 Peterson, *Province of Freedom*, pp.1–45.

26 Crooks, *History of Sierra Leone*, p.184. See also for the history of the Creoles (now known as Krio), Akintola Wyse, *The Krio of Sierra Leone: An Interpretive History* (London, 1989).

27 Fyfe, *History of Sierra Leone*, pp.48, 70–2.

28 *House of Commons Papers*, vol. XXXIV, p.166.

29 Crooks, *History of Sierra Leone*, pp.184, 317–28.

30 Harry A. Gailey, *A History of the Gambia* (London, 1964), pp.1–3.

31 ibid., passim, and p.70.

32 A.G. Hopkins, *An Economic History of West Africa* (London, 1973), pp.129–30, 134, 157–64, 172–86; Gailey, *History of the Gambia*, pp.81–111; Michael

Crowder, *Senegal* (London, 1962), pp.1–20.

33 J.D. Fage, *Ghana, A Historical Interpretation* (Maddison, 1961), p.74.

34 M.A. Havinden, 'The History of Crop Cultivation in West Africa: A Bibliographical Guide', *Economic History Review*, 2nd ser., XXIII (1970), 532–55; Fage, *Ghana*, pp.78–85.

35 Kwamina B. Dickson, *A Historical Geography of Ghana* (Cambridge, 1969), pp.1–30, 115–17.

36 J.D. Fage and Maureen Verity, *An Atlas of African History*, 2nd edn (London, 1978), map 34; Dickson, *Historical Geography of Ghana*, p.116.

37 Edward Reynolds, *Trade and Economic Change on the Gold Coast, 1807–74* (London, 1974), pp.167–8; Dickson, *Historical Geography of Ghana*, p.201.

38 Fage, *Ghana*, pp.76–8.

39 'Despatch from the Governor of the Gold Coast, April 7, 1851', *Reports of Her Majesty's Colonial Possessions 1850*, PP 1851, XXXIV (1421), p.197.

40 ibid., p.198.

41 Reynolds, *Trade and Economic Change on the Gold Coast*, pp.107–8.

42 McIntyre, *Imperial Frontier in the Tropics*, pp.281–2.

43 ibid., pp.282–4.

44 A.S. Kanya-Forster, 'French Expansion in Africa: The Mythical Theory' in Roger Owen and Bob Sutcliffe (eds), *Studies in the Theory of Imperialism* (London, 1972), pp.277–94.

45 Michael Crowder, *The Story of Nigeria* (2nd edn, London, 1966) passim; R. Olufemi Ekundare, *An Economic History of Nigeria, 1860–1960* (London, 1973), pp.31–99; Elizabeth Isichei, *A History of Nigeria* (Harlow, 1983) and J.U.J. Asiegbu, *Nigeria and its British Invaders, 1851–1920: A Thematic Documentary History* (New York, 1984).

46 C.D. Cowan, *Nineteenth-Century Malaya*, pp.270–1.

47 'Report on the Straits Settlements Blue Book for the Year 1881', *Papers Relating to Her Majesty's Colonial Possessions. Reports for 1880, 1881 and 1882*, PP 1883, XLV (3642), pp.168–9.

48 ibid., p.151.

49 McIntyre, *Imperial Frontier in the Tropics*, pp.211–59, 317–18.

50 *Encyclopaedia Britannica*, 1955 edn, vol.9, p.232.

51 McIntyre, *Imperial Frontier in the Tropics*, pp.331–2.

52 'Fiji Governor's Speech on Leaving the Colony', *Reports for 1880, 1881 and 1882* (3642), p.4.

53 ibid., p.13.

54 The average of the Rousseaux index for 1852, 1853 and 1854 was 100 while for 1882, 1883 and 1884 it was 99. For the same periods the Sauerbeck-Statist index fell from 92 to 81. See B.R. Mitchell and Phyllis Deane, *Abstract of British Historical Statistics* (Cambridge, 1962), pp.472–5.

4 THE COLONIAL 'SCRAMBLE' AND JOSEPH CHAMBERLAIN'S DEVELOPMENT PLANS, 1885–1903

1 See J.D. Fage and Maureen Verity, *An Atlas of African History* (2nd edn, London, 1978), esp. maps 47–56.

2 Ronald Robinson and John Gallagher with Alice Denny, *Africa and the Victorians: The Official Mind of Imperialism* (London, 1961), pp.160–209, 379–409; Harry A. Gailey, *A History of the Gambia* (London, 1964), passim; and Michael Crowder, *West Africa under Colonial Rule* (London, 1968), passim.

3 Vincent Harlow, E.M. Chilver and Alison Smith (eds), *History of East Africa*, vol. II (Oxford, 1965), esp. pp.543–624. See also Walter FitzGerald, *Africa, A Social, Economic and Political Geography* (2nd edn, London, 1936), pp.218 and 263.

4 George Bennett, 'Settlers and Politics in Kenya, Up to 1945', in Harlow, Chilver and Smith (eds), *East Africa*, II, pp.309–18.

5 See for example, G.N. Sanderson, 'The European Partition of Africa: Coincidence or Conjuncture?', *Journal of Imperial and Commonwealth History*, III (1974), 1–54, and Bernard Porter, 'Imperialism and the Scramble', *Journal of Imperial and Commonwealth History*, IX (1980), 76–81, for discussion of the literature and the issues involved. See also John D. Hargreaves, *West Africa Partitioned*, vol. II, *The Elephants and the Grass* (London, 1985) and Adu Boahen (ed.), *Unesco General History of Africa (1880–1935)*, vol. 7 (1985) for African reactions and resistance to colonial expansion.

6 See A.G. Hopkins, 'The Victorians and Africa: A Reconsideration of the Occupation of Egypt, 1882', *Journal of African History*, 227 (1986), 390; and M.E. Chamberlain, 'Clement Hill's Memoranda and the British Interest in East Africa', *English Historical Review*, LXXXVII (1972), 533–47, for a discussion of the importance of economic factors in British East African policy.

7 Gailey, *History of the Gambia*, esp. pp.203–9.

8 R. Olufemi Ekundare, *An Economic History of Nigeria, 1860–1960* (London, 1966), pp.134–209.

9 John E. Flint, *Sir George Goldie and the Making of Nigeria* (Oxford, 1960).

10 Margery Perham, *Lugard, The Years of Adventure, 1858–1898* (London, 1956), pp.623–713, and *Lugard, The Years of Authority, 1898–1945* (London, 1960), pp.21–203 and 247–6; but for critical views of Lugard's activities see Peter K. Tibenderana, *Sokoto Province Under British Rule, 1903–1939: A Study of Institutional Adaptation and Culturalisation of a Colonial Society in Northern Nigeria* (Zaria, Nigeria, 1988) who argues that indirect rule was a sham; and Marion Johnson, 'Cotton Imperialism in West Africa', *African Affairs*, 73, 291 (1974), 178–87, who shows that Lugard tried to induce raw cotton production by trying to crush the Northern Nigerian cotton weaving industry in 1906. Fortunately he failed.

11 Michael Crowder, *The Story of Nigeria* (London, 1966), esp. pp.210–30.

12 B.R. Mitchell, *International Historical Statistics, Africa and Asia* (London, 1982), pp.37–46; Nigerian population figures are subject to some uncertainty, but a recent UN estimate for Nigeria's population was 95.2 million in 1985. See *United Nations Monthly Bulletin of Statistics*, XLI, No. 5 (May 1987), p.4.

13 Margery Perham (ed.), *The Native Economies of Nigeria*; vol. I, *The Economics of a Tropical Dependency* by Daryll Forde and Richenda Scott (London, 1946); and vol. II *Mining, Commerce and Finance*, by P.A. Bower, A.J. Brown, C. Leubuscher, J. Mars and Sir Allan Pim (London, 1948); Keith M. Buchanan and J.C. Pugh, *Land and People in Nigeria: the Human Geography of Nigeria and its Environmental Background* (London, 1958); Sir Alan Burns, *History of Nigeria* (London, 1969); and the *Nigerian Handbook* (2nd edn, Crown Agents, London, 1954). See also Roland Oliver and G.N. Sanderson (eds), *The Cambridge History of Africa*, vol. 6, *From 1870 to 1905* (Cambridge, 1985).

14 J.D. Fage, *Ghana: A Historical Interpretation* (Madison, 1959), p.64.

15 *The Gold Coast Handbook 1923* (Accra 1923), p.2. Kwamina B. Dickson, *A Historical Geography of Ghana* (Cambridge, 1969); R. Szereszewski, *Structural Changes in the Economy of Ghana, 1891–1911* (London, 1965); and William E.F. Ward, *A History of Ghana* (London, 1967).

16 *The Gold Coast Handbook, 1923* (Accra, 1923), p.62.
17 ibid., pp.60–1.
18 Dickson, *Historical Geography of Ghana*, p.163.
19 Fage, *Ghana*, p.106, n.15 cited from S.H. Frankel, *Capital Investment in Africa* (London, 1938), pp.162–3; see also R.F. Burton and V.L. Cameron, *To the Gold Coast for Gold* (London, 1883).
20 Polly Hill, *Migrant Cocoa Farmers of Southern Ghana, A Study in Rural Capitalism* (Cambridge, 1963). See also M.A. Havinden, 'The History of Crop Cultivation in West Africa: A Bibliographical Guide', *Economic History Review*, 2nd ser., XXIII (1970), pp.543–8, for a discussion of the literature on the rise of cocoa farming in West Africa.
21 See Roland Oliver and Gervaise Mathew (eds), *History of East Africa*, vol. I (Oxford, 1963) and Harlow, Chilver and Smith (eds), vol. II; RT. Van Zwanenberg and Anne King, *An Economic History of Kenya and Uganda, 1800–1970* (Macmillan, 1975); Sir Charles Eliot, *The East Africa Protectorate* (London, 1905, Frank Cass, 1966); C.W. Hobley, *Kenya, From Chartered Company to Crown Colony* (London, 1929, 2nd edn, Frank Cass, 1970); and Perham, *Lugard*, vol. I.
22 Zwanenberg and King, *Kenya and Uganda*, pp.79–102. See also William R. Ochieng (ed.), *A History of Modern Kenya* (London, 1989) and Charles H. Ambler, *Keynan Communities in the Age of Imperialism: The Central Region in the Late Nineteenth Century* (New Haven, 1988), which shows how the great famine of 1897–1901 assisted the British conquest.
23 Kenneth Ingham, *The Making of Modern Uganda* (London, 1958), pp.36–105 and F. D. Lugard, *The Rise of our East African Empire*, 2 vols. (London, 1893).
24 Eliot, *East Africa Protectorate*, p.29.
25 Cited by Cyril Ehrich in 'The Uganda Economy, 1903–45', in Harlow, Chilver and Smith (eds), *History of East Africa*, II, p.397.
26 Ingham, *The Making of Modern Uganda*, p.100.
27 Perham, *Lugard*, I, pp.193–210.
28 Eliot, *East Africa Protectorate*, p.131; and Hobley, *Kenya from Chartered Company to Crown Colony*, pp.76–96.
29 Eliot, *East Africa Protectorate*, p.v.
30 ibid., pp.309–10.
31 ibid., p.310.
32 Robert L. Tignor, *The Colonial Transformation of Kenya: The Kamba, Kikuyu and Maasai from 1900–1939* (Princeton, 1976), pp.15–41, 94–110; Zwanenberg and King, *Kenya and Uganda*, pp.25–43; E.A. Brett, *Colonialism and Underdevelopment in East Africa: The Politics of Economic Change, 1919–1939* (London, 1973), pp.20–30; M.P.K. Sorrenson, *Origins of European Settlement in Kenya* (Nairobi and London, 1968), pp.1–141, 271–88, 295–6; Gavin Kitching, *Class and Economic Change in Kenya* (London, 1980), pp.16–22.
33 The economic origins of the conflict are examined in Robin Palmer and Neil Parsons (eds), *The Roots of Rural Poverty in Southern Africa* (London, 1977). See also M. Meredith, *The Past is Another Country: Rhodesia, 1890–1979* (London, 1979).
34 See C.D. Cowan, *Nineteenth Century Malaya. The Origins of British Political Control* (Oxford, 1961); James C. Jackson, *Planters and Speculators. Chinese and European Agricultural Enterprise in Malaya, 1786–1921* (Kuala Lumpur, 1968); H.C. Belfield (ed.), *Handbook of the Federated Malay States* (2nd edn., London, 1904); Sir Frank Swettenham, *British Malaya: An Account of the Origin and Progress of British Influence in Malaya* (London, 1906); Wang Gungwu, *A Short*

History of the Nanyang Chinese (Singapore, 1959); Chai Hon-Chan, *The Development of British Malaya, 1896–1909* (Kuala Lumpur, 1964).

35 See Teck Ghee Lim, *Peasants and Their Agricultural Economy in Colonial Malaya 1874–1941* (Kuala Lumpur and London, 1977), pp.12–23, 27–49.

36 ibid., p.245.

37 Cowan, *Nineteenth-Century Malaya*, pp.238–71.

38 R.G. Cant, 'Historical Reasons for the Retarded Development of Pahang State, Eastern Malaya, *New Zealand Geographer*, 21 (1965), .26–37.

39 Cowan, *Nineteenth-Century Malaya*, pp.257–8.

40 ibid., pp.259–62.

41 Swettenham, *British Malaya*, passim.

42 J.G. Pike, *Malawi: A Political and Economic History* (London, 1965); R.L. Rotberg, *The Rise of Nationalism in Central Africa: The Making of Malawi and Zambia, 1873–1964* (Cambridge, Mass., 1965); A.J. Wills, *An Introduction to the History of Central Africa* (Oxford, 1973); and Margery Perham, *Lugard*, vol. I, pp.59–160.

43 J.I. Clarke (ed.), *Sierra Leone in Maps* (London, 1966); John Levi with Michael Havinden, Omotunde Johnson and Gerald Karr, *African Agriculture: Economic Action and Reaction in Sierra Leone* (London, 1976), pp.1–85; John Levi and Michael Havinden, *The Economics of African Agriculture*, (Harlow, 1982), pp.43–5; and T.J. Allridge, *A Transformed Colony. Sierra Leone As It Was And Is* (London, 1910).

44 Julian Amery and J.L. Garvin, *Life of Joseph Chamberlain*, vol. 4 *At the Height of His Power* (London, 1951), pp.234–55.

45 *Government Handbook, The Colony of Fiji, 1874–1924* (Suva, 1924), pp.71–2.

46 Richard M. Kesner, *Economic Control and Colonial Development. Crown Colony Financial Management in the Age of Joseph Chamberlain* (London, 1981), pp.11 and 29.

47 *C.H.B.E.*, III, pp.143–9.

48 Colin N. Crisswell, *Rajah Charles Brooke. Monarch of All He Surveyed* (Oxford, 1978), esp. pp.1–39; and Leigh R. Wright, *The Origins of British Colonialism in Borneo* (Hong Kong, 1970).

49 *C.H.B.E.*, III, p.149.

50 James L. Garvin, *The Life of Joseph Chamberlain*, vol. 3, 1895–1900: *Empire and World Policy* (London, 1934), p.5.

51 William G. Hynes, *The Economics of Empire*: *Britain, Africa and the New Imperialism* (London, 1979), pp.111–29.

52 Andrew Porter, 'In Memoriam Joseph Chamberlain: A Review of Periodical Literature, 1960–73', *Journal of Imperial and Commonwealth History*, III (1975), .292–7. On the uncertainty of Chamberlain's motivations he notes C.L. Mowat's view in 1968 that Chamberlain's career 'still needs a good deal of explanation if he is to be considered one of the great Victorians' (p.296).

53 Kesner, *Economic Control*, p.72.

54 See Paul Kennedy, *The Realities Behind Diplomacy*: *Background Influences on British External Policy, 1865–1980* (London, 1981), esp. pp.32–6. Military expenditure rose from £23.2 to £31.7 million between 1870 and 1890–1, soared to £121.2 million in 1900–1 during the Boer War, and stood at £67.7 million in 1910–11 (p.35).

55 Garvin, *Life of Chamberlain*, vol. 3, p.19.

56 ibid., pp.19–20.

57 Kesner, *Economic Control*, pp.70–2.

58 Garvin, *Life of Chamberlain*, vol. 3, pp.176–7.

59 Kesner, *Economic Control*, pp.72–6; Garvin, *Life of Chamberlain*, vol. 3, p.177.
60 Kesner, *Economic Control*, pp.76–81.
61 S.B. Saul, 'The Economic Significance of "Constructive Imperialism"', *Journal of Economic History*, XVII, 2 (1957), 173–92 and David Jessop, 'The Colonial Stock Act of 1900: A Symptom of the New Imperialism?', *Journal of Imperial and Commonwealth History*, IV, 2 (1976), 254–63.
62 Porter, 'In Memoriam Joseph Chamberlain', p.293.
63 Kesner, *Economic Control*, pp.216–17. See also Robert V. Kubicek, *The Administration of Imperialism: Joseph Chamberlain at the Colonial Office* (Durham, N.C., 1969) and Andrew Porter, 'Joseph Chamberlain: A Radical Reappraisal?', *Journal of Imperial and Commonwealth History*, VI, 3 (1978), 330–6.
64 See Angus Maddison, *Phases of Capitalist Development* (Oxford, 1982), pp.85–91.

5 FIRST FRUITS

1 See Richard Kesner, *Economic Control and Colonial Development* (London, 1981) esp. pp.217–25; and Sir Keith Hancock, *Survey of British Commonwealth Affairs, 1918–38* (London, 1942), esp. vol. II, part 2.
2 There is an immense literature on this subject. A useful analysis is provided by Angus Maddison, *Phases of Capitalist Development* (Oxford, 1982), esp. 80–95. See also W.A. Lewis, *Growth and Fluctuations, 1870–1913* (London, 1978).
3 The Rousseaux index of agricultural and industrial prices rose from an average of 99 in 1882–4 to an average of 101 in 1910–12; while the Sauerbeck–Statist index of food and raw material prices remained stationary at an average of 81 in both periods. B.R. Mitchell and Phyllis Deane, *Abstract of British Historical Statistics* (Cambridge, 1962), pp.472–5.
4 Gerald K. Helleiner, *Peasant Agriculture, Government and Economic Growth in Nigeria* (Homewood, Illinois, 1966), p.492.
5 Margery Perham, *Lugard, The Years of Authority* (London, 1960), pp.247–65.
6 A.G. Hopkins, *An Economic History of West Africa* (London, 1973), pp.231–6. An alternative to 'peasant' production would have been concessions for plantations as sought by William Lever, but the Nigerian government regarded this as disruptive and defeated it, see K. Dike Nworah, 'The Politics of Lever's West African Concessions, 1907–13, *International Journal of African Historical Studies*, V, 2 (1972), 248–64.
7 ibid., pp.194–5.
8 ibid., p.220
9 ibid., p.220. For more details, see J.S. Hogendorn, 'The Origins of the Groundnut Trade in Northern Nigeria'. Unpublished Ph.D. thesis, University of London, 1966.
10 Hopkins, *Economic History of West Africa*, p.194.
11 R. Olufeme Ekundare, *An Economic History of Nigeria, 1860–1960* (London, 1973) p.137; and Kesner, *Economic Control*, p.86
12 Helleiner, *Peasant Agriculture*, pp.13–15.
13 See Robert Szereszewski, *Structural Changes in the Economy of Ghana 1891–1912* (London, 1965), and Polly Hill, *Migrant Cocoa Farmers of Southern Ghana. A Study in Rural Capitalism* (Cambridge, 1963), for the most illuminating and perceptive accounts of the spread of cocoa cultivation and its effects on the Ghanaian economy.

14 Gustof A. Wanner, *The First Cocoa Trees in Ghana, 1858–68* (Basle, 1962), pp.13–21.
15 Hill, *Migrant Cocoa Farmers*, passim.
16 Szereszewski, *Structural Changes*, p.53.
17 Hill, *Migrant Cocoa Farmers*, passim
18 G.B. Kay (ed.), *The Political Economy of Colonialism in Ghana*, (Cambridge, 1972), p.334.
19 ibid., p.41
20 Cyril Ehrlich, 'The Uganda Economy, 1903–1945' in Vincent Harlow, E.M. Childer and Alison Smith, *History of East Africa*, vol. II (Oxford, 1965), p.406.
21 ibid., pp.399–406.
22 ibid., pp.419–22.
23 ibid., p.421; and Ronald Hyam, *Elgin and Churchill at the Colonial Office, 1905–1908, the Watershed of Empire – Commonwealth* (London, 1968), pp.436–44.
24 Ehrlich, 'The Uganda Economy', p.474.
25 *The Oxford Survey of the British Empire*, vol. II, Asia (Oxford, 1914), p.474; and Kesner, *Economic Control*, pp.21 and 87.
26 Elsie K. Cook, *Ceylon, its Geography, its Resources and its People* (London, 1951), pp.170–96; *Oxford Survey, Asia*, pp.338–71.
27 Kesner, *Economic Control*, p.212.
28 ibid., pp.99–100.
29 Leonard Woolf, *Growing, an Autobiography of the Years*, 1904–1911 (London, 1961) p.180.
30 ibid., p.245.
31 Sir Frank Swettenham, *British Malaya, An Account of the Origin and Progress of British influence in Malaya* (3rd edn., London, 1948, first published in 1906), passim and esp. pp.272–305.
32 *Oxford Survey, Asia*, p.481. See also J.F. Hennart, 'Internationalization in Practice: Early Foreign Direct Investment in Malayan Tin Mining', *Journal of International Business Studies*, 127 (1986), 131–43.
33 John H. Drabble, *Rubber in Malaya, 1876–1922* (Oxford, Kuala Lumpur, 1973), p.213. See also R.T. Stillson, 'The Financing of Malayan Rubber', *Economic History Review*, 2nd ser., XXIV (1971), 589–98.
34 ibid., pp.28, 215–18
35 Swettenham, *British Malaya*, pp.293–8.
36 ibid., pp.299–301. For a critical view of Swettenham's role in Malaya, see D.R. Sardesai, *British Trade and Expansion in Southeast Asia*, 1830–1914 (New Delhi, 1977), esp. pp.220–80. See also John Benyon, 'Overlords of Empire? British "Proconsular Imperialism" in Comparative Perspective', *Journal of Imperial and Commonwealth History*, XIX, 2 (1991), 164–202.
37 B.R. Mitchell, *International Historical Statistics, Africa and Asia* (New York, 1982) p.505.
38 Swettenham, *British Malaya*, p.302. See also Teck Ghee Lim, *Peasants and their Agriculture Economy in Colonial Malaya, 1874–1941* (Oxford, 1977), passim.
39 Drabble, *Rubber in Malaya*, pp.207–11.
40 CO 884/12. No 194 (1913) West Indian (confidential) Negotiations about Oil Concessions in Trinidad, pp.1–25; and CAB 37/115, No 39 (Secret) Paper by Winston Churchill, First Lord of the Admiralty on Oil Fuel supply for His Majesty's Navy, 16 June 1913.
41 CO 884/12. No 202. British Guiana: Correspondence concerning bauxite

deposits, 21 July 1914 to 1 January 1916.

42 Bernard Porter, *The Lion's Share: A Short History of British Imperialism, 1850–1970* (London, 1975), pp.224–5; D.K. Fieldhouse, *Unilever Overseas. The Anatomy of a Multinational* (London, 1978), pp.499–507.

43 Porter, ibid., p.225; Fieldhouse, ibid., pp.494–526; W.K. Hancock, *Survey of British Commonwealth Affairs*, vol. II, pt. 2 (London, 1942), pp.173–200.

44 Porter, ibid., esp. pp.220–8 and 278–82. For the positive side of development, see also C.C. Wrigley in Andrew Roberts (ed.), *The Cambridge History of Africa*, vol. 7: *1905–14* (Cambridge, 1986) and Richard M. Kesner, 'Builders of Empire: The Role of the Crown Agents in Imperial Development, 1880–1924', *Journal of Imperial and Commonwealth History*, V, 3 (1977), 310–30; but for a critical view, see W. Evan Nelson, 'The Gold Standard in Mauritius and the Straits Settlements between 1850 and 1914', *Journal of Imperial and Commonwealth History*, XVI, 1 (1987), 48–76.

6 THE IMPACT OF THE FIRST WORLD WAR AND ITS AFTERMATH

1 For the effects of the war on the British economy see: Sidney Pollard, *The Development of the British Economy*, 1914–1967 (2nd edn London, 1969), pp.42–91. For wartime controls see: E.M.H. Lloyd, *Experiments in State Control at the War Office and the Ministry of Food* (Oxford, 1924); J. Arthur Salter, *Allied Shipping Control an Experiment in International Administration* (Oxford, 1921); C. Ernest Fayle, *History of the Great War: Seaborne Trade*, vol. II (London, 1923); R.H. Tawney, 'The Abolition of Economic Control, 1918–1921', *Economic History Review*, XIII (1943), 1–30.

2 W. Arthur Lewis, *Growth and Fluctuations 1870–1913* (London, 1978), pp.225–45.

3 For example, Ceylon Legislative Council, 18 Dec. 1914, CO 57/186; East Africa Protectorate Executive Council, 31 Dec. 1915, CO 544/13; Gold Coast, *Annual Report 1916*, p.7; Nigeria, *Report on the Blue Book for the Year 1917*, CO 657/4, p.26.

4 Nigeria, Nigerian Council, 29 Dec. 1915, CO 657/11, p.6.

5 The Federated Malay States government increased the rates of taxes on tin and rubber output, import duties, stamp duty and opium and liquor sales; the government of the Straits Settlements introduced income tax for the first time in 1916; export taxes were extended and the rates increased in Ceylon in 1915; Nigeria introduced an import surtax of 25 per cent in January 1915 and imposed export taxes for the first time in 1916; head tax was extended from Northern Nigeria to some provinces of Southern Nigeria in 1916; the Gold Coast government also imposed export taxes. For a detailed study of public finance in one colony during the war see: N.A. Cox-George, 'Studies in Finance and Development – The Gold Coast (Ghana) Experience 1914–18', *Public Finance*, XIII, 1 (1958), 146–77.

6 *Colonies' War Contribution. Treasury Minute*, PP (1918), XVII (Cd 9183), 365.

7 In Malaya, Ceylon, Fiji, Kenya, the Gold Coast and Jamaica.

8 Silver coin was replaced by tokens in Nigeria, for example. On the currency problems faced by colonies using the Indian rupee, see: Robert M. Maxon, 'The Kenya Currency Crisis 1919–21 and the Imperial Dilemma', *Journal of Imperial and Commonwealth History*, XVII, 3 (1989), 323–48.

9 W.H. Beveridge, *British Food Control* (London, 1928) pp.113–37; Lloyd,

Experiments in State Control, pp.201–28, 303, 313; Slater, *Allied Shipping Control*, pp.69–97. Colonial exports adversely affected from time to time by British import controls included tea (Ceylon), cocoa (Ceylon, Nigeria, Gold Coast, Trinidad), coconuts (Ceylon), coffee (Kenya, Jamaica), hides and skins (Kenya), groundnuts (Nigeria, Sierra Leone), rum (Jamaica), asphalt (Trinidad).

10 Richard Rathbone, 'World War 1 and Africa', *Journal of African History*, XIX, 1 (1978), 7; see also, Melvin E. Page (ed.), *Africa and the First World War* (New York, 1987).

11 Melvin E. Page, 'The War of *Thangata*: Nyasaland and the East African Campaign, 1914–1918', *Journal of African History*, XIX, 1 (1978), 87–100.

12 For example, in Malaya, Ceylon, Fiji, Nigeria, Trinidad. See also: J. Forbes Munro, *Africa and the International Economy 1800–1960* (London, 1976), p.123.

13 Especially in Kenya and Nigeria.

14 Federated Malay States, *Annual Report 1918*, p.20; Straits Settlements, *Annual Report 1917*, p.38; Fiji, *Annual Report 1916*, p.15; Gold Coast, *Annual Report 1919*, p.7; Trinidad, *Annual Report 1917*, p.20.

15 Munro, *Africa and the International Economy*, p.124.

16 For example, Governor Clifford's address to the Nigerian Legislative Council, 29 Dec. 1919, CO 657/11.

17 Paul Guinn, *British Strategy and Politics 1914 to 1918* (Oxford, 1965), p.6; Peter J. Yearwood, 'Great Britain and the Repartition of Africa, 1914–19', *Journal of Imperial and Commonwealth History*, XVIII, 3 (1990), 319–20.

18 W.O. Henderson, *Studies in German Colonial History* (London, 1962), pp.96–111; Sir Charles Lucas (ed.), *The Empire at War*, vol. IV (London, 1924); Mary E. Townsend, *The Rise and Fall of Germany's Colonial Empire* (New York, 1930), pp.365–8; Gaddis Smith, 'The British Government and the Disposition of the German Colonies in Africa, 1914 to 1918', in Prosser Gifford and Wm. Roger Louis (eds), *Britain and Germany in Africa, Imperial Rivalry and Colonial Rule* (New Haven, 1967), pp.275–7, 283–4.

19 Heinrich Schnee, *German Colonization Past and Future: The Truth About German Colonies* (London, 1926) pp.74–6.

20 H.C. O'Neil, *The War in Africa and the Far East* (London, 1918); Edmund Dane, *British Campaigns in Africa and the Pacific 1914–1918* (London, 1919); Rev. W.A. Crabtree, 'The Conquest of Togoland', *Journal of the African Society*, XIV (1914–15), 386–91; Lucas, *Empire at War*, pp.20–5.

21 Wm. Roger Louis, *Great Britain and Germany's Lost Colonies, 1914 to 1919* (Oxford, 1967), pp.36–76; W.D. Downes, *With the Nigerians in German East Africa* (London, 1919).

22 G.W.T. Hodges, 'African Manpower Statistics for the British Forces in East Africa, 1914 to 1918', *Journal of African History*, XIX, 1 (1978), 101–16; Roger Thomas, 'Military Recruitment in the Gold Coast During the First World War', *Cahiers D'Études Africaines*, XV, 57 (1975), 57–84; see also E.J. Yorke, 'A Crisis of Colonial Control: War and Authority in Northern Rhodesia, 1914–1919', unpublished PhD thesis, University of Cambridge, 1984.

23 Jan Smuts, *The British Commonwealth of Nations: A Speech Made by General Smuts, 15 May 1917* (London, 1917), p.4.

24 V.H. Rothwell, *British War Aims and Peace Diplomacy 1914 to 1918* (Oxford, 1971); See also: John S. Galbraith, 'British War Aims in World War I: A Commentary on "Statesmanship"', *Journal of Imperial and Commonwealth History*, XIII, I (1984), 25–45; Yearwood, 'Great Britain and the Repartition',

pp.323–5.

25 Ray Stannard Baker, *Woodrow Wilson and World Settlement*, vol. I (Gloucester, Mass., 1922), p.54; Quincy Wright, *Mandates under the League of Nations* (Chicago, 1930), p.3.

26 David Lloyd George, *The Truth About the Peace Treaties*, vol. II (London, 1938), p.765; Baker, *Woodrow Wilson*, I, p.55.

27 CAB23/40, I.W.C. 13, 1 May 1917; see also, *Manchester Guardian*, editorial, 25 May 1917.

28 Louis, *Great Britain and Germany's Lost Colonies*, p.77.

29 CAB23/40, W.C. 280, 22 Nov. 1917.

30 *Manchester Guardian*, 16 June 1917; see also speech by Commander Wedgewood, House of Commons, 16 May 1917, *Hansard*, Commons, 93, 1683.

31 CAB23/40, I.W.C. 13, 1 May 1917; see also Ernst B. Haas, 'The Reconciliation of Conflicting Colonial Policy Aims: Acceptance of the League of Nations Mandates System', *International Organisation*, VI (1952), 521–36; P.S. Gupta, *Imperialism and the British Labour Movement* (London, 1975), p.35; Smith, 'British Government and the Disposition of the German Colonies', p.289.

32 CAB23/5 W.C. 312, 3 Jan. 1918.

33 CAB35/5 W.C. 314, 4 Jan. 1918.

34 Seth P. Tillman, *Ango-American Relations at the Paris Peace Conference* (Princeton, 1961), p.28.

35 Charles Seymour, *The Intimate Papers of Colonel House*, vol. IV (New York, 1928), p.153.

36 United States, State Department, *Foreign Relations: The Paris Peace Conference 1919* (Washington D.C, United States Government Printing Office, 1943), vol. III, p.718; Louis, *Great Britain and Germany's Lost Coloniese*, p.4.

37 US, *Foreign Relations*, III, p.719.

38 US, *Foreign Relations*, III, pp.720–1; See also: R.C. Snelling, 'Peacemaking, 1919: Australia, New Zealand and the British Empire Delegation at Versailles', *Journal of Imperial and Commonwealth History*, IV, 2 (1975), 15–28; Colin Newbury, 'Spoils of War: Sub-Imperial Collaboration in South West Africa and New Guinea, 1914–20', *Journal of Imperial and Commonwealth History*, XIV, 3 (1988), 88–106.

39 US, *Foreign Relations*, III, p.763.

40 US, *Foreign Relations*, III, p.771; Wilson's adviser, George Louis Beer, however, supported the dominions' claims for exemption from the mandates system: *African Questions at the Paris Peace Conference* (New York, 1923), pp.443–44, 456–8.

41 Wm. Roger Louis, 'The Origins of the "Sacred Trust"', in Ronald Segal and Ruth First (eds), *South West Africa: Travesty of Trust* (London, 1967), p.74; Paul Clyde, *Japan's Pacific Mandate* (Port Washington, 1935), p.32.

42 Louis, *Great Britain and Germany's Lost Colonies*, pp.134–5.

43 Up to 10 Jan. 1919, Under Secretary of State for Foreign Affairs.

44 W.J. Hudson, *Billy Hughes in Paris: The Birth of Australian Diplomacy* (Melbourne, Australian Institute of International Affairs, 1978), pp.22–3; Baker, *Woodrow Wilson*, I, p.272; Yearwood, 'Great Britain and the Repartition', p.330.

45 Hudson, *Billy Hughes*, pp.21–3; H. Duncan Hall, 'The British Commonwealth and the Founding of the League Mandate System', in K. Bourne and D.C. Watt (eds), *Studies in International History* (London, 1967),

p.346.

46 US, *Foreign Relations*, III, p.796.

47 US, *Foreign Relations*, V, pp.472–3.

48 Nancy Viviani, *Nauru, Phosphate and Political Progress* (Canberra, 1970), p.44. See also, Barrie Macdonald, *Cinderellas of the Empire: Towards a History of Kiribati and Tuvalu* (Canberra, 1982).

49 Louis, *Great Britain and Germany's Lost Colonies*, pp.74–5, 124; Haas, 'Reconciliation of Conflicting Colonial Aims', p.531.

50 Wright, *Mandates Under the League*, p.629.

51 H.M.V. Temperley (ed.), *A History of the Peace Conference of Paris* (London, Royal Institute of International Affairs, 1920), vol. II, p.234.

52 Henry Noel Brailsford, *After the Peace* (London, 1920), p.166; on the 'open-door' see: Raymond L. Buell, *International Relations*, rev. edn (New York, 1929), pp.437–62.

53 Julius Stone, *Colonial Trusteeship in Transition* (Sydney, Australian Institute of International Affairs, 1944), pp.16–17.

54 Rothwell, *British War Aims*, p.290; Hudson, *Billy Hughes*, p.17; Wright, *Mandates Under the League*, p.94; Louis, *Great Britain and Germany's Lost Colonies*, pp.97–9; Smith, 'Disposition of the German Colonies', p.295; *Correspondence Relating to the Wishes of the Natives of the German Colonies as to Their Future Government*, PP., 1918, XVII (Cd.9210), 379.

55 John H. Harris, 'The Mandatory System After Five Years' Working', *Contemporary Review*, CXXVII, Feb. 1925, 171–8; Elizabeth Maanen-Helmer, *The Mandates System in Relation to Africa and the Pacific Islands* (London, 1929); Wm. Roger Louis, 'Great Britain and International Trusteeship: The Mandate System', in R.W. Winks (ed), *The Historiography of the British Empire-Commonwealth* (Durham, North Carolina, 1966), p.304; Frederick Lugard, 'The Mandate System and the British Mandates', *Journal of the Royal Society of Arts*, LXXII (June, 1924); Raymond Leslie Buell, 'Backward' Peoples Under the Mandate System', *Current History*, XX (June, 1924), 386–95.

56 *Recommendations of the Economic Conference (Paris) of the Allies*, P.P. 1916, XXXIV (Cd.8271), 11.

57 Guinn, *British Strategy and Politics*, pp.192–3. Curzon was a member of the inner War Cabinet of five to seven ministers throughout the period 6 Dec. 1916 to 31 Oct. 1919 and Milner was a member to 18 Apr. 1918.

58 Great Britain, P.P., *Extracts from Proceedings and Papers Laid Before the Conference*, P.P. 1917–18, XXIII (Cd.8566), pp.111, 114.

59 CAB23/40, I.W.C. 11, 12, 24 and 26 Ap. 1917; *Extracts from Proceedings and Papers Laid Before the Conference*, P.P. 1918, XVI (Cd.9177) 691; Ian M. Drummond, *Imperial Economic Policy 1917 to 1939: Studies in Expansion and Protection* (London, 1974), p.26.

60 Frederic Benham, *Great Britain Under Protection* (New York, 1941), p.88; Rixford Kinney Synder, *The Tariff Problem in Great Britain, 1918–1923* (Stanford, 1944), pp.40–56.

61 *Copy of Resolutions Passed by the Committee on Commercial and Industrial Policy After the War on the Subject of Imperial Preference*, P.P. 1917–18, XXIII (Cd.8582), p.4; see also, *Final Report of the Committee on Commercial and Industrial Policy After the War*, P.P. 1918, XIII (Cd.9035), p.27.

62 CAB23/40, W.C. 152, 31 May 1917.

63 H. Wilson Fox, 'Payment of War Debt by Development of Empire Resources', *United Empire*, IX, Jan. 1918, p.175; see also, Fox, 'The Development of Imperial Resources', *Journal of the Royal Society of Arts*, LXV

(Dec. 1916), 78–91.
64 Alfred Bigland, *Call of Empire* (London, 1926), p.91.
65 H. Wilson Fox, 'The Development of the Empire's Resources', *The Nineteenth Century and After*, Oct. 1917, p.836.
66 Alfred Bigland, 'The Empire's Assets and How to Use Them', *Journal of the Royal Society of Arts*, LXV, 1917, 359.
67 Fox, 'Development of the Empire's Resources', 847.
68 Fox, 'Payment of War Debt', 175; *The Times*, 30 Jan. 1917.
69 Bigland, 'Empire's Assets', 358.
70 Bigland, 'Empire's Assets', 358.
71 Quoted by Sir Frederick Lugard, 'The Crown Colonies and the British War Debt', *The Nineteenth Century and After*, LXXXVIII (1920), 241.
72 *Hansard*, Commons, 112, 13 Feb. 1919, 433.
73 Lugard, 'Crown Colonies and British War Debt'; E.D. Morel, *Africa and the Peace of Europe* (London, 1917), p.xxiii; W.K. Hancock, *Survey of British Commonwealth Affairs, II, Problems of Economic Policy*, Pt 1 (London, Royal Institute of International Affairs, 1940), pp. 106–10; David Killingray, 'The Empire Resources Development Committee and West Africa', *Journal of Imperial and Commonwealth History*, 10, 2 (1982), 194–210; Gupta, *Imperialism and the British Labour Movement*, pp.20–21.
74 CAB23/10, CAB.580, 18 June 1919.
75 Colonial Office, 'Economic Development in the Colonies and Protectorates' (Misc. No. 348, Jan. 1922), CO 885/26; Stephen Constantine, *The Making of British Colonial Development Policy 1914 to 1940* (London, 1984), p.47.
76 Hancock, *Problems of Economic Policy*, pp.125–6; Frederick V. Meyer, *Britain's Colonies in World Trade*, (London, Royal Institute of International Affairs, 1948), pp.10–11.
77 Hancock, *Problems of Economic Policy*, pp.116–17; Final Report on Commercial and Industrial Policy, p.25.
78 Hancock, *Problems of Economic Policy*, pp.121–2; The differential export duty on palm kernels was abolished in July 1922.
79 'Research Into Economic Resources of the British Empire', Colonial Office, circular despatch, 11 June 1919.

7   THE ECONOMICS OF 'TRUSTEESHIP'

1 Lord Milner was a member of the inner War Cabinet from December 1916 to April 1918 and secretary of state for the colonies from January 1919 to February 1921; Leopold Amery was parliamentary under secretary of state for the colonies from January 1919 to February 1921 and secretary of state from November 1924 to June 1929; William Ormsby-Gore (later Lord Harlech) was parliamentary under secretary of state for the colonies from October 1922 to January 1924 and from November 1924 to June 1929; J.H. Thomas was secretary of state for the colonies from January to October 1924.
2 For surveys of British unemployment policy and its relation to British colonial development policy in the 1920s see: E.A. Brett, *Colonialism and Underdevelopment in East Africa* (London, 1973), chaps. 4 and 5; Stephen Constantine, *The Making of British Colonial Development Policy, 1914–1940* (London, 1984), chaps. 5, 6 and 7; W.R. Garside, *British Unemployment 1919–1939* (Cambridge, 1990), chap. 7.
3 CAB 27 120 CU 268; CAB 24 129 CP 3415.
4 CP 1345. See Cabinet conclusions, 17 Oct. 1921.

5 CAB 27 179 TP 13.
6 CAB 27 179 TP 43.
7 *Imperial Economic Conference, Record of Proceedings and Documents* (PP 1924, X, (Cmd 2009), p.169.
8 CAB 27 191 69/5.
9 CAB 27 191 70/6.
10 CAB 27 191 71/7; CAB 27 195 CU 610; CAB 27 191 72/1.
11 CAB 24 164 CP 15.
12 *Hansard* (Commons), 5th ser., CLXX, 25 Feb. 1924, col. 185. The programme of works included railway construction to the value of £3.5 million and port installations to cost £4.5 million. The British government was to lend £3.5 million and the remaining sum of £4.5 million was to be raised publicly by the Kenyan government.
13 *Private enterprise in British Tropical Africa* PP 1924, VIII (Cmd 2016).
14 ibid., pp.5–6.
15 ibid., p.25.
16 *Report of the East Africa Commission, 1924–25* PP 1025, IX (Cmd 2387).
17 CAB 27 1965 CU 667.
18 CAB 24 174 CP 366.
19 *Report of the East Africa Commission, 1924–25*, p.182.
20 ibid., p.192.
21 *Hansard* (Commons), 5th ser., CLXXXIII, 11 May 1925, col. 1426; and CLXXXVII, 27 July 1925, col.; *Memorandum, by the Committee on Trade and Industry, on transport development and cotton growing in East Africa, 1924–25*, PP 1925, XXI, (Cmd 2463); P.S. Gupta, *Imperialism and the British Labour Movement, 1914–1964* (London, 1975), pp.71–85.
22 CAB 24 175 CP 434.
23 Cabinet conclusions, 23 Oct. 1925.
24 CAB 24 179 CP 129.
25 CAB 24 207 CP 27; CAB 24 201 CP 37.
26 CAB 24 202 CP 53.
27 CAB 24 202 CP 87; CAB 24 203 CP 104.
28 CAB 24 203 CP 110.
29 *Report of the East Africa Guaranteed Loan Committee 1926–29* PP 1929–30, VIII (Cmd 3494).
30 *Hansard* (Commons), 5th ser., CCXXVII, 30 Apr. 1929, col. 1414; see also *The Times*, 19 Apr. and 26 Apr. 1929.
31 CAB 26 12. See also: Neal R. Malmsten, 'The British Labour Party and the West Indies, 1918–39', *Journal of Imperial and Commonwealth History*, V, 2 (1977), 185–7.
32 *Hansard* (Commons), 5th ser., CCXXX, 17 July 1929, col. 475, 478.
33 *Statement on works approved for grants in connection with unemployment under the Development (Loan Guarantees and Grants) Act 1929, and the Colonial Development Act 1929, and from the Road Fund* PP 1929–30, XXV (Cmd 3449); *Hansard* (Commons), 5th ser., CCXXV, 24 Feb. 1930, col. 1952, 1960–1.
34 CAB 24 211 CP 134; *Statement on works approved for Government financial assistance in connection with unemployment* PP 1929–30, XXV (Cmd 3616); Robert Skidelsky, *Politicians and the Slump: the Labour Government of 1929–1931* (London, 1967), p.337.
35 *Report of the Committee on National Expenditure* PP 1930–31, XVI (Cmd 3920), p.133.
36 ibid., p.134.

37 Ian M. Drummond, *Imperial Economic Policy 1917–1939* (London, 1974), pp.43–144; *Report of the Empire Cotton Growing Committee* PP 1920, XVI (Cmd 523); *Report of the Tropical Agricultural College Committee* PP 1920, XXV (Cmd. 562); *Report on the Imperial Institute Committee of Enquiry* PP 1923, XII, Pt. 1 (Cmd 1997).

38 The Coalition Manifesto, 1918, cited in Benjamin Gerig, *The Open Door and the Mandates System* (London, 1930), p.79.

39 *Resolutions relating to Imperial Preference* PP 1924, XVIII (Cmd 2084).

40 *Imperial Economic Conference 1923, Summary of Conclusions* PP 1923, XXI, Pt. 1 (Cmd 1990), p.3.

41 *Imperial Economic Conference 1923, Record of Proceedings and Documents* PP 1924, X (Cmd 2009), p.150.

42 ibid., p.185.

43 *Hansard* (Commons), 5th ser., CLXXII, 29 Apr. 1924, col. 1597; *Statement of the position of His Majesty's Government in regard to the resolution of the Imperial Economic Conference 1923, and the proposals laid before the Conference by His Majesty's late Government* PP 1924, XVIII (Cmd 2115).

44 *Hansard* (Commons), 5th ser., CLXXIX, 17 Dec. 1924, col. 1665.

45 ibid., col. 1666–7.

46 Imperial Economic Committee, *Report on marketing and preparing for market of foodstuffs produced in the overseas parts of the Empire* PP 1924–5, XIII (Cmd 2493).

47 There were also some miscellaneous activities, one of which was the establishment of a chair in imperial economic relations at the London School of Economics in 1929, held by Professor J. Coatman.

48 Empire Marketing Board, *Note on the work of the Board and statement of research grants approved by the Secretary of State from July 1926 to May 1927* PP 1927, XVIII (Cmd 2898).

49 *First and Second Reports from the Select Committee on Estimates* PP 1931–2 (55, 90), IV, 699.

50 *First and Second Reports from the Select Committee on Estimates* PP 1928 (71, 114), VI, 181, and reply by Sir Stephen Tallents, Secretary to the EMB, pp.118–19; *Select Committee on Estimates, 1931–2*, pp.vi, 33; *Report of the Committee on National-Expenditure*, p.133; Memorandum by the British Poster Advertising Association, 9 Dec. 1929, CO 760 22 PC 126; *Hansard* (Commons), 5th ser., CCXII, 13 Feb. 1928, col. 651–2.

51 David Meredith, 'Imperial images: the Empire Marketing Board, 1926–32', *History Today*, 37 (Jan. 1987), 30–6.

52 For the African colonies, see Ralph A. Austen, *African Economic History: Internal Development and External Dependency* (London, 1987), chap. 6 and 7.

53 Greg Lanning, *Africa Undermined: Mining Companies and the Underdevelopment of Africa* (London, 1979), chap. 4.

54 Peter Bauer, *The Rubber Industry: A Study in Competition and Monopoly* (London, 1948).

55 David Meredith, 'Government and the decline of the Nigerian oil-palm export industry, 1919–1939', *Journal of African History*, 25 (1984), 311–29.

56 R.E. Wraith, *Guggisberg* (London, 1967), pp.98–128; David Meredith, 'The construction of Takoradi Harbour in the Gold Coast 1919 to 1930: a case study in colonial development and administration', *Transafrican Journal of History*, 5 (1976), 134–49.

57 Lim, Teck Ghee, *Peasants and Their Agricultural Economy in Colonial Malaya 1874–1941* (Kuala Lumpur and New York, 1977); Lim, Teck Ghee, 'Malayan

365

Peasant Smallholders and the Stevenson Restriction Scheme, 1922–28', *Journal of the Malaysian Branch of the Royal Asiatic Society*, 47, 2 (1974); John Drabble, 'Investment in the Rubber Industry in Malaya c.1900–1922', *Journal of South East Asian Studies*, 3, 2 (1972), 247–61; P.T. Bauer, 'The Working of Rubber Regulation', *The Economic Journal*, 56 (1946), 391–414.

58 E.A. Brett, *Colonialism and Underdevelopment in East Africa*, pp.186–90, 208–11; John Iliffe, *A Modern History of Tanganyika* (Cambridge, 1979), pp.289–90.

59 Siok Hwa Cheng, 'The rice industry of Malaya: a historical survey', *Journal of the Malayan Branch of the Royal Asiatic Society*, 42 (1969), p.132; Sir Hugh Clifford, 'Life in the Malay Peninsular: as it was and is', *Proceedings of the Royal Colonial Institute*, XXX (1898–9), p.386.

60 David Meredith, 'The Colonial Office, British business interests and the reform of cocoa marketing in West Africa, 1937–1945', *Journal of African History*, 29 (1988), 285–300.

61 John Iliffe, *The Emergence of African Capitalism* (London, 1983), p.37.

62 'Relation on Road Transport to Railway Development in the Colonies', Colonial Office Confidential Prince (Misc.) No. 489, 1936–37, CO 885 84.

8 DEPRESSION AND DISILLUSION

1 For a detailed analysis of the work of the CDAC see: David Meredith, 'The British Government and Colonial Economic Development, with particular reference to British West Africa, 1919–1939', unpublished Ph.D. thesis, University of Exeter, 1976, chap. 3; 'The British Government and Colonial Economic Policy, 1919–39', *Economic History Review*, 2nd ser., XXVIII, 3 (1975), 484–499; Stephen Constantine, *The Making of British Colonial Development Policy, 1914–1940* (London, 1984), chap. 8.

2 *Hansard* (Commons) 5th ser., CCXXIX, 107–8, 3 July 1929.

3 *Report on Labour Conditions in the West Indies*, PP 1938–39, XV (Cmd 6070); *Report of the Advisory Council on Nutrition in the Colonial Empire*, PP 1938–9, X (Cmd 6050, 6051).

4 Circular despatch 16 Sept. 1930. CO 854 78 1930.

5 *First, Second and Third Reports of the CDAC, 1929–1932*.

6 Calculated from the *Reports of the CDAC 1929–1934*.

7 Sir Alan Rae Smith, who had sat on the committee since its inception, succeeded Sir Basil Blackett on the latter's death in Sept. 1935.

8 CO 137 807 68564 1935 (Jamaica); CO 67 268 90153 1936 (Cyprus).

9 CO 295 590 70127 1935.

10 CO 831 42 77093/8 1937.

11 Minutes of the 117–125 meetings of the CDAC, April 1939 to July 1940, CO 970 3.

12 CO 536 204 40251 1939.

13 For an opposing view, i.e. that the CDAC did put much emphasis on the proportion of their expenditure to be spent in the United Kingdom, see, George C. Abbott, 'A re-examination of the 1929 Colonial Development Act', *Economic History Review*, 2nd ser., XXIV (1971), pp.68–81, and for a comment on Abbott's view see, Meredith, 'The British Government and Colonial Economic Policy, 1919–1939', p.487; Constantine, *The Making of British Colonial Development Policy*, p.211; W.R. Garside, *British Unemployment 1919–1939* (Cambridge, 1990), p.200.

14 *Hansard* (Commons) 5th ser., CCXXIX, 1259, 12 July 1929.

15 *Hansard* (Commons) 5th ser., CCXXXV, 1960, 24 Feb. 1930.
16 F.V. Meyer, *Public Works in the British Colonies* (Colonial Office, 1946), p.3.
17 Of all the colonial governors in the inter-war period only Sir Gordon Guggisberg, governor of the Gold Coast 1919–1927, has been the subject of a biography: R.E. Wraith, *Guggisberg* (London, 1967). It could be claimed that Guggisberg was the most imaginative governor in British Africa in the inter-war period and the only one to devote much attention to economic development, as he instituted a ten-year development programme for the Gold Coast in 1919. However, even he, as Wraith shows, spent most of his energy on reforming the political and administrative machinery of the Gold Coast government and drafting a new constitution.
18 L.P. Mair, *Native Policies in Africa* (London, 1936).
19 CO 852 250 15606/2 1939.
20 *Imperial Conference 1926. Appendices to the Summary*, PP 1926, xi (Cmd 2769).
21 *Hansard* (Commons) 5th ser. CCVII, 1411, 30 Apr. 1929.
22 CO 23 81, Cabinet conclusions, 3 Oct. 1934, Cabinet 33 (34)5.
23 'Report of the Inter-Departmental Committee on the industrial development of the Empire' PRO CAB 249 CP 145 Mar. 1934. See a letter from J.H. Campbell to the Colonial Office, 2 June 1939, alleging the use of sweated labour in Hong Kong: 15212/4 1939.
24 Chamberlain to Secretary of State for the Colonies, 28 Feb. 1936, PRO CO 852 17 15212/25 1935.
25 Davies to Macdonald, 22 July 1935, 15212/25 1935.
26 CO 852 105 15212/36; 15212/B/37.
27 CO 852 164 15212/B 1938.
28 15212/B 1938; see also, P.S. Gupta, *Imperialism and the British Labour Movement 1914–1964* (London, 1975), pp.244–6.
29 CO 852 250 15606/11/39.
30 15212/35.
31 15606/1/39.
32 ibid.
33 CAB 23 80, Cabinet conclusions, 3 Oct. 1934, Cabinet 33(34)6.
34 The governor of Nigeria to the secretary of state for the colonies, 5 April 1939; this was part of a long dispatch in which Governor Bourdillon expressed a certain degree of bitterness at the failure of the British Government – supposedly a trustee of the people of Nigeria – to come to terms with the colony's severe economic and social problems. CO 859 41 12901/1 1939.
35 CO 852 173 15279/9 1938.
36 For a discussion see S.H. Frankel, *Capital Investment in Africa: Its Course and Effects* (London, 1938), pp.173–91.
37 For the impact of the depression on one highly vulberable export economy – Mauritius, see: Richard B. Allen, 'The Slender, Sweet Thread: Sugar, Capital and Dependency in Mauritius, 1860–1936', *Journal of Imperial and Commonwealth History*, XVI, 2 (1988), pp.192–4.
38 For a discussion of the Nigerian case see Penelope Bower, 'The Balance of Payments in 1936' in M. Perham, (ed.), *Mining, Commerce and Finance in Nigeria* (London, 1948), and *The Balance of Payments of Nigeria in 1936* (Oxford, 1949).
39 The import values were measured on a cost insurance freight basis which meant that the 'unit values' used in Table 8.9 do not reflect changes in import duties. As discussed in Chapter Nine, in the 1930s most colonies raised their

import duties quite considerably, both to protect their public revenue and to enable them to give a greater margin of tariff preference to British goods. The deterioration in the 'terms of trade' for the average consumer in these colonies is, therefore, understated by Table 8.9. See also, S.M. Martin, 'The Long Depression: West African Export Producers and the World Economy, 1914–1945', in Ian Brown (ed.), *The Economies of Africa and Asia in the Inter-War Depression* (London, 1989).

40 On the rubber regulation scheme see P.T. Bauer, 'The Working of Rubber Regulation', *The Economic Journal*, LVI, No. 223 (1946), 391–414; P. Lamartine Yates, *Commodity Control: A Study of Primary Products* (London, 1943), pp.105–29. On the tin scheme see: Yates, *Commodity Control*, pp.130–56; see also, *The Colonial Empire in 1937–38: Statement to Accompany the Estimates for Colonial and Middle Eastern Services 1938*, PP 1937–38, XX (Cmd, 5760), pp.14–16.

41 F.V. Meyer, *Britain's Colonies in World Trade* (London, 1948), pp.67–85; K.S. Lomax, 'Colonial Demand for Cotton Goods', *Yorkshire Bulletin of Economic and Social Research*, 4, 1 (1952), p.70.

9 THE 'COLONIAL QUESTION' AND TOWARDS COLONIAL REFORM, 1930–40

1 I. M. Drummond, *Imperial Economic Policy 1917–1939: Studies in Expansion and Protection* (London, 1974).
2 F. V. Meyer, *Britain's Colonies in World Trade* (London, 1948), p.80.
3 Cameron to CO, 23 Feb. 1933, CO 32312261108119/1.
4 Extract from Proceedings of East Africa Governors' Conference, 1933, on 1108119/1.
5 Clementi to CO, 3 Apr. 1933, 1108119/1.
6 Petition to CO from Manchester cotton manufacturers, 24 Mar. 1933, 1108119/1.
7 Circular despatch, 13 Apr. 1934, CO 32312893180123.
8 CO to Ceylon, 3 June 1934, CO 3231305319383.
9 CO 32312903180123H.
10 Secretary of state, semi-official letter to Lord Stanley (a junior minister in the Treasury whose constituency was in Lancashire), 26 Nov. 1934, CO 323130431838.
11 *The Economist*, 12 May 1934, p.1019.
12 Calculated from the *Statistical Abstract for the British Empire*.
13 A. R. Peters, *Anthony Eden at the Foreign Office 1931–1938* (New York, 1986), pp.89–90; The Earl of Avon, *The Eden Memoirs: Facing the Dictators* (London, 1962), p.137.
14 League of Nations, *Report of the Committee for the Study of the Problem of Raw Materials* (No. A.27, 1937, IIB, Geneva, 8 Sept. 1937).
15 Keith Middlemas, *Diplomacy of Illusion: the British Government and Germany, 1937–39* (London, 1972), p.111; Royal Institute of International Affairs, *Documents on International Affairs 1937* (London, 1939), pp.214 ff.
16 Middlemas, *Diplomacy of Illusion*, p.111.
17 Committee of Imperial Defence, 'Transfer of a Colonial Mandate or Mandates to Germany', Report of a Sub-committee, CAB 16/145–146, June 1936, p.36. See also, A. Edho Ekoko, 'The British attitude towards Germany's colonial irredentism in Africa in the inter-war years', *Journal of*

Contemporary History, 14 (1979), 287–307; For Schacht's views on the economic problem Germany faced in obtaining tropical raw materials from colonies see his article, 'Germany's Colonial Demands', *Foreign Affairs*, 15, 2 (Jan. 1937), 223–34.

18 W. N. Medlicott and Douglas Dukin (eds.), *Documents on British Foreign Policy 1919–1939*, second series, vol. XVIII (London, 1980), p.434.

19 The Earl of Halifax, *Fulness of Days* (London, 1957), pp.184, 190; The Earl of Birkenhead, *Halifax: the Life of Lord Halifax* (London, 1965), p.365. Middlemas, *Diplomacy of Illusion*, pp.115–16.

20 Cabinet Committee on Foreign Policy, 24 Jan. 1938, CAB 27623.

21 ibid.

22 Sir Nevile Henderson, *Failure of a Mission: Berlin 1937–1939* (London, 1940), p.114.

23 ibid. pp.116–18.

24 Middlemas, *Diplomacy of Illusion*, p.447; Martin Gilbert and Richard Gott, *The Appeasers* (London, 1963), p.220; P.S. Gupta, *Imperialism and the British Labour Movement, 1914–1964* (London, 1975), pp.237–43.

25 Wolfe W. Schmokel, *Dream of Empire: German Colonialism, 1919–1945* (Westport, Connecticut, 1964, repr. 1980), p.125.

26 Middlemas, *Diplomacy of Illusion*, pp.115–16, 169; Keith Feiling, *The Life of Neville Chamberlain* (London, 1946), p.300; Royal Institute of International Affairs, *Documents*, pp.216, 235–7.

27 Sir Bernard Bourdillon to Malcolm MacDonald, 5 Apr. 1939, CO 8594112901/1 p.1.

28 George W. Baer, *The Coming of the Italo-Ethiopian War* (Cambridge Mass., 1967), chaps. 1–3; Avon, *The Eden Memoirs*, p.297; Halford L. Hoskins, 'The Suez Canal in Time of War', *Foreign Affairs*, 14, 1 (Oct. 1935), 93–101; Frank Hardie, *The Abyssinian Crisis* (London, 1974), chap. 16; Esmonde M. Robertson, *Mussolini as Empire-Builder* (London, 1977), pp.184–9.

29 Correlli Barnett, *The Collapse of British Power* (London, 1972), p.380.

30 Roy Douglas, *World Crisis and British Decline, 1929–1956* (New York, 1986), p.84.

31 Daniel Waley, *British Public Opinion and the Abyssinian War 1935–36* (London, 1975); Brice Harris Jr., *The United States and the Italo-Ethiopian Crisis* (Stanford, Calif., 1964). The dominion governments also apparently had little influence over British policy, see: David Carlton, 'The Dominions and British Policy in the Abyssinian Crisis', *Journal of Imperial and Commonwealth History*, I, 1 (1972), 59–77.

32 M. Rubens, 'Non-white reaction to the Italo-Ethiopian crisis, 1934–36', unpublished PhD thesis, Oxford University, 1978, p.iv; see also, William R. Scott, 'Black nationalism and the Italo-Ethiopian conflict 1934–1936', *Journal of Negro History*, 63 (1978), 118–34; W. E. Burghardt Du Bois, 'Inter-racial Implications of the Ethiopian Crisis: a Negro View', *Foreign Affairs*, 14, 1 (Oct. 1935), 82–92.

33 S. K. B. Asante, *Pan-African Protest: West Africa and the Italo-Ethiopian Crisis, 1934–1941* (London, 1977), chap. 6; see also, J. Ayodele Langley, *Pan-Africanism and Nationalism in West Africa 1900–1945* (Oxford, 1973), pp.327–37; Immanuel Geiss, *The Pan-African Movement* (London, 1974), p.354; Ali A. Mazrui and Michael Tidy, *Nationalism and New States in Africa* (London, 1984), chap. 1.

34 Rubens, 'Non-White reaction', pp.175–89.

35 ibid., pp.190–208; Morley Ayearst, *The British West Indies: the Search for*

Self-Government (London, 1960), pp.38–41; John La Guerre, 'The Moyne Commission and the West Indian intelligentsia, 1938–39', *Journal of Commonwealth Political Studies*, IX, 2 (1971), 137; J. M. Kenyatta, 'Hands off Abyssinia!', *The Labour Monthly*, 17, 9 (Sept. 1935), 535–36; Basil Davidson, *Black Star: a View of the Life and Times of Kwame Nkrumah* (London, 1973) p.31.

36 N. J. Ryan, *The Making of Modern Malaysia and Singapore* (Kuala Lumpur, 1971), pp.209–11; Rupert Emerson, *From Empire to Nation: the Rise to Self-Assertion of Asian and African Peoples* (Boston, 1960), p.29; see also, Raymond Callahan, 'The Illusion of Security: Singapore 1919–42', *Journal of Contemporary History*, 9, 2 (1974), 69–92; Richard Storry, *Japan and the Decline of the West in Asia 1894–1943* (London, 1979), p.7.

37 *Report of the Commission appointed to Enquire into the Disturbances in the Copperbelt of Northern Rhodesia*, PP 1934–5, VII (Cmd 5009), Oct. 1935, p.26; See also: Ian Henderson, 'Early African Leadership: The Copperbelt Disturbances of 1935 and 1940', *Journal of Southern African Studies*, 2, 1 (1975), 83–97; Charles Perrings, 'Consciousness, Conflict and Proletarianization: An Assessment of the 1935 Mineworkers' Strike on the Northern Rhodesian Copperbelt', *Journal of Southern African Studies*, 4, 1 (1977), 31–51.

38 *Labour Conditions in Northern Rhodesia*, Colonial No. 150 (London, 1938), pp.32–3.

39 *The Times*, 3–16 Sept. 1938.

40 David Meredith, 'The Colonial Office, British Business Interests and the Reform of Cocoa Marketing in West Africa, 1937–1945', *Journal of African History*, 29 (1988), 285–300.

41 *Report of the Commission on the Marketing of West African Cocoa*, PP 1937–8, IX (Cmd 5845), Sept. 1938.

42 E. Burnet and W. R. Aykroyd, 'Nutrition and Public Health', *Quarterly Bulletin of the Health Organization of the League of Nations*, IV, 2 (June 1935).

43 Economic Advisory Council, Committee on Nutrition in the Colonial Empire, First Report, Part I, *Nutrition in the Colonial Empire*, PP 1938–9, X (Cmd 6050), July 1939, pp.33, 38; Part II, *Summary of Information Regarding Nutrition in the Colonial Empire* (Cmd 6051), July 1939.

44 R. N. Chowdhuri, *International Mandates and Trusteeship Systems* (The Hague, 1955), pp.23–27.

45 W.M. MacMillan also contributed to the debate on colonial reform in the Heath Clark Lectures, 1939, published in C.K. Meek, W. M. MacMillan and E. R. J. Hussey, *Europe and West Africa: Some Problems and Adjustments* (London, 1940), and published an article, 'The Real Colonial Question', *Fortnightly Review*, CXL VIII, July-Dec. 1940, pp.548–57.

46 For an account of the West Indies riots see *The Times*, 25, 26 and 27 May, 1938; *Trinidad and Tobago Disturbances, 1937, Report of Commission*, PP 1937–8, XV (Cmd 5641); W. M. MacMillan, *Warning from the West Indies: a Tract for the Empire* (London, 1938), pp.5–15; K.W.J. Post, 'The Politics of Protest in Jamaica, 1938: Some Problems of Analysis and Conceptualisation', *Social and Economic Studies*, XVIII, 4 (1969), 374–90; Selwyn D. Ryan, *Race and Nationalism in Trinidad and Tobago: A Study of Decolonisation in a Multiracial Society* (Toronto, 1972), pp.44–67; Paul Blanshard, *Democracy and Empire in the Caribbean* (New York, 1947), pp.21–40; Neal R. Malmsten, 'The British Labour Party and the West Indies, 1918–39', *Journal of Imperial and Commonwealth History*, V, 2 (1977), 190–8; Stephen Constantine, *The Making of British Colonial Development Policy, 1914–40* (London, 1984), pp.234–8. On the threat posed to Trinidad's oil industry, regarded as important for

Britain's defence strategy, see: Howard Johnson, 'Oil, Imperial Policy and the Trinidad Disturbances, 1937', *Journal of Imperial and Commonwealth History*, IV, I (1975), 29–54.

47 *Hansard* (Commons) 5th series, vol. 338, col 110, 14 June 1938.

48 *West India Royal Commission Report*, PP 1944–45, X (Cmd 6607), June 1945, p.424. See also: John La Guerre, 'The Moyne Commission and the West Indian Intelligensia, 1938–39', *Journal of Commonwealth Political Studies*, IX, 2 (1971), 134–57.

49 Major Orde-Browne, the labour adviser to the secretary of state, produced three detailed reports on labour conditions in Northern Rhodesia, West Africa and the West Indies between 1937 and 1940; *Labour Conditions in Northern Rhodesia* (Colonial No. 150, May 1938); *Report on Labour Conditions in the West Indies*, PP 1938–9, XV (Cmd 6070), 721; *Report on Labour Conditions in West Africa, by Major G. St J. Orde-Browne*, PP 1940–1, IV (Cmd 6277), 1. See also, *The Colonial Empire, 1939*, PP 1938–39, XX (Cmd 6023), pp.18–37.

50 Charles Jeffries, *The Colonial Empire and its Civil Service* (Cambridge U.K., 1938); Harold Laski, 'The Colonial Civil Service', *Political Quarterly*, IX, 4 (1938), 541–51; Arthur Creech Jones, 'The Colonial Office', *Political Quarterly*, XIV, 1 (1943) 19–32; Anon, 'A Service in Transition: Administrators for a Changing Empire', *Round Table*, 26 (1946), 356–8; Colonial Office, *Organization of the Colonial Civil Service* (Colonial No. 197, London, 1946); Colonial Office, *Post-war Training for the Colonial Service* (Colonial No. 198, London, 1946); Sir Cosmo Parkinson, *The Colonial Office from Within, 1909–1945* (London, 1947); J. M. Lee and M. Petter, *The Colonial Office, War and Development Policy: Organization and the Planning of a Metropolitan Initiative, 1939–45* (London, 1982).

51 Minutes of a meeting of the Departmental Committee on Colonial Development, 27 June 1938, CO 85219015606.

52 ibid.

53 Meeting of the Committee, 4 July 1938; Minute by Dufferin and Ava, 19 Sept. 1938.

54 CO 85219015606.

55 ibid.

56 Treasury to CO, 8 June 1939, CO 8521891545314.

57 CO 32316987450/1.

58 ibid., 4 Sept. 1939. See also: Rosaleen Smyth, 'Britain's African Colonies and British Propaganda During the Second World War', *Journal of Imperial and Commonwealth History*, XIV, 1 (1985), 65–82.

59 ibid.

60 ibid.

61 CO 859/19/7475.

62 Minutes of a meeting held between the CO and the Treasury, 27 Nov. 1939; and Treasury to CO, 5 Jan. 1940, CO 859197475.

63 ibid.

64 CO 8522991545314.

65 CAB 674, WP(G) (4) 44; Cabinet minutes, 15 Feb. 1940, CAB 655.

66 WP(G) (4) 44.

67 ibid.

68 *Statement of Policy on Colonial Development and Welfare*, PP 1939–40, X (Cmd 6175), Mar. 1940; see also Constantine, *Colonial Development Policy*, pp.238–45.

69 Lord Hailey, *An African Survey: a Study of the Problems Arising in Africa South of*

the Sahara (London, 1938), p.1629.

70 Leonard Barnes, *Empire or Democracy? A Study of the Colonial Question* (London, 1939); Alfred Viton (pseud.), *Great Britain, an Empire in Transition* (New York, 1940); W.E. Burghardt Du Bois, 'The Realities in Africa: European Profit or Negro Development', *Foreign Affairs*, 21, 4 (1943), 720–32; George Padmore, *How Britain Rules Africa* (New York, 1936, repr. 1969); Nnamdi Azikwe, *Renascent* Africa (London, 1937, repr. 1969).

10   A NEW SENSE OF URGENCY

1 *The Colonial Empire (1939–1947)*, PP 1946–47, X (Cmd 7167), p. 10.
2 ibid., p. 8.
3 On wartime marketing, see: Charlotte Leubuscher, *Bulk Buying from the Colonies* (London, 1956), pp. 1–66; Nicholas Westcott, 'The East African Sisal Industry, 1929–1949: The Marketing of a Colonial Commodity during Depression and War', *Journal of African History*, 25, 4 (1984), 445–61; Raymond Dumett, 'Africa's Strategic Minerals during the Second World War', *Journal of African History*, 26, 4 (1985), 381–408; David Meredith, 'State Controlled Marketing and Economic Development: The Case of West African Produce during the Second World War', *Economic History Review*, 2nd ser., XXXIX, 1 (1986), 77–91. On the role of the state in the economies of the African colonies during the war, see: Michael Cowan and Nicholas Westcott, 'British Imperial Economic Policy during the war', in David Killingray and Richard Rathbone (eds), *Africa and the Second World War* (London, 1986). On inflation, see: A.R. Prest, *War Economics of Primary Producing Countries* (Cambridge, 1948), pp. 1–27, 241–82.
4 *Colonial Empire (1939–1947)*, p. 15; see also: R.D. Pearce, *The Turning Point in Africa, British Colonial Policy 1938–48* (London, 1982); Ali A. Mazrui and Michael Tidy, *Nationalism and New States in Africa* (London, 1984), pp. 10–30; Killingray and Rathbone, *Africa and the Second World War*; N.J. Westcott, 'Closer Union and the Future of East Africa, *1939–1948*: A Case Study in the "Official Mind of Imperialism"', *Journal of Imperial and Commonwealth History*, X, 1 (1981), 67–88; Ian Spencer, 'Settler Dominance, Agricultural Production and the Second World War in Kenya', *Journal of African History*, 27, 4 (1980), 497–514; A.N. Porter and A.J. Stockwell, *British Imperial Policy and Decolonization, 1938–1964, vol. 1, 1938–51* (London, 1987); John Darwin, *Britain and Decolonization: the Retreat from Empire in the Post-War World* (London, 1988) pp. 34–68.
5 *Hansard* (Commons), 5th ser., 361, 11 June 1940, col. 1205; Stephen Constantine, *The Making of British Colonial Development Policy, 1914–1940* (London, 1984), pp. 246–256; J.M. Lee, '"Forward Thinking" and War: The Colonial Office During the 1940s', *Journal of Imperial and Commonwealth History*, VI, 1 (1977), 64–79.
6 CO 967 13/41; CO 852 503/1.
7 Wm. Roger Louis, *Imperialism at Bay 1941–1945: The United States and the Decolonization of the British Empire* (Oxford, 1977); Darwin, *Britain and Decolonization*, pp. 34–68.
8 T 160 1111 18424/42.
9 6 May 1941, CO 967 13/41.
10 On Hailey's work with the Colonial Economic Advisory Council 1943 to 1945, see: D.J. Morgan, *The Official History of Colonial Development, vol. 1, The Origins of British Aid Policy, 1924–1945* (London, 1980), chap. 14; J.M. Lee

and Martin Petter, *The Colonial Office, War and Development Policy* (London, 1982), pp. 206–18; Porter and Stockwell, *British Imperial Policy*, pp. 212–24. On reform of the colonial civil service, see: Harold Laski, 'The Colonial Civil Service', *Political Quarterly*, IX, 4 (1938) 541–51; CAB 65 26 WM(42)49, 15 June 1942; CAB 66 25 WP(42)249; *Report of a Committee on the System of Appointment in the Colonial Office and the Colonial Services*, PP 1929–30, VIII (Cmd. 3554); Charles Jeffries, *The Colonial Empire and its Civil Service* (London, 1938); Lee and Petter, *The Colonial Office*, p. 152. On morale in the Colonial Civil Service, see: R.D. Pearce, 'Morale in the Colonial Service in Nigeria During the Second World War', *Journal of Imperial and Commonwealth History*, XI, 2 (1983), 175–96.

11 *Colonial Development and Welfare, Report on the Operation of the Act to 31 October 1942*, PP 1942–3, IX (Cmd 6422) 601, p. 4.

12 *Despatch from the Secretary of State for the Colonies to the Colonial Governments regarding certain aspects of colonial policy in war time*, PP 1940–1, VIII (Cmd 6299) 1, June 1941, para. 15

13 *Colonial Development and Welfare Report to 31 Oct. 1942*

14 *Colonial Development and Welfare, Return of Schemes, 1 Nov. 1942 to 31 Mar. 1943*, PP 1942–3, IX (Cmd 6457) 615.

15 *Colonial Development and Welfare, Return of Schemes, 1 Apr. 1943 to 31 Mar. 1944*, PP 1943–4, VII (Cmd 6532) 601.

16 *Colonial Development and Welfare, Return of Schemes, 1 Apr. 1944 to 31 Mar. 1945*, PP 1944–5, IX (106) 597.

17 *Colonial Development and Welfare, Return of Schemes, 1 Apr. 1945 to 31 Mar. 1946*, PP 1945–6, XIX (150) 1.

18 *Colonial Research Committee Progress Report 1942–43*, PP 1942–3, IX (Cmd 6486) 619.

19 CAB 66 57, WP 643, 1944; Porter and Stockwell, *British Imperial Policy*, vol. 1, pp. 202–11; Morgan, *Official History, 1*, chap. 15.

20 CAB 65 44.

21 CAB 66 60, WP 753, 1944.

22 Sidney Pollard, *The development of the British economy, 1914–1967*, second edition (London, 1969), pp. 356–63.

23 Minute by Caine, 7 June 1945; minute by Creasy, 3 July 1945; CO 852/555/16489/1945.

24 ibid.

25 'Financial results of the war in the United Kingdom', CO Circular to Colonies, June 1945, CO 852/555/16489.

26 Mike Cowen, 'Early Years of the Colonial Development Corporation: British State Enterprise Overseas During Late Colonialism', *African Affairs*, 83, 330, 1984, pp. 63–75.

27 'Development of Colonial Resources', CAB 129 19 CP(47)175, 6 June 1947; 'Production of Foodstuffs and Raw materials in the Colonies', CAB 129 19 CP(47)177, 8 June 1947.

28 CP 177.

29 CP 175.

30 'East African Groundnuts Scheme', Memorandum by the Minister of Food, CAB 129 19 CP(47)176, 8 June 1947; Porter and Stockwell, *British Imperial Policy, 1*, pp.307–31.

31 'East African Groundnuts Scheme'.

32 'Production of Dollar-Earning Colonial Commodities', CAB 129 20 CP(47)242, 23 Aug. 1947; See also, Sir Stafford Cripps, 'Colonies'

Contribution to World Trade Stability, *Crown Colonist*, Jan. 1948, 7–8; Ivor Thomas, 'Dollar-Saving by Colonial Development', *Crown Colonist*, Dec. 1949, 739–41; 'Dollar-Earning by Colonial Development', *New Commonwealth*, Apr. 1951, 482–3, 565–7.

33 *The Times*, 13 Nov. 1947, p. 3c; for full text of Cripps' speech, see: Porter and Stockwell, *British Imperial Policy*, vol. 1, pp. 278–83. Cripps was appointed Chancellor of the Exchequer on 13 Nov. 1947.

34 *Hansard* (Commons) 5th ser., 443, 6 Nov. 1947, col. 2034.

35 Viscount Montgomery, *The Memoirs of Field Marshal the Viscount Montgomery of Alamein, K.G.* (London, 1958), p. 462.

36 'Memorandum by the Secretary of State for the Colonies commenting on certain aspects of a report by the Chief of the Imperial General Staff in his tour in Africa in November-December, 1947', CAB 21/1690, 9 June 1948.

37 'Colonial development', note by Brook, 16 Jan. 1948, CAB 21/1690.

38 'Report by the Chief of the Imperial General Staff on his visit to Africa', Minutes of a Meeting of Ministers, 9 Jan. 1948, GEN 210/21st meeting, CAB 21/1690

39 'Memorandum by the Secretary of State', 9 Jan. 1948.

40 'Organisation for Colonial development', memorandum to Cabinet by the Secretary of State for the Colonies, 2 Mar. 1948 CAB 21/1690.

41 Note by Brook, 16 Jan. 1948. See also: E.R. Wicker, 'Colonial Development and Welfare 1929–1957: The Evolution of a Policy', *Social and Economic Studies*, 7, 4 (1958), 170–92.

42 'Organisation for Colonial Development', p. 5.

11   AN IMPOSSIBLE TASK?

1 *British Dependencies in the Far East 1945–1949*, PP 1948–9, XIII (Cmd. 7709), pp. 8–29.

2 P.T. Bauer, 'Marketing Monopoly in British Africa', *Kyklos*, 9 (1956), 164–176; David Meredith, 'State Controlled Marketing and Economic Development: The Case of West African Produce during the Second World War', *Economic History Review*, 2nd ser., XXXIX, 1 (1986), 77–91; 'Prices of Colonial Export Products', in A.N. Porter and A.J. Stockwell, *British Imperial Policy and Decolonization, 1938–64, vol. 1, 1938–51* (London, 1987), pp. 274–275.

3 Michael P. Todaro, *Economic Development in the Third World, fourth edition* (New York, 1989), pp. 190–191.

4 *Fifth Report from the Select Committee on Estimates, Colonial Development, June 1948*, PP 1947–48, VIII (181-I) pp. ix–xi.

5 *Colonial Development and Welfare: Despatch dated 12 November 1945, from the Secretary of State for the Colonies to Colonial Governments*, PP 1945–46, XIX (Cmd. 6713), p. 3; see also: D.J. Morgan, *The Official History of Colonial Development, vol. 2, Developing British Colonial Resources, 1945–1951* (London, 1980), chap. 2.

6 *Report on the Colonial Empire (1939–1947)* PP 1946–47, X (Cmd. 7167), p. 104. Approximately £11.3m of old public debt was written off, mainly for East African colonies, under the 1940 CD & W Act, see: *Financial and Explanatory Memorandum of the Colonial Development and Welfare Bill*, PP 1939–40 (40), I, p. 403.

7 *Report 1939–1947*, p. 28; *Despatch Nov. 1945*, p. 10; *Progress Report on the Colonial Territories (1949–50)*, VIII (Cmd. 7958), p. 87.

8 *Fifth Report from the Select Committee* (181-I), p. xviii; see also: P.N.C. Okigbo, *National Development Planning in Nigeria, 1900–1992* (London, 1989), p. 32; D.J. Morgan, *The Official History of Colonial Development, vol. 1, The Origins of British Aid Policy, 1924–1945* (London, 1980), chap. 16.

9 Secretary of State for the Colonies to Chancellor of the Exchequer, 30 Sept. 1954 and Chancellor of the Exchequer to Secretary of State for the Colonies, 17 Nov. 1954, in A.N. Porter and A.J. Stockwell, *British Imperial Policy and Decolonization, 1938–64, vol. 2, 1951–64* (London, 1989), pp. 343–354.

10 ibid, pp 348–351.

11 Annual Reports on Colonial Development and Welfare, 1946–70.

12 *Commonwealth Economic Conference, Final Communique*, PP 1952–3, XXIII (Cmd. 8717), para. 10.

13 Hansard (Commons) 5th ser., 458, 19 Nov. 1948, col. 752.

14 The East African High Commission was established in 1948 to coordinate and administer a number of services common to Kenya, Uganda and Tanganyika such as transport and communications, defence, scientific research, customs and excise and income tax.

15 *Report on the Use of Funds Provided Under the Colonial Development and Welfare Acts and Outline of the Proposal for Exchequer Loans to the Colonial Territories*, PP 1958–9, X (Cmnd 672), p. 8; see also: D.J. Morgan, *The Official History of Colonial Development, vol. 3, A Re-assessment of British Aid Policy, 1951–1965* (London, 1980), chap. 5.

16 *Report on the Use of Funds*, p. 9.

17 Gerrard Clauson, 'The British Colonial Currency System', *Economic Journal*, LIV, 213 (1944), 1–25; H.A. Shannon, 'The Modern Colonial Sterling Exchange Standard', *IMF Staff Papers*, 2 (1952), 318–362; Arthur Hazlewood, 'The Economics of Colonial Monetary Arrangements', *Social and Economic Studies*, 3 (1954), 291–315; A.F. Earle, 'Colonial Monetary Theory', *Social and Economic Studies*, 3 (1954), 97–108; A. Hasib, 'Money and Banking Problems in the British Colonies', *Indian Journal of Economics*, 38 (1957), 73–81.

18 *The Colonial Territories, 1954–55*, PP 1955–6, XIII (Cmd 9489) p. 62.

19 Colonial Office, *Memorandum on the Sterling Assets of the British Colonies* (Colonial No. 298, 1953), p. 3.

20 W.T. Newlyn, 'The Colonial Empire', in R.S. Sayers (ed.), *Banking in the British Commonwealth* (London, 1952), p. 440.

21 *Colonial Territories, 1954–55*, p. 62. See also P.T. Bauer, *West African Trade: A Study of Competition, Oligopoly and Monopoly in a Changing Economy* (1954); E.K. Hawkins, 'Marketing Boards and Economic Development in Nigeria and Ghana', *Review of Economic Studies*, 26 (1958), 51–62; R.H. Green, 'Ghana Cocoa Marketing Policy, 1938–1960', Nigerian Institute of Social and Economic Research, Conference Proceedings (Dec. 1960), pp.132–60; G.K. Helleiner, 'The Fiscal Role of the Marketing Boards in Nigerian Economic Development, 1947–61', *Economic Journal*, 74 (1964), 582–610; G.K. Helleiner, *Peasant Agriculture, Government and Economic Growth in Nigeria* (Homewood, III. 1966); A. Killick, 'The Economics of Cocoa' in W. Birmingham et al. (eds), *A Study of Contemporary Ghana, I, The Economy of Ghana* (London, 1967), pp. 365–71.

22 *The Colonial Territories, 1961–62*, PP 1961–2, XI (Cmnd 1751), p. 87. There were also small amounts made available to British colonies from Marshall Aid, see: Anon, 'What Marshall Aid Means to British Colonies', *Crown Colonist*, Sept. 1950, p. 548; Scott Newton, 'Britain, the Sterling Area and

European integration, 1945–50', in A.N. Porter and R.F. Holland (eds), *Money, Finance and Empire, 1790–1960* (London, 1985). Private capital, especially US private capital, was not very interested in the tropical colonies because of their lack of basic infrastructure, see: Porter and Stockwell, *British Imperial Policy*, vol. 2, pp. 176–7.

23 D.E. Moggridge, 'From War to Peace: the Sterling Balances', *Banker*, 122 (1972), 1032–5; A.R. Conan, *The Rationale of the Sterling Area* (London, 1961), pp. 65–6; *The Problem of Sterling* (London, 1966), pp. 78–87; Philip W. Bell, *The Sterling Area in the Post-War World* (Oxford, 1956), pp. 39–44; B.R. Tomlinson, 'Indo-British Relations in the Post-Colonial Era: the Sterling Balances Negotiations, 1947–49', in Porter and Holland (eds), *Money*; Morgan, *Official History*, vol. 3, chap 4; Porter and Stockwell, *British Imperial Policy*, pp. 127–33. For a full account, written from official sources, see L.S. Pressnell, *External Economic Policy Since the War*, vol. 1, *The Post-War Financial Settlement* (London, 1987).

24 See Chapter Ten, p. 22.

25 D.J. Morgan, *The Official History of Colonial Development*, vol. 2, *Developing British Colonial Resources, 1945–1951* (London, 1980), pp.54–6.

26 H.A. Shannon, 'The Sterling Balances of the Sterling Area 1939–49', *Economic Journal*, 60 (1950), 531–51; Ida Greaves, 'The Sterling Balances of the Colonial Territories', *Economic Journal*, 61 (1951), 433–9; Arthur Hazlewood, 'Sterling Balances and the Colonial Currency System', *Economic Journal*, 62 (1952), 942–5; Ida Greaves, 'Sterling Balances and the Colonial Currency System: A Comment', *Economic Journal*, 63 (1953), 921–3; Arthur Hazlewood, 'Sterling Balances and the Colonial Currency System: A Reply', *Economic Journal*, 64 (1954), 616–17; Ida Greaves, *The Colonial Sterling Balances, Essays in International Finance, No. 20* (Princeton, 1954).

27 *Commonwealth Economic Conference*, para. 9.

28 Ida Greaves, *Colonial Monetary Conditions* (Colonial Research Studies, No. 10, 1953), p.92; see also: Wadan Lal Narsey, 'A Re-interpretation of the History and Theory of Colonial Currency Systems', unpublished Ph.D. thesis, University of Sussex, 1988, chaps. 7, 8.

29 *Memorandum on the Sterling Assets*, p.15.

30 *Memorandum on the Sterling Assets*, pp.7–9; W.T. Newlyn and D.C. Rowan, *Money and Banking in British Colonial Africa* (Oxford, 1954), p.196.

31 *Memorandum on Sterling Assets*, p.14.

32 Arthur Hazlewood, 'Memorandum on the Sterling Assets of British Colonies: A Comment', *Review of Economic Studies*, 22 (1954), p.74. For a detailed discussion see: Allister E. Hinds, 'Sterling and Imperial Policy, 1945–51', *Journal of Imperial and Commonwealth History*, XV, 2 (1987), 148–69.

33 Judd Polk, *Sterling: Its Meaning in World Finance* (New York, 1956), pp.205–6; Susan Strange, *Sterling and British Policy* (London, 1972), p.67; Narsey, 'A Re-interpretation', pp.319–21; Porter and Stockwell, *British Imperial Policy*, vol. 2, pp.102–14; Allister E. Hinds, 'Imperial Policy and Colonial Sterling Balances, 1943–56', *Journal of Imperial and Commonwealth History*, XIX, 1 (1991), 24–44.

34 On Malaya's importance, see: A.J. Stockwell, 'British Imperial Policy and Decolonisation in Malaya, 1942–52', *Journal of Imperial and Commonwealth History*, XIII, 1 (1984), p.78.

35 Polk, *Sterling*, p.137; see also: Ivor Thomas, 'Dollar-Saving by Colonial Development', *Crown Colonist* (Dec. 1949) 739–41; 'Dollar-Earning by Colonial Development', *New Commonwealth* (Apr. 1951) 482–3, 565–5; P.S.

Gupta, *Imperialism and the British Labour Movement, 1914–64* (London, 1975), pp.312–13; P. Ady, 'The Future of the Sterling Area: Ghana', *Bulletin of the Oxford University Institute of Statistics*, 21, 4 (1959), 313–24.

36 Malaya epitomised this problem: it earned large amounts of US dollars and had considerable reconstruction costs as a result of Japanese occupation, yet was forced to restrict imports from both the dollar area and Britain: Martin Rudner, 'Financial Policies in Post-War Malaya: The Fiscal and Monetary Measures of Liberation and Reconstruction', *Journal of Imperial and Commonwealth History*, III, 3 (1975), 326–7.

12 THE TRIUMPH OF THE CHAMBERLAIN VIEW

1 John Iliffe, *A Modern History of Tanganyika* (Cambridge, 1979), p.436. On the history of the Tanganyika Groundnut Scheme see also Alan Wood, *The Groundnut Affair* (London, 1950); S. Herbert Frankel, *The Economic Impact on Under-Developed Societies* (Oxford, 1953), chap. 8; D.J. Morgan, *The Official History of Colonial Development, vol. 2, Developing British Colonial Resources, 1945–51* (London, 1980), chap. 5; A.N. Porter and A.J. Stockwell, *British Imperial Policy and Decolonisation, 1938–64, vol. 1, 1938–51* (London, 1987), pp.307–31; Paul Fordham, *The Geography of African Affairs* (London, 1965), pp.87–8.

2 *A Plan for the Mechanized Production of Groundnuts in East and Central Africa*, PP 1946–7, X (Cmd 7030), pp.18–20.

3 R. Miller, director of agricultural production, Tanganyika to C. Christie, United Africa Co., 15 Mar. 1946, and to G.F. Clay, Colonial Office, 27 Mar. 1947, CO 852 912/4A; D.K. Fieldhouse, *Unilever Overseas: The Anatomy of a Multinational 1895–1965* (London, 1978), pp.494–555. Unilever's African plantations were labour-intensive rather than mechanised.

4 Plan, p.18; 'Project for Growing Groundnuts in East and Central Africa', Memorandum to Cabinet by the secretary of state for the colonies and the minister of food, 29 Oct. 1946, C.P. (46) 402, CAB 129/14.

5 ibid., pp.28–29. In fact, the peasants who cultivated groundnuts in the vicinity of Kongwa obtained yields per acre several times higher than those obtained by the groundnut scheme: 1200–2000 lbs of shelled groundnuts per acre according to Plan, p.26. The Tanganyika Groundnut Scheme at Kongwa managed over three seasons: 375 lb, 144 lb and 244 lb, Wood, p.99; *Overseas Food Corporation, Annual Report and Statement of Accounts for the Year Ended 31 March 1950*, PP 1950, XIII (1947), p.15; *Overseas Food Corporation, Annual Report and Statement of Accounts for the Year Ended 31 March 1951*, PP 1951–2, XVII (1), p.11.

6 Plan, pp.6–7.

7 Wood, pp.50, 85; Colonial Office, 'Note on the Report of the Groundnut Mission to East and Central Africa', 24 Oct. 1946, para. 27, CO 852 603/7.

8 'East African Groundnut Project', Memorandum to Cabinet by the minister of food, 4 Jan. 1947, C.P. (47) 10, CAB 129/16.

9 *Second Report from the Committee of Public Accounts, May 1950*, PP 1950, III (70), p.85; Memorandum by minister of food, 4 Jan. 1947, C.P. (47) 4, CAB 129/16.

10 Wood, p.99; Memorandum by minister of food, 14 Jan. 1948, C.P. (48) 18, CAB 129/23.

11 OFC, *Annual Report, 1949–50*.

12 OFC, *Annual Report 1950–1*.

13 ibid., p.14.
14 Wood, p.208.
15 *Overseas Food Corporation, Annual Report and Statement of Accounts for the Year Ended 31 March 1955*, PP 1955–6, XXVI (195).
16 OFC, *Annual Report, 1950–51*, p.2.
17 *Overseas Food Corporation, Annual Report and Statement of Accounts for the Year Ended 31 March 1953*, PP 1953–4, XVIII (30).
18 *The Future of the Overseas Food Corporation, January 1951*, PP 1950–1, XXVII (Cmd 8125), p.10.
19 ibid., p.10.
20 ibid., pp.5,10.
21 *Overseas Food Corporation, Annual Report and Statement of Accounts for the Year Ended 31 March 1952*, PP 1952–3, XVI (51), p.2; OFC, *Annual Report 1954–55*, p.2.
22 OFC, *Annual Report 1954–55*, p.11; *The Future of the Overseas Food Corporation, May 1954*, PP 1953–54, XXVI (Cmd 9158), Appendix 1.
23 *Future of the OFC*, 1954, Appendix 1.
24 ibid. See also D.J. Morgan, *The Official History of Colonial Development, vol. 4, Changes in British Aid Policy, 1951–70* (London, 1980), chap. 4; W.P. Cocking and R.F. Lord, 'The Tanganyika Agricultural Corporation's Farming Settlement Scheme', *Tropical Agriculture*, 35, 2 (1958), 85–101.
25 *Hansard* (Commons) 5th ser., 446, 20 Jan. 1948, cols. 142, 154; (Lords) 5th ser., 161, 13 Apr. 1949, cols. 1175–1182.
26 *Overseas Food Corporation, First Annual Report and Statement of Accounts for the Period Ended March 31, 1949*, PP 1948–9, XIX (252), p.10; Public Accounts, p.89; 'British Food Supplies', Memorandum by the minister of food, 22 Oct. 1946, C.P. (46) 396, CAB 129/13.
27 *East African Groundnuts Scheme, Review of Progress to the End of November, 1947*, PP 1947–8, XI (Cmd 7314), p.9.
28 Public Accounts, p.85; and see p.89.
29 ibid., pp.64, 88–89.
30 ibid., p.70.
31 ibid., p.xii.
32 ibid., p.xi.
33 ibid., p.104.
34 ibid., p.44. On the engineering and transport aspects, see: Major General Desmond Harrison, 'Civil Engineering Problems of the East African Groundnuts Scheme', *Engineer*, 30 July 1948, 120–2; Medwyn Ormerod, 'The Transport Problems of the East African Groundnut Scheme', *Journal of the Institute of Transport*, 23, 11 (1950), 351–8.
35 *Colonial Development Corporation, Annual Report and Statement of Accounts for the Year Ended 31 Dec. 1948*, PP 1948–9, XIII (185), Appendix A; *Colonial Development Corporation, Annual Report and Statement of Accounts for the Year Ended 31 Dec. 1949*, PP 105, VIII (1905), p.45; *Colonial Development Corporation, Annual Report and Statement of Accounts for the Year Ended 31 Dec. 1950*, PP 1950–1, X (161), p.40. See also: Morgan, *Official History, vol. 2* chap. 6; *vol 4*, chaps. 5–8; Sir William Rendell, *The History of the Commonwealth Development Corporation 1948–72* (London, 1976), chaps. 1–9.
36 CDC, *Annual Report 1948*, p.6.
37 CDC, *Annual Report 1948*, pp.6,7.
38 ibid., p.8.
39 ibid., p.10.

40 CDC, *Annual Report 1949*, p.10.
41 CDC, *Annual Report 1949*, pp.66–67; CDC, *Annual Report 1950*, p.49.
42 CDC, *Annual Report 1950*, p.4.
43 ibid., p.2.
44 *Colonial Development Corporation, Annual Report and Statement of Accounts for the Year Ended 31 Dec. 1951*, PP 1951–2, IX (167), p.30.
45 ibid., p.4.
46 ibid., p.4.
47 *Colonial Development Corporation, Annual Report and Statement of Accounts for the Year Ended 31 Dec. 1952*, PP 1952–3, VIII (158), pp.4–5.
48 *Colonial Development Corporation, Annual Report and Statement of Accounts for the Year Ended 31 Dec. 1953*, PP 1953–4, X (148), p.6.
49 *Colonial Development Corporation, Annual Report and Statement of Accounts for the Year Ended 31 Dec. 1954*, PP 1954–5, IV (113), p.7.
50 CDC, *Annual Report 1953* p.6.
51 *Colonial Development Corporation, Annual Report and Statement of Accounts for the Year Ended 31 Dec. 1955*, PP 1955–6, XII (160), p.6.
52 *Report of the Committee of Enquiry into the Financial Structure of the Colonial Development Corporation, Sept. 1959*, PP 1958–9, X (Cmd 786).
53 *Colonial Development Corporation, Annual Report and Statement of Accounts for the Year Ended 31 Dec. 1961*, PP 19 (201), p.8.
54 *Colonial Development Corporation, Annual Report and Statement of Accounts for the Year Ended 31 Dec. 1958*, PP 1958–9, X (214), p.9; See also: CDC, *Annual Report 1955*, p.9 and *Colonial Development Corporation, Annual Report and Statement of Accounts for the Year Ended 31 Dec. 1956*, PP 1956–7, IX (151), p.5; P.E. Witlam, 'Change of Method Needed in Colonial Development', *New Commonwealth*, 6 July 1953, pp.5–6; C.J.M. Alport, 'Suggestions for a Reformed Colonial Development Corporation', *New Commonwealth*, 14 Sept. 1953, pp.273–4; J. Dugdale, 'Can the Colonial Development Corporation do Better?', *New Commonwealth*, 31 Oct. 1955, pp.412–13.
55 Morgan, *Official History*, vol. 4, chap. 7; Rendell, *History of the Commonwealth Development Corporation*, chaps. 10–13.
56 CDC, *Annual Report 1948*, p.22; *1949*, pp.12–14.
57 CDC, *Annual Report 1949*, p.31.
58 On the Niger Agricultural Project see: K.D.S. Baldwin, *The Niger Agricultural Project* (Cambridge, Mass., 1957).
59 *Hansard* (Commons) 5th ser., 478, 19 Oct. 1950, col. 2370.
60 CDC, *Annual Report 1949*, p.22.
61 CDC, *Annual Report 1948*, p.22.
62 CDC, *Annual Report 1954*, p.27.
63 See Oliver Lyttelton, Viscount Chandos, *The Memoirs of Lord Chandos*, (London, 1962), p.201; Andrew Boyle, *Only the Wind Will Listen: Reith of the BBC* (London, 1972), pp.335–7.

13   DEVELOPING THE 'GREAT ESTATE'

1 *The Colonial Empire (1947–1948)*, PP, 1947–48, XI (Cmd 7433), p.4.
2 *The Colonial Territories (1948–1949)*, PP, 1948–49, XIII (Cmd 7715), pp.1–2.
3 *Hansard* (Commons) 5th ser/. 477, 12 July 1950, col. 1369, James Griffiths, secretary of state for the colonies.
4 *The British Colonial Territories in 1950: A Regional Review of Progess* (British Information Services, I.D. 1050, New York, Mar. 1951), p.7.

5 *The Colonial Territories 1953–4*, PP, 1953–4, XXV (Cmd 9169), p.2.
6 United Nations, *Methods of Financing Economic Development in Under-Developed Countries* (New York, 1949), pp.6–21. Domestic savings in British colonies were low partly because the inhabitants were mostly very poor, but it was also due to the undeveloped state of savings institutions and the tendency for savings arising in the export sector to accumulate abroad.
7 For a discussion of the theory of exports as an engine of growth, see: Alfred Maizels, *Exports, and Economic Growth of Developing Countries* (Cambridge, 1962), chaps. 1–3; Irving B. Kravis, 'Trade as a Handmaiden of Growth: Similarities between the Nineteenth and Twentieth Centuries', *Economic Journal*, 80 (Dec. 1970), 850–72; W.A. Lewis, 'The Slowing Down of the Engine of Growth', *American Economic Review*, 70, 4 (Sept. 1980), 555–64; James Riedel, 'Trade as the Engine of Growth in Developing Countries, Revisited', *Economic Journal*, 94 (Mar. 1984), 56–73.
8 This cannot be shown statistically for the colonial period and obviously varied between colonies and over time. A.R. Prest and I.G. Stewart commented in 1953: 'A frequent remark in the past about West African colonies, and Nigeria in particular, has been that they are dominated by their export trades, and consequently exhibit a quite unusual degree of fragility. It appears from out [*sic*] figures that in fact exports were something like a sixth of Gross Domestic Product in 1950–51 and imports something like a tenth. It would seem therefore that assertions that Nigeria is even more dependent on international trade than Britain and similarly situated countries (and, a fortiori, judgements about the whole economy on the basis of the foreign sector) cannot be substantiated, even at a time of extremely high world prices for Nigerian export staples', *The National Income of Nigeria, 1950–51* (London, 1953) p.85. Frederic Benham's estimates indicate an export: GDP ratio for Malaya in 1947 of approximately one fifth: *The National Income of Malaya, 1947–49* (Singapore, 1951), pp.194, 208. Phyllis Deane indicated ratios of 15 per cent and 24 per cent for Jamaica in 1933 and 1938 respectively and of 23 per cent for Nyasaland in 1938: *The Measurement of Colonial National Incomes* (Cambridge, 1948), pp.130, 93–4; Alan Peacock and Douglas Dosser calculated the national income of Tanganyika which showed an average export: NI ratio of 28 per cent for the years 1952–4: *The National Income of Tanganyika 1952–1954* (London, 1958), p.45. See also: Phyllis Deane, *Colonial Social Accounting* (Cambridge, 1953).
9 Maizels, *Exports and Economic Growth*, p.85.
10 Robert E. Baldwin, 'Patterns of Development in Newly Settled Regions', *The Manchester School of Economic and Social Studies*, XXIV, 2 (May 1956), 161–79; Melville H. Watkins, 'A Staple Theory of Economic Growth', *Canadian Journal of Economics and Political Science*, XXIX, 2 (May 1963), 141–77; K.N. Raj, 'Linkages in industrialization and development strategy: some basic issues', *Journal of Development Planning*, 8 (1975), 105–19; John T. Thoburn, *Primary Commodity Exports and Economic Development* (London, 1977), chaps. 5–7.
11 W. Arthur Lewis, 'Colonial Development', *Transactions of the Manchester Statistical Society*, 116 (Jan. 1949), 1–30; see also, Lewis, 'Developing colonial agriculture', *Three Banks Review*, 2 (1949), 3–21.
12 ibid., p.9
13 John Spraos, 'The Statistical Debate on the Net Barter Terms of Trade between Primary Commodities and Manufactures', *Economic Journal*, 90 (Mar. 1980), 107–128; the proposition was first advanced by Prebisch and

Singer in 1950: R. Prebisch, *The Economic Development of Latin America and its Principal Problems* (United Nations, Economic Commission for Latin America, New York, 1950); H.W. Singer, 'The Distribution of Gains between Investing and Borrowing Countries', *American Economic Review, Papers and Proceedings*, 5, Supplement (May, 1950), 473–485; United Nations, *Special Study on Economic Conditions in Non-self-governing territories* (New York, 1960), pp.7–16.

14 W. Arthur Lewis, *Report on Industrialisation and the Gold Coast* (Accra, 1953), p.2. See also: A.N. Hakam, 'Impediments to the growth of indigenous industrial entrepreneurship in Ghana, 1946–1968', *Economic Bulletin of Ghana*, 2, 2 (1972), 3–31; Jaleel Ahmad, *Import Substitution, Trade and Development* (Greenwich, 1978), pp.41–60.

15 *Fifth Report from the Select Committee on Estimates, Colonial Development, June 1948*, PP, 1947–48, VIII (181–I), p.ix.

16 W. Arthur Lewis, 'A Review of Economic Development', *American Economic Review*, LV, 2 (May, 1965), p.10.

17 Chapter One, pp.19–20.

18 Estimates of private capital flows made in the 1950s were published in *The Colonial Territories* and in the *Commonwealth and Sterling Area Statistical Abstract*. The average annual net flow of private long-term capital to the entire colonial empire between 1954 and 1959 was £81 million; half of this went to the Caribbean and one-fifth to East Africa. Private capital flows were three times larger than public capital flows in these years. See also, W.M. Clarke, *Private Enterprise in Developing Countries* (London, 1966), p.22

19 Bernard Braine, 'U.K. income tax and colonial industrial development', *New Commonwealth*, 17 Mar. 1952, 256–257; C.J.M. Alport, 'The colonial investor and U.K. taxation', *New Commonwealth*, 24 Jan. 1955, 60–1.

20 Lewis, 'Review of Economic Development', p.9; see also, John Iliffe, *The Emergence of African Capitalism* (London, 1983), chap. 2.

21 John Dugdale, 'Should Britain have a bilateral colonial policy?', *New Commonwealth*, 5 Sept. 1955, 213–14.

22 P.S. Gupta, *Imperialism and the British Labour Movement 1914–1964* (London, 1975); David Goldsworthy, *Colonial Issues in British Politics 1945–1961* (Oxford, 1971); see also: D.N. Pritt, *The Labour Government 1945–51* (London, 1963); Rita Hinden, *Empire and After: A Study of British Imperial Attitudes* (London, 1949).

23 Leopold Amery, *My Political Life*, vol. II, *War and Peace, 1914–1929* (London, 1953), p.340.

24 *First and Second Reports from the Select Committee on Estimates, 30 Apr. and 19 Jul. 1928*, PP, 1928, VI (71, 114) [Empire Marketing Board]; *First and Second Reports from the Select Committee on Estimates, 21 Mar. and 20 Jun. 1932*, PP, 1931–2, IV (55,90) [Empire Marketing Board and Colonial Development Fund]; *Select Committee, Colonial Development, 1948; Fourth Report from the Select Committee on Estimates, Colonial Office*, PP, 1959–60.

25 Cyril Ehrlich, 'Building and Caretaking: Economic Policy in British Tropical Africa, 1890–1960', *Economic History Review*, 2nd ser., XXVI, 4 (1973), 649–67.

26 Lord Lugard, *The Dual Mandate in British Tropical Africa* (London, 1922, reprinted by Frank Cass, London, 1965). For post-war official references to Lugard's views see: *Colonial Empire (1947–8)*, p.4 and *The Colonial Territories 1952–3*, PP, 1952–3, XXIII (Cmd 8856), p.1.

27 Lugard, *Dual Mandate*, pp.615–17; Benjamin Kidd, *Control of the Tropics* (New

York, 1898).

28 'Organization for Colonial Development', memorandum to Cabinet by the Secretary of State for the Colonies, 2 Mar. 1948, CAB 21 1690.

29 See pp.152–159, chap. 7.

30 Alan Wood, *The Groundnut Affair* (London, 1950), p.27.

31 See pp.215–217, chap. 10.

32 There were fourteen secretaries of state for the colonies in the eight ministries between 1922 and 1945, and nine in the three ministries, 1945–1964.

33 W.K. Hancock, *Survey of British Commonwealth Affairs, II, Problems of Economic Policy 1918–1939*, part 2 (London, 1942), p.142.

34 See pp.264–266, chap. 11.

35 See: Arthur Hazlewood (ed.), *African Integration and Disintegration* (London, 1967); Arthur Hazlewood, *Economic Integration: the East African Experience* (London, 1975).

36 D.K. Fieldhouse, *Black Africa, 1945–1980: Economic Decolonization and Arrested Development* (London, 1986); John Darwin, *Britain and Decolonisation: The Retreat from Empire in the Post-War World* (London, 1988).

Bibliography

Abbott, George C. 'A Re-examination of the 1929 Colonial Development Act', *Economic History Review*, 2nd ser., XXIV (1971), 68–81.

Ady, P. 'The Future of the Sterling Area: Ghana', *Bulletin of the Oxford University Institute of Statistics*, 21, 4 (1959), 313–24.

Ahmad, Jaleel. *Import Substitution, Trade and Development* (Greenwich, 1978).

Allan, William. *The African Husbandman* (London, 1965).

Allen, Richard B. 'The Slender, Sweet Thread: Sugar, Capital and Dependency in Mauritius, 1860–1936', *Journal of Imperial and Commonwealth History*, XVI, 2 (1988), 177–200.

Allridge, T.J. *A Transformed Colony. Sierra Leone As It Was And Is* (London, 1910).

Alport, C.J.M. 'Suggestions for a Reformed Colonial Development Corporation', *New Commonwealth*, 14 Sept. 1953, 273–4.

Alport, C.J.M. 'The Colonial Investor and U.K. Taxation', *New Commonwealth*, 24 Jan. 1955, 60–1.

Ambler, Charles H. *Kenyan Communities in the Age of Imperialism: The Central Region in the Late Nineteenth Century* (New Haven, 1988).

Amery, Julian and Garvin, J.L. *Life of Joseph Chamberlain*, vol. 4: *At the Height of His Power* (London, 1951).

Amery, Leopold. *My Political Life*, vol. II. *War and Peace, 1914–1929* (London, 1953).

Anon. 'A Service in Transition: Administrators for a Changing Empire', *Round Table*, 26 (1946), 356–8.

Anon. 'What Marshall Aid Means to British Colonies', *Crown Colonist*, Sept. 1950, 548–9.

Asante, S.K.B. *Pan-African Protest: West Africa and the Italo-Ethiopian Crisis, 1934–1941* (London, 1977).

Asiegbu, J.U.J. *Nigeria and its British Invaders, 1851–1920: A Thematic Documentary History* (New York, 1984).

Austen, Ralph A. *African Economic History: Internal Development and External Dependency* (London, 1987).

The Earl of Avon, *The Eden Memoirs: Facing the Dictators* (London, 1962).

Ayearst, Morley. *The British West Indies: The Search for Self-Government* (London, 1960).

Azikwe, Nnamdi. *Renascent Africa* (London, 1937, repr. 1969).

Baer, George W. *The Coming of the Italo-Ethiopian War* (Cambridge Mass., 1967).

Baker, Ray Stannard. *Woodrow Wilson and World Settlement*, vol. I (Gloucester, Mass., 1922).

Baldwin, K.D.S. *The Niger Agricultural Project* (Cambridge, Mass., 1957).

383

Baldwin, Robert E. 'Patterns of Development in Newly Settled Regions', *The Manchester School of Economic and Social Studies*, XXIV, 2 (May 1956), 161–79.

Barnes, Leonard. *Empire or Democracy? A Study of the Colonial Question* (London, 1939).

Barnett, Correlli. *The Collapse of British Power* (London, 1972).

Bauer, P.T. 'The Working of Rubber Regulation', *Economic Journal*, 56 (1946), 391–414.

Bauer, P.T. *The Rubber Industry: A Study in Competition and Monopoly* (London, 1948).

Bauer, P.T. *West African Trade: A Study of Competition, Oligopoly and Monopoly in a Changing Economy* (London, 1954).

Bauer, P.T. 'Marketing Monopoly in British Africa', *Kyklos*, 9 (1956), 164–76.

Beer, George Louis. *African Questions at the Paris Peace Conference* (New York, 1923).

Belfield, H.C. (ed.). *Handbook of the Federated Malay States* (London, 2nd edn, 1904).

Bell, Philip W. *The Sterling Area in the Post-War World* (Oxford, 1956).

Benham, Frederic. *Great Britain Under Protection* (New York, 1941).

Benham, Frederic. *The National Income of Malaya, 1947–49* (Singapore, 1951).

Benians, E.A., Butler, J., Carrington, C.E. (eds). *The Cambridge History of the British Empire*, vol. III. *The Empire-Commonwealth 1870–1919* (Cambridge, 1959).

Bennett, George 'Settlers and Politics in Kenya, Up to 1945', in Harlow, Chilver and Smith (eds), *East Africa, II*, pp.309–18.

Benyon, John 'Overlords of Empire? British "Proconsular Imperialism" in Comparative Perspective', *Journal of Imperial and Commonwealth History*, 19, 2 (1991), 164–202.

Beveridge, W.H. *British Food Control* (London, 1928).

Biebuyck, Daniel (ed.), *African Agrarian Systems* (Oxford, 1963).

Bigland, Alfred. 'The Empire's Assets and How to Use Them', *Journal of the Royal Society of Arts*, LXV, 1917, 355–65.

The Earl of Birkenhead, *Halifax: The Life of Lord Halifax* (London, 1965).

Blakeley, Brian L. *The Colonial Office, 1868–1892* (Durham, N.C., 1972).

Blanshard, Paul. *Democracy and Empire in the Caribbean* (New York, 1947).

Boahen Adu (ed.). *Unesco General History of Africa*, vol. 7. 1880–1935 (Paris, 1985).

Bodelsen, C.A. *Studies in Mid-Victorian Imperialism* (Copenhagen, 1924).

Bourne, K. and Watt D.C. (eds). *Studies in International History* (London, 1967).

Bower, Penelope. 'The Balance of Payments in 1936' in M. Perham (ed.), *Mining, Commerce and Finance in Nigeria* (London, 1948) (Oxford, 1949).

Bower, Penelope. *The Balance of Payments of Nigeria in 1936* (Oxford, 1949).

Boyle, Andrew. *Only the Wind Will Listen: Reith of the BBC* (London, 1972).

Brailsford, Henry Noel. *After the Peace* (London, 1920).

Braine, Bernard. 'U.K. Income Tax and Colonial Industrial Development', *New Commonwealth* (17 Mar. 1952), 256–7.

Brett, E.A. *Colonialism and Underdevelopment in East Africa: The Politics of Economic Change, 1919–1939* (London, 1973).

Brodie, Fawn M. *The Devil Drives: A Life of Sir Richard Burton* (London, 1967).

Brown, Ian (ed.). *The Economies of Africa and Asia in the Inter-War Depression* (London, 1989).

Buchanan, Keith M. and Pugh, J.C. *Land and People in Nigeria: The Human Geography of Nigeria and its Environmental Background* (London, 1958).

Buckley, Suzann. The Colonial Office and the Establishment of an Imperial Development Board: The Impact of World War I, *Journal of Imperial and Commonwealth History*, II, 3 (1974), 308–15.

Buell, Raymond Leslie. '"Backward" Peoples Under the Mandate System', *Current History*, XX (*June, 1924*), *386–95*.

Buell, Raymond Leslie. International Relations, rev. edn (New York, 1929).

Burghardt Du Bois, W.E. 'Interracial Implications of the Ethiopian Crisis: A Negro View', *Foreign Affairs*, 1–4, 1 (Oct. 1935), 82–92.

Burghardt Du Bois, W.E. 'The Realities in Africa: European Profit or Negro Development', *Foreign Affairs*, 21, 4, (1943), 720–32.

Burnet, E. and Aykroyd, W.R. 'Nutrition and Public Health:', *Quarterly Bulletin of the Health Organisation of the League of Nations*, IV, 2 (June 1935).

Sir Alan Burns, *History of Nigeria* (London, 1969).

Burton, R.F. and Cameron, V.L. *To the Gold Coast for Gold* (London, 1883).

Callahan, Raymond. 'The Illusion of Security: Singapore 1919–42', *Journal of Contemporary History*, 9, 2 (1974), 69–92.

Cain, P.J. and Hopkins, A.G. 'Gentlemanly Capitalism and British Expansion Overseas II: New Imperialism, 1850–1945', *Economic History Review*, 2nd ser., XL, 1, 40 (1987), 1–26.

Cant, R.G. Historical Reasons for the Retarded Development of Pahang State, Eastern Malaya, *New Zealand Geographer*, 21 (1965).

Carlton, David. 'The Dominions and British Policy in the Abyssinian Crisis', *Journal of Imperial and Commonwealth History*, I, 1 (1972), 59–77.

Chamberlain, M.E. 'Clement Hill's Memoranda and the British Interest in East Africa', *English Historical Review*, LXXXVII (1972), 533–47.

Chapman, S.D. 'British-based Investment Groups Before 1914', *Economic History Review*, 2nd ser., XXXVIII, 2 (1985), 230–51.

Cheng, Siok Hwa. 'The Rice Industry of Malaya: A Historical Survey', *Journal of the Malayan Branch of the Royal Asiatic Society*, 42, 2 (1969), 130–44.

Chowdhuri, R.N. *International Mandates and Trusteeship Systems* (The Hague, 1955).

Clarke, J.I. (ed.). *Sierra Leone in Maps* (London, 1966).

Clarke, W.M. *Private Enterprise in Developing Countries* (London, 1966).

Clauson, Gerrard. 'The British Colonial Currency System', *Economic Journal*, LIV, 213 (1944), 1–25.

Clifford, Hugh. 'Life in the Malay Peninsular: As It Was And Is', *Proceedings of the Royal Colonial Institute*, XXX (1898–99), 369–401.

Clyde, Paul. *Japan's Pacific Mandate* (Port Washington, 1935).

Cocking, W.P. and Lord, R.F. 'The Tanganyika Agricultural Corporation's Farming Settlement Scheme', *Tropical Agriculture*, 35, 2 (1958), 85–101.

Conan, A.R. *The Problem of Sterling* (London, 1966).

Conan, A.R. *The Rationale of the Sterling Area* (London, 1961).

Constantine, Stephen. '"Bringing the Empire Alive": The Empire Marketing Board and Imperial Propaganda, 1926–33', in John M. Mackenzie (ed.), *Imperialism and Popular Culture* (Manchester, 1986).

Constantine, Stephen. *The Making of British Colonial Development Policy 1914 to 1940* (London, 1984).

Cook, Elsie K. *Ceylon, Its Geography, Its Resources and Its People* (London, 1951).

Cottrell, Philip L. *British Overseas Investment in the Nineteenth Century* (London, 1975).

Cowan, C.D. *Nineteenth Century Malaya* (Oxford, 1961).

Cowen, Michael. 'Early Years of the Colonial Development Corporation: British

State Enterprise Overseas During Late Colonialism', *African Affairs*, 83, 330 (1984), 63–75.

Cowen, Michael and Westcott, Nicholas. 'British Imperial Economic Policy During the War', in David Killingray and Richard Rathbone (eds.), *Africa and the Second World War* (London, 1986).

Cox-George, N.A. 'Studies in Finance and Development – The Gold Coast (Ghana) Experience 1914–1918', Public Finance, XIII, 1 (1958), 146–77.

Crabtree, W.A. 'The Conquest of Togoland', *Journal of the African Society*, XIV (1914–15), 386–91.

Cripps, Stafford. '"Colonies" Contribution to World Trade Stability', *Crown Colonist*, (Jan. 1948), 7–8.

Crisswell, Colin N. *Rajah Charles Brooke. Monarch of All He Surveyed* (Kuala Lumpur, 1978).

Crooks, J.J. *A History of the Colony of Sierra Leone, West Africa* (Dublin, 1903).

Crowder, Michael. *Senegal* (London, 1962).

Crowder, Michael. *The Story of Nigeria* (2nd edn., London, 1966).

Crowder, Michael. *West Africa Under Colonial Rule* (London, 1968).

Curtin, Philip. *The Atlantic Slave Trade: A Census* (Madison, Wisconsin, 1969).

Dane, Edmund. *British Campaigns in Africa and the Pacific 1914–1918* (London, 1919).

Darwin, John. *Britain and Decolonization: The Retreat from Empire in the Post-War World* (London, 1988).

Davidson, Basil. *Black Star: A View of the Life and Times of Kwame Nkrumah* (London, 1973).

Davies, Peter N. *Trading in West Africa, 1840–1920* (London, 1976).

Davis, Lance E. and Huttenback, Robert A. 'The Export of British Finance, 1865–1914', in A.N. Porter and R.F. Holland (eds), *Money, Finance and Empire, 1790–1960* (London, 1985).

Davis, Lance E. and Huttenback, Robert A. *Mammon and the Pursuit of Empire: the Economics of Imperialism, 1869–1912* (Cambridge, 1986).

Deane, Phyllis. *The Measurement of Colonial National Incomes* (Cambridge, 1948).

Deane, Phyllis. *Colonial Social Accounting* (Cambridge, 1953).

Dickson, Kwamina B. *A Historical Geography of Ghana* (Cambridge, 1969).

Dilke, Charles. *Greater Britain* (London, 1868).

Douglas, Roy. *World Crisis and British Decline, 1929–1956* (New York, 1986).

Downes, W.D. *With the Nigerians in German East Africa* (London, 1919).

Drabble, John. 'Investment in the Rubber Industry in Malaya c.1900–1922', *Journal of South East Asian Studies*, 3, 2 (1972), 247–61.

Drabble, John H. *Rubber in Malaya, 1876–1922*, (Oxford, Kuala Lumpur, 1973).

Drummond, Ian M. *Imperial Economic Policy 1917 to 1939: Studies in Expansion and Protection* (London, 1974).

Dugdale, J. 'Can the Colonial Development Corporation do Better?', *New Commonwealth* (31 Oct. 1955) 412–13.

Dugdale, J. 'Should Britain Have a Bilateral Colonial Policy?', *New Commonwealth* (5 Sept. 1955) 213–14.

Dumett, Raymond. 'Africa's Strategic Minerals During the Second World War', *Journal of African History*, 26, 4 (1985), 381–408.

Earle, A.F. 'Colonial Monetary Theory', *Social and Economic Studies*, 3 (1954), 97–108.

Eckstein, A.M. 'Is There a "Hobson-Lenin Thesis" on Late Nineteenth Century Colonial Expansion?', *Economic History Review*, 2nd ser., XLIV, 2 (1991), 297–318.

Edelstein, Michael. *Overseas Investment in the Age of High Imperialism: The United Kingdom, 1850–1914* (New York, 1982).

Ehrlich, Cyril. 'Building and Caretaking: Economic Policy in British Tropical Africa, 1890–1960', *Economic History Review*, 2nd ser., XXVI, 4 (1973), 649–67.

Ehrlich, Cyril. 'The Uganda Economy, 1903–45', in Harlow, Chilver and Smith (eds), *East Africa, II* (Oxford, 1965).

Ekoko, A. Edho. 'The British Attitude Towards Germany's Colonial Irredentism in Africa in the Inter-War Years', *Journal of Contemporary History*, 14 (1979), 287–307.

Ekundare, R. Olufemi. *An Economic History of Nigeria, 1860–1960* (London, 1973).

Sir Charles Eliot, *The East Africa Protectorate* (London, 1905, Frank Cass, 1966).

Emerson, Rupert. *From Empire to Nation: The Rise to Self-Assertion of Asian and African Peoples* (Boston, 1960).

Fage, J.D. *Ghana, A Historical Interpretation* (Maddison, 1961).

Fage, J.D. and Verity, Maureen. *An Atlas of African History*, 2nd edn (London, 1978).

Fayle, C. Ernest. *History of the Great War: Seaborne Trade*, vol. II (London, 1923).

Feiling, Keith. *The Life of Neville Chamberlain* (London, 1946).

Fieldhouse, D.K. *Black Africa, 1945–1980: Economic Decolonisation and Arrested Development* (London, 1986).

Fieldhouse, D.K. *Unilever Overseas. The Anatomy of a Multinational, 1895–1965* (London and Stanford, USA 1978).

Fiji, The Colony of, 1874–1924 (Suva, 1924).

Fitzgerald, Walter. *Africa, A Social, Economic and Political Geography* (London, 2nd edn, 1936).

Flint, John E. *Sir George Goldie and the Making of Nigeria* (Oxford, 1960).

Fordham, Paul. *The Geography of African Affairs* (London, 1965).

Fox, H. Wilson. 'The Development of Imperial Resources', *Journal of the Royal Society of Arts*, LXV (Dec. 1916), 78–91.

Fox, H. Wilson. 'The Development of the Empire's Resources', *The Nineteenth Century and After* (Oct. 1917), 835–58.

Fox, H. Wilson. 'Payment of War Debt by Development of Empire Resources', *United Empire*, IX (Jan. 1918), 169–88.

Frenkel, S.H. *Capital Investment in Africa: Its Course and Effects* (London, 1938).

Frenkel, S.H. *The Economic Impact on Under-Developed Societies* (Oxford, 1953).

Fyfe, Christopher. *A Short History of Sierra Leone* (London, 1962).

Gailey, Harry A. *A History of the Gambia* (London, 1964).

Galbraith, John S. 'British War Aims in World War I: A Commentary on "Statesmanship", *Journal of Imperial and Commonwealth History*', XIII, 1 (1984), 25–45.

Gallagher, John and Robinson, Ronald. 'The Imperialism of Free Trade', *Economic History Review*, 2nd ser., VI, I (1953), 1–15.

Garside, W.R. *British Unemployment 1919–1939* (Cambridge, 1990).

Garvin, James L. *The Life of Joseph Chamberlain*, vol. 3. *1895–1900: Empire and World Policy* (London, 1934).

Geiss, Immanuel. *The Pan-African Movement* (London, 1974).

George, David Lloyd. *The Truth About the Peace Treaties*, vol. II (London, 1938).

Gerig, Benjamin. *The Open Door and the Mandates System* (London, 1930).

Gifford, Prosser and Louis, Wm. Roger (eds). *Britain and Germany in Africa, Imperial Rivalry and Colonial Rule* (New Haven, 1967).

Gilbert, Martin and Gott, Richard. *The Appeasers* (London, 1963).

The Gold Coast Handbook, 1923 (Govt. Printer, Accra, 1923).

Goldsworthy, David. *Colonial Issues in British Politics 1945–1961* (Oxford, 1971).

Greaves, Ida. 'The Sterling Balances of the Colonial Territories', *Economic Journal*, 61 (1951), 433–9.

Greaves, Ida. *Colonial Monetary Conditions* (Colonial Research Studies, No. 10, 1953).

Greaves, Ida. 'Sterling Balances and the Colonial Currency System: A Comment', *Economic Journal*, 63 (1953), 921–3.

Greaves, Ida. *The Colonial Sterling Balances, Essays in International Finance, No. 20* (Princeton, 1954).

Green, R.H. 'Ghana Cocoa Marketing Policy, 1938–60', *Nigerian Institute of Social and Economic Research, Conference Proceedings* (Dec. 1960), 132–60.

Grimble, Arthur. *A Pattern of Islands* (London, 1952).

Guinn, Paul. *British Strategy and Politics 1914 to 1918* (Oxford, 1965).

Gungwu, Wang. *A Short History of the Nanyang Chinese* (Singapore, 1959).

Gupta, P.S. *Imperialism and the British Labour Movement* (London, 1975).

Haas, Ernst B. 'The Reconciliation of Conflicting Colonial Policy Aims: Acceptance of the League of Nations Mandates System', *International Organisation*, VI (1952), 521–36.

Lord Hailey, *An African Survey: A Study of the Problems Arising in Africa South of the Sahara* (London, 1938).

Hakam, A.N. 'Impediments to the Growth of Indigenous Industrial Entrepreneurship in Ghana, 1946–1968', *Economic Bulletin of Ghana*, 2, 2 (1972), 3–31.

Hall, A.R. (ed.). *The Export of Capital from Britain 1870–1914* (London, 1968).

Hall, H. Duncan 'The British Commonwealth and the Founding of the League Mandate System', in K. Bourne and D.C. Watt (eds), *Studies in International History* (London, 1967).

Hancock, W.K. *Survey of British Commonwealth Affairs*, vol. I. *Problems of Nationality, 1918–1936* (London, 1937); vol. II. *Problems of Economic Policy, 1918–1939*; part 1 (London, 1940), part 2 (London, 1942).

Hardie, Frank. *The Abyssinian Crisis* (London, 1974).

Hargreaves, John D. *Prelude to the Partition of West Africa* (London, 1963).

Hargreaves, John D. *West Africa Partitioned*, vol. II. *The Elephants and the Grass* (London, 1985).

Harlow, V.T. *A History of Barbados, 1625–1685* (Oxford, 1926).

Harlow, Vincent, Chilver, E.M. and Smith, Alison (eds). *History of East Africa*, vol. II (Oxford, 1965).

Harris Jr., Brice. *The United States and the Italo-Ethiopian Crisis* (Stanford, Calif., 1964).

Harris, John H. 'The Mandatory System After Five Years' Working', *Contemporary Review*, CXXVII (Feb. 1925), 171–8.

Harrison, Desmond 'Civil Engineering Problems of the East African Groundnuts Scheme', *Engineer* (30 July 1948), 120–2.

Hasib, A. 'Money and Banking Problems in the British Colonies', *Indian Journal of Economics*, 38 (1957), 73–81.

Havinden, M.A. 'The History of Crop Cultivation in West Africa: A Bibliographical Guide', *Economic History Review* 2nd ser., XXIII (1970), 532–55.

Hawkins, E.K. 'Marketing Boards and Economic Development in Nigeria and Ghana', *Review of Economic Studies*, 26 (1958), 51–62.

Hazlewood, Arthur. 'Sterling Balances and the Colonial Currency System',

Economic Journal, 62 (1952), 942–5.

Hazlewood, Arthur. 'The Economics of Colonial Monetary Arrangements', *Social and Economic Studies*, 3 (1954), 291–315.

Hazlewood, Arthur. 'Memorandum on the Sterling Assets of British Colonies: A Comment', *Review of Economic Studies*, 22, 1 (1954), 72–4.

Hazlewood, Arthur. 'Sterling Balances and the Colonial Currency System: A Reply', *Economic Journal*, 64 (1954), 616–17.

Hazlewood, Arthur (ed.). *African Integration and Disintegration* (London, 1967).

Hazlewood, Arthur. *Economic Integration: The East African Experience* (London, 1975).

Headrick, Daniel R. *The Tools of Imperialism* (Oxford, 1982).

Helleiner, G.K. 'The Fiscal Role of the Marketing Boards in Nigerian Economic Development, 1947–61', *Economic Journal*, 74 (1964), 582–610.

Helleiner, G.K. *Peasant Agriculture, Government and Economic Growth in Nigeria* (Homewood, Illinois, 1966).

Henderson, Ian. 'Early African Leadership: The Copperbelt Disturbances of 1935 and 1940', *Journal of Southern African Studies*, 2 1 (1975), 83–97.

Henderson, Nevile. *Failure of a Mission: Berlin 1937–1939* (London, 1940).

Henderson, W.O. *Studies in German Colonial History* (London, 1962).

Hennart, J.F. 'Internationalisation in Practice: Early Foreign Direct Investments in Malayan Tin Mining', *Journal of International Business Studies*, 17 (1986), 131–43.

Herbertson A.J. and Howarth, O.J.R. (eds). *The Oxford Survey of the British Empire*, vol. II. *Asia* (Oxford, 1914).

Hettiarachchy, Tilak. *The Sinhala Peasant* (Lake House Investments Ltd, Colombo, 1982).

Hill, Polly. *Migrant Cocoa Farmers of Southern Ghana, A Study in Rural-Capitalism* (Cambridge, 1963).

Hinden, Rita. *Empire and After: A Study of British Imperial Attitudes* (London, 1949).

Hinds, Allister E. 'Imperial Policy and Colonial Sterling Balances, 1943–56', *Journal of Imperial and Commonwealth History*, XIX, 1 (1991), 24–44.

Hinds, Allister E. 'Sterling and Imperial Policy, 1945–51', *Journal of Imperial and Commonwealth History*, XV, 2 (1987), 149–69.

Hobley, C.W. *Kenya, From Chartered Company to Crown Colony* (London, 1929, 2nd edn, Frank Cass, 1970).

Hobsbawm, E.J. *The Age of Empire, 1875–1914* (London, 1987).

Hobson, John A. *Imperialism*: A Study (3rd edn, London, 1988).

Hodges, G.W.T. 'African Manpower Statistics for the British Forces in East Africa, 1914 to 1918', *Journal of African History*, XIX, 1, 1978, 101–16.

Hon-Chan, Chai. *The Development of British Malaya, 1896–1909* (Kuala Lumpur, 1964).

Hopkins, A.G. *An Economic History of West Africa* (London, 1973).

Hopkins, A.G. 'The Victorians and Africa: A Reconsideration of the Occupation of Egypt, 1882', *Journal of African History*, 27, 2 (1986), 363–91.

Hopkins, A.G. 'Accounting for the British Empire', *Journal of Imperial and Commonwealth History*, XVI, 2 (1988), 234–42.

Hoskins, Halford L. 'The Suez Canal in Time of War', *Foreign Affairs*, 14, 1 (Oct. 1935), 93–101.

Hudson, W.J. *Billy Hughes in Paris: The Birth of Australian Diplomacy* (Melbourne, 1978).

Hyam, Ronald. *Elgin and Churchill at the Colonial Office, 1905–1908, The Watershed of Empire – Commonwealth* (London, 1968).

Hyam, Ronald. 'Empire and Sexual Opportunity', *Journal of Imperial and Commonwealth History*, XIV, 2 (1986), 34–90.

Hynes, William G. *The Economics of Empire Britain, Africa and the New Imperialism* (London, 1979).

Iliffe, John. *A Modern History of Tanganyika* (Cambridge, 1979).

Iliffe, John. *The Emergence of African Capitalism* (London, 1983).

Ingham, Kenneth. *The Making of Modern Uganda* (London, 1958).

Isichei, Elizabeth. *A History of Nigeria* (Harlow, 1983).

Jackson, James C. *Planters and Speculators, Chinese and European Agricultural Enterprise in Malaya, 1786–1921* (Kuala Lumpur and Singapore, 1968).

Jeffries, Charles *The Colonial Empire and its Civil Service* (Cambridge, 1938).

Jessop, David 'The Colonial Stock Act of 1900: A Symptom of the New Imperialism?', *Journal of Imperial and Commonwealth History*, IV, 2 (1976), 155–63.

Johnson, Howard 'Oil, Imperial Policy and the Trinidad Disturbances, 1937', *Journal of Imperial and Commonwealth History*, IV, 1 (1975), 29–54.

Johnson, Marion 'Cotton Imperialism in West Africa', *African Affairs*, 73, 291 (1974), 178–87.

Jones, Arthur Creech. 'The Colonial Office', *Political Quarterly*, XIV, 1 (1943), 19–32.

Jones, Arthur Creech and Hinden, Rita. *Plan for Africa* (London, 1941)

Kanya-Forster, A.S. 'French Expansion in Africa: The Mythical Theory' in Roger Owen and Bob Sutcliffe (eds), *Studies in the Theory of Imperialism* (London, 1972).

Kay, G.B. (ed.). *The Political Economy of Colonialism in Ghana* (Cambridge, 1972).

Kennedy, Paul. *The Realities Behind Diplomacy: Background Influences on British External Policy, 1865–1980* (London, 1981).

Kenyatta, J.M. 'Hands Off Abyssinia!', *Labour Monthly*, 17, 9 (Sept. 1935), 535–6.

Kesner, Richard M. 'Builders of Empire: The Role of the Crown Agents in Imperial Development, 1880–1914', *Journal of Imperial and Commonwealth History*, V, 3 (1977), 310–30.

Kesner, Richard M. *Economic Control and Colonial Development. Crown Colony Financial Management in the Age of Joseph Chamberlain* (London, 1981).

Kidd, Benjamin *Control of the Tropics* (New York, 1898).

Killick, A. 'The Economics of Cocoa' in W. Birmingham et al. (eds), *A Study of Contemporary Ghana, I, The Economy of Ghana* (London, 1967).

Killingray, David. 'The Empire Resources Development Committee and West Africa', *Journal of Imperial and Commonwealth History*, 10, 2 (1982), 194–210.

Killingray David and Rathbone Richard (eds), *Africa and the Second World War* (London, 1986).

Kitching, Gavin. *Class and Economic Change in Kenya* (London, 1980).

Kravis, Irving B. 'Trade as a Handmaiden of Growth: Similarities Between the Nineteenth and Twentieth Centuries', *Economic Journal*, 80 (Dec. 1970), 850–72.

Kubicek, Robert V. *The Administration of Imperialism: Joseph Chamberlain at the Colonial Office* (Durham, N.C., 1969).

Kubicek, Robert V. 'The Colonial Steamer and the Occupation of West Africa by the Victorian State, 1840–1900', *Journal of Imperial and Commonwealth History*, XVIII, 1 (1991), 9–32.

La Guerre, John. 'The Moyne Commission and the West Indian Intelligentsia, 1938–9', *Journal of Commonwealth Political Studies*, IX, 2 (1971), 134–7.

Langley, J. Ayodele *Pan-Africanism and Nationalism in West Africa 1900–1945*

(Oxford, 1973).

Lanning, Greg. *Africa Undermined: Mining Companies and the Underdevelopment of Africa* (London, 1979).

Laski, Harold. 'The Colonial Civil Service', *Political Quarterly*, IX, 4 (1938), 541–51.

League of Nations, *Report of the Committee for the Study of the Problem of Raw Materials*, (No. A.27, 1937, IIB (Geneva, 8 Sept. 1937).

League of Nations, *Industrialisation and Foreign Trade* (Geneva, 1945).

Lee, J.M. '"Forward Thinking" and War: The Colonial Office During the 1940s', *Journal of Imperial and Commonwealth History*, VI, 1 (1977), 64–79.

Lee, J.M. and Petter, M. *The Colonial Office, War and Development Policy: Organisation and the Planning of a Metropolitan Initiative, 1939–45* (London, 1982).

Leubuscher, Charlotte. *Bulk Buying from the Colonies* (London, 1956).

Lever, William H. *Viscount Leverhulme by his Son* (London, 1927).

Levi, John, and Havinden, Michael. *The Economics of African Agriculture* (Harlow, UK, 1982).

Levi J., Havinden M., Johnson, O. and Karr, G.. *African Agriculture: Economic Action and Reaction in Sierra Leone* (London, 1976).

Lewis, W.A. 'Colonial Development', *Transactions of the Manchester Statistical Society*, 116 (Jan. 1949), 1–30.

Lewis, W.A. 'Developing Colonial Agriculture', *Three Banks Review*, 2 (1949), 3–21.

Lewis, W.A. *Report on Industrialisation and the Gold Coast* (Accra, 1953).

Lewis, W.A. 'A Review of Economic Development', *American Economic Review*, LV, 2 (May, 1965), 1–15.

Lewis W.A. (ed.), *Tropical Development 1880–1913* (London, 1970).

Lewis, W.A. *Growth and Fluctuations*, 1870–1913 (London, 1978).

Lewis, W.A. 'The Slowing Down of the Engine of Growth', *American Economic Review*, 70, 4 (Sept. 1980), 555–64.

Lim, Teck Ghee. 'Malayan Peasant Smallholders and the Stevenson Restriction Scheme, 1922–8', *Journal of the Malaysian Branch of the Royal Asiatic Society*, 47, 2 (1974), 105–22.

Lim, Teck Ghee. *Peasants and Their Agricultural Economy in Colonial Malaya 1874–1941* (Kuala Lumpur and London, 1977).

Lloyd, E.M.H. *Experiments in State Control at the War Office and the Ministry of Food* (Oxford, 1924).

Lomax, K.S. 'Colonial Demand for Cotton Goods', *Yorkshire Bulletin of Economic and Social Research*, 4, 1 (1952), 67–71.

Louis, Wm. Roger. 'Great Britain and International Trusteeship: The Mandate System', in R.W. Winks (ed.), *The Historiography of the British Empire-Commonwealth* (Durham, North Carolina, 1966).

Louis, Wm. Roger. *Great Britain and Germany's Lost Colonies, 1914 to 1919* (Oxford, 1967).

Louis, Wm. Roger. 'The Origins of the "Sacred Trust"', in Ronald Segal and Ruth First (eds), *South West Africa: Travesty of Trust* (London, 1967).

Louis, Wm. Roger. *Imperialism at Bay 1941–1945: The United States and the Decolonisation of the British Empire* (Oxford, 1977).

Lucas Charles (ed.), *The Empire at War*, vol IV (London, 1924).

Lugard, Frederick. *The Rise of Our East African Empire* (London, 1893).

Lugard, Frederick. 'The Crown Colonies and the British War Debt', *Nineteenth Century and After*, LXXXVIII (Aug. 1920), 239–55.

Lugard, Frederick. *The Dual Mandate in British Tropical Africa* (London, 1922, repr. by Frank Cass, 1965).

Lugard, Frederick. 'The Mandate System and the British Mandates', *Journal of the Royal Society of Arts*, LXXII (June, 1924).

Lynn, Martin. 'The "Imperialism of Free Trade" and the Case of West Africa, c.1830–c.1870', *Journal of Imperial and Commonwealth History*, XV, 1 (1986), 22–40.

Lynn, Martin. 'From Sail to Steam: The Impact of Steamship Services on the British Palm Oil Trade with West Africa, 1850–1890', *Journal of African History*, 30, 2 (1989), 227–45.

Lyttelton, Oliver. 'Viscount Chandos', *The Memoirs of Lord Chandos* (London, 1962).

Maanen-Helmer, Elizabeth. *The Mandates System in Relation to Africa and the Pacific Islands* (London, 1929).

Macdonald, Barrie. *Cinderellas of the Empire: Towards a History of Kiribati and Tuvalu* (Canberra, 1982).

MacIntyre, W.D. *The Imperial Frontier in the Tropics, 1865–1875* (London, 1967).

Mackenzie, John M. (ed.), *Imperialism and Popular Culture* (Manchester, 1986).

MacMillan, W.M. *Warning from the West Indies: A Tract for the Empire* (London, 1938).

MacMillan, W.M. 'The Real Colonial Question', *Fortnightly Review*, CXLVIII (July-Dec. 1940, 548–57).

McPhee, Allan. *The Economic Revolution in British West Africa* (London, 1926).

Maddison, Angus. *Phases of Capitalist Development* (Oxford, 1982).

Mair, L.P. *Native Policies in Africa* (London, 1936).

Maizels, Alfred. *Exports, and Economic Growth of Developing Countries* (Cambridge, 1962).

Malmsten, Neal R. 'The British Labour Party and the West Indies, 1918–39', *Journal of Imperial and Commonwealth History*, V, 2 (1977), 177–205.

Martin, S.M. 'The Long Depression: West African Export Producers and the World Economy, 1914–1945', in Ian Brown (ed.), *The Economies of Africa and Asia in the Inter-War Depression* (London, 1989).

Maxon, Robert M. 'African Production and the Support of European Settlement in Kenya: The Uasin Gishu-Mimias Railway Scheme', *Journal of Imperial and Commonwealth History*, XIV, 1 (1985), 52–64.

Maxon, Robert M. 'The Kenya Currency Crisis 1919–21 and the Imperial Dilemma', *Journal of Imperial and Commonwealth History*, XVII, 34 (1989), 323–48.

Mazrui, Ali A. and Tidy, Michael. *Nationalism and New States in Africa* (London, 1984).

Medlicott W.N. and Dakin Douglas (eds). *Documents on British Foreign Policy, 1919–1939*, Second series, vol. XVIII, *European Affairs, January 2-June 3, 1937* (London, 1980).

Meek, C.K., MacMillan, W.M. and Hussey, E.R.J. Europe and West Africa: Some Problems and Adjustments (London, 1940).

Meredith, David. 'The British Government and Colonial Economic Policy 1919–1939', *Economic History Review*, 2nd ser., XXVIII, 3 (1975), 484–499.

Meredith, David. 'The Construction of Takoradi Harbour in the Gold Coast 1919 to 1930: A Case Study in Colonial Development and Administration', *Transafrican Journal of History*, 5 (1976), 134–49.

Meredith, David. 'Government and the Decline of the Nigerian Oil-Palm Export Industry, 1919–1939', *Journal of African History*, 25 (1984), 311–29.

Meredith, David. 'State Controlled Marketing and Economic Development: The Case of West African Produce During the Second World War', *Economic History Review*, 2nd ser., XXXIX, 1 (1986), 77–91.

Meredith, David. 'Imperial Images: The Empire Marketing Board, 1926–32', *History Today*, 37 (Jan. 1987), 30–6.

Meredith, David. 'The Colonial Office, British Business Interests and the Reform of Cocoa Marketing in West Africa, 1937–1945', *Journal of African History*, 29 (1988), 285–300.

Meredith, M. *The Past is Another Country: Rhodesia, 1890–1979* (London, 1979).

Meyer, Frederick V. *Britain's Colonies in World Trade* (London, 1948).

Middlemas, Keith. *Diplomacy of Illusion: The British Government and Germany, 1937–39* (London, 1972).

Viscount Milner, *Questions of the Hour* (London, 1923).

Mitchell, B.R. *International Historical Statistics, Africa and Asia* (London, 1982).

Mitchell, B.R. and Deane, Phyllis. *Abstract of British Historical Statistics* (Cambridge, 1962).

Moggridge, D.E. 'From War to Peace: The Sterling Balances', *Banker*, 11 (1972), 1032–35.

Moneypenny, W.F. and Buckle, G.E. *The Life of Bejamin Disraeli, Earl of Beaconsfield*, vol. III, *1846–1855* (London, 1914).

Viscount Montgomery, *The Memoirs of Field Marshal the Viscount Montgomery of Alamein, K.G.* (London, 1958).

Morel, E.D. *Africa and the Peace of Europe* (London, 1917).

Morgan, D.J. *The Official History of Colonial Development*, vol. 1. *The Origins of British Aid Policy, 1924–1945* (London, 1980).

Morgan, D.J. *The Official History of Colonial Development*, vol. 2. *Developing British Colonial Resources, 1945–1951* (London, 1980).

Morgan, D.J. *The Official History of Colonial Development*, vol. 3. *A Re-assessment of British Aid Policy, 1951–1965* (London, 1980).

Morgan, D.J. *The Official History of Colonial Development*, vol. 4. *Changes in British Aid Policy, 1951–1970* (London, 1980).

Munro, J. Forbes. *Africa and the International Economy 1800–1960* (London, 1976).

Munro, J. Forbes. 'Shipping Subsidies and Railway Guarantees; William Mackinnon, East Africa and the Indian Ocean', *Journal of African History*, XXVIII, 2 (1987), 209–230.

Musson, A.E. *The Growth of British Industry* (London, 1978).

Nelson, W. Evan. 'The Gold Standard in Mauritius and the Straits Settlements Between 1850 and 1914', *Journal of Imperial and Commonwealth History*, XVI, 1 (1987), 48–76.

Newbury, Colin. 'Spoils of War: Sub-imperial Collaboration in South West Africa and New Guinea, 1914–20', *Journal of Imperial and Commonwealth History*, XIV, 3 (1988), 88–106.

Newlyn, W.T.. 'The Colonial Empire', in R.S. Sayers (ed.), *Banking in the British Commonwealth* (London, 1952).

Newlyn, W.T. and Rowan, D.C. *Money and Banking in British Colonial Africa* (Oxford, 1954).

Newton, Scott. 'Britain, the Sterling Area and European Integration, 1945–50', in A.N. Porter and R.F. Holland (eds), *Money, Finance and Empire, 1790–1960* (London, 1985).

Nigerian Handbook 2nd edn, London, 1954).

Nworah, K. Dike. 'The Politics of Lever's West African Concessions, 1907–1913',

International Journal of African Historical Studies, V, 2 (1972), 248–64.

Ochieng, William R. (ed.), *A History of Modern Kenya* (London, 1989).

Okigbo, P.N.C. *National Development Planning in Nigeria, 1900–1992* (London, 1989).

Oliver, Roland and Mathews, Gervaise (eds). *History of East Africa*, vol. 1 (Oxford, 1963).

Oliver, Roland and Sanderson, G.N. (eds). *The Cambridge History of Africa*, vol. 6. *From 1870 to 1905* (Cambridge, 1985).

Ormerod, Medwyn. 'The Transport Problems of the East African Groundnut Scheme', *Journal of the Institute of Transport*, 23, 11 (1950), 351–8.

O'Neil, H.C. *The War in Africa and the Far East* (London, 1918).

Owen, Roger, and Sutcliffe, Bob (eds). *Studies in the Theory of Imperialism* (London, 1972).

Padmore, George. *How Britain Rules Africa* (New York, 1936, repr. 1969).

Page, Melvin E. 'The War of *Thangata*: Nyasaland and the East Africa Campaign, 1914–1918', *Journal of African History*, XIX, 1 (1978), 87–100.

Page, Melvin E. (ed.). *Africa and the First World War* (New York, 1987).

Palmer, Robin and Parsons, Neil (eds). *The Roots of Rural Poverty in Southern Africa* (London, 1977).

Parkinson, Cosmo *The Colonial Office from Within, 1909–1945* (London, 1947).

Peacock, Alan and Dosser, Douglas. *The National Income of Tanganyika 1952–1954* (London, 1958).

Pearce, R.D. *The Turning Point in Africa, British Colonial Policy 1938–48* (London, 1982).

Pearce, R.D. 'Morale in the Colonial Service in Nigeria During the Second World War', *Journal of Imperial and Commonwealth History*, XI, 2 (1983), 175–96.

Perham, Margery (ed.). *The Native Economies of Nigeria* vol. 1. *The Economics of a Tropical Dependency* by Daryll Forde and Richenda Scott (London, 1946); and vol 2, *Mining, Commerce and Finance*, by P.A.. Bower, A.J. Brown, C. Leubuscher, J. Mars and Sir Allan Pim (London, 1948).

Perham, Margery. *Lugard, The Years of Adventure, 1858–1898* (London, 1956).

Perham, Margery. *Lugard, The Years of Authority, 1898–1945* (London, 1960).

Perrings, Charles. 'Consciousness, Conflict and Proletarianisation: An Assessment of the 1935 Mineworkers' Strike on the Northern Rhodesian Copperbelt', *Journal of Southern African Studies*, 4, 1 (1977), 31–51.

Peters, A.R. *Anthony Eden at the Foreign Office 1931–1938* (New York, 1986).

Peterson, John. *Province of Freedom, A History of Sierra Leone, 1787–1870* (London, 1969).

Pike, J.G. *Malawi: A Political and Economic History* (London, 1965).

Polk, Judd. *Sterling: Its Meaning in World Finance* (New York, 1956).

Pollard, Sidney. *The Development of the British Economy, 1914–1967* (2nd edn London, 1969).

Porter, Andrew. 'In Memoriam Joseph Chamberlain: A Review of Periodical Literature, 1960–73', *Journal of Imperial and Commonwealth History*, III (1975), 292–7.

Porter, Andrew. 'Joseph Chamberlain: A Radical Reappraisal?', *Journal of Imperial and Commonwealth History*, VI, 3 (1978), 330–6.

Porter, Andrew. 'The Balance Sheet of Empire, 1850–1914', *Historical Journal*, 31, 3 (1988), 685–99.

Porter, Andrew. '"Gentlemanly Capitalism" and Empire: The British Experience Since 1750?', *Journal of Imperial and Commonwealth History*, XVIII, 3 (1990), 265–95.

Porter, Andrew (ed.). *Atlas of British Overseas Expansion* (London, 1991).

Porter, A.N. and Holland R.F. (eds). *Money, Finance and Empire, 1790–1960* (London, 1985).

Porter, A.N. and Stockwell, A.J. *British Imperial Policy and Decolonisation, 1938–1964*, vol. 1. *1938–51* (London, 1987).

Porter, A.N. and Stockwell A.J., *British Imperial Policy and Decolonisation, 1938–64*, vol. 2, *1951–64* (London, 1989).

Porter, Bernard. *The Lion's Share. A Short History of British Imperialism, 1850–1970* (London, 1975).

Porter, Bernard. 'Imperialism and the Scramble', *Journal of Imperial and Commonwealth History*, IX (1980), 76–80.

Post, K.W.J. 'The Politics of Protest in Jamaica, 1938: Some Problems of Analysis and Conceptualisation', *Social and Economic Studies*, XVIII, 4 (1969), 374–90.

Prebisch, R. *The Economic Development of Latin America and its Principal Problems* (New York, 1950).

Pressnell, L.S. *External Economic Policy Since the War*, vol. 1. *The Post-War Financial Settlement* (London, 1987).

Prest, A.R. *War Economics of Primary Producing Countries* (Cambridge, 1948).

Prest, A.R. and Stewart, I.G. *The National Income of Nigeria, 1950–51* (London, 1953).

Pritt, D.N. *The Labour Government 1945–51* (London, 1963).

Raj, K.N. 'Linkages in Industrialisation and Development Strategy: Some Basic Issues', *Journal of Development Planning*, 8 (1975), 105–19.

Rathbone, Richard. 'World War I and Africa', *Journal of African History*, XIX, 1 (1978), 1–9.

Rendell, William. *The History of the Commonwealth Development Corporation 1948–1972* (London, 1976).

Reynolds, Edward. *Trade and Economic Change on the Gold Coast, 1807–1874* (London, 1974).

Riedel, James. 'Trade as the Engine of Growth in Developing Countries, Revisited', *Economic Journal*, 94 (Mar. 1984), 56–73.

Roberts, Andrew (ed). *The Cambridge History of Africa*, vol. 7, *1905–1914* (Cambridge, 1986).

Robertson, Esmonde M. *Mussolini as Empire-Builder* (London, 1977).

Robinson, Ronald and Gallagher, John with Denny Alice, *Africa and the Victorians. The Official Mind of Imperialism* (London, 1961).

Rose, J. Holland, Newton A.P., Benians E.A. (eds). *The Cambridge History of the British Empire*, vol. II *The Growth of the New Empire* (Cambridge, 1940).

Rotberg, R.L. *The Rise of Nationalism in Central Africa: The Making of Malawi and Zambia, 1873–1964* (Cambridge, Mass, 1965).

Rothwell, V.H. *British War Aims and Peace Diplomacy 1914 to 1918* (Oxford, 1971).

Royal Institute of International Affairs. *The Colonial Problem* (London, 1937).

Royal Institute of International Affairs. *Documents on International Affairs 1937* (London, 1939).

Royal Institute of International Affairs, *Germany's Claims to Colonies* (London, 1938, 2nd edn., 1939).

Royal Institute of International Affairs, *Raw Materials and Colonies* (London, 1936).

Rudner, Martin. 'Financial Policies in Post-War Malaya: The Fiscal and Monetary Measures of Liberation and Reconstruction', *Journal of Imperial and Commonwealth History*, III, 3 (1975), 323–46.

Ryan, N.J. *The Making of Modern Malaysia and Singapore* (Kuala Lumpur, 1971).

Ryan, Selwyn D. *Race and Nationalism in Trinidad and Tobago: A Study of Decolonisation in a Multiracial Society* (Toronto, 1972).

Salter, J. Arthur., *Allied Shipping Control an Experiment in International Administration* (Oxford, 1921).

Sayers, R.S. (ed.), Banking in the British Commonwealth (London, 1952).

Sanderson, G.N. 'The European Partition of Africa: Coincidence or Conjuncture?', *Journal of Imperial and Commonwealth History*, III (1974), 1–54.

Sardesai, D.R. *British Trade and Expansion in Southeast Asia, 1830–1914* (New Delhi, 1977).

Saul, S.B. 'The Economic Significance of "Constructive Imperialism", *Journal of Economic History*, XVII, 2 (1957), 173–92.

Schacht, H. 'Germany's Colonial Demands', *Foreign Affairs*, 15, 2 (Jan. 1937), 223–34.

Schedvin, C.B. 'Staples and Regions of Pax Britannica', *Economic History Review*, 2nd ser., XLIII, 4 (1990), 533–50.

Schmokel, Wolfe W. *Dream of Empire: German Colonialism, 1919–1945* (Westport, Connecticut, 1964, repr. 1980).

Schnee, Heinrich., *German Colonisation Past and Future: The Truth About German Colonies* (London, 1926).

Scott, William R. 'Black Nationalism and the Italo-Ethiopian Conflict 1934–36', *Journal of Negro History*, 63 (1978).

Segal Ronald, and First Ruth (eds). *South West Africa: Travesty of Trust* (London, 1967).

Seymour, Charles. *The Intimate Papers of Colonel House*, vol. IV (New York, 1928).

Shannon, H.A. 'The Modern Colonial Sterling Exchange Standard', *IMF Staff Papers*, 2 (1952), 318–62.

Shannon, H.A. 'The Sterling Balances of the Sterling Area 1939–49', *Economic Journal*, 60 (1950), 531–51.

Simon, Matthew 'The Pattern of New British Portfolio Foreign Investment, 1865–1914', in A.R. Hall (ed.), *The Export of Capital from Britain 1870–1914* (London, 1968).

Singer, H.W. 'The Distribution of Gains Between Investing and Borrowing Countries', *American Economic Review, Papers and Proceedings*, 5, Supplement (May, 1950), 473–85.

Skidelsky, Robert *Politicians and the Slump: The Labour Government of 1929–1931* (London, 1967).

Smith, Gaddis. 'The British Government and the Disposition of the German Colonies in Africa, 1914 to 1918', in Prosser Gifford and Wm. Roger Louis (eds), *Britain and Germany in Africa, Imperial Rivalry and Colonial Rule* (New Haven, 1967).

Smuts, Jan., *The British Commonwealth of Nations: A Speech Made by General Smuts, 15 May 1917* (London, 1917).

Smyth, Rosaleen. 'Britain's African Colonies and British Propaganda During the Second World War', *Journal of Imperial and Commonwealth History*, XIV, 1 (1985), 65–82.

Snelling, R.C. 'Peacemaking, 1919: Australia, New Zealand and the British Empire Delegation at Versailles', *Journal of Imperial and Commonwealth History*, IV, 2 (1975), 15–28.

Sorrenson, M.P.K. *Origins of European Settlement in Kenya* (Nairobi and London, 1968).

Spencer, Ian. 'Settler Dominance, Agricultural Production and the Second World War in Kenya', *Journal of African History*, 27, 4 (1980), 497–514.

Stillson, R.T. 'The Financing of Malayan Rubber', *Economic History Review*, 2nd Ser., XXIV (1991), 589–98.

Stockwell, A.J. 'British Imperial Policy and Decolonisation in Malaya, 1942–52', *Journal of Imperial and Commonwealth History*, XIII, 1 (1984), 68–87.

Stone, Julius. *Colonial Trusteeship in Transition* (Sydney, Australian Institute of International Affairs, 1944).

Spraos John, 'The Statistical Debate on the Net Barter Terms of Trade Between Primary Commodities and Manufactures', *Economic Journal*, 90 (Mar. 1980), 107–128.

Storry, Richard. *Japan and the Decline of the West in Asia 1894–1943* (London, 1979).

Strange, Susan. *Sterling and British Policy* (London, 1972).

Supple, B.E. 'Income and Demand, 1860–1914', in Roderick Floud and Donald McCloskey (eds), *The Economy History of Britain Since 1700*, vol. 2, *1860 to the 1970s* (Cambridge, 1981).

Sir Frank Swettenham, *British Malaya: An Account of the Origin and Progress of British Influence in Malaya* (London, 1906).

Synder, Rixford Kinney. *The Tariff Problem in Great Britain, 1918–1923* (Stanford, 1944).

Szereszewski, R. *Structural Change in the Economy of Ghana 1891–1911* (London, 1965).

Tawney, R.H. 'The Abolition of Economic Control, 1918–1921', *Economic History Review*, XIII (1943), 1–30.

Temperley, H.M.V. (ed.), *A History of the Peace Conference of Paris* (London, 1920).

Thoburn, John T. *Primary Commodity Exports and Economic Development* (London, 1977).

Thomas, Ivor. 'Dollar-Saving by Colonial Development', *Crown Colonist* (Dec. 1949), 739–41.

Thomas, Ivor. 'Dollar-Earning by Colonial Development', *New Commonwealth* (Apr. 1951), 482–83, 565–67.

Thomas, Roger. 'Military Recruitment in the Gold Coast During the First World War', *Cahiers D'Etudes Africaines*, XV, 57 (1975), 57–84.

Tibenderana, Peter K. *Sokoto Province Under British Rule, 1903–1939: A Study of Institutional Adaption and Culturalisation of a Colonial Society in Northern Nigeria* (Zaria, Nigeria, 1988).

Tignor, Robert L. *The Colonial Transformation of Kenya: The Kamba, Kikuyu and Maasai from 1900–1939* (Princeton, 1976).

Tillman, Seth P. *Anglo-American Relations at the Paris Peace Conference* (Princeton, 1961).

Tinbergen, J. *Business Cycles in the United Kingdom 1870–1914* (London, 1956, 2nd edn).

Todaro, Michael P. *Economic Development in the Third World* (4th edn, New York, 1989).

Tomlinson, B.R. 'Indo-British Relations in the Post-Colonial Era: The Sterling Balances Negotiations, 1947–9', in A.N. Porter and R.F. Holland (eds), *Money, Finance and Empire, 1790–1960* (London, 1985).

Townsend, Mary E. *The Rise and Fall of Germany's Colonial Empire* (New York, 1930).

Trollope, Anthony. *The West Indies and the Spanish Main* (1859, repr. Alan Sutton, Gloucester, 1985).

Turnbull, C.M. *A History of Singapore 1819–1988* (2nd ser., Oxford, 1989).

Turrell, R.V. and Van-Helten, J.J. 'The Investment Group: The Missing Link in British Overseas Expansion Before 1914', *Economic History Review*, 2nd Ser., XL, 2 (1987), 267–74.

United Nations, *Methods of Financing Economic Development in Under-Developed Countries* (New York, 1949).

United Nations, *Special Study on Economic Conditions in Non-self-governing Territories* (New York, 1960).

United Nations, *Yearbook of International Trade Statistics, 1952–1964*.

United Nations, *Yearbook of International Trade Statistics, 1958–1964*.

United States, State Department, *Foreign Relations: The Paris Peace Conference 1919* (Washington D.C., United States Government Printing Office, 1943).

Van Zwanenberg, R.T. and King Anne. *An Economic History of Kenya and Uganda, 1800–1970* (London, 1975).

Viton, Alfred (pseud.). *Great Britain, An Empire in Transition* (New York, 1940).

Viviani, Nancy. *Nauru, Phosphate and Political Progress* (Canberra, 1970).

Waley, Daniel. *British Public Opinion and the Abyssinian War 1935–36* (London, 1975).

Wanner, Gustof A. *The First Cocoa Trees in Ghana, 1858–1869* (Basle, 1962).

Ward, J.R. *Poverty and Progress in the Caribbean, 1800–1960* (London, 1985).

Ward, William E.F. *A History of Ghana* (London, 1967).

Watkins, Melville H. 'A Staple Theory of Economic Growth', *Canadian Journal of Economics and Political Science*, XXIX, 2 (May 1963), 141–77.

Westcott, N.J. 'Closer Union and the Future of East Africa, 1939–1948: A Case Study in the "Official Mind of Imperialism"', *Journal of Imperial and Commonwealth History*, X, 1 (1981), 67–88.

Westcott, Nicholas. 'The East African Sisal Industry, 1929–1949: The Marketing of a Colonial Commodity During Depression and War', *Journal of African History* 25, 4 (1984), 445–461.

Wicker, E.R. 'Colonial Development and Welfare 1929–1957 The Evolution of a Policy', *Social and Economic Studies*, 7, 4 (1958), 170–192.

Williams, Eric. *Capitalism and Slavery* (London, 1944).

Williams, Harry. *Ceylon, Pearl of the East* (2nd edn., London, 1863).

Williamson, James. *A Short History of British Expansion, The Modern Empire and Commonwealth* (2nd edn, London, 1934).

Wills, A.J. *An Introduction to the History of Central Africa* (Oxford, 1973),

Winks, R.W. (ed.), *The Historiography of the British Empire-Commonwealth* (Durham, N.C., 1966).

Witlam, P.E. 'Change of Method Needed in Colonial Development', *New Commonwealth*, (6 July 1953), 5–6.

Wood, Alan. *The Groundnut Affair* (London, 1950).

Woolf, Leonard. *Growing, An Autobiography of the Years, 1904–1911* (London, 1961).

Wraith, R.E. *Guggisberg* (London, 1967).

Wright, Leigh R. *The Origins of British Colonialism in Borneo* (Hong Kong, 1970).

Wright, Quincy. *Mandates Under the League of Nations* (Chicago, 1930).

Wyse, Akintola. *The Krio of Sierra Leone: An Interpretive History* (London, 1989).

Yates, P. Lamartine. *Commodity Control: A Study of Primary Products* (London, 1943).

Yearwood, Peter J. 'Great Britain and the Repartition of Africa, 1914–19', *Journal of Imperial and Commonwealth History*, XVIII, 3 (1990), 316–41.

BIBLIOGRAPHY

OFFICIAL BRITISH PUBLICATIONS

Reports of Committees, Commissions, etc.

'Despatch from the Governor of British Guiana, May 1851', *Reports of Her Majesty's Colonial Possessions, 1850*, PP 1851, XXXIV (1421).

'Despatch from the Governor of the Gold Coast, April 7, 1851', XXXIV (1421).

'Despatch from Governor John Higginson to Colonial Secretary', 16 May 1851, XXXIV (1421).

'Despatch from the Governor of Jamaica, December 31, 1851', *Reports of Her Majesty's Colonial Possessions, 1851*, PP 1852, XXXI (1539).

A Return of the Area and Population of Each Division of Each Presidency of India from the Latest Inquiries. PP 1857, XXIX (215.Ser.2), 83.

Report from the Select Committee Appointed to Consider the State of the British Settlements on the Western Coast of Africa, PP 1865, 1 (412).

'Report on the Straits Settlements Blue Book for the Year 1881', *Papers Relating to Her Majesty's Colonial Possessions. Reports for 1880, 1881 and 1882*, PP 1883, XLV (3642).

Recommendations of the Economic Conference (Paris) of the Allies, PP 1916, XXXIV (Cmd 8271), 11.

Copy of Resolutions Passed by the Committee on Commercial and Industrial Policy After the War on the Subject of Imperial Preference, PP 1917–18, XXIII (Cmd 8482), 315.

Extracts from Proceedings and Papers Laid Before the Imperial War Conference, PP 1917–18, XXIII (Cmd 8566), 319.

Final Report of the Committee on Commercial and Industrial Policy After the War, PP 1918, XIII (Cmd 9035), 239.

Colonies' War Contribution. Treasury Minute, PP 1918, XVII (Cmd 9183), 365.

Correspondence Relating to the Wishes of the Natives of the German Colonies as to their Future Government, PP 1918, XVII (Cmd 9210), 379.

Report of the Empire Cotton Growing Committee, PP 1920, XVI (Cmd 523), 13.

Report of the Tropical Agricultural College Committee, PP 1920, XXV (Cmd 562), 521.

Imperial Economic Conference 1923, Summary of Conclusions, PP 1923, XXI, Pt. 1 (Cmd 1990), 197.

Report on the Imperial Institute Committee of Enquiry, PP 1923, Pt. 1 (Cmd 1997), 197.

Imperial Economic Conference 1923, Record of Proceedings and Documents, PP 1924, X (Cmd 2009), 313.

Private Enterprise in British Tropical Africa: Report of the Committee appointed by the Secretary of State for the Colonies, to consider and report whether, and if so, what measures could be taken to encourage Private Enterprise in the development of the British Dependencies in East and West Tropical Africa, with special reference to existing and projected schemes of transportation, PP 1924, VIII (Cmd 2016), 195.

Resolutions Relating to Imperial Preference at the Imperial War Conference, 1917 and the Imperial Economic Conference, 1923, with detailed Statements of the Proposals laid before the Conference of 1023, and of the Preference in force from 1919 to 1924 PP 1924, XVIII (Cmd 2084), 45.

Statement of the Position of His Majesty's Government in Regard to the Resolution of the Imperial Economic Conference 1923, and the Proposals laid before the Conference by His Majesty's late Government, PP 1924, XVIII (Cmd 2115), 55.

Report on the East Africa Protectorate 1924,25, 1924–25, IX (Cmd 2387), 855.

Memorandum, by the Committee on Trade and Industry, on Transport Development and Cotton Growing in East Africa, 1924–25, PP 1925, XXI (Cmd 2463), 39.

Imperial Economic Committee, *Report on Marketing and Preparing for Market of Foodstuffs Produced in the Overseas Parts of the Empire*, PP 1924–5, XIII (Cmd 2493), 799.

Imperial Conference 1926. Appendices to the Summary, PP 1926, xi (Cmd 2769), 607.

Empire Marketing Board, Note on the Work of the Board and Statement of Research Grants Approved by the Secretary of State from July 1926 to May 1927, PP 1927, XVIII (Cmd 2898), 23.

First and Second Reports from the Select Committee on Estimates, 30 April and 19 July 1928, PP 1928, VI (71, 114) [Empire Marketing Board].

Statement on Works Approved for Grants in Connection with Unemployment under the Development (Loan Guarantees and Grants) Act 1929, and the Colonial Development Act 1929, and from the Road Fund, PP 1929–30, XXV (Cmd 3449), 929.

Report of the East Africa Guaranteed Loan Committee 1926–9, PP 1929–30, VIII (Cmd 3494), 589.

Report of a Committee on the System of Appointment in the Colonial Office and the Colonial Services, PP 1929–30, VIII (Cmd 3554), 677.

Statement on Works Approved for Government Financial Assistance in Connection with Unemployment, PP 1929–30, XXV (Cmd 3616), 947.

Report of the Committee on National Expenditure, PP 1930–1, XVI (Cmd 3920), 1.

First and Second Reports from the Select Committee on Estimates, 21 March and 20 June 1932, PP 1931–2, IV (55, 90) [Empire Marketing Board and Colonial Development Fund].

Report of the Commission Appointed to Enquire into the Disturbances in the Copperbelt of Northern Rhodesia, October 1935, PP 1934–5, VII (Cmd 5009), 587.

Trinidad and Tobago Disturbances, 1937, Report of Commission, PP 1937–8, XV (Cmd 5641), 537.

Report of the Commission on the Marketing of West African Cocoa, PP 1937–8, IX (Cmd.5845), 191.

Nutrition in the Colonial Empire, Report of the Economic Advisory Council, PP 1938–9, X (Cmd 6050), 55.

Summary of Information Regarding Nutrition in the Colonial Empire Report of the Economic Advisory Council, Part II, PP 1938–9, X (Cmd 6051), 265.

Report on Labour Conditions in the West Indies, PP 1938–9, XV (Cmd 6070), 721.

Colonial Office, *Labour Conditions in Northern Rhodesia* (Colonial No. 150 HMSO, London, 1938).

Statement of Policy on Colonial Development and Welfare, PP 1939–40, X (Cmd 6175), 25.

Financial and Explanatory Memorandum of the Colonial Development and Welfare Bill, PP 1939–40 (40), I.

Despatch from the Secretary of State for the Colonies to the Colonial Governments Regarding Certain Aspects of Colonial Policy in Wartime, PP 1940–1, VIII (Cmd 6299), 1.

Colonial Research Committee Progress Report 1942–3, PP 1942–3, IX (Cmd 6486), 619.

West India Royal Commission Report, PP 1944–5, VI (Cmd 6607), 245.

Colonial Development and Welfare: Despatch Dated 12 November 1945, from the Secretary of State for the Colonies to Colonial Governments, PP 1945–6, XIX (Cmd 6713), 35.

Colonial Office, *Organisation of the Colonial Civil Service* (Colonial No. 197,

London, 1946).

Colonial Office, *Post-War Training for the Colonial Service* (Colonial No. 198, London, 1946).

Enquiry into the Cost of Living and Control of the Cost of Living in the Colony and Protectorate of Nigeria (1946, Colonial No. 204).

Fifth Report from the Select Committee an Estimates, Colonial Development, June 1948, PP 1947–8, VIII (181–1), 1.

British Dependencies in the Far East 1945–1949, PP 1948–9, XIII, (Cmd 7709), 371.

A Plan for the Mechanised Production of Groundnuts in East and Central Africa, PP 1946–7, X (Cmd 7030), 279.

East African Groundnuts Scheme, Review of Progress to the End of November 1947, PP 1947–8, XI (Cmd 7314), 1.

The Future of the Overseas Food Corporation, January 1951, PP 1950–1, XXVII (Cmd 8125), 925.

Second Report from the Committee of Public Accounts, May 1950, PP 1950, III (70).

Commonwealth Economic Conference, Final Communique, PP 1952–3, XXIII (Cmd 8717), 387.

The Future of the Overseas Food Corporation, May 1954, PP 1953–4, XXVI (Cmd 9158).

Colonial Office, *Memorandum on the Sterling Assets of the British Colonies* (Colonial No. 298, 1953).

Report on the Use of Funds Provided Under the Colonial Development and Welfare Acts and Outline of the Proposal for Exchequer Loans the Colonial Territories, PP 1958–9, X (Cmd 672), 107.

Report of the Committee of Enquiry into the Financial Structure of the Colonial Development Corporation, September 1959, PP 1958–9, X (Cmd 786), 77.

Fourth Report from the Select Committee on Estimates, Colonial Office, PP 1959–60, VI (260).

The British Colonial Territories in 1950: A Regional Review of Progress (British Information Services, ID, 1050, New York, March 1951).

Annual Reports

Colonial Development

First interim report of the Colonial Development Advisory Committee, Aug. 1929 – Feb. 1930, PP 1929–30, VIII (Cmd 3540), 609.

Second, 1930–31, PP 1930–31, X (Cmd 3876), 959.

Third, 1931–32, PP 1931–32, VI (Cmd 4079), 485.

Fourth, 1932–33, PP 1932–33, X (Cmd 4316), 481.

Fifth, 1933–34, PP 1933–34, IX (Cmd 4634), 819.

Sixth, 1934–35, PP 1934–35, VII (Cmd 4916), 681.

Seventh, 1935–36, PP 1935–36, VII (Cmd 5202) 965.

Eighth, 1936–37, PP 1936–37, IX (Cmd 5537) 509.

Ninth, 1937–38, PP 1937–38, IX (Cmd 5789) 421.

Tenth, 1938–39, PP 1938–39, X (Cmd 6062) 7.

Eleventh and final report, 1 Apr. 1939 to 17 Jul. 1940, PP 1940–41, IV (Cmd 6298), 189.

Colonial Development Fund

Abstract Account of the Colonial Development Fund for the year ended 31st March, 1931, PP 1931–32, XVIII (24), 753.
31st March, 1932, PP 1932–33, XX (34), 657.
31st March, 1933, PP 1933–34, XX (29), 667.
31st March, 1934, PP 1934–35, XVI (36), 677.
31st March, 1935, PP 1935–36, XIX (29), 693.
31st March, 1936, PP 1936–37, XX (35), 721.
31st March, 1937, PP 1937–38, XX (31), 817.
31st March, 1938, PP 1938–39, XX (37), 939.
31st March, 1939, PP 1939–40, X (34), 1.
31st March, 1940, PP 1940–41, V (40), 125.
31st March, 1941, PP 1941–42, V (18), 131.

Colonial Development and Welfare

Report on the operation of the Act to 31st October, 1942, PP 1942–43, IX (Cmd 6422), 601.
Return of schemes under the Act in the period 1st November, 1942 to 31st March, 1943, PP 1942–43, IX (Cmd 6457), 615.
1 Apr. 1943 to 31 Mar. 1944, PP 1943–44, VII (Cmd 6532), 601.
1 Apr. 1944 to 31 Mar. 1945, PP 1944–45, XIX (105), 597.
1 Apr. 1945 to 31 Mar. 1946, PP 1945–46, XIX (150), 1.
1 Apr. 1946 to 31 Mar. 1947, PP 1946–47, XIX (127), 73
1 Apr. 1947 to 31 Mar. 1948, PP 1947–48, XXI (166), 11.
1 Apr. 1948 to 31 Mar. 1949, PP 1948–49, XXIX (211), 1.
1 Apr. 1949 to 31 Mar. 1950, PP 1950, XIX (107), 9.
1 Apr. 1950 to 31 Mar. 1951, PP 1950–51, XXVI (189), 473.
1 Apr. 1951 to 31 Mar. 1952, PP 1951–52, XXIV (211). 267.
1 Apr. 1952 to 31 Mar. 1953, PP 1952–53, XXIII (189), 361.
1 Apr. 1953 to 31 Mar. 1954, PP 1953–54, XXV (181), 209.
1 Apr. 1954 to 31 Mar. 1955, PP 1955–56, XXXV (5), 1.
1 Apr. 1955 to 31 Mar. 1956, PP 1955–56, XXXV (309), 33.
1 Apr. 1956 to 31 Mar. 1957, PP 1956–57, XXVI (200), 1.
1 Apr. 1957 to 31 Mar. 1958, PP 1957–58, XXIV (223), 1.
1 Apr. 1958 to 31 Mar. 1959, PP 1958–59, XXV (240), 1.
1 Apr. 1959 to 31 Mar. 1960, PP 1959–60, XXVII (244)
1 Apr. 1960 to 31 Mar. 1961, PP 1960–61, XXVII (240)
1 Apr. 1961 to 31 Mar. 1962, PP 1961–62, XXX (232)
1 Apr. 1962 to 31 Mar. 1963, PP 1962–63, XXX (342)
1 Apr. 1963 to 31 Mar. 1964, PP 1963–64, XXV (313)
1 Apr. 1964 to 31 Mar. 1965, PP 1964–65, XXVIII (305)
1 Apr. 1965 to 31 Mar. 1966, PP 1966–67, LII (160)
1 Apr. 1966 to 31 Mar. 1967, PP 1966–67, LII (587)
1 Apr. 1967 to 31 Mar. 1968, PP 1967–68, XXXVIII (424)
1 Apr. 1968 to 31 Mar. 1969, PP 1968–69, LII (393)
1 Apr. 1969 to 31 Mar. 1970, PP 1970–71, VIII (92)
Colonial Development and Welfare Acts 1929–70: A Brief Review. PP 1970–71, VIII (Cmd 4677), 575.

Colonial Development Corporation

Annual Report and Statement of Accounts for the year ended 31 December 1948, PP 1948–49, XIII (188), 471.
31 December 1949, PP 1950, VIII (105) 171.
31 December 1950, PP 1950–51, X (161), 571.
31 December 1951, PP 1951–52, IX (167), 95.
31 December 1952, PP 1952–53, VIII (158), 685.
31 December 1953, PP 1953–54, X (148), 783.
31 December 1954, PP 1954–55, IV (113), 279.
31 December 1955, PP 1955–56, XII (260), 839.
31 December 1956, PP 1956–57, IX (151), 889.
31 December 1957, PP 1957–58, IX (164), 1.
31 December 1958, PP 1958–59, X (214), 1.
31 December 1959, PP 1959–60, X (211), 207.
31 December 1960, PP 1960–61, X (199), 1.
31 December 1961, PP 1961–62, IX (201), 1.
31 December 1962, PP 1962–63, X (226), 1.

OVERSEAS FOOD CORPORATION

Annual Report and Accounts for the period ended 31 March 1949, PP 1948–49, XIX (252), 1.
31 March 1950, PP 1950, XIII (147), 95.
31 March 1951, PP 1951–52, XVII (1), 697.
31 March 1952, PP 1952–53, XVI (51), 123.
31 March 1953, PP 1953–54, XVIII (30), 45.
31 March 1954, PP 1953–54, XVIII (296), 143.
31 March 1955, PP 1955–56, XXVI (195), 1.

Colonial Territories

Statement to Accompany the Estimates for Colonial and Middle Eastern Services, 1938, PP 1937–8, XX (Cmd 5760), 841.
Statement to Accompany the Estimates for Colonial and Middle Eastern Services, 1939, PP 1938–9, XX (Cmd 6023), 965.
Report on the Colonial Empire (1939–47), PP 1946–47, X (Cmd 7167), 403.
Report on the Colonial Empire, 1947–8, PP 1947–48, XI (Cmd 7433), 47.
Progress Report on the Colonial Territories, 1948–49, PP 1948–49, XIII (Cmd 7715), 641.
1949–50, PP 1950, VIII (Cmd 7958), 415.
The Colonial Territories, 1950–1, PP 1950–1, XXVI (Cmd 8243), 1.
1951–52, PP 1951–2, XXIV (Cmd 8553), 1.
1952–53, PP 1952–3, XXIII (Cmd 8856), 1.
1953–54, PP 1953–4, XXV (Cmd 9169), 1.
1954–55, PP 1955–6, XIII (Cmd 9489), 1.
1955–56, PP 1955–6, XIII (Cmd 9769), 197.
1956–57, PP 1956–7, X (Cmd 195), 315.
1957–58, PP 1957–8, IX (Cmd 451), 393.
1958–59, PP 1958–9, X (Cmd 780), 475.
1959–60, PP 1959–60, X (Cmd 1065)

1960–61, PP 1960–1 (Cmd 1407)
1961–62, PP 1961–2 XI (Cmd 1751)

Statistical Abstracts

Statistical Abstract for the several British Colonies, Possessions, and Protectorates in Each year from 1896 to 1910, Forty-eighth Number, PP 1911, XCVIII (Cmd 6003), 711.

1897 to 1911, Forty-ninth Number, PP 1912–13, CIII (Cmd 6533), 599.

1898 to 1912, Fiftieth Number, PP 1914, XCVI (Cmd 7165), 313.

1899 to 1913, Fifty-first Number, PP 1914–16, LXXIX (Cmd 7786) 1.

1900 to 1914, Fifty-second Number, PP 1916, XXXII (Cmd 8329), 1.

1901 to 1915, Fifty-third Number, PP 1918, XXV (Cmd 9051), 131.

Statistical Abstract for British Self-governing Dominions, Colonies, Possessions, and Protectorates in Each Year from 1903 to 1917. Fifty-fourth Number, PP XLIX (Cmd 664), 233.

To 1919, Fifty-fifth Number, PP 1922, XXII (Cmd 1630), 463.

To 1921, Fifty-sixth Number, PP 1924, XXIV (Cmd 2247), 365.

To 1923, Fifty-seventh Number, PP 1926, XXVIII (Cmd 2738), 311.

To 1925, Fifty-eighth Number, PP 1928–9, XXI (Cmd 3198), 395.

Statistical Abstract for the several British Oversea Dominions and Protectorates in each of the years 1913 and from 1922 to 1927. Fifty-ninth Number, PP 1929–30, XXX (Cmd 3434), 1.

1913 and from 1924 to 1929, Sixtieth Number, PP 1930–1, XXIX (Cmd 3919), 419.

1924 to 1930, Sixty-first Number, PP 1931–2, XXIV (Cmd 4102), 421.

1925 to 1931, Sixty-second Number, PP 1932–3, XXV (Cmd 4393), 421.

1924 to 1933, Sixty-third Number, PP 1934–5, XXII (Cmd 4819), 433.

1925 to 1934, Sixty-fourth Number, PP 1935–6, XXVI (Cmd 5016) 1.

1926 to 1935, Sixty-fifth Number, PP 1936–7, XXVII (Cmd 5298), 1.

1927 to 1936, Sixty-sixth Number, PP 1937–8 XXVIII (Cmd 5582), 285.

1928 to 1937, Sixty-seventh Number, PP 1937–8, XXVIII (Cmd 5872), 529.

1929 to 1938, Sixty-eighth Number, PP 1939–40, xi (Cmd 6140), 1.

Statistical Abstract for the British Commonwealth for each of the ten years 1936 to 1945 (Trade and Commerce Section). Sixty-ninth Number, PP 1946–7, XV (Cmd 7224), 497

Statistical Abstract for the British Commonwealth for the years 1933 to 1939 and 1945 to 1947. Seventieth Number. PP 1950 (Cmd 8051)

Statistical Abstract for the Commonwealth (Trade Statistics, with an appendix for the Sterling Area), Seventy-first Number, 1947, 1948, 1949 and the first half of 1950 (HMSO, London, 1951).

Statistical Abstract for the Commonwealth (Trade Statistics), Seventy-second Number, 1948–51 (HMSO, London, 1952).

The Commonwealth and the Sterling Area, 73rd Statistical Abstract, 1949–52 (HMSO, London, 1953).

No. 74, 1950–1953 (HMSO, London, 1955).

No. 75, 1951–1954 (HMSO, London, 1955).

No. 76, 1952–1955 (HMSO, London, 1956).

No. 77, 1956 (HMSO, London, 1957).

No. 78, 1957 (HMSO, London, 1958).

No. 79, 1958 (HMSO, London, 1959).

No. 80, 1959 (HMSO, London, 1960).

No. 81, 1960 (HMSO, London, 1961).

No. 82, 1961 (HMSO, London, 1962).
No. 83, 1962 (HMSO, London, 1963).
No. 84, 1963 (HMSO, London, 1964).
No. 85, 1964 (HMSO, London, 1965).
No. 86, 1965 (HMSO, London, 1966).

Economic Surveys

Economic Surveys of the Colonial Empire, 1932 (Colonial No. 95, HMSO, London, 1934).
Economic Survey of the Colonial Empire, 1933 (Colonial No. 109, HMSO, London, 1935).
Economic Survey of the Colonial Empire, 1935 (Colonial No. 126, HMSO, London, 1937).
Economic Survey of the Colonial Empire, 1936 (Colonial No. 149, HMSO, London, 1938).
Economic Survey of the Colonial Empire, 1937 (Colonial No. 179, HMSO, London, 1940).
51, I: Northern Rhodesia, Nyasaland, Basutoland, Bechuanaland and Swaziland (281[1], HMSO, London, 1952).
II: The East African Territories: Kenya, Tanganyika, Uganda, Zanzibar, Somaliland, Aden, Mauritius, Seychelles (Colonial No. 281[2], HMSO, London, 1954).
III: West Africa: Gambia, Gold Coast, Nigeria, Sierra Leone, St Helena (Colonial No. 281[3], HMSO, London, 1952).
IV: America and the West Indies: Barbados, British Guiana, British Honduras, Jamaica, Leeward Islands, Trinidad and Tobago, Windward Islands, Bahamas, Bermuda, Falkland Islands (Colonial No. 281[4], HMSO, London, 1953).
V: Far East: Federation of Malaya, Singapore, Hong Kong, Brunei, North Borneo, Sarawak (Colonial No. 281[5], HMSO, London, 1955).
VI: Mediterranean and Pacific: Malta, Cyprus, Gibraltar, Fiji, Tonga, British Solomon Islands, Gilbert and Ellice Islands, New Hebrides (Colonial No. 281[6], HMSO, London, 1953).
VII: The Products of the Colonial Territories (Colonial No. 281[7], HMSO, London, 1952).

Index